SEXUALLY COERCIVE BEHAVIOR

UNDERSTANDING AND MANAGEMENT

ANNALS OF THE NEW YORK ACADEMY OF SCIENCES
Volume 989

SEXUALLY COERCIVE BEHAVIOR

UNDERSTANDING AND MANAGEMENT

*Edited by Robert A. Prentky, Eric S. Janus,
and Michael C. Seto*

*The New York Academy of Sciences
New York, New York
2003*

Library of Congress Cataloging-in-Publication Data

Sexually coercive behavior : understanding and management / edited by Robert A. Prentky, Eric S. Janus, and Michael C. Seto
    p. cm. -- (Annals of the New York Academy of Sciences; v. 989)
"Result of a conference . . . sponsored by the New York Academy of Sciences and the National Institute of Justice, held on June 7–9, 2002 in Washington, DC."
Includes bibliographical references and index.
    ISBN 1-57331-398-X (cloth : alk. paper) — ISBN 1-57331-399-8 (pbk. : alk. paper)
    1. Sex crimes--United States--Prevention--Congresses. 2. Sex offenders--United States--Psychology--Congresses. 3. Sex offenders--Rehabilitation--United States--Congresses. 4. Sex offenders--Legal status, laws, etc.--United States--Congresses. I. Prentky, R. A. II. Janus, Eric S. III. Seto, Michael C. IV. Series.
    Q11.N5 vol. 989
    [[HV6592]]
    500 s—dc21
    [364.151   2003011374

GYAT / PCP
Printed in the United States of America
ISBN 1-57331-398-X (cloth)
ISBN 1-57331-399-8 (paper)
ISSN 0077-8923

ANNALS OF THE NEW YORK ACADEMY OF SCIENCES

Volume 989
June 2003

SEXUALLY COERCIVE BEHAVIOR

UNDERSTANDING AND MANAGEMENT

Editors
ROBERT A. PRENTKY, ERIC S. JANUS, AND MICHAEL C. SETO

This volume is the result of a conference entitled **Understanding and Managing Sexually Coercive Behavior** held on June 7–9, 2002 in Washington, DC by the New York Academy of Sciences and cosponsored by the National Institute of Justice.

CONTENTS

Financial assistance was received from:

Cosponsor

• NATIONAL INSTITUTE OF JUSTICE

Supporters
• NATIONAL INSTITUTE OF MENTAL HEALTH, NIH
• NATIONAL COUNCIL OF JUVENILE AND FAMILY COURT JUDGES

Introduction

ROBERT A. PRENTKY,[a] ERIC S. JANUS,[b] AND MICHAEL C. SETO[c]

[a]*Justice Resource Institute, Bridgewater, Massachusetts 02324, USA*

[b]*William Mitchell College of Law, St. Paul, Minnesota 55105, USA*

[c]*Centre for Addiction and Mental Health, University of Toronto, Toronto, Ontario, M5T 1R8 Canada*

In 1987 the Academy sponsored a conference entitled Human Sexual Aggression: Current Perspectives.[d] The meeting was well attended (by approximately 300 people) and well received. As one of the co-chairs of the conference, Robert Prentky received very positive feedback from Academy staff, as well as an informal invitation from the Academy to revisit the same topic in the future. Fifteen years have passed, and the field has clearly evolved so that another meeting and resulting volume has merit. We will introduce this 15-year follow-up conference by highlighting some of the major statutory, social policy, and empirical landmarks of the past decade and a half.

Beginning with the American Psychological Association's first Task Force on Male Violence against Women in 1991, the 1990s have witnessed increasing attention to the scope, the magnitude, and the effects of crimes involving sexually deviant, coercive, and aggressive behavior (e.g., Goodman, Koss & Russo, 1993a and 1993b; Goodman, Koss, Fitzgerald, Russo & Keita, 1993; Koss, 1990, 1993a). This increased attention in the social science community paralleled an increased profile in the public sector as well as wide-reaching state and federal legislation, such as, the Wetterling Act in 1994 (42 U.S.C. 14071), the 1996 amended Wetterling Act, known as "Megan's Law" (P. L. No. 104-145, 110 St. 1345), the 1995 amendments to the Federal Rules of Evidence allowing admissibility of prior sexual crimes (Pub. L. No. 103-322, sec. 320935(a)), the 1996 Lychner Sexual Offender Tracking and Identification Act (42 U.S.C. 14072), and the new wave of civil commitment laws for "sexual predators." Although not a direct result of federal legislation, one of the more remarkable achievements of the past decade was the creation of the Center for Sex Offender Management (CSOM) in June 1997, as a joint effort of the Office of Justice Programs (Department of Justice), the National Institute of Corrections, and the State Justice Institute. This highly concentrated statutory focus on sexual violence over the past decade has, if nothing else, underscored the ubiquity and diversity of the problem.

As far as *ubiquity* is concerned, our incidence/prevalence data have improved in the last ten years. The National Victim Center and the National Crime Victims Research and Treatment Center reported in 1992 that 13% of all adult American

---

[d]See *Human Sexual Aggression: Current Perspectives*, Vol. 528 of the *Annals of the New York Academy of Sciences*, edited by Robert A. Prentky and Vernon L. Quinsey and published in 1988.

Ann. N.Y. Acad. Sci. 989: ix–xiii (2003). © 2003 New York Academy of Sciences.

women had been the victim of forcible rape at some time in their lives. The NVC/ CVRTC Report estimated that there were 683,000 forcible rapes during 1992. The American Psychological Association's Task Force on Male Violence against Women concluded that "Between 14% and 25% of adult women have endured rape according to its legal definition" (Goodman, Koss, Fitzgerald et al., 1993). Goodman et al. (1993) remarked that, "Perhaps the most startling theme to emerge from these articles is the extraordinarily high prevalence of male violence against women" (p. 1055). Although numerous methodological problems clearly preclude any definitive conclusions (cf. Koss, 1993a, 1993b), a diverse cross-section of studies spanning several decades suggest that approximately 25% of adult women have experienced some form of sexual victimization, and somewhere between 10% and 15% of women have been raped.

The assumption that sexual crimes against children and teenagers are drastically underreported is now well accepted. One of the strongest sources of evidence for this assumption comes from offenders themselves, some of whom report vastly more victims than their court records reflect. Perhaps the most dramatic self-report data on victimization rates from offenders comes from the research of Abel and his colleagues. Abel et al. (1987) recruited 561 subjects through a variety of different sources (e.g., health care workers, media advertising, and presentations at meetings). The subjects were given a confidential structured clinical interview about their history of deviant sexual behavior. The 561 subjects reported a total of 291,737 "paraphilic acts" committed against 195,407 victims.

Rather than relying on the veracity of adults' reports of highly socially disapproved behavior, Finkelhor and Dziuba-Leatherman (1994a) conducted a national telephone survey of children between the ages of 10 and 16. Sexual abuse involving physical contact was reported by 3.2% of the girls and 0.6% of the boys, revealing "levels of child victimization that far exceed those reported in official government victimization statistics" (Finkelhor and Dziuba-Leatherman, 1994a, p. 415). The rape rate, for example, was about five times higher than the estimate of 0.1% reported in the National Crime Survey. The overall rate for sexual abuse among children and teenagers (ages 0–17) in 1991 was 6.3 per 1000, a threefold increase since 1986, when the rate was determined to be 2.1 (Finkelhor and Dziuba-Leatherman, 1994b).

Finkelhor (1994) surveyed the estimates of child sexual abuse in 21 countries, including the United States and Canada. All studies reported rates of abuse that were quite comparable to the rates in North America, ranging from 7% to 36% for women and 3% to 29% for men. In general, females are abused 1.5 to 3 times more frequently than males. Given the methodological problems that compromise the accuracy of frequency estimates of child sexual abuse, the ranges provided in these studies, particularly the studies employing national probability samples, are probably our "best guesses" at this time.

The National Survey of Adolescents (NSA) conducted telephone interviews with 4023 male and female adolescents and parents or guardians (Kilpatrick and Saunders, 1997). Extrapolating from the NSA sample to the national population of adolescents, Kilpatrick and Saunders (1997) concluded that of the 22.3 million adolescents (ages 12–17) living in the United States, roughly 1.8 million have been the victim of a serious sexual assault.

Although it is impossible to measure with precision the *actual* incidence of sexual coercion, it is reasonable and defensible to conclude that an extraordinarily large number of children, teenagers, and adults are the victims of sexual coercion and sexual assault each year. Senator Joseph Biden's (1993) observation is well-taken: "If the leading newspapers were to announce tomorrow a new disease that, over the past year, had afflicted from three to four million citizens, few would fail to appreciate the seriousness of the illness. Yet, when it comes to the three to four million women who are victimized by violence each year, the alarms ring softly" (p. 1059).

With respect to *diversity*, we have moved well beyond our earlier focus on impulsive, antisocial criminals serving time in prison for felony sexual assaults on strangers. Sexual coercion and sexual aggression is expressed or manifest in a remarkably wide range of behaviors, further underscoring the seriousness of the problem. Specialized populations that have been the target of empirical inquiry include (a) children, referred to as "abuse reactive," who have sexually assaulted other children; (b) elderly victims, some in their nineties, who have been sexually assaulted by family members or by residents or staff in nursing homes; (c) college women, who have been reporting sexual assault in increasing numbers, prompting universities to take preemptive steps to increase security; (d) "impaired professionals," individuals such as clergy, physicians, teachers, and therapists, who exploit positions of power and/ or authority to sexually victimize congregants, patients, students, and clients; and (e) sexual "harassers," individuals who exploit positions of power and/or authority to sexually victimize subordinates.

Despite the remarkable diversity and heterogeneity of sexual coercion, considerable progress has been made on several scientific fronts. The sheer volume of laws that seek to manage sexual offenders has created a virtual army of practitioners to implement the laws, which has, in turn, driven the science of *risk assessment*. Since most of these laws require some form of risk assessment, there has been a dramatic increase in the development, validation, and revision of risk assessment procedures during the past decade. The most notable developments in the area of risk assessment include the development of valid actuarial risk assessment instruments, consideration of acute and stable dynamic risk factors, and the assessment of risk among younger offenders.

A second area of empirical scrutiny where progress has been exciting is *etiology*. The prospect of developing unified theoretical models to explain rape and child molestation was once considered bleak at best. Lack of optimism was driven primarily by the heterogeneity of sexual offenders, particularly those who assault adult victims. Within the last ten years, however, models developed on markedly dissimilar samples of rapists have yielded surprising overlap in explanatory constructs. These studies have increased the confidence of scientists that it may indeed be possible in the near future to set forth working theoretical models to explain sexual coercion of adult women. Although comparable models for explaining sexual coercion of children remain elusive, the same methodologies brought to bear on rape will, we trust, sort out the etiologic riddles of child molestation.

A third area in which noteworthy progress has been made is *management*. Development of increasingly effective management strategies for sexual offenders is essential to the overarching goal of reducing victimization rates. We use the term *management* to refer, collectively, to the laws that govern convicted sexual offenders; the systems of supervision that are used to monitor sexual offenders in the community; the psychophysiological (e.g., polygraphy and penile plethysmography) and electronic (e.g., GPS) adjuncts to supervision; outpatient and inpatient treatment;

and the adjunctive use of medication. Overall, these management models have not been tested. Testing such models prospectively is time-consuming and quite expensive. Although grant support has not been readily available for such efforts, the field has borrowed from the public health sector, and the models that have been developed represent major advancements.

The legal system provides the framework for the management of sexual offenders. Beginning three decades ago, criminal laws were revised in order to broaden and modify the substantive definitions of rape and sexual assault to reflect new understandings of the nature, etiology, and social meaning of sexual coercion. These laws continue to evolve. Complementing those changes were reforms in legal and law enforcement policies and procedures, designed to facilitate the participation of victims of sexual assault and rape in the criminal justice process and to reflect the potential severity of harm caused by sexual assault. A third wave of reforms, beginning in the early 1990s, sought to identify and manage directly the future risk of sexual assault by expanding to the civil (regulatory) system. A decade after these latest reforms, researchers and policymakers are beginning to understand the need for more nuanced approaches to the management of sexual offenders, offering a more graduated and flexible continuum of interventions.

The past 15 years has seen an increased level of public discourse with a concomitant rise in the role of public policy in shaping the societal response to sexual violence. Many of the significant legislative reforms of the 1990s had their beginnings in public outrage over specific instances of sexual violence. Driven far more by public sentiment than science, the reforms have pushed at conventional constitutional boundaries and have constituted a new public policy characterized by an aggressive, empirically *un*informed stance toward sexual violence. This public policy has shaped all aspects of the management of sexual offenders, from local decisions about whether to parole or transfer a sexual offender, to national decisions by federal agencies about funding research on sexual violence. The legislative fruits of this public policy have triggered contentious constitutional challenges, often resulting in badly split court decisions. In the end, the courts have consistently refused to impose significant constitutional limits on the activist legislative agenda, leaving the shape and boundaries of the legal response to sexual violence squarely in the hands of policymakers. With a decade and a half of experience, policymakers ought now to turn their attention to empirically informed evaluations of the reforms, aimed at judging whether they are the best possible means for achieving the goal that has driven the new public policy, the reduction of sexual violence.

The gravity of the problem of human sexual coercion demands constructive social responses, and constructive social responses require empirical input. Significant achievements in scientific research on sexual coercion have been made within the past fifteen years. Thus, from a scientific standpoint, as well as from a social and legal standpoint, we felt that it was timely to convene major scholars in this area to set forth an agenda for future scientific, policy, and legal directions to reduce the level of sexual coercion and sexual violence in society. We hope these proceedings will serve as a blueprint for such an agenda by informing legislation and policy, and for guiding and stimulating future research.

REFERENCES

ABEL, G.G., BECKER, J.V., MITTELMAN, M.S., CUNNINGHAM-RATHNER, J., ROULEAU, J.L. & MURPHY, W.D. (1987). Self-reported sex crimes of nonincarcerated paraphilics. *Journal of Interpersonal Violence, 2,* 3–25.

BIDEN, J.R. (1993). Violence against women. The Congressional response. *American Psychologist, 48,* 1059–1061.

FINKELHOR, D. (1994). The international epidemiology of child sexual abuse. *Child Abuse & Neglect, 18,* 409–417.

FINKEHOR, D. & DZIUBA-LEATHERMAN, J. (1994a). Children as victims of violence: A national survey. *Pediatrics, 94,* 413–420.

FINKEHOR, D. & DZIUBA-LEATHERMAN, J. (1994b). Victimization of children. *American Psychologist, 49,* 173–183.

GOODMAN, L.A., KOSS, M.P. & RUSSO, N.F. (1993a). Violence against women: Physical and mental health effects. Part I: Research findings. *Applied and Preventive Psychology, 2,* 79–89.

GOODMAN, L.A., KOSS, M.P. & RUSSO, N.F. (1993b). Violence against women: Mental health effects: Part II. Conceptualizations of post-trauma stress. *Applied and Preventive Psychology, 2,* 123–130.

GOODMAN, L.A., KOSS, M.P., FITZGERALD, L.F., RUSSO, N.F. & KEITA, G.P. (1993). Male violence against women. Current research and future directions. *American Psychologist, 48,* 1054–1058.

KOSS, M.P. (1990). The women's mental health research agenda: Violence against women. *American Psychologist, 45,* 374–380.

KOSS, M.P. (1993a). Rape. Scope, impact, interventions, and public policy responses. *American Psychologist, 48,* 1062–1069.

KOSS, M.P. (1993b). Detecting the scope of rape. A review of prevalence research methods. *Journal of Interpersonal Violence, 8,* 198–222.

KILPATRICK, D.G & SAUNDERS, B.E. (1997, April). The prevalence and consequences of child victimization. *Research Preview.* Washington, DC: U.S. Department of Justice, National Institute of Justice.

PRENTKY, R.A. & QUINSEY, V.L. (1988). *Human sexual aggression: Current perspectives* (Vol. 528). New York: The New York Academy of Sciences.

Sex Offender Management

The Public Policy Challenges

LAURIE O. ROBINSON

Distinguished Senior Scholar, Lee Center of Criminology,
University of Pennsylvania (Washington Office),
Washington, DC 20036, USA

ABSTRACT: Few issues within the crime policy arena are as volatile as those involving sex offending, yet there is an enormous "knowledge gap" between research, science, and clinical practice, on the one hand, and the policy and criminal justice practitioner communities, on the other. Recent highly publicized cases involving sex offending, which have elevated the issue in the public eye, provide an opportunity for experts in this field to play an aggressive role in informing this debate. In particular, high priority should be given to developing more effective means of communicating to policymakers, practitioners, the media, elected officials, and the public what is known from science and clinical practice about sex offending and about what works in addressing it. A strong commitment to greater cross-disciplinary collaboration is also needed, as is federal leadership, particularly in supporting a cross-department research agenda. Researchers and other experts in this field can play a valuable role in helping ensure rational and effective public policy relating to sex offending that can achieve public safety and help reduce future victimization.

KEYWORDS: sex offender; crime policy; public policy; victimization

INTRODUCTION

Public policy relating to crime is clearly central to the foundations of a civil society; effective governance in this area demands deliberate and informed consideration of options. Within the broad arena of crime policy, few issues are as volatile, or as likely to trigger emotion in elected officials and the public, as the question of sex offending. The goal of encouraging responsible and measured public policy in this area is thus a special challenge.

The recent spate of allegations concerning the Catholic clergy has made this issue a timely one on the national policy agenda. Significant questions have been thrown into the public forum for discussion: Why do some human beings engage in this behavior? How should we, as a society, deal with the perpetrators? What about the victims? And—most important—how do we prevent the creation of future sex offenders and avert future victimization?

Address for correspondence: Laurie O. Robinson, President, CSR, Inc., 2107 Wilson Blvd., Suite 1000, Arlington, VA 22201. Voice: 703-312-5220; fax: 703-312-5230.
lrobinson@csrincorporated.com

Ann. N.Y. Acad. Sci. 989: 1–7 (2003). © 2003 New York Academy of Sciences.

This storm of attention provides an opportunity for experts to help inform the ongoing policy dialogue.

BACKGROUND

In 1993, it seemed clear that the issue of sex offending demanded the attention of the U.S. Department of Justice. At that time, a number of well-publicized criminal case "horror stories" (like those involving Polly Klaas in California and Megan Kanka in New Jersey) were spurring public officials to institute "three strikes" laws, new mandatory minimum sentences, and sex offender registration and community notification statutes, among other measures. In addition, public leaders, as well as citizens, were questioning the capacity of the criminal justice system to meet its core mission of providing public safety.

Much of the public's *general* disenchantment about the criminal justice and sentencing systems, I believed, was being driven by fears *in specific* about how sex offenders in these high-profile cases were being handled. It thus seemed crucial to better understand this subset of criminal offenders and what measures were being, or could be, used to address (and prevent) this behavior. A number of experts in the field, such as Robert Prentky and Fred Berlin, were requested to educate the U.S. Department of Justice and to provide counsel on what the Department could do to address this issue constructively.

What was learned from those consultations was that, as experts in this field are well aware, much is known about sex offending from research, science, and clinical practice. But, just as clearly, there was a huge "knowledge gap" on the part of those in criminal justice and the policy arena charged with finding solutions to the problem. Also, it was noted that multidisciplinary approaches were needed and punitive criminal justice solutions *alone*—longer, tougher sentences—would not solve the problem. Experts underscored that "you can't punish sex offending away."

As a result of these consultations, a National Summit on Promoting Public Safety Through the Effective Management of Sex Offenders in the Community was convened by the U.S. Department of Justice in late 1996. Two goals were envisioned for this gathering: first, to highlight promising practices and research on the topic, assess the "state of the art," and identify gaps in existing practice and research; and, second, to serve as a forum for developing recommendations on potential action steps for the Justice Department's Office of Justice Programs (OJP), which I headed.

The 180 participants at the Summit, a diverse group of criminal justice practitioners, legislators, policymakers, victim advocates, treatment specialists, and researchers, made three recommendations:

(1) That more knowledge needed to be developed and disseminated;
(2) That technical assistance and training were needed for every part of the criminal justice system;
(3) That broad public education was esstential, including establishment of a national resource center as a repository of best practices, treatment strategies, and research findings (http://www.csom.org/about/about.html).

Spurred by these recommendations, grant funding was set aside through the OJP to launch a Center for Sex Offender Management, headed then and now by Madeline

Carter. The mission of this center was to provide information, training, and technical assistance on this issue. (Since 1999, the center has also taken on the function of supporting Justice Department–funded pilot sex offender management programs around the country.)

PUBLIC POLICY CHALLENGES

Numerous public policy issues surround the problem of how our society, and its criminal justice system, should handle sex offenders. From my experience as Assistant Attorney General, I see six key challenges requiring attention from academics, researchers, clinicians, and other experts in this field.

First, and perhaps most centrally, is the issue of education, communication, and translation. Despite the fact that research knowledge about sexually coercive behavior and treatment approaches has grown tremendously over the last decade (Becker & Hunter, 1997; Gilligan & Talbot, 2000; Hanson, 1998; Gallagher, Wilson, Hirschfield, Coggeshall & MacKenzie, 1999), the fact remains that policymakers, elected officials, the media, and criminal justice practitioners still know *relatively little* about sex offending and how to deal with it. In fact, the response by government officials is still too often driven by anecdote and rhetoric rather than by facts, research, and successful practice.

Experts in this field thus have a critical leadership role to play in aggressively informing this national discussion. Policymakers and the press need solid information. But the research community has not done enough to communicate to that audience— in plain-language explanations—what is known about sex offending and what works in treating it.

In my current work with the University of Pennsylvania's Lee Center of Criminology, I see the value of, and need for, better bridging between academia, on the one hand, and policymakers and practitioners, on the other. These worlds speak different languages, work at different paces, and value different things. Researchers in any field are good at talking to each other, but often are less effective—or interested—in communicating with those outside the academic realm. Yet it is clear that publishing in scholarly journals is not a successful route to educating legislators and busy practitioners and prompting them to embrace, and act on, new research findings.

This step of *translation* must therefore be a high priority if the important work emerging in this field is going to have a broad impact. For every research study undertaken, the question of how its findings will be communicated must be an integral part of the undertaking. Professionals in this field should give focused, ongoing attention to questions like these: How can key research findings better reach decision makers and opinion leaders? How can research findings be distilled into language that those audiences can understand and "own"? Even where, ideally, one would await the results of additional research, is there more that can be done *now* to summarize for policymakers what *is* known, recognizing that public officials do not have the luxury of waiting years for more refined research to emerge?

Public education—to help dispel the myths and misunderstandings about sex offending—also has to be an essential piece of this. The public (and its elected representatives) need to understand, for example, that all sex offenders will not be locked up for life; that most of them will return to the community; and that much *is* known about risk assessment, treatment, and management options. The National Institute of Justice is to be commended for requiring as a product of this conference a practitioner-friendly summary of the proceedings for publication and dissemination.

New approaches are also needed in how key issues are framed. Every Washington policy debate on crime is still haunted by the ghost of Willie Horton, and the label every politician most fears is that of "soft on crime." So, as policy proposals regarding sex offending are discussed, it is important to articulate explicitly the overarching goal of public safety and to acknowledge openly the powerful reality of public fear.

Language, too, is important: In encouraging treatment for sex offenders, for example, it is helpful to clarify its use as a tool to help reduce future victimization, and not to describe it as a therapeutic service to be provided to offenders.

This is thus an opportune time for experts in this field to play a leadership role, whether nationally or in their local communities, in shaping wise and science-based approaches in this emotionally charged public policy area.

CROSS-DISCIPLINARY APPROACHES

A second public policy challenge is the need for greater cross-disciplinary collaboration. Reflecting progress that is being made, representation at the conference included a broad cross section of attendees from the academic and treatment communities, law, social work, criminal justice, and public health.

Yet have we done enough? Are experts on the academic and research side talking with judges, prosecutors, public defenders, state corrections directors, and probation officials? Are public health professionals regularly part of the discussion? What about local elected officials, victim advocates, and juvenile justice experts? While few would dispute the value of comprehensive collaborations, implementation of such approaches is often not easy; they require breaking out of the comfort zone of professional niches and embracing new ways of doing business. The rewards, however, can be substantial. Experts in this field can do much to help inform the work of law enforcement leaders, elected prosecutors, and local judges in their communities. Local police chiefs, in particular, are an important group to which outreach should be made; many law enforcement leaders around the country today are public servants with advanced degrees and with a strong commitment to problem solving, community policing, and citizen-responsive government. They can be important allies in this work.

The sex offender management demonstration programs currently underway with U.S. Department of Justice OJP funding underscore the importance of cross-disciplinary work. The Center for Sex Offender Management has identified 19 "resource sites" around the country, jurisdictions that have implemented promising practices and innovative sex offender management and supervision techniques (http://www.csom.org/resource/resource.html). The underlying principle at each of these sites is their collaborative, multidisciplinary and multiagency approach to both case management and policy development.

Reflecting the adage of thinking globally, but acting locally, these demonstration sites are serving as creative laboratories for work with managing sex offenders in the community.

FEDERAL LEADERSHIP ROLE

A third public policy challenge is that of ensuring a strong federal leadership role on this issue. No one jurisdiction, whatever its deep commitment, is going to fund national research or provide technical assistance nationally to practitioners. These are uniquely federal, and federally supported, roles. But attention to the problem of sex offending should not be a political issue. At base, it is a "public safety for communities" issue. All appropriate federal agencies should thus be encouraged, if they have not done so already, to place the subject of sexually coercive behavior high on their agendas.

The federal role is particularly important in the area of research. Yet it is my view, from my years in government, that there is insufficient coordination between the Departments of Justice and Health and Human Services in this area, and even—within the Justice Department's OJP—between the National Institute of Justice and the Office of Juvenile Justice and Delinquency Prevention. With federal budgets in this area likely to diminish in coming years, it becomes all the more important that there be a strong commitment to developing a cross-agency/cross-department research agenda on the range of issues relating to sex offending and response to it.

PRISONER REINTEGRATION

With growing national attention to the challenge of prisoner reentry (Travis, Robinson & Solomon, 2002), it is important that emerging initiatives in this area do not overlook the special challenges presented in dealing with the sex offender population as it returns postprison to the community. It would be easier for these programs to *exclude* sex offenders, believing them a difficult and risky group. One major reentry demonstration program in a large eastern city, for example, includes *every offender* returning to a small number of zip code areas—except sex offenders. It is unclear if the program's leadership believes these offenders do not need services or help, or whether the hope is that they will somehow disappear!

There are promising developments, however. In Chittenden County, Vermont, for example, work is underway to encourage effective transition of incarcerated sex offenders back into the community (Little & Lyon, 2001). As part of a comprehensive statewide sex offender supervision and treatment program, Chittenden County's approach couples the use of relapse prevention with an innovative program using trained community volunteers to support offender reintegration.

LISTENING TO VICTIMS

A fifth public policy challenge is the importance of ensuring that victim groups are part of the policy development process. Because of their powerful voice in helping shape crime policy in this country, victims should be drawn into both policy formulation and planning for programs and research.

When planning was underway for the Justice Department's 1996 Summit, the strategic—and moral—importance of making the victim advocate community a key ally and focusing on the goal of reducing victimization became evident. Groups like the National Center for Victims of Crime and the National Organization for Victim Assistance should be partners in this work. Equally important, state and local crime victim advocate groups can play a vital role.

Innovative efforts are underway to ensure victims a voice in community-based sex offender management initiatives. In New Haven, for example, a unique collaboration exists among the probation office, a sex offender treatment provider, and a victim advocate, with the advocate actually playing an integral role on the supervision team (Little & Lyon, 2001, p. 44). In order to ensure that we build knowledge about how this works, a researcher is documenting the process.

UNINTENDED CONSEQUENCES

Finally, it is crucial, as new policies are considered, that the potential for unintended consequences be examined.

When the Clinton Administration and Congress in the 1990s rushed to pass Megan's Law (1996) and similar statutes (The Jacob Wetterling Act, 1994; The Pam Lychner Act, 1996; CSJA Amendments, 1998), it reflected the familiar Washington race to see who can be tougher on crime. While definitive research is still lacking on whether these laws have increased public safety, there are incidents of vigilantism and harassment reported in almost every state (Matson, 2001), and anecdotal reports that, following the implementation of community notification requirements, some sex offenders may have gone "underground" (Matson, 2001, p. 14).

While no rigorous evaluations of these initiatives are apparently underway (it is curious why the National Institute of Justice is not supporting one), steps of this kind, like any other single response, are not a successful "quick fix." Instead, comprehensive, multidisciplinary approaches are needed.

As civil commitment proposals are now being considered around the country, potential consequences of such statutes should also be carefully examined.

CONCLUSION

Experts in this field have an opportunity to make important and much needed contributions to the ongoing public policy debate regarding sex offending. Working collectively, these experts can help ensure adoption of rational and effective approaches that can achieve public safety and also reduce the likelihood of future suffering.

REFERENCES

BECKER, J.V. & HUNTER, J.A. (1997). Understanding and treating child and adolescent sex offenders. In T.H. Ollendick & R.J. Prinz (Eds.), *Advances in clinical child psychology* (Vol. 19). New York: Plenum Press.
CJSA Amendments: Section 115 of the General Provisions of Title I of the Departments of Commerce, Justice and State, the Judiciary, and Related Agencies Appropriations Act, Pub. L. 105-119, 111 Stat. 2440, 2461 (1998).
GALLAGHER, C., WILSON, D., HIRSCHFIELD, P., Coggeshall, M. & MacKenzie, D. (1999). A quantitative review of the effects of sex offender treatment on sexual reoffending. *Corrections Management Quarterly, 3*, 19–29.

GILLIGAN, L. & TALBOT, T. (2000). *Community supervision of the sex offender: An overview of current and promising practices.* Silver Spring, MD: Center for Sex Offender Management.

HANSON, R.A. 1998. What do we know about sex offender risk assessment? *Psychology, Public Policy, and Law, 4*, 50–72.

LITTLE, K. & LYON, E. (2001). *Case studies on the center for sex offender management's national resource sites* (2nd ed.). Silver Spring, MD: Center for Sex Offender Management.

MATSON, S. (2001). *Community notification and education.* Silver Spring, MD: Center for Sex Offender Management.

Megan's Law, Pub. L. 104-145, 110 Stat. 1345 (1996).

The Jacob Wetterling Act: Title XVII of the Violent Crime Control and Law Enforcement Act, 42 U.S.C.A. Sec. 14071 (1994).

The Pam Lychner Sexual Offender Tracking and Identification Act, Pub.L. 104-236, 110 Stat. 3093 (1996).

TRAVIS, J., SOLOMON, A. & WAUL, M. (2001). *From prison to home: The dimensions and consequences of prisoner reentry.* Washington, DC: Urban Institute.

TRAVIS, J., ROBINSON, L. & SOLOMON, A. (2002). Prisoner reentry: Issues for practice and policy. *Criminal Justice, 17*, 12–18.

The Role of Citizen Education and Political Engagement in Framing the Issues

SCOTT HARSHBARGER

President and CEO, Common Cause
1250 Connecticut Avenue, NW #600
Washington, DC 20036, USA

I appreciate the opportunity to speak with you today as you gather together to share your expertise on the very difficult, complex topic of sexual abuse and how to manage offenders. Throughout my career, I've been proud to have been known as an advocate for victims. It's also a special privilege to appear here with Laurie Robinson, with whom I've worked over the years and who did so much as a leader in the Justice Department to advance a tough but smart, multidisciplinary approach to this often controversial issue.

Much of what I have to say echoes what Laurie Robinson eloquently described for you about the challenges we face in addressing this issue. Like many of you, I have worked on this issue for many years—though from a very different perspective. I would like to share some of my perspective as a former district attorney and attorney general, as the current president of Common Cause, a national citizens' lobbying group, and as someone who has worked both within and outside of the system to bring attention to these difficult issues, to hold people and systems accountable, and to create and effect social change.

As relevant and important as my criminal justice and treatment background may seem to be, I hope to convince you that my position with Common Cause is the most significant role that will help me achieve my goal today—to convince you to become actively engaged in the political and civic fray as a citizen and as a professional.

Here's my reason for having this goal: In a democracy, our public values and public policies are played out and developed through the political process. So if you care about the policies that are being made, you need to get involved and participate. Citizens—real people and experts on the particular issues—are often the missing ingredients in most policy debates involving criminal justice issues, especially the treatment of sexual crimes and offenders.

We need rational policies and laws that reflect what we know about sex offenders. But that can only happen if you—the experts, the ones who know the most about the complex issues related to sexual abuse—get involved. I challenge you to view it as your obligation as public citizens and your responsibility as professionals.

In sharing the perspective that I have gained over the years, I want to address four main points: (1) the problem of sexual abuse and institutional response and resis-

Address for correspondence: Scott Harshbarger, Murphy, Hesse, Toomey & Lehane LLP, Two Seaport Lane, Boston MA 02210. Voice: 617-479-5000; fax: 617-338-1324.
sharshbarger@mhtl.com

Ann. N.Y. Acad. Sci. 989: 8–12 (2003). © 2003 New York Academy of Sciences.

tance; (2) real progress through taking tough, smart action; (3) building on what we know works; and (4) sharing your expertise and getting involved.

THE PROBLEM OF SEXUAL ABUSE AND INSTITUTIONAL RESPONSE AND RESISTANCE

You gather here at a time when sexual abuse is, once again, prominent in the public arena. Yet I am sure that, as professionals who have worked on this issue for years, the fact that the abuse happened, with its impact on both the victims and the Roman Catholic Church, does not come as a surprise to you—as it has to many uninformed citizens.

As an aside, the unfolding Wall Street story of the misdeeds of Enron and Arthur Andersen is a parallel example of exactly the same kind of institutional resistance and failure to respond—and of a tragic situation that has already befallen millions of people because of decisions and actions made by a few.

Why are these stories prominent now? It's *not* because any individual offender or victim has gotten everyone's attention. It's because the *system* has come into question. Institutional resistance to openness and change has been exposed, and citizens— average people—feel and see the effect in their lives.

The press is raising fundamental questions—questions that need to be asked— about the scope of the problem, the process by which these sexual abuse reports and the perpetrators were handled within the Roman Catholic Church, and just how much people both inside and outside the Church knew.

Make no mistake about the Roman Catholic Church and the crisis that they are confronting. It's no accident. Responsible individuals made choices. They chose the institution over the victims—the system over the people—and that's why they are under scrutiny and are being criticized for their secrecy. It's also important to remember that these are not just criminal justice issues—they are political and civic issues as well.

REAL PROGRESS THROUGH TAKING TOUGH, SMART ACTION

One thing I have learned throughout my tenure as a public official is that crises can be opportunities if they are used as teachable moments to advance well-thought-out policies. You need to be tough, but you also need to be smart.

Well-meaning legislation has been enacted in response to cries from victims and their advocates that legislators need to do something. But do legislators have the correct information? Were their proposals developed in conjunction with respected research? If the answer is no, then why not?

As a prosecutor, I can tell you that the facts matter. Policymakers and legislators need to rely on research to develop the best methods of management of offenders and protection of victims, rather than responding quickly to allay the concerns for public safety. And research is also needed to evaluate the efficacy of these interventions and to inform policies and laws that embrace these efforts. Your knowledge is being used every day in decisions being made in the criminal justice system. You need to keep on sharing it so that law enforcement can use it to protect victims and make the wisest and safest decisions about perpetrators.

The pressure on legislators, policymakers, and the press to respond immediately is extraordinary. It is easy to criticize legislators and policymakers for enacting "knee-jerk" laws or instituting myopic practices that don't consider the complexity of the problem or potential ramifications. However, you can only hold them accountable for bad choices if the right people—the experts in the field, be they victims, researchers, or practitioners—are willing to step up and get involved.

Let me share with you a few examples from my work on sexual abuse within the Massachusetts criminal justice system. When I became district attorney in 1983, there were 40 pending cases of child sexual abuse; 8 years later, there were 732 cases. This "increase" was not a result of a dramatic surge in the 1980s in crimes against children; nor was it an accident. It was a function of required reporting of conduct heretofore cloaked in secrecy, acted out behind closed doors, and protected by adult and professional privilege. We made choices. We paid attention and investigated cases thoroughly and responded to victims and tried to do something about what had happened to them. They saw that the system could be responsive. However, our work was not done in isolation. It was greatly enhanced by the larger public movement for victims' rights and by the passing of the Child Abuse Reporting Law in the Massachusetts legislature in 1982. The courage of many victims to speak out and the advocacy of professionals gave me the support and tools that I needed as a prosecutor to respond effectively.

Perhaps the most basic sign of progress is that it is now commonly acknowledged that sexual abuse of children by "family" members or other adults in positions of trust occurs and is a crime. It sounds simple now, but do not forget how much this progress represents. We need to acknowledge our victories, even if they are "quick" ones or not complete.

In 1996, when I was attorney general, as a result of several serious, well-publicized crimes, the idea of a Massachusetts Sexual Offender Registry was proposed as a "solution," in large part due to the political climate, which resulted from Megan's Law. I proposed a six-point, comprehensive plan for taking action to manage sexual offenders. In addition to extended probation periods and a broad registry of offenders, the plan recommended intervening differently at the various stages of the case and early identification of juvenile offenders as an essential component of prevention and protection. These recommendations now seem like obvious policies to focus on, but back then they were viewed as moving beyond the narrow debate on identifying offenders in the community. I relied upon the expert advice of treatment professionals and others in the criminal justice field to advance the public and legislative discussion about what needed to be done. Yet, with all the gains that we have seen, we all know significant work still needs to be done.

John Gardner, the founder of Common Cause, made a statement that certainly applies here. He said, "Reform is not for the short-winded." No one knows this better than each of you sitting here today.

BUILDING ON WHAT WE KNOW WORKS

From my perspective, sexual abuse is one of the toughest issues to deal with because it is so complex and there are no quick fixes or easy answers. The reality is that most offenders will not be locked up, and those who are will not be in jail forever—and so will be back in our communities. We need to deal with that fact creatively and not just say that incarceration is the answer. We need to have the courage to risk making mistakes in our efforts to solve the problem. We need to acknowledge that false cases sometimes occur and be aware that they can jeopardize all the good work that we do and the credibility that victims have worked so hard to achieve. We do know what needs to be done. In most cases, we know who the predators are—they're in our families, our communities, and our workplaces. We need to have comprehensive policies that are coherent, creative, and multilayered to address the complexity of the problem. But this will not happen unless you enter the fray of public debate.

SHARING YOUR EXPERTISE AND GETTING INVOLVED

Bill Moyers tells a story about a conversation that he had with a cab driver, who remarked to him, "Political leaders think we're stupid; they're wrong. We're usually just uninformed."

I share this story to make this point: Do not assume that everyone knows what you know. By "everyone," I mean the people in positions of power who can implement policies, your colleagues in the treatment field and other professions, and the public—who need to be educated and involved in advancing the best policies.

As district attorney and attorney general, I convened many conferences to promote the multidisciplinary collaboration that Laurie Robinson spoke about earlier—by bringing together police officers, prosecutors, therapists, probation officers, child welfare workers, and school personnel to talk about these issues and learn from each other. It's not rocket science. It just made sense to me that all the people who interact with a family, with an offender, with a victim—as well as the people who are the experts on the particular issue—get together to develop a comprehensive, informed plan. Yet I constantly heard, through the training, the meetings, and information sharing, that it was the first time that all of these professionals were in the same room together. I saw firsthand the achievements that could happen if they all started working together—the most important aspect being that it helped the victims of abuse and held their perpetrators accountable. Yet I know that it still is not accepted as common practice.

As someone in law enforcement who tried to surround himself with the voices of those from many different, but equally important, disciplines, I must tell you that you have to be willing to come to the table, to share your expertise, and to advocate for changes that you think are wise—and to do so even if you are not invited. You know that there are no simple solutions. You need to enter the public arena and make the arguments for more comprehensive change.

It is also critical to support "those who brung you." As a former elected official, I greatly appreciated support from advocacy groups when I took positions that reflected the right thing to do but perhaps were not the most popular positions, or were not the easiest or cheapest plans to implement.

You have a crucial role to play in making all of this happen. I would like to challenge you today to view this increased political and media attention to the issue of sexual abuse as an opportunity for you to advance understanding and increase more effective responses and interventions.

SUMMARY

First, in order to make any significant progress, social change needs to happen. Second, a popular movement of victims, treatment providers, and other citizens needs to get the attention of the policymakers, legislators, and those who are in a position to make changes. Third, systemic reform needs to occur, and systems and professionals who work within them need to be held accountable. This reform needs to be tough but smart. Fourth, change will not happen unless you decide to get involved. Finally, everything that I have learned throughout my career as a prosecutor and public official and from my time in Washington at Common Cause has shown me that to create change, you need some heroes within the system fighting for your issues. You need outside advocacy to help these insiders make the case for implementing real change. You need to share what you know, you need to be persistent, and you need to believe that you can make a difference.

John Gardner once remarked, "I run into able, successful Americans who aren't doing a blinking thing for their communities, and I want to say, 'Who gave you permission to stand aside?'"

You have an unprecedented opportunity to make a difference and to achieve real understanding and progress in the quest to keep all citizens safe from sexual abuse. It is not only your obligation as a citizen, it is your responsibility as a professional. And if you do not get into the fray, who will?

I urge you to continue to stay the course, and engage and enter the fray with skill and passion, being tough but smart, and helping any of those leaders at any level who stand with and for you. I wish you the best of luck as you grapple with these very challenging and complex problems.

A 15-Year Retrospective on Sexual Coercion: Advances and Projections

ROBERT A. PRENTKY

Justice Resource Institute, Bridgewater, Massachusetts 02324, USA

ABSTRACT: This paper surveys the clinical and legal literature in the area of sexual offender law, policy, and research from 1987 through 2001. Eleven clinical journals, yielding approximately 12,858 articles were screened, as well as 1196 articles in law journals. Content trends over fifteen years are reported. In addition, five major areas within the sexual offender field (etiology, risk assessment, legislative management, remediation, and public policy) are examined for noteworthy changes over the past fifteen years. Advances and projections for future developments are discussed.

KEYWORDS: sexual coercion research; risk assessment; public policy; etiology; treatment; sexual offender laws

INTRODUCTION

The past 15 years has witnessed a marked increase in the political and social "profile" of sexual offenders and the general problem posed by sexual violence. Beginning with The Community Protection Act adopted by the Washington State legislature in 1990 (WA Laws of 1990, ch. 3), there has been a plethora of new state and federal laws intended to manage the problem of sexual violence. Congress passed the Violence against Women Act (VAWA) of 1994, with an explicit goal of providing greater safeguards for victims of domestic violence and sexual assault. The VAWA legislation was expanded with the Violence Against Women Act of 2000 (Pub. L. 106-386). Congress passed The Wetterling Act in 1994 (42 U.S.C. 14071). Later amended in 1996, The Wetterling Act became known as "Megan's Law" (P. L. No. 104-145, 110 St. 1345). By 1997, every state had some variant of a sexual offender public notification law pursuant to The Wetterling Act. The Federal Rules of Evidence were amended in 1995, allowing admissibility of prior sexual crimes (Pub. L. No. 103-322, sec. 320935(a)). The Pam Lychner Sexual Offender Tracking and Identification Act (42 U.S.C. 14072) was passed in 1996, and the much-debated Child Online Protection Act/Children's Internet Protection Act was passed in 1998 and subsequently overturned in federal court. The Victims of Trafficking and Violence Prevention Act was passed in 2000. The highest profile legislation, however, has been the new wave of civil commitment laws, referred to as Sexually Violent

Address for correspondence: Robert Prentky, Research Department, Justice Resource Institute, 63 Main Street, Suite 6, Bridgewater, MA 02324. Voice: 508-697-2744, ext. 205; fax: 508-697-2738.

rprentky@jri.org

Ann. N.Y. Acad. Sci. 989: 13–32 (2003). © 2003 New York Academy of Sciences.

Predator (SVP) statutes, christened in 1990 when the State of Washington enacted the first such statute (Community Protection Act, 1990 WA Laws, ch. 3). By August, 1999, sixteen states had new or revised civil commitment laws. A remarkable achievement at the federal level was the creation of the Center for Sex Offender Management in June 1997, a joint effort of the Office of Justice Programs (Department of Justice), the National Institute of Corrections, and the State Justice Institute.

Given this highly concentrated legislative focus on sexual assault over the past 15 years, it seemed reasonable to examine other commensurate landmarks during the same time period. In this overview, I have attempted to accomplish two goals: (a) report trends in the clinical and legal literatures from 1987 to 1991, and (b) examine the major empirical, theoretical, and practice-based accomplishments over that same time period and offer projections for propitious changes on the horizon.

A REVIEW OF THE CLINICAL LITERATURE

The clinical literature on sexual coercion over the past 15 years was surveyed in 11 journals [cf. Appendix]. All issues over the past 15 years (1987–2001) for all 11 journals were screened, yielding approximately 12,858 articles. Of these articles, 926 (7%) could be classified into one of 19 *a priori* content categories (cf. Appendix). Two of the eleven journals (Journal of Abnormal Psychology (JAP) and Journal of Clinical and Consulting Psychology (JCCP)) accounted for a vastly disproportionate number of screened articles (8100 of the 12,858), but very few classified articles (69, <1%). Although the American Psychological Association initiated its first Task Force on Male Violence Against Women in 1991, this presumptively significant expression of concern quite apparently did not translate into an increase in scholarly papers in two of its flagship journals. By eliminating those two journals, the "adjusted" total number of articles was 4758, and the number that was classifiable rose to 18% (857/4758). Moreover, of the 857 classified papers, 205 (24%) involved Victim Impact, not, strictly speaking, a content area having to do with sexual offenders *per se.* Thus, the number of articles on sexual offenders (652) represented approximately 14% of the total number published in nine journals (minus JAP and JCCP) over 15 years.

The number of articles published per year for the 15 years is depicted in FIGURE 1, and the number of articles published in three 5-year blocks is presented in FIGURE 2. By visual inspection, there is a linear increase in published papers from 1987 to 1998, with a slight drop in 1999, and a marked drop in 2000. Although there was a rebound in 2001, the total did not approach 1998. The classification of articles by content area is presented in TABLE 1. Four content areas accounted for >10% of the articles. Five content areas accounted for 4%–9% of the articles, and all other content areas accounted for <4%.

One area, in particular, that accounted for a very small number of published papers was recidivism (2.4%). That was a particularly striking finding, since there has been a considerable focus over the past decade on the development of actuarial risk assessment scales and treatment efficacy, both of which rely on estimates of recidivism rates. To look at this question more closely, I borrowed (courtesy of K. Hanson and K. Morton) the list of 177 studies that were employed in the 2002 meta-analysis on risk factors for sexual recidivism. These 177 studies ranged from 1943 to the present (i.e., in press). Since most of these articles were not picked up in the earlier

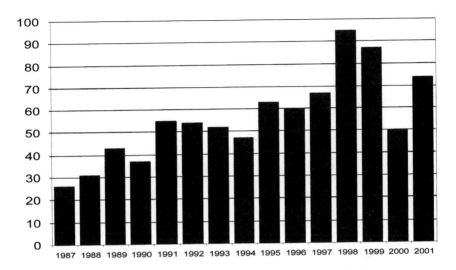

FIGURE 1. Clinical articles published per year.

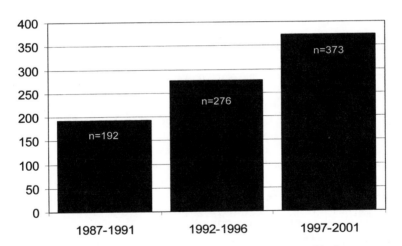

FIGURE 2. Clinical articles published in three 5-year blocks.

review of the published scientific literature, the task was to determine where they appeared. The 177 studies were classified into one of eight citation categories (journal articles, chapters, books, internal reports, theses/dissertations, talks, unpublished papers, and papers submitted for publication). Over half of the articles (53%) had *not* been published in journals. Of this group, 37 (21%) were presented as talks, 31 (18%) were internal reports, and 9 (5%) were cited as unpublished papers. The 83 papers that were published in journals (47% of the total) appeared in 37 different periodicals, only three of which were included in the general review of the literature just described. Most of the 37 periodicals were quite obscure, not peer-reviewed, and

TABLE 1. Classification frequency by content area

>10%		4%–9%		<4%	
Clinical/descriptive	28.6	Assessment: general	7.4	Classification	2.9
Victim impact	28.0	Treatment: empirical	5.7	Recidivism	2.4
Treatment: clinical	15.0	General theory	4.6	Risk assessment (general)	2.4
PPG-Sexual Arousal	11.0	Prevention	4.6	Bio/neuro/hormonal	2.2
		Date rape	4.2	Attitudes	1.9
				Risk assessment (ARA)	1.8
				Pornography	1.8
				Etiology	1.4
				Incidence	1.4
				Treatment: drugs	1.0

not part of the corpus of scientific literature that researchers in the field are generally acquainted with. It would appear that much of the literature, at least in the area of recidivism, is not published in peer-reviewed journals. Moreover, what is published, is scattered in a large number of relatively obscure periodicals that are off the radar screen for most researchers.

A REVIEW OF THE LEGAL LITERATURE

The legal literature on sexual coercion over the past 15 years (1987–2001) was surveyed using Index to Legal Periodicals (Westlaw database). A total of 1196 articles were identified using three different content searches: (1) general terms (rape, sexual abuse, sexual assault, sexual violence, child molestation), (2) civil commitment laws (sex predator, sex psychopath, sexual offender commitment, etc.), (3) community notification (registration, Megan's law, etc.). *Category 1* accounted for 1010 articles (85% of total); *Category 2* accounted for 74 articles (6%); and *Category 3* accounted for 112 articles (9%). FIGURE 3 depicts the distribution of these 1196 articles over the 15-year span. FIGURES 4 and 5 depict the distribution of Category 2 (civil commitment laws) and Category 3 (community notification) articles, respectively, over the 15-year span.

As is evident in FIGURE 3, a period of five years, from 1994 through 1998, accounts for almost half of all of the published papers in the legal literature over the past 15 years. After the peak in 1997, the number of papers consistently declined, with fewer papers published in 2001 than in 1987. The distribution of the subgroup of articles on civil commitment reflects precisely the enactment of the new SVP laws. The first law was passed in Washington in 1990. The marked elevation observed in 1992 presumably is a function of the papers written in response to that first piece of legislation, which took two years to eventually appear in journals. Similarly, beginning in 1994 and over the next several years 13 more laws were passed, reflecting the increase in published papers from 1995 through 1998. Indeed, this four-year period accounted for 58% of all papers published. There was a marked decline in 1999, consistent with the general decline in interest in these laws. In 1999, 13 additional states had active SVP bills that were expected to pass that year. By the end of

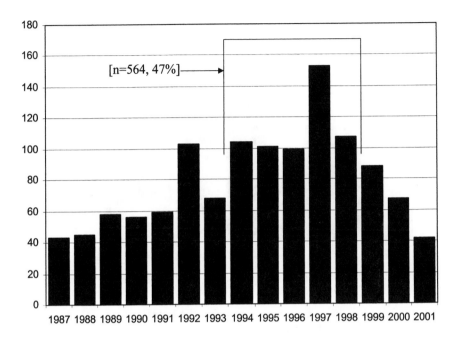

FIGURE 3. Law articles published per year.

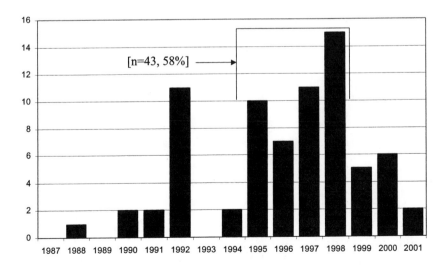

FIGURE 4. Articles on civil commitment.

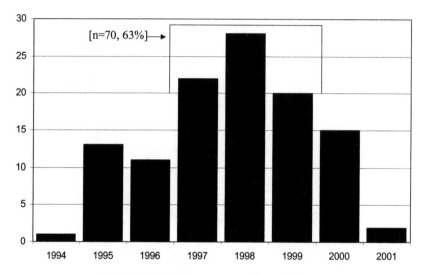

FIGURE 5. Articles on cummunity notification.

the year, only 3 of the 13 bills passed, and since the last law was enacted in August 1999, no new SVP law has been enacted.

The distribution of the subgroup of articles on community notification reflects the same phenomenon. In 1996, federal legislation required states to adopt community notification laws or risk losing 10% of their federal law enforcement funding. Within approximately one year, 47 states had complied. As can be seen in FIGURE 5, the increase in published papers on community notification began in 1997, and a brief three-year period, 1997–1999, accounted for 63% of all papers published on the topic. Just as interest in civil commitment legislation has waned since 1999, so has interest in community notification.

ETIOLOGY

Although considerable progress has been made over the past 15 years in the development of etiologic models for explaining rape behavior in diverse samples of adult males (e.g., Kafka, 1997; Knight & Sims-Knight, 2003; Malamuth, 2003, 1998; Malamuth, Heavey & Linz, 1993), the inordinate complexity and interactivity of adverse life experiences that antecede and contribute in unique ways to different manifestations of sexually coercive outcomes defy any reductionistic explanations.

An apt metaphor that seems to capture the challenges that face us in developing models for explaining sexually coercive behavior is Gleick's (1988) chaos theory. Gleick (1988) spoke of the "butterfly effect," the notion that a tiny, insignificant insect fluttering its wings in the air over London could affect storm systems the following month in New York. In scientific terms, the butterfly effect refers to "sensitive dependence on initial conditions." In the present context, the butterfly effect is a metaphor for the subtlety, complexity, and interactivity of the "initial conditions" that foster outcomes of sexually coercive behavior.

One of the most persistent conundrums in the empirical literature on etiology is the role of childhood abuse in general and sexual abuse in particular. A prevailing view, and a reasonable hypothesis, during the 1980s was that sexual crimes in adolescence or adulthood represented a "recapitulation" of the offender's own experience of sexual victimization (Finkelhor et al., 1986; Garland & Dougher, 1990; Kempe & Kempe, 1984; Lanyon, 1986; Rogers & Terry, 1984). The recapitulation hypothesis tarnished under empirical scrutiny as studies failed to find reliable evidence for the antecedent role of sexual abuse (cf. Prentky, 1999). Although some studies offered partial support (e.g., Knight & Prentky, 1993; Prentky & Knight, 1993), it became clear that simply noting the presence of sexual victimization in the history of an offender was overly parsimonious as an explanation for the resulting sexually abusive behavior.

In earlier research, childhood abuse was typically examined as an encapsulated, homogeneous group of aggravating, equally weighted life experiences. The profound complexity of the proximal, as well as the distal, effects of child abuse is a truism at this point. It is clear that child abuse varies in its predictive importance according to the presence of a number of morbidity factors (Kaufman & Zigler, 1987; Prentky, 1999), such as the age of onset of the abuse, the duration of the abuse, the violence and/or invasiveness in the abuse, and the child's relationship to the perpetrator. The more recent programmatic research of Burton (e.g., 2000) underscores the predictive criticality of invasiveness, or more specifically penetration, for dire outcomes. Any or all of these factors, including interaction with other adverse life experiences, may be moderators of outcome. Indeed, Prentky, Knight, Sims-Knight, Rokous, and Cerce (1989) reported that the *co-occurrence* of caregiver inconstancy and sexual abuse in childhood was a powerful predictor of the degree of sexual aggression in adulthood.

One potential moderator of child abuse that thus far has *not* been embraced by the researchers developing etiologic models of sexual coercion concerns brain damage. A wide range of replicated studies have demonstrated that child abuse can cause permanent damage to the neural structure and function of the developing brain (De Bellis et al., 1999; Teicher, 2000, 2002). It is speculated that protracted stress from an ongoing abusive home life may result in chronically elevated cortisol levels, which has its greatest impact on limbic structures, particularly the hippocampus. The hippocampus is uniquely vulnerable to stress in that (a) it develops slowly, (b) it is one of the few brain regions that continues to develop after birth, and (c) it has a higher density of cortisol receptors than almost any other area of the brain (Teicher, 2002). Teicher (2002) pointed out that prolonged or excessive exposure to cortisol can significantly change the shape of the largest neurons in the hippocampus and can kill them; moreover, cortisol can suppress production of new granule cells (small neurons) that normally continue to develop after birth. In sum, severe, prolonged abuse in childhood has the potential to cause permanent brain damage, most notably in the temporal limbic region.

The potential relevance for the etiology of many forms of sexually coercive behavior in humans is clear. As Perry, Pollard, Blakley, Baker, and Vigilante (1995) commented, "Unlike broken bones, irreversible maldevelopment of brain areas mediating empathy resulting from emotional neglect in infancy and childhood is not readily observable" (p. 276). Perry et al. (1995) went on to remark that "Some of the most powerful clinical examples of this phenomenon are related to lack of attachment experience early in life. The child who has been emotionally neglected early in life will exhibit profound attachment problems that are extremely insensitive to any replacement experiences later, including therapy. Examples of this include feral children, children in orphanages observed by Spitz and Wolf (1945) and, often, the remorseless, violent child" (pp. 276–277). The biological imprint of severe, prolonged child abuse may not only be permanent, but may simultaneously damage areas of the brain that are critical for development of the capacity for empathy, critical for socialization, and perhaps even critical for the internalization of values (i.e., conditionability), as well as acting as a catalyst for increasingly severe maladjustment in development of social and interpersonal skills, problem-solving skills, and impulse control. In these worst-case scenarios, we may be setting in motion an increasingly disruptive attachment disorder, resulting in intractable emotional detachment, incapacity for empathy, and lack of "conscience" (Prentky, 2003). The relevance of attachment for sexual offenders, who, as a group, appear to be distinguished by their maladaptive interpersonal relationships, would seem transparent. Although there has been considerable attention to disorders of attachment or intimacy deficits in the sexual offender literature (e.g., Cortoni & Marshall, 2001; Marshall, 1993; Marshall, Hudson & Hodkinson, 1993; Marshall, Serran & Cortoni, 2000; Smallbone & Dadds, 2000; Ward, Hudson & McCormack, 1997), thus far it has not been incorporated into comprehensive, unified, theoretical models of rape. Thus, the next generation of etiologic models must embrace a much more sensitive analysis of the "initial life conditions," including biological parameters associated with abuse and the evolution of various expressions of malattachment, in proximal as well as distal outcomes of sexual coercion.

In sum, there have been remarkable advances in understanding the fundamental constructs that undergird and motivate sexual assault of adult women and, most importantly, how those constructs relate to one another. The best that we could do, only a decade ago, was to describe what those constructs might be (Prentky & Knight, 1991). Given the advances in this domain, it is all the more remarkable how *little* progress has been made in developing comparable models for child molestation, or more specifically pedophilia. The etiology of pedophilia remains, in my estimation, a black box. This reality reveals one of the most profound "disconfirmations" of a logical working hypothesis. Twenty years ago, prevailing wisdom was that child molestation would yield its taxonomic and etiologic secrets far faster and much easier than rape. Rape and proneness to rape, it was thought, was so pervasive throughout the general population, that it would be exceptionally difficult to develop models that embraced all manifestations of the behavior. By contrast, those with sexualized interest in children represent a relatively small, stable, encapsulated group that would be readily amenable to empirical scrutiny. It appears, at this point, that the opposite has been the case.

RISK ASSESSMENT

The Catalyst

The spate of federal and state legislation during the decade of the 1990s seeking to manage sexual offenders resulted in a concomitant and marked increase in efforts to develop and validate risk assessment instruments. In addition to the programmatic research on risk assessment scales for adult offenders, there have been more recent trends to focus on the problems of assessing risk with children and juveniles, and on the development of valid acute and stable dynamic risk indicators. Law clearly has driven science in this case. One of the collateral developments has been an increasing recognition of the greater utility of a public health model than a strict criminal justice model. One such sign has been the replacement of "dangerousness" with "risk." Risk implies the presence of a potential hazard, and the probability of occurrence of that hazard. Risk *reduction* implies reduction in the probability of the occurrence of the hazard. Risk has greater utility and more flexibility than dangerousness. First, risk is clearly thought of as dimensional and continuous, whereas dangerousness is too often (and too easily) thought of in dichotomous terms (i.e., either the offender *is* dangerous or *is not* dangerous). It is much easier to pose the question "What degree of risk does the offender present?" than "What degree of dangerousness does the offender present?" Second, dangerousness captures a narrow swath of human behavior, typically acts of interpersonal violence, whereas risk captures a much broader range of behaviors (e.g., we might speak about an offender's risk of eloping, of violating parole, of specific "lapses," of abusing substances, of depression, and/or suicide, etc.). Third, the occurrence of risk is more likely to be seen as some calculable probability, whereas dangerousness is more likely to be thought of in absolute terms. Fourth, the use of risk brings criminology "in line" with numerous other disciplines, from measuring health care outcomes (where the term "risk adjustment" is used) and environmental protection (environmental health risk management) to meteorology (Monahan & Steadman, 1996).

In sum, there is a clear, if not urgent, mandate for risk-relevant decisions within the criminal justice system, and an equally clear path to follow in developing and testing sophisticated assessment procedures guided by methods successfully employed in other fields. If there is any question about the ubiquity of risk-relevant decisions about sexual offenders within the court system, the following list was prepared by Heilbrun et al. (1998):

> (a) *civil commitment* (in which a sex offender had a co-occurring diagnosis that would meet the criterion for mental disorder and whose risk for sexual offending was linked to the disorder and provided evidence of danger to others), (b) *sentencing* (following the conviction of a sex offense in some jurisdictions, the issue of aggravating and mitigating circumstances generally, or the questions of specialized treatment needs and sexual offense risk more specifically, are invoked), (c) *postsentence commitment* (as in a *Hendricks* context—whether a convicted inmate at the end of a sentence, without mental illness but nonetheless presenting a significant risk for sexual reoffending, can be civilly committed), (d) *postsentence community notification* (involving informing the local police and community members that a convicted sexual offender is about to be released and plans to reside in their community), (e) *the granting and conditions of probation or parole*, and (f) *child custody*. (p. 153)

The Polemic

The literature generally discusses two methods of risk assessment: clinical and actuarial. Based on considerable, unambiguous evidence, it is reasonable and readily defensible to conclude that the predictive efficacy of actuarial methods of risk assessment are superior to clinically derived assessments of risk (e.g., Dawes, Faust & Meehl, 1989, 1993; Grove, Zald, Lebow, Snitz & Nelson, 2000; Grove & Meehl, 1996; Monahan et al., 2001; Swets, Dawes & Monahan, 2000). Despite what scientists might regard as a *fait accompli*, there has been considerable resistance to the adoption of actuarial risk assessment (Dvoskin & Heilbrun, 2001). Litwack (2001), for example, argued that "research to date has not demonstrated that actuarial methods of risk assessment are superior to clinical methods," and that even the best of the actuarial risk assessment tools are not sufficiently validated "for use in determining when individuals should be confined on the grounds of their dangerousness." This would seem to be a rather specious argument, since the question, at least at the present time, is *not* whether examiners should assess the risk posed by potentially dangerous sexual offenders, but how to do it best, given that it will be done. The only ethical conclusion that we are left with, assuming that we have elected to participate in the adjudication of risk, is that the liberty-interest decisions made by SVP courts *must* be done with the highest reliability and the lowest error rates possible, given current state-of-the-art methods for rendering these decisions.

Although the precise reasons for the resistance to use of actuarial risk assessment are debatable, the relative superiority of actuarial over clinical methods of assessing risk is not. It would seem prudent to avow the most authoritative opinion on the matter expressed by Monahan et al. (2001), who concluded that, "The general superiority of statistical over clinical risk assessment in the behavioral sciences has been known for almost half a century." The "half century" noted by Monahan et al. (2001) undoubtedly refers to the seminal paper of Meehl and Rosen (1955). Although somewhat more colorfully expressed, Meehl reissued the same verdict in 1998, remarking that:

> The clinical-statistical problem ("What is the optimal method of combining data for predictive purposes?") has also been solved, although most clinicians haven't caught on yet…I do not know of any controversy in the social sciences in which the evidence is so massive, diverse, and consistent. It is a sad commentary on the scholarly habits of our profession that many textbooks persist in saying that the question is still open.

Recommendations

The following general recommendations are intended to advance the field of risk assessment. First, we must avoid parochialism by embracing models and methods that are used by more "mature" disciplines, far more seasoned in the ways of assessing risk. By defining sexual violence as a public health hazard, not unlike occupational hazards, environmental hazards, health-care-related hazards, and meteorological hazards, we can benefit from an abundance of experience assessing risk of hazards in other domains.

Second, we must, in the scientific vernacular, strive to reduce "uncertainty." That is, we must focus on improving our understanding of the sources and nature of uncertainty in risk assessment with sexual offenders. Clearly, one such area is *change*. As the "organism" changes over time, risk factors that were valid at time 1 may cease to be valid or may be suboptimal at time 2. The most recent frontier, testing acute and stable dynamic risk factors, addresses the issue of change. There are, however, many other sources of uncertainty, such as the conditions or circumstances under which the assessment of risk is taking place. Risk assessments often occur in forensic environments under forensic conditions, wherein meaningful confidentiality does not exist.

Third, focal attention to risk-relevant interventions is essential. We must place the highest priority on external control of behavior through sophisticated aftercare models that target critical high-risk factors, thereby reducing reliance on internal behavior change.

Fourth, our ultimate goal must be risk *management*, not risk assessment. There are a number of excellent prototypes for such risk management models, such as the one set forth in the two volumes of the Final Report of The Presidential/Congressional Commission on Risk Assessment and Risk Management (1997) entitled *Framework for Environmental Health Risk Management*, and *Risk Assessment and Risk Management in Regulatory Decision-Making*.

The Interface of Risk Assessment with Law and Policy

We are currently in a health care era of assessment and accountability in which costs as well as clinical outcomes are emphasized. Risk assessment inevitably becomes intertwined with law and policy. The most obvious example is civil commitment law, which is driven by policy and must rely on risk assessment. From a public health framework, civil commitment law should, at least in theory, place the highest premium on outcomes-based measures of the reduction in the public health hazard of sexual violence. Hazard reduction (i.e., clinical outcomes) is then examined relative to the costs of the civil commitment strategy, and both can be compared with the efficacy of other strategies. It is the very inextricable nature of law, public policy, and assessment that demands an operational public health model.

One novel method for beginning to operationalize a public health approach to managing sexual violence is the application of "diagnosis-related groups" or DRGs. A procedure adopted by Medicare about 15 years ago, DRGs provided a linkage between the severity of a diagnosis and the magnitude of resources required for optimal intervention. Severity is equitable risk. The higher the severity, the greater the likelihood of a poor outcome. A sexual offender risk management model of the future may use precisely defined categories of behavior (i.e., the equivalent of DRGs) that correspond to severity (or risk) *and* intensiveness of remedial interventions (i.e., costs).

LEGISLATIVE MANAGEMENT

As noted at the outset, the decade of the 1990s produced an extraordinary increase in state and federal legislation designed to manage sexual offenders, most notably the nationwide public notification laws and the new civil commitment laws. Between 1990 and 1999, 16 states adopted a new or revised civil commitment statute. As of September 2001, however, the same 16 states had civil commitment laws. No state has passed a new civil commitment law since the Commonwealth of Massachusetts in August 1999. Although a total of 1200 men have been committed under these laws (as of September 2001), three-quarters of them were committed in just four states (California, Minnesota, New Jersey, and Wisconsin) (S. Matson, personal communication, May 2002). An additional 866 men were waiting trial for possible commitment, and a total of 61 men had been released or discharged (S. Matson, personal communication, May 2002). Only four states are *actively* committing men (California, Minnesota, New Jersey, Wisconsin), while other states are proceeding more cautiously. As of September 2001, Florida had committed 35 men over a period of two years, and

Massachusetts has committed 20 men in a period of about two and a half years. North Dakota has used their law to commit only three men. Despite no apparent resistance from the mental health community, and despite no apparent resistance from the courts, these new civil commitment laws seem to have ground to a rapid standstill. Although this interesting sociolegal phenomenon is worthy of further consideration, it appears at the present time that cost is the delimiting factor (Fitch, 1998; La Fond,1998; Lieb & Matson, 1998; Prentky & Burgess, 2001).

Prentky and Burgess (2001) noted that, "Sex offender-specific legislation over the past 60 years can be described metaphorically as waxing in tidal waves of revulsion and protest over well-publicized crimes and waning in response to egregious violations of constitutional safeguards. The marriage of sexual offenders and civil commitment law clearly is imperfect, characterized by an unremitting tension, and, thus far, refractory to conventional legal 'remedies'" (p. 159). As Janus (1997, pp. 72–73) observed, civil commitments for sexual offenders do

> not arise out of a benign, *parens patriae* motive. The subjects of sex offender commitments are *not*, for the most part, incompetent to make decisions about their own mental health treatment. And they have not been found incompetent to stand trial or not guilty by reason of insanity. Sex offender commitments possess many of the qualities that elicit condemnation of preventive detention. Most centrally, unlike standard civil commitments, sex offender commitments are aimed directly at those guilty of criminal acts, and are explicitly intended to circumvent the traditional strict constitutional limitations on the state's power to incarcerate. In addition, though courts may categorize them as *civil commitment as usual*, sex offender commitments are well outside the traditional boundaries for standard civil commitment. For these reasons, sex offender commitment schemes need special justification or legitimization, ...

The justification is, of course, community safety. Civil commitment of sexual offenders uses preventive detention to accomplish the same purpose that has previously been reserved exclusively for criminal matters (cf. Janus, 1997). Whereas a criminal sentence will, almost inevitably, return the offender to the community, a civil commitment provides some sense of comfort that the offender may never return to the community. Thus, community safety is pitted against protection of constitutional rights. The result is an inexorable tension that has been most visibly manifest in the pendulum of enactment and repeal. Janus (1996) concluded with the following plea: "Sex offender commitment laws confuse too many important values. Obscuring the critical role that mental disorder plays in defining the state's police powers, these laws embrace a dangerous jurisprudence of prevention. We must find other, more truthful and more principled ways to prevent sexual violence" (p. 213). It is our responsibility, indeed it is our mandate as professionals in this field, to provide constructive options that substantially increase community safety while not abridging basic constitutional rights. As Prentky and Burgess (2001) observed, "There is little evidence, thus far, that litigation in response to the current wave of sexual predator laws will shed light on the ambiguity of the critical elements that comprise these laws, *or*, for that matter, provide the legal architecture for a comprehensive risk reduction model that could effectively promote community safety" (p. 160). The chain of events is clear. Informed professionals must inform public policy, which in turn informs legislation. It would appear at this point that *informed* law designed to manage sexual offenders and control sexual coercion should be our primary goal. Such law *must* embody the principle of sexual autonomy and be dispassionate and constructive in discretionary and regulatory decisions. Based on past experience, enacting such law will be our most challenging, elusive goal.

REMEDIATION AND MANAGEMENT

Remediation embraces a variety of interventions and strategies that are employed to reduce risk of reoffense, particularly when offenders are returned to the community. Here, I address only two of the higher profile concerns over the past 15 years: (1) treatment efficacy, and (2) aftercare models.

Treatment models have not changed substantially over the last 20 years. Essentially, the same cognitive-behavioral, relapse-prevention model adopted in the early 1980s (Pithers, Marques, Gibat & Marlatt, 1983) continues, with revisions and adaptations (Laws, Hudson & Ward, 2000), to be used today. Perhaps the most significant change has been the increasing acceptance of the importance of medication as an adjunct to therapy. The pharmacological regimen includes three categories of drugs: (1) the antiandrogens, with the agent of choice in the United States being medroxyprogesterone acetate (MPA; Provera, Upjohn); (2) the selective serotonin reuptake inhibitors (SSRIs); and (3) gonadotropin releasing hormone agonists (GnRH), with the agents of choice being being two long-acting analogues of naturally occurring GnRH or LH-RH (leuprolide, Lupron and goserelin, Zoladex).

The conventional criterion for the effectiveness of treatment with sexual offenders is a reduction in sexual recidivism rates as a function of treatment (i.e., the reoffense rates were higher among those not treated than among those treated). Variations in recidivism rates reported by different treatment programs, however, are extremely difficult to interpret. Differences among recidivism rates across studies are confounded with legal jurisdiction, duration of follow-up, offender characteristics, different attrition rates, differences in program integrity and amount of treatment, amount and quality of posttreatment supervision, and a host of other variables (Prentky, Lee, Knight & Cerce, 1997). In addition, recidivism measures tend to be noisy and result in comparisons of low statistical power. Even without commenting on variations in recidivism rates that may be attributable to treatment program characteristics, the variation in recidivism rates attributable only to methodological differences, such as length of follow-up, sources of data used to estimate recidivism, and the definition of what constitutes recidivism, is truly remarkable (Prentky et al., 1997).

In an excellent paper on the critical role of base rates for recidivism in treatment outcome studies, Barbaree (1997) concluded that "recidivism studies were found to be quite insensitive to the effects of treatment" (p. 111). The problem is a relatively simple one. As Barbaree noted, the base rates for sexual recidivism in most studies range from 0.10 to 0.40. Sample sizes in most studies are generally small, rarely more than 200 offenders. With a low base rate and a small sample, the treatment effect would have to be very large (>0.50) to observe significant differences between treated and untreated offenders. In other words, the difference in sexual recidivism rates between treated and untreated sexual offenders would have to be 50% or more. It is quite unrealistic to expect treatment effects of that magnitude. Consequently, as Barbaree (1997) demonstrated, it is not surprising that the conventional treatment outcome studies of the past have failed to demonstrate significant treatment effects.

In a widely reported meta-analysis on 12 studies of treated sexual offenders ($N = 1313$), Hall (1995) found a small but significant overall effect size for treatment versus comparison conditions ($R = 0.12$). The *effect size for treatment*, or simply *treatment effect*, is the observed decrease in sexual recidivism rates as a direct function of treatment. The overall recidivism rate for treated sexual offenders was 0.19, compared with the overall recidivism rate of 0.27 for untreated sexual offenders. The effect sizes were larger in those samples with higher base rates of recidivism, those samples with follow-up periods that were greater than 5 years, those samples that included outpatients, and those studies that used cognitive-behavior therapy or antiandrogen medication. Cognitive-behavior therapy and antiandrogen medication were significantly more effective than behavioral techniques, such as covert sensitization or aversion. Cognitive-behavior therapy and antiandrogen medication appeared to be of equal efficacy (i.e., there was no difference in effectiveness between the two).

A General Accounting Office study identified and summarized 22 reviews of research on sexual offender treatment (GAO, 1996). The reviews, which were published between 1977 and 1996, covered 550 studies. The gist of the GAO (1996) report was that the results are promising but inconclusive. The report concluded that "the most optimistic reviews concluded that some treatment programs showed promise for reducing deviant sexual behavior. However, nearly all reported that definitive conclusions could not be drawn because methodological weaknesses in the research made inferences about what works uncertain. There was consensus that to demonstrate the effectiveness of sexual offender treatment more and better research would be required" (GAO, 1996, p. 11).

The only longitudinal treatment outcome study with random assignment was California's Sex Offender Treatment and Evaluation Project (SOTEP). Stationed at Atascadero State Hospital, SOTEP operated from 1985 to June 1995, with the final data panel collected in 2000. This study was also supported by a five-year grant from the National Institute of Mental Health, awarded in 1989 and ending in 1996. The most recent recidivism data, reported by Marques and Day in 1998, indicated that, with an average of five years at risk, the 167 subjects who completed treatment had a nonsignificantly lower sexual reoffense rate (10.8%) than the 225 volunteer control subjects (13.8%) or the 220 nonvolunteer controls (13.2%). Marques, Nelson, Alarcon, and Day (2000) provided a realistic postmortem review of the strengths and weaknesses of SOTEP.

Perhaps the most noteworthy finding from SOTEP was *not* the low, highly respectable sexual recidivism rate of 10.8% for treated offenders but the low sexual recidivism rate of 13–14% for the untreated offenders. This finding raises precisely the problem described by Barbaree (1997). With a five-year sexual reoffense base rate of 13–14% for untreated sexual offenders, a sample would have to be enormous to demonstrate a significant treatment effect.

Sample size was addressed by the Collaborative Outcome Data Project on the Effectiveness of Psychological Treatment for Sex Offenders (Hanson et al., 2002). Hanson et al. (2002) reported on a meta-analysis of 43 studies with a total of 9454 subjects (5078 treated and 4376 untreated). Although the average period at risk was 46 months, follow-up periods ranged from 12 months to 16 years. Averaged across all studies, the sexual recidivism rates were 12.3% for treated and 16.8% for untreated subjects. A microanalysis that selected only "modern" treatment studies, presumably employing the relapse prevention model, the sexual recidivism rates were 9.9% for treated and 17.4% for untreated subjects. Thus, the treatment effect ranged from 4.5% in the aggregate analysis to 7.5% in the subsample that was selected for modern studies.

Given the sample sizes in the Hanson et al. (2002) study, there is little question at this point that treatment reduces sexual recidivism. How much remains uncertain.

The most reasonable estimate at this point is that treatment will reduce sexual recidivism over a 60-month period by 7–8%. This, nevertheless, must be regarded as a crude estimate, because it collapses across a markedly heterogeneous population of offenders with widely varying base rates. The simple use of dimensions known to differentiate between recidivists and nonrecidivists, such as psychopathy or impulsivity among rapists and degree of sexual preoccupation with children or incest vs. nonincest among child molesters, would bring considerable clarity to estimates of treatment effects.

Aftercare is undoubtedly the single most critical management tool for sexual offenders in the community. Aftercare is typically operationalized as an interdisciplinary, individualized, case management model that draws upon the resources and the collaborative input from probation or parole officers and their supervisors, treatment providers, victim services, social services, law enforcement, judges, and a variety of specialized personnel, such as polygraphers. The most well-known model, the "containment approach," was developed by English and her colleagues (English, Pullen & Jones, 1996). Although none of the models have been subjected thus far to rigorous empirical scrutiny, prevailing wisdom suggests that this is potentially the most important management strategy and the one that should be the focus of our scientific efforts. In sum, my *first* recommendation is the testing of containment-type management models that focus on risk-relevant acute and stable dynamic factors, not punitive factors.

One common component of aftercare is some form of surveillance. Traditional surveillance techniques have been fairly cumbersome and suboptimal in effectiveness. A potentially more reliable, effective, and flexible procedure makes use of Global Positioning System (GPS) technology. Thus, my *second* recommendation would be to increasingly incorporate GPS surveillance into aftercare. Although GPS already has obvious advantages in speed, precision, and coverage, there are simple improvements that can further advance this technology: (a) miniaturizing the "personal tracking device" (PTD); currently cumbersome and weighing 3–4 pounds, it could be as small as a pocket cell phone; this would reduce the "false alarms" resulting from offenders setting the PTD down and unintentionally walking out of range; (b) extending the battery life in the PTD and the bracelet, which would also reduce false alarms; (c) replacing telephone lines with fiber-optic cable.

Two final recommendations for improving aftercare would be (1) assured-compliance drug treatment, that is, developing better strategies for assuring full compliance with medication, including, if necessary, screening for steroids; and (2) triaging (i.e., initial screening for intensiveness of services based on presenting static risk).

PUBLIC POLICY AND MANAGEMENT

Public policy is the overarching umbrella that covers all aspects of the treatment, management, and research on sexual coercion. Public policy is also the principal driving force that influences the enactment of laws, authorizes state-sponsored treatment programs, influences the amount and direction of funding for federally sponsored research, and affects most management and discretionary decisions. Of the innumerable issues that are subject to, or influenced by, policy, some of the more obvious include (1) registration and community notification laws, (2) civil commitment laws, (3) downward classification of incarcerated sexual offenders, (4) parole of sexual offenders, (5) state-mandated interventions, such as castration, (6) state-mandated assessment procedures, such as polygraphy, (7) state-mandated surveillance procedures, and (8) research funding.

Given the pervasive, dendritic nature of the problem of sexual abuse, with branches that insinuate into and directly affect all aspects of society, I have recommended earlier in this article that we reframe the problem as a public health issue. Similar recommendations, made by others over the past several years (Becker, 2000; English, Pullen & Jones, 1997; McMahon, 2000; McMahon & Puett, 1999; Mercy, 1999; Prentky & Burgess, 2000), underscore the very *public*, and by extension policy-oriented, nature of the problem. In speaking specifically about aftercare, English et al. (1997) stated that, "No matter how good the design and implementation of sexual offender–specific containment practices, these cannot function at peak effectiveness without the support of informed, clear, and consistent public policies" (p. 6). As noted previously, sophisticated models have been developed that address many serious "hazards" that potentially have an impact, in a nondiscriminating fashion, on large segments of society. Public health models are designed to manage, contain, and reduce these potential hazards. Sexual abuse, in all of its myriad manifestations, clearly represents a public health hazard that directly effects the lives of a substantial proportion of the most vulnerable members of our society, women and children. As the Honorable Charles Gill (1992) observed, "The fundamental documents that bestowed the blessings of liberty on our founding fathers excluded slaves, children, and women" (p. 4). Similarly, as Prentky and Burgess (2000) commented, "The bequeathing of unalienable rights to other than adult white males comes at an agonizingly unhurried pace. One of the tragic consequences of this legacy is the relative absence of rights to sexual autonomy for women and children" (p. 243).

In sum, public health hazards, such as sexual abuse, pose significant risks to health and safety. Public health models that target specific hazards are designed to attenuate the associated risks. The foci of the model are typically risk-relevant interventions and risk management. The conditions that we face with sexual abuse fall precisely into this framework. As Mercy and O'Carroll (1988) noted 15 years ago, "Injury resulting from interpersonal violence is now recognized as an important public health problem" (p. 285). Sexual abuse clearly qualifies as *injury* resulting from *interpersonal* violence. Although the criminal model may be more viscerally satisfying, and thus have greater appeal, the public health model is far more likely to reduce the magnitude of the problem.

ACKNOWLEDGMENT

The author gratefully acknowledges the assistance of Jackie Diamond, Debbie Cavanaugh, and Jeff Egge with literature reviews and manuscript preparation.

REFERENCES

BARBAREE, H.E. (1997). Evaluating treatment efficacy with sexual offenders: The insensitivity of recidivism studies to treatment effects. *Sexual Abuse: A Journal of Research and Treatment, 9,* 111–128.

BECKER, J.V. (2000). Editorial. *Sexual Abuse: A Journal of Research and Treatment, 12*, 1.

BURTON, D. (2000). Were adolescent sexual offenders children with sexual behavior problems? *Sexual Abuse: A Journal of Research and* Treatment, *12*(1), 112–141.

CORTONI, F. & MARSHALL, W.L. (2001). Sex as a coping strategy and its relationship to juvenile sexual history and intimacy in sexual offenders. *Sexual Abuse: A Journal of Research and Treatment, 13*, 27–43.

DAWES, R.M., FAUST, D. & MEEHL, P.E. (1989). Clinical versus actuarial judgment. *Science, 243*, 1668–1674.

DAWES, R.M., FAUST, D. & MEEHL, P.E. (1993). Statistical prediction versus clinical prediction: Improving what works. In G. Keren & C. Lewis (Eds.), *A handbook for data analysis in the behavioral sciences: Methodological issues* (pp. 351–367). Hillsdale, NJ: Erlbaum.

DE BELLIS, M.D., KESHAVAN, M.S., CLARK, D.B., CASEY, B.J., GIEDD, J.N., et al. (1999). Developmental traumatology part II: Brain development. *Biological Psychiatry, 45*, 1271–1284.

DVOSKIN, J.A. & HELIBRUN, K. (2001). Risk assessment and release decision making: Toward resolving the great debate. *Journal of American Academy of Psychiatry and Law, 29*, 6–10.

ENGLISH, K., S. PULLEN & L. JONES (Eds.). (1996). *Managing adult sex offenders: A containment approach.* Lexington, KY: American Probation and Parole Association.

ENGLISH, K., PULLEN, S. & JONES, L. (1997). *Managing adult sex offenders in the community: A containment approach. Research in Brief.* Washington, DC: National Institute of Justice, U.S. Department of Justice.

FINKELHOR, D., ARAJI, S., BARON, L., BROWNE, A., PETERS, S. D. & WYATT, G.E. (1986). *A sourcebook on child sexual abuse.* Beverly Hill, CA: Sage.

FITCH, W.L. (1998). Sex offender commitment in the United States. *The Journal of Forensic Psychiatry, 9*, 237–240.

GARLAND, R.J. & DOUGHER, M.J. (1990). The abused-abuser hypothesis of child sexual abuse: A critical review of theory and research. In J.R. Feierman (Ed.), *Pedophilia: Biosocial dimensions* (pp. 488–509). New York: Springer-Verlag.

GENERAL ACCOUNTING OFFICE. (1996). *Sex offender treatment.* Report to The Chairman, Subcommittee on Crime, Committee on the Judiciary, U.S. House of Representatives. Washington, DC: General Accounting Office.

GILL, C.D. (1992). Essay on the status of the American child, 2000 AD: Chattel or constitutionally protected child-citizen? In A.W. Burgess (Ed.), *Child trauma I: Issues & research* (pp. 3–48). New York: Garland Publishing.

GLEICK, J. (1988). *Chaos: Making a new science.* New York: Penguin Press.

GROVE W.M. & MEEHL, P. (1996). Comparative efficacy of informal (subjective, impressionistic) and formal (mechanical, algorithmic) prediction procedures: The clinical-statistical controversy. *Psychology, Public Policy, and Law, 2*, 293–323.

GROVE, W.M., ZALD, D.H., LEBOW, B.S., SNITZ, B.E. & NELSON, C. (2000). Clinical versus mechanical prediction: A meta-analysis. *Psychological Assessment, 12*, 19–30.

HALL, G.C.N. (1995). Sexual offender recidivism revisited: A meta-analysis of recent treatment studies. *Journal of Consulting and Clinical Psychology, 63*, 802–809.

HANSON, R.K., GORDON, A., HARRIS, A.J.R., MARQUES, J.K., MURPHY, W., et al. (2002). First report of the collaborative outcome data project on the effectiveness of psychological treatment for sex offenders. *Sexual Abuse: A Journal of Research and Treatment, 14*, 169–194.

HEILBRUN, K., NEZU, C.M., KEENEY, M., CHUNG, S. & WASSERMAN, A.L. (1998). Sexual offending: Linking assessment, intervention, and decision-making. *Psychology, Public Policy, and Law, 4*, 138–174.

JANUS, E.S. (1996). Preventing sexual violence: Setting principled constitutional boundaries on sex offender commitments. *Indiana Law Journal, 72*(1), 157–213.

JANUS, E.S. (1997). Sex offender commitments: Debunking the official narrative and revealing the Rules-in-Use. *Stanford Law & Policy Review, 8*, 71–102.

KAFKA, M.P. (1997). Hypersexual desire in males: An operational definition and clinical implications for males with paraphilias and paraphilia-related disorders. *Archives of Sexual Behavior, 26*, 505–526.

KAUFMAN, J. & ZIGLER, E. (1987). Do abused children become abusive parents? *American Journal of Orthopsychiatry, 57*, 186–192.

KEMPE, R.S. & KEMPE, C.H. (1984). *The common secret: Sexual abuse of children and perpetrators.* New York: Freeman.

KNIGHT, R.A. & PRENTKY, R.A. (1993). Exploring characteristics for classifying juvenile sex offenders. In H.E. Barbaree, W.L. Marshall & S. M. Hudson (Eds.), *The juvenile sex offender* (pp. 45–83). New York: Guilford Press.

KNIGHT, R.A. & SIMS-KNIGHT, J.E. (2003). The developmental antecedents of sexual coercion against women: Testing alternative hypotheses with structural equation modeling. In R.A. Prentky, E.S. Janus & M.C. Seto (Eds.), *Sexually coercive behavior: Understanding and management.* New York: Annals of the New York Academy of Sciences. This volume.

KNIGHT, R.A. & SIMS-KNIGHT, J.E. (in press). The developmental antecedents of sexual coercion against women in adolescents. In R. Geffner & K. Franey s(Eds.), *Sex offenders: Assessment and treatment.* New York: Haworth Press.

LA FOND, J.Q. (1998). The costs of enacting a sexual predator law. *Psychology, Public Policy, and Law, 4*, 468–504.

LANYON, R.I. (1986). Theory and treatment in child molestation. *Journal of Consulting and Clinical Psychology, 54*, 176–182.

LAWS, D.R., HUDSON, S.M. & WARD, A. (Eds.). (2000). *Remaking relapse prevention with sex offenders: A sourcebook.* Thousand Oaks, CA: Sage Publishers.

LIEB, R. & MATSON, S. (1998). *Sexual predator commitment laws in the United States: 1998 update.* Olympia, WA: Washington State Institute for Public Policy.

LITWAK, T.R. (2001). Actuarial versus clinical assessments of dangerousness. *Psychology, Public Policy, and Law, 7*, 409–443.

MALAMUTH, N.M. (2003). Criminal and noncriminal sexual aggressors: Integrating psychopathy in a hierarchical-mediational confluence model. In R.A. Prentky, E.S. Janus & M.C. Seto (Eds.), *Sexually coercive behavior: Understanding and management.* New York: Annals of the New York Academy of Sciences. This volume.

MALAMUTH, N.M. (1998). An evolutionary-based model integrating research on the characteristics of sexually coercive men. In J.G. Adair, D. Belanger & K.L. Dion (Eds.), *Advances in psychological science: Social, personal, and cultural aspects.* (Vol. 1). Hove, England: Psychology Press.

MALAMUTH, N.M., HEAVEY, C. & LINZ, D. (1993). Predicting men's antisocial behavior against women: The interaction model of sexual aggression. In G.N. Hall, R. Hirschman, J. Graham & M. Zaragoza (Eds.), *Sexual aggression: Issues in etiology, assessment and treatment* (pp. 63–97). Washington, DC: Hemisphere Publishing Corp.

MARQUES, J.K. & DAY, D.M. (1998). *Sex offender treatment evaluation project: Progress report (May, 1998).* Sacramento, CA: California Department of Mental Health.

MARQUES, J.K., NELSON, C., ALARCON, J.-M. & DAY, D.M. (2000). Preventing relapse in sex offenders: What we have learned from SOTEP's experimental treatment program. In D.R. Laws, S.M. Hudson & T. Ward (Eds.), *Remaking relapse prevention with sex offenders: A sourcebook.* Thousand Oaks, CA: Sage.

MARSHALL, W.L. (1993). The role of attachments, intimacy, and loneliness in the etiology and maintenance of sexual offending. *Sexual and Marital Therapy, 8*, 109–121.

MARSHALL, W.L., HUDSON, S.M. & HODKINSON, S.M. (1993). The importance of attachment bonds in the development of juvenile sex offending. In H.E. Barbaree, W.L. Marshall & S.M. Hudson (Eds.), *The juvenile sex offender* (pp. 164–181). New York: Guilford Press.

MARSHALL, W.L., SERRAN, G.A. & CORTONI, F.A. (2000). Childhood attachments, sexual abuse, and their relationship to adult coping in child molesters. *Sexual Abuse: A Journal of Research and Treatment, 12*(1), 17–26.

MCMAHON, P.M. (2000). The public health approach to the prevention of sexual violence. *Sexual Abuse: A Journal of Research and Treatment, 12*(1), 27–36.

MCMAHON, P.M. & PUETT, R.C. (1999). Child sexual abuse as a public health issue: Recommendations of the expert panel. *Sexual Abuse: A Journal of Research and Treatment, 11*(4), 257–266.

MEEHL, P.E. (1998). The power of quantitative thinking. Presentation upon receiving the Cattell Award by the American Psychological Society. Meehl, P.E. & Rosen, A. (1955). Antecedent probability and the efficiency of psychometric signs, patterns, or cutting scores. *Psychological Bulletin, 52*, 194–216.

MERCY, J.A. (1999). Having new eyes: Viewing child sexual abuse as a public health problem. *Sexual Abuse: A Journal of Research and Treatment, 11*(4), 317–325.

MERCY, J.A. & O'CARROLL, P.W. (1988). New directions in violence prediction: The public health arena. *Violence and Victims, 3*, 285–301.

MONAHAN, J. & STEADMAN, H.J., (1996). Violent storms and violent people. *American Psychologist, 51*, 931–938.

MONAHAN, J., STEADMAN, H., SILVER, E., APPLEBAUM, A., ROBBINS, et al. (2001). *Rethinking risk assessment: The MacArthur study of mental disorder and violence.* New York: Oxford University Press.

PERRY, B.D., POLLARD, R.A., BLAKLEY, T.L., BAKER, W.L. & VIGILANTE, D. (1995). Childhood trauma, the neurobiology of adaptation, and "use-dependent" development of the brain: How "states" become "traits." *Infant Mental Health Journal, 16*(4), 271–291.

PITHERS, W.D., MARQUES, J.K., GIBAT, C.C. & MARLATT, G.A. (1983). Relapse prevention with sexual aggressives: A self-control model of treatment and maintenance of change. In J.G. Greer & I.R.Stuart (Eds.), *The sexual aggressor: Current perspectives on treatment.* New York: Van Nostrand Reinhold.

PRENTKY, R.A. (1999). Child sexual molestation. In V.B. Van Hasselt & M. Hersen (Eds.), *Handbook of psychological approaches with violent offenders* (pp. 267–300). New York: Kluwer Academic/Plenum Publishers.

PRENTKY, R.A. (2003). Remediation of coercive sexual behavior. In B.K. Schwartz (Ed.), *Handbook of correctional psychology.* Kingston, N.J.: Civic Research Institute, Inc.

PRENTKY, R.A. & BURGESS, A.W. (2000). *Forensic management of sexual offenders.* New York: Kluwer Academic/Plenum Publishers.

PRENTKY, R.A. & KNIGHT, R.A. (1991). Identifying critical dimensions for discriminating among rapists. *Journal of Consulting and Clinical Psychology, 59*, 643–661.

PRENTKY, R.A. & KNIGHT, R.A. (1993). Age of onset of sexual assault: Criminal and life history correlates. In G.C.N. Hall, R. Hirschman, J.R. Graham & M.S. Zaragoza (Eds.), *Sexual aggression: Issues in etiology, assessment, and treatment* (pp. 43–62). Washington, DC: Taylor & Francis.

PRENTKY, R.A., KNIGHT, R.A., SIMS-KNIGHT, J.E., STRAUS, H., ROKOUS, F. & CERCE, D. (1989). Developmental antecedents of sexual aggression. *Development and Psychopathology, 1*, 153–169.

PRENTKY, R.A., LEE, A.F.S., KNIGHT, R.A. & CERCE, D. (1997). Recidivism rates among child molesters and rapists: A methodological analysis. *Law and Human Behavior, 21*, 635–659.

PRESIDENTIAL/CONGRESSIONAL COMMISSION ON RISK ASSESSMENT AND RISK MANAGEMENT. (1997). *Framework for Environmental Health Risk Management.* Final Report, Vol. 1. Washington, DC: U.S. Government Printing Office.

PRESIDENTIAL/CONGRESSIONAL COMMISSION ON RISK ASSESSMENT AND RISK MANAGEMENT. (1997). *Risk Assessment and Risk Management in Regulatory Decision-Making.* Final Report, Vol. 2. Washington, DC: U.S. Government Printing Office.

ROGERS, C.M. & TERRY, T. (1984). Clinical interventions with boy victims of sexual abuse. In I. Stuart & J. Greer (Eds.), *Victims of sexual aggression* (pp. 91–104). New York: Van Nostrand Reinhold.

SMALLBONE, S.W. & DADDS, M.R. (2000). Attachment and coercive sexual behavior. *Sexual Abuse: A Journal of Research and Treatment, 12*(1), 3–15.

SPITZ, R.A. & WOLF, K.M. (1946). Anaclitic depression: An inquiry into the genesis of psychiatric conditions in early childhood. II. *Psychoanalytic Study of the Child, 2*, 313–342.

SWETS, J.A., DAWES, R.M. & MONAHAN, J. (2000). Psychological science can improve diagnostic decisions. *Psychological Science, 1*, 1–26.

TEICHER, M.H. (2000). Wounds that time won't heal: The neurobiology of child abuse. *Cerebrum, 2*(4), 50–67.

TEICHER, M.H. (March, 2002). Scars that won't heal: The neurobiology of child abuse. *Scientific American*, 68–75.
WARD, T., HUDSON, S.M. & MCCORMACK, J. (1997). Attachment style, intimacy deficits, and sexual offending. In B. K. Schwartz & H.R. Cellini (Eds.), *The sex offender: New insights, treatment innovations, and legal developments* (pp. 2.1–2.11). Kingston, NJ: Civic Research Institute.

APPENDIX

Journals Surveyed	Content Areas Coded
Archives of Sexual Behavior	Assessment (general)
Criminal Justice and Behavior	Attitudes
International Journal of Offender Therapy	Bio/neuropsych/hormonal
Journal of Interpersonal Violence	Classification
Journal of Abnormal Psychology	Clinical and descriptive
Journal of Consulting and Clinical Psychology	Date rape
Journal of Offender Rehabilitation	Etiology
Law and Human Behavior	Incidence
Sexual Addiction and Compulsivity	Prediction
Sexual Abuse: A Journal of Research and Treatment	Prevention
Violence and Victims	Pornography
	PPG/sexual arousal
	Recidivism
	Risk assessment (general)
	Risk assessment (ARA)
	Treatment—clinical
	Treatment—drugs
	Treatment—empirical
	Victim impact

Criminal and Noncriminal Sexual Aggressors

Integrating Psychopathy in a Hierarchical-Mediational Confluence Model

NEIL M. MALAMUTH

University of California, Los Angeles, Los Angeles, California 90095-1538

ABSTRACT: In contrast to widely held beliefs, I suggest that research conducted with either criminal or noncriminal samples of sexually aggressive men actually reveals many similar characteristics shared by both groups. The Hierarchical-Mediational Confluence (HMC) model is presented here to integrate these findings. As relatively distal risk factors, it includes personality and behavioral characteristics associated with psychopaths and predictive of antisocial behavior generally. As more proximate risk factors, it includes personality and behavioral characteristics specifically associated with sexual aggression, such as attitudes condoning sexual aggression, dominance for sexual arousal, and heavy pornography consumption. In addition, the model predicts that the interactive combination of the various risk factors results in higher sexual aggression than expected by the additive combination of these risk factors, a prediction similar to the distinction between "primary" and "secondary" psychopaths. A series of studies supporting the HMC model is presented. Finally, some differences between criminal and noncriminal sexual aggressors are also noted. In particular, criminal sexual aggressors have often committed various other antisocial acts in addition to sexual aggression. In contrast, noncriminals primarily reveal only some elevation in personality characteristics potentiating such nonsexual antisocial behaviors, but report having committed only sexual aggression.

KEYWORDS: sexually aggressive criminals; noncriminal sexual aggressors; structural equation modeling; Confluence Model; psychopathy

INTRODUCTION AND OVERVIEW

Identifying the key factors[a] that distinguish male sexual aggressors from nonsexual aggressors is likely to elucidate the causes of such aggression. In pursuit of this goal, research has focused on two groups of sexual aggressors and compared their characteristics to those of nonaggressors. The first group were identified as sexual aggressors by the judicial system and incarcerated for their crimes. We will refer to

Address for correspondence: Neil Malamuth, Communication Studies, 334 Kinsey Hall, UCLA, Los Angeles, CA 90095-1538. Voice: 310-206-8868; fax:310-206-8901.

nmalamut@ucla.edu

[a]The term *factors* is used here to encompass such aspects as personality traits, developmental experiences, and behavioral characteristics that have been identified as correlated among men with increased risk for committing sexually aggressive acts.

Ann. N.Y. Acad. Sci. 989: 33–58 (2003). © 2003 New York Academy of Sciences.

this group as "sexually aggressive criminals." The second group are men who self-reported on research questionnaires that they had committed acts of sexual aggressors; they will therefore be referred to herein as "noncriminal sexual aggressors."

Are the characteristics of these two types of sexual aggressors similar or different? One might expect considerable differences since noncriminals and criminals are likely to differ in many other respects, such as socioeconomic levels, intelligence and educational attainment, and likelihood of committing other antisocial acts. If, despite these differences, the research reveals similar characteristics in both groups of sexual aggressors, it would add considerable confidence in the validity of those factors as important in the etiology of sexual aggression.

Research conducted with criminals found that such men were relatively high in characteristics such as impulsivity and callousness, traits often encompassed within the label of psychopathy. Initially, studies conducted with noncriminals sought to find similar characteristics in these self-identified sexual aggressors as were found with criminal sexual aggressors. Generally, researchers concluded that these psychopathic traits were not defining characteristics of noncriminal sexual aggressors, but that other characteristics, such as attitudes accepting of sexual aggression, were the important discriminators between sexual aggressors and nonaggressors within the noncriminal population. Believing, then, that criminal and noncriminal sexual aggressors exhibited different traits, researchers, in subsequent studies, focused primarily on only one or the other of these populations.

The following examination of important findings from studies of criminal or noncriminal sexual aggressors reveals that far from being dissimilar, there are actually many remarkably similar characteristics shared by both groups of sexual aggressors. Furthermore, it will be shown that a model we have labeled the "hierarchical-mediational" Confluence (HMC)[b] model provides an effective integration of the findings from studies of both criminal and noncriminal samples. This model yields more fruitful prediction because it incorporates both general hostile/antisocial personality characteristics associated with psychopathy in conjunction with those characteristics more specifically associated with sexual aggression. A series of studies supporting the utility of this model are presented here. The HMC model's tailored approach to the prediction of sexual aggression is compared not only to psychopathy research but also to the "broad band" Five-Factor Model of personality.

STUDIES OF CRIMINAL SEXUAL AGGRESSORS

Studies seeking to identify the attributes of criminal sexual aggressors (e.g., Prentky & Knight, 1991) have often emphasized characteristics associated with antisocial criminals generally, such as "lifestyle impulsivity" (Prentky, Knight, Lee & Cerce, 1995). In keeping with this emphasis, Hare, Clark, Grann, and Thorton (2000) argued that construct of psychopathy may be useful for the study of sexual aggressors as well as other criminals.

Cleckley (1941) described psychopaths as individuals who appeared sane and charming but were actually disturbed, particularly lacking remorse, shame, and sin-

---

[b]This model will interchangeably be referred to as either HMC or the Confluence Model.

cerity. He referred to them as wearing "masks of sanity." Although there have been various measures of psychopathy used, perhaps the most widely used one was developed by Hare (1991). Although Hare (1991) based some of his ideas on Cleckley's earlier writings, he expanded considerably the characteristics involved within this construct to emphasize individuals who are impulsive and frequently engage in exploitative, antisocial acts. He developed a 20-item scale entitled the Psychopathy Checklist-Revised (PCL-R) to assess prototypical characteristics of psychopathy (Hare, 1991). Hare et al. (2000) describe psychopathy as a personality disorder that includes three major components: the interpersonal, affective, and behavioral/lifestyle components. In describing the characteristics measured by this scale, Hare et al. (2000) note that

> on the interpersonal level, individuals with this disorder typically present as grandiose, arrogant, callous, dominant superficial, deceptive and manipulative. Affectively, they are short-tempered, unable to form strong emotional bonds with others, and lacking in empathy, guilt, remorse, or deep-seated emotions. These interpersonal and affective features are associated with a socially deviant lifestyle that includes irresponsible and impulsive behavior, and a tendency to ignore or violate social conventions and morals. (p. 626)

In empirical assessments using factor analyses, this scale has been shown to largely yield two rather than three majors factors, with the first including the interpersonal and affective items, whereas the second the lifestyle ones (see Hare et al., 2000, for a summary). In addition there are a few items that do not load on either of the factors. The detailed elements of this scale will be described later in this chapter when the model underlying psycohpathy research is compared to the HMC model.

Harpur, Hart, and Hare (2002) contend that "psychopathy as assessed by the PCL is perhaps the most reliable and well-validated diagnostic category in the field of personality disorders" (p. 319). With regard to its predictive utility, Hare et al. (2000) summarize a wide range of findings across many studies in various countries, indicating that a large number of those who commit antisocial behaviors, including sexual aggression, show elevated scores on the PCL scale. He notes that research indicates that in a recent study by Porter et al. (2000), it was found that 35.9% of rapists and 64% of rapists/child molesters scored high (30 or above) on the PCL-R scale of psychopathy. Further, Hare et al. emphasized that "the joint presence" of psychopathy and deviant sexual arousal appears to particularly characterize adult and adolescent sex offenders. He referred to a study by Rice and Harris (1997) who found that sexual reoffending was predicted by the interaction of high PCL-R scores and high sexual arousal to rape (as indicated by penile tumescence). As described below, this finding fits exceptionally well with the predictions of the HMC model.

STUDIES OF NONCRIMINAL SEXUAL AGGRESSORS

With awareness that many sexual aggressors escape identification by the criminal system, researchers attempted to identify their characteristics among noncriminal populations. Whereas criminal samples often included aggressors against strangers, noncriminal samples more typically included aggressors against acquaintances. Some of the earliest empirical work on the characteristics of noncriminal sexual aggressors assessed psychopathic traits such as impulsivity, callousness, and hostility in light of findings that these are common among criminal aggressors. Interestingly, these studies compared the discriminant ability of measures of psychopathy to measures hypothesized to be more specific to sexual aggression, such as attitudes legitimizing such aggression. Some of these studies found support only for the latter type of measure as a correlate of sexual aggression. For example, Koss, Leonard, Beezley, and Oros (1985) conducted a discriminant analysis (a variant of regression analysis) that included various types of measures, including Scale 4 of the MMPI (Minnesota Multiphasic Personality Inventory), which assesses psychopathic deviance. Although they found that adherence to rape-supportive attitudes differentiated between sexual aggressors and nonaggressors, they also found that "measures of psychopathy did not contribute to the differentiation of self-reported forms of sexually aggressive behavior in this study. The lack of differentiation is inconsistent with published literature on incarcerated rapists" (pp. 989–990).

This conclusion that men who aggress against complete strangers (typically criminal samples) differ from those who aggress against acquaintances (typically noncriminals) led to the emergence of largely independent research literatures, which appeared to yield substantially different profiles of sexual aggressors. The prevailing view has been that the attributes associated with sexual aggressors in criminals and noncriminals differ fundamentally.

Nevertheless, the seeds for the integrative approach advocated in the present chapter (that includes both the characteristics associated with psychopathy and those more specific to predicting sexual aggression) can be found in some of the early studies with noncriminal samples. One of these studies will be described in some detail because it yielded findings that are quite informative to the present analysis: Rapaport and Burkhart (1984) administered a questionnaire to 201 undergraduate males that included measures designed to assess a lack of social conscience and irresponsibility. They chose these instruments "… based on previous findings that convicted sex offenders received elevated scores on measures of psychopathic/antisocial characteristics" (p. 218). Specifically, the measures used were the Responsibility, Socialization, and Empathy scales from the California Psychology Inventory (CPI, Gough, 1957). Similar to the Koss et al. (1985) study mentioned above, Rapaport and Burkhart also included various scales measuring characteristics with different degrees of specific relevance to sexual aggression. These consisted of two types of measures: (1) those assessing general sex role beliefs, attitudes toward women, and sexual attitudes, and (2) those measuring attitudes about male antagonism and violence toward women. As part of this assessment, the authors included a scale designed to measure men's endorsement of the use of force on the part of the male to obtain sexual acts. The dependent measure consisted of a self-reported scale of the extent to which the man had used various coercive tactics to engage in sexual acts.

The data were analyzed by correlational and regression analyses. Of the psychopathic personality measures, the Responsibility and Socialization, but not the Empathy, scales significantly correlated with coercive sexuality. Of the attitudinal measures, there was no relationship between the general sex role attitudinal measures and coercive sexuality. In contrast, the scales measuring attitudes about male antagonism and sexual violence did consistently relate to coercive sexuality. The researchers further found that an equation that combined both the psychopathic personality and the attitude measures did significantly relate to sexual aggression, although the form in which the data are presented limits the reader's ability to evaluate the independent and/or interactive contribution of each measure. Similar findings have been recently reported by Hersh and Gray-Little (1998). However, when these latter investigators compared the ability of attitude measures alone to discriminate between sexual aggressors and nonaggressors versus the discriminative ability of attitudes plus psychopathic personality characteristics, they found no greater discriminative ability with the addition of the psychopathy measures. Taken together, these studies present a somewhat ambiguous picture, but they do suggest that it may be useful to examine the role of both general antisocial characteristics (e.g., psychopathic personality characteristics) and factors more specific to sexual aggression, such as measures of attitudes endorsing the use of sexual coercion. This is, in fact, a central feature of the HMC model.

THE CONFLUENCE MODEL OF THE CHARACTERISTICS OF SEXUAL AGGRESSORS

Background to Development of Model

The development of the HMC model began with the research of Malamuth (1986) who studied a noncriminal sample of men in order to develop a coherent model capable of integrating the attributes of sexual aggressors. Malamuth's study was conducted completely independently of and without awareness of Hare's (1991) psychopathy scale and related research. It did, however, include one personality measure of the type of risk factor typically used to assess general antisocial tendencies, namely Psychoticism. In contrast, the other risk variables chosen for Malamuth's study were selected because they had been hypothesized to or shown to be specifically discriminative of sexual aggressors. These included sexual arousal to

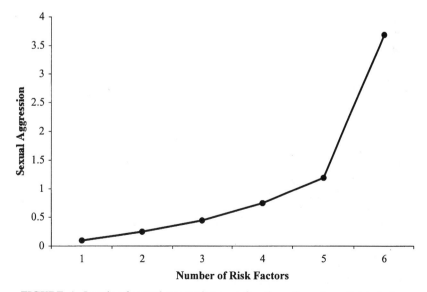

FIGURE 1. Levels of sexual aggression as a function of number of risk factors on which the men scored relatively high. (Adapted from Malamuth, 1986.)

rape (as revealed in penile tumescence assessment), callous attitudes about violence against women, dominance as a motive for sex, hostility toward women, and early sexual experience.

As revealed in simple correlations, all of these attributes discriminated between sexual aggressors and nonaggressors, except that the correlation with psychoticism only approached statistical significance. Most importantly, it was found that although these variables individually related to aggressive sexual behavior, a regression equation that included the interactive combination of all these variables was much better in predicting sexual aggression than each of the risk variables alone or even than the additive combination of all of the risk variables. This finding is illustrated in FIGURE 1, which shows the average level of sexual aggression as a function of the number of risk factors on which the man scored relatively high. As indicated in the relatively steep rise between having four and five of the risk factors (see FIG. 1), the effect is clearly more than a simple additive one. This type of effect has been continuously replicated in the series of studies described below.

These findings were the basis for the more developed version of the Confluence Model, emphasizing the importance of the interactive confluence of the relevant risk factors and the inclusion in a "hierarchical-mediational" of both general antisocial characteristics and related factors more specific and proximate to sexual aggression.

Using Structural Equation Modeling

Subsequent studies on the Confluence Model used some variant of "causal" or "structural equation" statistical modeling (Kaplan, 2000). Before proceeding to describe key follow-up Confluence Model research, it is useful to summarize this well-established statistical modeling approach because it is integrally related to the structure of the HMC model. In simple terms, structural equation modeling combines aspects of both "factor analysis" and "path analysis." It enables several types of analyses. First, the factor analytic part enables organizing several facets of a broader factor within a hierarchical framework. For example, the "shared variance" of facets such as grandiosity, impulsivity, short-tempered, and low empathy may be modeled within a broader construct that might be labeled "general antisocial personality characteristics," "psychopathy," or "general hostile personality." Statistical tests are included that indicate the degree to which the level of organization used is appropriate or not. Second, the path analytic part enables the relationship among several such hierarchically organized broader constructs to be represented statistically. At the same time, it is feasible to represent a unique variance from a facet to another factor (although this is done relatively infrequently). Third, mediation and moderation (Barron & Kenny, 1986) effects among factors and between factors and the outcome (e.g., sexual aggression) may be fully considered.

Such possible interrelationships have generally not been tested in other research on the characteristics of sexual aggressors in criminal and noncriminal populations. As noted above, some of the early research seeking to identify the characteristics of noncriminal sexual aggressors first considered general antisocial and/or psychopathic characteristics but has largely moved away from including such characteristics in favor of focusing on characteristics more specific to sexual aggression (e.g., attitudes justifying sexual aggression). This was partly due to use of the most common form of regression analysis, which includes the assessment of "main effects" only without explicitly testing interaction and/or indirect effects. The typical outcome was that the more specific predictor (e.g., attitude legitimizing sexual aggression) significantly entered the equation but not the more general psychopathic predictor. This often led the investigators to conclude that the more specific predictor was of primary importance and that the more general psychopathic predictor was not, since it had "dropped out" once control for overlap between the two types of predictors had been accomplished by using the regression analyses.

Such conclusions based on regression analyses can easily lead to potential errors, as illustrated in the following statistical example given by Fergusson and Howood (1988):

> Let us assume that we are concerned to study the relationships between three variables: annual rainfall, annual pasture growth and the live weight of sheep at the point of slaughter. The causal model that links these three variables is intuitively clear: Rainfall → Pasture growth → Sheep weight. Next let us assume that...an investigator elects to examine these relationships by the application of a multiple regression equation in which sheep weight is regressed upon pasture growth and rainfall. The results of this analysis are predictable and will show that pasture growth is a significant predictor of sheep weight but rainfall is not. ...The next step is likely to be the conclusion that while pasture growth is an important causal factor, rainfall is not." (p. 331)

Similar specious conclusions may have been reached in the research on the characteristics of sexual aggressors. By analogy, general psychopathic characteristics may be equivalent to the "rainfall," in the above example and more specific characteristics, such as attitudes legitimizing sexual aggression, may be the "pasture growth." In a regression analysis wherein only direct effects are assessed, attitudes would be found to be the only significant predictor of sexual aggression. Similarly, an analysis that compared the discriminant ability of attitudes alone versus attitudes plus psychopathic characteristics may show the same discriminative success (e.g., Hersh & Gray-Little, 1998), potentially leading to the specious conclusion that psychopathic characteristics are not important. In fact, as the above analogy suggests, general "psychopathic" characteristics may substantially affect the development of callous attitudes toward violence against women via potential processes discussed later in this chapter. Equally important, research with criminal samples that included only assessment of general psychopathic characteristics and did not include measures of characteristics potentially more proximate to sexual aggression (e.g., attitudes justifying sexual coercion) may have also missed a critical aspect of a comprehensive model of the characteristics of sexual aggressors.

In the series of studies described here, we have developed the HMC model, which enables avoidance of the type of specious conclusions exemplified above. Our model is "hierarchical," in that certain higher-order constructs or factors that encompass several components or facets are included at the level designed to best encompass the variance shared by the components in their overlap and their ability to predict the outcome of sexual aggression. This has been accomplished via the modeling of "latent" constructs and/or via the creation of composites combining individual scales or measures. It is "mediational" in that some constructs or factors have proximate or direct paths into the sexual aggression outcome (e.g., components of the hostile masculinity constellation), whereas others relate to the outcome only via mediation by the more proximate factors. We will now describe some of the other key studies that led to the development of this model and elaborate here upon some key issues not discussed in previous publications.

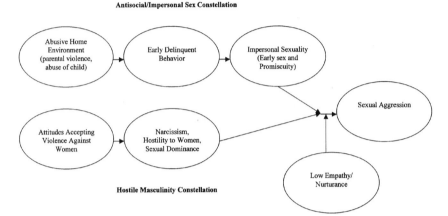

FIGURE 2. The two major constellations of factors comprising the Confluence Model as reported by Malamuth et al. (1991). (Adapted from Malamuth et al., 1991).

Development of Key Constellations

Using structural equation modeling, Malamuth, Sackloskie, Koss, and Tanaka (1991) concluded that the attributes of sexual aggressors (including the key ones studied by Malamuth, 1986) actually coalesce into two major constellations rather than being a set of unrelated independent variables. The first constellation included callous, manipulative attitudes toward women; grandiose, narcissistic personality characteristics; hostility toward women; and dominance as a motive for sex. This constellation of attributes was labeled the Hostile Masculinity path. It was also found to be associated with social isolation. The second constellation included early experiences of abusive/conflictual home environments, general antisocial tendencies reflected in adolescent delinquency, and relatively high levels of promiscuous/impersonal sex. It was labeled the Sexual Promiscuity/Impersonal Sex path (see FIG. 2). It is noteworthy that the characteristics that constitute the Hostile Masculinity path are personality traits, whereas those of the Impersonal Sex path are experiential/behavioral ones (i.e., early experience of abuse, engaging in early antisocial and sexual behavior and sexually promiscuous behavior).

In keeping with Malamuth (1986), the data of Malamuth et al. (1991) showed that the interaction of the two constellations of characteristics predicted sexual aggression most successfully. (They also found that in contrast to sexual aggression, nonsexual aggression is best predicted by the characteristics of the Hostile Masculinity path alone.) Malamuth et al. formally labeled the model integrating these constellations of characteristics the "Confluence Model," to emphasize that the interactive confluence of the set of characteristics included in both of these two constellations best discriminated between sexual aggressors and nonaggressors.

Inclusion of General Hostile Personality Characteristics

The next key study in this line of research on the Confluence Model was a longitudinal study by Malamuth, Linz, Heavey, Barnes, and Acker (1995). Three general hypotheses were empirically tested in this research:

(1) The same two-path "causal structure" would be useful not only for cross-sectional "prediction" but also for the longitudinal prediction of sexual aggression, above and beyond the prediction achieved by earlier sexual aggression alone.

(2) A particular subset of the same characteristics used to predict sexual aggression would also predict general dysfunction and violence in relationships with women.

(3) In keeping with the "hierarchical-mediation" approach, certain general personality and behavioral characteristics would only indirectly contribute to sexual aggression via mediation by more specific factors.

This study followed up approximately 150 men for whom we had collected data from approximately ten years earlier. All three hypotheses were supported, but I will elaborate here only on the third one. These investigators incorporated in their assessment of the men's characteristics several additional scales designed to measure general "hostile" personality characteristics not previously assessed in this line of research. The hierarchical approach emphasized here predicts that these relatively general characteristics would indirectly contribute to sexual aggression via mediation by some of the more specific factors incorporated within the Confluence Model. A particularly important general construct to consider here was labeled Proneness to General Hostility. It was a composite of four reliable and validated scales, each with multiple items (ranging from 16 to 40). More detailed descriptions of these scales are presented in Malamuth et al. (1995). Two of these scales measured impulsive tendencies. The first was the Irritability scale, assessing individual differences in reacting impulsivity or rudely to slight provocations or disagreements (characteristics likely to lead to impulsive aggression). A second related measure was the Impulsivity scale shown previously to affect various types of antisocial behavior in many populations and settings. The other two scales measured intensity of emotional reactions, with particular focus on "emotional dyscontrol." One of these was the Emotional Susceptibility scale, measuring feelings of discomfort, inadequacy, and vulnerability. The other was the Affective Intensity scale, assessing affective responses to emotion-provoking and threatening life events.

The findings of this research provided support for the HMC model. Specifically, the Proneness to General Hostility composite indirectly predicted sexually aggressive behavior only via mediation by the more proximate predictor of Hostile Masculinity (see FIG. 3).[c] In contrast, nonsexual aggression against women was directly predicted by the Proneness to General Hostility composite. Vega and Malamuth (2003) recently replicated and extended the HMC model's set of findings in another sample of noncriminals and found support for virtually all of the features of the model in FIGURE 3.

---

[c]Similarly, another factor, Sex Role Stress (i.e., the extent to which a person experienced stress when perceived in ways inconsistent with traditional male sex roles) indirectly predicted sexual aggression, again mediated via the Hostile Masculinity construct. Because it is less germane to the perspective presented here, it is not included in the relevant graph.

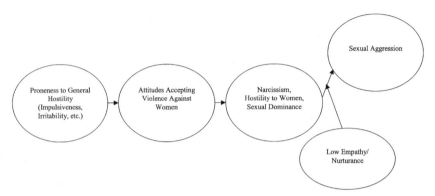

FIGURE 3. The relationship between general hostile/antisocial personality character-istics and ones more specific to sexual aggression, constituting a key aspect of the develop-ment of the hierarchical-mediational version of the Confluence Model. (Adapted from Malamuth et al., 1995).

Inclusion of Nurturance/Empathy as an Attenuator

The factors described heretofore are risk factors increasing the likelihood of sex-ual aggression. The next study pertaining to the development of the HMC model, by Dean and Malamuth (1997), sought, in contrast, to examine the role of empathic, nurturant personality characteristics, hypothesized as attenuators of risk. Therefore, in addition to assessing the risk factors, the investigators measured the broad person-ality dimensions of dominance (egotistical, self-oriented) versus nurturance (other-oriented, empathic). As predicted, Dean and Malamuth (1997) found that such a "self-centered" versus "other-concerned" dimension indeed moderated sexually ag-gressive behavior. These data confirmed that when a man had the risk characteristics included in the Confluence Model but was also high on his compassion and empathy for others, there was only a weak relationship between the risk factors and actual sexually aggressive behavior. When a person was relatively low on their compassion or empathy for others, there was a strong link between the risk factors and actual sex-ually aggressive behavior.

Replications and Extensions of Confluence Model's Findings by Other Investigators

There have been several studies by independent researchers that have successful-ly replicated the findings of the Confluence Model as well as elaborating on certain aspects of the constellations constituting this model. For example, Christopher, Owens, and Stecker (1996) successfully replicated and elaborated on this model with a noncriminal sample. In particular, they assessed more fully an aspect of the Hostile Masculinity dimension, namely the feelings of antagonism, anger, rejection, and hurt vis a vis relations with women. In another study, Wheeler, George, and Dahl (2002) replicated and extended the findings of Dean and Malamuth (1997) using a different measure of the nurturance/empathy dimension. Additional support for the key aspects of the Confluence Model was found in research by Hall, Sue, Narang, and Lilly (2000).

Lim and Howard (2001) replicated the Confluence Model in Singapore and also included measures of such general constructs as Antisociality (i.e., lack of concern about how others react to one's behaviors) and Belligerence (impulsiveness and general antisocial behavior). Taken together, these closely parallel key components of Hare PCL-R Psychopathy scale. The investigators found that Belligerence had only indirect effects on sexual aggression, mediated by more specific factors, such as attitudes supportive of sexual aggression. Similarly, Antisociality exerted indirect effects on both sexual aggression (via sexual promiscuity and attitudes accepting violence against women) and on nonsexual aggression (via belligerence). In contrast, and in keeping with findings of Malamuth et al. (1995), using the similar measure of Proneness to General Hostility, Belligerence had direct effects on nonsexual aggression against women. Similarly, Bourg (2001) used a general antisocial construct composed of Nonconformity, Hypermasculinity, and Aggressiveness. The link between this relatively general construct and sexual aggression was mediated by a "specific construct" that included key aspects of Hostile Masculinity, namely Hostility toward Women, Dominance as a Motive for Sex, and Adversarial Sexual Beliefs. In addition, in a recent meta-analysis, Murnen, Wright, and Kaluzny (2002) found very strong reliability in the correlation across various studies between the various components of hostile masculinity and men's self-reported levels of sexual aggression.

There have also been some successful replications and extensions of the HMC model with criminal samples. Johnson and Knight (2000) studied a sample of 122 juvenile offenders from five treatment centers. They examined the relevance of the Confluence Model with this sample and found that the key elements replicated very well: The investigators concluded that "...the present study does uncover commonalities between the paths leading to sexually coercive behavior in our sample of juvenile offenders and Malamuth et al.'s (1991) sample of college males" (p. 176). Knight and Sims-Knight (in press) conducted a similar analysis in a sample of 275 adult male sexual offenders and found support for a model similar to the Confluence Model. These investigators suggested that there may be a third constellation of characteristics more specific to "callous, unemotional" characteristics. However, in our view the model they presented very closely supports the two-path hierarchical-mediational model we have emphasized since they found that the Callous/Unemotional construct only indirectly affected sexual aggression, via elements of the Hostile Masculinity constellation (specifically, aggressive-sexual fantasy). Yet, I acknowlege that in Malamuth (1998) I had also suggested a similar conceptualization using a third interacting constellation with a person's scores of Dominance/Narcissism versus Nurturance/Empathy. There is clearly a need for further clarification at both the conceptual and empirical levels regarding whether the dimension of nurturance/empathy is best considered as part of the General Proneness to Hostility (or psychopathy) set of characteristics, a separate moderator dimension of such general antisocial characteristics, or a third interacting constellation with the other two constellations encompassed within the Confluence Model.[d]

Confluence Model as a Unifying Framework

The HMC model enables the unification of much research that has investigated portions of this model, though often using other labels for the same or similar constructs. For example, Kosson, Kelly, and White (1997) studied noncriminal men who completed the Socialization scale mentioned above (Gough, 1957), assessing impulsive antisocial behavior. This factor corresponds to the HMC model's Delinquency factor, an aspect of the Impersonal Sex constellation. Kosson et al. also administered the Narcissistic Personality Inventory (Raskin & Hall, 1981), assessing traits that closely correspond to aspects of Hostile Masculinity (e.g., see Malamuth et al., 1993).

In keeping with what we would expect based on the HMC model, Kosson et al. (1997) found that both the Socialization scale and the Narcissistic Personality Inventory as well as their interaction contributed to the prediction of sexual aggression.

Essentially, this was a test of key elements of the HMC model, although the investigators did not specifically refer to this model. We believe that this is illustrative for a great deal of the published work in this area, which may be readily positioned within the HMC framework.

Moreover, by identifying certain key factors of the profile of sexually aggressive men, the HMC model can serve as a useful framework for examining the role of other potentially relevant factors. This is due to the ability to include in the model and therefore "control" for what has already been identified as reliably associated with the characteristics of sexual aggressors prior to the addition of other factors that may simply be spurious correlates or redundant factors. This is well illustrated by the findings of Malamuth, Addison, and Koss (2000) (replicated by Vega & Malamuth, 2003). They examined the relationship between pornography and sexual aggression by embedding their assessment within the Confluence Model. With a national random sample of men, these investigators first classified participants, on the basis of the Confluence Model's dimensions, into varying levels of risk for sexually aggressing. Within these differing levels of risk they then examined the predictive utility of pornography consumption. (This is somewhat similar to the "classification tree" approach used by Steadman et al., 2000.) It was found that among those classified at relatively low risk, there was only a small difference in sexual aggression as a function of pornography use. In contrast, pornography use was indeed a very good discriminator among those previously determined to be at high risk for sexually aggressing. Among high-risk men, those who additionally were very frequent users of pornography were much more likely to have engaged in sexual aggression than

---

[d]An additional issue raised by similarities among HMC model research, extensions by Knight and associates, and development of actuarial scales predicting recidivism (e.g., Hanson & Harris, 2001) concerns the sexuality components of a risk model. Our own work has emphasized both aspects of the Impersonal Sexuality constellation (e.g., early sexual intercourse, multiple sexual partners, and fantasizing about strangers) and aspects that we believe are more related to the Hostile Masculinity constellation aspect of aggressive-sexual fusion, such as rape fantasies, dominance as a motive for sexuality, and penile tumescence to rape depictions. Knight and Sims-Knight (in press) have also emphasized sexual drive and sexual preoccupation. To evaluate the extent to which each of these is related to sexual aggression, we conducted an analysis of relevant scales using the database gathered by Malamuth et al. (1995). It was found that measures of impersonal sexuality, aggression-sexual fusion, sex drive, and sexual preoccupation all correlated with self-reported sexual aggression. Assessing the unique links between these factors and sexual aggression via computation of "beta" weights in a regression equation indicated that some components of each still remained significant contributors, although with sex drive the findings suggested more of a dissatisfaction with how much sex the person experienced rather than actual differences in amount of sexual experiences.

their counterparts who consumed pornography less frequently. The researchers suggested that the links between pornography consumption and aggressiveness toward women may be circular, whereby aggressive men are drawn to those images in pornography that reinforce their impersonal and hostile orientation to sexuality.

COMPARING THE CONFLUENCE AND PSYCHOPATHY MODELS

Similarities between Models

There is a remarkable correspondence between factors identified in the HMC model research and the characteristics within Hare's Psychopathy scale[e] (see TABLE 1). Both models have two major constellations, one encompassing personality traits and the other behavioral or lifestyle characteristics. Although the Confluence Model has

TABLE 1. Similarity between characteristics of sexual aggressors identified in Confluence Model research and in factor analysis of Hare's Psychopathy scale

Confluence Model Research (Primarily Noncriminal Samples)	Psychopathy Based Research (Primarily Criminal Samples)
A. Personality	
Proneness to General Hostility/Antisociality Impulsivity, Irritability, Emotional Dyscontrol **Hostile Masculinity Constellation** 1. Grandiose, arrogant, self-centered 2. Callous attitudes justifying violence against women 3. Dominance/power in sex 4. Hostility toward women 5. Social isolation **Factor Included as Moderator Variable** 6. Low empathy/nurturance	**Factor 1 within Hare's Scale** *Interpersonal*: Grandiose, arrogant, callous, dominant, superficial, deceptive, and manipulative *Affective*: Short-tempered; unable to form strong emotional bonds; social isolation; lacking guilt, remorse, deep seated emotion, or empathy
B. Behavioral History	
Impersonal Sex Constellation 1. Victimized in childhood by sexual and/or physical abuse and/or experiencing parental violence 2. Adolescent delinquency 3. Promiscuous/impersonal sex (includes many short-term relationships)	**Factor 2 within Hare's Scale** Irresponsible and impulsive behavior **Additional Items/Factors for Total Score** 1. Criminal versatility 2. Promiscuous sexual behavior 3. Many short-term martial relationships

[e]I would like to acknowledge others who have pointed to some of the similarities I will amplify upon here. In particular, I am grateful to Raymond Knight and associates (e.g., Johnson and Knight, 2000; Knight and Cerce, 1999; Knight & Sims-Knight, in press). Those investigators successfully replicated and suggested some elaborations to our Confluence Model (described below) with both criminal and noncriminal samples.

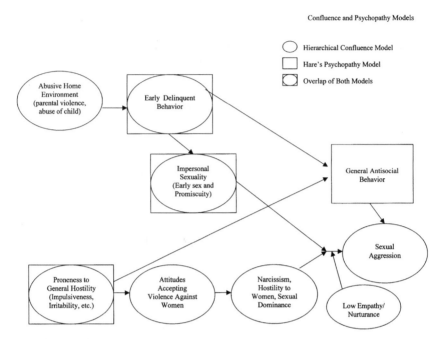

FIGURE 4. Correspondence in the characteristics identified by research on HMC model and Hare's Psychopathy research. Circles within boxes indicate overlap of models.

been tailored more to characteristics predicting sexual aggression (e.g., callous attitudes to women rather than callous attitudes generally), several of the major personality factors identified by this model are also incorporated within Hare's Psychopathy scale (see FIG. 4).[f] This should be encouraging to researchers in both lines of investigation, particularly in light of the differences in the samples used (e.g., criminal versus noncriminal). Note that in HMC research, characteristics such as Impulsivity are represented at the personality level, whereas in Psychopathy research, these are included in actual "Irresponsible and impulsive behavior." This distinction may be important in that the former line of research has been conducted primarily with noncriminal samples (who only have some elevated personality potential, but have not actually committed much general antisocial behavior), whereas the latter research has more often been conducted with actual criminals, who may have both higher elevations in the personality risk factors and have actually engaged in various types of antisocial and criminal acts.

On a conceptual level, both models emphasize that the impact of a combination of risk factors is greater than simply adding the effect of each factor individually. In psychopathy research, this has been reflected in distinctions between "primary" and

---

[f]Low empathy is clearly also part of the set of characteristics included in Hare's Psychopathy Model. It is not shown in FIG. 4 as part of the overlap because it is depicted in this figure as a moderator variable, as suggested by Dean & Malamuth (1997).

"secondary" psychopaths. In HMC model research, this has been consistently demonstrated in the finding that the interactive model produces a better prediction than the additive combination of each of the relevant factors. In other words, these data show that once the same individual scores relatively high on all of the relevant risk factors, their sexual aggression is much higher than would be expected by computing the additive risk from each of the risk factors individually. Recently, psychopathy researchers have also begun to more formally translate their emphasis on psychopathy as a "distinct class" into hypotheses and data supporting interaction effects of the relevant dimensions (i.e., Harpur et al., 2002).

Differences between Models and Suggested Future Research

Despite the overwhelming similarity, some differences between the Psychopathy and the HMC models are noteworthy. First, the Confluence Model approach has typically assessed each of the risk factors by using separate, reliable, multiple-item scales. In contrast, the various components of Hare's Psychopathy scale are measured by a small subset of items or even one item. Each of these approaches has certain merits. The former enables a more comprehensive assessment of each risk factor, whereas the latter enables a more practical single scale.

The second difference between the models lies in the fact that Confluence Model research gives a clear separation of the components constituting the total risk score, whereas the Psychopathy approach relies primarily on a total score. It may be that part of the ability of the Psychopathy scale to predict diverse antisocial behaviors reflects the fact that within a single PCL-R score various traits are being assessed simultaneously. Varied traits assessed by this scale may actually be predicting different behaviors. While some individuals indeed show marked elevations on all three of the relevant clusters, it is also apparent that some individuals may show elevations on some facets of this measure and not on others. The same overall score may be obtained by people who differ quite dramatically in different facets of the scale. Levenson, Patrick, Bradley, and Lang (2000) similarly note that "… individuals high in overall psychopathy are likely to differ from nonpsychopaths on a variety of traits (e.g., dominance, aggressiveness, impulsivity, sensation seeking, and harm avoidance)…. Different facets of psychopathy might have accounted for different group effects. Further research incorporating groups selected for elevations on one or the other PCL-R factor … and measures of potential trait mediators will be needed to resolve this issue." (p. 383)

Third, the HMC model has emphasized more specific predictors relevant to sexual aggression, whereas the Psychopathy research has relied on more general characteristics relevant to a wide variety of antisocial behaviors. This issue will be addressed in more detail below in comparing various approaches to assessment. It is noteworthy here, though, to comment on the emphasis in HMC research on using structural equation modeling. As noted earlier, this statistical modeling approach has several advantages. Because it combines aspects of both "factor analysis" and "path analysis" it enables several facets of a broader factor to be organized within a hierarchical framework and to relate to other relevant higher-order factors. For example, the relevant shared variance within variables such as impulsivity, irritability, and low empathy load on the "broader band" "General Hostile Personality" factor, which is linked to the more specific construct of Hostile Masculinity (which is indicated by such measures as Hostility toward Women and Sexual Dominance). In addition, mediation and moderation (Barron & Kenny, 1986) effects may be fully considered.

Fourth, although many of the personality characteristics of both the HMC and Psychopathy Models are distinctly similar (even if different labels and assessments have been used), one key component has been emphasized in the Confluence Model but has not been included in the PCL-R assessment of Psychopathy. In the HMC model research, it has been operationalized in such measures as the penile tumescence index (assessing arousal to rape as compared to mutually consenting depictions; e.g., Malamuth, 1986), the Sexual Dominance scale (e.g., Malamuth et al., 1991, 1995), and sexually coercive fantasies (e.g., Malamuth & Dean, 1997). As noted above, when the Psychopathy scale has been used to predict sexual aggression, it has been found to be most useful when combined with measures of dominance/power in sexuality (Hare et al., 2000), as revealed in research such as that of Rice and Harris (1997), who reported that the interaction of high PCL-R scores and the penile tumescence index was particularly predictive of offenders' recidivism in sexual aggression. This is essentially comparable to using some of the key elements of the HMC model (also see Seto & Lalumiere, 2000, who point to such correspondence). The major difference is that the more specific facets relevant to sexual aggression (e.g., assessment of callous attitudes toward women rather than callous attitudes generally) were not included by Rice and Harris (1997). If they had been included we would expect even better prediction.

A fifth key difference is greater emphasis on general antisocial behavior in Psychopathy research. This is understandable in light of the types of populations typically studied in both lines of research. Confluence Model studies have been conducted primarily (but not exclusively) with noncriminals, whereas Psychopathy Model studies have been conducted primarily (but not exclusively) with criminals. Obviously, the latter samples are likely to have a higher level of general antisocial behavior. This aspect merits further concentration in future research. One issue is the extent to which general antisocial behavior can be considered a "causal" factor in the development of sexual aggression, a "marker" of some of the underlying characteristics that lead to both general antisocial and sexually aggressive behaviors or a characteristic that may help distinguish among different "types" of offenders, some more persistently antisocial in general, whereas others more "specialists" in sexually aggressive behaviors (Hunter, 2002; Moffitt, 1993; Monson & Langhinrichsen-Rohling, 2002).

An additional issue concerns the distinction between "successful" versus "unsuccessful" psychopaths. Ishikawa (2000; also see Ishikawa et al., 2001) conducted a study that demonstrated that there are "...individuals, who can be identified as psychopathic based on the traditional notion of disrupted emotional and interpersonal functioning...who show intact autonomic nervous system and frontal functioning, and also manage to avoid being convicted for their crimes. ..." (p. 88) Lynam (2002) suggests that successful psychopaths are people who have some of the "... facets of psychopathy...but lack others (particularly the facets of low Conscientiousness) that are likely to contribute to occupational failures or arrests" (p. 342). Perhaps the noncriminals studied in the HMC research are more similar to "successful psychopaths," whereas those among "criminal samples" are the unsuccessful psychopaths. However, Ishikawa's (2000) research also raises questions about the conceptualization of psychopathy in terms of certain underlying physiological deficits. It therefore raises questions about the utility of applying the label of "psychopathy" *per se*. Future studies should conduct a systematic comparison among criminals and noncriminals using the measures typically used in the HMC model and in the psychopathy lines of research to directly compare these and to also study some of the underlying mechanisms (e.g., Ishikawa, 2000) hypothesized to have caused the manifest characteristics.

In addition, better understanding of the causes of coalescing characteristics, suggested by HMC and Psychopathy lines of research, is needed. Vasqiez and Figueredo (2002) described several alternative models: One model argues that the combination of characteristics included within psychopathy may actually constitute a "package" on which evolutionary selection pressures operated, creating a "niche" that enabled successful exploitative behavior (Mealey, 1995). A second model is that, through "assortative mating," individuals with "bad" characteristics were more likely to mate with similar others who had other "bad" characteristics, eventually leading to a group of individuals who were more likely to have offspring who combine several such "bad" characteristics. Lalumiere, Harris, and Rice (2001) similarly distinguished between a model suggesting that psychopathy is the outcome of defective or perturbed development versus the successful exploitative behavior model (Mealey, 1995). In comparing various groups of offenders to nonoffenders, they found greater support for the latter model, but the findings were not unequivocal.

Finally, we do not as yet have sufficiently good comparisons on whether criminal sexual aggressors score particularly high on certain "specific" characteristics encompassed within the HMC model research. Although research has shown that traits such as Sexual Dominance and Narcissism are Hostile Masculinity characteristics on which both criminal and noncriminal sexual aggressors score high on, this has not been adequately examined with some other characteristics, namely attitudes accepting of violence against women and hostility toward women. Recall that the PCL-R Psychopathy scale, on which sexual aggressors score high, includes characteristics such as "callousness" and "short-tempered," suggesting that they would also be high on similar characteristics when the relevant targets are women and the aggression is sexual aggression. It would be useful though to assess whether they are particularly high in these characteristics when women are the targets. The limited research available at this point does suggest that sexual aggressors hold attitudes more accepting of the use of sexual and of nonsexual physical aggression, generally, but not particularly of sexual aggression or other acts of violence against women (e.g., Spaccarelli, Bowden, Coatsworth & Kim, 1997). This study also suggests that sexual aggressors are more likely to use aggression as a means of influencing or controlling others in various situations. Clearly, though, this issue requires additional more precise investigation.

COMPARING DIFFERING ASSESSMENT STRATEGIES

Different Levels of Generality

It is particularly revealing to compare the Five-Factor Model (FFM) of personality, Hare's Psychopathy PCL-R scale, and the Confluence Model on assessment and prediction issues. Each represent different levels of generality and were developed for somewhat differing purposes. Yet, they share some properties and some common goals.

The FFM approach is a broad-band approach that attempts to encompass as much of the variance across all of the descriptors of personality as possible by extracting a few higher-order factors. If one's purpose is to predict across a wide range of behaviors or criteria, then this may be the best and most parsimonious strategy (for discussions of the advantages and disadvantages of different levels of "broad band" vs. "narrow band" assessment strategies, see Paunonen & Adelheid, 2001 and Paunonen & Ashton, 2001).

The HMC model represents a relatively narrow band approach but also encompasses some broad-band aspects. It was designed to develop the best prediction for a particular outcome, namely sexual aggression. Consequently, researchers using this strategy attempted to (1) identify all of the risk factors shown to predict this particular outcome, (2) to organize them in the most coherent and parsimonious manner, and (3) create a replicable predictive model of the characteristics of sexual aggressors. Therefore, "higher order" factors were extracted and used only to the extent that they effectively encompassed common variance of the risk factors shown to predict sexual aggression. For example, scales such as Hostility toward Women, Adversarial Sexual Beliefs and Sexual Dominance were found to consistently have key common variance that could be encompassed in a latent construct or alternatively in a composite labeled Hostile Masculinity. By using structural equation modeling, we not only used the factor analysis strategy (represented by the FFM approach encompassing a much wider range of characteristics), but also incorporated "mediation," whereby certain more general factors (e.g., our General Hostility) are included as predictors of sexual aggressors only if the man also has certain attributes (e.g., Hostile Masculinity) more proximate to sexual aggression.

Hare's psychopathy approach may be thought of as a strategy of predicting a specific class of behaviors (i.e., antisocial behavior) rather than a particular behavior only (i.e., sexual aggression). It "bundles together" in a single scale (1) the most relevant parts of the broader bands of personality and (2) previous antisocial behavior. Using an FFM analysis, Lynam (2002) argued that psychopathy correlates with a diverse set of behaviors because it is, in fact, a collection of diverse traits that has not been adequately shown to constitute a taxon. He notes that there has been evidence for the taxonicity of the antisocial lifestyle and childhood antisocial behavior items (Factor 2 of Hare's Psychopathy scale) but not for the taxonicity of the interpersonal and affective items of Factor 1 of this scale. He suggests that "… the differences observed between psychopathic and nonpsychopathic individuals are matters of degree rather than differences in kind" (p. 344). He further notes that

> … certain individuals seem to have little control over their actions. On this basis, these individuals may ask how can such a disorder be a collection of facets? Is this not evidence for the distinctiveness of psychopathy? I believe it is not evidence for the taxonicity of psychopathy. Instead, I believe that psychopathy consistently comes to the attention of mental health professionals and criminal justice workers because it is such a virulent collection of traits… high Antagonism, low Conscientiousness, and low anxiety. … In its most full-blown form, the psychopathic individual is not restrained by fear, concern for others, or the ability to reflect on the longer term outcomes of his or her behavior. (pp. 343–344)

In contrast, Harpur et al. (2002) argue that "the prototypical characteristics of the psychopath combine several dimensions of the FFM. … These characteristics form a unified whole when seen in a psychopathic inmate but are presented by distinct dimensions in the FFM" (p. 316). The debate therefore focuses on the question of

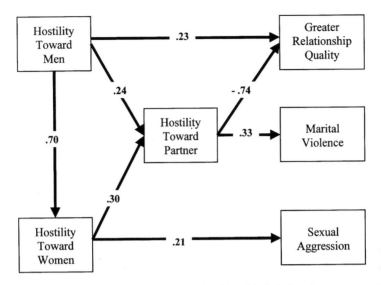

FIGURE 5. Men's reported quality of relationship with their female partner as a function of three types of hostility: Hostility toward Men, Hostility toward Women, and Hostility toward Partner. (Note: Numbers indicate path coefficient values, all of which are statistically significant.)

whether, when the various risk factors combine in the same individual, they create more risk than expected based on an additive combination of the risk factors? The view that there is a "synergistic" or "interactive" effect has been an important emphasis in HMC Model research. Indeed, it is what led to the use of the term *confluence*. Research on the Confluence Model has repeatedly demonstrated such an interaction (e.g., Malamuth, 1986; Malamuth et al. 1991; 1995). Psychopathy researchers have also recently begun to turn their attention to examining interaction effects (e.g., Harpur et al., 2002). Also, some researchers claim to have obtained other types of evidence for psychopathy as a discrete class (Harris, Rice & Quinsey, 1994; Skilling, Harris, Rice & Quinsey, 2002).

Each of these three approaches (FFM, Psychopathy, and HMC) may be best suited for particular purposes: the FFM approach for a parsimonious assessment strategy for predicting a wide variety of behaviors; the PCL-R Psychopathy scale for predicting across a variety of antisocial behaviors only; and the HMC Model for predicting sexual aggression. The HMC approach emphasizes the selection of predictors at a level of specificity or broadness that is most suited for a particular criteria or outcome. To illustrate the potential importance of such differentiation, we conducted analyses on the database used by Malamuth et al. (1995). Participants in this research had been administered several variants of the Hostility toward Women (HTW) scale embedded within a much larger set of questions. The referent of each scale item (e.g., "women," "men," or "your partner") was altered to reflect different relationships. For example, the HTW item "I am not easily angered by women" was phrased as "I am not easily angered by men" in the Hostility toward Men version, and "I am not easily angered by my partner" on the Hostility toward Partner version.[g]

TABLE 2. Mean quality of marital relationships as a function of men's scores on three types of hostility: Hostility to Men, Hostility to Women, and Hostility to Partner

		Low Hostility to Men		High Hostility to Men	
		Hostility to Women		Hostility to Women	
		Low	High	Low	High
Hostility to Partner	Low	1.50 ($n = 43$)	1.60 ($n = 10$)	1.20 ($n = 10$)	2.30 ($n = 12$)
	High	−1.40 ($n = 14$)	−2.20 ($n = 11$)	−0.40 ($n = 8$)	−1.60 ($n = 46$)

FIGURE 5 shows the findings of path analyses using these scales to predict several outcomes: Relationship quality with the man's female partner, nonsexual violence against the man's partner, or sexual aggression against women generally. As expected, these analyses show that while Hostility toward Men (used here as an indicator of general hostile tendencies) and Hostility toward Women are highly correlated, the relationship between Hostility toward Men and sexual aggression against women is mediated via the more proximate predictor of Hostility toward Women. Similarly, while both Hostility toward Men and Hostility toward Women had an indirect influence on violence toward his female partner, the version of the scale that specifically assessed Hostility toward the Partner was the more proximate, direct predictor. It mediated the effects of the other versions of the hostility scale.

Interestingly, relationship quality had a strong direct link from Hostility toward the Partner in the expected direction (i.e., the more hostility toward the partner the lower the quality of the relationship), but, surprisingly, there was an additional pathway suggesting a positive association between Hostility toward Men and relationship quality with the partner. To explore this unexpected association further, we classified the men as high or low in hostility based on median splits. TABLE 2 shows the mean scores on relationship quality based on these classifications. In general, the results reflect what we expected. Men high on all three types of hostility ($x = -1.6$, $n = 46$) reported much lower relationship quality with their spouses than men low on all three types of hostility ($x = 1.5$, $n = 43$). Yet, men high in hostility toward other men and women but low in hostility toward their partner actually report the highest quality of partner relationship ($x = 2.3$, $n = 12$). Perhaps these individuals have dif-

---

gWe believe that the different versions of the hostility scales we developed correlate highly with key aspects of the conceptualization of psychopathy (particularly the superficial, manipulative pretense of sincerity) and that they reflect both some common variance and unique variance relevant to different targets. To assess this, we also created modified versions of the Machiavelianism Scale, which is designed to assess a dispositional inclination to manipulate and exploit others (Christie, 1968). An example of an item on this scale is "Never tell women (or men) the real reason you did something unless it is useful to do so." We found that the Hostility toward Women and the Machivialiianism toward Women scales correlated very highly ($R = .73$, $P < .0001$), as did the Hostility toward Men and the Machivialilianism toward Men scales ($R = .69$, $P < .0001$). As expected, when comparing "across targets," the correlations are somewhat lower but still strong: The Hostility toward Men and the Machivialianism toward Women scales correlated .58 ($P < .0001$), and the Hostility toward Women scale and the Machivalianism toward Men correlated .52 ($P < .0001$).

ficulty in their relations with people generally but have found a particularly suitable partner with whom they get along with very well. These data reveal the usefulness of assessing varying levels of broadness and specificity, depending on the particular processes and outcome of interest.

Related data have also been reported by Anderson (1996) who assessed both laboratory aggression and self-reported naturalistic aggression. She found that "under conditions of high provocation, hostility toward women predicted increases in male aggression against women and decreases in male aggression against men. This effect remained even after general hostility was controlled for" (p. iii). These findings provide further support for the importance of assessing constructs at a level of specificity tailored to the outcome (e.g., particular target) under investigation.[h]

Assessing Levels Within a Hierarchy

The various research findings described in this chapter suggest that a comprehensive model of the characteristics of sexual aggressors needs to include various levels of "broad band" and more "narrow band" characteristics. As indicated above, the Five-Favor Personality Model, the Psychopathy Model, and the Confluence Model represent different levels of assessment, moving from the more general to the more specific (although the latter includes some general and some specific). Recent developments in personality theory and assessment may provide some relevant guidance regarding the utility of assessment at each of these levels:

> Description based on a few higher-order traits offers a convenient and parsimonious way to communicate about personality. ... Specific treatment decisions, however, seem to require the detailed evaluation of personality provided by description of the lower-order traits. ... It is not clear whether the lower-order traits are simply subcomponents of the higher-order traits or whether they are separate entities that co-occur to create the higher-order trait. ... Behavior-genetic analyses of twin study data are beginning to provide an answer to this question... that the specific facet traits of the five-factor model have substantial residual variance when the effects of the five higher-order dimensions are removed. ...Personality phenotypes are based on a large number of genetic building blocks that have relatively specific effects and a few factors with more widespread effects. ... For this reason, the most important level in the hierarchy for coding relevant traits is in the basic or lower-order level. (Livesley, 2001, p. 32)

The above quote not only strengths the rationale for the relatively "lower-order" level of the HMC model but also highlights the need for research to more precisely elucidate the mechanisms that link "higher-order" general hostile/antisocial factors

---

[h]In a wide-ranging analysis, Felson (2002) recently argued that sexual coercion specifically, and aggression against women generally, is caused by the same factors that cause other forms of antisocial behaviors. In contrast to the integrative approach suggested here, he therefore argues that there is little need for consideration of "specialization." In one part of this analysis, Felson (2002) discusses our research using self-reported likelihood of raping (e.g., Malamuth, 1981). Felson (2002) writes that "... there is no attempt to compare the likelihood measure for rape to likelihood measures for other crimes to see if some men have a special proclivity to rape." (p. 139) Unfortunately, Felson has overlooked research that has precisely done what he argues is needed, namely in Malamuth (1989a; 1989b). That research indicates that although there is indeed some variance common to various forms of self-reported likelihood to antisocial behavior generally (e.g., theft and murder), there is also clearly unique variance to reports of likelihood of engaging in sexual aggression. Further, the mechanisms leading to acts of sexual aggression may share some properties with those leading to other forms of antisocial behavior, but the data presented indicate that there may also be certain unique factors of considerable importance (Malamuth, 1989a; 1989b; Anderson, 1996, Malamuth, 1988).

(or traits) to the "narrower" more proximate factors directly predictive of sexual aggression. A full description of the various possibilities is beyond the scope of this chapter, but for illustrative possibilities, two will be highlighted. One possibility is that the presence of relatively general antisocial attributes may increase "receptivity" to more specific, related ones. For example, a person who has more general hostile emotions may be more open to cultural or other messages that encourage hostility, and domination of and prejudice toward certain "outgroups," such as minorities, women, and gays. The particular subgroups toward which particular hostile feelings become directed may vary dramatically from one cultural (and/or individual developmental) context to another. Therefore, a person possessing general hostile personality characteristics may in one context develop hostile feelings toward one group and not another, whereas in a different context, a totally different group may become the "legitimate" target for developing those hostile emotions and related characteristics. Therefore, it may be only partially informative to determine whether an individual has general hostile characteristics. It may also be critical to evaluate whether these have become directed toward women, thereby possibly increasing the likelihood of sexual aggression.

A second possibility is "combinatorial," both additive and interactional. For example, high levels of hostility alone may result in greater likelihood of various forms of general antisocial behavior, including but not particularly, sexual aggression. However, high hostility combined with high sexual dominance may be particularly likely to result in high levels of sexual aggression and only the same increase in various forms of other antisocial behaviors as suggested in the previous sentence. High sexual dominance without high hostility may result in engagement in some forms of sexual expression and fantasy (e.g., sadomasochism) but may not be expressed in physical sexual aggression. Also relevant would be the combination with attenuating factors such as empathy.

Hypothesized combinatorial effects are illustrated in the following newspaper description of a recent study by Dr. Christian Guilleminault of "violent sex sleep" (appearing in the *Journal of Psychosomatic Medicine,* Vol. 64, 2002, pp. 328–336), in which people commit violent sexual acts in their sleep:

> Each of the patients in their study had additional emotional problems, which Guilleminault said influenced the form the sleep disorder took. Had the patients not had emotional problems—which included obsessive-compulsive personality disorder, generalized anxiety disorder, and major depressive disorders—the sleep disorder, he said, would still have existed but might have emerged as sleepwalking, sleep eating or sleep talking." (*Los Angeles Times Newspaper,* August 19, 2002, S Section, p. 1)

Attention to combinatorial analyses in future research may also help clarify the differences between criminal and noncriminal sexual aggressors. Although I am suggesting that members of both groups will often show some elevations on both general hostile/antisocial characteristics (i.e., psychopathic) and the more specific factors pertaining to sexual aggression (e.g., hostile masculinity characteristics), they may differ in the degree to which each group is high on one or the other set of characteristics. The criminal samples may be particularly high on the hostile/antisocial characteristics and only show relative moderate elevations on some of the specific characteristics, whereas the noncriminals may show the opposite pattern. Moreover, the criminal samples are likely to have other relevant combinatorial factors (e.g., lower intelligence and social skills, and higher comorbidity of other negative factors).

CLOSING COMMENTS

The examples given above are possibilities, but clearly there is much work to be done. This work may be guided by three features of the HMC Confluence Model discussed here. In closing, it is worth summarizing and highlighting these points.

The first concerns the relationship among the predicting factors themselves: They are organized into two major interrelated constellations. The probability of the occurrence of various factors within a constellation is affected by the presence or absence of other factors. For example, the likelihood that a person will exhibit sexual promiscuity is affected by the extent to which he has shown evidence of delinquent tendencies in adolescence, which, in turn, is affected by the likelihood that he came from a home where there was child abuse and violence between the parents.

The second feature of the HMC concerns the relationship between the predictor factors and sexual aggression: The presence of each additional risk factor increases the probability that a male will be sexually aggressive. However, the presence of all of the risk factors creates a considerably greater likelihood of sexual aggression than the simple additive combination of each of the risk factors. This is reflected in the reliable interaction effect consistently found (e.g., Malamuth, 1986; Malamuth et al., 1991). At the same time, the presence of certain "protective" factors (e.g., high levels of nurturance/empathy) may attenuate the association between risk factors and actual sexual aggression.

The third feature that has been highlighted here is that it is a "hierarchical-mediational" model. For example, the link between more broad or general factors (e.g., Proneness to General Hostility) and the outcome of sexual aggression is mediated by more specific factors (e.g., Hostile Masculinity). We suggest that this approach leads to more accurate accounting for the relationships among general factors, more specific facets and factors, and specific outcomes than by typical regression or discriminate analyses, such as those used by Hersh and Gray-Little (1998). As noted above, those investigators found that the combination of psychopathic personality and "specific" attitudinal measures was not preferable to the use of the attitudinal measures alone. However, the comparable "hierarchical-mediational" Confluence Model's analyses enable the inclusion within a coherent framework of both general psychopathic (or hostile) personality characteristics that create the potential for sexual aggression (e.g., high impulsivity/irritability and/or low empathy) and factors more specific to sexual aggression (e.g., hostile masculinity, impersonal sex) that affect whether the potential actually leads to sexual aggression.

Finally, the striking similarity between the characteristics of sexual aggressors in criminal and noncriminal populations identified independently by the HMC model and the findings of psychopathy research is worth restating: Both models (1) have yielded two major constellations (or factors): antisocial personality and behavioral characteristics; (2) include early sexual experience/promiscuous sexual behavior component; and (3) have found that "Dominance/Power" as a source of sexual arousal is an important aspect of the characteristics of sexual aggressors. In addition, both models suggest that the interactive combination of the various factors results in a higher risk than a simple additive model, a prediction that has received considerable support. All in all, the remarkable correspondence between the findings of these two lines of research is very encouraging, for it provides independent verification that such characteristics are likely to provide a reliable basis for prediction, prevention, and treatment.

ACKNOWLEDGMENT

I appreciate the very helpful suggestions made by Dr. Eugenie Dye on an earlier draft of this paper.

REFERENCES

ANDERSON, K.B. (1996). *Cognitive and personality predictors of male-on-female aggression: An integration of theoretical perspectives.* Unpublished doctoral dissertation. University of Missouri-Columbia.

BARRON, R.M. & KENNY, D.A. (1986). The moderator-mediator variable distinction social psychological research: Conceptual, strategic, and statistical considerations. *Journal of Personality and Social Psychology 51,* 1173–1182.

BOURG, S.N. (2001). *Sexual and physical aggression within a dating/acquaintance relationship: Testing models of perpetrator characteristics.* Unpublished doctoral dissertation, Auburn University.

CHRISTOPHER, F.S., OWENS, L.A. & STECKER, H.L. (1993). Exploring the darkside of courtship: A test of a model of male premarital sexual aggressiveness. *Journal of Marriage & the Family, 55,* 469–479.

CLECKLEY, H. (1941). *The mask of sanity.* St. Louis: C. V. Mosby.

COHEN, J. & COHEN, P. (1983). *Applied multiple regression/correlation for the behavioral sciences.* Hillsdale, NJ: Erlaum.

DEAN, K. & MALAMUTH, N.M. (1997). Characteristics of men who aggress sexually and of men who imagine aggressing: Risk and moderating variables. *Journal of Personality and Social Psychology, 72,* 449–455.

FELSON, R.B. (2002). *Violence and Gender Reexamined.* Washington, D.C.: American Psychological Association.

FERGUSSON, D.M. & HORWOOD, L.J. (1988). Structural equation modeling of measurement processes in longitudinal data. In M. Rutter (Ed.), *Studies of psychosocial risk: The power of longitudinal data.* (pp. 325–353). Cambridge: Cambridge University Press.

GOUGH, H.G. (1994). Theory, development, and interpretation of the CPI Socialization Scale. *Psychological Reports*, Monograph Supplement 1-V75.

HALL, G.C.N., SUE, S., NARANG, D.S. & LILLY, R.S. (2000). Culture-specific models of men's sexual aggression: Intra- and interpersonal determinants. *Cultural Diversity & Ethnic Minority Psychology, 6,* 252–268

HANSON, R.K. & HARRIS A.J.R. (2001). A structured approach to evaluating change among sexual offenders. *Sexual abuse: A journal of research and treatment, 13,* 105–122.

HARE, R.D. (1991). *Manual for the psychopathy checklist-revised.* Toronto, Ontario, Canada: Multi-health systems.

HARE, R.D., CLARK, D., GRANN, M. & THORTON, D. (2000). Psychopathy and the predictive validity of the PCL-R: An international perspective. *Behavioral Sciences and the Law, 18,* 623–645.

HARPUR, T.J., HART, S. & HARE, R.D. (2002). Personality of the psychopath. In P.T. Costa Jr. & T. A. Widiger, (Eds.), *Personality disorders and the five-factor model of personality (2nd ed.).* (pp. 299–324). Washington, D. C.: American Psychological Association.

HERSH, K. & GRAY-LITTLE, B. (1998). Psychopathic traits and attitudes associated with self-reported sexual aggression in college men. *Journal of Interpersonal Violence,* 13, 456–471.

HUNTER, J. (2002). Youth Aggression: Subtypes and trajectories. Proposal submitted to the National Institute of Mental Health.

ISHIKAWA, S.S. (2000). *Psychophysiological, neurophysiological, and psychosocial differences between psychopaths with and without a history of criminal conviction.* Unpublished doctoral dissertation, UCLA.

ISHIKAWA, S.S., RAINE, A., LENCZ, T., BIHRLE, S. & LACASSE, L. (2001). Autonomic stress reactivity and executive functions in successful and unsuccessful criminal psychopaths from the community. *Journal of Abnormal Psychology, 110,* 423–432.

JOHNSON, G.M. & KNIGHT, R.A. (2000). Developmental antecedents of sexual coercion in juvenile sexual offenders. *Sexual Abuse: A Journal of Research and Treatment, 12,* 165–178.

KAPLAN, D. (2000). *Structural equation modeling: foundations and extensions.* Thousand Oaks, Calif.: Sage.

KNIGHT, R.A. & SIMS-KNIGHT, J.E. (in press). The developmental antecedents of sexual coercion against women in adolescents. In R. Geffner & K. Franey (Eds.), *Sex offenders: Assessment and treatment.* New York: Haworth Press.

KOSS, M.P., LEONARD, K.E., BEEZLEY, D.A. & OROS, C.J. (1985). Non-stranger sexual aggression: A discriminant analysis of psychological characteristics of nondetected offenders. *Sex Roles, 12,* 981–992.

KOSSON, D.S., KELLY, J.C. & WHITE, J.W. (1997). Psychopathy-related traits predict self-reported sexual aggression among college men. *Journal of Interpersonal Violence, 12,* 241–254.

LALUMIERE, M., HARRIS, G.T. & RICE, M.E. (2001). Psychopathy and developmental instability. *Evolution & Human Behavior, 22,* 75–92.

LIM, S. & HOWARD, R. (1998). Antecedents of sexual and non-sexual aggression in young Singaporean men. *Personality and Individual Differences, 25,* 1163–1182.

LIVESLEY, W.J. (2001). Conceptual and taxonomic issues. In W.J. Livesley (Ed.), *Handbook of personality disorders: Theory, research and treatment* (pp.3–38). New York, NY: The Guilford Press.

LYNAM, D.R. (2002). Psychopathy from the perspective of the five-factor model of personality. In P.T. Costa Jr. & T.A. Widiger (Eds.), *Personality disorders and the five-factor model of personality (2nd ed.)* (pp. 325–348). Washington, DC: American Psychological Association.

MALAMUTH, N.M. (1981). Rape proclivity among males. *Journal of Social Issues. 37,* 138–157.

MALAMUTH, N.M. (1988). Predicting laboratory aggression against female vs. male targets: Implications for research on sexual aggression. *Journal of Research in Personality, 22,* 474–495.

MALAMUTH, N.M. (1998). An evolutionary-based model integrating research on the characteristics of sexually coercive men. In J.G. Adair & D. Belanger (Eds.), *Advances in psychological science, Vol. 1* (pp. 151–184). Psychology Press: Erlbaum (UK).

MALAMUTH, N.M. (1986). Predictors of naturalistic sexual aggression. *Journal of Personality and Social Psychology, 50,* 953–962.

MALAMUTH, N.M. (1989). The attraction to sexual aggression scale: Part one. *The Journal of Sex Research, 26,* 26–49.

MALAMUTH, N.M., (1989). The attraction to sexual aggression scale: Part two. *The Journal of Sex Research, 26,* 324–354.

MALAMUTH, N.M., LINZ, D., HEAVEY, C.L., BARNES, G. & ACKER, M. (1995). Using the confluence model of sexual aggression to predict men's conflict with women: A ten-year follow-up study. *Journal of Personality and Social Psychology, 69,* 353–369.

MALAMUTH, N.M., SACKLOSKIE, R., KOSS, M. & TANAKA, J. (1991). The characteristics of aggressors against women: Testing a model using a national sample of college students. *Journal of Consulting and Clinical psychology, 59,* 670–681.

MALAMUTH, N.M., ADDISON, T. & KOSS, M. (2000). Pornography and sexual aggression: Are there reliable effects and can we understand them? *Annual Review of Sex Research, 11,* 26–91.

MEALEY, L. (1995). The sociobiology of sociopathy: An integrated evolutionary model. *Behavioral & Brain Sciences, 3,* 523–599.

MOFFITT, T.E. (1993). Adolescence-limited and life-course-persistent antisocial behavior: A developmental taxonomy. *Psychological Review, 4,* 674–701.

MONSON, C.M. & LANGHINRICHSEN-ROHLING, J. (2002). Sexual and nonsexual dating violence perpetration: Testing an integrated perpetrator typology. *Violence and Victims, 17,* 403–428.

MURNEN, S.K., WRIGHT, C. & KALUZNY, G. (2002). If "boys will be boys" then girls will be victims? A meta-analytic review of the research relating masculine ideology to sexual aggression. *Sex Roles, 46,* 359–375.

PAUNONEN, S.V. & ADELHEID, A.A.M. (2001). The personality hierarchy and the prediction of work behaviors. In B.W. Roberts & R. Hogan (Eds.), *Personality psychology in the workplace.* (pp. 161–191). Washington, DC: APA.

PAUNONEN, S.V. & ASHTON, M.C. (2001). Big Five factors and facets and the prediction of behavior. *Journal of Personality & Social Psychology, 3,* 524–539.

PORTER, S., FAIRWEATHER, D., DRUGGE, J., HERVÉ, H., BIRT, A. & BOER, D.P. (2000). Profiles of psychopathy in incarcerated sexual offenders. *Criminal Justice and Behavior, 27,* 216–233.

PRENTKY, R.A., KNIGHT, R., LEE, A.F.S. & CERCE, D. (1995). Predictive validity of lifestyle impulsivity for rapists. *Criminal Justice and Behavior, 22,* 106–128.

PRENTKY, R.A. & KNIGHT, R.A. (1991). Dimensional and categorical discrimination among rapists. *Journal of Consulting and Clinical Psychology, 59,* 643–661.

RAPAPORT, K. & BURKHART, B.R. (1984). Personality and attitudinal characteristics of sexually coercive males. *Journal of Abnormal Psychology, 93,* 216–221.

RICE, M.E. & HARRIS, G.T. (1997). Cross-validation and extension of the Violence Risk Appraisal Guide for child molesters and rapists. *Law and Human Behavior, 21,* 231–241.

SPACCARELLI, S., BOWDEN, B., COATSWORTH, J.D. & KIN, S. (1997). Psychosocial correlates of male sexual aggression in a chronic delinquent sample. *Criminal Justice and Behavior, 24,* 71–95.

STEADMAN, H.J., SILVER, E., MONAHAN, J., APPELBAUM, P.S., ROBBINS, P.C., MULVEY, E.P., GRISSO, T., ROTH, L.H. & BANKS, S. (2000). A classification tree approach to the development of actuarial violence risk assessment tools. *Law and Human Behavior, 24,* 83–100.

VASQIEZ, G & FIGUEREDO, A.J. (2002). The "dark side" of assortative mating: The "genetic dregs" hypothesis. Paper presented at the Annual Meetings of the Human Behavior and Evolution Society. Rutgers University, New Jersey.

VEGA, V. & MALAMUTH, N.M. (2003, May) *A hierarchical-mediational model of sexual aggression.* Paper presented at the International Communication Association Meetings, San Diego, CA.

WHEELER, J.G., GEORGE, W.H. & DAHL, B.J. (2002). Sexually aggressive college males: Empathy as a moderator in the "Confluence Model" of sexual aggression. *Personality and Individual Differences, 33,* 759–775.

The Development of Sexual Aggression through the Life Span

The Effect of Age on Sexual Arousal and Recidivism among Sex Offenders

HOWARD E. BARBAREE, RAY BLANCHARD, AND CALVIN M. LANGTON

Centre for Addiction and Mental Health, and the University of Toronto, Toronto, Ontario, Canada, M6J 1H4

ABSTRACT: There is a strong belief in the field that sexual aggression persists unabated into old age. If libido is one of the important determinants of sexual aggression, as has been theorized, and if libido decreases with aging, then it follows that sexual aggression should show similar aging effects. The present study examines the effects of age on sexual arousal and sexual recidivism in sex offenders. In the first study, 1431 sex offenders' erectile responses were measured using volumetric phallometry during presentations of visual and auditory depictions of prepubescent, pubescent, and adult males and females. The maximum degree of arousal was plotted over the age of the offender at the time of the test. Age was a powerful determinant of sexual arousal and a line-of-best-fit indicated that arousal decreased as a reciprocal of the age-at-test. In the second study, 468 sex offenders released into the community were followed for an average period of over five years. The effects of age-at-release were examined using Kaplan-Meier survival curves plotted for subjects in different age-at-release cohorts. Results indicated that offenders released at an older age were less likely to recommit sexual offenses and that sexual recidivism decreased as a linear function of age-at-release. Age-related decreases were confirmed while controlling for other risk factors using Cox regression analysis. The implications of reductions in sexual aggression with age are discussed in relation to our understanding of the etiology of sexual aggression and our use of actuarial risk assessments.

KEYWORDS: sexual aggression; age effects; recidivism; volumetric phallometry

INTRODUCTION

There is a strong belief in the field that sexual aggression persists unabated into old age. In their meta-analytic review of 61 data sets, representing over 23,393 sex offenders, Hanson and Bussière (1998) found that indicators of deviant sexual interests—number of prior sexual offences, phallometrically measured sexual arousal to children—consistently predicted sexual recidivism. Age was identified as a moderate predictor ($r = .13$) of sexual recidivism, with younger offenders recidivating at a

Address for correspondence: Howard Barbaree, Law and Mental Health Program, Centre for Addiction and Mental Health, Unit 3, 1001 Queen Street West, Toronto, Ontario, Canada, M6J 1H4. Voice: 416-535-8501 ext. 2919; fax: 416-583-4327.
Howard_Barbaree@camh.net.

Ann. N.Y. Acad. Sci. 989: 59–71 (2003). © 2003 New York Academy of Sciences.

higher rate. Selecting variables that correlated with sexual recidivism at $r = .10$ or above, Hanson (1997) developed a brief actuarial scale with four items, representing the best independent predictors of sexual reoffending. Across seven development samples, comprising a total of 2592 sex offenders, Hanson found that the Rapid Risk Assessment of Sex Offender Recidivism (RRASOR) scores accurately predicted sexual recidivism. The predictive validity of the RRASOR has been replicated in a number of studies (e.g., Barbaree, Seto, Langton & Peacock, 2001; Sjöstedt & Lång-ström, 2001). One of the four items on the RRASOR coded the age of the offender at release from custody as being younger than 25 years (signifying higher risk), and older than 25 years (signifying lower risk). The implication was that risk for sexual recidivism does not change after the age of 25.

There are good reasons to question the notion that sexually motivated behaviors of any type—paraphilic or conventional—would continue unabated throughout a man's middle years and into old age. Such an expectation is at variance with the known facts of human endocrinology, specifically, findings concerning testosterone and age. Numerous studies have established that bioavailable testosterone peaks in early adulthood and thereafter decreases with age through the remainder of the life span (e.g., Denti et al., 2000; Jankowska, Rogucka, Medras & Welon, 2000). There is also evidence that testosterone receptor sites may become less sensitive with age, so that the threshold concentration of testosterone necessary to maintain libido may increase with age (e.g., Baker & Hudson, 1983).

Testosterone is necessary or at least important in maintaining libido. The popula-tions in which a significant relationship between serum testosterone levels and libido has been found include normal men, normal adolescent boys, men in or past middle-age, men complaining of loss of sexual interest, men with erectile dysfunction, and hypogonadal men (e.g., Udry, Billy, Morris, Groff & Raj, 1985; Schiavi, 1999). Based on this well-established relationship, one would therefore expect that the nor-mal decline in testosterone levels with age would be accompanied by a concomitant decrease in libido, over and above any decreases in libido attributable to health prob-lems in later life.

Studies of human sexuality and aging indicate a general decline in male sexual behavior through the life span. For example, Rowland, Greenleaf, Dorfman, and Davidson (1993) examined sexual arousal and behavior of 39 healthy sexually func-tional men ranging in age from 21 to 82. These authors recorded erectile responses to visual erotic stimulation and found that the magnitude of erectile responses de-creased and their latency increased with advanced age. These authors also collected data on self-reported sexual activity and functioning in these same subjects. Results indicated significant age-related decreases in the frequency of sexual activity, in-cluding intercourse and masturbation.

The present paper presents two studies of the effects of advancing age on sexual behavior in the sex offender. The first examined the magnitude of sexual arousal, while the second examined rates of sexual recidivism.

STUDY 1

Introduction

The current literature supports the notion that sexual arousal decreases with age in sex offenders. Hall (1991) examined the relationship between age and erectile responses measured by circumferential penile plethysmography in 169 inpatient adult male sex offenders ranging in age from 20 to 66 years of age. Age accounted for a significant proportion of the variance in arousal, and arousability was inversely related to age. This reduction in sex offender arousability seems to begin at an early age. Kaemingk, Koselka, Becker, and Kaplan (1995) examined the relationship between age and erectile responses measured by circumferential penile plethysmography in 104 adolescent sex offenders ranging in age from 13 to 17 years. Age accounted for a significant proportion of the variance in arousal, with the younger adolescents showing erectile responses to a greater number of stimulus presentations, and demonstrating a greater mean percentage full erection score across stimulus presentations. The present study examined the magnitude of erectile responses of sex offenders as a function of age.

Method

Subjects

Between December 1995 and January 2002, 1460 male patients underwent the same phallometric test for erotic gender and age preferences at the Kurt Freund Laboratory at the Centre for Addiction and Mental Health (Toronto, Ontario, Canada). In every case, the presenting complaint concerned illegal or disturbing sexual behavior. Parole and probation officers, lawyers, correctional institutions, and children's protective societies referred the majority of subjects. Physicians referred subjects who had no involvement with the criminal justice system. The data of 29 subjects were spoiled by technical problems with the test; the data of the remaining 1431 were used for the present study.

These patients comprised 14% with no known sexual offenses, 54% with offenses against children under age 12, 31% with offenses against pubescents age 12–14, 16% with offenses against teenagers age 15–16, and 28% with offenses against adults age 17 and older. These percentages add up to more than 100, because some patients had offenses against victims in more than one age range. The mean age of the patients was 37.17 years (SD = 13.32). The median educational level was high school graduation. The patients were predominantly of European descent, with 82% describing themselves as White.

Materials and Procedure

The Kurt Freund Laboratory is equipped for volumetric phallometry; that is, the apparatus measures penile blood volume change rather than penile circumference change. The volumetric method measures penile tumescence more accurately at low levels of response (Kuban, Barbaree & Blanchard, 1999). A photograph and schematic drawing of the volumetric apparatus are given in Freund, Sedlacek, and Knob (1965). The major components include a glass cylinder that fits over the penis and an inflatable cuff that surrounds the base of the penis and isolates the air inside the cylinder from the outside atmosphere. A rubber tube attached to the cylinder leads to a pressure transducer, which converts air pressure changes into voltage output changes. Increases in penile volume compress the air inside the cylinder and thus produce an output signal from the transducer. The apparatus is calibrated so that known quantities of volume displacement in the cylinder (e.g., 2 cc) correspond to known changes in transducer voltage output. The apparatus is very sensitive and can reliably detect changes in penile blood volume much less than 1 cc.

The specific test used in this study has been described in detail by Blanchard, Klassen, Dickey, Kuban, and Blak (2001). The test stimuli were audio-taped narratives presented through headphones and accompanied by slides. There were seven categories of narratives, which described sexual interactions with prepubescent girls, pubescent girls, adult women, prepubescent boys, pubescent boys, and adult men, and also solitary, nonsexual activities ("neutral" stimuli). The accompanying slides showed nude models corresponding in age and sex to the topic of the narrative. Neutral narratives were accompanied by slides of landscapes. The test stimuli were presented as discrete trials, each 54 s in duration, with intertrial intervals as long as necessary for penile blood volume to return to baseline. The full test consisted of four blocks of seven trials, with each block including one trial of each type in fixed pseudorandom order.

The same laboratory technician administered all phallometric tests in this study. The time required to complete these tests was usually about one hour.

Results

The dependent measure of penile response was the *Output Index* or OI (Freund, 1967). This is the average of the three greatest responses to any stimulus category except "neutral," where penile response is expressed in cubic centimeters (cc) of blood volume increase from the start of a trial. As measured by the authors' laboratory equipment, full erection for the average patient corresponds to a blood volume increase of 20–25 cc.

FIGURE 1 shows the relationship between penile response and age. The bars represent the mean observed blood volume increase for patients of every age from 13 to 77. The amplitude of penile response declines steeply from adolescence to about age 30; it continues to decline after that, but at a lower rate. It is clear from the observed data that the decrease would be better described by a curved than by a straight line.

The curve that best fit the data was an inverse function of the form, $Y = b_0 + (b_1/X)$. In other words, penile response is better described as a function of $1/age$ than of age. The line plotted in the figure is the predicted blood volume increase for every age, as generated by the regression equation, penile response $= b_0 + (b_1/age)$. The correlation between penile response and the inverse of age, $r_{(1429)} = .47$, was statistically significant, $t_{(1429)} = 20.09$, $P < .001$.

Discussion

The data suggest that the male libido is highest in adolescence and declines thereafter. The observed decline is perhaps earlier and steeper than one would predict from the data on serum testosterone alone. The curve might therefore represent a combined effect of decreasing testosterone levels and decreasing target tissue sensitivity, or an interaction of hormonal phenomena and maturational variables. It is also probable that other factors, essentially unrelated to libido or testosterone, further contributed to the age-related decrease in penile erection in this study. Examples include age-related vascular insufficiency and neuropathy (Feldman, Goldstein, Hatzichristou, Krane & McKinlay, 1994). One would not expect these to be predominant factors for men aged 20–35, however, which is the age range where most of the ob-

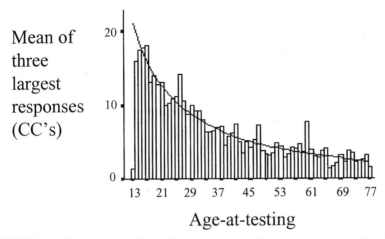

Mean of three largest responses (CC's)

Age-at-testing

FIGURE 1. The average of the three largest erectile responses (cc's of volume increase) as a function of age at test.

served decrease in arousability occurred. It is therefore likely that the curve depicted in FIGURE 1 primarily reflects a true decrease in erotic responsiveness and not merely a decrease in the validity of penile erection as an indicator of erotic responsiveness.

STUDY 2

Introduction

If sex offenders demonstrate reductions in sexual arousal and concomitant reductions in libido with advancing age, it follows that they would demonstrate similar reductions in the frequency of sexual behavior. The present study focuses on the effects of age on sex offender recidivism as an example of sex offenders' sexual behavior. Hanson (2001) has examined the rates of sexual recidivism at different ages at release in a large sample of sex offenders. The results indicated that sex offender's risk for recidivism decreases with age-at-release. According to Hanson (2001), the patterns of decline differ among rapists, child molesters, and incest offenders: In incest offenders, from an initial peak at ages 18–24, there is a rapid decline to below 10% at ages 25–29, with a continuing gradual decline to age 60, after which there are no incidents of reoffense in these samples; in nonfamilial child molesters, the rate of recidivism peaks when offenders are released at ages 25–29, then gradually declines to release at age 50, at which time the rate of decline increases markedly to release at age 70; rapists show a gradual decline in rates of recidivism from 18 years to 60 years.

In examining the plotted rates of recidivism over age-at-release (see Figure 2 in Hanson, 2001), there are two issues that require mention and clarification, one minor, the other more important. The minor issue is that the age intervals on the abscissa are unequal and therefore the plots Hanson (2001) uses are somewhat distorted.

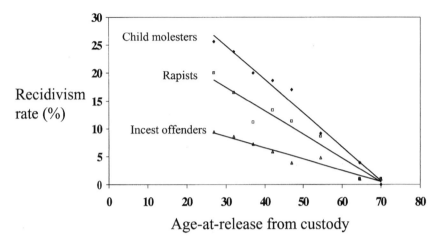

FIGURE 2. Recidivism rates (%) replotted as a function of age-at-release from custody in child molesters, rapists, and incest offenders aged 25 and older. (Data from Hanson, 2001.)

The more important issue concerns the fact that the statistically significant differences between groups in pattern of decline identified by Hanson (2001) are entirely due to performance in the youngest age group (18–24 years) of extrafamilial child molesters. While only linear trends were evident in the rapists and incest offenders, logistic regression identified a significant curvilinear component to the trend of recidivism over age-at-release in extrafamilial child molesters. Examination of Figure 2 in Hanson (2001) indicates that recidivism rates increase from the youngest (18–24) to the next youngest age group (24–29) in these offenders. Thereafter, from age 25 on, rates of recidivism among the extrafamilial child molesters decrease in an approximately linear fashion. Hanson (2001) presents a theoretical combination of deviant sexual interest, self-control, and opportunity to explain the differences between offender subgroups, but the explanation is somewhat speculative. Our focus in the present paper is on changes in behavior that occur with later age. For these reasons, and for the sake of simplicity, our discussion of the Hanson (2001) data will exclude consideration of the youngest age groups.

In the present paper, FIGURE 2 presents a replotting of the Hanson (2001) data for offenders released between the ages of 25 and 70+. The recidivism rate for each offender subgroup (child molesters, rapists, incest offenders) is plotted over the midpoint of the appropriate age interval. For each group, a regression line is plotted, and the regression constants (slope and y-intercept) are presented in TABLE 1. TABLE 1 also presents the correlations between observed and predicted rates of recidivism; the correlations are all above 0.97, indicating that the regression lines are good fits to the observed data. A number of aspects of these data become very clear from this replotting. In the Hanson (2001) data set (1) recidivism in sex offenders declined from the late twenties, (2) the decline can be best characterized as a linear decline over age-at-release in all offender subgroups, (3) the decline ended at age 70, and at that age the estimated recidivism rate is zero for all subgroups, and (4) in their youth,

TABLE 1. Slopes and y-intercepts for regression lines plotting recidivism (%) over age-at-release for the three offender groups and total sample in Hanson (2001)

Subset	Slope	y-Intercept	Pearson r
Child molesters	−0.607	43.172	.99
Rapists	−0.451	31.203	.97
Incest	−0.227	15.607	.98
Full sample	−0.429	29.995	.99

NOTE: Correlations between actual and predicted recidivism rates are presented in the final column.

sex offender subgroups differed in the rate at which they recidivated, with child molesters showing the highest rate and incest offenders showing the lowest rate. Therefore, we disagree with Hanson (2001) that the offender subgroups differ in the pattern of decline in recidivism with age at release. Our interpretation is that all offender groups show a linear decrease in recidivism with age. The offender subgroups are only different in the level of recidivism exhibited in their youth.

There are two potential confounds in the Hanson (2001) study. First, time-at-risk may have varied among the age-at-release groupings. The present study will address this potential confound by comparing age-at-release cohorts using Kaplan-Meier survival analysis, which controls for time-at-risk. Second, age-at-release groups may vary in their level of risk due to other risk factors. The present study compared age-at-release cohorts on other risk factors, then controlled for non-age-related risk factors using actuarial risk assessment and Cox regression analysis.

Scientific research has consistently shown that actuarial methods of risk assessment are more accurate than clinical judgements alone in predicting future violence and sexual assault among individuals released into the community. A number of actuarial instruments for use with sex offenders have been made available in recent years, which are objectively scored and provide probabilistic estimates of risk based on the empirical relationships between their combination of items and recidivism. The probabilistic estimates indicate the percentage of people with the same score who would be expected to reoffend within a defined period of opportunity. Barbaree et al. (2001) recently conducted a comparison among available actuarial instruments on 215 sex offenders released from prison for an average of 4.5 years and found the RRASOR (Hanson, 1997) to have a moderately high level of predictive accuracy (see also Langton, 2003). For the purposes of the present study, the RRASOR will be used to assess and control for non-age-related risk factors.

The present study examined sexual recidivism in a sample of sex offenders released from a Canadian federal penitentiary. It was hypothesized that sexual recidivism would decrease in a linear fashion as a function of age-at-release. Regression constants derived from Hanson (2001) (shown previously) and presented in TABLE 1 (full sample) provided a basis for making a prediction of the values of the regression constants in the present study. Addressing the potential confounds in the Hanson (2001) study, the present study will control for time-at-risk and non-age-related risk factors.

Method

Subjects

The sample consisted of 468 adult sex offenders who were assessed and treated at the Warkworth Sexual Behaviour Clinic (WSBC), a prison-based sex offender treatment program at the Warkworth Institution (Ontario, Canada), between June 1989 and December 2001. All sex offenders housed at Warkworth Penitentiary were eligible for treatment at the WSBC and were actively encouraged to participate by their case managers and treatment staff. All offenders who sought treatment were admitted to the program on a priority basis, depending on their projected release date, with earlier release leading to earlier admission. The sample of 468 sex offenders constituted 175 rapists (offenders who had sexually assaulted unrelated females, aged 16 years of age and older, exclusively), 155 child molesters (offenders who had sexually assaulted unrelated or extrafamilial children), 93 familial offenders (offenders who had sexually assaulted biologically related and/or step-children, exclusively), and 45 mixed offenders (offenders who had sexually assaulted both adult females and children). Many of these offenders were involved in earlier published follow-up studies (Barbaree et al., 2001, $n = 199$; Seto & Barbaree, 1999, $n = 201$). The average age of the sample at release was 40 years (ranging from 21 to 83 years). Participants had an average grade 10–level of education (ranging from grade 1 to high school graduation). For additional sample information, see Langton (2003).

Measures

Rapid Risk Assessment for Sexual Offense Recidivism (RRASOR). The RRASOR has four items: number of prior charges or convictions for sexual offenses; age upon release from prison, or anticipated opportunity to reoffend in the community; any male victims, coded as yes or no; and any unrelated victims, coded as yes or no (Hanson, 1997). Total scores can range from 0 to 6; the item weights reflect the magnitude of the item's independent relationship with sexual recidivism.

Data Collection

Participants gave written consent for the use of their information for research purposes at the time of their assessment at the Warkworth program. The clinical files contained the following information: (1) a review of institutional files, including police reports, court records, previous psychological reports, and case management reports; (2) a semistructured interview with the offender; (3) psychological test results; and (4) treatment reports cowritten by the group therapist and the program director. The RRASOR was scored retrospectively from file information in 2000 and 2001. All instrument coding was completed by individuals who were unaware of the recidivism outcomes. Interrater reliability for the RRASOR was good (Langton, 2003). Recidivism information was obtained in December 2001 from the Canadian Police Information Centre database maintained by the Royal Canadian Mounted Police; this national database records criminal charges and convictions incurred in Canada. Sexual recidivism was defined as a conviction for a new contact sexual offense following release.

TABLE 2. *N*, five-year failure rates, and actuarial risk scores for four age-at-release cohorts

Age-at-Release Cohort	*n*	5-Year Failure Rate	RRASOR Mean	SD
21–30	105	16.78	1.69	1.02
31–40	160	11.21	1.53	1.28
41–50	116	7.64	2.11	1.40
51+	87	3.82	1.62	1.62
Full sample	468	10.19	1.72	1.35

Results

The average follow-up period was 5.9 years. Subtracting time returned to custody for parole violations and new nonsexual criminal convictions produced an average time-at-risk for sexual reoffense of 5.6 years (SD = 3 years, range 1 day to 11.7 years). The sexual recidivism rate was 11.3%.

The sample was divided into age at release cohorts as follows: those that were released when they were 21–30, 31–40, 41–50, and 51+ years of age. TABLE 2 presents the resulting *n* in each age-at-release cohort. The cohorts were then compared on sexual recidivism in two separate tests. In the first of these, time-at-risk was controlled. In the second of these, time-at-risk and actuarial risk were controlled.

Controlling for Time-at-Risk

FIGURE 3 presents Kaplan-Meier survival functions for sex offenders in the four age-at-release cohorts. As can be seen from the figure, the ultimate failure rate was ordered according to age-at-release, with the youngest aged cohort exhibiting a failure rate of over 20%, and the oldest age-at-release cohort exhibiting an ultimate failure rate of approximately 5%. The major observed differences between survival functions for age-at-release cohorts were statistically significant. The over 51-aged cohort showed fewer failures compared with the 21- to 30-year-old cohort (Log Rank Statistic = 7.02, P = .008), and the 31- to 40-year old cohort (Log Rank Statistic = 4.12, P = .052), controlling for time-at-risk.

Five-year failure rates were calculated from these survival functions. Failure rates for the four age-at-release cohorts are presented in TABLE 2. These failure rates were regressed over the midpoint of the age intervals defining the age-at-release cohorts. The resulting regression analysis indicated that five-year failure rates showed a linear decrease with age-at-release according to the equation $Y = (-.425 * X) + 27.06$, where Y is the predicted failure rate and X is age-at-release. The correlation between observed and predicted failure rates was 0.99, indicating that the regression line is a very good fit to the observed data. These regression coefficients are remarkably similar to those calculated from the Hanson (2001) data set (slope = −.425 vs. −.429; and y-intercept = 27.06 vs. 29.99). Therefore, the hypothesis was supported that recidivism rates decrease in a linear fashion with age-at-release, replicating Hanson (2001), when time-at-risk was controlled.

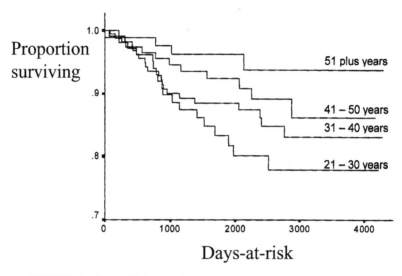

FIGURE 3. Kaplan-Meier survival curves for four age-at-release cohorts.

Controlling for Other Risk Factors

The mean score on the RRASOR was calculated for the four age-at-release cohorts. These are presented with their respective standard deviations in TABLE 2. Between groups ANOVA found significant differences among the age-at-release cohorts ($F_{(3,464)} = 4.680$, $P < .01$). Examination of the means revealed no pattern of risk over age-at-release that would indicate a potential confound with age (e.g., decreasing risk scores in older cohorts). Bonferroni multiple comparisons confirmed that the only significant difference between mean RRASOR scores among the age cohorts was that between 31- to 40-year-olds and the 41- to 50-year-olds. To control for actuarial risk, a Cox regression analysis was conducted. Cox regression is a survival analytic procedure that is suitable for use with both continuous and categorical variables that controls for time-at-risk. In Cox regression, predictor variables can be entered in blocks in a step-wise fashion, and subsequent blocks are tested for significance having taken the earlier block into account. For the Cox regression analysis presented in TABLE 3, the actuarial score for the RRASOR was entered in the first block, and age-at-release was forced into the model in the second block.

As was expected, the RRASOR was found to be a significant predictor of sexual recidivism. In support of the hypothesis being tested here, when age-at-release was entered as a second block, it was found to be a significant predictor of recidivism also. The hazard ratio for age-at-release was 0.953 (with a 95% confidence interval of 0.926–0.980).

Discussion

On the basis of our replotting of the Hanson (2001) data, we predicted that recidivism would decrease in a linear fashion over age-at-release. The results of Study 2

TABLE 3. Cox regression analysis using the RRASOR and age-at-release to predict sexual recidivism ($N = 468$)

	B	SE	e^B	95% CI for e^B	
				Lower	Upper
Block 1					
RRASOR	0.43***	0.09	1.53	1.28	1.83
Block 2					
RRASOR	0.51***	0.10	1.67	1.37	2.03
Age at release (in years)	−0.05**	0.01	0.95	0.93	0.98

NOTE: $\chi^2(1) = 23.370$ at Block 1, $P < .001$; $\Delta\chi^2(1) = 12.611$ at Block 2, $P < .001$; for the final equation, $\chi^2(2) = 32.426$, $P < .001$.
** $P < .01$***; $P < .001$

supported the hypothesis. Using survival analysis and calculating five-year failure rates for each of the four age-at-release cohorts, failure rate was found to be a decreasing linear function of age-at-release. While age-at-release cohorts were found to differ according to actuarial risk, the age-at-release effect was found to be significant when actuarial risk was controlled using Cox regression. The resulting hazard ratio indicates that for each successive year of age-at-release, the recidivism risk was estimated to be 95% of the risk posed during the previous year.

GENERAL DISCUSSION

There are a number of reasons why we might expect that sexual aggression decreases with age. First, bioavailable testosterone, the male sex hormone peaks in the early twenties and decreases thereafter. Studies of human sexuality and aging indicate that sexual arousal and libido decrease with age in men. The present study has shown that sexual arousal and recidivism decreases with age in sex offenders, confirming previously published findings.

The present studies as well as previous studies have been cross-sectional in design rather than longitudinal. When we infer changes in arousal and recidivism over age in the individual sex offender, we are making an important assumption that the cross-sectional comparisons reflect the effects of aging and not other confounding cohort effects.

Nevertheless, these apparent effects of aging in the sex offender reported in this paper have important implications for the field. In general terms, the research literature is replete with findings from samples of sex offenders who were in their youth to their middle years, on average. The extent to which these general findings in the literature extend to the elderly sex offender remains to be confirmed. More specifically, the samples of sex offenders that have been used in the development and validation of the actuarial instruments have included a preponderance of younger offenders (Hanson, 2001). The average age-at-release in these samples varies from approximately 30 to 39 years of age. Moreover, the distribution of age in these samples was positively skewed. In positively skewed distributions, other measures of central tendency are lower than the value of the arithmetic mean. Therefore, these samples are overweighted with individuals whose ages are even younger than the averages. If sexual aggression decreases with age, the actuarial estimates of probability of reoffense used routinely in offender assessments are based on samples of men who were released at a time in their lives when they were relatively more likely to reoffend. It follows that the estimates for rates of recidivism given by actuarial methods will overestimate rates for older men.

The results reported here have implications for sex offender policy and law. Sexually Violent Predator legislation in the United States, and Dangerous Offender legislation in Canada are most often applied to offenders when they have a substantial history of sexual offenses, and usually when they are older. The result is that the most stringent methods of legal control are applied as the offender's risk for reoffense is decreasing.

ACKNOWLEDGMENTS

We would like to thank our research assistants Michelle Adams, Leigh Harkins, and Heidi Marcon; Sylvia Kim and Thomas Blak for assistance with graphics presentations; Ed Peacock, Robin Wilson, and Shelley Hassard for assistance with access to file material; Martin Lalumière, Michael Seto, Grant Harris, Marnie Rice, and Bill Marshall for comments on an earlier draft; and the Ontario Mental Health Foundation, and the Centre for Addiction and Mental Health for financial support for this research.

REFERENCES

BAKER, H.W.G. & HUDSON, B. (1983). Changes in the pituitary-testicular axis with age. *Monographs on Endocrinology, 25,* 71–83.

BARBAREE, H.E., SETO, M.C., LANGTON, C.M. & PEACOCK, E. J. (2001). Evaluating the predictive accuracy of six risk assessment instruments for adult sex offenders. *Criminal Justice and Behavior, 28,* 490–521.

BLANCHARD, R., KLASSEN, P., DICKEY, R., KUBAN, M.E. & BLAK, T. (2001). Sensitivity and specificity of the phallometric test for pedophilia in nonadmitting sex offenders. *Psychological Assessment, 13,* 118–126.

DENTI, L., PASOLINI, G., SANFELICI, L., BENEDETTI, R., CECCHETTI, A., et al. (2000). Aging-related decline of gonadal function in healthy men: Correlation with body composition and lipoproteins. *Journal of the American Geriatrics Society, 48,* 51–58.

FELDMAN, H.A., GOLDSTEIN, I., HATZICHRISTOU, D.G., KRANE, R.J. & MCKINLAY, J.B. (1994). Impotence and its medical and psychosocial correlates: Results of the Massachusetts male aging study. *Journal of Urology, 151,* 54–61.

FREUND, K. (1967). Diagnosing homo- or heterosexuality and erotic age-preference by means of a psychophysiological test. *Behaviour Research and Therapy, 5,* 209–228.

FREUND, K., SEDLACEK, F. & KNOB, K. (1965). A simple transducer for mechanical plethysmography of the male genital. *Journal of the Experimental Analysis of Behavior, 8,* 169–170.

HALL, G.C.N. (1991). Sexual arousal as a function of physiological and cognitive variables in a sexual offender population. *Archives of Sexual Behavior, 20,* 359–369.

HANSON, R.K. (1997). *The development of a brief actuarial risk scale for sexual offense recidivism* (User report 1997–04). Ottawa: Department of the Solicitor General of Canada.

HANSON, R.K. (2001). *Age and sexual recidivism: A comparison of rapists and child molesters* (User report 2001–01). Ottawa: Department of the Solicitor General of Canada.

HANSON, R.K. & BUSSIÈRE, M.T. (1998). Predicting relapse: A meta-analysis of sexual offender recidivism studies. *Journal of Consulting and Clinical Psychology, 66,* 348–362.

KAEMINGK, K.L., KOSELKA, M., BECKER, J.V. & KAPLAN, M.S. (1995). Age and adolescent sexual offender arousal. *Sexual Abuse: A Journal of Research and Treatment, 7,* 249–257.

KUBAN, M., BARBAREE, H.E. & BLANCHARD, R. (1999). A comparison of volume and circumference phallometry: Response magnitude and method agreement. *Archives of Sexual Behavior, 28,* 345–359.

LANGTON, C.M. (2003). *Contrasting approaches to risk assessment with adult male sexual offenders: An evaluation of recidivism prediction schemes and the utility of supplementary clinical information for enhancing predictive accuracy.* Unpublished doctoral dissertation. University of Toronto.

ROWLAND, D.L., GREENLEAF, W.J., DORFMAN, L.J. & DAVIDSON, J.M. (1993). Aging and sexual function in men. *Archives of Sexual Behavior, 22,* 545–557.

SETO, M.C. & BARBAREE, H.E. (1999). Psychopathy, treatment behavior and sex offender recidivism. *Journal of Interpersonal Violence, 14,* 1235–1248.

SCHIAVI, R.C. (1999). *Aging and male sexuality.* Cambridge, UK: Cambridge University Press.

SJÖSTEDT, G. & LÅNGSTRÖM, N. (2001). Actuarial assessment of sex offender recidivism risk: A cross-validation of the RRASOR and the Static-99 in Sweden. *Law and Human Behavior, 25,* 629–645.

UDRY, J.R., BILLY, J.O.G., MORRIS, N.M., GROFF, T.R. & RAJ, M.H. (1985). Serum androgenic hormones motivate sexual behavior in adolescent boys. *Fertility and Sterility, 43,* 90–94.

The Developmental Antecedents of Sexual Coercion against Women: Testing Alternative Hypotheses with Structural Equation Modeling

RAYMOND A. KNIGHT[a] AND JUDITH E. SIMS-KNIGHT[b]

[a]Department of Psychology, Brandeis University, Walham, Massachusettes 02454, USA

[b] Department of Psychology, University of Massachusetts Dartmouth,
North Dartmouth, Massachusetts 02747-2300, USA

ABSTRACT: A unified model of the origin of sexual aggression against women on both adult and juvenile sexual offender samples has been developed and successfully tested. This model proposed three major causal paths to sexual coercion against women. In the first path, physical and verbal abuse was hypothesized to produce callousness and lack of emotionality, which disinhibited sexual drive and sexual fantasies. These in turn disinhibited hostile sexual fantasies, and led to sexual coercion. In the second causal path, sexual abuse contributed directly to the disinhibition of sexual drive and sexual fantasies, which through hostile sexual fantasies led to sexual coercion. The third path operated through early antisocial behavior, including aggressive acts. It developed as a result of both physical/verbal abuse and callousness/lack of emotion. It in turn directly affected sexual coercion and worked indirectly through the hostile sexual fantasies path. In the present study, the anonymous responses of a group of 168 blue-collar, community males to an inventory (the Multidimensional Assessment of Sex and Aggression) were used in a structural equation model to test the validity of this model. Moreover, this model was pitted against Malamuth's (1998) two-path model. Whereas the three-path model had an excellent fit with the data (CFI = .951, RMSEA = .047), the two-path model fit less well (CFI = .857, RMSEA = .079). These results indicate the superiority of the three-path model and suggest that it constitutes a solid, empirically disconfirmable heuristic for the etiology of sexual coercion against women.

KEYWORDS: sexual abuse; physical abuse; sexual coercion; sexual aggression; antisocial behavior; adult sexual offender; juvenile sexual offender

INTRODUCTION

Although questions about the etiology and the course of sexually aggressive behavior are crucial, research studies specifically addressing these issues have been seriously neglected. This gap in our knowledge constitutes a formidable roadblock to any attempts to adopt a public health model of sexual aggression (McMahon &

Address for correspondence: Raymond Knight, Ph.D., Department of Psychology, MS 062, Brandeis University, Waltham, MA 02454-9110. Voice: 781-736-3259; fax: 781-736-3291.
Knight2@Brandeis.edu

Ann. N.Y. Acad. Sci. 989: 72–85 (2003). © 2003 New York Academy of Sciences.

Puett, 1999; Mercy, 1999; Wurtele, 1999). Early detection, prevention, and intervention have the potential to avoid considerable victim trauma and to interrupt the engraining of treatment-resistant behavioral patterns in perpetrators. The practical implementation of a primary prevention perspective requires, however, well-founded models of etiology and course to guide policies and interventions.

Only one developmental model of sexual aggression against women has had any significant empirical validation—the two-path confluence model proposed by Neil Malamuth, which he has tested on men when they were undergraduate students and ten years later (Malamuth, 1998; Malamuth, Heavey & Linz, 1993). Essentially, the model proposed that the confluence of two factors increases the probability of sexually coercive behavior: (a) sexual promiscuity or sociosexuality (Simpson & Gangestad, 1991), which is the frequency of impersonal sex, and (b) negative masculinity, which includes risk-taking, honor defending, and competitive attitudes and behavior (Malamuth, 1998). Malamuth did not have very extensive measures of early developmental antecedents of these two paths. For instance, his measure of delinquency was having friends who got into trouble with the law and running away.

Testing the Malamuth Model

In our initial explorations of Malamuth's model (Knight, 1993) we administered the Multidimensional Assessment of Sex and Aggression (the MASA; Knight & Cerce, 1999; Knight, Prentky & Cerce, 1994) to both sexual offenders and college students. Because our research program had evolved from the clinical literature and research on sexual offenders, and had initially been designed to generate and assess typological models of sexual coercion (Cohen, Garofalo, Boucher & Seghorn, 1971; Freund, 1988, 1990; Knight, Rosenberg & Schneider, 1985), we focused on the sexual drive, preoccupation, compulsivity, and deviance aspects of the sexual path (i.e., on "sexualization"), rather than on sociosexuality per se. We found that (a) different developmental antecedents than those proposed by Malamuth accounted for the two paths, with sexual abuse in childhood anteceding sexualization and physical abuse predicting negative masculinity, and (b) the two-path model accounted for only a small proportion of the variance of sexual coercion.

Revising Malamuth's Model

These preliminary studies led to a revision of Malamuth's model. The data suggested that the purported homogeneous dimension of negative masculinity was really masking two separate processes. Both factor analytic studies of the Psychopathy Checklist (PCL, see Hare, Harpur, Hakstian, Forth, Hare & Newman, 1990; Harpur, Hakstian & Hare 1988; Harpur, Hare & Hakstian, 1989) and some new creative experimental work on psychopathy (Patrick, 1994; Patrick & Zempolich, 1998) have not only identified two distinct descriptive subcomponents of psychopathy, but there are now some speculations about what constitute their underlying processes. These subcomponents captured different aspects of negative masculinity and mapped nicely onto the data in our revised model. Their incorporation into the model greatly improved the fit of the model.

The revised, three-path model of the origins of sexual aggression (see FIG. 1) comprised two distinct early environmental causes—physical/verbal abuse and sex-

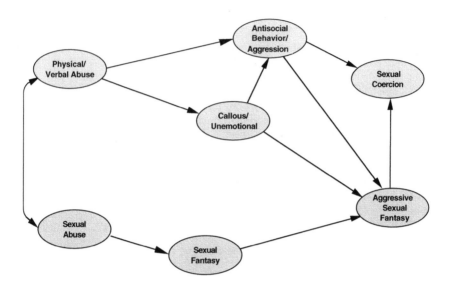

FIGURE 1. *A priori* three-component theoretical structural model predicting sexual coercion against women in adult males.

ual abuse. Physical/verbal abuse was hypothesized to have two roles. First, it increased the likelihood of arrogant, deceitful personality/emotional detachment [Callous/Unemotional (CU) trait in the figure], the first of Hare's two factors on the PCL. Second, it served as a model of aggression, thus increasing the likelihood of the manifestation of aggressive behavior and antisocial, impulsive acting out, similar to Factor 2 of the PCL. Behavioral genetic research suggests that this second factor has high heritability and low environmental influence (Edelbrock, Rende, Plomin & Thompson, 1995; Krueger, 2000; Mason & Frick, 1994; Depue, 1996, but see Livesley, 1998, for contrary evidence), but it is also purported to be influenced by physical/verbal abuse.

Sexual abuse was hypothesized to lead to sexual preoccupation and compulsivity, which in turn increased the risk of aggressive sexual fantasies. Thus, early abuse experiences plus personality predispositions were hypothesized to combine to produce three latent traits that predict sexual aggression—arrogant, deceitful personality/ emotional detachment, impulsivity/antisocial behaviors, and sexual preoccupation/ hypersexuality.

Testing of the Three-Path Model on Adult and Juvenile Sexual Offenders

Adult Sexual Offenders

The predictive power of the revised three-path model was first tested on a new sample of 275 incarcerated male sexual offenders from a variety of prisons in Minnesota and New Jersey, using both computerized and paper-and-pencil versions of the MASA. The scale construction paralleled that described for the present study.

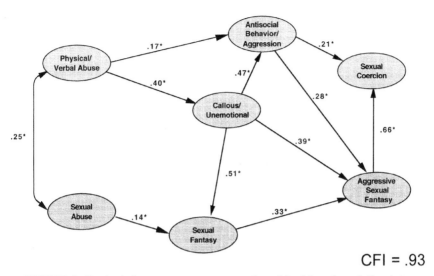

FIGURE 2. Revised three-component structural model adding the relation between Callousness/Unemotional and Sexual Fantasy.

These scales and their latent traits were fashioned into the three-path causal model presented in FIGURE 1 and analyzed using EQS (Bryne, 1994). The fit of the data to the original *a priori* model, presented in FIGURE 1, was good (Comparative Fit Index [CFI] = .91), supporting the hypothesis that the three paths interacted in the proposed manner to predict sexually coercive behavior. As suggested by the R^2 Lagrange Multiplier Test (Bryne, 1994), the model was significantly improved, however, by adding a path from CU to Sexual Fantasy (CFI = .93). In this adjusted model, which is the one presented in FIGURE 2, 65% of the variance of both Sexual Coercion and Aggressive Sexual Fantasy (i.e., = .65 for each) was accounted for, and each of the three paths contributed to the prediction of sexual coercion.

Juvenile Sexual Offenders

The revised model developed on adult sexual offenders was then used to predict sexually coercive behavior against women and girls in a sample of 218 juvenile sexual offenders, using the computerized version of the MASA. The juveniles in this new sample came from inpatient juvenile sexual offender treatment facilities in Maine, Massachusetts, Minnesota, and Virginia. All participants had been adjudicated for sexual offenses involving sexual contact with a victim. The mean age of the sample was 15.97, and including the present offense, these offenders had been incarcerated an average of 3.06 times. The sample was ethnically diverse.

The confirmatory analysis of the revised adult model showed a reasonable fit to the data, as indicated by a CFI of .90 (Byrne, 1994, 2001) and a root-mean-square error of approximation (RMSEA) of .070 (Brown & Cudeck, 1993: a RMSEA below .08 indicates a reasonable fit). The two-path alternative, which required the restructuring of the model to closely match Malamuth's model, did not fit the data as well (CFI = .80; RMSEA = .096). The most notable differences between the juvenile and adult models were: (a) the smaller percent of variance of both Aggressive Sexual Fantasies and Sexual Coercion accounted for in the juvenile results, $R^2 = .44$ and .37, respectively, and (b) three paths that were significant in the adults' solution failed to yield significant standardized betas in the juvenile data—Physical/Verbal Abuse to Antisocial Behavior/Aggression, Antisocial Behavior/Aggression to Aggressive Sexual Fantasy, and Sexual Abuse to Sexual Fantasy. Modification indices suggested a significant direct effect of Sexual Abuse on Sexual Coercion ($\beta = .25$). When a revised *post hoc* model was calculated with this new path added and nonsignificant paths eliminated, the CFI increased only slightly to .91.

The cross-sample consistency of the three-path model provides support for a unified theory of sexual aggression against women. The comparison with the two-path model suggests that the three-path model is a superior model, at least among sexual offenders. It was important to test this revised three-model on a non–sex offender sample. Consequently, the purpose of the present study was to test this same three-path model on a noncriminal, community sample that closely matched the adult sexual offenders in socioeconomic status.

METHOD

Participants

The 168 community controls in this study were all sampled from the Mummers, a male club in Philadelphia, Pennsylvania. A large portion of the local chapter of the club volunteered because their payment for participation, $25.00 each, was donated to the organization. Some characteristics of this adult sample are presented in TABLE 1. In age, marital status, and years of education these community controls were comparable to, and did not differ significantly from the adult criminal sample we had tested earlier. The distribution of races in this sample was, however, limited—97.6% Caucasian. This was considerably different from both criminal samples, which had significantly more African-Americans, Hispanics, and Asians. As can be seen in TABLE 1, the salary levels of the community sample indicated a preponderance of lower-middle class and middle class participants.

Procedure

Test Administration

All participants were administered the paper-and-pencil version of the MASA in groups of 12 to 25 participants. As in the testing of the adult and juvenile sexual offenders, the participants were assured that all of their responses were completely anonymous. Respondents did not put their names on any test forms. Moreover, a Certificate of Confidentiality from NIMH protected the assurance of confidentiality and anonymity.

The MASA

The MASA was originally developed to supplement our coding of archival records, which we had found significantly lacking in the area of sexual behavior, cognitions, and fantasies. As we expanded our subject pool to include institutions

TABLE 1. Descriptive data for the participants

Characteristic		
Age	M	35.20
	SD	12.68
Number of arrests	M	0.83
	SD	1.47
Years of education	M	12.24
	SD	1.88
Percent married		51%
Race	African-American	0.6%
	Asian	0%
	Caucasian	97.6%
	Hispanic	0%
	Other	1.8%
Salary	None	9.6%
	<$5000	3.6%
	$5000–$10,000	5.4%
	$10,000–$25,000	21.0%
	$25,000–$40,000	31.1%
	$40,000–$50,000	19.2%
	>$50,000	10.2%

other than the Massachusetts Treatment Center, we had to expand the coverage of the MASA, because the records at these institutions lacked the information that we needed for our typological investigations. Consequently, in the first version of the MASA we assessed the following ten domains—social competence, juvenile and adult antisocial behavior, sexualization, paraphilias, pornography exposure, offense planning, sadism, expressive aggression, and pervasive anger. We have factor analyzed the items in each of these domains. The factors yielded have been replicated on new samples and the factor scores show both high internal consistency and test–retest reliability (Knight & Cerce, 1999).

The MASA has been revised six times and is now only administered in a computerized format. It has been administered to over 2000 males and 200 females. As we continued to revise the MASA, we added assessments of other components of thought and behavior that were hypothesized to be critical in the development and assessment of sexual coercion. In the present study we have added to the ten original domains sexual abuse, physical abuse, emotional detachment, and arrogant and deceitful personality.

RESULTS

Scale Construction

For the community adult sample, the observed measures (depicted as rectangles in FIG. 3) for each of the latent traits (depicted as ovals) were exactly the same mea-

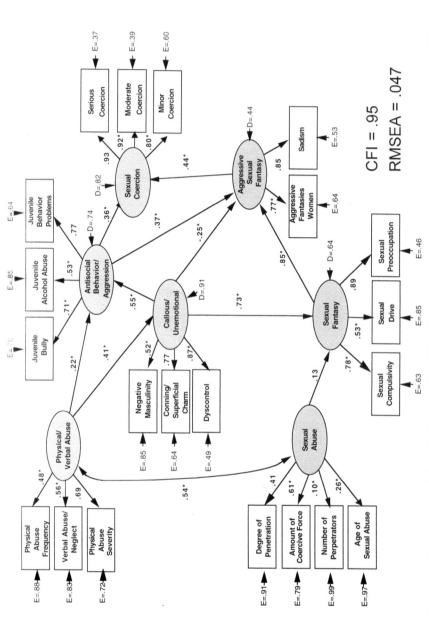

FIGURE 3. *A priori* three-component theoretical structural model predicting sexual coercion against women, tested in a sample of 168 adult community workers.

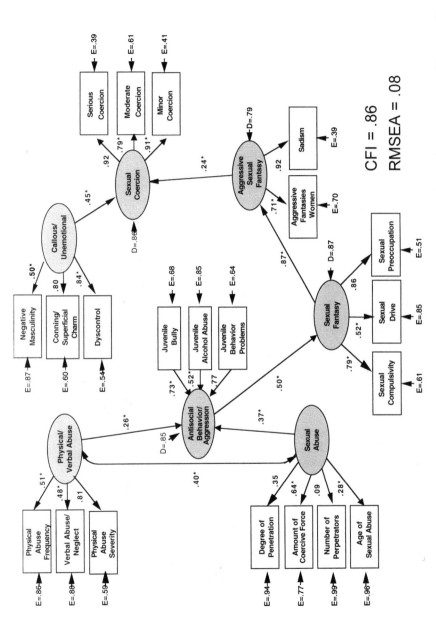

FIGURE 4. Malamuth's two-path component theoretical structural model predicting sexual coercion against women, tested in a sample of 168 adult community blue-collar workers.

sures as those created for the juvenile model. The internal consistencies of all summative scales were tested to provide an indication of whether these components cohered in community participants the way that they did in the juveniles. Of the 15 scales so tested, only one, Sexual Drive ($\alpha = .38$), had an alpha that fell below .70. Seven scales had alphas between .70 and .79, and the remaining seven were equal to or greater than .80. An additional six scales in the model, all early developmental scales, were calculated either as a maximum, minimum, or count over a number of responses or response categories (e.g., physical abuse frequency) or as a complex algorithm over a number of responses (e.g., degree of penetration).

For both the adult and juvenile sexual offenders we had calculated factor analyses of both the early developmental antecedents and the psychopathy-related scales. For both samples the analysis of childhood abuse scales yielded two separate, theoretically clean factors, one for Physical/Verbal Abuse and the other for Sexual Abuse. The analysis of the psychopathy-related scales yielded different results for the two samples. Whereas for the adult sexual offenders two factors emerged—CU and Impulsive, Aggressive Behavior, the juvenile factor analysis yielded three separate factors that corresponded more closely to Cooke and Michie's (2001) three-factor solution. Because the Empathy, Perspective-taking, Guilt factor was completely independent of the Callousness factor, we decided in the juvenile model not to force it into the CU trait. The community sample analysis also yielded three factors and was treated in the same way. Also, the juvenile analysis had included a scale of items from Monroe's (1978) Dyscontrol Scale, a self-report measure of impulsivity. Because it loaded highly on the CU factor, and significantly less on the Antisocial Behavior/Aggression factor in both the juvenile and community samples, we left the scale on the CU factor in both analyses.

The three sexual coercion outcome observable measures were differentiated in terms of the sexual acts in the coercive sexual behavior against a woman. Serious coercion involved attempted or completed intercourse. Moderate coercion involved oral sex or anal penetration. Mild coercion included touching, feeling, kissing, or petting. The victim was defined as a woman if she was older than 16 years. The dependent measure was the maximum number of the specific sexual acts against an age-appropriate or older female, regardless of the method of coercion (plying with alcohol, manipulation against their will, verbal threats, or physical force). Sexually coercive acts against males and younger females were not counted in these measures of sexual coercion.

Confirmatory Analysis

As can be seen in FIGURE 3, the confirmatory analysis of the revised three-path model showed a very good fit to the data, as indicated by a CFI of .95 (Byrne, 1994, 2001) and a RMSEA of .047 (Brown & Cudeck, 1993: a RMSEA below .05 indicates an excellent fit). The three paths accounted for a greater percent of the variance of Aggressive Sexual Fantasies ($R^2 = .81$) than they did for Sexually Coercive behavior ($R^2 = .33$). This model was compared to a two-path model designed to match Malamuth's (Malamuth et al., 1993) as closely as possible. His delinquency to sexual promiscuity path was approximated by our sexual and physical/verbal abuse to antisocial behaviors to sexual fantasy to aggressive sexual fantasy. His attitudes supporting violence to negative masculinity path was approximated by our CU trait, for which negative masculinity is one of the three observed indicators. This alternative two-path model did not fit the data as well (CFI = .86; RMSEA = .080). This model also accounted for a slightly lower percent of Sexual Coercion variance (R^2 = .26) than the three-path model, and a considerably lower percent of the variance of Aggressive Sexual Fantasies (R^2 = .38). This alternative model is presented in FIGURE 4.

The most notable differences on the confirmatory, three-path model between the community adults and the adult sexual offenders were: (a) the smaller percent of variance of Sexual Coercion (behavior) accounted for in the community sample and the greater percent of variance of Aggressive Sexual Fantasies accounted for in the community sample; (b) only in the community sample did the CU latent trait have no zero-order correlation with Aggressive Sexual Fantasy, and consequently it served as a suppressor variable for predicting that latent trait; and (c) the Sexual Abuse latent trait did not cohere as well in the community sample as it did in the two sexually aggressive samples, especially the observed variables—the number of perpetrators and the age of sexual abuse.

DISCUSSION

The most important finding in the present study was the high congruence between the results for the adult sexual offenders and the community sample. The ability of the model to predict across criminal and noncriminal samples and across juvenile and adult developmental stages strongly supports the possibility that a unified theory of sexual aggression can be fashioned to explain a considerable portion of the variance of sexually coercive behavior against women. This consistency suggests that we will be able to identify basic processes in the form of specific dispositions and identifiable developmental experiences that increase the potential for sexual coercion. Such identification is the first step toward primary prevention. Having a validated model of the etiology of sexual aggression is the cornerstone of any public health approach to sexual aggression and a necessary prerequisite for implementation of a primary prevention perspective.

It is important to emphasize that the three traits that define the three paths— sexual drive/preoccupation, antisocial behavior, and callousness/unemotionality— correspond to core theoretical processes identified in both the experimental and psychometric research on psychopathy and in the personality literature. In addition, it can be argued that these same three traits account for a considerable proportion of the variance of factors identified as predictors of general recidivism (Gendreau, Little & Goggin, 1996), and more specifically of factors that predict recidivism for a sexual crime in adults (Hanson & Bussière, 1998). These variables play a prominent role in the risk assessment scales that have been fashioned to predict recidivism in adult sexual offenders (Hanson, 2000). Similarly, for juveniles the first two factors for the Juvenile Sex Offender Risk Assessment Schedule (J-SOAP) are sexual drive/ sexual preoccupation and impulsive, antisocial behavior (Prentky, Harris, Frizzel & Righthand, 2000). Moreover, the J-SOAP's third scale, "Intervention," with its emphasis on failing to accept responsibility, lacking internal motivation, empathy, remorse, and guilt, and maintaining cognitive (callous?) distortions corresponds well to the CU factor (Knight & Zakireh, 2002). These three components, or their related behavioral correlates, constitute key targets of therapeutic intervention for sexual aggression (e.g., Righthand & Welch, 2001). Thus, these three components appear to play a critical role in the etiology of sexual coercion and in the modulation of such behavior across the life span.

This study compared the three-component model to one analogous to Malamuth's two-path model. Even giving considerable leeway in predicting aspects of the data not explicitly specified by that model, that model still accounted less well for the data than the three-path model. In fairness to Malamuth's model, it is important to point out that Malamuth's conceptualization of the sexual path is quite different from the one included in this model. Malamuth (1998) argued that sexual promiscuity (or sociosexuality) fits the available data better than sexual drive. We agree that they are different variables, but our data suggest that sexual drive is a potent variable. In addition to the data reported here, Knight and Prentky (2003) compared rapists to community and criminal controls and divided the controls into subgroups of self-admitted sexual aggressors and coercion deniers on the basis of their anonymous answers to questions about their sexually coercive behavior. Sexually aggressive males (criminal and noncriminal) reported significantly higher frequencies of sexual preoccupation and compulsivity, sexual drive, and paraphilic fantasies and behaviors than the noncoercive males. In addition, Knight (in press) presented evidence that this same cluster of sexual variables produced patterns in taxometic analyses (see Meehl, 1999) that suggested that hypersexuality was distributed as a taxon rather than a dimension. These data suggest that sexualization or hypersexuality (Kafka, 1997) may be the core sexual component involved in sexual coercion against women. We are currently collecting data in which both sexualization and sociosexuality are measured, so that we can compare their relative contributions to sexual coercion.

This difference is important to resolve, because the two conceptions of sexuality have different implications for evolutionary theorizing. Clearly, if promiscuity (or sociosexuality) is the operative variable, then the specific theory proposed by several authors (e.g., Malamuth, 1998; Quinsey & Lalumière, 1995 Thornhill & Thornhill, 1992) would be supported, because of the congruity of the specific design of this variable and the theoretical model (Andrews, Gangestad & Matthews, in press). These models have proposed that the proclivity for sexual coercion is related to particular divergent mating tactics, such as a preference for short-term relationships, a propensity for extra-pair romances, and a desire to engage in impersonal or uncommitted sexual behavior (i.e., to sociosexuality) that hypothetically provide a reproductive, and therefore evolutionary benefit for males. Consequently, the proclivity for impersonal sex has been hypothesized to be adaptive for and naturally selected for males. If, however, sexual drive is the more predictive variable, it would be consistent with a variety of mating strategies, monogamy, polygamy, promiscuity, or combinations of pair-bonding and extra-bond mating, and would not necessarily be differentially selected for males. Men with high sex drives who are callous and unemotional might express exclusively short-term mating strategy, whereas men with high sex drives who are also driven by attachment needs or constrained by their sociocultural environment, might express that sexuality in one of the other mating strategies.

The model presented here is only a preliminary structure; problems and inconsistencies still remain. Other developmental antecedents must be measured and explored. It must be determined whether the callous, arrogant, and deceitful personality and emotional detachment are better conceived as a single factor or two separate traits. The core processes underlying the traits in the model must be explored, and behavioral/performance-based, psychometrically sound measures of these processes must be developed. There are many questions that remain unanswered, but the model provides a solid, empirically disconfirmable beginning.

ACKNOWLEDGMENT

Research Grants R01-MH54263 from the National Institute of Mental Health, and 94-IJ-CX-0049 and 92-IJ-CX-K032 from the National Institute of Justice supported the research reported in this paper.

REFERENCES

ANDREWS, P.W., GANGESTAD, S.W. & MATTHEWS, D. (in press).. Adaptationism—How to carry out an exaptationist program. *Behavioral and Brain Sciences.*

BROWN, M.W. & CUDECK, R. (1993). Alternative ways of assessing model fit. In K.A. Bollen & J.S. Long (Eds.), *Testing structural equation models* (pp. 445–455). Newbury Park, CA: Sage Publications.

BYRNE, B.M. (1994). *Structural equation modeling with EQS and EQS/Windows: Basic concepts, applications, and programming.* Thousand Oaks, CA: Sage Publications.

BYRNE, B.M. (2001). *Structural equation modeling with AMOS: Basic concepts, applications, and programming.* Mahwah, NJ: Lawrence Erlbaum.

COHEN, M.L., GAROFALO, R.F., BOUCHER, R. & SEGHORN, T. (1971). The psychology of rapists. *Seminars in Psychiatry, 3,* 307–327.

COOKE, D.J. & MICHIE, C. (2001). Refining the construct of psychopathy: Towards a hierarchical model. *Psychological Assessment, 13,* 171–188.

DEPUE, R.A. (1996). A neurobiological framework for the structure of personality and emotion: Implications for personality disorders. In J.F. Clarkin & M.F. Lenzenweger (Eds.), *Major theories of personality disorder* (pp. 347–390). New York: Guilford Press.

EDELBROCK, C., RENDE, R., PLOMIN, R. & THOMPSON, L.A. (1995). A twin study of competence and problem behavior in childhood and early adolescence. *Journal of Child Psychology and Psychiatry, 36,* 775–785.

FREUND, K. (1988). Courtship disorder: Is this hypothesis valid? In R.A. Prentky & V. Quinsey (Eds.), *Human sexual aggression: Current perspectives* (Vol. 528, pp. 172–182). New York: Annals of the New York Academy of Sciences.

FREUND, K. (1990). Courtship disorder. In W.L. Marshall, D.R. Laws & H.E. Barbaree (Eds.), *The handbook of sexual assault: Issues, theories, and treatment of the offender* (pp. 195–207). New York: Plenum Press.

GENDREAU, P., LITTLE, T. & GOGGIN, C. (1996). A meta-analysis of the predictors of adult offender recidivism: What works! *Criminology, 34,* 575–607.

HANSON, R.K. (2000). *Risk assessment.* Beaverton, OR: Association for the Treatment of Sexual Abusers.

HANSON, R.K. & BUSSIÈRE, M.T. (1998). Predicting relapse: A meta-analysis of sexual offender recidivism studies. *Journal of Consulting and Clinical Psychology, 66,* 348–362.

HARE, R.D., HARPUR, T.J., HAKSTIAN, A.R., FORTH, A.E., HART, S.D. & NEWMAN, J.P. (1990). The revised Psychopathy Checklist: Reliability and factor structure. *Psychological Assessment, 2,* 338–341.

HARMAN, H.H. (1967). *Modern factor analysis.* Chicago: University of Chicago Press.

HARPUR, T.J., HAKSTIAN, A. & HARE, R.D. (1988). Factor structure of the Psychopathy Checklist. *Journal of Consulting and Clinical Psychology, 56,* 741–747.

HARPUR, T.J., HARE, R.D. & HAKSTIAN, A. (1989). Two-factor conceptualization of psychopathy: Construct validity and assessment implications. *Psychological Assessment: A Journal of Consulting and Clinical Psychology, 1*, 6–17.

KAFKA, M.P. (1997). Hypersexual desire in males: An operational definition and clinical implications for males with paraphilias and paraphilia-related disorders. *Archives of Sexual Behavior, 26*, 505–526.

KNIGHT, R.A. (in press). Typologies/profiles of rapists. In J.R. Conte (Ed.), *Handbook on trauma and abuse*. New York: Sage Publications.

KNIGHT, R.A. (1993, November). *The developmental and social antecedents of sexual aggression*. Invited presentation to the 12th Annual Conference of The Association for the Treatment of Sexual Abusers, Boston, MA.

KNIGHT, R.A. & CERCE, D.D. (1999). Validation and revision of the Multidimensional Assessment of Sex and Aggression. *Psychologica Belgica, 39*(2/3), 187–213.

KNIGHT, R.A. & PRENTKY, R.A. (2003). The role of sexual motivation in sexually coercive behavior. Manuscript submitted for publication.

KNIGHT, R.A., PRENTKY, R.A. & CERCE, D. (1994). The development, reliability, and validity of an inventory for the multidimensional assessment of sex and aggression. *Criminal Justice and Behavior, 21*, 72–94.

KNIGHT, R.A., ROSENBERG, R. & SCHNEIDER, B. (1985). Classification of sexual offenders: Perspectives, methods, and validation. In A.W. Burgess (Ed.), *Research handbook on rape and sexual assault* (pp. 222–293). New York: Garland Publishing.

KNIGHT, R.A. & SIMS-KNIGHT, J.E. (in press). The developmental antecedents of sexual coercion against women in adolescents. In R. Geffner & K. Franey (Eds.), *Sex offenders: Assessment and treatment*. New York: Haworth Press.

KNIGHT, R.A. & ZAKIREH, B. (2002, October). *Assessing juvenile sexual offenders using the multidimensional assessment of sex and aggression*. Paper presented at the 20th Annual Meeting of the Association for the Treatment of Sexual Abusers, Montreal, Canada.

KRUEGER, R.F. (2000). Pheontypic, genetic, and non-shared environmental parallels in the structure of personality: A view from the Multidimensional Personality Questionnaire. *Journal of Personality and Social Psychology, 79*, 1057–1067.

LIVESLEY, W.J. (1998). The phenotypic and genotypic structure of psychopathic traits. In D.J. Cooke, A. Forth & R.D. Hare (Eds.), *Psychopathy: Theory, research and implications for society* (pp. 69–79). Dordtrecht: Kluwer Academic Publishers.

MALAMUTH, N.M. (1998). An evolutionary-based model integrating research on the characteristics of sexually coercive men. In J. Adair, K. Dion & D. Belanger (Eds.), *Advances in psychological science: Vol. 1. Social, personal, and developmental aspects* (pp. 151–184). Hove, UK: Psychology Press/Erlbaum.

MALAMUTH, N.M., HEAVEY, C.L. & LINZ, D. (1993). Predicting men's antisocial behavior against women: The interaction model of sexual aggression. In G.C. Nagayama Hall, R. Hirschman, J.R. Graham & M.S. Zaragoza (Eds.), *Sexual aggression: Issues in etiology and assessment, treatment and policy* (pp. 63–97). Washington, DC: Hemisphere Publishing.

MASON, D.A. & FRICK, P.J. (1994). The heritability of antisocial behavior: A meta-analysis of twin and adoption studies. *Journal of Psychopathology and Behavioral Assessment, 16*, 301–323.

MCMAHON, P. & PUETT, R. (1999). Child sexual abuse as a public health issue: Recommendations of an expert panel. *Sexual Abuse: A Journal of Research and Treatment, 11*, 257–266.

MEEHL, P.E. (1999). Clarifications about taxometric method. *Applied & Preventive Psychology, 8*, 165–174.

MERCY, J.A. (1999). Having new eyes: Viewing child sexual abuse as a public health problem. *Sexual Abuse: A Journal of Research and Treatment, 11*, 317–322.

MONROE, R.R. (1978). The medical model in psychopathy and dyscontrol syndromes. In W.H. Reid (Ed.), *The psychopath*. New York: Bruner/Mazel.

PATRICK, C.J. (1994). Emotion and psychopathy: Startling new insights. *Psychophysiology, 31*, 319–330.

PATRICK, C.J. & ZEMPOLICH, K.A. (1998). Emotion and aggression in the psychopathic personality. *Aggression and Violent Behavior, 3*, 303–338.

PRENTKY, R.A., HARRIS, B., FRIZZEL, K. & RIGHTHAND, S. (2000). An actuarial procedure for assessing risk with juvenile sex offenders. *Sexual Abuse: A Journal of Research and Treatment, 12,* 71–93.

QUINSEY, V.L. & LALUMIÈRE, M.L. (1995). Evolutionary perspectives on sexual offending. *Sexual Abuse: A Journal of Research and Treatment, 7,* 301–315.

RIGHTHAND, S. & WELCH, C. (2001). *Juveniles who have sexually offended: A review of the professional literature.* Washington, DC: Office of Juvenile Justice and Delinquency Prevention.

SIMPSON, J.A. & GANGESTAD, S.W. (1991). Individual differences in sociosexuality: Evidence for convergent and discriminant validity. *Journal of Personality and Social Psychology, 60,* 870–883.

THORNHILL, R. & THORNHILL, N.W. (1992). The evolutionary psychology of men's coercive sexuality. *Behavioral and Brain Sciences, 15,* 363–421.

WURTELE, S.K. (1999). Comprehensiveness and collaboration: Key ingredients of an effective public health approach to preventing child sexual abuse. *Sexual Abuse: A Journal of Research and Treatment, 11,* 323–325.

The Monoamine Hypothesis for the Pathophysiology of Paraphilic Disorders: An Update

MARTIN P. KAFKA

Department of Psychiatry, Harvard Medical School, Boston, Massachusetts 02115, USA, and McLean Hospital, Belmont, Massachusetts 02478, USA

ABSTRACT: A monoamine hypothesis for the pathophysiology of paraphilic disorders was first articulated in 1997 by Kafka. This hypothesis was based on four converging lines of empirical evidence. First, the monoamine neurotransmitters, dopamine, norepinephrine, and serotonin serve a modulatory role in human and mammalian sexual motivation, appetitive, and consummatory behavior. Second, the sexual effects of pharmacological agents that affect monoamine neurotransmitters can have both significant facilitative and inhibitory effects on sexual behavior. Third, paraphilic disorders appear to have Axis I comorbid associations with nonsexual psychopathologies that are associated with monoaminergic dysregulation. Last, pharmacological agents that enhance central serotonergic function in particular, have been reported to ameliorate paraphilic sexual arousal and behavior. Contemporary data supporting or refuting a monoaminergic hypothesis as a biological component associated with paraphilic sex offending behaviors will be reviewed. Particular attention will be given to pharmacological–metabolic probe studies, reports of Axis I comorbidity, the proposed role of disinhibited sexual motivation or sexual appetitive behavior, and cumulative pharmacological treatment data sets.

KEYWORDS: serotonin; neurotransmitters; sexual behavior; psychopathology; monoaminergic dysregulation; paraphilic disorders; sex offender; Axis I comorbidity; medical therapy

INTRODUCTION

Any attempt to organize a theory of etiology or pathophysiology to explain a complex set of behaviors must first define a syndrome or taxon of behaviors that can be consistently and uniformly characterized. Although the reliability, validity, and operational definition of some paraphilic disorders has been challenged (O'Donohue, Regev & Hagstrom, 2000), the core clinical features of paraphilias described during the past 20 years by consensus panels of experts include the following: paraphilias, found predominantly in males, are repetitive, compelling, socially deviant sexual behaviors that are associated with personal distress, harm to others, or

Address for correspondence: Martin P. Kafka, M.D., Senior Attending Psychiatrist, McLean Hospital, 115 Mill Street, Belmont, MA 02478. Voice: 617-855-3191; fax: 617-855-2272.
mpkafka@aol.com

Ann. N.Y. Acad. Sci. 989: 86–94 (2003). © 2003 New York Academy of Sciences.

other expressions of significant psychosocial impairment (American Psychiatric Association, 1980, 2000).

Sex offenders are a very heterogeneous group of men. Indeed, the taxonomic classification of incarcerated rapists and pedophiles has served to highlight the remarkable diversity of sex offender subtypes (Prentky & Burgess, 2000). In this paper, I will attempt to synthesize recent research specifically delineating clinical psychopathology and neurobiological correlates associated with that group of male sex offenders who also meet diagnostic criteria for paraphilic diagnoses. Inasmuch as adult sexual coercion is not currently included under the paraphilic diagnostic umbrella, this theoretical formulation does not specifically include adult rapists, although some serial rapists have been considered to have a paraphilic rape disorder (Abel & Osborn, 1992).

Approximately 5 years ago, Kafka suggested that paraphilic disorders may be associated with monoaminergic dysregulation in the central nervous system (Kafka, 1997a). This hypothesis, advanced to explain a possible role for monoamines in the pathophysiology of repetitive, socially deviant sexual behaviors, was based on four converging lines of evidence and associated with the clinical observation that paraphilias can be characterized as sexual appetitive behavior disorders (Kafka. 1997b). First, the monoaminergic neurotransmitters—norepinephrine, dopamine, and serotonin—are important neuroregulators associated with human and animal sexual motivation/appetite (Meston & Frolich, 2000). Second, data gathered from studies of the sexual "side effect" profiles of commonly prescribed antidepressants, psychostimulants, and neuroleptics strongly suggested that these pharmacological agents can significantly affect sexual appetitive behavior, including both sexual motivation and consummatory behaviors (Crenshaw & Goldberg, 1996). Third, data in support of this hypothesis was presented that correlated monoamine neurotransmitter dysregulation with the specific dimensions of psychopathology associated with studies of paraphilic sexual aggressors. These clinical dimensions included antisocial impulsivity, anxiety, depression, and hypersexuality. Last, clinical reports that pharmacological agents that enhance central serotonin neurotransmission could reduce paraphilic sexual arousal and behavior were reviewed, as these studies supported the espoused theory (Greenberg & Bradford, 1997).

Any theory that is initially proposed to explain a complex set of behaviors must be subject to further empirical validation by various lines of clinical and biological investigation. I will try to "update" the monoamine hypothesis by reviewing data predominantly published since the 1997 report that support, extend, limit, or refute the putative role of monoamine neuromodulators in the pathophysiology of paraphilias.

MONOAMINE STUDIES OF PARAPHILIC MALES

There are now several research reports that support the basic concept that monoaminergic dysregulation may be associated with deviant sexual arousal and paraphilic status. Kogan and colleagues (1995) reported higher levels of catecholamine metabolites (norepinephrine and dopamine) in a mixed group of sex offenders, including "compulsive" paraphiliacs. Maes and associates (2001a, b) intensively studied eight pedophiles (with no other comorbid Axis I or II psychopathology) and compared them to 11 normal controls in two neurobiological studies. A series of differences between controls and pedophiles were reported, including that pedophiles had lower baseline cortisol and prolactin, higher baseline body temperature, higher baseline epinephrine levels, and a more exaggerated response to pharmacological provocation of serum cortisol and epinephrine with m-CCP, a pharmacological probe with affinity for CNS serotonergic receptors (Maes et al., 2001a). The authors concluded that pedophilia, a paraphilic disorder, might be associated with a dysregulation of serotonergic receptor sensitivity. They speculated that pedophilia may be associated with decreased presynaptic serotonergic activity accompanied by a compensatory up-regulation of postsynaptic serotonin 2A/2C receptors.

The central serotonergic system modulates many different neurobiological functions, but biological evidence is consistent that diminished serotonergic neurotransmission is associated with a propensity toward behavioral disinhibition (Soubrie, 1986), and specifically with violence and impulsive aggression (Kavoussi, Armstead & Coccaro, 1997). It is possible, then, that the biological correlates that were reported in these studies were not specific for pedophilia, but more generally associated with behavioral disinhibition. These data, while far from definitive, certainly support a monoaminergic biological component associated with repetitive socially deviant sexual behavior, even in the absence of apparent Axis I psychopathology.

AXIS I COMORBIDITY AND PARAPHILIAS

Despite extensive and methodologically sound data characterizing the importance and prevalence of psychiatric comorbidity in clinical and community populations, the systematic study of Axis I comorbid diagnoses in sex offenders paraphiliacs is still under-studied in comparison to other Axis I disorders. On the other hand, the number and quality of such investigations has increased in recent years, and these data consistently suggests that certain psychiatric diagnoses may be more prevalent among sex offender paraphiliacs. In particular, mood disorders (dysthymic disorder, major depression, and bipolar subtypes), anxiety disorders (social phobia, panic disorder, posttraumatic stress disorder), psychoactive substance abuse (especially alcohol abuse), conduct disorder and attention deficit hyperactivity disorder may be more prevalent among adolescent and adult male paraphilic sex offenders (Kafka & Prentky, 1998; Kafka & Hennen, 2002; Fago, 1999; Raymond, Coleman, Ohlerking, Christenson & Miner, 1999; McElroy, Soutello, Taylor, et al., 1999; Gali, McElroy, Soutello, et al., 1999). Although monoaminergic dysregulation has consistently been reported in many of the aforementioned Axis I psychiatric syndromes (Comings, 2001; Ressler & Nemeroff, 2000; Yates, 2001), neurobiological perturbations of central monoamine neuroregulation have been implicated in most of the major Axis I psychiatric illnesses that have been recently systematically investigated, including many not specifically associated with paraphilic conditions. In this case, then, the more salient clinical question is whether putative monoaminergic abnormalities associated with consistently identified nonsexual Axis I psychopathological states comorbidly occurring with sexual aggression would share specific pathophysiological associations with paraphilic syndromes and whether treatments specifically targeting these monoaminergic pathways could ameliorate both paraphilic disorders and their associated Axis I comorbidity.

PARAPHILIAS, SEXUAL APPETITE, AND MONOAMINES

Paraphilias are considered as primary sexual disorders (American Psychiatric Association, 1994, 2000), but they are reserved for a separate category distinct from the sexual dysfunctions and gender-identity disorders. As sexual disorders, the pathophysiology associated with paraphilias could have some neurobiological representation associated with the human sexual response cycle, but any specific relationship between paraphilias and other sexual "dysfunctions" have not been consistently elucidated. The operational definition of paraphilias as conditions associated with "recurrent, intense sexually arousing fantasies, sexual urges or behaviors" (American Psychiatric Association, 1980, 2000) implies that these disorders affect both sexual arousal and sexual motivation, characteristics associated with the desire phase of the human sexual response (American Psychiatric Association, 2000; Levin, 1994). Indeed, there are some data that paraphilias are frequently associated with persistently increased sexual appetitive behavior (both engaging in overt sexual behavior as well as sexual preoccupation) across the adolescent and adult lifecycle and that this appetitive dysregulation or hypersexual desire is most apparent in males with multiple paraphilic diagnoses (Kafka, 1997a; Hanson & Harris, 2000; Kafka & Hennen, in press). Clinical indicators associated with "hypersexuality" have also been reported in a large sample of sexually coercive males as well ($n = 212$), independent of their paraphilic status (Knight & Cerce, 1999; R. Knight, personal communication, 4/7/02). If we consider, based on the aforementioned data, that paraphilias could be sexual desire phase disorders associated with disinhibited sexual appetitive behavior in contrast to inhibited sexual desire (hypoactive sexual desire disorder), then a putative pathophysiology for paraphilic behavior should be associated with neurophysiological perturbations affecting sexual motivation or sexual desire.

The specific neurobiological substrate for human sexual appetitive behavior is still largely unexplored. Studies of male rats, the "typical" mammal extensively studied as the mammalian model of sexual behavior, suggest that androgenic hormones, monoaminergic neurotransmitters, and neuropeptides have the most profound effects on sexual motivation and appetitive behavior (Hull, Lorrain, Du, et al. 1999; Mas, 1995). It has been cogently argued that the appetitive/motivational phase of sexual behavior in male rats has some homology with human sexual motivation (Everitt & Bancroft, 1991; Pfaus, 1996) as well. In current animal models of sexual appetitive behavior, a neurobiological substrate associated with male sexual motivation/appetite is apparently determined by the presence of sufficient testosterone in association with the increased release of dopamine in some limbic (e.g., medial amygdala, nucleas accumbens) and hypothalamic nuclei (medial preoptic, lateral hypothalamic) when an external stimulus (e.g., an estrous female) is presented (Everitt, 1995). Dopamine increases both during sexual approach in anticipation of genital behavior (appetitive phase) and during copulation (consummatory phase) as well (Mas, Fumero, Fernandez-Vera & Gonzalez-Mora, 1995). In male rats, dopamine release and turnover increases in both the hypothalamic medial preoptic area (mPOA) and the nucleas accumbens (NA) during conditions associated with increased sexual motivation and copulatory behavior. At the time of ejaculation, however, serotonin is released in the lateral hypothalamic area (but not the mPOA), and this release is associated with the inhibition of limbic NA dopamine release (Lorrain, Matuszewich, Friedman & Hull, 1997). The release of serotonin and the inhibition of dopamine are associated with impaired copulation, suggesting a model for sexual "satiety" (Lorrain, Riolo, Matuszewich & Hull, 1999). Indeed, the administration of serotonergic enhancing agents, including fluoxetine, suppress sexual behavior in male rats (Baum & Starr, 1980; McKenna, 2001). Studies in other nonhuman primates suggest there is a more complex interaction between monoaminergic receptor subtypes and either the facilitation or inhibition of masculine sexual behavior, although most investigators cite an inhibitory role for serotonin and an excitatory role for dopamine (Pomerantz, 1995) in sexual appetitive behavior.

If we apply a sexual motivation/desire model to human paraphilic sexual behavior, it would follow that enhancing limbic and hypothalamic serotonergic neurotransmission, suppressing dopaminergic neurotransmission, or inhibiting the central effects of testosterone and its metabolites should reduce sexual motivation in human males. It is well known that serotonin reuptake inhibitors can affect both the incentive/motivational phase of the human male sexual response (diminished sexual desire) as well as the consummatory phase (delayed ejaculation/anorgasmia) (Montejo, Llorca, Izquierdo & Rico-Villadermos, 2001). While these are considered as "side effects" during the course of treatment of depressive and anxiety disorders, the ability to diminish sexual appetitive behavior can be a "therapeutic" effect for a subject afflicted with sexual appetitive disinhibition or hypersexuality.

There are now over 200 case examples of the positive prescriptive use of serotonin-enhancing "antidepressants," primarily serotonin reuptake inhibitors and nefazodone for the treatment of paraphilias or paraphilia-related disorders (Greenberg & Bradford, 1997; Bradford & Gratzer, 1995; Kafka, 1991a, b, 1992, 1994; Kafka & Hennen, 2000; Greenberg, Bradford, Curry & O'Rourke, 1996; Abouesh & Clayton, 1999; Levitsky & Owens, 1999; Galli, Raute, McConnville & McElroy, 1998; Rubinstein & Engel, 1996; Zohar, Kaplan & Benjamin, 1994; Kruesi, Fine, Valladares, Phillips & Rapoport, 1992). In most of these reports, the successful reduction of paraphilic arousal and behavior is usually accomplished without substantially mitigating normophilic sexual arousal and behavior. The current absence of any double-blind placebo-controlled studies supporting (or refuting) the efficacy of serotonin reuptake inhibitors for paraphilic sex offenders is a major limitation to a wider acceptance of their prescriptive use for violent sex offender paraphiliacs (Bradford, 2001).

It is important to mention that in the past 5 years, there have been additional advances in the prescriptive use of medications affecting the hypothalamic–pituitary–testicular axis to treat sexual aggression. The slow but growing use of gonadotropin-releasing hormone (GnRH) agonists, medications whose net effect is to markedly diminish physiologically active testosterone, has been reported as effective in case series of sexual aggressors, including paraphiliacs (Rosler & Witztum, 1998; Thibaut, Cordier & Kuhn, 1993; Briken, Nika & Berner, 2001; Krueger & Kaplan, 2001). While it is presumed that the primary pharmacological effects of these medications are not directly on monoaminergic synapses, testosterone has been noted to enhance sexual appetitive behavior in postadolescent male rats by specifically increasing the sensitivity of hypothalamic dopamine receptors and concomitantly reducing the sensitivity of hypothalamic serotonergic receptors (Everitt, 1983, 1995; Kendall & Tonge, 1976). Such monoaminergic effects would diminish sexual appetitive behavior. Additional laboratory studies of the hypothalamic nuclei of newborn male rats have demonstrated that, in comparison to female rats, neonatal masculinization of the hypothalamus by testosterone was associated with both lower content and uptake of serotonin, and that castration was associated with both increased serotonergic content and uptake resembling intact females (Borisova, Proshlyakova, Sapronova & Ugrumov, 1996; Zhang, Ma, Barker & Rubinow, 1999). Last, immunizing male rats against gonadotrophin-releasing hormone (the hormone that stimulates the release of luteinizing hormone) was associated with marked decrease in follicle-stimulating hormone, luteinizing hormone, and testosterone, the same physiological effects associated with GnRH agonists. This immunization increased serotonin, but not dopamine in the hypothalamus, olfactory tubercles, and corpus striatum of male rats (Juorio, Li, Gonzalez, Chedrese & Murphy, 1991). All these data suggest that inhibiting testosterone's physiological effects by either antiandrogens, GnRH agonists, or surgical castration would substantially mitigate monoaminergic signals usually associated with the amplification of sexual stimuli and motivation.

At this juncture, after reviewing the aforementioned data on studies of monoamines and sexual aggression, Axis I comorbidity, sexual appetitive behavior, and psychopharmacology, it is certainly premature to conclude that monoaminergic neuroregulatory perturbations are definitively involved in the pathophysiology of paraphilic sexual aggression. Indeed, most of data reviewed thus far suggest that, while perturbations involving serotonergic or dopaminergic central neurotransmission do appear important in the pathophysiology of aggression and impulsivity as well as sexual appetitive and copulatory behaviors, a specific role for these neuromodulators in the paraphilic condition remains neither proven nor rejected. Nevertheless, in such an important field of investigation as the multidimensional etiology of sexual violence, the monoamine hypothesis of paraphilic disorders can still be used to suggest viable lines of clinical as well as laboratory investigation of the biological component associated with sexual deviance and aggression.

REFERENCES

ABEL, G.G. & OSBORN, C. (1992). The paraphilias: The extent and nature of sexually deviant and criminal behavior. In *Psychiatric Clinics of North America: Clinical forensic psychiatry* (Vol. 15, pp. 675–687). Philadelphia, PA: W.B. Saunders.

ABOUESH, A. & CLAYTON, A. (1999). Compulsive voyeurism and exhibitionism: A clinical response to paroxetine. *Archives of Sexual Behavior, 28*, 23–30.

AMERICAN PSYCHIATRIC ASSOCIATION. (1980). *Diagnostic and statistical manual of mental disorders* (3rd ed.). Washington, DC: American Psychiatric Association.

AMERICAN PSYCHIATRIC ASSOCIATION. (2000). *Diagnostic and statistical manual of mental disorders* (4th ed., Text Rev.). Washington, DC: American Psychiatric Association.

AMERICAN PSYCHIATRIC ASSOCIATION (1994). Sexual and gender identity disorders. In *Diagnostic and Statistical Manual of Mental Disorders* (4th ed., pp. 493–538). Washington, DC: American Psychiatric Association.

BAUM, M.J. & STARR, M.D. (1980). Inhibition of sexual behavior by dopamine antagonists or serotonin agonist drugs in castrated male rats given estradiol or dihydrotestosterone. *Pharmacology, Biochemisrty, and Behavior, 13*, 47–67.

BORISOVA, N.A., PROSHLYAKOVA, E.V., SAPRONOVA, A.Y. & UGRUMOV, M.V. (1996). Androgen-dependent sex differences in the hypothalamic serotoninergic system. *European Journal of Endocrinology, 134*, 232–235.

BRIKEN, P., NIKA, E. & BERNER, W. (2001). Treatment of parapahilia with luteinizing hormone-releasing hormone agonists. *Journal of Sex and Marital Therapy, 27*, 45–55.

BRADFORD, J.M.W. (2001). The neurobiology, neuropharmacology, and pharmacological treatment of paraphilias and compulsive sexual behavior. *Canadian Journal of Psychiatry, 46*, 26–33.

BRADFORD, J.M. & GRATZER, T.G. (1995). A treatment for impulse control disorders and paraphilia: A case report. *Canadian Journal of Psychiatry, 40*, 4–5.

COMINGS, D.E. (2001). Clinical and molecular genetics of ADHD and Tourette's Syndrome. In J. Wasserstein, L.E. Wolf & F.F. Lefever (Eds.), *Adult attention deficit disorder: Brain mechanisms and life outcomes* (Vol. 931, pp. 50–83). New York. New York Academy of Sciences.

CRENSHAW, T.L. & GOLDBERG, J.P. (1996). *Sexual pharmacology: Drugs that affect sexual function.* New York. W.W. Norton.

EVERITT, B.J. (1983). Monoamines and the control of sexual behavior. *Psychological Medicine, 13*, 715–720.

EVERITT, B.J. (1995). Neuroendocrine mechanisms underlying appetitive and consummatory elements of masculine sexual behavior. In J. Bancroft (Ed.), *The pharmacology of sexual function and dysfunction* (pp. 15–31). Amsterdam: Elsevier Science.

EVERITT, B.J. & BANCROFT, J. (1991). Of rats and men: The comparative approach to male sexuality. In J. Bancroft, C.M. Davis & H.J. Ruppel, Jr. (Eds.), *Annual Review of Sex Research* (Vol. 2, pp. 77–118). Mt. Vernon, IA: Society for the Scientific Study of Sex.

FAGO, D.P. (1999). Comorbidity of attention deficit hyperactivity disorder in sexually aggressive children and adolescents. In B. Schwartz (Ed.), The sex offender: Theoretical advances, treating special populations and legal developments (Vol. 3. pp.16.1–16.15). Kingston, NJ. Civic Research Institute.

GALLI, V.B., RAUTE, N.J., MCCONNVILLE, B.J. & MCELROY, S.L. (1998). An adolescent male with multiple paraphilias treated successfully with fluoxetine. *Journal of Child and Adolescent Psychopharmacology, 8*, 195–197.

GALLI, V., MCELROY, S.L., SOUTELLO, C.A., et al. (1999). The psychiatric diagnoses of twenty two adolescents who have sexually molested other children. *Comprehensive Psychiatry, 40*, 85–87.

GREENBERG, D.M. & BRADFORD, J.M.W. (1997).Treatment of the paraphilic disorders: A review of the role of the selective serotonin reuptake inhibitors. *Sexual Abuse: Journal of Treatment and Research, 9*, 349–360.

GREENBERG, D.M., BRADFORD, J.M.W., CURRY, S. & O'ROURKE, A. (1996). A comparison of treatment of paraphilias with three serotonin reuptake inhibitors: A retrospective study. *Bulletin of the American Acadamy of Psychiatry Law, 24*, 525–532.

HANSON, R. & HARRIS, A. (2000). Where should we intervene? Dynamic predictors of sexual offense recidivism. *Criminal Justice and Behavior, 27*, 6–35.

HULL, E.M., LORRAIN, D.S., DU, J., et al. (1999). Hormone-neurotransmitter interactions in the control of sexual behavior. *Behavioural Brain Research, 105*, 105–116.

JUORIO, A.V., LI, X.M., GONZALEZ, A., CHEDRESE, P.J. & MURPHY, B.D. (1991). Effects of active immunization against gonadotrophin-releasing hormone on theconcentrations of noradrenaline, dopamine, 5-hydroxytryptamine and some of their metabolites in the brain and sexual organs of male rats. *Neuroendocrinology, 54*, 49–54.

KAFKA, M.P. (1991a). Successful antidepressant treatment of nonparaphilic sexual addictions and paraphilias in men. *Journal of Clinical Psychiatry, 52*, 60–65.

KAFKA, M.P. (1991b). Successful treatment of paraphilic coercive disorder (a rapist) with fluoxetine hydrochloride. *British Journal of Psychiatry, 158*, 844–847.

KAFKA, M.P. (1994). Sertraline pharmacotherapy for paraphilias and paraphilia-related disorders; An open trial. *Annals of Clinical Psychiatry, 6*,189–195.

KAFKA, M.P. (1997a). A monoamine hypothesis for the pathophysiology of paraphilic disorders. *Archives of Sexual Behavior, 26*, 337–352.

KAFKA, M.P. (1997b). Hypersexual desire in males: An operational definition and clinical implications for men with paraphilias and paraphilia-related disorders. *Archives of Sexual Behavior, 26*, 505–526.

KAFKA, M.P. & HENNEN, J. (2000). Psychostimulant augmentation during treatment with selective serotonin reuptake inhibitors in males with paraphilias and paraphilia-related disorders: A case series. *Journal of Clinical Psychiatry, 61*, 664–670.

KAFKA, M. & HENNEN, J. (2002). A DSM IV Axis I comorbidity study of males (n=120) with paraphilias and paraphilia-related disorders. *Journal of Sexual Abuse, 14,* 347–366.

KAFKA, M.P. & HENNEN. J. (in press). Hypersexual desire in males: Are males with paraphilias different from males with paraphilia-related disorders? *Sexual Abuse.*

KAFKA, M.P. & PRENTKY, R. (1992). Fluoxetine treatment of nonparaphilic sexual addictions and paraphilias in men. *Journal of Clinical Psychiatry, 52,* 351–358.

KAFKA, M.P. & PRENTKY, R,A. (1998). Attention deficit hyperactivity disorder in males with paraphilias and paraphilia-related disorders: A comorbidity study. *Journal of Clinical Psychiatry, 59,* 388–396.

KAVOUSSI, R., ARMSTEAD, P. & COCCARO, E. (1997). The neurobiology of impulsive aggression. *Psychiatric Clinics of North America, 20,* 395–403.

KENDALL, D. & TONGE, S. (1976). Monoamine concentrations in eight areas of the brain of mature and immature male rats and the effects of injected hormones [proceedings]. *Journal of Pharmacy and Pharmacology, 28(Suppl.),* 37P.

KNIGHT, R. & CERCE, D. (1999). Validation and revision of the Multidimensional Assessment of Sex and Aggression. *Psycholigica Belgica, 39,* 135–161.

KOGAN, B.M., TKACHENKO, A.A., DROZDOV, A.Z., et al. (1995). Monoamine metabolism in different forms of paraphilia [In Russian]. *Zhurnal Nevropatologii i Psikhiatrii Imeni S S Korsakova, 95,* 52–56.

KRUEGER, R.B. & KAPLAN, M.S. (2001). Depot-leuprolide for treatment of paraphilias: A report of 12 cases. *Archives of Sexual Behavior, 30,* 409–422.

KRUESI, M.J.P., FINE, S., VALLADARES, L. PHILLIPS, R.A. & RAPOPORT, J.L. (1992). Paraphilias: A double-blind crossover comparison of clomipramine versus desipramine. *Archives of Sexual Behavior, 21,* 587–593.

LEVIN, R.J. (1994). Human male sexuality; Appetite and arousal, desire and drive. In C.R. Legg & D. Booth (Eds.), *Appetite: Neural and behavioral bases* (pp. 128–164). Oxford: Oxford University Press.

LEVITSKY, A.M. & OWENS, N.J. (1999). Pharmacologic treatment of hypersexuality and paraphilias in nursing home residents. *Journal of the American Geriatrics Society, 47,* 231–234.

LORRAIN, D.S., MATUSZEWICH, L., FRIEDMAN, R.D. & HULL, E.M. (1997). Extracellular serotonin in the lateral hypothalamic area is increased during the postejaculatory interval and impairs copulation in male rats. *Journal of Neuroscience, 17,* 9361–9366.

LORRAIN, D., RIOLO, J., MATUSZEWICH, L. & HULL, E. (1999). Lateral hypothalamic serotonin inhibits nucleas accumbens dopamine: Implications for sexual satiety. *Journal of Neuroscience, 19,* 7648–7652.

MAES, M., DE VOS, N., VAN HUNSEL, F., et al. (2001a). Pedophilia is accompanied by increased plasma concentrations of catecholamines, in particular epinephrine. *Psychiatry Research, 103,* 43–49.

MAES, M., VAN WEST, D., DE VOS, N., et al. (2001b). Lower baseline plasma cortisol and prolactin together with increased body temperature and higher m-CPP-induced cortisol responses in men with pedophilia. *Neuropsychopharmacology, 24,* 37–46.

MAS, M. (1995). Neurobiological correlates of masculine sexual behavior. *Neuroscience and Biobehavioral Reviews, 19,* 261–277.

MAS, M., FUMERO, B., FERNANDEZ-VERA, J.R. & GONZALEZ-MORA, J.L. (1995). Neurochemical correlates of sexual exhaustion and recovery as assessed by in vitro microdialysis. *Brain Research, 675,*13–19.

MCELROY, S.L., SOUTELLO, C.A., TAYLOR, P., et al. (1999). Psychiatric features of 36 convicted sexual offenses. *Journal of Clinical Psychiatry, 60,* 414–420.

MCKENNA, K.E. (2001). Neural circuitry involved in sexual function. *Journal of Spinal Cord Medicine, 24,* 148–154.

MESTON, C.M. & FROLICH, P.F. (2000). The neurobiology of sexual functioning. *Archives of General Psychiatry, 57,* 1012–1032.

MONTEJO, A.L., LLORCA, G., IZQUIERDO, J.A. & RICO-VILLADERMOS, F. (2001). Dysfunction. Incidence of sexual dysfunction associated with antidepressant agents: A prospective multicenter study of 1022 patients. *Journal of Clinical Psychiatry, 62(Suppl. 3),* 10–20.

O'DONOHUE, W., REGEV, L.G. & HAGSTROM, A. (2000). Problems with the DSM IV diagnosis of pedophilia. *Sex Abuse, 12,* 95–106.

PFAUS, J.G. (1996). Homologies of animal and human sexual behaviors. *Hormones and Behavior, 30,* 187–200.

POMERANTZ, S.M. (1995). Monoamine influences on male sexual behavior of nonhuman primates. In J. Bancroft (ed.), *The pharmacology of sexual function and dysfunction* (pp. 201–211). Amsterdam: Elsevier Science.

PRENTKY, R.A. & BURGESS, A.W. (2000). Diagnosis and classification. In R.A. Prentky & A.W. Burgess (Eds.), *Forensic management of sexual offenders* (pp. 25–70). New York: Kluver Academis/Plenum.

RAYMOND, N.C., COLEMAN, E., OHLERKING, F., CHRISTENSON, G.A. & MINER, M. (1999). Psychiatric comorbidity in pedophilic sex offenders. *American Journal of Psychiatry, 156,* 786–788.

RESSLER, K.J. & NEMEROFF, C.B. (2000). Role of serotonergic and noradrenergic systems in the pathophysiology of depression and anxiety disorders. *Depression and Anxiety, 12(Suppl. 1),* 2–19.

ROSLER, A. & WITZTUM, E. (1998). Treatment of men with paraphilia with a long-acting analogue of gonadotropin-releasing hormone. *New England Journal of Medicine, 338,* 416–422.

RUBINSTEIN, E.B. & ENGEL, N.L. (1996). Successful treatment of transvestic fetishism with sertraline and lithium. *Journal of Clinical Psychiatry, 57,* 92.

SOUBRIE, P. (1986). Reconciling the role of central serotonin neurons in human and animal behavior. *Behavioural Brain Research, 9,* 319–364.

THIBAUT, F., CORDIER, B. & KUHN, J.M. (1993). Effect of a long-lasting gonadotrophin hormone-releasing agonist in six cases of severe male paraphilia. *Acta Psychiatrica Scandinacica, 87,* 445–450.

YATES, A. (2001). Conduct disorder. In G.O. Gabbard (Ed.), *The treatment of psychiatric disorders* (3rd ed., Vol. 1, pp. 177–190). Washington, DC: American Psychiatric Publishing.

ZHANG, L., MA, W., BARKER, J.L. & RUBINOW, D.R. (1999). Sex differences in expression of serotonin receptors (subtypes 1A and 2A) in rat brain: A possible role of testosterone. *Neuroscience, 94,* 251–259.

ZOHAR, J., KAPLAN, Z. & BENJAMIN, J. (1994). Compulsive exhibitionism successfully treated with fluvoxamine: A controlled case study. *Journal of Clinical Psychiatry, 55,* 86–88.

Sexual Behavior Problems in Preteen Children

Developmental, Ecological, and Behavioral Correlates

W. N. FRIEDRICH,[a] W. HOBART DAVIES,[b] ELEONORA FEHER,[a]
AND JOHN WRIGHT[c]

[a]Mayo Clinic, Rochester, Minnesota 55905, USA

[b]University of Wisconsin-Milwaukee, Milwaukee, Wisconsin 53201, USA

[c]University of Montréal, Montréal, Canada

ABSTRACT: A large sample of 2–12 year old children ($N = 2311$) was studied to determine the relationship between three sexually intrusive behavior items (SIBs) measured by the Child Sexual Behavior Inventory (CSBI) and a range of developmental, ecological, and behavioral correlates. The variables studied included age, gender, race, family income, single parent status, maternal education, family sexual behaviors, physical abuse, sexual abuse, domestic violence, social competence of the child, and three scales from the CBCL (Internalizing, Externalizing, and PTSD). Sexual abuse was not the primary predictor of SIB, but a model incorporating family adversity, modeling of coercive behavior, child behavior, and modeling of sexuality predicted a significant amount of variance.

KEYWORDS: sexual behavior; family sexuality; sexual abuse

Three papers were published in short succession in 1988 and 1989 which drew attention to the previously undiscovered phenomenon of children with sexual behavior problems (Friedrich & Luecke, 1988; Johnson, 1988; 1989). Sexual behavior that appeared temporally reactive to sexual abuse had already been noted in the literature (Friedrich, Urquiza & Beilke, 1986), but this behavior typically took the form of increased masturbatory behavior, sexual interest, boundary problems, and sexual knowledge. A different set of behaviors, best described as persistently sexually intrusive, were evident in the three studies noted above. These behaviors consisted of children sexually touching other children and adults, and even attempting acts more typically thought to be adult-like, (e.g., cunnilingus, fellatio), and attempted or actual intercourse.

Sexual abuse, however, was not demonstrated as the sole presumptive causal agent of these behaviors, even in the first samples, and particularly for males (Friedrich & Luecke, 1988; Johnson, 1988). A high degree of comorbid family relational problems

Address for correspondence: William Friedrich, Ph.D., Mayo Clinic, 200 S.W. First Street, Rochester, MN 55905. Voice: 507-255-7164; fax: 507-255-7383.

friedrich.william@mayo.edu

Ann. N.Y. Acad. Sci. 989: 95–104 (2003). © 2003 New York Academy of Sciences.

were noted to be routine in the families of sexually aggressive children (Friedrich & Luecke, 1988). This suggested that while sexual abuse might predispose children to behave sexually, family factors potentiated this predisposition.

In fact, under close scrutiny, sexual abuse appears to be a frequent but not essential contributor to sexual behavior problems in both teens and adults (Chaffin & Friedrich, 2000). Unfortunately, the clinical community, who often react to a child caught in an adult-like sexual act as if she/he must be a sexual abuse victim, only variably absorbs this knowledge.

Recent research on sexual behavior problems in sexually abused children has focused on the establishment of risk factors related to the emergence of sexually intrusive behavior (Hall, Mathews & Pearce, 1998). These risk factors include aspects of the child's abuse experience, (e.g. sadistic, eroticizing, enacted by multiple perpetrators), as well as characteristics of the child, (e.g., sense of hopelessness, general boundary problems, sexually focused), the child's history, (e.g., frequent moves, physical abuse), the parent–child relationship, (e.g., sexualized, intrusive), and caregiver characteristics, (e.g., PTSD in the mother, attachment problems in the mother's history).

These risk factors are applicable to sexually abused children. However, a recent study with preschoolers exhibiting sexually intrusive behavior found that less than half of them have a definite sexual abuse history. Given the problems disadvantaged preschoolers have in reporting sexual abuse, the number is probably higher (Silovsky & Niec, 2002). Consequently, a different perspective is needed to understand those children who exhibit sexually intrusive behavior (SIB). Is sexual abuse an etiologic agent for some children, but another variable is the etiologic agent for nonsexually abused children who exhibit SIB?

While up to 40% of sexually abused children do not exhibit overt behavior problems per parent report, the remaining symptomatic children differ on more than the sexual abuse experience (Kendall-Tackett, Finkelhor & Williams, 1993). Recent data suggest that sexually abused children who are symptomatic are significantly more likely than asymptomatic sexually abused children to have experienced more overall life stress, come from more troubled and disrupted families, and have experienced more maternal rejection (Friedrich & Fehrer, under review). This suggests that the presence of symptoms is due at least in part to predisposing or risk factors. This conclusion is supported by research on the development of PTSD in children. Symptomatic children were more likely to have experienced more violent and prolonged abuse, had a closer relationship with the perpetrator, and blamed themselves for the abuse (Wolfe, Sas & Wekerle, 1994).

Given that SIBs are not generic or developmentally expected symptoms, it is also likely that either sexual abuse or exposure to sexuality is a necessary feature. However, the expression of symptoms subsequent to the abuse or exposure must be potentiated by other variables. Literature on disruptive behavior problems in children can illuminate our understanding of SIB. For example, Patterson and colleagues (2000) have suggested that "child problem behaviors, such as hyperactivity, antisocial [behavior], peer rejection, depressed mood, achievement failure, substance abuse, and police arrest, are all manifestations of a single process" (p. 91). This process is described as coercive parenting, and is characterized by rejection, poor monitoring, and the modeling of coercive and aggressive interpersonal strategies.

Sexual behavior problems secondary to sexual abuse are associated with both cumulative distress and proneness to acting out. In addition, sexual behavior is associated with overt family sexuality (Friedrich, 1997). A model that integrates these components could help us understand the emergence of SIB in children, regardless of history of sexual abuse. The components of the model might include family adversity, which could include cumulative life stress, exposure to a coercive interactional style, modeling of and/or exposure to sexuality, and a child substrate that is either socially inept or interpersonally disruptive.

This paper set out to examine several questions. The first pertains to the relative importance of sexual abuse in predicting SIB. The second seeks to identify other potentiating variables to SIB. Thirdly, we sought to determine whether SIB in preteens could be understood as a combination of the ingredients described in the above paragraph, (i.e., family adversity, modeling of sexuality and coercion, and a child prone to social problems).

A large and diverse sample was used to examine these questions. It included a strictly normative subsample that was screened for the absence of sexual abuse, developmental problems, and utilization of mental health services. Large psychiatric outpatient and sexually abused subsamples were also available and have been described elsewhere (Friedrich, Fisher, Dittner, et al., 2001).

METHOD

Participants

Normative Subsamples

Normative data for the Child Sexual Behavior Inventory (CSBI) represent 1114 children, combined from three nonclinical samples: (a) 723 children who were in the waiting area of a Community Pediatrics Clinic in Rochester, Minnesota; (b) 111 children who were in the waiting area of a Community Family Medicine Clinic in Rochester, Minnesota; and (c) 280 children from public day-care settings in the Los Angeles, California area, the majority of whom were lower income and of minority status.

The total sample of 1114 included 49.7% female and several races (77.7% Caucasian, 7.7% Black, and 11.6% Hispanic). Additional information about these samples is reported in Friedrich et al. (2001).

Outpatient Psychiatric Subsamples

A sample of 577 2–12-year-old children, who presented for an outpatient psychological or psychiatric evaluation, but whose primary female caregiver denied any suspicion of possible sexual abuse, were included. They came from six clinical settings in the United States and one in Germany. Typically these children were consecutively admitted to the clinics involved. The most common referral questions reflected concerns about attention, learning, adjustment problems, and rule-violating behaviors. Additional information about these samples is reported in Friedrich et al. (2001).

Sexual Abuse Subsamples

The sexual abuse sample totaled 620 children, aged 2 to 12 years, with a confirmed history of sexual abuse, usually with the last incident having occurred within the previous 12 months. In each case, abuse was confirmed by the appropriate social services or child protection agency in the area, as well as by the clinic evaluating the child. Abuse was confirmed through the child's statements, perpetrator confession, medical evidence, and/or eyewitness testimony. These children came from 13 clinical settings in the United States, Canada, and Europe. The majority of these children were consecutive referrals for assessment to their respective agency or clinic, but others represented convenience samples of sexually abused children (e.g., children in therapy). This was not a representative sample of sexually abused children, and was biased to include sexually abused children seen as in need of services. As a result, their overall behavior was likely to be more severe than that of a random sample of sexually abused children. Data on the nature and onset of sexual abuse was available for 394 of these children. Information was available on the following dichotomously scored variables: penetration, more than one perpetrator, medical evidence, whether the perpetrator was an adult, and whether the perpetrator was an immediate family member. In addition, information on age of onset, duration in months, and time elapsed since last abuse was also calculated. The mean age at onset of the abuse for this subsample was 5.9 years (SD = 2.4). The duration of abuse was typically one month or less (median = 1 month), although the mean was 10.5 months (SD = 13.5). Additional information about these samples is reported in Friedrich et al. (2001).

Measures

Child Sexual Behavior Inventory (CSBI)

The child's mother or primary female caregiver (e.g., foster mother) completed this 38-item checklist in each case. The CSBI presented the primary female caregiver with a list of behaviors they had observed in the prior six months. Each item was rated on a four-point scale anchored at 0 (never) and 3 (at least once per week). The CSBI requires a fifth-grade reading level (Friedrich, 1997). For the purposes of this study, three items were selected as representative of sexually intrusive behavior: # 9, "Touches another child's sex parts" (endorsed for 10.4 % of the sample, M = .15, SD = .49); # 10, "Tries to have sexual intercourse with another child or adult" (endorsed for 4.5 % of the sample, M = .07, SD = .35); and # 11, "Puts mouth on another child/adult's sex parts" (endorsed for 3.1% of the sample, M = .04, SD = .28). These three items had the highest loading on a factor of the CSBI labeled Sexual Intrusiveness (Trane & Friedrich, under review). Reliability analysis of these three items resulted in a Cronbach's alpha of .74. They were summed and labeled SIB.

Demographic Data Sheet

The demographic information obtained included the age, sex, and race of the child; the marital, financial, and educational status of the parent(s); family size; the quality of the child's peer relationships; hours/week in day care, an 11-item life events checklist; and 8 questions pertaining to family sexuality. Individual items from both the life events and family sexuality measures were used in the correlational and regressional analyses. These were physical abuse (14.1%), and domestic violence (18%) from the life events checklist, and three items from the family sexuality measure ["My child has watched naked adults on TV or in a movie" (30.2%); "My child has seen adults having sex on TV or in a movie" (16.5%); and "My child has seen his/her parents having sex (7.6%)"]. An additional 7 items from the life events checklist were summed to create a measure of total life stress (LE TOT).

Child Behavior Checklist (CBCL)

The behavior problem portion of the CBCL consists of a large number of behavior problems answered in a three-point scale (i.e., never, sometimes, often). It is a well-validated and widely used measure of a range of behavior problems in children. Two versions were used: the 99-item version for children 2 to 3 years old (Achenbach, 1988) and the 113-item version for children 4 to 16 years old (Achenbach, 1991). Internalizing and Externalizing T scores were calculated for each child. These are widely used summary scores, the first reflecting the degree of problems related to depression, anxiety, and somatic concerns, and the latter reflecting aggression, overactivity, and antisocial behaviors. In addition, a seven-item empirically derived PTSD subscale was also scored for the 4–12 year olds (Friedrich, Trane, Lengua, et al., under review). Scores from the CBCL allowed us to examine the relationship of sexual behaviors in children to generic and PTSD-related child behavior problems.

Subjects were excluded if key items were missing in the demographic data sheet (e.g., family income, maternal education) or more than one item was missing for either the CSBI or the CBCL.

RESULTS

Correlational analyses were first completed with the sum of the three CSBI items (SIB) and a range of demographic, family sexuality, and CBCL variables. The sample size insured that those values of at least .10 and higher were likely to be significant. The correlations with SIB were as follows: age ($R = -.10$), gender ($R = .04$), race ($R = .11$), maternal education ($R = -.25$), single parent ($R = .24$), family income ($R = -.37$), total life stress ($R = .23$), naked adults ($R = .15$), adults having sex ($R = .11$), parents having sex ($r = .15$), physical abuse ($R = .22$), domestic violence ($R = .23$), sexual abuse ($R = .22$), social competence ($R = .40$), internalizing ($R = .64$), externalizing ($R = .68$), and PTSD ($R = .63$). The fact that gender was not significant deserves comment, since this finding is clearly different than the literature on adolescents and adults, where male perpetrators dominate. In addition, younger children were more likely to exhibit this behavior, and again this does not easily correspond to SIB in preteens preceding sexual aggression in teenagers.

The largest correlations with SIB are the scales from the CBCL, followed by an inverse relationship with income and family education, single-parent status, domestic violence, physical abuse, and sexual abuse. The three family sexuality items were also correlated, but at a very low level.

TABLE 1. Multiple regression analyses with SIB as the dependent variable and sexual abuse status entered first

Block	Step	Variable	R^2	R^2 Change
1	1	Sex abuse	.071	.071
2	2	Income	.171	.10
	3	LE TOT	.189	.018
	4	Gender	.196	.007
	5	Age	.202	.006
3	6	Social competence	.290	.088
	7	Naked adults	.298	.008
4	8	Internalizing	.522	.224
	9	Externalizing	.571	.049
	10	PTSD	.584	.013

$F = 168.6$ (10, 1203); $P < .000$

Excluded variables: maternal education, race, family size, marital status, physical abuse, domestic violence, watched adults having sex, watched parents having sex.

ABBREVIATIONS: LE TOT = measure of total life stress; PTSD = posttraumatic stress disorder.

Family income was significantly related to each of the demographic and behavioral variables as was SIB, including male gender ($R = .07$). Lower family income is strongly related to maternal education ($R = -.57$), being a single parent ($R = -.56$), total life stress ($R = -.38$), externalizing behavior ($R = .38$), sexual abuse ($R = .31$) and physical abuse ($R = .23$). Family income is clearly a strong, "summary" variable for several aspects of family adversity.

After controlling for family income, partial correlations with SIB were calculated for the demographic and behavioral variables listed above. Although most correlations were slightly attenuated, the relationship between SIB and the measures of child behavior problems derived from the CBCL remained essentially the same, that is, externalizing ($R = .63$), internalizing ($R = .61$), and PTSD ($R = .60$). The correlations between SIB and single-parent status, maternal education, age, and race became insignificant after family income was partialled out. Sexual abuse ($R = .11$), physical abuse ($R = .15$), and domestic violence ($R = .13$) were still significantly correlated.

The next series of analyses examined the relationship between sexual abuse, demographic variables, and CBCL scores in predicting SIB using stepwise multiple regression analyses. Four blocks of variables were entered separately (TABLE 1). Sexual abuse status was the sole variable entered in Block 1. Block 2 included age, gender, race, family size, maternal education, family income, total life stress, and single parent status. Block 3 comprised physical abuse, domestic violence, family sexuality, and a single item related to the social competence of the child. Block 4 contained the three CBCL subscales. Sexual abuse accounted for roughly 7% of the variance in an overall equation that was significant, $F = 168.6$, (10, 1203), $P < .000$. Significant Block 2 variables, and their respective R^2 were family income (.10), total life stress (.018), gender (.007), and age (.006). For Block 3, significant variables

TABLE 2. Multiple regression analyses with SIB as the dependent variable and sexual abuse status entered last

Block	Step	Variable	R^2	R^2 Change
1	1	Income	.163	.163
	2	LE TOT	.182	.019
	3	Age	.188	.006
	4	Gender	.192	.004
	5	Maternal education	.195	.003
2	6	Social competence	.283	.088
	7	Naked adults	.291	.008
	8	Physical abuse	.294	.003
3	9	Internalizing	.523	.229
	10	Externalizing	.573	.050
	11	PTSD	.586	.013
4	12	Sexual abuse	.586	.000

$F = 141.90$ (10, 1201); $P < .000$
Excluded variables: race, family size, marital status, domestic violence, watched adults having sex, watched parents having sex.
ABBREVIATIONS: LE TOT = measure of total life stress; PTSD = posttraumatic stress disorder.

were social competence (.088) and watching naked adults on TV/movie (.008). For Block 4, CBCL Internalizing (.224), CBCL Externalizing (.049), and CBCL PTSD (.013) emerged as significant predictors.

When sexual abuse is entered in Block 4, to allow the examination of the unique contribution of sexual abuse status after controlling for the influence of other variables, it accounted for minimal unique variance and was no longer significant ($R^2 = .001, F = 1.71.$ (1, 1201), $P < .19$) (TABLE 2). However, the overall equation remained significant, $F = 141.90$ (12, 1201), $P < .000$, and relatively similar to the regression analysis in TABLE 1 in terms of the independent variables that were entered. Block 1 included family income (.163), total life stress (.019), age (.006), gender (.004), and maternal education (.003). Block 2 variables were social competence (.088), watching naked adults on TV/movie (.008), and physical abuse (.003). Block 3 variables were CBCL Internalizing (.229), CBCL Externalizing (.050), and CBCL PTSD (.013).

The next analysis examined the validity of a model based on literature pertaining to the development of disruptive behavior and the prediction of SIB. Four blocks of variables were created: family adversity (consisting of family income, marital status, maternal education, and total life stress); modeling of coercive behavior (physical abuse, domestic violence); exposure to sexuality (sexual abuse, family sexuality); and child substrate (externalizing behavior and social competence). We conceptualized family adversity as temporally primary relative to the other three variables and therefore it was the first block entered. Exposure to sexuality was conceptualized as the unique contributor to the emergence of SIB, and thus was entered last. Modeling of coercive behavior and child substrate were entered second and third, respectively.

TABLE 3. Four-part model predicting SIB

Block	Step	Variable	R^2	R^2 Change
1	1	Family income	.164	.164
	2	LE TOT	.186	.022
2	3	Physical abuse	.199	.013
	4	Domestic violence	.203	.004
3	5	Externalizing	.499	.296
	6	Social competence	.506	.007
4	7	Sexual abuse	.512	.006

$F = 190.74$ (7,1287); $P < .000$.
ABBREVIATION: LE TOT = measure of total life stress.

The variables in each block were entered in a stepwise manner and the results of this analysis are presented in TABLE 3.

The overall multiple regression equation was significant, $F = 190.74$ (7, 1287), $P < .000$, $R^2 = .512$, with each block contributing unique variance. Significant Block 1 variables and their R^2 were family income (.164) and total life stress (.022). Block 2 variables were physical abuse (.013) and domestic violence (.004). Both of the Block 3 variables were entered (i.e., CBCL Externalizing [.296] and social competence [.008]), and the sole significant variable in Block 4 was sexual abuse (.006). These results support the model that was derived from the literature and ,together, the independent variables account for the majority of the variance (87.7%) that was accounted for in the equations summarized in TABLES 1 and 2.

A subsample of the sexually abused children ($N = 379$) had additional information on the nature of their sexual abuse. Correlations between SIB and these sexual abuse features are small, but they are theoretically sound in that all are related to more serious abuse. For example, the largest correlation, ($R = .20$), is between SIB and penetration having occurred, and the victims were typically younger at the time of the abuse ($R = -.14$), which was incestuous ($R = .15$), or involved multiple perpetrators ($R = .14$), and lasted longer ($R = .14$). In addition, sexually abused children with SIB were more likely to have a history of physical abuse ($R = .14$).

DISCUSSION AND SUMMARY

These results provide support for the multiple determinants of SIB in preteens. In addition, the relative absence of gender effects is just one indication that SIB in children must not be considered as parallel to intrusive sexual behavior in adolescents or adults. In addition, SIB was correlated inversely with age. While the correlation was small, it does suggest that at least some of this behavior is associated with both immaturity and reactivity to the child's circumstances, be it abuse or other adversity.

SIB was most strongly correlated with the CBCL subscales of Externalizing, Internalizing, and PTSD, and secondarily to family income, a variable that appears to be an important summary of family adversity. Additional significant correlations were noted for social competence of the child, maltreatment experiences including sexual abuse, and exposure to domestic violence. While sexual abuse was not the primary correlate of SIB, features of the sexual abuse experience that reflected earlier, longer, and more serious abuse were significantly related to SIB.

The complexity of the multiple potential factors related to the emergence of SIB is considerable. If sexual abuse is not the only variable, what other factors in the child's life model sexuality, and more importantly, intrusive and adult-like sexuality? Are children with SIB prone to aggressive behavior, but well-socialized, or are they less socially competent and more passive? It is likely that they are a heterogenous group (Hall et al., 2002).

It does appear that a four-component model has heuristic validity. As demonstrated with the current data, the elements are family adversity, modeling of coercion, modeling of sexuality, and a vulnerable/predisposed child substrate. This model accounted for more than 50% of the variance of the three-item SIB dependent variable, and indicated that variables from each of these components added relevant variance. These were family income, total life stress, physical abuse, domestic violence, and externalizing behavior and social competence for the first three components. The relevant modeling-of-sexuality variable was sexual abuse.

There are many limitations to these findings. They rely only on parent report and represent single points in time. Observational data or input from other observers, as well as multiple sampling times, would greatly enhance our understanding of this behavior. Older children may be able to provide valuable information as well about the degree to which they think about sexual matters, (cf. the Sexual Concerns subscale from the Trauma Symptom Checklist–Children (Briere, 1996).

Analyses with a behavior, SIB, that has a relative low frequency, also reduce the stability of the findings. In addition, we do not know what the precursor variables are to persistent sexual behavior disturbance. Are they the more active behaviors captured in the SIB variable created for this study, or are they a function of sexual knowledge and interest? For example, some individuals may have unusual thinking about sexuality but they rarely act on it or do so only when the circumstances of their life change.

Additional issues pertain to the diversity of SIB in children. Who are those children who do not have adversity or modeling of coercion in their lives, but yet are persistently sexual with other children? Are they more likely to be sexually abused? Are their issues more fleeting? The behaviors subsumed under SIB do not provide information as to whether this behavior stopped quickly with limit-setting, or occurred in a context in which there were other triggers or potentiating factors.

Developmental issues are primary as well. We cannot understand who among preteens with SIB desist as they move into adolescence and who persist until research studies sample across this critical developmental period.

Until these data emerge, it does seem clear that SIB in preteens can be measured by adult report. These problems are related to a range of potentiating factors that parallel the results of other research with disruptive children. However, it may be that SIB needs either a sexual event and/or modeling to activate this behavior into the form of SIB that was measured in this study. Until further research is completed, it is quite likely that utilizing adolescent or adult treatment protocols for these behaviors is not appropriate.

REFERENCES

ACHENBACH, T. M. (1988). *Child Behavior Checklist for Ages 2–3*. Burlington, VT: University of Vermont Department of Psychiatry.

ACHENBACH, T.M. (1991). *Manual for the Child Behavior Checklist/4-18 and 1991 Profile*. Burlington, VT: University of Vermont Department of Psychiatry.

BRIERE, J. (1996). *Trauma Symptom Checklist Children*. Odessa, FL: Psychological Assessment Resources.

CHAFFIN, M. & FRIEDRICH, W.N. (2000). Developmental-systemic perspectives on children with sexual behavior problems. Keynote speech presented at the annual meeting of ATSA, November, San Diego, CA.

FRIEDRICH, W.N. (1997) *Child Sexual Behavior Inventory*. Odessa, FL: Psychological Assessment Resources.

FRIEDRICH, W.N. & FEHRER, E. Correlates of behavior problems in a clinical sample of sexually abused children. (Under review).

FRIEDRICH, W.N., FISHER, J., DITTNER, C., ACTON, R., BERLINER, L., BUTLER, J., DAMON, L., DAVIES, W.H., GRAY, A. & WRIGHT, J. (2001). Child Sexual Behavior Inventory: Normative, psychiatric and sexual abuse comparisons. *Child Maltreatment, 6*, 37–49.

FRIEDRICH, W.N. & LUECKE, W.J. (1988). Young school-age sexually aggressive children. *Professional Psychology, 19*, 155–164.

FRIEDRICH, W.N., LENGUA, L., TRANE, S., FISHER, J., DAVIES, W. H., PITHERS, W. & TRENTHAM, B. Parent report of PTSD and Dissociation Symptoms: Normative, psychiatric, and sexual abuse comparisons. (Under editorial review).

FRIEDRICH, W.N., URQUIZA, A.J. & BEILKE, R.L. (1986). Behavior problems in sexually abused young children. *Journal of Pediatric Psychology, 11*, 47–57.

HALL, D.K., MATHEWS, F. & PEARCE, J. (1998). Factors associated with sexual behavior problems in young sexually abused children. *Child Abuse and Neglect, 22*, 1045-1063.

HALL, D.K., MATHEWS, F. & PEARCE, J. (2002). Sexual behavior problems in sexually abused children: A preliminary typology. *Child Abuse and Neglect, 26*, 289–312.

JOHNSON, T.C. (1988). Child perpetrators: Children who molest other children: Preliminary findings. *Child Abuse & Neglect, 12*, 219–229.

JOHNSON, T. (1989). Female child perpetrators: Children who molest other children. *Child Abuse and Neglect, 13*, 571–585.

KENDALL-TACKETT, K., WILLIAMS, L.M. & FINKELHOR, D. (1993). Impact of sexual abuse on children: A review and synthesis of recent empirical studies. *Psychological Bulletin, 113*, 164–180.

PATTERSON, G.R., DEGARMO, D.S. & KNUTSON, N. (2000). Hyperactive and antisocial behaviors: Comorbid or two points in the same process? *Development and Psychopathology, 12*, 91–106.

SILOVSKY, J. & Niec, L. 2002. Characteristics of young children with sexual behavior problems: A pilot study. *Child Maltreatment, 7*, 187–197.

TRANE, S. & FRIEDRICH, W.N. Dimensions of sexual behavior in children: Factor analysis of the CSBI. (In preparation).

WOLFE, D.A. SAS, L. & WEKERLE, C. (1994). Factors associated with the development of post-traumatic stress disorder among child victims of sexual abuse. *Child Abuse & Neglect, 18*, 37–50.

The Etiology of Anomalous Sexual Preferences in Men

VERNON L. QUINSEY

Psychology Department, Queen's University, Kingston, Ontario, K7L 3N6, Canada

ABSTRACT: People discover rather than choose their sexual interests. The process of discovery typically begins before the onset of puberty and is associated with an increase in the secretion of sex hormones from the adrenal glands. However, the determinants of the direction of sexual interest, in the sense of preferences for the same or opposite sex, are earlier. These preferences, although not manifest until much later in development, appear to be caused by the neural organizational effects of intrauterine hormonal events. Variations in these hormonal events likely have several causes and two of these appear to have been identified for males. One cause is genetic and the other involves the sensitization of the maternal immune system to some aspect of the male fetus. It is presently unclear how these two causes relate to each other. The most important question for future research is whether preferences for particular-aged partners and parts of the male courtship sequence share causes similar to those of erotic gender orientation.

KEYWORDS: paraphilia; sex offenders; hormones; neural development; pedophilia; homosexuality

THE ETIOLOGY OF ANOMALOUS SEXUAL PREFERENCES IN MEN

Variations in sexual preferences have both proximate and ultimate causes. Proximate causes include genetically initiated events, brain structures, and learning (experience-induced neural changes). Ultimate causes refer to the features of ancestral environments that were the agents of selection producing the species-typical reproductive behavior we observe today. Many of the findings relevant to ultimate causation concern cross-culturally invariant similarities of and differences between the sexual psychologies of men and women. Current human sexual interests and desires appear to be exquisitely designed to foster reproductive success in ancestral environments.

Sexual preferences refer to how an individual would like to reach orgasm (Langevin, 1983). Thus, an individual can have sexual preferences for particular sexual activities or types of partners that are not behaviorally expressed. Sexual preferences are termed anomalous if they are associated with activities or partner types that are reproductively irrelevant or harmful to the individual's fitness interests. Reproductively irrelevant behaviors include masturbation, fetishism, voyeurism, and so

Address for correspondence: Vernon L. Quinsey, Ph.D., Professor of Psychology and Psychiatry, Psychology Department, Queen's University, Kingston, Ontario, K7L 3N6. Voice: 613-533-6538; fax: 613-533-2499.

quinsey@psyc.queensu.ca

Ann. N.Y. Acad. Sci. 989: 105–117 (2003). © 2003 New York Academy of Sciences.

forth; reproductively irrelevant partners are those who are of a different species, the same sex, of pre- or postreproductive age, or dead. It is the *preference* for these activities or types of partners that is anomalous, not merely finding them erotic or involving them in sexual behavior. Masturbation may keep a man fit for intercourse or eliminate tired sperm, fetishism may be involved in foreplay; in time, a prepubertal child is likely to become fertile. The idea, however, is that anomalous sexual preferences would be expected to have decreased personal Darwinian fitness in ancestral environments. This paper discusses anomalous sexual preferences involved in male homosexuality and pedophilia. Before turning to these topics, however, the evidence for a male sexual preference system that focuses male attention on reproductively relevant stimuli will be presented.

THE MALE SEXUAL PREFERENCE SYSTEM

Heterosexual men prefer young adult females as sexual partners. The evidence comes from studies of the sexual attractiveness of stimulus persons who vary in age and sex measured by ratings, covertly measured viewing time, and changes in penile tumescence (Freund, Langevin, Cibiri and Zajac, 1973; Harris et al., 1992, 1996; Jankowiak, Hill & Donovan, 1992; Quinsey & Chaplin, 1988a; Quinsey et al., 1975, 1993, 1996; Silverthorne & Quinsey, 2000). Men prefer features that are associated with fertility and health, including symmetrical faces with particular neotenous features (Johnston, 1999) and average weight figures with hip to waist ratios typical of young adult women (Singh, 1993). There is very strong agreement among observers' ratings of the beauty of female faces (Johnston, 1999) and as far as known, these preferences occur across cultures (Bradshaw, Bubier & Sullivan, 1994; Cunningham, Roberts, Barbee, Druen & Wu, 1995; Johnston, 1999; Korthase & Trenholme, 1982; Singh & Luis, 1995). Preferred partner age remains constant over age among adult men (Bradshaw, Bubier & Sullivan, 1994; Korthase & Trenholme, 1982; Silverthorne & Quinsey, 2000).

Heterosexual men are more interested in sexually novel partners than are women, giving rise to what can be termed a "male courtship pattern" characterized by greater male interest in pictures of nudes and erotic movies, desiring a greater number of sexual partners, greater male striving for actual sexual encounters, less discrimination among potential sexual partners in short-term mating contexts, and so forth (for reviews see Buss, 1989; Buss & Schmitt, 1993; and Hamida, Mineka & Bailey, 1998). The ultimate explanation for these features of the male sexual preference system turns on the observation that the principal limiting factor on male reproductive success in ancestral environments was the number of a man's sexual partners, whereas the principal limiting factor on female reproductive success was the resources a woman could obtain to raise the offspring she had, not the number of her sexual partners.

Sexually dimorphic anatomical features are associated with the different sexual psychologies of men and women. In addition to sex-typical primary and secondary sexual characteristics and body sizes, there are reproductively relevant differences in brain structures. The preoptic hypothalamus is both sexually dimorphic and involved in reproduction across the vertebrates, in part through its production of gonadotropin releasing hormone (Grober, 1997). In humans, sex differences have been found in the sexually dimorphic nucleus of the preoptic hypothalamus, the second and third interstitial nucleus of the anterior hypothalamus (INAH-2 and 3), the suprachiasmatic nucleus, and the bed nucleus of the stria terminalis (Allen et al., 1989; LeVay, 1994; Swaab, Zhou, Fodor & Hofman, 1997). With respect to the latter structure, Zhou et al. (1995) found that the central nucleus of the bed nucleus of the stria terminalis was larger in heterosexual and homosexual men than in women and male-to-female transsexuals, suggesting that this area is involved in gender identity but not sexual orientation.

Other sexually dimorphic neuroanatomical traits are not obviously related to reproductive behavior. These include a larger anterior commissure in women than men (Allen & Gorski, 1991) and a more bulbous-shaped posterior corpus callosum (the splenium) in men than women (Allen, Richey, Chai & Gorski, 1991). A variety of other sex differences appear to result from differences in early neurodevelopment. Men show greater rightward dermatoglyphic (fingerprint ridge count) asymmetry than women (Hall & Kimura, 1994), are more likely to be left-handed (Coren, 1993), and to suffer differentially from a large number of non–sex chromosome–linked neurodevelopmental problems known as "selective male afflictions" (Gualtieri & Hicks, 1985). The sexes are also differentiated by their occupational preferences (Lippa, 2002) and their performance in many cognitive and motor tasks (for reviews, see Collaer & Hines, 1995; Halpern & Crothers, 1997; Kimura, 2000).

MALE HOMOSEXUALITY

The sexual dimorphism of anatomical structures results from the influence of hormones during the development of a wide variety of species. Often these hormones organize neural tissues that guide subsequent development and behavior. For example, the quality of male copulatory behaviors in a number of vertebrate species is affected by prenatal hormonal influence. More importantly in the present context, sex-typical preferences for opposite sex partners can sometimes be reversed by interventions in the organizational phase of neurodevelopment, for example, in rats (Brand et al., 1991) and zebra finches (Adkins et al., 1997). The organizational effects of prenatal hormones are also important in the development of erotic gender preference in humans (Ellis & Ames, 1987; Meyer-Bahlburg et al., 1995) and the resulting erotic preferences in males appear to be relatively fixed, probably pre-pubertally (Beckstead, in press; Bell, Weinberg & Hammersmith, 1981; Green, 1988; McClintock & Herdt, 1996). Male sexual gender preferences are highly bimodal whether measured by questionnaire (Ellis, Burke & Ames, 1987; Kinsey et al., 1953) or phallometric assessment (Freund & Costell, 1970; Freund et al., 1973). Bisexual behaviors among men are very common, but bisexual preferences are rare.

Although homosexual men, like heterosexual women, prefer masculine-appearing male sexual partners (Bailey et al., 1997), they nevertheless display a typically male courtship pattern. Homosexual men are as interested in partner variety as heterosexual men, though they succeed in having more partners than heterosexual men, presumably because heterosexual men have to compromise with the preferred courtship pattern of women (Bailey et al., 1994; Symons, 1979). The male-typical mating effort of male homosexuals is strong evidence for the modularity of the male sexual preference system because it shows that courtship pattern and preferred partner sex are dissociable. The typically male interest in mating effort of male homosexuals invalidates Wilson's (1975) evolutionary "helper at the nest" explanation of male homosexuality which argues that homosexuality was selected for by the inclusive fitness advantages accrued by heterosexually disadvantaged men providing care for their siblings' children; contemporary American homosexual men do not invest more than heterosexual men in their relatives, including their siblings' children (Bobrow & Bailey, 2001). In a related vein, LeVay (1994) has pointed out that the inclusive fitness explanation does not account for homosexual preferences, only the lack of heterosexual mating effort.

Male homosexuality is partly heritable (Bailey, Dunne & Martin, 2000; Bailey et al., 1999; Bailey & Pillard, 1991; Whitam, Diamond & Martin, 1993) and there is evidence that the genetic transmission is maternal (Hamer & Copeland, 1994; Turner, 1995). Certainly the great majority of adult sons of male homosexuals are themselves heterosexual (Bailey et al., 1995). Hamer et al. (1993) found a link between a locus on the X chromosome (Xq28) and homosexuality in men but not among women (Hu et al., 1995), although there has been a failure to replicate this finding (Rice et al., 1999). Homosexuals and male-to-female transsexuals have more maternally related aunts than uncles (Green & Keverne, 2000; Turner, 1995). This observation again suggests the involvement of the X chromosome as well as genomic imprinting (imprinted genes are those that are expressed differently depending upon whether they are maternally or paternally derived). The inheritance of male homosexuality is puzzling given the relatively poor reproductive success of homosexual men (e.g., Hamer & Copeland, 1994).

Adult male homosexual orientation is strongly linked to cross-sex-typed behavior in childhood in both prospective and retrospective studies (Bailey & Zucker, 1995; Bell, Weinberg & Hammersmith, 1981). The observation that prehomosexual boys prefer to play with girls challenges theories of sexual orientation, such as that of Storms (1981), that depend upon differential interaction of boys with other boys. However, childhood gender nonconformity is not a cause of homosexuality in itself; rather, it reflects earlier events. Evidence for this proposition comes from studies of 5-alpha reductase-2 deficiency androgen-insensitivity syndrome. Boys with this syndrome have female external genitalia until puberty, when they develop in a typically masculine fashion. Although these boys are raised as girls prepubertally, the majority appear to have heterosexual preferences as adults (Imperato-McGinley et al., 1979), providing strong evidence that cross-sex-typed childhood behavior is not a sufficient cause of adult homosexual preference.

Male homosexuals resemble women more than heterosexual men on many sexually dimorphic characteristics in addition to childhood play preferences. Females reach puberty earlier than males and homosexual men reach puberty earlier than heterosexual men (Bogaert, Friesen & Klentrou, 2002). Homosexual men have been found to exhibit less rightward dermatoglyphic asymmetry than heterosexual men (Hall & Kimura, 1994), although there have been failures to replicate this result (Mustanski, Bailey & Kaspar, 2002). The size of the anterior commissure is smaller (Allen & Gorski, 1992) and that of INAH-III larger (LeVay, 1991) in heterosexual than in homosexual men. In contrast to these characteristics in which homosexual men tend to resemble women, a greater proportion of homosexual than heterosexual men are non-right handers (Lalumière, Blanchard & Zucker, 2000). Homosexual men also score like women or intermediate between heterosexual men and women on cognitive tasks that differentiate between the sexes: visuospatial abilities (Sanders & Ross-Field, 1986a; Wegesin, 1998), left visual field bias (Sanders & Ross Field, 1986b), throwing to a target (Hall & Kimura, 1995), a lexical decision/semantic monitoring task (Wegesin, 1998), but not fine motor skills (Hall & Kimura, 1995). Male homosexuals prefer female-typical occupations as adults (Lippa, 2002).

Male homosexuals have more older brothers than male heterosexuals (Blanchard, 1997, 2001; Blanchard et al., 1995; Blanchard & Zucker, 1994). Each older brother increases the odds of homosexuality by 33 percent (Blanchard & Bogaert, 1996), which means about 14% of homosexuals owe their sexual orientation to the fraternal birth-order effect (Cantor, Blanchard, Paterson & Bogaert, 2002). Blanchard and Klassen's (1997) maternal immune hypothesis asserts that Y (male) chromosome-linked minor histocompatibility antigens (H-Y antigens) on the surface of male fetal cells progressively sensitize the maternal immune system with each male fetus. The resulting maternally produced anti-H-Y antibodies disrupt the masculinization of the fetal brain.

Several observations lend credence to the maternal immune hypothesis of male homosexuality. Placental cells do not express H-Y antigens, suggesting that the placenta plays a role in hiding the foreign paternal genome from the maternal immune system (Bodmer & McKie, 1994). Intra-uterine mortality is higher for males than females (Gualtieri & Hicks, 1985). Neurodevelopmental anomalies are more common in males than females and occur more frequently in males born later in a sibline (Gualtieri & Hicks, 1985). Left-handedness, thought to reflect perturbations in neurodevelopment, is more common in males than females and in homosexual males than heterosexual males (Lalumière, Blanchard & Zucker, 2000) and fluctuating asymmetry, another reflection of neurodevelopmental difficulty, correlates positively with fraternal birth order (Lalumière, Harris & Rice, 1999). Males with older brothers are smaller at birth than those with older sisters (Côté, Blanchard & Lalumière, in press; Ellis & Blanchard, 2001). Finger ridges develop during the time that the brain is masculinized *in utero*, explaining the feminized pattern of dermatoglyphic asymmetry displayed by male homosexuals. Homosexual males' small INAH-III more directly reflects interference with the masculinization of the brain. It is, however, apparent that the hypothalamus of male homosexuals is not simply a feminized structure, but rather a different one: For example, there is no difference in the sexually dimorphic nucleus of the preoptic hypothalamus between heterosexual and homosexual men, but a large difference in the nonsexually dimorphic number of vasopressin neurons in the suprachiasmatic nucleus (Swaab et al., 1997). Hypothalamic structures appear to be formed differentially by paternally imprinted genes (Goos & Silverman, 2001). Thus the structures involved in sexual motivation are expected to reflect the father's rather than the mother's genetic interest and be designed to extract resources from the mother and her kin. If male homosexual preference results from selective pressures, these are likely to be complicated and partly reflect genetic conflict.

The fraternal birth order effect does not explain all male homosexuality: for example, some homosexuals are first-born. There may be several etiological paths that converge on a disruption of the masculinization of the brain: one genetic path, one via sensitization of the maternal immune system, and perhaps others having to do with stress (Kinsley, Lambert & Jones, 1997), maternal ingestion of toxic substances, and so forth. The most interesting question, however, involves the relationship between the inheritance of male homosexuality and the maternal immune hypothesis. If these etiological paths are not independent, the genetic link could be provided by the inheritance of variations in the sensitivity of the maternal immune system (Quinsey & Lalumière, 1995). The attractiveness of this conjecture is that it provides a countervailing maternal benefit (decreased likelihood of dying from an infectious disease) to the maternal fitness cost incurred by the poor reproductive performance of homosexual men. This countervailing benefit could explain why, if partly heritable, homosexuality is not bred out of the population.

PEDOPHILIA

By definition, pedophilic men prefer prepubertal children as the object of their sexual interest. This definition excludes men who opportunistically engage in sexual activity with children, but prefer adult partners (Freund, Watson & Dickey, 1991). Phallometric measures of sexual interest discriminate men who are known to have had sex with children from those who have not and, among those who have sexually contacted children, the sex of the children involved (e.g., Freund & Blanchard, 1989; Freund & Watson, 1991; Harris et al., 1992; Quinsey et al., 1975).

A very limited amount of evidence suggests that pedophilic age preferences develop prepubertally. Freund and Kuban (1993) found that a greater proportion of pedophiles than men who preferred adults reported childhood curiosity about seeing children but not adults in the nude. These retrospective self-reports suggested that erotic gender preferences were established prior to age preferences. A companion study showed that among heterosexual men who were erotically oriented toward adults (gynephiles), interest in children of the preferred sex disappeared around the time of puberty, suggesting an active devaluation of the nonpreferred age category.

The origins of variations in sexual age preferences are not known, but a number of potential causes can be ruled out. Childhood sexual experience has been an intuitively appealing and popular etiological candidate but can be rejected on several grounds. Within- and between-gender sex play among children is extremely common, whereas pedophilic preferences are uncommon in men and perhaps nonexistent among women. The fact that almost all sex offenses against children are committed by men and most of these against female children (Carlstedt, Forsman & Soderstrom, 2001) rules out any simple etiological role of early sexual experience in the development of pedophilia. In the most ambitious and best-controlled study of adjudicated offenders, Gebhard et al. (1965) found that a minority of sex offenders reported sexual contact with adults and the proportion so reporting was no higher among men who sexually offended against children than men who had committed nonsexual offenses. In societies where sex between boys and men is very common, the boys take wives and have children as adults (Herdt, 1984), suggesting that they develop male-typical sex and age erotic preferences. The evidence supporting the early sexual experiences hypothesis is very weak, mostly consisting of the retrospective reports of identified offenders contrasted with inadequate comparison groups (Garland & Dougher, 1990).

Conditioning interpretations of the presumed effects of early sexual experience have frequently been advanced. Experimental attempts to condition sexual arousal to neutral or nonpreferred stimuli in adult subjects (e.g., Lalumière & Quinsey,

1998), however, suffer from the same ambiguities of interpretation as the treatment literature that uses conditioning techniques to eliminate arousal to preferred stimuli because it is entirely unclear whether the changes observed actually reflect changes in enduring underlying preferences, and there is good reason to believe from studies of instructional control that they do not (Quinsey & Chaplin, 1988b).

The failure to find experiential determinants of pedophilic preferences, their early appearance, and their apparent stability encourage the development of a neurohormonal explanation. The central idea is that the male sexual preference system comprises a number of neurally based modules that correspond to ancestrally recurring reproductive problems. These include determining the appropriate sex and age of partner, as well as particular courtship patterns. We have seen how male homosexuality can be interpreted as resulting from a perturbation in the masculinization of the brain. Pedophilia could develop from a variant of the same process.

If a variant of the neurohormonal theory of sexual orientation explains pedophilic age preferences, we would expect links between age and gender preferences. Among men and women who prefer adult partners, there is some evidence that age and gender preferences develop independently of each other. Silverthorne and Quinsey (2000) found in a rating study of sexual attractiveness that homosexual and heterosexual men preferred younger partners of their preferred sex than did homosexual and heterosexual women. In contrast to all other groups, the homosexual women rated older persons of their preferred sex as more attractive than younger. However, this study included no children as stimuli. In a study that did include child stimuli, Freund, Watson, and Rienzo (1989) found that the phallometrically measured age preferences of male heterosexuals was very similar to those of male homosexuals for their preferred sexes. However, comparisons of the age preferences of men who prefer adult partners with those who prefer children indicate that age and gender preferences are linked. Whereas 2 to 4% of men who prefer adults have homosexual preferences, 25 to 40% of pedophiles do (Blanchard et al., 2000). There is also more bisexual interest among pedophiles than among men who prefer adults in phallometric assessments (Freund & Langevin, 1976; Freund & Watson, 1992; Quinsey & Chaplin, 1988a).

There is a strong fraternal birth-order effect for sexual orientation among homosexual pedophiles just as there is among men who erotically prefer adult men, or androphiles (Blanchard et al., 2000). But the correlates of homosexual pedophilia are not all the same as those of androphilia. Homosexual pedophiles do not reach puberty earlier like androphiles (Blanchard & Dickey, 1998) and retrospectively reported cross-gender childhood behavior has not been linked with homosexual preference among pedophiles as it has with androphiles (Freund & Blanchard, 1987).

The correlates of homosexual pedophilia are also not identical to those of heterosexual pedophilia. On average, homosexual pedophiles prefer older children than do heterosexual pedophiles (for a review see Quinsey, 1986). Homosexual pedophiles report having engaged in less boyhood aggression than heterosexual pedophiles, who in turn report less than heterosexual controls (Freund & Blanchard, 1987). More importantly, a fraternal birth-order effect has not been demonstrated for heterosexual pedophiles (Blanchard et al., 2000), even though such an effect has been shown in mixed groups of sexual offenders, including officially identified rapists (Coté, Earls & Lalumière, 2002; Lalumière et al., 1998). Nevertheless, in support of the application of the neurohormonal theory to heterosexual pedophiles, Cantor et al. (2002)

found a greater prevalence of left-handedness among both heterosexual and homosexual pedophiles than among men who had committed sex offenses against adults. This same study found a relationship between lower intelligence and younger preferred victim age in both heterosexual and homosexual pedophiles.

Progress in understanding the etiology of pedophilia will be facilitated by investigations of the same genetic and neuroanatomical factors that are involved in other anomalies of the male sexual preference system.

SUMMARY AND CONCLUSIONS

The direction of erotic gender preference in men appears to be determined by neurohormonal intrauterine events, although the details of this process remain to be established. Both genetic and developmental (the fraternal birth order effect) antecedents to these neurohormonal changes have been found, but the relationship between these classes of antecedents remains obscure. The neurohormonal events involved in producing male homosexual erotic preferences also result in behavioral, cognitive, and neuroanatomical features that are often, but not always, more typical of women than men. The clearest example of the fact that the characteristics of homosexual men are not all feminized and that the male sexual preference system is modular is that homosexual men show the male-typical interest in partner novelty.

The origins of variations in erotic age preferences are essentially unknown, although there is some circumstantial evidence favoring a neurohormonal developmental hypothesis. The neurohormonal theory applies to the sexual orientation of pedophiles because homosexual pedophiles are, like androphiles, born later among brothers. The theory has not been shown to apply to erotic age orientation *per se* because there is no fraternal birth-order effect for heterosexual pedophilia. Nevertheless, the causes of variations in gender and age orientation are likely to be related, as indicated by the much higher proportion of men with homosexual interests among pedophiles than men who prefer adult partners. It is unknown whether pedophilia is associated with the X chromosome because there have yet been no genetic studies of pedophiles.

Given the evidence for the modularization of the male sexual preference system and the influence of prenatal hormones on its development, neurohormonal developmental theories may be capable of explaining other anomalies and variations in sexual preferences. There are some encouraging data for rapists in this respect. A small proportion of rapists are extremely persistent (Walker, personal communication, 1998), a larger proportion exhibit a preference for descriptions of brutal rapes over consensual sex in phallometric assessment (e.g., Lalumière & Quinsey, 1994; Quinsey, Chaplin & Upfold, 1984), and a fraternal birth-order effect among rapists has been found twice (Coté, Earls & Lalumière, 2002; Lalumière et al., 1998).

ACKNOWLEDGMENTS

Preparation of this article was facilitated by a Senior Research Fellowship from the Ontario Mental Health Foundation. I wish to thank Jill Atkinson, Martin Lalumière, and Michael Seto for commenting on an earlier version of this manuscript.

REFERENCES

ADKINS, R.E., MANSUKHANI, V., THOMPSON, R. & YANG, S. (1997). Organizational actions of sex hormones on sexual partner preference. *Brain Research Bulletin, 44*, 497–502.

ALLEN, L.S. & GORSKI, R.A. (1991). Sexual dimorphism of the anterior commissure and massa intermedia of the human brain. *Journal of Comparative Neurology, 312*, 97–104.

ALLEN, L.S. & GORSKI, R.A. (1992). Sexual orientation and the size of the anterior commissure in the human brain. *Proceedings of the National Academy of Sciences of the United States of America, 89*, 7199–7202.

ALLEN, L.S., HINES, M., SHRYNE, J.E. & GORSKI, R.A. (1989). Two sexually dimorphic cell groups in the human brain. *Journal of Neuroscience, 9*, 497–506.

ALLEN, L.S., RICHEY, M.F., CHAI, Y.M. & GORSKI, R.A. (1991). Sex differences in the corpus callosum of the living human being. *Journal of Neuroscience, 11*, 933–942.

BAILEY, J.M., BOBROW, D., WOLFE, M. & MIKACH, S. (1995). Sexual orientation of adult sons of gay fathers. *Developmental Psychology, 31*, 124–129.

BAILEY, J.M., DUNNE, M.P. & MARTIN, N.G. (2000). Genetic and environmental influences on sexual orientation and its correlates in an Australian twin sample. *Journal of Personality and Social Psychology, 78*, 524–536.

BAILEY, J.M. & PILLARD, R.C. (1991). A genetic study of male sexual orientation. *Archives of General Psychiatry, 48*, 1089–1096.

BAILEY, J.M., PILLARD, R.C., DAWOOD, K., MILLER, M.B., FARRER, L.A., TRIVEDI, S. & MURPHY, R.L. (1999). A family history study of male sexual orientation using three independent samples. *Behavior Genetics, 29*, 79-86.

BAILEY, J.M., GAULIN, S., AGYEI Y. & GLADUE, B. (1994). Effects of gender and sexual orientation on evolutionarily relevant aspects of human mating psychology. *Journal of Personality and Social Psychology, 66*, 1081–1093.

BAILEY, J.M., KIM, P.Y., HILLS, A. & LINSENMEIER, J.A.W. (1997). Butch, femme, or straight acting? Partner preferences of gay men and lesbians. *Journal of Personality and Social Psychology,73*, 960–973

BAILEY, J.M. & ZUCKER, K.J. (1995). Childhood sex-typed behavior and sexual orientation: A conceptual analysis and quantitative review. *Developmental Psychology, 31*, 43–55.

BECKSTEAD, A.L. (in press). Cures versus choices: Agendas in sexual reorientation therapy. *Journal of Gay and Lesbian Psychotherapy.*

BELL, A.P., WEINBERG, M.S. & HAMMERSMITH, S.K. (1981). *Sexual preference: Its development in men and women.* Bloomington: Indiana University Press.

BLANCHARD, R. (1997). Birth order and sibling sex ratio in homosexual versus heterosexual males and females. *Annual Review of Sex Research, 8*, 27–67.

BLANCHARD, R. (2001). Fraternal birth order and the maternal immune hypothesis of male homosexuality. *Hormones and Behavior, 40*, 105–114.

BLANCHARD, R., BARBAREE, H.E., BOGAERT, A.F., DICKEY, R., KLASSEN, P., KUBAN, M.E. & ZUCKER, K.J. (2000). Fraternal birth order and sexual orientation in pedophiles. *Archives of Sexual Behavior, 29*, 463–478.

BLANCHARD, R. & BOGAERT, A.F. (1996). Homosexuality in men and number of older brothers. *Archives of General Psychiatry, 153*, 27–31.

BLANCHARD, R. & DICKEY, R. (1998). Pubertal age in homosexual and heterosexual sexual offenders against children, pubescents, and adults. *Sexual Abuse, 10*, 273–282.

BLANCHARD, R. & KLASSEN, P. (1997). H-Y antigen and homosexuality in men. *Journal of Theoretical Biology, 187*, 373–378.

BLANCHARD, R. & ZUCKER, K.J. (1994). Reanalysis of Bell, Weinberg, and Hammersmith's data on birth order, sibling sex ratio, and parental age in homosexual men. *Amrican Journal of Psychiatry, 151*, 1375–1376.

BLANCHARD, R., ZUCKER, K.J., HUME, C.S. & BRADLEY, S.J. (1995). Birth order and sibling sex ratio in homosexual male adolescents and probably prehomosexual feminine boys. *Developmental Psychology, 31*, 22–30.

BOBROW, D. & BAILEY, J.M. (2001). Is male homosexuality maintained via kin selection? *Evolution and Human Behavior, 22*, 361–368.

BODMER, W. & MCKIE, R. (1994). *The book of man: The quest to discover our genetic heritage.* Toronto: Penquin.

BOGAERT, A.F., FRIESEN, C. & KLENTROU, P. (2002). Age of puberty, and sexual orientation in a national probability sample. *Archives of Sexual Behavior, 31*, 73–82.

BRADSHAW, R.H., BUBIER, N.E. & SULLIVAN, M. (1994). The effects of age and gender on perceived facial attractiveness: A reply to McLellan and McKelvie. *Canadian Journal of Behavioural Science, 26*, 199–204.

BRAND, T., KROONEN, J., MOS, J. & SLOB, K. (1991). Adult partner preference and sexual behavior of male rats affected by perinatal endocrine manipulations. *Hormones and Behavior, 25*, 323–341.

BUSS, D.M. (1989). Sex differences in human mate preferences: Evolutionary hypotheses tested in 37 cultures. *Behavioral and Brain Sciences, 12*, 1–49.

BUSS, D.M. & SCHMITT, D. P. (1993). Sexual Strategies Theory: An evolutionary perspective on human mating. *Psychological Review, 100*, 204–232.

CANTOR, J.M, BLANCHARD, R., PATERSON, A.D. & BOGAERT, A.F. (2002). How many gay men owe their sexual orientation to fraternal birth order? *Archives of Sexual Behavior, 31*, 63–72.

CARLSTEDT, A., FORSMAN, A. & SODERSTROM, H. (2001). Sexual child abuse in a defined Swedish area 1993-97: A population-based survey. *Archives of Sexual Behavior, 30*, 483–493.

COLLAER, M.L. & HINES, M. (1995). Human behavioral sex differences: A role for gonadal hormones during early development? *Psychological Bulletin, 118*, 55–107.

COREN, S. (1993). *The left-hander syndrome.* New York: Vintage.

CÔTÉ, K., BLANCHARD, R. & LALUMIÈRE, M.L. (in press). The effect of birth order on birth weight: Does the sex of preceding siblings matter? *Journal of Biosocial Science.*

CÔTÉ, K., EARLS, C.M. & LALUMIÈRE, M.L. (2002). Birth order, birth interval, and deviant sexual preferences among sex offenders. Sexual Abuse, 14, 67–81.

CUNNINGHAM, M.R., ROBERTS, A.R., BARBEE, A.P., DRUEN, P.B. & WU, C. (1995). Their ideas of beauty are, on the whole, the same as ours: Consistency and variability in cross-cultural perception of female attractiveness. *Journal of Personality and Social Psychology, 68*, 261–279.

ELLIS, L. & AMES, M.A. (1987). Neurohormonal functioning and sexual orientation: A theory of homosexuality-heterosexuality. *Psychological Bulletin, 101*, 233-258.

ELLIS, L. & BLANCHARD, R. (2001). Birth order, sibling sex ration, and maternal miscarriages in homosexual and heterosexual men and women. Personality and Individual Differences, 30, 543–552.

ELLIS, L., BURKE, D. & AMES, M.A. (1987). Sexual orientation as a continuous variable: A comparison between the sexes. *Archives of Sexual Behavior, 16*, 523–529.

FREUND, K. & BLANCHARD, R. (1987). Feminine gender identity and physical aggressiveness in heterosexual and homosexual pedophiles. *Journal of Sex and Marital Therapy, 13*, 25–34.

FREUND, K. & BLANCHARD, R. (1989). Phallometric diagnosis of pedophilia. *Journal of Consulting and Clinical Psychology, 57*, 100–105.

FREUND, K. & COSTELL, R. (1970). The structure of erotic preference in the nondeviant male. *Behaviour Research and Therapy, 8*, 15–20.

FREUND, K. & KUBAN, M. (1993). Toward a testable developmental model of pedophilia: The development of erotic age preference. *Child Abuse and Neglect, 17*, 315–324.

FREUND, K. & LANGEVIN, R. (1976). Bisexuality in homosexual pedophilia. *Archives of Sexual Behavior, 5*, 415–423.

FREUND, K. LANGEVIN, R., CIBIRI, S. & ZAJAC, Y. (1973). Heterosexual aversion in homosexual males. *British Journal of Psychiatry, 122*, 163–169.

FREUND, K. & WATSON, R.J. (1991). Assessment of the sensitivity and specificity of a phallometric test: An update of phallometric diagnosis of pedophilia. *Psychological Assessment, 3*, 254-260.

FREUND, K. & WATSON, R.J. (1992). The proportions of heterosexual and homosexual pedophiles among sex offenders against children: An exploratory study. *Journal of Sex and Marital Therapy, 18*, 34–43.

FREUND, K., WATSON, R.J. & DICKEY, R. (1991). Sex offenses against female children perpetrated by men who are not pedophiles. *Journal of Sex Research, 28*, 409–423.

FREUND, K., WATSON, R.J. & RIENZO, D. (1989). Heterosexuality, homosexuality, and erotic age preference. *Journal of Sex Research, 26,* 107–117.

GARLAND, R.J. & DOUGHER, M.J. (1990). The abused/abuser hypothesis of child sexual abuse: A critical review of theory and research. In J.R. Feierman (Ed.). *Pedophilia: Biosocial dimensions* (pp. 488–509). London: Springer-Verlag.

GEBHARD, P.H., GAGNON, J.H., POMEROY W.B. & CHRISTENSON, C.V. (1965). *Sex offenders: An analysis of types.* New York: Harper & Row.

GOOS, L.M. & SILVERMAN, I. (2001). The influence of imprinting on brain development and behavior. *Evolution and Human Behavior, 22,* 385–408.

GREEN, R. (1988). The immutability of (homo)sexual orientation: Behavioral science implications for a constitutional (legal) analysis. *Journal of Psychiatry and Law, 16,* 537–575.

GREEN, R. & KEVERNE, E.B. (2000). The disparate maternal aunt-uncle ratio in male transsexuals: An explanation invoking genomic imprinting. *Journal of Theoretical Biology, 202,* 55–63.

GROBER, M.S. (1997). Neuroendocrine foundations of diverse sexual phenotypes in fish. In L. Ellis & L.Ebertz (Ed.), *Sexual orientation. Toward biological understanding* (pp. 3–20). Westport, CT: Praeger.

GUALTIERI, T. & HICKS, R.E. (1985). An immunoreactive theory of selective male affliction. *The Behavioral and Brain Sciences, 8,* 427–441.

HALL, J.A.Y. & KIMURA, D. (1994). Dermatoglyphic asymmetry and sexual orientation in men. *Behavioral Neuroscience,108,* 1203–1206.

HALL, J.A.Y. & KIMURA, D. (1995). Sexual orientation and performance on sexually dimorphic motor tasks. *Archives of Sexual Behavior, 24,* 395-407.

HALPERN, D.F. & CROTHERS, M. (1997). Sex, sexual orientation, and cognition. In L. Ellis & L. Ebertz (Eds). *Sexual orientation: Toward biological understanding.* (pp. 181–197). London: Praeger.

HAMER, D. & COPELAND, P. (1994). *The science of desire: The search for the gay gene and the biology of behavior.* Toronto: Simon & Schuster.

HAMER, D.H., HU, S., MAGNUSON, V.L., HU, N. & PATTATUCCI, A.M.L. (1993). A linkage between DNA markers on the X chromosome and male sexual orientation. *Science, 261,* 321–327.

HAMIDA, S.B., MINEKA, S. & BAILEY, J.M. (1998). Sex differences in perceived controllability of mate value: An evolutionary perspective. *Journal of Personality and Social Psychology, 75,* 953–966.

HARRIS, G.T., RICE, M.E., QUINSEY, V.L. & CHAPLIN, T.C. (1996). Viewing time as a measure of sexual interest among child molesters and normal heterosexual men. *Behaviour Research and Therapy, 34,*389–394.

HARRIS, G.T., RICE, M.E., QUINSEY, V.L., CHAPLIN, T.C. & EARLS, C. (1992). Maximizing the discriminant validity of phallometric data. *Psychological Assessment, 4,* 502–511.

HERDT, G.H. (Ed.). (1984). *Ritualized homosexuality in Melanesia.* Berkeley: University of California Press.

HU, S., PATTATUCCI, A.M.L., PATTERSON, C., LI, L., FULKER, D.W., CHERNY, S.S., KRUGLYAK, L. & HAMER, D.H. (1995). Linkage between sexual orientation and chromosome Xq28 in males but not in females. *Nature Genetics, 11,* 248-256.

IMPERATO-MCGINLEY, J., PETERSON, R.E., GAUTIER, T. & STURLA, E. (1979). Androgens and the evolution of male-gender identity among male pseudohermaphrodites with 5 alpha-reductase deficiency. *New England Journal of Medicine, 300,* 1233–1237.

JANKOWIAK, W., HILL, E. & DONOVAN, J. (1992). The effect of sex and sexual orientation on attractiveness judgments: An evolutionary interpretation. *Ethololology and Sociobiliology, 13.* 73–85.

JOHNSTON, V.S. (1999). *Why we feel: The science of human emotions.* Reading, MA: Perseus.

KIMURA, D. (2000). *Sex and cognition.* Cambridge: MIT Press.

KINSEY, A.C., POMEROY, W.B., MARTIN, C.E. & GEBHARD, P.H. (1953). *Sexual Behavior in the Human Male.* Philadelphia: Saunders.

KINSLEY, C.H., LAMBERT, K.G. & JONES, H.E. (1997). Experimental alterations of prenatal determinants of sexual orientation and sex-typical behavior in nonhuman mammals.

In L. Ellis & L. Ebertz (Eds). *Sexual orientation: Toward biological understanding.* (pp. 21–40). London: Praeger.

KORTHASE, K.M. & TRENHOLME, I. (1982). Perceived age and perceived physical attractiveness. *Perceptual and Motor Skills, 54,* 1251–1258.

LALUMIÈRE, M.L., BLANCHARD, R. & ZUCKER, K.J. (2000). Sexual orientation and handedness in men and women: A meta-analysis. *Psychological Bulletin, 126,* 575–592.

LALUMIÈRE, M.L., HARRIS, G.T., QUINSEY, V.L. & RICE, M.E. (1998). Sexual deviance and number of older brothers among sexual offenders. *Sexual Abuse, 10,* 5–15.

LALUMIÈRE, M.L., HARRIS, G.T. & RICE, M.E. (1999). Fluctuating asymmetry and fraternal birth order: A first look. *Proceedings of the Royal Society of London, B, 266,* 2351–2354.

LALUMIÈRE, M.L. & QUINSEY, V.L. (1994). The discriminability of rapists from non-sex offenders using phallometric measures: A meta-analysis. *Criminal Justice and Behavior, 21,* 150–175.

LALUMIÈRE, M.L. & QUINSEY, V.L. (1998). Pavlovian conditioning of sexual interests in human males. *Archives of Sexual Behavior, 27,* 241-252.

LANGEVIN, R. (1983). *Sexual strands: Understanding and treating sexual anomalies in men.* Hillsdale, N.J.: Erlbaum.

LEVAY, S. (1991). A difference in hypothalamic structure between heterosexual and homosexual men. *Science, 253,* 1034–1037.

LEVAY, S. (1994). *The sexual brain.* Cambridge, MA: MIT Press.

LIPPA, R.A. (2002). Gender-related traits of heterosexual and homosexual men and women. *Archives of Sexual Behavior, 31,* 83–98.

MCCLINTOCK, M.K. & HERDT, G. (1996). Rethinking puberty: The development of sexual attraction. *Current Directions in Psychological Science, 5,* 178–183.

MEYER-BAHLBURG, H.F.L., EHRHARDT, A.A., ROSEN, L.R. & GRUEN, R.S. (1995). Prenatal estrogens and the development of homosexual orientation. *Developmental Psychology, 31,* 12–21.

MUSTANSKI, B.S., BAILEY, J.M. & KASPAR, S. (2002). Dermatoglyphics, handedness, sex, and sexual orientation. *Archives of Sexual Behavior, 31,* 113–122.

QUINSEY, V.L. (1986). Men who have sex with children. In D.N. Weisstub (Ed.), *Law and mental health: International perspectives, 2,* (pp. 140–172). New York: Pergamon.

QUINSEY, V.L. & CHAPLIN, T.C. (1988a). Penile responses of child molesters and normals to descriptions of encounters with children involving sex and violence. *Journal of Interpersonal Violence, 3,* 259–274.

QUINSEY, V.L. & CHAPLIN, T.C. (1988b). Preventing faking in phallometric assessments of sexual preference. In R.A. Prentky and V.L. Quinsey (Eds.), *Human sexual aggression: Current perspectives. Annals of the New York Academy of Sciences, 528,* 49–58.

QUINSEY, V.L., CHAPLIN, T.C. & UPFOLD, D. (1984). Sexual arousal to nonsexual violence and sadomasochistic themes among rapists and non-sex offenders. *Journal of Consulting and Clinical Psychology, 52,* 651–657.

QUINSEY, V.L., EARLS, C., KETSETZIS, M. & KARAMANOUKIAN, A. (1996). Viewing time as a measure of sexual interest. *Ethology and Sociobiology, 17,* 341–354.

QUINSEY, V.L. & LALUMIÈRE, M.L. (1995). Evolutionary perspectives on sexual offending. *Sexual Abuse, 7,* 301–315.

QUINSEY, V.L., RICE, M.E., HARRIS, G.T. & REID, K.S. (1993). Conceptual and measurement issues in the phylogenetic and ontogenetic development of sexual age preferences in males. In H.E. Barbaree, W.L. Marshall & S.M. Hudson (Eds.), *The juvenile sex offender.* (pp.143–163). New York: Guilford.

QUINSEY, V.L., STEINMAN, C.M., BERGERSEN, S.G. & HOLMES, T.F. (1975). Penile circumference, skin conductance, and ranking responses of child molesters and "normals" to sexual and nonsexual visual stimuli. *Behavior Therapy, 6,* 213–219.

RICE, G., ANDERSON, C., RISCH, N. & EBERS, G. (1999). Male homosexuality: Absence of linkage to microsatellite markers at Xq28. *Science, 284,* 665–667.

SANDERS, G. & ROSS-FIELD, L. (1986a). Sexual orientation and visuo-spatial ability. *Brain & Cognition, 5,* 280–290.

SANDERS, G. & ROSS-FIELD, L. (1986b). Sexual orientation, cognitive abilities and cerbral asymmetry: A review and a hypothesis tested. *International Journal of Zoology, 20,* 459–470.

SILVERTHORNE, Z.A. & QUINSEY, V.L. (2000). Sexual partner age preferences of homosexual and heterosexual men and women. *Archives of Sexual Behavior, 29,* 67–76.

SINGH, D. (1993). Adaptive significance of female physical attractiveness: Role of waist-to-hip ratio. *Journal of Personality and Social Psychology, 65,* 293–307.

SINGH, D. & LUIS, S. (1995). Ethnic and gender consensus for the effects of waist-to-hip ratio on judgment of women's attractiveness. *Human Nature, 6,* 51–65.

STORMS, M.D. (1981). A theory of erotic orientation development. *Psychological Review, 88,* 340–353.

SWAAB, D.F., ZHOU, J.-N., FODOR, M. & HOFMAN, M.A. (1997). Sexual differentiation of the human hypothalamus: Differences according to sex, sexual orientation, and transsexuality. In L. Ellis & L. Ebertz (Eds). *Sexual orientation: Toward biological understanding.* (pp.129–150). London: Praeger.

SYMONS, D. (1979). *The evolution of human sexuality.* New York: Oxford University Press.

TURNER, W.J. (1995). Homosexuality, Type 1: An Xq28 phenomenon. *Archives of Sexual Behavior, 24,* 109–134.

WEGESIN, D.J. (1998). A neuropsychologic profile of homosexual and heterosexual men and women. *Archives of Sexual Behavior, 27,* 91–108.

WHITAM, F.L., DIAMOND, M. & MARTIN, J. (1993). Homosexual orientation in twins: A report of 61 pairs and three triplet sets. *Archives of Sexual Behavior, 22,* 187–206.

WILSON, E.O. (1975). *Sociobiology: The new synthesis.* Cambridge, MA: Belknap Press.

ZHOU, J.N., HOFMAN, M.A., GOOREN, L.J.G. & SWAAB, D.F. (1995). A sex difference in the human brain and its relation to transsexuality. *Nature, 378,* 68–70.

Detecting Anomalous Sexual Interests in Juvenile Sex Offenders

MICHAEL C. SETO,[a] WILLIAM D. MURPHY,[b] JACQUELINE PAGE,[c]
AND LIAM ENNIS[d]

[a]Centre for Addiction and Mental Health, University of Toronto,
Toronto, Ontario, M5T 1R8 Canada

[b]Department of Psychiatry, University of Tennessee, Memphis, Tennessee 38105, USA

[c]University of Tennessee Science Center, Memphis, Tennessee 38105, USA

[d]Department of Counseling, Educational Psychology and Research,
University of Memphis, Memphis, Tennessee 38152, USA

ABSTRACT: Phallometric studies suggest that some adolescent sex offenders exhibit anomalous sexual interests. However, there have been ethical and practical objections to the phallometric testing of adolescents. Alternative measures may be needed if we are to understand the role of anomalous sexual interests in adolescent sexual offending. The Screening Scale for Pedophilic Interests (SSPI) was designed as a brief measure of pedophilic interests based on sexual offense history variables: any male victims, more than one victim, any victims under age 12, and any unrelated victims. Score on the SSPI is significantly and positively correlated with phallometrically measured pedophilic interests among adult offenders against children. In this study, the SSPI was scored in three samples of adolescent sex offenders who underwent phallometric testing for pedophilic interests. Scores on the SSPI were positively correlated with a phallometric index of relative sexual arousal to children in all three samples. This relationship was strongest using visual stimuli. The positive relationship between SSPI scores and pedophilic responding held up despite the use of different penile measures, stimulus sets, procedures, and scoring methods. The usefulness of the SSPI as a proxy measure among adolescents is discussed.

KEYWORDS: phallometric studies; anomalous sexual interests; adolescents; SSPI; pedophilia

Recent phallometric studies suggest that some adolescent sex offenders exhibit anomalous sexual interests. Robinson, Rouleau, and Madrigano (1997) compared 27 adolescent sex offenders and 28 young adult controls, and found that adolescents had

Address for correspondence: Michael Seto, Law and Mental Health Program, Centre for Addiction and Mental Health, Unit 3-1001 Queen Street West, Toronto, Ontario, Canada, M6J 1H4. Voice: 416-535-8501 X2966.
michael_seto@camh.net

Ann. N.Y. Acad. Sci. 989: 118–130 (2003). © 2003 New York Academy of Sciences.

significantly higher relative responses to auditory stimuli depicting sexual interactions with children or rape. Seto, Lalumière, and Blanchard (2000) studied 40 adolescent sex offenders, all between 14 and 17 years of age, who had child victims. Adolescents with only female victims did not differ from the comparison group of young adults aged 18 to 21, while adolescents with male victims were significantly more sexually aroused by depictions of children than the young adults.

There have been ethical and practical objections, however, to the phallometric testing of adolescents (see Seto, 2001, for counter-arguments). Alternative measures are likely to be needed if the role of anomalous sexual interests in adolescent sexual offending is to be understood. Important questions include the following: Do anomalous sexual interests distinguish adolescent sex offenders from others? Do anomalous sexual interests predict sexual recidivism among adolescent sex offenders? When do anomalous sexual interests emerge?

Promising alternatives to phallometry include unobtrusively recorded viewing time and proxy measures comprising correlates of phallometrically measured sexual arousal to children. Among adult offenders against children, relative sexual arousal to children is associated with the following sexual offense history variables: having a male victim, having more than one victim, having a prepubescent victim, and having an extrafamilial victim (Freund & Watson, 1991; Seto, Lalumière & Kuban, 1999). Follow-up studies also show that these variables are associated with a greater likelihood of sexual reoffending (Hanson & Bussière, 1998).

Drawing from this research, Seto and Lalumière (2001) developed a brief scale, the Screening Scale for Pedophilic Interests (SSPI), composed of four sexual offense history items, each of which contributed to the prediction of phallometrically measured sexual arousal to children: any male victims, more than one victim, any victim under age 12, and any unrelated victims. We operationally defined pedophilic interests as equal or more sexual arousal to prepubescent children than to adults. Total scale score was significantly associated ($r = .34$) with sexual arousal in children in a sample of 1113 sex offenders with child victims. The proportion of offenders identified as having pedophilic interests was linearly related to SSPI score, so that offenders with the highest possible score were almost five times as likely to be identified as offenders with the lowest possible score. Moreover, we have unpublished data showing that SSPI score is a significant predictor of sexual recidivism among adult offenders against children.

The applicability of the SSPI to adolescent sex offenders is unclear. Victim sex is a significant predictor of sexual interest in children, with adolescents who had male victims responding more to child stimuli than adolescents who had only female victims (Becker, Hunter, Stein & Kaplan, 1989; Hunter, Goodwin & Becker, 1994). However, Becker et al. (1989) found that adolescents did not significantly differ in their relative sexual interest in children according to their relationship with the victim (familially related vs. unrelated) or victim age (less than 8 years of age vs. older). Hunter et al. (1994) found that neither number of victims nor relationship to victim were significantly associated with relative sexual interest in children. The present study was conducted to determine whether the SSPI is significantly correlated with phallometrically measured sexual interest in children across three samples of adolescent sex offenders.

TABLE 1. Adolescent sample characteristics

	Sample 1 (N = 45)	Sample 2 (N = 141)	Sample 3 (N = 67)
Biographic			
Offender age	15.9 (1.2)	15.0 (1.4)	15.0 (1.2)
	12 to 17	12 to 17	13 to 17
Education	8th grade	—	9th grade
Race	Predominantly White	32% Black	49% Black
		65% White	49% White
Criminal history			
Number of sexual victims	3.0 (3.0)	2.4 (2.8)	3.0 (2.9)
Number of nonsexual charges	—	1.5 (3.5)	—
SSPI Items			
Total score	3.7 (1.1)	3.0 (1.6)	2.7 (1.6)
% Any male victims	76	48	37
% Multiple victims	42	53	61
% Victim under age 12	91	80	79
% Unrelated victim	84	66	55

NOTE: Means and ranges are provided for offender age. Standard deviations are provided in brackets.

METHOD

Participants

Sample 1

This sample consisted of 45 adolescent sex offenders between the ages of 12 and 17, referred for an evaluation at the phallometric laboratory at the former Clarke Institute of Psychiatry in Toronto, Canada. These adolescents participated in the phallometric testing as part of their clinical assessment between 1985 and 1996. This particular phallometric test was discontinued in 1996. Data from 40 of these adolescents were previously reported (Seto et al., 2000). Characteristics of this sample are reported in TABLE 1.

Thirty-eight percent of the sample had male victims only, 24% had female victims only, and 38% had both male and female victims. With regard to victim age, 44% had a victim under the age of 6, 73% had a victim between the ages of 6 and 11, and 24% had a victim aged 12 and over (the values do not add up to 100% because some offenders had victims in different age categories). With regard to relationship to the victim, 18% offended against a family member and 84% offended against an extrafamilial child (the values do not add up to 100% because some offenders had victims in different relationship categories). All of the adolescents had committed a sexual offense involving physical contact with a person under the age of 14.

Sample 2

This sample consisted of 158 adolescent sex offenders between the ages of 12 and 17, referred for an evaluation at a specialized adolescent sex offender program based at the Department of Psychiatry, University of Tennessee at Memphis, who underwent a phallometric assessment. Participants were referred for evaluations from different sources, including criminal justice, mental health, or legal professionals. Psychometric data from these participants were included in a previous report and are not discussed here (Cooper, Murphy & Haynes, 1996). Of these 158 adolescents, 141 had data on their phallometrically measured responses to slides depicting targets of both sexes, and 41 had data on their responses to audiotaped vignettes describing sexual interactions with targets of both sexes.

Twenty-three percent had male victims only, 52% had female victims only, and 25% had both female and male victims. With regard to victim age, 38% had victims aged 5 or younger, 58% had victims between the ages of 6 and 11, and 39% had victims aged 12 or older. With regard to relationship to victim, 29% offended against an immediate family member, 27% offended against an extended family member, and 66% offended against an extrafamilial child. All but four adolescents had committed a sexual offense that involved physical contact with the victim. Approximately half of the hands-on sexual offenses involved vaginal or anal penetration; the remainder consisted of fondling or oral sex.

Sample 3

This sample consisted of 69 adolescent sex offenders between the ages of 12 and 17, evaluated at an adolescent sex offender program based at the Department of Psychiatry, University of Tennessee at Memphis. Data from these adolescents were previously reported in Murphy, DiLillo, Haynes, and Steere (2001). Phallometric data were missing for two adolescents, so the analyses were based on 67 adolescents between the ages of 13 and 17.

Fifteen percent had male victims only, 63% had female victims only, and 22% had both female and male victims. With regard to victim age, 52% had victims aged 5 or younger, 55% had victims between the ages of 6 and 11, and 42% had victims aged 12 or older. With regard to relationship to victim, 40% offended against an immediate family member, 43% offended against an extended family member, and 52% offended against an extrafamilial child. Ten percent of the adolescents had committed a hands-off sexual offense, and all had committed a sexual offense involving physical contact with a victim.

Materials and Apparatus

Sample 1

The sexual stimuli were film clips that depicted nude male or female individuals from four age categories walking towards the camera: very young prepubescent children (5–7 years old), prepubescent children (8–11 years old), pubescent children (12–13 years old), and young adults (early to mid-20s). Sexually neutral film clips of landscapes were also shown. Clips depicting individuals were accompanied by audiotapes describing these individuals as involved in nonsexual activities such as swimming. The audiotaped third-person narratives emphasized features of the individuals' body shapes; narratives about females were all read by the same adult woman, while narratives about males were all read by the same adult man. Clips depicting landscapes were accompanied by narratives describing the scenery; half were read by the female narrator and the other half were read by the male narrator. Film clips were presented using three Eiki SNT-0 Slim Line 16-mm film projectors while audiotapes were presented using a Tiffen Pro-Corder System II audiotape player and headphones. The film clips were shown on three screens located approximately 3 m in front of the participant's chair. Each screen was 1.5 m² in area, while the projected images were approximately 1.2 m by 1.5 m in size.

Changes in penile volume were recorded in the laboratory. A schematic diagram and drawing of the volumetric apparatus is provided by Freund, Sedlacek, and Knob (1965), and a comparison of volumetric and circumferential phallometry is found in Kuban, Barbaree, and Blanchard (1999). The apparatus included a glass cylinder that fit over the participant's penis and an inflatable latex cuff that surrounded the base of his penis and isolated the air inside the cylinder from the air outside. The cylinder was connected by a rubber tube to a Rosemount Model 831A pressure transducer, which converted changes in air pressure into changes in voltage output. An increase in penile volume compressed the air inside the cylinder and thus produced transducer output; known quantities of volume displacement in the cylinder corresponded to known changes in voltage output. Transducer signals were recorded using a 12-bit analog/digital converter housed in an IBM-compatible microcomputer (Data Translation Inc. DT 2811-PGH, 8-input board).

Sample 2

The slide stimuli were the same as those described by Murphy, Haynes, Stalgaitis, and Flanagan (1986). There were two slides in each of seven age categories: 5, 9, 12, 15, 18, 25, and 35 years. There were two sets of these slide stimuli, one depicting female targets and the other depicting male targets.

Audio stimuli consisted of two sets of 2-minute audiotapes, one describing interactions with a male and the other describing interactions with a female (see Abel, Becker, Murphy & Flanagan, 1981; Murphy et al., 1986). The female set consisted of eight categories: (1) child-initiated, (2) child mutual, (3) child nonphysical coercion, (4) child physical coercion, (5) child sadism, (6) child nonsexual assault, (7) adult female mutual, and (8) incest with a relative of unspecified age. The male set consisted of the same child stimuli and an adult male mutual stimulus; there was no incest stimulus. There were two exemplars of each category.

Participants' erectile responses were recorded using a Barlow strain gauge (Barlow, Becker, Leitenberg & Agras, 1970) connected to a Grass Model 7 polygraph (Grass-Telefactor, Astro-Med Industrial Park, 600 East Greenwich Avenue, West Warwick, RI, 02893).

Sample 3

The auditory stimuli used with this sample were developed by Becker, Hunter, Goodwin, Kaplan, and Martinez (1992). The stimuli are 2-min long and describe dyadic interactions that vary according to the age and gender of the target person depicted, as well as the nature of the behavior involved ("consenting" or nonconsenting). Each participant received two complete presentations of 21 tapes. There were 18 sexual tapes and 3 nonsexual tapes: (1) 10–11-year old male, consenting; (2) male adolescent, consenting; (3) male adult, consenting; (4) male child, incestuous; (5) 6–7-year old male, with force; (6) 10–11-year old male, with force; (7) male peer, with force; (8) 10–11 year old female, consenting; (9) female peer, consenting; (10) female adult, consenting; (11) female child, incestuous; (12) 6–7-year old female, with force; (13) 10–11-year old female, with force; (14) female peer, with force; (15) adult, with force; (16) exhibitionism; (17) frottage; (18) voyeurism; (19 physical assault of male; (20) physical assault of female; and (21) a nonsexual, nonviolent social interaction. As in Sample 2, erectile responses were recorded using a Barlow strain gauge connected to a Grass Model 7 polygraph.

Procedure

Sample 1

Each participant provided informed consent after the procedure was explained to them at the beginning of the test session. The test session consisted of 3 blocks of 9 trials, each trial lasting 28 seconds. The nine trials consisted of one trial for each age–sex category and one neutral landscape scene; the order of trials in each block was randomized and then the same order was presented to every participant within each block. Film clips of different individuals from the same age–sex category were simultaneously presented on three screens during each trial. The next stimulus was not presented until participants had returned to within 1.0 cc of their baseline volume. Participants were monitored by a low-light Sony Shibaden HV-15 video camera trained on their upper body during the testing, in order to inhibit such faking tactics as looking away or tampering with the sensor. Participants who did not comply with the testing procedures were not included in the database. The entire testing session took approximately an hour. Participants also underwent an interview and completed a questionnaire as part of their evaluation. The interview and questionnaire included questions about family background, schooling, criminal history, and sexual behavior. Information about victims of sexual offenses were coded from the interview, questionnaire, and official records.

Sample 2

Many of the evaluations took place over two consecutive days, with most completed within one week. After providing their consent, participants and family members participated in a structured interview with a doctoral-level psychologist. A few participants were interviewed by a doctoral student or psychology intern. The interview contained questions about family background, schooling, criminal and delinquent behavior, mental health history, substance use, peer relationships, and sexual behavior. Information about victims of sexual offenses was coded from these interviews and from official records when available (e.g., police synopsis, court referral). Following the structured interview, participants completed a psychosexual evaluation that included paper-and-pencil questionnaires and phallometric testing.

The phallometric procedures using in this study are similar to those described by Murphy et al. (1986). Participants began with an adaptation phase during which they watched a sexually explicit videotape for 15 minutes. Each participant underwent up to four phallometric test sessions. Each session lasted approximately one hour, with a break of at least two hours between sessions and no more than two sessions per day. There were separate sessions for the female slides, male slides, female audio-tapes, and male audiotapes, respectively. The standard procedure in the laboratory was to present slides first. Seventeen participants saw only female slides or male slides. The reasons for the incomplete slide presentations were not recorded, but participants usually did not view both sets of slide stimuli because the participants missed a laboratory session or because of time constraints. Only data from participants who saw both male and female slides were analyzed in this study.

Most participants did not receive both sets of audiotapes because of time constraints. The tapes they did hear corresponded to the sex of their victims: 77 heard only the female set, and 32 heard only the male set. Because only 41 participants heard both male and female audiotapes, and because those participants had already been assessed using slide stimuli, data from the audiotaped stimuli were not analyzed for this study.

Participants were instructed to attend to the stimuli and to refrain from interfering with their responding. Participants were asked to estimate their response in terms of percentage of full erection after each stimulus presentation. All stimuli were presented in a predetermined, random order. There was an interval of at least 30 seconds between each stimulus presentation, or until the participant had returned to within 5 mm of their baseline circumference.

Sample 3

These participants underwent the same structured interview and psychosexual evaluation as described for Sample 2, except that they listened to two audiotapes describing adult sexual interactions, one involving a male and female and the other involving two males, during the adaptation phase. These audiotapes were drawn from the Abel et al. (1981) stimulus set. Each participant heard all of the Becker et al. (1992) tapes twice. The first presentation took place on the same day, over two hour-long sessions that were separated by at least two hours to avoid participant fatigue. The second presentation took place on a different day, usually the next day, in two hour-long sessions separated by at least two hours. Auditory stimuli were presented in a predetermined, random order. The interstimulus interval was at least 30 seconds, or until the participant's arousal returned to within 5 mm of baseline circumference.

Scoring of the Screening Scale for Pedophilic Interests (SSPI)

The items for the SSPI were scored from information about the participants' sexual offense histories, obtained from self-report and official records. Each item was coded dichotomously, as absent or present: Any male victims (0 = no, 2 = yes); more than one victim (0 = no, 1 = yes); any victim under the age of 12 (0 = no, 1 = yes); and any extrafamilial victims, defined in this study as a child who was not the adolescent's sibling, step-sibling, nephew or niece, or cousin (0 = no, 1 = yes). Total SSPI scores could range from 0 to 5.

Scoring of Phallometric Data

For all the phallometric indices reported here, positive scores indicate a preference for children, while negative scores indicate a preference for adults. Consistent with the recommendation of Harris, Rice, Quinsey, Chaplin, and Earls (1992), individuals who minimally responded in the laboratory were retained in the analysis of phallometric data.

Sample 1

Consistent with previous studies from this laboratory, changes in penile volume were measured by the peak response and the total area under the response curve for each stimulus presentation (Seto et al., 1999, 2000). Both scores were standardized within each participant and then averaged. These scores were used to calculate a Pedophilic Film Index, defined as the largest response to stimuli depicting very young or prepubescent children minus the largest response to stimuli depicting adults. Stimuli depicting 12- or 13-year-olds were excluded from the analysis because they could be considered peers of the youngest adolescents.

Sample 2

Participants' responses to the stimuli were recorded in terms of mm change in penile circumference. These scores were converted to percentages of full erection. A full erection was determined based on a participant's report of obtaining a full erection either during the adaptation phase or during any of the test sessions. If a participant did not report getting a full erection, the circumference change at full erection was estimated from his largest recorded response during a stimulus presentation and his self-reported level of response. For example, if a participant's greatest response to a sexual stimulus was 10 mm change in circumference, and he reported that this represented 50% of full erection, his full erection response was estimated as 20 mm change in circumference.

Responses to slides depicting 12-year-olds were excluded from the analysis because the depicted individuals could be perceived as peers by the youngest adolescents in the sample. Responses to each stimulus type were averaged and then a Pedophilic Slide Index was calculated as the difference between the highest response to pictures of male or female children aged 5 or 9, and the highest response to pictures of male or female individuals aged 15 or older.

Sample 3

Responses to stimuli describing 10- or 11-year-olds were excluded from the analysis because the depicted individuals could be perceived as peers by the youngest adolescent offenders in the sample. A Pedophilic Audio Index was calculated for the 67 adolescents as the difference between the maximum response to audiotapes describing aggressive sexual interactions with children and the maximum response to audiotapes describing sexual interactions with peers. This Pedophilic Audio Index is not a pure index of pedophilic interests because coercive interactions were included in its calculation. Audiotapes describing nonaggressive interactions with young children are not part of this stimulus set.

TABLE 2. Relationships between the Screening Scale for Pedophilic Interests and phallometric indices of relative sexual arousal to children

SSPI Item	Development $N = 1,113$	Sample 1 Film ($N = 45$)	Sample 2 Slide ($N = 141$)	Sample 3 Audio ($N = 67$)
SSPI total score	.34**	.46**	.24**	.23‡
Any male victim	.25*	.29‡	.16‡	.11
Multiple victims	.17*	.39*	.20*	.34*
Any young victims	.12*	.07	.08	.11
Any unrelated victims	.19*	.14	.17*	.06

‡ $P < .10$
* $P < .05$.
** $P < .005$

RESULTS

Sample 1

In terms of difference in standardized scores, the average Pedophilic Film Index was 1.32 (SD = 1.04, range = −1.82 to 1.75). Forty-two percent of the adolescents responded equally or more to film clips of children compared to film clips of adults. The SSPI was significantly and positively correlated with the Film Index, $r(43) = .46, P < .005$. The area under the Receiver Operating Characteristic (AUC) curve for the Film Index was .83 (SE = .07), $P < .01$. The correlations between individual SSPI items and the Film Index are shown in TABLE 2.

Sample 2

In terms of difference in percentage of full erection, the average Pedophilic Slide Index was −22.7 (SD = 22.6, range = −70 to +28). Fourteen percent of the adolescents responded equally or more to slides of children compared to slides of adults. The SSPI was significantly and positively correlated with the Slide Index, $r(139) = .24, P < .005$. The AUC was .60 (SE = .07), which was not significantly better than chance (AUC = .50). The correlations between individual SSPI items and the Slide Index are shown in TABLE 2.

Offenders received a point on the SSPI if any of their sexual victims was under the age of 12. This meant 12- and 13-year-old adolescents who offended against a victim who was one or two years younger could receive a point on the SSPI, whereas 17-year-old adolescents with a victim who was 5 years younger would not. Using Sample 2, our largest sample of adolescent sex offenders, we modified the young victim item on the SSPI so that there was a minimum three year difference between offenders and their victims. This modified SSPI had very similar correlations with the Slide Index, $r(139) = .22, P = .01$. The correlation was also similar when we calculated another modified SSPI counting only victims under the age of 6 as "young victims": $r(139) = .24, P = .005$. Overall, offender age was not significantly related to SSPI score, $r(139) = −.15, P = .08$, or the Slide Index, $r(139) = −.05$, n.s.

Sample 3

In terms of percentage full erection, the average Pedophilic Audio Index was −1.7 (SE = 28.4, range = −76 to 63). Fifty-five percent of the sample responded equally or more to audiotapes of sexual interactions involving children compared to audiotapes of sexual interactions involving adults. The SSPI was positively and almost significantly correlated with the Pedophilic Audio Index, $r(65) = .22$, $P = .06$. The AUC was .65 (SE = .07), $P < .05$. The correlations between individual SSPI items and the Audio Index are also shown in TABLE 2.

All Three Samples

The samples differed in their sexual offense histories, with the Clarke adolescents being more likely to have male victims than Samples 2 and 3, $z = 3.29$, $P < .005$, and $z = 4.05$, $P < .001$, respectively. The Clarke adolescents were also more likely to have unrelated victims than the other two samples, $z = 2.30$, $P < .05$, and $z = 3.19$, $P < .005$, respectively.

The proportion of adolescents who responded equally or more to stimuli depicting children, compared to stimuli depicting adults, at each SSPI score, is shown in FIGURE 1. Excluding a score of zero, which only seven adolescents across all three samples obtained, there was a linear relationship between SSPI score and the proportion of adolescents who were identified as having pedophilic interests. Higher scores were associated with greater proportions of adolescents being identified, although the proportions of adolescents identified at each score were smaller than found among adult offenders against children in Seto and Lalumière (2001).

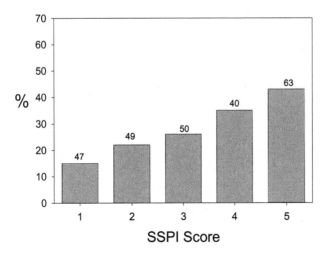

FIGURE 1. Proportion of adolescent sex offenders across all three samples who responded equally or more to stimuli depicting children over adults. Number of adolescents with each score are indicated above each bar.

DISCUSSION

In all three samples, SSPI scores were positively related to phallometrically measured sexual interests in children among adolescent sex offenders. It is worth noting that these positive relationships were found despite the use of different penile measures, stimulus sets, procedures, and scoring methods. These data suggest that the SSPI could be a useful proxy measure of pedophilic interests among adolescents. Excluding the small number of adolescents ($n = 7$) who received a score of 0, there was a linear relationship between SSPI score and the proportion of participants who responded equally or more to stimuli depicting children, compared to stimuli depicting adults, so that the adolescents who received the highest possible score were approximately three times as likely as the adolescents who received a score of 1 to be identified as having pedophilic interests.

The correlations found between SSPI scores and phallometrically measured interest in children, ranging from .23 to .46, can be compared to previously reported correlations of .18 between self-reported deviant sexual fantasizing and phallometric responding (Hunter et al., 1994) and .28 between self-reported sexual interest in nonaggressive sex with a child and phallometric responding (Hunter, Becker & Kaplan, 1995). Although the correlations for the SSPI are not distinctly greater than for self-report, the SSPI is relatively easy to score and can be used for individuals who deny any deviant sexual fantasies or interests. It would be interesting to determine whether self-reported interests and the SSPI independently contribute to the identification of pedophilic interests.

In contrast to the development sample described by Seto and Lalumière (2001), number of victims was a stronger correlate of phallometrically measured pedophilic responding than sex of victim among adolescent sex offenders. However, switching the weights assigned to sex of victim and number of victims had only a small effect on the areas under the ROC curve. This suggests the item weights of the SSPI are relatively robust and, as shown in TABLE 2, the correlates of phallometrically measured pedophilic responding represented in the scale are similar for adolescent and adult offenders against children. It should be noted, however, that 40 of the adolescents in the Clarke sample were part of the large development sample used by Seto and Lalumière (2001), so these correlations are not independent of each other.

The development and validation of measures of anomalous sexual interests among adolescent sex offenders is necessary to further our understanding of the etiology of anomalous sexual interests, onset of sexual offending, adolescent risk assessment, and intervention. Recent research suggests that antisociality and anomalous sexual interests are important factors to consider in adolescent sexual offending, just as they are in adult sexual offending (see Becker, 1988; Butler & Seto, 2002). For example, Långström and Grann (2000) found that sex of victim and number of victims were significantly related to sexual recidivism (but having victims younger than 12 and having stranger victims were not). Worling and Curwen (2000) found that sexual recidivists scored higher on a self-report measure of sexual interest in children and lower on self-reported delinquency than adolescents who did not sexually reoffend, while nonsexual recidivists scored higher on well-established risk factors such as self-reported delinquency, aggression, and prior criminal charges. Finally, Gretton, McBride, Hare, O'Shaughnessy, and Kumka (2001) found that adolescents who were both high in psychopathy and anomalous sexually on phallometric testing were more likely to commit new offenses of any kind during follow-up. This relationship was not detected for sexual recidivism, which might be partly attributed to the lower base rate for this outcome (15% sexual vs. 51% general recidivism). The predictive validity among adolescent sex offenders of both phallometric testing and the SSPI should be examined in future research.

It would also be important to determine how early in life pedophilic interests can be detected. In the present study, across all three samples, one 12-year-old and nine 13-year-old adolescent sex offenders responded equally or more to stimuli depicting prepubescent children, compared to stimuli depicting adults. It is plausible that, like heterosexual or homosexual interests in peer- or adult-aged individuals, pedophilic interests emerge in late childhood or early adolescence. Based on evidence regarding the development of heterosexual or homosexual preferences, Herdt and McClintock (2000) suggest that these sexual interests typically emerge by the age of 10, overlapping with the age of onset for gonadal puberty.

The SSPI is obviously not an appropriate measure for studying the emergence of pedophilic interests, because it requires offending behavior to be scored. Nonbehavioral, unobtrusive measures such as viewing time or neurological recordings of evoked potentials might be more useful in this regard. Some juveniles may have pedophilic interests, but have not had sufficient opportunity to commit offenses that reflect their interests. One would therefore expect their SSPI scores to increase over time. This argument also implies that young adolescents with high scores on the SSPI may have particularly strong pedophilic interests, with clinical implications for risk assessment and intervention planning.

ACKNOWLEDGMENTS

We would like to thank Martin Lalumière, Vern Quinsey, and Marnie Rice for their helpful comments on an earlier version of this manuscript.

REFERENCES

ABEL, G.G., BECKER, J.V., MURPHY, W.D. & FLANAGAN, B. (1981). Identifying dangerous child molesters. In R. B. Stuart (Ed.), *Violent behavior: Social learning approaches to prediction, management and treatment* (pp. 116–138). New York: Brunner/Mazel.

BARLOW, D.H., BECKER, R., LEITENBERG, H. & AGRAS, W.S. (1970). A mechanical strain gauge for recording penile circumference change. *Journal of Applied Behavior Analysis, 3,* 73–76.

BECKER, J.V. (1988). Adolescent sex offenders. *The Behavior Therapist, 11,* 185–187.

BECKER, J.V., HUNTER, J A., GOODWIN, D., KAPLAN, M.S. & MARTINEZ, D. (1992). Test-retest reliability of audio-taped phallometric stimuli with adolescent sex offenders. *Annals of Sex Research, 5,* 45–51.

BECKER, J.V., HUNTER, J., STEIN, R. & KAPLAN, M.S. (1989). Factors associated with erectile response in adolescent sex offenders. *Journal of Psychopathology and Behavioral Assessment, 11,* 353–362.

BECKER, J.V., KAPLAN, M.S., & TENKE, C.E. (1992). The relationship of abuse history, denial and erectile response profiles of adolescent sexual perpetrators. *Behavior Therapy, 23,* 87–97.

BUTLER, S.M., & SETO, M.C. (2002). Distinguishing two types of juvenile sex offenders. *Journal of the American Academy of Child and Adolescent Psychiatry, 41,* 83–90.

COOPER, C.L., MURPHY, W.D., & HAYNES, M.R. (1996). Characteristics of abused and non-abused adolescent sexual offenders. *Sexual Abuse, 8,* 105–119.

FREUND, K., SEDLACEK, F. & KNOB, K. (1965). A simple transducer for mechanical plethysmography of the male genital. *Journal of the Experimental Analysis of Behavior, 8,* 169–170.

FREUND, K., & WATSON, R.J. (1991). Assessment of the sensitivity and specificity of a phallometric test: An update of phallometric diagnosis of pedophilia. *Psychological Assessment, 3,* 254–260.

GRETTON, H.M., MCBRIDE, M., HARE, R.D., O'SHAUGHNESSY, R. & KUMKA, G. (2001). Psychopathy and recidivism in adolescent sex offenders. *Criminal Justice and Behavior, 28,* 427–449.

HANSON, R.K., & BUSSIÈRE, M.T. (1998). Predicting relapse: A meta-analysis of sexual offender recidivism studies. *Journal of Consulting and Clinical Psychology, 66,* 348–362.

HARRIS, G.T., RICE, M.E., QUINSEY, V.L., CHAPLIN, T.C. & EARLS, C. (1992). Maximizing the discriminant validity of phallometric assessment data. *Psychological Assessment, 4,* 502–511.

HERDT, G., & MCCLINTOCK, M. (2000). The magical age of 10. *Archives of Sexual Behavior, 29,* 587–606.

HUNTER, J.A., BECKER, J.V., & KAPLAN, M.S. (1995). The Adolescent Sexual Interest Card Sort: Test-retest reliability and concurrent validity in relation to phallometric assessment. *Archives of Sexual Behavior, 24,* 555–561.

HUNTER, J.A., GOODWIN, D.W. & BECKER, J.V. (1994). The relationship between phallometrically measured deviant sexual arousal and clinical characteristics in juvenile sexual offenders. *Behaviour Research and Therapy, 32,* 533–538.

KUBAN, M., BARBAREE, H.E. & BLANCHARD, R. (1999). A comparison of volume and circumference phallometry: Response magnitude and method agreement. *Archives of Sexual Behavior, 28,* 345–359.

LÅNGSTRÖM, N. & GRANN, M. (2000). Risk for criminal recidivism among young sex offenders. *Journal of Interpersonal Violence, 15,* 855–871.

MURPHY, W.D., DILILLO, D., HAYNES, M.R. & STEERE, E. (2001). An exploration of factors related to deviant sexual arousal among juvenile sex offenders. *Sexual Abuse, 13,* 91–103.

MURPHY, W.D., HAYNES, M.R., STALGAITIS, S.J., & FLANAGAN, B. (1986). Differential sexual responding among four groups of sexual offenders against children. *Journal of Psychopathology and Behavioral Assessment, 8,* 339–353.

ROBINSON, M.-C., ROULEAU, J.-L., MADRIGANO, G. (1997). Validation of penile plethysmography as a psychophysiological measure of the sexual interests of adolescent sex offenders/Validation de la pléthysmographie pénienne comme mesure psychophysiologique des intérêts sexuels des agresseurs adolescents. *Revue Québécoise de Psychologie, 18,* 111–124.

SETO, M.C. (2001). The value of phallometry in the assessment of male sex offenders. *Journal of Forensic Psychology Practice, 1,* 65–75.

SETO, M.C., & LALUMIÈRE, M.L. (2001). A brief screening scale to identify pedophilic interests among child molesters. *Sexual Abuse, 13,* 15–25.

SETO, M.C., LALUMIÈRE, M.L., & BLANCHARD, R. (2000). The discriminative validity of a phallometric test for pedophilic interests among adolescent sex offenders against children. *Psychological Assessment, 12,* 319–327.

SETO, M.C., LALUMIÈRE, M.L., & KUBAN, M. (1999). The sexual preferences of incest offenders. *Journal of Abnormal Psychology, 108,* 267–272.

WORLING, J.R., & CURWEN, T. (2000). Adolescent sexual offender recidivism: Success of specialized treatment and implications for risk prediction. *Child Abuse and Neglect, 24,* 965–982.

The Cultural Context of Sexual Aggression

Asian American and European American Perpetrators

GORDON C. NAGAYAMA HALL,[a] ANDRA L. TETEN,[a] AND STANLEY SUE[b]

[a]*Department of Psychology, University of Oregon, Eugene, Oregon 94703, USA*

[b]*Department of Psychology, University of California, Davis, Davis, California 95616, USA*

ABSTRACT: Attention paid to culture in theories of sexual coercion has been limited. This failure to include culture in these theories implies that culture does not have an important role in sexually coercive behavior. Recent conceptual and empirical work supports the existence of culture-specific models of sexual coercion. Sexual coercion has been characterized in much of the literature as an individual phenomenon. However, cultural norms are influential in collectivist cultural groups. Whereas European American men's sexual coercion is primarily determined by misogynous beliefs, Asian American men's sexual coercion is determined by a combination of misogynous beliefs and cultural considerations. These findings underscore the need to consider cultural context in the development of theoretical models and interventions for sexually coercive behavior.

KEYWORDS: cultural context; misogynous beliefs; Asian Americans; European Americans

THE CULTURAL CONTEXT OF SEXUAL COERCION

Culture is not a consideration in most psychological theories. These theories are typically assumed to be theories of human behavior rather than specific to the European American contexts in which most have been developed and tested (Sue, 1999). Cross-cultural validation can help reveal what is generalizable about scientific theories. Moreover, investigation of phenomena in multiple cultural contexts may reveal aspects of theories that are culturally specific, in that different explanations may be required from culture to culture. Similar to this general monocultural state of the field of psychology, only limited attention has been paid to culture in theories of sexual coercion.

Sexual coercion has been characterized in much of the literature as an individual phenomenon. Evolutionary, psychophysiological, and social-learning theories all have conceptualized factors within the individual that contribute to the propensity for sexual coercion (Hall & Teten, in press). Evolutionary theory emphasizes that sexual coercion may be a vestige of genetic selection in which some sexually coer-

Address for correspondence: Gordon C. Nakayama Hall, Ph.D., Professor, Department of Psychology, 1227 University of Oregon, Eugene, OR 97403-1227. Voice: 541-346-4969; fax: 541-346-4911.

gnhall@darkwing.uoregon.edu

Ann. N.Y. Acad. Sci. 989: 131–143 (2003). © 2003 New York Academy of Sciences.

cive men were able to produce progeny (Malamuth & Heilmann, 1998). Sexual coercion persists because it was potentially adaptive. Psychophysiological approaches focus on sexually coercive men who appear to have a sexual preference for sexual coercion, as measured by sexual arousal patterns (Barbaree & Marshall, 1991). Some sexually coercive men exhibit greater sexual arousal to coercive sexual stimuli, such as rape, than to consenting sexual stimuli. In social-learning models, direct experiences, such as being sexually victimized, or vicarious experiences, such as media portrayals of rape, are processed cognitively and may lead to an increased risk for becoming sexually coercive (Hall & Barongan, 1997). Men who are sexually coercive may be imitating these direct or vicarious experiences via sexual coercion. These three theories are interrelated. For example, psychophysiological sexual arousal has an evolutionary basis insofar as it is associated with reproductive fitness. Similarly, sexual arousal to coercive stimuli may be conditioned via social learning processes. The common thread across these theories is that intraindividual variables are considered to be the basis of sexual coercion.

Feminist theories of sexual coercion consider the individual in a societal context. Feminist approaches contend that sexual coercion exists because of societal acceptance of patriarchy and misogyny (Bohner & Schwartz, 1996; Koss et al., 1994). Many men internalize these patriarchal and misogynous beliefs, and some men act on these beliefs in the form of sexual coercion toward women. Although sexual coercion is maladaptive, some feminist scholars view it as normative insofar as it is tolerated in society and relatively common.

None of the preceding theories of sexual coercion has been adequately investigated outside European American contexts. Moreover, the failure to include ethnocultural factors in these theories implies that culture does not have an important role in sexually coercive behavior. However, recent conceptual and empirical work supports the existence of culture-specific models of sexual coercion.

CULTURE-SPECIFIC MODELS OF SEXUAL COERCION

Similar to feminist theories, cultural theories address contextual issues in sexual coercion. Most cultures include elements of patriarchy and misogyny (Sanday, 1997). However, cultural groups vary to the extent to which their behavior is influenced by intrapersonal and interpersonal determinants. For example, European Americans tend to be more individualistic and less collectivistic than persons of Chinese ancestry (Oyserman, Coon & Kemmelmeier, 2002). Thus, the behavior of a person of Chinese ancestry may be more influenced by how it might have an impact on group harmony than would the behavior of a European American person, which may be more influenced by concerns about establishing independence from others. However, constructs such as individualism and collectivism are broad and may be distal to specific behaviors, including sexual coercion (Hall & Phung, 2001). Individualism or collectivism does not put an individual at risk for becoming sexually coercive. Nevertheless, the determinants of sexual coercion may vary across individualist and collectivist cultural contexts.

In individualist contexts, personal beliefs concerning the permissibility of sexual coercion may determine an individual's risk for becoming sexually coercive (Hall & Phung, 2001). For example, misogynous beliefs have been demonstrated to be associated with men's sexual coercion against women (Malamuth et al., 1991, 1995). Although misogynous beliefs may be transmitted at the societal level, as feminist theorists emphasize, sexually coercive men in individualist contexts do not necessarily seek a consensus concerning their misogynous beliefs or sexually coercive behavior. Individual beliefs that justify sexual coercion may outweigh concerns about its acceptability to others (Ward, Hudson, Johnston & Marshall, 1997). In cultural contexts in which independence is valued, the individual is the primary arbiter of whether to engage in a behavior.

Perceived consensus is critical in decision making in collectivist contexts. Fitting in with the group is valued and standing out as an individual is discouraged (Markus & Kitayama, 1991). Although it could be argued that the individual makes the final decision about behavior even in collectivist contexts, this decision is heavily influenced by the wishes of others. The reference group for one's behavior may be a protective or risk factor for sexual coercion (Hall & Barongan, 1997; Hall & Phung, 2001). A prosocial reference group may discourage sexual coercion, whereas a misogynous reference group may encourage it. Being a member of a group is taken seriously in collectivist contexts and groups may be delineated more carefully than they are in individualist contexts (Nagata, 1997). Therefore the reference groups that are most likely to be influential are those with which a person feels a sense of connection and commitment, such as the family or ethnic community. Although a collectivist person may be part of a larger group (e.g., men, Americans), "local" group norms (e.g., family, ethnic community) will be more relevant than "nonlocal" group norms. Broad societal values which feminist theorists view as influential may be less influential than local reference group norms. For example, collectivist individuals may hold higher or lower levels of misogynous beliefs than most of society, depending on the level of misogynous beliefs in their reference group.

Hall, Sue, Narang, and Lilly (2000) proposed a model of sexual coercion that incorporates cultural contextual influences. The model moves from variables that are distal to sexual coercion to variables that are more proximal to sexual coercion. Ethnicity was the most distal variable in the model. Ethnicity *per se* does not create a risk for sexually coercive behavior. The next variable was individualism/collectivism. Persons in particular ethnic groups may be relatively individualistic (e.g., European Americans) or collectivistic (e.g., Asian Americans). For relatively individualistic persons, intrapersonal variables, including misogynous beliefs, are most directly associated with sexually coercive behavior. For relatively collectivistic persons, interpersonal variables, including concern about the effects on one's social reputation of perpetrating sexual coercion, are most directly associated with sexually coercive behavior. Moreover, many ethnic-minority Americans are bicultural in that they are both individualistic and collectivistic. Sexual coercion among bicultural persons would be influenced by both intrapersonal and interpersonal variables.

METHODOLOGICAL ISSUES IN CULTURAL RESEARCH ON SEXUAL COERCION

The investigation of the cultural context of sexual coercion presents many methodological challenges. A major issue involves varying definitions of sexual coercion across cultural groups. For example, many Asian women may not view sexual coercion as a serious problem, and hence may be unlikely to report being sexually victimized (Dussich, 2001). Given the known disparities in victim and perpetrator perceptions of what qualifies as sexually coercive behavior (Koss et al., 1994), if victims do not perceive sexual coercion as a serious problem, perpetrators are even less likely to view it as such. Thus, behavior that is perceived as sexually coercive in one culture will not necessarily be perceived similarly in other cultures.

In addition to definitional issues, there are language and cultural barriers. Translating and back-translating a measure does not insure that the constructs assessed by the measure are culturally equivalent (Okazaki & Sue, 1995). Manifestations of problem behaviors may vary according to cultural context, such as culture-bound psychological disorders (Mezzich, Kleinman, Fabrega & Parron, 1996). Moreover, even the same problem behaviors may have differing impacts across cultural contexts (Hall, Bansal & Lopez, 1999). Therefore the definition of sexual coercion and its effects are unlikely to be consistent across cultures.

Most of the cross-cultural methodological issues discussed above pertain to cross-national research. Some of these issues are less problematic when multiple cultural groups are studied within a single national context. In the United States, for example, multiple cultural groups coexist and share some common cultural characteristics, such as language. Moreover, definitions among cultural groups of problem behaviors, such as sexual coercion, are more likely to be similar within a nation than between nations.

It could be argued that groups that share a geographic space also share a culture that makes them more alike than different. The assumption is that immigrant groups quickly acculturate to mainstream norms. This assumption is supported by empirical evidence that suggests the relative absence of ethnic differences in the United States on measures of development and personality (Hall et al., 1999; Rowe, Vazsonyi & Flannery, 1994). However, traditional psychological measures do not assess culturally relevant constructs that may be the basis of important cultural differences.

Many ethnic-minority Americans are bicultural. While they may share many characteristics with other Americans, they may simultaneously adhere to cultural characteristics that are specific to their ethnic group (LaFromboise, Coleman & Gerton, 1993). Thus, the assessment of those characteristics that ethnic-minority Americans share with other Americans without also assessing culturally specific characteristics may yield an incomplete explanation of ethnic-minority behavior. In a positive sense, bicultural groups that share elements of two cultures may allow the identification of culturally universal and culturally specific characteristics to be more accessible than when monocultural groups are studied in different national contexts in which there is limited cultural overlap.

One issue that arises when multiple cultural groups share a geographic context that is not an issue in cross-national research is the minority status of some of the cultural groups. In most multicultural settings, one group is relatively dominant and creates pressure to assimilate (LaFromboise et al., 1993). Minority status can influence a group's behavior in addition to the effects of the group's culture. For example, minority status can cause group cohesion because of group similarities and because the majority treats minority individuals as if they belong to the group (Gaines et al., 1997). Minority groups also face discrimination, which can have negative health outcomes (Clark, Anderson, Clark & Williams, 1999). Discrimination may also have specific effects on sexual coercion. Some ethnic-minority men may feel that they cannot directly address their resentment about discrimination with the majority persons who are responsible for it, so they may displace this resentment by victimizing persons who are perceived as weaker and less likely to retaliate, including ethnic-minority women and children (Comas-Diaz, 1995). Therefore it is important to assess the effects of minority status, as well as cultural influences, with ethnic-minority populations.

ASIAN AMERICAN AND EUROPEAN AMERICAN SEXUAL COERCION

We have conducted a series of studies with Asian American and European American men in which we have identified culture-specific models of sexual coercion. Asian Americans are relevant for studies of cultural differences because many have cultural ties to Asia. Sixty percent of persons of Asian ancestry in the United States were born in Asia <http://www.census.gov/Press-Release/www/2002/cb02-18.html>. However, 80% of Asian Americans are able to communicate in English, which allows the possibility of conducting research using English language measures for many Asian Americans. Asian Americans are the most collectivistic and least individualistic of American ethnic groups (Oyserman et al., 2002).

Our studies on sexual coercion have involved college students. Among Asian Americans of college age, 88% attend college (Hsia & Peng, 1998). These data suggest that college populations are representative of Asian American early adults, but may be less representative of European American early adults. Nevertheless, college populations are relevant in that sexual coercion is relatively common because of opportunities for social contact in college (Koss et al., 1994).

It could be contended that Asian American college students are acculturated and may not retain an Asian identity. However, in a large sample of Asian American college students, the majority retained an Asian or bicultural identity (Abe-Kim, Okazaki & Goto, 2001). Forty-seven percent self-identified as assimilated into European American culture, 29% as having a traditional Asian orientation, and 24% as having a bicultural orientation.

Intrapersonal and Interpersonal Determinants of Sexual Coercion

Hall, Sue, Narang, and Lilly (2000) contended that determinants of sexual coercion in individualist cultures are primarily intrapersonal. Such intrapersonal determinants include personal beliefs that may be misogynous. The Confluence Model of Malamuth et al. (1991, 1995), which posits the confluence of hostile masculinity and impersonal sex as determinants of sexual coercion, was characterized by Hall et al. (2000) as an intrapersonal model. Hostile masculinity involves misogynous beliefs and impersonal sex involves a willingness to engage in multiple sexual relations without closeness or commitment.

In collectivist contexts, determinants of sexual coercion include interpersonal influences (Hall et al., 2000). Because conformity to group norms is valued, personal beliefs may be moderated by the social context. Thus the impact on one's reputation of engaging in sexually coercive behavior may be a determinant of sexual coercion. Behaviors that have a negative impact on one's reputation result in loss of face.

Intrapersonal and interpersonal determinants of sexual coercion were examined in samples of 377 European American and 91 Asian American college men from the West Coast and Midwest (Hall et al., 2000). There was not a significant ethnic difference in self-reported frequency of engaging in sexually coercive acts, as measured by the Sexual Experiences Survey (Koss & Gidycz, 1985). Thirty-eight percent of European American men and 33% of Asian American men had engaged in some form of sexual coercion. However, there were clear ethnic differences in path models of sexual coercion. In the European American model, a path from rape-myth acceptance to hostility toward women to sexual coercion was identified (Hall et al., 2000). Rape-myth acceptance involves attitudes and generally false beliefs about rape that function to deny and justify male sexual coercion (Lonsway & Fitzgerald, 1994). Hostility toward women involves a tendency to perceive hostile intent in women's actions (Lonsway & Fitzgerald, 1994). This path is consistent with the hostile masculinity path of the Confluence Model (Malamuth et al., 1991, 1995). The Asian American model also included rape-myth acceptance and hostility toward women, but was more complex than the European American model. In one path, loss of face was associated with hostility toward women, which was associated with use of alcohol before or during sex. Use of alcohol before or during sex was associated with sexual coercion. These data suggest that misogynous beliefs were risk factors for sexual coercion among Asian American men who were concerned about loss of face and used alcohol before or during sex. A second path in which number of consenting sexual partners was associated with alcohol use before or during sex, which was associated with sexual coercion, is similar to the impersonal sex path of the Confluence Model (Malamuth et al., 1991, 1995). A third path suggested that the perceived negative impact of sexual coercion was a deterrent to sexually coercive behavior. Perceived negative impact of sexual coercion involved perceptions that peers and parents would disapprove of sexual coercion and that being arrested for rape would ruin one's reputation.

These results suggest that misogynous beliefs are determinants of sexual coercion for both European American and Asian American men. However, the consideration of misogynous beliefs alone offers an incomplete explanation of Asian American men's sexual coercion. In addition to misogynous beliefs, loss of face, perceived impact of sexual coercion on one's reputation, number of sexual partners, and alcohol use were components of Asian American men's sexual coercion. These additional variables were also tested for European Americans but did not add to the predictive utility of the model. These results support the contention that European American men's sexual coercion is primarily a function of intrapersonal variables. Conversely, Asian American men's sexual coercion is a combination of intrapersonal variables (rape-myth acceptance, hostility toward women), interpersonal variables (loss of face, perceived impact of sexual coercion on one's reputation), and situational variables (availability of sexual partners, alcohol use). It was concluded that there are bicultural influences on Asian American sexual coercion, in that there was ethnic overlap in intrapersonal determinants, but ethnic specificity in interpersonal and situational determinants (Hall et al., 2000).

It is possible that the ethnic-specific aspects of Asian American men's sexual coercion may be at least partially a function of their ethnic minority status. Concerns about loss of face and the impact of deviant behavior on one's reputation may result from the increased societal scrutiny of members of ethnic minority groups. Because Asian Americans were the only ethnic minority group in the Hall et al. (2000) study, it is unclear whether the findings were a function of cultural variables, ethnic-minority status, or both.

Ethnicity, Culture, Minority Status, and Sexual Coercion

We are currently conducting a multisite study of Asian American and European American men's sexual coercion. The sample ($N = 865$) consists of men from three West coast universities, one Northeast university, and one university in Hawaii. This is the largest study to date of Asian American men's sexual coercion. The large sample allows the investigation of potential within-group variability, as well as the use of multiple measures and structural equation modeling. The inclusion of a Hawaii performance site allows the analysis of Asian Americans in a context in which they are part of the majority group. Similarities between minority (i.e., mainland) and majority (i.e., Hawaiian) Asian Americans would suggest a cultural basis of behavior, if these behaviors are different from the behaviors of mainland European Americans. Similarities between Hawaiian Asian Americans and European Americans that are different from mainland Asian Americans would suggest that a mainland Asian American-European American difference may be based on minority status.

The large sample also allowed the creation via factor analysis of latent constructs, which consisted of multiple measures. Multiple measures of a construct are typically more accurate in measuring latent constructs than single measures. The latent constructs that were created for the study with their component measures are presented in TABLE 1. The ethnic-identity construct includes involvement with and attitudes toward an ethnic group. Perceived minority status involves identification as a member of an ethnic minority group and perceived maltreatment as a result of ethnic minority status. Loss of face involves awareness and concern about one's social standing. Although the Sexual Dominance Scale (Nelson, 1979) has multiple subscales, the factor analyses indicated that the Sexual Submission subscale loaded highly on a dominance factor and was a better indicant of dominance than the other subscales. Sexual dominance in this case was indicated by a desire not to be sexually submissive. The misogynous beliefs construct involves negative attitudes toward women, including the acceptance of violence against women including sexual violence, acceptance of gender role stereotypes, and the belief that heterosexual relationships are inherently adversarial. The measure of sexual coercion was the Sexual Experiences Survey (Koss & Gidycz, 1985).

In that ethnicity *per se* does not place a person at risk for sexual coercion, we initially investigated a structural model including the whole sample ($N = 865$). The best-fitting model involved two paths. In the first, sexual dominance was associated with misogynous beliefs, which was associated with sexual coercion. The second path involved a negative association between loss of face and sexual coercion. Inclusion of the perceived ethnic minority status construct did not improve model fit in this or any other model that was tested. The ethnic identity construct also did not improve model fit. The fit of this model with the data was adequate, with a comparative fit index of .87, but the model accounted for only 6% of the shared variance among the constructs and sexual coercion.

In an effort to improve comparability between the mainland and Hawaiian Asian American samples, participants having both parents of the following ethnicities were identified: Chinese American, Filipino American, Japanese American, Korean American, Vietnamese American, and a combination of Asian backgrounds. This resulted in samples of 214 mainland Asian Americans, 116 Hawaiian Asian Americans, and 374 European Americans from the mainland and Hawaii. There were no

TABLE 1. Factor-analytically derived latent constructs and their component measures

Latent construct	Component measures
Ethnic identity	Multigroup Ethnic Identity Measure (Phinney, 1992); Stephenson (2000) Multigroup Acculturation Scale; Ethnocultural Identity Behavioral Index (Yamada, Marsella & Yamada, 1998)
Perceived minority status	Perceived minority status (Sidanius, Pratto & Rabinowitz, 1994); Stigma Consciousness Scale (Pinel, 1999)
Loss of face	Loss of Face Scale (Zane, 1991); Public Self- Consciousness Scale (Fenigstein, Scheier & Buss, 1975)
Sexual dominance	Sexual Submission subscale (Nelson, 1979)
Misogynous beliefs	Attitudes Toward Violence Scale; Hostility Toward Women Scale; Adversarial Heterosexual Beliefs, Rape Myth Scale (Lonsway & Fitzgerald); Machismo Scale (Cuéllar, Arnold & Gonzalez, 1995)

significant differences in percentages of each sample who admitted perpetrating sexual coercion. Thirty-two percent of mainland Asian American men, 31% of Hawaiian Asian American men, and 29% of European American men had engaged in some form of sexual coercion. There were no significant differences on the other measures in the study among the European Americans or among the Asian American groups for the mainland sample. However, there were significant overall differences between mainland Asian Americans vs. Hawaiian Asian Americans vs. European Americans.

European Americans exhibited higher scores than the two Asian American groups on the Ethnocultural Behavior Index, Ethnic Society Immersion, and Dominant Society Immersion. These measures assess participation in activities (e.g., language, friendships, dating, music, eating) with other persons from the same ethnic group. The higher scores for European Americans may be a function of their majority status. There may be more opportunities for European Americans to participate in activities with other European Americans than there may be for Asian Americans to participate in activities with other Asian Americans. Conversely, mainland Asian Americans showed higher scores of Multigroup Ethnic Identity than the other two groups. In contrast to the Ethnocultural Behavior Index and Stephenson Multigroup Acculturation Scale, which assess participation in activities, the Multigroup Ethnic Identity assesses the meaning of ethnic group memberships and how ethnic group membership affects one's life.

Consistent with previous research (Hall et al., 2000), mainland and Hawaiian Asian Americans scored higher on the loss of face measure than did European Americans. On the related measure of self-consciousness, mainland Asian Americans showed higher scores than Hawaiian Asian Americans and European Americans. Thus, concerns about social standing are more critical for Asian Americans, particularly those from the mainland, than for European Americans.

Asian Americans tended to endorse greater levels of misogynous beliefs than did European Americans. Mainland Asian Americans and Hawaiian Asian Americans were significantly more accepting of adversarial heterosexual beliefs and violence than were European Americans. Mainland Asian Americans had significantly higher scores than the other two groups on the Machismo scale.

Despite there being more European American women than Asian American women in most of the contexts of the samples, most sexual coercion involved same-ethnicity perpetrators and victims. This could be interpreted as support for the hypothesis that ethnic minority men displace their resentment over societal discrimination onto ethnic minority women because these women are perceived as relatively weak and unable to retaliate (Comas-Diaz, 1995). However, it is more likely that same-ethnicity sexual coercion is a function of same-ethnic social networks.

Given the differences on the measures between mainland Asian Americans, Hawaiian Asian Americans, and European Americans, would ethnic-specific models of sexual coercion explain the data better than a general model? In a structural model for mainland Asian Americans, three paths to sexual coercion were included. Ethnic identity was negatively associated with sexual coercion in one path. In a second path, ethnic identity was positively associated with loss of face, which was negatively associated with sexual coercion. These data suggest that Asian American identity was a protective factor against sexual coercion. In the third path, sexual dominance was positively associated with misogynous beliefs, which was positively associated with sexual coercion. This model fit the data well, with a comparative fit index of .90, and it accounted for 29% of the variance in sexual coercion, which is a large statistical effect (Cohen, 1988). A structural model for Hawaiian Asian Americans mirrored the model for mainland Asian Americans, except that there was not a direct path from ethnic identity to sexual coercion. The comparative fit index was good at .88, and the variance in sexual coercion that was accounted for by the model was .09, which is a small statistical effect.

A structural model for European American men also included the dominance → misogynous beliefs → sexual coercion path, and a path in which loss of face was negatively associated with sexual coercion. However, the loss of face path was weaker than it was in the mainland and Hawaiian Asian American models. The comparative fit index was .87 for the European American model and the amount of variance accounted for in sexual coercion was only 4%, which is less than was accounted for by the general model that was not ethnic specific. Inclusion of the ethnic identity construct did not improve model fit or variance explained.

Taken together, these findings suggest that ethnic-specific models of sexual coercion are more relevant for Asian American than for European American men. General models of sexual coercion provided a poorer fit with the data and accounted for less of the variance in sexual coercion than did the mainland Asian American and Hawaiian Asian American models. Conversely, the fit of the general models was not different from the fit of the European American model, and the amount of variance accounted for in sexual coercion in the European American model was less than in the general models.

Ethnic identity appears to be a protective factor against sexual coercion for Asian American but not for European American men. Being Asian American is a prosocial identity for most Asian Americans. These results suggest that being European American is neither a prosocial nor an antisocial identity for European Americans. The failure of ethnic identity to improve the predictive power of the European American model of sexual coercion is not because ethnic identity was not salient. European

Americans were more ethnically identified on some measures than Asian Americans. However, it appears that identification and involvement with members of one's own ethnic group has a greater impact on behavior for Asian Americans than it does for European Americans. Perhaps this is because it is more effortful for Asian Americans to be involved with other Asian Americans because Asian Americans are relatively few in number.

Interestingly, concern about social standing is a protective factor for both Asian American and European American men, although this protective effect appears to be stronger among Asian American men. Loss of face was not associated with European American sexual coercion in the Hall et al. (2000) study, but it was assessed with a single measure. Perhaps the treatment of loss of face as a latent construct in the current results more accurately depicted its influence on European American sexual coercion. This finding is consistent with other work that suggests peer influences on deviant behavior (Dishion, McCord & Poulin, 1999). Losing face may be a risk or protective factor, depending on whether the reference group is prosocial or antisocial (Hall et al., 2000).

CONCLUSIONS

Asian American sexual coercion may not be considered as a serious problem because of the unwillingness of victims to report sexual coercion to authorities and the low rates of arrests that result from such limited reporting. However, across studies and settings, approximately 30% of Asian American men perpetrated sexual coercion, which is not significantly different from the rates of sexual coercion among European American men. Thus, sexual coercion appears to be as serious a problem in Asian American communities as it is in others.

The studies reviewed in this chapter suggest that sexual coercion should be considered in ethnocultural contexts. Intrapersonal misogynous beliefs, which have commonly been offered as an explanation of sexual coercion, were associated with European American and Asian American men's sexual coercion. However, Asian American men's sexual coercion was most completely explained by a combination of intrapersonal and ethnocultural factors. Ethnic group identification and concern about losing social standing were protective factors against Asian American men's sexual coercion. These findings appear to be culturally based rather than the result of ethnic minority status. The mainland Asian American model was the best-fitting model for Asian Americans in Hawaii, where Asian Americans are the majority. Moreover, perceived minority status was not associated with the constructs leading to sexual coercion. Although the effect was weaker than it was for Asian American men, concern about social standing was a protective factor against European American men's sexual coercion. Thus, social context may be important for both Asian American and European American men's sexual coercion, and models that solely consider intrapersonal influences may be inadequate.

Models that did not include ethnicity were less adequate to explain mainland Asian American sexual coercion than an ethnic-specific model. Models of sexual coercion may need to be tailored to different ethnic groups. Nevertheless, it is not membership in an ethnic group that is the basis of ethnic differences. Conceptualization and identification of constructs that may underlie ethnic-specific effects is needed.

It is unknown whether these findings involving Asian Americans apply to other cultural or minority groups. Asians and Asian Americans are among the most collectivist groups worldwide (Oyserman et al., 2001). Therefore ethnocultural effects might be expected to be attenuated in less collectivistic groups.

The findings in the studies on Asian American men's sexual coercion are cross-sectional. However, across two studies it was found that Asian American men's sexual coercion was associated with both misogynous beliefs and cultural factors. We are currently involved in a longitudinal project to determine the predictive utility of models of Asian American and European American sexual coercion. Another limitation of these studies is that they have solely relied on self-report. Part of our current research involves supplementing self-report with a laboratory analogue of sexual imposition that we have developed (Hall & Hirschman, 1994).

The findings in our work imply that context must be considered in the prevention of sexual coercion. The results of the studies reviewed in this chapter, as well as treatment outcome studies with sexual offenders (Hall, 1995), suggest that modifying misogynous beliefs is a basic element of any effective prevention program. However, for men who are concerned about their social standing, peer group influences may be equally important. Interventions may need to involve leaving a deviant peer group (Hall & Phung, 2001). Nevertheless, for a person who is group oriented, it may be difficult to disidentify with a group. Thus, changing peer group norms might be attempted. Another solution might involve association with a new prosocial peer group, such as one that celebrates ethnic or cultural heritage. Although such interventions at the peer group level may be most important for Asian American men, they may also be important for many European American men.

Ethnocultural context will become increasingly important in research on sexual coercion and in psychology more generally. Non-European Americans already make up 30% of the U.S. population and are projected to be the majority within 50 years <http://www.census.gov/prod/cen2000/dp1/2kh00.pdf>. Monocultural research on sexual coercion and in psychology risks becoming obsolete (Hall, 1997). The issue is not simply a matter of studying diverse research samples using traditional methods, but of innovative conceptualizations of theory and research from multicultural perspectives.

ACKNOWLEDGMENTS

Work on this chapter was supported by National Institute of Mental Health Grants R01 MH58726 and R25 MH62575.

REFERENCES

ABE-KIM, J., OKAZAKI, S. & GOTO, S.G. (2001). Unidimensional versus multidimensional approaches to the assessment of acculturation for Asian American populations. *Cultural Diversity and Ethnic Minority Psychology, 7,* 232–246.

BARBAREE, H.E. & MARSHALL, W.L. (1991). The role of male sexual arousal in rape: Six models. *Journal of Consulting and Clinical Psychology, 59,* 621–630.

BOHNER G. & SCHWARZ, N. (1996) The threat of rape: Its psychological impact on nonvictimized women. In D. M. Buss and N. M. Malamuth (Eds.). *Sex, power, conflict: Evolutionary and feminist perspectives.* (pp. 162–175). New York: Oxford University Press.

CLARK, R., ANDERSON, N.B., CLARK, V.R. & WILLIAMS, D.R. (1999). Racism as a stressor for African Americans: A biopsychosocial model. *American Psychologist, 54*, 805–816.

COHEN, J. (1988). *Statistical power analysis for the behavioral sciences.* Hillsdale, NJ: Erlbaum.

COMAS-DIAZ, L. (1995). Puerto Ricans and sexual child abuse. In L.A. Fontes (Ed.), *Sexual abuse in nine North American cultures: Treatment and prevention* (pp. 31–66). Thousand Oaks, CA, USA: Sage.

CUÉLLAR, I., ARNOLD, B. & GONZALEZ, G. (1995). Cognitive referents of acculturation: Assessment of cultural constructs in Mexican Americans. *Journal of Community Psychology, 23*, 339–356.

DISHION, T.J., MCCORD, J. & POULIN, F. (1999). When interventions harm: Peer groups and problem behavior. *American Psychologist, 54*, 755–764.

DUSSICH, J.P.J. (2001). Decisions not to report sexual assault: A comparative study among women living in Japan who are Japanese, Korean, Chinese and English-speaking. *International Journal of Offender Therapy and Comparative Criminology, 45*, 278–301.

FENIGSTEIN, A., SCHEIER, M.F. & BUSS, A.H. (1975). Public and private self-concsiousness: Assessment and theory. *Journal of Consulting and Clinical Psychology, 43*, 522–527.

GAINES, S.O., MARELICH, W.D., BLEDSOE, K.L., STEERS, W.N., HENDERSON, M.C., GRANROSE, C.S., BARAJAS, L., HICKS, D., LYDE, M., TAKAHASHI, Y., YUM, N., RIOS, D.I., GARCIA, B.F., FARRIS, K.R. & PAGE, M.S. (1997). Links between race/ethnicity and cultural values as mediated by racial/ethnic identity and moderated by gender. *Journal of Personality and Social Psychology, 72*, 1460–1476.

HALL, C.C.I. (1997). Cultural malpractice: The growing obsolescence of psychology with the changing U.S. population. *American Psychologist, 52*, 642–651.

HALL, G.C.N. (1995). Sexual offender recidivism revisited: A meta-analysis of recent treatment studies. *Journal of Consulting and Clinical Psychology, 63*, 802–809.

HALL, G.C.N. BANSAL, A. & LOPEZ, I.R. (1999). Ethnicity and psychopathology: A meta-analytic review of 31 years of comparative MMPI/MMPI-2 research. *Psychological Assessment, 11*, 186–197.

HALL, G.C.N. & BARONGAN, C. (1997). Prevention of sexual coercion: Sociocultural risk and protective factors. *American Psychologist, 52*, 5–14.

HALL, G.C.N. & HIRSCHMAN, R. (1994). The relationship between men's sexual aggression inside and outside the laboratory. *Journal of Consulting and Clinical Psychology, 62*, 375–380.

HALL, G.C.N. & PHUNG, A. (2001). Cognitive enculturation and sexual abuse. In J. Schumaker & T. Ward (Eds.), *Cultural cognition and psychopathology* (pp. 107–118). Westport, CT: Greenwood.

HALL, G.C.N., SUE, S., NARANG, D.S. & LILLY, R.S. (2000). Culture-specific models ofmen's sexual coercion: Intra- and interpersonal determinants. *Cultural Diversity and Ethnic Minority Psychology, 6*, 252–267.

HALL, G.C.N. & TETEN, A.L. (in press). Understanding rape behavior. In J. Conte (Ed.), *Encyclopedia of trauma and abuse.* Thousand Oaks, CA: Sage.

HSIA, J. & PENG, S.S. (1998). Academic achievement and performance. In L. C. Lee & N. W. S. Zane (Eds.), *Handbook of Asian American psychology* (pp. 325–357). Thousand Oaks, CA: Sage.

KOSS, M.P. & GIDYCZ, C.A. (1985). Sexual Experiences Survey: Reliability and validity. *Journal of Consulting and Clinical Psychology, 53*, 422-423.

KOSS, M.P., GOODMAN, L.A., BROWNE, A., FITZGERALD, L.F., KEITA, G.P. & RUSSO, N.F. (1994*). No safe haven: Male violence against women at home, at work, and in the community.* Washington, DC: American Psychological Association.

LAFROMBOISE, T., COLEMAN, H.L.K. & GERTON, J. (1993). Psychological impact of biculturalism: Evidence and theory. *Psychological Bulletin, 114*, 395-412.

LONSWAY, K.A., & FITZGERALD, L.F. (1994). Rape myths: In review. *Psychology of Women Quarterly, 18*, 133–164.

LONSWAY, K.A. & FITZGERALD, L.F. (1995). Attitudinal antecedents of rape myth acceptance: A theoretical and empirical reexamination. *Journal of Personality and Social Psychology, 68*, 704–711.

MALAMUTH, N.M. & HEILMANN, M.F. (1998). Evolutionary psychology and sexual coercion. In C. Crawford and D. L. Krebs (Eds.). *Handbook of evolutionary psychology: Ideas, issues, and applications* (p.515–542). Mahwah, NJ: Erlbaum.

MALAMUTH, N.M., LINZ, D., HEAVEY, C.L., BARNES, G. & ACKER, M. (1995). Using the confluence model of sexual coercion to predict men's conflict with women: A 10-year follow-up study. *Journal of Personality and Social Psychology, 69*, 353–369.

MALAMUTH, N.M., SOCKLOSKIE, R.J., KOSS, M.P. & TANAKA, J.S. (1991). Characteristics of aggressors against women: Testing a model using a national sample of college students. *Journal of Consulting and Clinical Psychology, 59*, 670–681.

MARKUS, H.R. & KITAYAMA, S. (1991). Culture and the self: Implications for cognition, emotion, and motivation. *Psychological Review, 98*, 224–253.

MEZZICH, J.E., KLEINMAN, A., FABREGA, H. & PARRON, D.L. (1996). *Culture and psychiatric diagnosis: A DSM-IV perspective*. Washington, DC: American Psychiatric Press.

NAGATA, D.K. (1997). The assessment and treatment of Japanese American children and adolescents. In J.T. Gibbs & L.N. Huang (Eds.), *Children of color: Psychological interventions with culturally diverse youth* (pp. 68–111). San Francisco: Jossey-Bass.

OKAZAKI, S. & SUE, S. (1995). Methodological issues in assessment research with ethnic minorities. *Psychological Assessment, 7*, 367–375.

OYSERMAN, D., COON, H.M. & KEMMELMEIER, M. (2002). Rethinking individualism and collectivism: Evaluation of theoretical assumptions and meta-analyses. *Psychological Bulletin, 128*, 3–72.

PHINNEY, J.S. (1992). The Multi-group Ethnic Identity Measure: A new scale for use with diverse groups. *Journal of Adolescent Research, 7*, 156–176.

PHINNEY, J. S. (1996). When we talk about American ethnic groups, what do we mean? *American Psychologist, 51*, 918–927.

ROWE, D.C., VAZSONYI, A.T. & FLANNERY, D.J. (1994). No more than skin deep: Ethnic and racial similarity in developmental process. *Psychological Review, 101*, 396–413.

SANDAY, P.R. (1997). The socio-cultural context of rape: A cross-cultural study. In L.L. O'Toole & J. R. Schiffman (Eds.), *Gender violence: Interdisciplinary perspectives* (pp. 52–66). New York: New York University Press.

STEPHENSON, M. (2000). Development and validation of the Stephenson Multigroup Acculturation Scale (SMAS). *Psychological Assessment, 12*, 77–88.

SUE, S. (1999). Science, ethnicity, and bias: Where have we gone wrong? *American Psychologist, 54*, 1070–1077.

WARD, T., HUDSON, S.M., JOHNSTON, L. & MARSHALL, W.L. (1997). Cognitive distoritons and sexual offending: An integrative review. *Clinical Psychology Review, 17*, 479–507.

YAMADA, A., MARSELLA, A.J. & YAMADA, S.Y. (1998). The development of the Ethnocultural Identity Behavioral Index: Psychometric properties and validation with Asian Americans and Pacific Islanders. *Asian American and Pacific Islander Journal of Health, 6*, 35–45.

ZANE, N. (1991, August*). An empirical examination of loss of face among Asian Americans*. Paper presented at the American Psychological Association Convention, San Francisco.

Etiology: Commentaries on the Session

[EDITORS' NOTE: Following are three commentaries, each of which, with editing to minimize overlap, pursues a distinct focus. In the first, discussant Marnie Rice, joined by colleague and conference participant Grant Harris, comments on a set of the papers presented in this first part of the symposium—the section exploring the causes of sexually coercive behavior. Rice and Harris point up the increase in attention to biological variables that has occurred since the first New York Academy of Science conference on sexual aggression was held some 16 years ago,[a] and they suggest that this broadening of variables considered in research will require a broadening of perspective as well among clinicians. In the second commentary, discussant Mary Koss, who at the conference voiced complete disagreement with Vernon Quinsey's presentation, provides a detailed critique of that paper. Hopefully, their respective articles in this volume will provide a foundation for a point–counterpoint interaction between these two scholars, who combine a vigorous advocacy for their positions with regard and respect for the other. In the final commentary, Jim Breiling, chair for the etiology session, presents several substantive comments that he made at the conference. He points out that research into etiology, with its focus on the cause(s) of onset, is the potential source for the scientific base for whatever may be possible in the way of research-based primary prevention of the first offense, and that the relationship of etiologic research to treatment to reduce the likelihood of re-offending is uncertain: The science base with a clear and direct link to treatment to prevent recidivism is research that identifies variables associated with a reduced likelihood of reoffending. He also suggests that available findings on the proximate initiation of serious violent offenses provide the basis for a primary prevention of sexual assault, especially date rape, that warrants evaluation.]

Overview of the session

MARNIE E. RICE AND GRANT T. HARRIS

Mental Health Centre, Penetanguishene, Ontario L9M 1G3, Canada

The papers in this session demonstrated the progress made since the previous New York Academy of Sciences conference on sexual aggression in 1986. At that time, social learning theory was a predominant viewpoint in psychology, and most of us would have said that the primary causes of aggression, including sexual aggression,

[a]See *Human Sexual Aggression: Current Perspectives*, Vol. 528 of the *Annals of the New York Academy of Sciences* (1988) edited by Robert A. Prentky and Vernon L. Quinsey.

Address for correspondence: Marnie Rice, Ph.D., Research Director Emerita, Research Department, Mental Health Center Penetanguishene, Penetanguishene, ON l9M 1G3, Canada. Voice: 705-549-3181 ext. 2614; fax: 705-549-3652.

riceme@mcmaster.ca

Ann. N.Y. Acad. Sci. 989: 144–153 (2003). © 2003 New York Academy of Sciences.

were interpersonal influences leading to antisocial predispositions and attitudes, and that deviant sexual interests were acquired through conditioning in which sexual arousal was repeatedly associated with deviant material and sexual fantasy. From the chapters in this section in the present volume, however, it is now clear that neurophysiological factors present at birth have a great deal to do with aggression and sexual deviance among adults.

Thus, Howard Barbaree suggested that sex offenders' recidivism rates vary with age, because bioavailable testosterone decreases with age. Of course, further longitudinal research is required before firm conclusions can be drawn. Sex offenders released at older ages are certainly different in many ways (in addition to age at release) from sex offenders released at young ages. For example, they are likely to have been older at the time they committed their offense. Thus, as Barbaree illustrated, age at release might add little to prediction after age at offense is taken into consideration. Nevertheless, the explanation offered for the age–recidivism relationship was physiological. Similarly, Martin Kafka discussed hypotheses for the pathophysiology of paraphilic disorders, suggesting that increased levels of monoamine neurotransmitters may be causally related to increased sexual aggression. Consistent with this hypothesis, Kafka related clinical experiences in which prescribing selective serotonin reuptake inhibitors seemed to reduce sexual aggression.

Vern Quinsey reviewed several lines of research suggesting that sexual preferences are laid down prenatally. Human males sometimes exhibit anomalous preferences, and pedophilia is one example of such an anomaly. The preferences are anomalous inasmuch as they could not have been reproductively viable in ancestral populations. Unlike child molesters, rapists target adult women, and, for the most part, women of reproductive ages. Thus, sexual coercion might be one component of a viable reproductive strategy among psychopaths in which the interests of partners/victims are simply ignored. On the other hand, rapists who *prefer* nonconsensual sex or prefer to see victims suffer probably also exhibit anomalous sexual interests because such preferences are unlikely to have been as reproductively viable as preferences for consenting sex. Quinsey suggested that anomalous sexual preferences are likely to be the result of disrupted neurodevelopment and constitute a paraphilia when they lead to criminal behavior.

Michael Seto described a valuable measure of deviant sexual preferences among adolescent child molesters. It is interesting to note that having male victims is more indicative of sexual deviance than is having female victims. These data are consistent with Quinsey's hypotheses that the neural organization of sexual preferences is modular, and that preference for male children indicates a malfunction in two modules (gender and age), and thus is more deviant than preferences for female children (where only the age "module" is malfunctioning).

Neil Malamuth described a two-path model to explain sexually coercive acts against adult women. Malamuth's model is silent on whether the paths are due to social learning or neurophysiological factors, but it has yielded strong empirical support. Ray Knight proposed a three-path model that is also silent on the role of social learning versus neurophysiological influences. Knight reported success in predicting sexually coercive behavior, but it is unclear whether the loss of parsimony in postulating a third path is justified by an improvement in variance accounted for. It will be interesting to see whether models that postulate causal paths that explicitly incorporate neurodevelopmental factors can improve on these models.

William Friedrich presented findings showing a correlation between childhood sexual victimization or witnessing sexual abuse, and becoming an adult perpetrator of sexual abuse. Such findings have traditionally been seen as support for social learning accounts of sexual aggression. Recent findings showing the heritability of antisociality admit of other possibilities, however. For example, antisocial fathers may be more likely than other fathers to abuse their children and spouses. Children of antisocial fathers might inherit antisocial tendencies in addition to suffering abuse at their fathers' hands. Longitudinal studies testing structural models of the development of sexual abuse hold promise for explicating etiology.

In conclusion, sex offender researchers, as they seek a comprehensive explanation, are paying more attention to genetic, prenatal, and biological factors. Within a neurodevelopmental model of sexual aggression, a main issue for future research will be the explanatory power of relatively general phenomena such as psychopathy (i.e., an extreme tendency to neglect, devalue, or ignore the interests of others under all circumstances), and such very specific phenomena as the failure of one or more sexual preference modules. In the case of pedophilia, Quinsey presents the provocative hypothesis that the latter phenomenon leads to a very specific sexual interest in prepubescent children. [See the subsequent critique of Quinsey's propositions in Mary Koss's commentary, ED.] In the case of sexual aggression toward women, however, psychopathy may be the more important phenomenon. Quinsey postulated that some rapists exhibit biastophilia—a sexual interest in the surprise/fear of a victim, and that this is probably the result of disruption to one sexual preference module pertaining to the carrying out of "courtship."

The emerging findings about the neuroanatomy and neurophysiology of sexual behavior, which represent an advance toward a more comprehensive account, have to be consistent with more established findings from the study of behavior and personality in general. Thus, social learning research, with its emphasize on the role of experience in the development and the remediation of antisocial behavior, continues as a more proximate factor. Genetics and very early biomedical events that lead to neurodevelopmental disruption may emerge as important distal factors. The inclusion of well-established genetic, biological, and psychiatric factors in the search for a comprehensive explanation of sexual aggression may well present challenges for clinicians to learn about and take these factors into account in their work as well as opportunities for new and better procedures.

Critique of Vernon Quinsey's paper

MARY KOSS

Mel and Enid Zuckerman Arizona College of Public Health, Tucson, Arizona 85719, USA

Vernon Quinsey's paper directed attention to biological/genetic/evolutionary influences that are not currently adequately represented in existing models. Later in this

Address for correspondence: Mary Koss, Ph.D., Professor, Public Health, Family and Community Medicine, Psychiatry and Psychology, Mel and Enid Zuckerman Arixona College of Public Health, University of Arizona, 1632 Lester Street, Tucson, AZ 85719. Voice: 520-626-9502; fax: 520-626-9511.
   mpk@u.arizona.edu

volume (Lalumière, Quinsey, Harris, Rice & Trautrimas), it is noted that male homosexuality is a sexual attraction that "is discovered," not developed, and has failed to yield to treatment, as has pedophilia. They reason that because empirical data suggest that male homosexuality is inherited, and homosexuality and pedophilia are both "anomalous sexual preferences," pedophilia may also prove to be heritable.

Quinsey's presentation, like the others, was constrained by a time limit. I appreciated how much material he covered even more after doing the background reading for this commentary. But it is probably not possible to convey a nuanced treatment of these complex issues within the proceeding's ground rules, neither in Quinsey's remarks, nor in my commentary. Nevertheless, I will try to identify certain issues including imprecision in terminology, uncritical presentation of existing literature, and insufficient discussion of how the concepts presented work within an interactionist perspective (Crowell & Burgess, 1996).

It might be helpful to clarify the term "homosexuality," which denotes sexual orientation, sexual identity, and sexual behavior. Sexual orientation refers to the pattern of sexual attraction, whether to women or to men (Bailey, 1995). The man who is attracted to men is homosexual and the man who is attracted to both men and women is bisexual, but these are psychological, not behavioral references. Many experts have noted the frequency of discordance of individuals' sexual orientation, sexual identity, and sexual behavior (Klein, 1990, cited in Bailey, 1995). It is far more likely that homosexual sexual attraction is related to biological causes than sexual identity or behaviors.

The use of the term "anomalous sexual preferences" to refer to homosexuality is problematic. According to the *Dictionary of Psychological and Psychoanalytic Terms*, the term *abnormal*, the root word of *anomalous*, must be reserved for "distorted if not morbid behavior" because its statistical meaning—any deviation from the norm—is not accepted in popular usage (English & English, 1958, p. 2). Homosexuality, although a departure from the norm, is not morbid or distorted as Quinsey clearly stated, whereas pedophilia is both a statistical departure and a mental disorder. Clustering both phenomena under the single heading, and the negative connotation of the particular term that is used, is not only incorrect, but also very likely to be misinterpreted by the public.

Quinsey relies on the standard set of biological studies to support his thesis. The neurohormonal approach views sexual orientation as dependent on early sexual differentiation of hypothalamic brain structures (for a review, see Harshbarger, 2001). In theory, gay men and heterosexual women have brain structures that are similar and different from heterosexual men and lesbians. Neurohomormally linked differences point to causal agents that are biological and innate, without necessarily being genetic. Most of the neuroendocrine studies involve rats and report that males exposed to low prenatal androgens demonstrate lordosis and infrequent mounting behavior. These studies fail to account for the fact that human male homosexuals do not display the copulatory pattern of the opposite sex and do not have a decreased level of mounting behavior (Bailey, 1995).

Evidence of hormonally linked neuroanatomical differences is also presented including: (1) the suprachiasmatic nucleus of the hypothalamus is larger in homosexual compared to heterosexual men; (2) the third interstitial nucleus of the anterior hypothalamus (INAH-3) is smaller in homosexual compared to heterosexual men; and (3) the anterior commissure of the corpus collosum is largest in homosexual men compared to both men and women (this brain structure is not recognized as contributing to sexual behavior, however). The central studies (Swaab & Hofman, 1990; LeVay, 1991; Allen & Gorski, 1992, cited in Bailey, 1995; Harshbarger, 2001) rest on small samples that were nonscientifically recruited and are unreplicated or in at least one case have failed to replicate.

Other neurohormonal work has focused on sexually dimorphic characteristics thought to be related to cerebral lateralization including spatial ability and handedness. Of 15 studies of hand dominance, eight found an excess of left-handedness among homosexual men and seven, including the largest study, found no differences (Zucker & Bradley, 1995, cited in Harshbarger, 2001). Bailey (1995) notes that it is counterintuitive for the field to associate male homosexuality with left-handedness and at the same time look for brain structures that have been feminized by low levels of testosterone. (*High* levels of fetal testosterone are thought to cause left-handedness). Other measures of cerebral asymmetry have shown more promise (reviewed in Hershberger, 2001).

Studies of cognitive abilities thought to be sexually dimorphic reveal that homosexual men significantly exceed heterosexual men on general intelligence, verbal intelligence, performance intelligence, vocabulary, logical reasoning, openness to experience, verbal fluency, and perceptual motor speed, and they are inferior in verbal memory, mental rotation, and psychomotor skill (Harshbarger & Pych, 1999, cited in Harshbarger, 2001). The validity of this entire line of inquiry rests on the existence of sexual dimorphism in cognitive abilities. The effect sizes for sex differences in math performance ($d = -0.05$) and verbal performance ($d = 0.11$) are below the .20 cutoff for a small effect and also cannot be measured free of gender socialization that affects men's and women's social cognitions about how well they should perform in these areas (see Hyde & Lynn, 1988 cited in Hyde & Oliver, 2001). That said, the studies of the results in homosexual men are sometimes consistent with known sex differences (mental rotation and spatial perception), while other results are inconsistent, including verbal memory, vocabulary, and logical reasoning (which are not usually sex-differentiated), and performance intelligence (which is modestly related to spatial ability and usually shows differences favoring men). Quinsey also presents sexual dimorphisms in reproductively relevant human characteristics omitting two large effects: frequency of masturbation and attitudes permissive of sex in casual relationships (see Hyde & Oliver, 2001).

From an evolutionary perspective, homosexuals have presumably been at a reproductive disadvantage, yet the rates of it exceed all estimates of mutation frequency. This pattern argues for low heritability, but the evidence from comparisons of MZ and DZ twins suggests moderate heritability. However, all the studies of this type could be biased if there is a tendency for gay twins with a gay co-twin to volunteer at a higher rate than those with a heterosexual co-twin. And the calculation of heritability depends on having an accurate estimate of population base rate. Due to government obstacles to collecting U.S. sexuality data, these studies rely on Kinsey's 1948 and 1953 data, despite their age, acknowledged severe sampling biases, and amenability to several different estimates for homosexuality. (HIV surveys are in process that will obtain new estimates.) The heritability calculation goes from trivial to fairly substantial, depending on whether a 10% or 4% estimate of homosexuality prevalence is used. Furthermore, none of the current biological theories predict the high discordance found in MZ co-twins (Bailey, 1995).

Two specific locations for genes for male homosexuality have been studied (Hu et al., 1993; 1995; Macke et al., 1993, reviewed in Harshbarger, 2001). One DNA sequence that controls the androgen receptor gene showed no difference between heterosexual and homosexual men. Working on the assumption that there is an excess of homosexuality among maternal relatives, the Xq28 region on the X chromosome was compared and showed differences between homosexual and heterosexual men, a finding that was replicated, but with a smaller effect size. Replication is crucial because of previous failures to reproduce initial findings in molecular genetic studies of depression, schizophrenia, and alcoholism.

Quinsey's evolutionary analysis of rape and pedophilia appeared to be drawn directly from Thornhill and Palmer (cited in Koss, 2003). The presentation does not reflect published critiques of that work (e.g., Figueredo, 1992 cited in Koss, 2003; Travis, 2003; or Ward & Siegert, 2002). There isn't space to repeat these criticisms, but the bottom line of evolutionary arguments is, "What do the genes do?" Two explanations for the persistence of putative gay genes have been proposed: (1) that they promote survival and reproductive success in nonaffected carriers, on the model of sickle-cell anemia; and (2) that homosexuals, although sacrificing their own reproductive success, promote the reproduction of their siblings, parents, nieces and nephews by investing time and resources. No empirical examination of these explanations has been attempted and the latter faces the problem of nondisclosure and familial rejection standing in the way of plausibility.

I conclude there is so much still to be learned about the biological factors that influence homosexuality that it is premature to use it as a strong case from which to base arguments about pedophilia's causes. Furthermore, when dealing with issues in which the general public has a great deal of interest, it is important to take care that one's remarks do not inadvertently support political agendas (see Veniegas & Conley, 2000). Finally, understanding of sexual coercion will be fostered to the extent that the field pursues the complementary influences that collectively and interactively determine behavior including genetic, all other biological, familial, social, psychological, and cultural factors (Patatucci, 1998).

Acknowledgments

I want to thank Professor Anthony R. D'Augelli of Pennsylvania State University for his guidance and editorial feedback; the responsibility for any errors is mine.

REFERENCES

BAILEY, J.M. (1995). Biological perspectives on sexual orientation. In A.R. D'Augelli & D.J. Patterson (Eds.), *Lesbian, gay, and bisexual identities in families: Psychological perspectives* (pp. 103–135). New York: Oxford University Press.

CROWELL, N.A.& BURGESS, A.W. (1996). *Understanding violence against women.* Washington, DC: National Academy Press

HARSHBARGER, S.L. (2001). Biological factors in the development of sexual orientation. In A.R. D'Augelli & D.J. Patterson (Eds.), *Lesbian, gay, and bisexual identities in families: Psychological perspectives* (pp. 27–51). New York: Oxford University Press.

HYDE, J.S., & OLIVER, M.B. (2000). Gender differences in sexuality: Results from meta-analysis. In C.B. Travis & J.W. White (Eds.), *Sexuality, society, and feminism.* Washington, DC: American Psychological Association.

Koss, M.P. (2003). Evolutionary models of why men rape: Acknowledging the complexities. In C. Travis (Ed.), *Evolution, gender and rape* (pp. 191–206). Boston, MA: MIT Press..

Pattatucci, M.L. (1998). Biopsychosocial interactions and the development of sexual orientation. In C.J. Patterson & A.R. D'Augelli (Eds.), *Lesbian, gay, and bisexual identities in families: Psychological perspectives* (pp. 19–39). New York: Oxford University Press.

Travis, C., Ed. (2003). *Evolution, gender, and rape.* Boston, MA: MIT Press.

Veniegas, R.C., & Conlney, T.D. (2000). Biological research on women's sexual orientations: evaluating the scientific evidence. *Journal of Social Issues, 56,* 267–282.

Ward, T. & Siegert, R. (2002) Rape and evolutionary psychology: A critique of Thornhill and Palmer's theory. *Aggression and Violent Behavior, 7,*145–168.

Etiology research as the route to science-based prevention

JIM BREILING

National Institute of Mental Health, NIH, Bethesda, Maryland 20892, USA

This commentary reflects the most important of the substantive comments that I made introducing the etiology session and during the ensuing discussion.

The etiology session represented remarkable progress for the comprehensive understanding of the young science of sexual aggression, both with respect to the factors related to the onset of sexual aggression and for providing support and guidance for science-based programs to prevent the initiation or first occurrence of sexual aggression. (Etiology, with its focus on the causes of onset, is of uncertain relevance for providing a scientific basis for treatment; for treatment, putative variables need to be identified for reducing reoccurrence.)

Sexual aggression is a young, sensitive, and controversial area of science, and has yet to receive attention from the research community commensurate with its prevalence and public health significance. Sexual aggression has only become an area of research sufficient for periodic volumes such as this one during the past several decades. While sex is a focus of explicit depiction in several media, it is still at best a sensitive topic for general discussion, even in the scientific community. Sex research is often controversial for addressing a private, emotionally and ideologically charged area. So, there are few investigators in academic and other settings who are situated so that they can develop and pursue viable research grant applications. As a result, grant support for this area of study has been modest. Yet, as the papers for the etiology session demonstrate, researchers in this area have done stupendous work with a modicum of support: they have generated a remarkable breadth of research, ranging from possible genetic effects to developmental research that reaches from childhood and adolescence to the decades of adulthood, considers the relation of psychiatric disorders to occurrence, encompasses attitudes, behaviors and disorders in models of development of various forms of sexual aggression, and addresses the possible ef-

Address for correspondence: Jim Breiling, National Institute of Mental Health, 6101 Executive Boulevard, Room 6-179, Bethesda, MD 20892-9651. Voice: 301-443-3527; fax: 301-443-4611. jbreilin@mail.nih.gov

fects of cultural and ethnic variation and the critical matter of adequate measurement of sexual interests. And if other etiology research, whose representation was sought for this session (and which I will briefly touch on in the latter part of these comments) is considered, the etiology research concerning sexual aggression has, at least for sexual assault, arguably provided scientific illumination and strength sufficient to justify launching primary prevention interventions. This represents astounding progress and achievement (consider for a moment how elusive the science base is for primary prevention of serious mental disorders).

The progress in this field of study reflects in part the extent to which the research on sexual aggression has been able to draw upon progress in the methods and findings in other relevant areas of study such as delinquency and criminology, psychiatry, and behavioral genetics. It also reflects in part the important contributions made by researchers of sexual aggression in other countries. For practical financial reasons, the substantial international contribution at this session is limited to Canada. which is explicitly represented by three of the eight presenters (Barbaree, Quinsey, and Seto) and by a fourth Canadian by birth and whose important research on sexually aggression developed significantly while he had an appointment in Canada (Malamuth). And it also reflects in part the notable abilities of the investigators in this area of study, irrespective of their nationality, their devotion to this important but so sensitive and controversial work, and their ability for accomplishing an incredible amount with minute resources. From this inspirational cadre of researchers has come a broad outline of a base and in some cases substantial structures for needed research through which the new researchers of tomorrow can make important contributions.

Unfortunately, the seeming rarity of bright new investigators (like Michael Seto) who are undertaking research in this area puts at risk the potential progress of tomorrow. Recruiting and nourishing the next generation of researchers might well be the most important immediate priority for the pioneers of research in this area, and who are now on the cusp of retirement age.

The proceedings of every conference are inherently limited to those whose participation can be obtained. As a result, the research findings concerning sexual assault from Del Elliott's National Youth Survey are not represented in the presentations. Because of their importance for etiology research and for science-based prevention, I will present the most salient of these and related findings, albeit in very abbreviated form because of space limitations.

Del Elliott's National Youth Survey is a prospective longitudinal study of the antisocial behaviors (delinquency, criminality, sexual assault, spousal assault) and of possible explanatory factors for such behavior with a national representative sample of American males and females from age 11 to, at present, adults in their late 30s and 40s Its prospective design allowed for temporal ordering that findings of putative causes require. With supplemental funding from NIMH's (long deceased) Center for the Study and Prevention of Rape, Elliott added sexual assault to the antisocial behaviors about which confidential self-reports and official records were sought. Three findings of special note for our purposes here are (1) that sexual assault was almost always preceded by instances of robbery and/or aggravated assault, and that in turn these serious violent offenses were preceded by a history of conduct problems (Elliott, 1994); (2) that associating with delinquent peers was a substantial risk factor for sexual assault, as it was for progressing to other, preceding serious violent offenses (Ageton, 1983; Elliott, 1993), and (3) that official records reflect only a minute portion of the actual acts of antisocial behavior, and indeed, that official records could entirely miss, or reflect only one or a few instances of minor offending from long careers of high rate and serious antisocial offending (Elliott et al., 1987).

The first two major findings support including sexual assault in primary prevention for serious violent offenses generally, and for a focus on minimizing associations with deviant peers as the lead engine in a primary prevention program model. The third finding points up the limitations of using official records to identify those youths who are at high risk for progressing to serious violent offenses, including sexual assault, and to whom, for reasons of cost-efficiency, the primary intervention should be targeted. Thus, the voluntary cooperation of the youths and a parent (or parents) in the screening will be necessary. I view this positively as engaging the youths in the program from the beginning, which should contribute to a successful intervention. The third finding also points to the importance for models of etiology including adequate measures of the perpetration of antisocial behaviors if these models are to adequately represent reality.

Since the engine of prevention for the program based on Elliott's findings would be minimizing associations with deviant peers, an affirmative answer to the question as to whether deviant associations can be prevented or, if they exist, can be substantially minimized, is a key to success. Changing policies that bring deviant youth together, e.g., in tracked and special school classes, undoubtedly presents a formidable challenge. However, in the community there are two intervention models—Scott Henggeler's Multisystemtic Therapy and Patti Chamberlain's Multidimensional Treatment Foster Care—whose focus on and success in minimizing associations with deviant peers have been key to their demonstrating significant reductions in recidivism with serious offending delinquents in rigorous evaluations. As a result, these two program models have been recognized as effective models by Del Elliott's Blueprint programs based on the assessment of their evaluation data by a panel of researchers. These two models also obtain significant benefit-to-cost results when only reductions in antisocial behavior are considered as benefits; other benefits, such as reduced teen parenting, greater progress in school, better employment outcomes, and reduced health care costs, would almost certainly more than double the already substantial short-term financial benefits. (For descriptions of these programs and their outcomes, see The Blueprint Programs of the Center for the Study and Prevention of Violence at http://www.colorado.edu/cspv/blueprints.)

So, a scientific foundation for primary prevention of the initiation of sexual assault and the basis for believing that a substantial impact can be obtained on a major risk factor for such violent offending clearly exist. What should occur now is the mounting of a primary prevention trial for serious violent offending, including sexual assault, that utilizes these scientific findings. If the intervention is well-implemented (targeted to high-risk youth and obtains significant impact on associations of deviant peers), strong positive effects can be expected. This would constitute a giant step down the research road to enabling a safer and more humane society that better protects and develops the human potential of its youth and its future. For this important step, we very probably need a bright, energetic investigator (or a team of investigators) from the ranks of the young scientists whose involvement is critical to the future of sexual aggression research and to progress toward a safer society.

REFERENCES

AGETON, S.S. (1983) *Sexual assault among adolescents.* Lanham, MA: Lexington Books.

ELLIOTT, D.S. (1994) Serious violent offenders: Onset, developmental course and termination. *Criminology, 32,* 1–22.

ELLIOTT, D.S. (1993) *Longitudinal research in criminology: Promise and practice,* pp. 189–202 in E. Weitenkamp & H. Kerner (eds.) *Cross-national longitudinal research on human development and criminal behavior.* Dordrecht: Kluwer.

ELLIOTT, D.S., B. MORSE & D. HUIZINGA (1993) Self-reported violent offending, pp. 119–145 in S. G. Millstein, A.C. Petersen and E.O. Nightengale (eds), *Promoting the health of adolescents.* New York: Oxford University Press.

Sexual Offender Recidivism Risk

What We Know and What We Need to Know

R. KARL HANSON, KELLY E. MORTON, AND ANDREW J. R. HARRIS

*Corrections Research, Department of the Solicitor General of Canada,
Ottawa, Ontario K1A 0P8, Canada*

ABSTRACT: If all sexual offenders are dangerous, why bother assessing their risk
to reoffend? Follow-up studies, however, typically find sexual recidivism rates
of 10%–15% after five years, 20% after 10 years, and 30%–40% after 20 years.
The observed rates underestimate the actual rates because not all offences are
detected; however, the available research does not support the popular notion
that sexual offenders inevitably reoffend. Some sexual offenders are more dangerous than others. Much is known about the static, historical factors associated with increased recidivism risk (e.g., prior offences, age, and relationship to
victims). Less is known about the offender characteristics that need to change
in order to reduce that risk. There has been considerable research in recent
years demonstrating that structured risk assessments are more accurate than
unstructured clinical assessments. Nevertheless, the limitations of actuarial
risk assessments are sufficient that experts have yet to reach consensus on the
best methods for combining risk factors into an overall evaluation.

KEYWORDS: sexual offender recidivism; risk assessment; actuarial; prediction

Sexual offenders are among those that invoke the most fear and concern: Children
are warned to avoid strangers; women are afraid to go out at night. The outcry over
well-publicized cases of horrific sexual crimes has led to special policies for sexual
offenders, such as registries, community notification, and post-sentence detention.
To the naïve public, all sexual offenders are equally dangerous. Those involved in
managing sexual offenders, however, recognize considerable variability. The drunk
college student who exposes himself at a party is quite different from the priest who
leaves a trail of child victims as he is shuffled across parishes or the serial rapist who
abducts women from the streets.

RECIDIVISM BASE RATES

The starting point for any risk assessment is the recidivism base rate. The recidivism base rate is the proportion of a group of sexual offenders who will reoffend af-

Address for correspondence: R. Karl Hanson, Corrections Research, Department of the Solicitor General of Canada, 10th Floor, 340 Laurier Avenue, West, Ottawa, Ontario K1A 0P8, Canada. Voice: 613-991-2840; fax: 613 990 8295.
hansonk@sgc.gc.ca

Ann. N.Y. Acad. Sci. 989: 154–166 (2003). © 2003 New York Academy of Sciences.

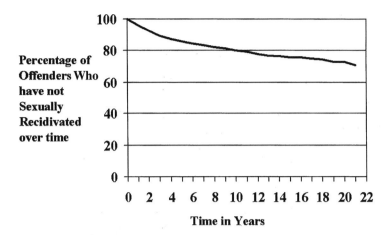

FIGURE 1. Sexual recidivism in a sample of 4724 sexual offenders over a twenty-year period.

ter a period of time (i.e., the follow-up period). If, for example, 20 out of 100 sexual offenders were reconvicted for a new sexual offence, the recidivism base rate would be 20%. This rate can be used to predict how many offenders will reoffend (e.g., 20 out of 100) as well as to estimate the probability that an individual offender will reoffend (i.e., the "typical" sexual offender has a 20% chance of reoffending).

FIGURE 1 summarizes the sexual recidivism rate in a mixed group of sexual offenders. This data set comprises 10 individual samples; the aggregated sample (n = 4724) is the largest presently available (Harris & Hanson, 2002). These samples range in size from 191 to 1138 offenders and were drawn from the following jurisdictions: California, Washington, Québec, Ontario, Manitoba, Alberta, Her Majesty's Prison Service (England & Wales), and the Correctional Service of Canada (3 distinct samples). Sexual recidivism was defined by a new charge in five samples and by a new conviction in the remaining five samples. The average follow-up period was seven years, with approximately 16% of the sample being followed for more than 15 years. FIGURE 1 expresses sexual recidivism as a "survival curve" (Greenhouse, Stangl & Bromberg, 1989).

As can be seen in FIGURE 1, the five-year recidivism rate was 14% (95% confidence interval of 13–15%), the 10-year recidivism rate was 20% (95% confidence interval of 19–21%), the 15-year rate was 24% (95% confidence interval of 22–26%) and the 20-year rate was 27% (95% confidence interval of 24–30%). Although the cumulative recidivism rates increase with time, the chances that an offender will eventually "recidivate" decreases the longer he remains offense-free in the community. The proportion of new recidivists was 14% in the first five years at liberty compared to only 3% during years 15 to 20.

The sexual recidivism rates for rapists (those who have offended against an adult victim) and child molesters are very similar (FIG. 2). Rapists, however, are much more likely than child molesters to recidivate with a nonsexual violent offence (Hanson & Bussière, 1998). Among child molesters, those most likely to sexually recid-

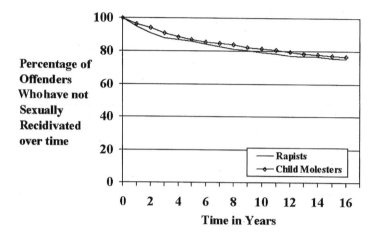

FIGURE 2. Sexual recidivism of rapists ($n = 1038$) and child molesters ($n = 2798$) over a fifteen-year period

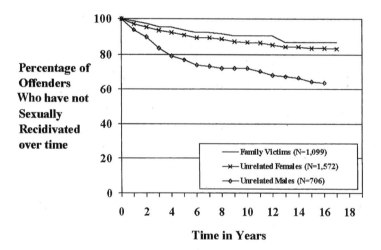

FIGURE 3. Sexual recidivism in a sample of child molesters.

ivate are those who offended against unrelated boy victims, followed by those who offended against unrelated girl victims and, finally, incest offenders (FIG. 3). Incest offenders were defined as those with victims within their own family, such as children, step-children, and nieces.

The available data suggest that most sexual offenders do not recidivate. It is important to remember, however, that many sexual offenses are never reported to police. The extent to which the undetected offenses should influence the observed recidivism rates is a matter of debate. If the typical sexual offender commits many offenses, then the observed rates should be close to the actual rates. High-frequency

TABLE 1. Predictors of sexual offence recidivism

Risk Factor	r	n (k)
Sexual deviance		
PPG sexual interest in children	.32	4853 (7)
Any deviant sexual preference	.22	570 (5)
Prior sexual offenses	.19	11,294 (29)
Any stranger victims	.15	465 (4)
Early onset	.12	919 (4)
Any related victims	.11	6889 (21)
Any boy victims	.11	10,294 (19)
Diverse sexual crimes	.10	6011 (5)
Criminal history/lifestyle		
Antisocial personality	.14	811 (6)
Any prior offenses	.13	8683 (20)
Demographic factors		
Age (young)	.13	6969 (21)
Single (never married)	.11	2850 (8)
Treatment history		
Treatment dropout	.17	806 (6)

NOTE: r is the average correlation coefficient from Hanson and Bussière (1998). k is the number of studies, and n is the total sample size.

offenders are likely to get caught, even if the probability of detection for any one offense is small. On the other hand, if the typical sexual offender commits only a few offences (e.g., 5 or less), then the observed recidivism rates would be expected to seriously underestimate the actual rates. All experts agree that the observed rates are minimal estimates, but specifying the amount of underestimation is difficult given that the phenomenon of interest is, by definition, unobservable. Nevertheless, a reasonable estimate would be that the actual recidivism rates are at least 10% to 15% higher than the observed rates (based on the assumptions that 60% (or less) of recidivists commit 5 (or fewer) new offenses over a 20-year period and that the probability of detection is 15% per offense). For example, given that the observed 20-year recidivism rate ranges from 25% to 40%, it is quite likely that the actual recidivism rates are in the range of 35% to 55%.

RISK FACTORS FOR SEXUAL RECIDIVISM

Not all sexual offenders are equally likely to reoffend. Considerable research has been conducted identifying those factors that are, and are not, predictive of sexual recidivism. Most of these studies were summarized in Hanson and Bussière's (1998) meta-analysis. This review examined 61 unique samples (making up a total of 28,972 sexual offenders), the main results of which are reported in TABLE 1. To be included in the table, each risk factor must have been examined in at least four stud-

TABLE 2. Factors unrelated to sexual offence recidivism

Risk Factor	r	n (k)
Victim empathy	.03	4670 (3)
Denial of sex offence	.02	762 (6)
Unmotivated for treatment	.01	435 (3)
General psychological problems	.01	655 (6)
Sexually abused as a child	−.01	5051 (6)
Degree of sexual contact	−.03	828 (6)

NOTE: r is the average correlation coefficient from Hanson and Bussière (1998). k is the number of studies, and n is the total sample size.

ies and have an average correlation with sexual recidivism of at least $r = .10$ (10% difference in recidivism rates for those with or without the characteristic).

The strongest predictors of sexual recidivism are factors related to sexual deviance and general criminality. Hanson and Bussière (1998) found the single biggest predictor of sexual offense recidivism was sexual interest in children as measured by phallometric assessment (penile plethysmograph or PPG). Phallometric assessment involves the direct monitoring of sexual response when viewing or listening to sexual stimuli (Launay, 1994). Other important predictors included clinical assessments of deviant sexual preferences, prior sexual offenses, and a history of selecting unrelated victims or male victims. General criminality, as measured by the total number of prior offenses and antisocial personality, is also an important risk factor. It is also worth noting that the sexual recidivists tend to be single and young (Hanson, 2001).

Hanson and Bussière (1998) also identified some characteristics not associated with sexual recidivism. Some of the findings in TABLE 2 were surprising. Clinical interviews are routinely used in risk assessment, but much of the information commonly assessed in these interviews, such as low victim empathy, denial, and lack of motivation for treatment, were unrelated to sexual offense recidivism. It may be difficult to assess sincere remorse given the obvious social pressures of the forensic setting.

COMBINING RISK FACTORS INTO AN OVERALL EVALUATION

No single risk factor is sufficient to predict whether a particular offender will reoffend or not. Consequently, all competent evaluations consider a range of factors, each of which could potentially increase or decrease the offender's recidivism potential. Offenders with all the risk factors are obviously high-risk, and those with no risk factors are low-risk, but what about the typical offender who has some risk factors?

There are several ways that individual factors can be organized into an overall evaluation. Evaluators using the *unstructured clinical* approach integrate diverse material based on theory and their experience with similar cases. In such evaluations, neither the risk factors considered nor the method of combining the risk factors are fixed, and are allowed to change from case to case. In *structured clinical* assessments, the evaluator specifies in advance the risk factors considered in the evalua-

TABLE 3. Average predictive accuracy of actuarial, empirically guided, and unstructured clinical assessments

	Average *d*	95% Confidence Interval	Q	Number of Findings	Total Sample Size
Actuarial	0.68	0.62–0.73	113.68***	50	7145
Empirically guided clinical	0.52	0.33–0.71	12.16*	6	703
Outlier removed	0.42	0.22–0.62	4.04	5	632
Unstructured clinical	0.28	0.14–0.42	20.93*	12	1851

*$P < .05$; ***$P < .001$.

tion. *Empirically guided clinical* assessments resemble structured clinical assessments in that both types of evaluation begin with an examination of an explicit list of risk factors. The distinct feature of the empirically guided clinical approach is that the risk factors considered are primarily restricted to those with empirical evidence supporting their relationship with sexual recidivism (e.g., Sexual Violence Risk–20; Boer, Wilson, Gauthier & Hart, 1997). In the empirically guided approach, the final evaluation of risk is left to the judgement of the clinician. In contrast, the *actuarial* approach not only specifies the risk factors to be considered, but also specifies the method of combining the factors into an overall evaluation (e.g., Static-99; Hanson & Thornton, 2000). The final method of evaluation, the *adjusted actuarial* approach, begins with an actuarial measure and then adjusts the estimated recidivism risk based on factors external to the actuarial scheme (e.g., Violence Prediction Scheme; Webster, Harris, Rice, Cormier & Quinsey, 1994) (TABLE 3).

Although actuarial scales have been used with general criminal populations for many years (e.g., Hoffman, 1994), actuarial scales specifically designed for sexual offenders have only recently become available (Epperson, Kaul & Huot, 1995; Hanson, 1997; Rice & Harris, 1997). Consequently, most of the early research examined clinical assessments that were either unstructured (e.g., Dix, 1976; Hall, 1988; Ryan & Miyoshi, 1990), structured (Smith & Monastersky, 1986), or empirically guided (Epperson et al., 1995). Hanson and Bussière's (1998) review of studies prior to 1996 identified only one study of an actuarial risk scale specifically designed for sexual offenders (Epperson et al., 1995). Since 1996, the research on actuarial risk scales has increased dramatically such that we are now able to identify at least 50 replication findings of sexual offender risk scales.

FIGURE 4 presents the predictive accuracy of various approaches to evaluating sexual offender recidivism risk. These studies examined sexual recidivism as the outcome criterion, typically defined as rearrest or reconviction. The results are reported in terms of Cohen's *d*, or the standardized mean difference (Hasselblad & Hedges, 1995). According to Cohen (1988, p. 40), *d* values of .80 are considered "large," *d* values of .50 are considered "medium," and *d* values of .20 are considered "small." In FIGURE 4, the *d* values are plotted against the inverse of their variances. The findings from studies with small samples, or few recidivists, would be expected to have more variability than the findings from large studies (i.e., a finding on the

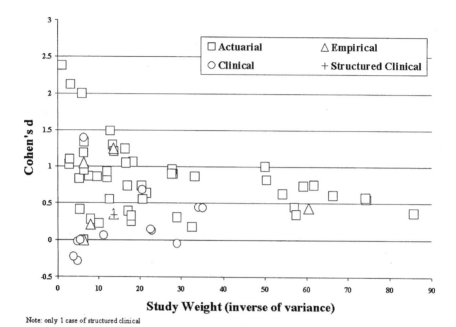

Note: only 1 case of structured clinical

FIGURE 4. Accuracy of different approaches to predicting sexual offense recidivism (k = 38, findings = 69, N = 8545).

right-hand side of the figure should be more reliable than those on the left-hand side).

Overall, actuarial risk assessments were significantly more accurate ($d = 0.68$, 95% confidence interval of 0.62 to 0.73) than unstructured clinical assessments ($d = 0.28$, 95% confidence interval of 0.14 to 0.42). The empirically guided clinical assessment had a level of predictive accuracy intermediate between the two other approaches ($d = 0.52$, 95% confidence interval of 0.33 to 0.71). There were relatively few tests of the empirically guided approach, however, and the findings were strongly influenced by the high level of predictive accuracy found in a single study by Dempster ($d = 1.25$; 1998). Removing this outlier resulted in an average predictive accuracy of $d = 0.42$ (95% confidence interval of 0.22 to 0.62), with a nonsignificant Q statistic indicating no more variability across studies than would be expected by chance. For comparison, a Cohen's d of 0.68 corresponds to a ROC area of 0.68 and a correlation coefficient of 0.26 (at a 20% base rate). A Cohen's d of 0.28 corresponds to a ROC area of 0.58 and a correlation coefficient of 0.11 (at a 20% base rate).

The scales with the most replication studies were the Rapid Risk Assessment for Sexual Offence Recidivism (RRASOR; Hanson, 1997), closely followed by Static-99 (Hanson & Thornton, 2000) then the Sex Offender Risk Appraisal Guide (SORAG) and the Violence Risk Appraisal Guide (VRAG; Quinsey, Harris, Rice & Cormier, 1998). We were able to locate only one or two replication studies for six other scales: Minnesota Sex Offender Screening Tool (MnSOST; Epperson et al.,

TABLE 4. Average accuracy of Static-99, RRASOR, VRAG, and SORAG for predicting sexual recidivism

	Average d	95% Confidence Interval	Q	Number of Findings	Total Sample Size
Static-99	0.76	.65 to .87	38.2***	15	4202
RRASOR	0.66	.58 to .75	41.2***	17	5004
VRAG	0.64	.50 to .79	7.65	5	1000
SORAG	0.68	.51 to .86	9.38	5	1104
Outlier removed	0.60	.42 to .78	0.39	4	1033

***$P < .001$.

1995); Minnesota Sex Offender Screening Tool–Revised (MnSOST-R; Epperson, Kaul & Hesselton, 1998); Vermont Assessment of Sex-Offender Risk (VASOR; McGrath & Hoke, 1994); Juvenile Sex Offender Assessment Protocol (J-SOAP; Prentky, Harris, Frizzell & Righthand, 2000); Violence Risk Scale: Sex Offender (VRS:SO; Wong, Olver, Wilde, Nicholaichuk & Gordon, 2000); and the Manitoba Secondary Risk Assessment (Hanson, 2002).

For the prediction of sexual recidivism, Static-99 appeared to have the greatest overall accuracy, followed closely by the SORAG, RRASOR, and VRAG (TABLE 4). The relative predictive accuracies should be interpreted cautiously, however, because the confidence intervals overlap and direct comparisons between Static-99 and SORAG have not typically found significant differences between the two measures (Barbaree, Seto, Langton & Peacock, 2001; Hanson & Thornton, 2000; Harris et al., in press; Nunes, Firestone, Bradford, Greenberg & Broom, 2002).

STATIC, STABLE, AND ACUTE RISK FACTORS

Most of the established risk factors for sexual recidivism are static, historical factors that are not amenable to deliberate intervention (e.g., prior offences, age). Such factors can be useful for evaluating long-term recidivism potential, but they provide no direction as to how to reduce that risk. Changing risk levels requires the consideration of dynamic (changeable) risk factors. Dynamic risk factors can be divided into stable and acute factors (Hanson & Harris, 2000). Stable factors tend to change slowly, over periods of months or years, or perhaps not at all. In contrast, acute factors can change rapidly, over a period of weeks, days, or even minutes. In order to understand the distinction between stable and acute risk factors, consider the differences between alcoholism (i.e., the chronic propensity to problem drinking) and intoxication. It is worth noting that certain factors can be acute risk factors, but not stable risk factors. For example, offenders with chronically negative mood are at no higher risk for recidivism than happy offenders, but both groups are at increased risk to reoffend when their mood declines (Hanson & Harris, 2000).

Interventions with sexual offenders require identifying and changing stable, dynamic risk factors. Consequently, stable dynamic risk factors are also called criminogenic needs—those problematic characteristics that need to change in order to prevent reoffending. Acute risk factors are most important for community supervision—being able to anticipate an imminent offense and intervene appropriately.

Although less is known about dynamic risk factors than static risk factors, recent research suggests that certain potentially changeable factors, such as intimacy deficits and attitudes tolerant of sexual assault, provide information that is not fully captured in the existing actuarial risk scales. Hanson and Harris (2001) found that the Sex Offender Need Assessment Rating (SONAR, now revised as two scales, the Stable–2000 and Acute–2000) significantly differentiated recidivists from nonrecidivists even after controlling for scores on the VRAG and Static-99. SONAR contains items related to negative social influences, intimacy deficits, sexual self-regulation, attitudes tolerant of sexual assault, and lack of cooperation with supervision. Among child molesters in community treatment, Beech, Friendship, Erikson, and Hanson (2002) found that a questionnaire measure of "deviance" significantly predicted sexual recidivism after controlling for Static–99 scores. Beech's deviance measure addressed attitudes tolerant of sexual assault and social-affective deficits (e.g., loneliness, emotional identification with children). Similarly, Thornton (2002) found that his "initial deviance" measure also significantly predicted sexual recidivism after controlling for Static–99 scores. Thornton's (2002) initial deviance assessment included three broad domains of distorted attitudes, socio-affective functioning, and low self-control.

EFFECTS OF TREATMENT

An important question is the extent to which treatment can influence recidivism rates of sexual offenders. There are few well-controlled studies of sexual offender treatment, and even fewer studies focussing on current forms of treatment. Despite more than 35 review papers since 1990, and a review of reviews (United States General Accounting Office, 1996), researchers and policymakers have yet to reach consensus on whether treatment effectively reduces sexual recidivism.

Furby, Weinrott, and Blackshaw's (1989) narrative review of the early (largely pre-1980) treatment outcome literature concluded that there was no evidence that treatment reduced recidivism for sexual offenders. Hall's (1995) meta-analysis of 12 treatment outcome studies, which appeared after Furby et al.'s (1989) review, found a small overall treatment effect ($r = .12$). Hall concluded that medical treatment and comprehensive cognitive-behavioral treatment were both effective and superior to purely behavioral treatments.

Hall's (1995) review, however, has been criticized for including studies that compared treatment completers to treatment dropouts. Such comparisons are difficult to interpret because those who drop out of treatment would be expected to have characteristics related to recidivism risk, such as youth, impulsivity, and antisocial personality (Wierzbicki & Pekarik, 1993). When the dropout studies were removed from Hall's (1995) meta-analysis, the treatment effect was no longer significant (Harris, Rice & Quinsey, 1998).

Gallagher et al.'s (1999) meta-analysis considered 25 studies examining psychological or hormonal treatments. Like Hall (1995), they concluded that there was a significant treatment effect for cognitive-behavioral treatments. Unlike Hall (1995), they found insufficient evidence to support medical/hormonal treatments. The apparent effectiveness of medical/hormonal treatments in Hall's (1995) review could be attributed to a single study of physical castration (Wille & Beier, 1989).

The most comprehensive review of psychological treatment for sexual offenders is that conducted by the Collaborative Outcome Data Project Committee (Hanson et al., 2002). This committee was formed in 1997 with the goals of organizing the existing outcome literature for sexual offenders and encouraging new evaluation projects to be conducted in a manner that contributes to cumulative knowledge. The first report of the Committee concluded that current psychological treatments are associated with reductions in both sexual and general recidivism. After an average 4–5 years of follow-up, 10% of the offenders in the treatment groups had sexually "recidivated" compared to 17% of the comparison groups ($n = 3,016$ from 15 studies). The reduction in general (any) recidivism was from 51% to 32%. The report also cautioned, however, that more and better research is required before firm conclusions can be reached (see Rice & Harris, this volume).

WHAT WE KNOW AND WHAT WE NEED TO KNOW

Considerable research has been conducted on the recidivism rates of sexual offenders. Overall, the observed rates are between 10% and 15% after 5 years and approximately 20% after 10 years. Given that these findings are from sufficiently large and diverse samples, new research studies are unlikely to change these estimates any time in the near future. How to interpret the observed rates, however, remains debatable given that most sexual offences never appear in official records.

Not all sexual offenders are equally likely to reoffend. Many characteristics have been reliably associated with increased recidivism risk, including prior sexual offences, deviant sexual preferences, unrelated victims, male victims, and general criminal history. As well, researchers have combined these risk factors into actuarial scales, which now have demonstrated validity for the prediction of sexual recidivism. Most of the established risk factors are static, historical characteristics. A promising development is that recent research has increasingly supported the relevance of potentially changeable characteristics, such as intimacy deficits and attitudes tolerant of sexual assault. Importantly, several studies have demonstrated that these dynamic factors provide information not captured by the existing actuarial scales.

Much, however, remains to be known. It is possible that many supposedly dynamic risk factors are actually proxies for enduring characteristics that are difficult, if not impossible, to change (e.g., intimacy deficits as a symptom of personality disorder). Further research is required that examines how changes in dynamic factors are associated with changes in recidivism risk. As it stands, evaluators have no empirically validated method for determining whether sexual offenders have benefited from treatment.

Perhaps the most contentious issue is how best to combine individual risk factors into an overall evaluation. Unguided clinical opinion is widely practiced and routinely accepted by the courts, but there is little justification for its continued use given the demonstrated superiority of structured, actuarial risk assessments. Empirically guided clinical assessments appear to have predictive accuracy intermediate between the unguided clinical and the actuarial approaches. The empirically guided approach, however, may be the best available option for many assessment questions (such as identifying treatment targets) because the available actuarial measures do not consider enough dynamic (changeable) risk factors

Quinsey et al. (1998) argue that evaluators should use actuarial measures and only actuarial measures: any attempt to consider other information would simply dilute a valid assessment. A contrasting position (and Quinsey's previous opinion) is that evaluators should base their evaluations on actuarial measures, but be willing to adjust their assessment on the basis of risk factors external to the actuarial scheme (Webster et al., 1994). Both approaches are plausible. Evaluators using a pure actuarial approach must deliberately ignore risk factors known to be associated with the risk of recidivism. Evaluators adjusting an actuarial prediction do so without empirical justification.

For the prediction of sexual recidivism, we were unable to locate any studies that compared unadjusted versus adjusted actuarial prediction. It is interesting to note, however, that this controversy has been examined and resolved in weather forecasting: the most accurate weather forecasters are those that adjust the actuarial predictions (Swets, Dawes & Monahan, 2000). Weather forecasting is an excellent domain in which to test prediction methods because the feedback is rapid, frequent, and obvious. As well, the prediction does not influence the outcome. It is difficult to conduct research that fairly tests the contribution of professional judgement in empirically informed risk assessments (Litwak, 2001). We believe, however, that it remains a worthy challenge for researchers hoping to improve the assessment and management of sexual offenders.

REFERENCES

BARBAREE, H.E., SETO, M.C., LANGTON, C.M. & PEACOCK, E.J. (2001). Evaluating the predictive accuracy of six risk assessment instruments for adult sex offenders. *Criminal Justice and Behavior, 28,* 490–521.

BEECH, A., FRIENDSHIP, C., ERIKSON, M. & HANSON, R. K. (2002). The relationship between static and dynamic risk factors and reconviction in a sample of U.K. child abusers. *Sexual Abuse: A Journal of Research and Treatment, 14,* 155–167.

BOER, D.P., WILSON, R.J., GAUTHIER, C.M. & HART, S.D. (1997). Assessing risk for sexual violence: Guidelines for clinical practice. In C.D. Webster & M.A. Jackson, (Eds.). *Impulsivity: Theory, assessment and treatment* (pp. 326–342). New York: Guilford.

COHEN, J. (1988). *Statistical power analysis for the behavioral sciences.* (1988). Hillsdale, NJ: Erlbaum.

DEMPSTER, R.J. (1998). *Prediction of sexually violent recidivism: A comparison of risk assessment instruments.* Unpublished masters thesis, Simon Fraser University, British Columbia.

DIX, G.E. (1976). Differential processing of abnormal sex offenders: Utilization of California's Mentally Disordered Sex Offender Program. *Journal of Criminal Law, Criminology, & Police Science, 67,* 233–243.

EPPERSON, D.L., KAUL, J.D. & HESSELTON, D. (1998, October). *Final report of the development of the Minnesota Sex Offender Screening Tool – Revised (MnSOST-R).* Presentation at the 17th Annual Research and Treatment Conference of the Association for the Treatment of Sexual Abusers, Vancouver, B.C., Canada.

EPPERSON, D.L., KAUL, J.D. & HUOT, S.J. (1995, October). *Predicting risk of recidivism for incarcerated sex offenders: Updated development on the Sex Offender Screening Tool (SOST).* Paper presented at the 14th Annual Research and Treatment Conference of the Association for the Treatment of Sexual Abusers, New Orleans, Louisiana.

FURBY, L., WEINROTT, M.R. & BLACKSHAW, L. (1989). Sex offender recidivism: A review. *Psychological Bulletin, 105,* 3–30.

GALLAGHER, C.A., WILSON, D.B., HIRSCHFIELD, P., COGGESHALL, M.B. & MACKENZIE, D.L. (1999). A quantitative review of the effects of sex offender treatment on sexual reoffending. *Corrections Management Quarterly, 3,* 19–29.

GREENHOUSE, J.B., STANGL, D. & BROMBERG, J. (1989). An introduction to survival analysis: Statistical methods for the analysis of clinical trial data. *Journal of Consulting and Clinical Psychology, 57,* 536–544.

HALL, G.C.N. (1988). Criminal behavior as a function of clinical and actuarial variables in a sexual offender population. *Journal of Consulting and Clinical Psychology, 56,* 773–775.

HALL, G.C.N. (1995). Sexual offender recidivism revisited: A meta-analysis of recent treatment studies. *Journal of Consulting and Clinical Psychology, 63,* 802–809.

HANSON, R.K. (2001). *Age and sexual recidivism: A comparison of rapists and child molesters.* (User Report 2001–01). Ottawa: Department of the Solicitor General of Canada.

HANSON, R.K. (1997). *The development of a brief actuarial risk scale for sexual offense recidivism.* (User Report 97–04). Ottawa: Department of the Solicitor General of Canada.

HANSON, R.K. (2002). *Evaluation of Manitoba's Secondary Risk Assessment.* Unpublished manuscript.

HANSON, R.K. & BUSSIÈRE, M.T. (1998). Predicting relapse: A meta-analysis of sexual offender recidivism studies. *Journal of Consulting and Clinical Psychology, 66 (2),* 348–362.

HANSON, R.K., GORDON, A., HARRIS, A.J.R., MARQUES, J.K., MURPHY, W., QUINSEY, V.L., et al. (2002). First report of the collaborative outcome data project on the effectiveness of psychological treatment for sex offenders. *Sexual Abuse: A Journal of Research and Treatment, 14,* 169–194.

HANSON, R.K. & HARRIS, A.J.R. (2000). Where should we intervene? Dynamic predictors of sex offense recidivism. *Criminal Justice and Behavior, 27,* 6–35.

HANSON, R.K. & THORNTON, D. (2000). Improving risk assessments for sex offenders: A comparison of three actuarial scales. *Law and Human Behavior, 24(1),* 119–136.

HARRIS, A.J.R. & HANSON, R.K. (2002). *Recidivism in sexual offenders.* Unpublished manuscript. Solicitor General Canada.

HARRIS, G.T., RICE, M.E. & QUINSEY, V.L. (1998). Appraisal and management of risk in sexual aggression: Implications for criminal justice policy. *Psychology, Public Policy, and Law, 4,* 73–115.

HARRIS, G.T., RICE, M.E., QUINSEY, V.L., LALUMIÈRE, M.L., BOER, D. & LANG, C. (in press). A multi-site comparison of actuarial risk instruments for sex offenders. *Psychological Assessment.*

HASSELBLAD, V. & HEDGES, L.V. (1995). Meta-analysis of screening and diagnostic tests. *Psychological Bulletin, 117(1),* 167–178.

HOFFMAN, P.B. (1994). Twenty years of operational use of a risk prediction instrument: The United States Parole Commission's Salient Factor Score. *Journal of Criminal Justice, 22,* 477–494.

LAUNAY, G. (1994). The phallometric assessment of sex offenders: Some professional and research issues. *Criminal Behaviour and Mental Health, 4,* 48–70.

LITWACK, T.R. (2001). Actuarial versus clinical assessments of dangerousness. *Psychology, Public Policy and Law, 7(2),* 409–443.

MCGRATH, R.J. & HOKE, S.E. (1994). *Vermont Assessment of Sex-Offender Risk.* Waterbury, VT: Author.

NUNES, K.L., FIRESTONE, P., BRADFORD, J.M., GREENBERG, D.M. & BROOM, I. (2002). A comparison of modified versions of the Static-99 and the Sex Offender Risk Appraisal Guide (SORAG). *Sexual Abuse: A Journal of Research and Treatment 14,* 253–269.

PRENTKY, R., HARRIS, B., FRIZZELL, K. & RIGHTHAND, S. (2000). An actuarial procedure for assessing risk with juvenile sex offenders. *Sexual Abuse: A Journal of Research and Treatment, 12,* 71–93.

QUINSEY, V.L., HARRIS, G.T., RICE, M.E. & CORMIER, C.A. (1998). *Violent offenders: Appraising and managing risk.* Washington, DC: American Psychological Association.

RICE, M.E. & HARRIS, G.T. (1997). Cross-validation and extension of the Violence Risk Appraisal Guide for child molesters and rapists. *Law and Human Behavior, 21*, 231–241.

RYAN, G. & MIYOSHI, T. (1990). Summary of a pilot follow-up study of adolescent sexual perpetrators after treatment. *Interchange, 1,* 6–8.

SMITH, W.R. & MONASTERSKY, C. (1986). Assessing juvenile sexual offenders' risk for reoffending. *Criminal Justice and Behavior, 13,* 115–140.

SWETS, J.A., DAWES, R.M. & MONAHAN, J. (2000). Psychological science can improve diagnostic decisions. *Psychological Science in the Public Interest, 1,* 1–26.

THORNTON, D. (2002). Constructing and testing a framework for dynamic risk assessment. *Sexual Abuse: A Journal of Research and Treatment, 14,* 139–153.

UNITED STATES GENERAL ACCOUNTING OFFICE. (1996). *Sex offender treatment: Research results inconclusive about what works to reduce recidivism.* Washington, DC: Author.

WEBSTER, C., HARRIS, G., RICE, M., CORMIER, C. & QUINSEY, V. (1994). *The Violence Prediction Scheme: Assessing dangerousness in high risk men.* Toronto: Centre of Criminology, University of Toronto.

WIERZBICKI, M. & PEKARIK, G. (1993). A meta-analysis of psychotherapy drop-out. *Professional Psychology: Research and Practice, 24,* 190–195.

WILLE, R. & BEIER, K.M. (1989). Castration in Germany. *Annals of Sex Research, 2,* 103–133.

WONG, S., OLVER, M., WILDE, S., NICHOLAICHUK, T.P. & GORDON, A. (2000, July). *Violence Risk Scale (VRS) & Violence Risk Scale-sex offender version (VRS-SO).* Presented at the 61st Annual Convention of the Canadian Psychological Association, Ottawa, Canada.

Principles of Forensic Mental Health Assessment

Implications for the Forensic Assessment of Sexual Offenders

KIRK HEILBRUN

Department of Psychology, Drexel University, and Villanova School of Law, Philadelphia, Pennsylvania 19102-1192, USA

ABSTRACT: Risk assessment with sexual offenders is generally performed for two purposes: to assist the court in deciding on a relevant legal question (in a legal context), or to plan treatment interventions (in a clinical context). Failure to make this distinction, and to accurately identify the context and purpose for which the assessment is being conducted, can result in significant problems. This chapter will begin by making this distinction. Then, focusing on evaluations done for legal decision making purposes, it will describe 29 recently derived broad principles of forensic mental health assessment and their application to evaluations done to assist legal decision making.

KEYWORDS: risk assessment; forensic mental health assessment; sexual offenders; legal decision making

INTRODUCTION

Our society has a particular concern with sexual offenders.[a] Even the tendency to describe a widely divergent range of behavior under a single rubric—sexual offender—provides evidence of this reality. To the extent that such concern makes us safer as a society, provides rehabilitation to offenders and lowers risk for reoffending, or enhances our understanding of sexual offending and thereby promotes better informed legislation and legal decision making, it is useful.

However, the tendency to set this cohort apart, with the implication that their needs for assessment and rehabilitation are different from those of nonsexual offenders, can also create significant problems. This chapter will address some of these problems. When sexual offenders are assessed in a forensic context—to assist

---

Address for correspondence: Kirk Heilbrun, Ph.D., Professor and Head, Department of Psychology, Drexel University, Philadelphia, PA 19102-1192. Voice: 215-762-3634; fax: 215-762-8625.

Kirk.Heilbrun@drexel.edu

[a]For the purposes of this chapter, "sexual offender" will refer to an individual who has been charged or convicted of an offense that has a sexual component. It will include both "hands off" offenses (e.g., peeping, possession of pornography) and "hands on" offenses (e.g., rape, child molestation).

Ann. N.Y. Acad. Sci. 989: 167–184 (2003). © 2003 New York Academy of Sciences.

TABLE 1. Differences between treatment and forensic roles for mental health professionals[a]

	Therapeutic	Forensic
Purpose	Diagnose and treat symptoms of illness	Assist decision maker or attorney
Examiner–examinee relationship	Helping role	Objective or quasi-objective stance
Notification of purpose	Implicit assumptions about purpose shared by doctor and patient	Assumptions about purpose not necessarily shared
	Formal, explicit notification typically not done	Formal and explicit notification
Who is being served	Individual patient	Variable; may be court, attorney, and client
Data sources	Self-report Psychological testing Behavioral assessment Medical procedures	Self-report Psychological testing Behavioral assessment Medical procedures Observations of others Relevant legal documents
Response style of examinee	Assumed to be reliable	Not assumed to be reliable
Clarification of reasoning and limits on knowledge	Optional	Very important
Written report	Brief, conclusory note	Lengthy and detailed Documents findings, reasoning, and conclusions
Court testimony	Not expected	Expected

[a]From Heilbrun, 2001; reproduced by permission from Kluwer/Academic Press.

the court in answering a legal question, or to provide evidence that an attorney might use in arguing a case on behalf of a client—then such evaluations are different (in some important respects) from diagnostic/therapeutic assessments performed with sexual offenders, and similar (in other important ways) to forensic evaluations performed with defendants charged with nonsexual offenses.

Several (Greenberg & Shuman, 1997; Heilbrun, 2001; Melton, Petrila, Poythress & Slobogin, 1997) have made the distinction between evaluations that are conducted for diagnostic or therapeutic purposes, and those performed in a forensic context. These differences may be seen in TABLE 1. In a total of nine areas, there are important and readily identifiable differences between these two kinds of evaluations. This suggests that some procedures that would be appropriate for one form of assessment would not be readily transferable to the other form (TABLE 1). We cannot assume, in other words, that expertise in treating sexual offenders, and conducting evaluations that help to plan such treatment, will necessarily yield expertise in performing forensic assessment with such offenders. Since forensic and therapeutic assessments are distinct activities, it is useful to consider principles and guidelines that might promote quality in forensic assessment. Further, it is helpful to consider how such principles and guidelines might apply to forensic assessment performed with sexual offenders. This chapter will describe how a set of recently derived principles of FMHA (forensic mental health assessment) applies to forensic assessment with this population. In this discussion, I will distinguish two categories of FMHA that might be performed with sexual offenders: (a) *sexual offender–specific*, which are only conducted with sexual offenders (e.g., sentencing enhancement upon classification as a Violent Sexual Predator, postsentence Hendricks commitment, and release from Hendricks commitment), and (b) *nonsexual offender–specific*, which are performed with defendants charged with all offenses and include questions described in the footnote below[b] among criminal evaluations. Finally, I will focus in this chapter on criminal evaluations, although additional discussion regarding civil and juvenile/family evaluations may also be noteworthy at another time.

PRINCIPLES OF FORENSIC MENTAL HEALTH ASSESSMENT AND APPLICATION TO SEX OFFENDERS

In recent years, several clinical-legal scholars have addressed the question of whether there are principles of forensic mental health assessment (FMHA) that are sufficiently broad to apply to a wide range of forensic evaluations, including those performed with sexual offenders. For example, Greenberg and Brodsky (in press) described various aspects of a model of civil forensic psychological evaluations, and Melton, Petrila, Poythress, and Slobogin (1997) offered a number of recommendations for conducting forensic assessments addressing a number of different legal questions. Heilbrun (2001) offered a detailed description of a set of 29 principles relevant to all types of FMHA. Following this, Heilbrun, Marczyk, and DeMatteo (2002) applied these principles to case reports on various forensic topics in criminal and civil law.

These 29 principles will serve as the basis for much of the discussion in this chapter. Applying these principles to forensic assessments of sexual offenders can serve a unifying purpose, emphasizing the ways in which such assessments are similar to other kinds of FMHA.

---

[b]There is a range of criminal and civil legal questions that might trigger a request for a forensic assessment by a mental health professional. Criminal questions include competencies to stand trial, plead guilty, waive right to counsel and confess, act as one's own attorney, refuse an insanity defense, testify, be sentenced, and be executed. They also include several aspects of mental state at the time of the offense (sanity, mens rea/diminished capacity, commitment following acquittal by reason of insanity, release from hospitalization after postinsanity commitment) and several aspects of sentencing (noncapital and capital) as well as parole eligibility. Civil questions include civil commitment, guardianship, competence to consent to treatment, competence to consent to research, testamentary capacity, Worker's Compensation or Americans with Disabilities Act eligibility, torts of emotional distress, malpractice, and Social Security disability eligibility. Juvenile and family questions include juvenile commitment, competence to stand trial, and waiver/reverse waiver, child custody, child abuse and neglect, and termination of parental rights. There are also some legal questions that apply only to sexual offenders: sentencing enhancement upon classification as a Violent Sexual Predator, postsentence Hendricks commitment, and release from Hendricks commitment.

These principles were derived and organized through a combination of reviewing the existing literature and considering the professional experience of those in the field. They are described sequentially, under four broad steps in the larger process of forensic assessment: (1) preparation, (2) data collection, (3) data interpretation, and (4) communication. Sources of support relevant to the fields of psychology and psychiatry (in law, ethics, science, and practice) were then applied to each principle, to determine its degree of applicability. These sources included psychology ethics (*The Ethical Principles of Psychologists and Code of Conduct*, American Psychological Association, 1992), forensic psychology ethics (*The Specialty Guidelines for Forensic Psychologists*, Committee on Ethical Guidelines for Forensic Psychologists, 1991), psychiatric ethics (*The Principles of Medical Ethics with Annotations Especially Applicable to Psychiatry*, American Psychiatric Association, 1998), and forensic psychiatric ethics (*The Ethical Guidelines for the Practice of Forensic Psychiatry*, American Academy of Psychiatry and the Law, 1995). The legal literature included federal statutes, federal administrative code, and federal case law (U.S. Supreme Court and federal appellate cases), as well as models such as the *Criminal Justice Mental Health Standards* (American Bar Association, 1989). Scientific support was drawn from the behavioral sciences and medicine. Standard of practice literature, addressing whether the principle was recognized and supported as desirable in FMHA (separate from the questions of ethics, law, and scientific support), was also applied to considering each principle.

Heilbrun (2001) then categorized each principle as either *established* (reasonably consistent support in research evidence, consistent with law and ethics, and accepted in practice) or *emerging* (support mixed or absent in some areas, and/or continuing significant disagreement among professionals regarding their application). I will now summarize each of these 29 FMHA principles and comment briefly on the application of each to forensic evaluations with sexual offenders (TABLE 2).

Identify relevant forensic issues. This principle addresses the focus of the evaluation: the capacities and behaviors that are of primary interest in FMHA. There is a distinction between the legal question, which defines the parameters of the evaluation under the law, and the included forensic issues, which are the capacities and abilities included within the legal question. The associated guideline for this principle involves citing the legal question and the included forensic issues in the first section of the report, which seems applicable to both criminal FMHA generally (middle column, TABLE 2) and nonspecific FMHA with sexual offenders (in which the sexual offending charge is not the specific reason for conducting the evaluation). For sex offender–specific FMHA, there is the additional caution about the importance of describing the status of current law under which the evaluation is being conducted; some laws have been subject to constitutional challenge when implemented at the state level, even when U.S. Supreme Court case law (e.g., *Kansas v. Hendricks*, 1997) is reasonably clear.

Accept referrals only within area of expertise. This principle describes forensic expertise as based in (1) training and experience with populations similar to that of the individual being evaluated, and (2) experience applying this expertise in conducting forensic assessment. The guideline for application involves describing the evaluator's expertise by citing relevant degrees, licensure, and board certification status, and providing even more detail on the CV (which should be available to attorneys upon request). When conducting FMHA with sexual offenders, there are

TABLE 2. Guidelines for applying principles to FMHA to nonsexual offenders, to sexual offenders nonspecifically, and to sexual offenders specifically

Principle	General Guideline for Administration in FMHA	Guideline for Administration in FMHA with Sexual Offenders
1. Identify relevant forensic issues	Cite legal question and included forensic issues in first section of report	*Nonspecific:* same as general guideline *Specific:* ensure that citation includes current status of the law, such as appeals or constitutional challenges, if they affect current FMHA procedures
2. Accept referrals only within area	Give degree and licensure, board certification status Provide CV and/or summary of qualifications if requested	*Nonspecific:* ensure that CV includes specific information about clinical and forensic experience with sexual offenders *Specific:* provide information describing basis for appointment in detail (e.g., member of panel appointed by governor to conduct such evaluations)
3. Decline the referral when evaluator impartiality is unlikely	Avoid involvement in cases in which there is substantial incentive for the forensic clinician (personal, professional, or monetary) to have case decided in a particular direction	*Nonspecific:* monitor own personal and professional reactions to punishment and treatment of sexual offenders *Specific:* monitor own personal and professional reactions to reoffense risk, treatment response, and change in sexual offenders
4. Clarify the evaluator's role with the attorney	Ensure that both the forensic clinician and the referral source are clear whether the clinician will serve as court-appointed evaluator, attorney-requested evaluator, or consultant	*Nonspecific:* same as general guideline *Specific:* same as general guideline
5. Clarify financial arrangements	Ensure that terms of payment for evaluation are understood by both the forensic clinician and the party responsible for payment	*Nonspecific:* same as general guideline *Specific:* same as general guideline
6. Obtain appropriate authorization	Cite basis for evaluation request (e.g., court-ordered, attorney-requested) Describe whether informed consent was obtained, if evaluation was not court-ordered	*Nonspecific:* Underscore the difference between the forensic evaluation and treatment, particularly if the offender has a history of specialized treatment *Specific:* same as above

TABLE 2. Guidelines for applying principles to FMHA to nonsexual offenders, to sexual offenders nonspecifically, and to sexual offenders specifically (*continued*)

Principle	General Guideline for Administration in FMHA	Guideline for Administration in FMHA with Sexual Offenders
7. Avoid playing the dual roles of therapist and forensic evaluator	Minimize the frequency of this combination. If such roles are combined, it should be with explicit justification, advance planning, and clear notification to the individual involved.	*Nonspecific:* same as general guideline *Specific:* be particularly cautious in specialized treatment programs that any combination of treatment and FMHA is planned and notification is clear to those involved
8. Determine the particular role to be played within forensic assessment if the referral is accepted	If report will be submitted into evidence, evaluator should be *impartial*—tone of report should reflect this	*Nonspecific:* same as general guideline *Specific:* remain within designated role and do not address treatment needs unless contained within forensic issues that constitute referral question(s)
9. Select the most appropriate model to guide data gathering, interpretation, and communication	Use the Morse model (mental disorder, functional abilities, and causal connection) or the Grisso model (functional, contextual, causal, interactive, judgmental, and dispositional characteristics)	*Nonspecific:* same as general guideline *Specific:* interpret "mental disorder" very broadly, to include components of personality and aspects of sexual functioning that act as risk factors and protective factors for sexual offending
10. Use multiple sources of information for each area being assessed	Obtain self-report, psychological testing data, third-party interviews, and collateral records data	*Nonspecific:* same as general guideline *Specific:* same as general guideline
11. Use relevance and reliability (validity) as guides for seeking information and selecting data sources	Use data sources with demonstrated reliability and validity (when this has been researched) and that will provide information relevant to the area being assessed	*Nonspecific:* same as general guideline *Specific:* same as general guideline
12. Obtain relevant historical information	In a separate section, document the individual's history and previous functioning in areas relevant to current clinical condition and functional legal capacities	*Nonspecific:* same as general guideline *Specific:* add historical information regarding both deviant and healthy sexual behavior

TABLE 2. Guidelines for applying principles to FMHA to nonsexual offenders, to sexual offenders nonspecifically, and to sexual offenders specifically (*continued*)

Principle	General Guideline for Administration in FMHA	Guideline for Administration in FMHA with Sexual Offenders
13. Assess clinical characteristics in relevant, reliable, and valid ways	Describe clinical characteristics using measures that are reliable, valid for the purpose used, and/or weighed against information from collateral sources	*Nonspecific:* same as general guideline *Specific:* define "clinical characteristics" broadly, to include components of personality and aspects of sexual functioning that act as risk factors and protective factors for sexual offending when risk assessment is part of FMHA
14. Assess legally relevant behavior	Document information collected from multiple sources regarding the individual's functional legal capacities	*Nonspecific:* focus on sexual offending only to the extent indicated by the referral questions *Specific:* distinguish between risk for future sexual offending and future nonsexual offending
15. Ensure that conditions for evaluation are quiet, private, and distraction-free	Note any deviation from reasonably quiet, private, and distraction-free conditions Describe impact on data collected	*Nonspecific:* same as general guideline *Specific:* same as general guideline
16. Provide appropriate notification of purpose and/or obtain appropriate authorization before beginning	Describe elements of notification of purpose or informed consent given to individual being evaluated and to third parties who are interviewed	*Nonspecific:* same as general guideline *Specific:* same as general guideline
17. Determine whether the individual understands the purpose of the evaluation and the associated limits on confidentiality	Document how the individual's understanding was assessed, and to what extent he/she understood the relevant information	*Nonspecific:* underscore distinction between FMHA and treatment evaluation and assess how this was understood, particularly if the individual has a history of involvement in specialized treatment for sexual offenders *Specific:* same as above
18. Use third-party information in assessing response style	Describe the consistency of third-party information with self-reported information, and be particularly cautious about self-report when it is significantly different from third-party accounts	*Nonspecific:* same as general guideline *Specific:* anticipate problem of potential underreporting of sexual offending because of private aspect of such behavior; focus on observable behaviors that are meaningful

TABLE 2. Guidelines for applying principles to FMHA to nonsexual offenders, to sexual offenders nonspecifically, and to sexual offenders specifically (*continued*)

Principle	General Guideline for Administration in FMHA	Guideline for Administration in FMHA with Sexual Offenders
19. Use testing when indicated in assessing response style	Administer test(s) sensitive to response style, particularly when there is concern about the accuracy of self-report	*Nonspecific:* same as general guideline *Specific:* consider measures specifically applicable to sexual offenders
20. Use case-specific (idiographic) evidence in assessing clinical condition, functional abilities, and causal connection	Describe the individual's clinical condition and functional legal abilities in the context of their history of symptoms and demonstrated capacities	*Nonspecific:* same as general guideline *Specific:* interpret "clinical condition" to include aspects of personality and behavior applicable to sexual offending
21. Use nomothetic evidence in assessing clinical condition, functional abilities, and causal connection	Describe the results of psychological tests, structured instruments, and specialized tools validated for assessing (1) clinical condition or (2) functional legal capacities	*Nonspecific:* same as general guideline *Specific:* consider measures specifically applicable to sexual offenders
22. Use scientific reasoning in assessing causal connection between clinical condition and functional abilities	Describe explanations for clinical condition and functional abilities that have the most supporting evidence and least disconfirming evidence When evidence is mixed, or competing explanations seem comparably well-supported, say so	*Nonspecific:* same as general guideline *Specific:* same as general guideline, with "clinical condition" interpreted as relevant for sexual offending
23. Do not answer the ultimate legal question	Present conclusions about forensic capacities but not the larger legal question(s)	*Nonspecific:* same as general guideline *Specific:* same as general guideline
24. Describe findings and limits so that they need change little under cross examination	Be careful, impartial, and thorough in presenting data and reasoning Consider alternative explanations	*Nonspecific:* same as general guideline *Specific:* same as general guideline
25. Attribute information to sources	Describe data so that the source(s) of any specific finding is clear	*Nonspecific:* same as general guideline *Specific:* same as general guideline
26. Use plain language; avoid technical jargon	Make minimal use of technical language, and define technical terms when they must be used	*Nonspecific:* same as general guideline *Specific:* same as general guideline

TABLE 2. Guidelines for applying principles to FMHA to nonsexual offenders, to sexual offenders nonspecifically, and to sexual offenders specifically (*continued*)

Principle	General Guideline for Administration in FMHA	Guideline for Administration in FMHA with Sexual Offenders
27. Write report in sections, according to model and procedures	Include sections on referral information, sources of information, relevant history, clinical functioning, relevant functional legal capacities, and conclusions Describe causal relationship between clinical symptoms and functional legal capacities	*Nonspecific:* same as general guideline *Specific:* same as general guideline
28. Base testimony on the results of the properly performed FMHA	Master the contents of the report, which contains thorough documentation of evaluation, and use report contents to guide testimony	*Nonspecific:* same as general guideline *Specific:* same as general guideline
29. Testify effectively	Use effective style in presenting substantive FMHA findings in testimony	*Nonspecific:* same as general guideline *Specific:* same as general guideline

several additional steps that could be taken. Even nonspecific FMHA could be improved by having the evaluator indicate the extent of his/her clinical and forensic experience with this population. In sex offender–specific FMHA, it may also be useful to have the forensic clinician indicate the basis for the appointment to the case. Some jurisdictions have panels from which evaluators are appointed, for example, and it is useful to indicate that one's appointment is on that basis (as contrasted with the more customary referral sources in FMHA: defense attorneys, prosecutors, or courts).

Decline the referral when evaluator impartiality is unlikely. Impartiality is important in FMHA. Even when a forensic clinician is asked by a prosecutor or defense attorney to conduct an evaluation, the clinician should resist the temptation to function as an advocate for the appointing side. Rather, when the evaluation is conducted impartially, the results may support the arguments of the appointing side (in which case the forensic clinician's report may be introduced into evidence and testimony sought), or they may not (depending on the rules of evidence in the jurisdiction, such findings may be treated as privileged attorney work product and not introduced into evidence). This principle underscores the importance of declining to accept a case for evaluation when there are personal, professional, or monetary influences that could substantially impede impartiality throughout the assessment. The guideline for application with sexual offender FMHA suggests that the forensic clinician monitor his/her own reactions to the issues of punishment and rehabilitation of sexual offenders, with extreme views (e.g., "sexual offenders should never be punished, only treated," or "sexual offenders should always receive the maximum possible sentence and should never receive specialized treatment") reflecting indicators of bias that could undermine impartiality. The questions of punishment, rehabilitation, and reoffense risk are in even sharper focus with sexual offender–specific FMHA, as risk level and capacity to respond to risk-reducing interventions are essential elements of evaluations of sentencing enhancement, postsentence commitment, and release from such commitment.

Clarify the evaluator's role with the attorney. This principle describes the problem of the evaluator's playing more than one role in a single FMHA case (e.g., treating therapist and forensic evaluator) and the potentially harmful results of such dual roles. In addition, as suggested by the general FMHA guideline for application, it is helpful to ensure that both the forensic clinician and the referring attorney or court understand and agree upon a single role for the evaluation. This does not appear any different for specific or nonspecific sexual offender FMHA than it does for general criminal FMHA.

Clarify financial arrangements. The hourly rate or total amount of billing for services, and how this will be paid, should be clarified and agreed upon in advance whenever financial arrangements for such evaluations are not described in jurisdictional law or policy. This principle and the general application guideline do not need modification for application to either kind of FMHA with sexual offenders.

Obtain appropriate authorization. The source of appropriate authorization in FMHA depends on the role being played by the forensic clinician. It may be the court (for court-ordered evaluations) or the retaining attorney (for defense- or prosecution-requested evaluations). A court-appointed referral typically requires a signed court order for authorization to proceed; a request from an attorney clearly conveys the consent of that attorney, but the forensic clinician must also obtain the consent of the defendant. Both the source of the request for the evaluation and the nature of the authorization obtained should be cited in the report, according to the criminal FMHA application guideline. This should be applied with a particular iteration when evaluating sexual offenders, either nonspecifically or specifically: the evaluator should ask whether the defendant has any history of specialized treatment. For those who do, it is important to emphasize strongly that FMHA is distinct from diagnostic/therapeutic evaluation.

Avoid playing the dual roles of therapist and forensic evaluator. This principle stresses that one particular aspect of dual role relationships—assuming the roles of both therapist and forensic evaluator with the same individual in the same FMHA case—should generally be avoided because of the potential for decreasing the quality of the forensic evaluation and potentially harming the client (TABLE 1). There may be some instances in which this principle does not apply, but those are invariably characterized by a justification to combine treatment and forensic assessment, advance planning to do so, and clear notification to the individual involved prior to commencing either. One such example involves individuals who are committed as incompetent to stand trial undergoing skills-based interventions to improve their relevant capacities for communication, reasoning, and understanding of information related to the legal system. It is unclear whether specialized treatment for sexual offenders could be combined in the same way with ongoing forensic assessment of continued need for hospitalization. If it is, however, then it should be planned in advance, justified, and done with the consent of those receiving both treatment and forensic assessment.

Determine the particular role to be played within forensic assessment if the referral is accepted. This principle emphasizes that forensic clinicians should typically choose a single role in the beginning of the case and maintain that role throughout. The possible exception to this general rule involves moving from a role requiring impartiality (e.g., defense, prosecution, or court-appointed expert expected to testify) to a role in which impartiality is not needed (e.g., consultant) if it is clear that the attorney will not request a report or testimony because of the findings of the evaluation. In all cases in which the forensic clinician may be responsible for providing evidence (report and testimony), however, the evaluator should strive to maintain impartiality and the report should reflect this. Nonspecific FMHA with sexual offenders does not differ from general criminal FMHA on this point. The particular challenge in specific FMHA with sexual offenders involves addressing treatment needs only when they are among the forensic issues being evaluated, and avoiding the temptation to offer heartfelt but irrelevant comments regarding treatment needs.

Select the most appropriate model to guide data gathering, interpretation, and communication. There are several models that can be applied to FMHA to guide the steps of data collection, interpretation, and communication. Two of the most prominent (Morse, 1978; Grisso, 1986) both identify functional legal abilities and the causal connection between deficits in such abilities and an area such as clinical symptoms, although the models differ somewhat in their complexity. Nonspecific sexual offender FMHA can be done using either of these models. For sex offender–specific FMHA, the area of "mental disorder" must be interpreted sufficiently broadly and flexibly to include a focus on the patterns of thinking, feeling, and arousal that contribute to criminally deviant sexual behavior and the risk that such behavior will recur.

Use multiple sources of information for each area being assessed. Multiple sources of information serve several important functions in forensic assessment: minimizing the error associated with a single source, assessing the impact of an evaluee's deliberate distortion of sensitive information, and providing a way to communicate the thoroughness of the evaluation. When information from multiple sources such as self-report, collateral records, and collateral interviews provides a consistent portrayal of an individual, it is more likely that this information is accurate. Conversely, inconsistency and disagreement across sources should alert the forensic clinician to the presence of inaccuracy in at least one of the sources. The principle is applicable in basically the same form for all types of FMHA being discussed—general, sexual offender–nonspecific, and sexual offender–specific.

Use relevance and reliability (validity) as guides for seeking information and selecting data sources. This principle emphasizes the importance of both relevance and reliability (two important legal criteria for admissibility of evidence) as guides for sources of information in FMHA. The legal term "reliability" encompasses both psychometric reliability and validity, so tests and tools that are used in FMHA should have demonstrated levels of reliability and validity that are documented in a manual accompanying the test, which should be commercially available or easily accessible. Like the last principle, this one is comparably applicable to each form of FMHA discussed in this chapter.

Obtain relevant historical information. The amount of historical information needed in FMHA is often greater than in therapeutic evaluation, but the need for history also depends on the nature of the legal question and associated forensic issues. Some evaluations, such as competence to stand trial, may require only a relatively limited history that includes criminal and mental health areas. The nature and extent of the history needed in nonspecific sexual offender FMHA, like that needed in more general FMHA, would vary according to the focus of the evaluation. However, with specific sex offender FMHA, there is consistently a question regarding the person's sexual offending and, often, the risk of its recurrence. More detailed history on previous sexual offending, on the patterns of thinking, feeling, arousal, and behavior associated with offending, and on protective factors, is therefore likely to be important.

Assess clinical characteristics in relevant, reliable, and valid ways. A previous principle addressed the importance of relevance and reliability in selecting sources of information. This principle expands on this, stressing the value of assessing clinical characteristics using tests and tools that have been derived and validated for this purpose, on a population similar to that of the individual being evaluated, and this validation process documented in published research and a test manual. This must be interpreted somewhat broadly for sexual offender–specific FMHA, with "clinical characteristics" including the patterns of thinking, feeling, arousal, and behavior associated with offending.

Assess legally relevant behavior. This principle refers to the capacities and behavior that are contained within the larger legal question that triggered the FMHA. Relevance and reliability are again considered as guides, allowing detailed documentation of information collected from multiple sources regarding these capacities. There are two iterations of this principle that are indicated for FMHA with sexual offenders. First, for nonspecific FMHA, there may be some need to focus on the offense itself (as, for example, in an evaluation of mental state at the time of the offense), or the need for offense-relevant information may be more limited (in competence to stand trial, for example). The extent of the particular focus on the offense as a sexual crime, however, should be driven by the referral questions. The second iteration applies to sexual offender-specific FMHA in which reoffense risk is addressed. If it is, the evaluator should be careful to distinguish between risk of reoffending for any kind of offense, and risk of sexual reoffending.

Ensure that conditions for evaluation are quiet, private, and distraction-free. The physical conditions under which FMHA is conducted have the potential to interfere with the effectiveness and validity of the evaluation if they are sufficiently poor. This principle stresses the need for a setting that is relatively quiet, free from auditory or visual distractions, and permitting an exchange between the forensic clinician and client that cannot be overheard by a third party. When there are deviations from a reasonable standard, this should be noted in the report and the potential impact upon the evaluation described. This principle applies comparably to all three forms of FMHA being discussed.

Provide appropriate notification of purpose and/or obtain appropriate authorization before beginning. Whether the forensic clinician begins with a notification of purpose to the individual being evaluated or obtains that person's informed consent depends on the forensic clinician's role and the associated authorization that was obtained. Either should include a description of the nature and purpose of the evaluation, who authorized it, the limits on confidentiality, and how the results might be used. When the individual's participation is not voluntary (e.g., for a court-ordered evaluation of competence to stand trial), it would not be appropriate for the forensic clinician to further seek the individual's informed consent. However, when the evaluation is conducted at the request of the defense attorney, it is *is* voluntary, and informed consent should be sought before beginning. Third parties who are interviewed as part of FMHA are doing so on a voluntary basis as well, so obtaining their consent before beginning the interview would also be appropriate. This principle also applies to general, sexual offender–nonspecific, and sexual offender–specific FMHA comparably.

Determine whether the individual understands the purpose of the evaluation and associated limits on confidentiality. The information conveyed as part of either the notification of purpose or informed consent process must be understood by the individual being evaluated in order to be meaningful. The evaluator should use a process to assess this understanding; further, the evaluator should describe the process and convey an apparent limits to the individual's comprehension of relevant information. This principle applies somewhat differently to either nonspecific or specific sexual offender FMHA in cases in which the individual has some history of specialized treatment. In such instances, there is a particular risk that the individual might confuse forensic assessment with that done for diagnostic and treatment-planning purposes, so the evaluator should pay particular attention to ensuring that this distinction is understood—and that the individual is aware that the present evaluation is for forensic purposes only.

Use third-party information in assessing response style. Third-party information is important in FMHA for a number of reasons. One of the most important is to assess the accuracy and completeness of an individual's self-report about sensitive areas, such as symptoms, behavior involved in offending, and the related motivation for such behavior. This principle stresses the value of using collateral documents and informants in establishing a picture of the individual's history and relevant behavior with multiple sources of information, and assessing whether self-reported information is consistent with other sources and therefore more likely to be accurate. In cases in which self-reported information about sensitive areas appears inconsistent with information in the same areas from collateral sources, one possibility is that the individual has deliberately distorted such information. There is one way in which this principle must be applied somewhat differently with sexual offender–specific FMHA: sexual offending, and related risk factors, are typically much less observable to third parties than, for example, symptoms of severe mental illness or temper problems. The forensic clinician must anticipate this problem, and compensate by focusing on behaviors that are more observable but still meaningful in the context of the evaluation.

Use testing when indicated in assessing response style. The use of psychological tests and specialized measures (e.g., measures specifically developed to assess exaggeration of symptoms or minimization of symptoms or deviant thoughts) can be very helpful in assessing an individual's response style. Among other justifications, the results of such testing can allow the evaluator to calculate how heavily to rely on self-report in the course of the assessment. Sexual offender–specific FMHA would need to consider specialized measures that are particularly applicable to sexual offenders, particularly those sensitive to defensiveness, but the two other forms of FMHA appear comparable in the extent to which this principle applies.

Use case-specific (idiographic) evidence in assessing clinical condition, functional abilities, and causal connection. Science can contribute to FMHA in three ways: idiographic data, nomothetic data, and scientific reasoning. This principle addresses the first of the three. In response to the "compared to what?" question, this principle promotes gathering information that allow the comparison of the individual to his/her own capacities and functioning at other times. "Clinical condition" must be interpreted broadly in sexual offender–specific FMHA, but the three forms of FMHA are otherwise comparable on this principle.

Use nomothetic evidence in assessing clinical condition, functional abilities, and causal connection. This principle is focused on the second way that science can contribute to FMHA: comparing the individual's functioning on relevant dimensions to that of similar populations, using tests and tools that have been developed and validated for that purpose on such populations. Using such tests facilitates the informed consideration of how similar such measured capacities are to those in "known groups." When conducting sexual offender-specific FMHA, it is useful to consider tests that have been validated for use with the sex offenders. This aside, however, the application of this principle is comparable across all three forms of FMHA being discussed in this chapter.

Use scientific reasoning in assessing causal connection between clinical condition and functional abilities. Scientific reasoning may be used by considering the results of one source of information, such as self-report, as yielding "hypotheses to be verified" through information obtained from other sources (e.g., psychological testing, record review, third-party interviews). The acceptance of a given hypothesis should also depend on how parsimonious it is, accounting for the most information with the simplest explanation. This principle applies reasonably well to all three forms of FMHA being discussed, although (as with several previous principles) it is important to adapt sexual offender–specific FMHA so that "clinical condition" is interpreted sufficiently flexibly to include characteristics and behavior particularly relevant to sexual offending.

Do not answer the ultimate legal question directly. The "ultimate legal question" to be answered by the court (such as competence to stand trial or child custody arrangement) has been the focus of much debate regarding whether it should be answered as part of FMHA. The arguments in favor of and opposing "ultimate issue" testimony have been offered (Rogers & Ewing, 1989; Slobogin, 1989) and summarized (Heilbrun, 2001; Melton et al., 1997). It has been argued, on the "pro" side, that courts and attorneys often expect an ultimate opinion, and that such opinions are permitted under the applicable rules of evidence in many jurisdictions. By contrast, those opposing answering the ultimate legal question in FMHA stress that there are moral, political, and community-value components that affect the answer to the ultimate legal question, considerations that should be outside the scope of FMHA. My own recommendation is to focus on the included forensic capacities (in sexual offender–specific FMHA, recidivism risk, and risk-reduction potential through available community conditions, among others) but avoid answering the ultimate legal question. The application of this principle seems comparable across all three forms of FMHA.

Describe findings and limits so that they need change little under cross examination. When FMHA results are presented, either in a report or testimony, the presentation should be careful, thorough, and reflect consideration of various alternative possibilities. The tone should be impartial, and the forensic clinician should communicate both the reasoning and the data supporting it. This applies as well to sexual offender–specific and –nonspecific FMHA as it does to FMHA more broadly.

Attribute information to sources. Attributing information to its source is important for at least two reasons. First, it indicates whether information is consistent across multiple sources, which in turn affects judgments about response style of the individual being evaluated. Second, it informs the judge or an attorney reading the report of the source of specific information. This principle applies equally well to all three forms of FMHA being discussed.

Use plain language; avoid technical jargon. Many of those who request and use the results of FMHA are not trained in medicine or behavioral science. Some are trained in law; others (e.g., jurors) may be trained in neither law nor behavioral science. It is thus useful to avoid using technical language, or at least to define technical terms if they must be used. This principle also applies comparably well to sexual offender–specific and –nonspecific FMHA as to more general criminal FMHA

Write report in sections, according to model and procedures. There are various ways to organize an FMHA report. I recommend an approach that incorporates one of the models described in an earlier principle, and conveys the procedures, findings, and reasoning of the evaluation. The following sections are recommended: (1) *Referral* (with identifying information concerning the individual, his/her characteristics, the nature of the evaluation, and by whom it was requested or ordered); (2) *Procedures* (times and dates of the evaluation, tests or procedures used, different records reviewed, and third-party interviews conducted, as well as documentation of the notification of purpose or informed consent and the degree to which the information was apparently understood); (3) *Relevant history* (containing information from multiple sources describing areas important to the evaluation); (4) *Current clinical condition* (broadly considered to include appearance, mood, behavior, sensorium, intellectual functioning, thought, and personality; with a specific population such as sexual offenders, it would also include the patterns of thinking, feeling, arousal, and behavior associated with that particular offense risk); (5) *Forensic capacities* (defined by the legal question); and (6) *Conclusions and recommendations* (focusing on forensic capacities rather than ultimate legal questions). With some adjustment for the particular aspects of clinical condition in sexual offender–specific FMHA, this principle applies well to all three kinds of FMHA.

Base testimony on the results of the properly performed FMHA. Linking testimony to the larger evaluation process can be greatly facilitated by using the report as both the mode of documenting the evaluation and the basis for the testimony. This allows the attorney to use the expert's findings effectively, the opposing attorney to challenge them, and the judge to understand them. This principle seems to apply well to all three forms of FMHA under discussion.

Testify effectively. This final principle describes two aspects of expert testimony: substantive and stylistic. Substantive aspects of expert testimony are linked with previous principles, which promote thoroughness, accuracy, impartiality, and consistency with sources of authority in law, ethics, science, and practice. Stylistic aspects of expert testimony involve how the forensic clinician presents, dresses, speaks, and otherwise behaves to make testimony more understandable and credible. Both the substance and style of expert testimony should be good to make such testimony maximally effective. This principle applies comparably well to all three kinds of FMHA.

DISCUSSION

Forensic mental health assessment blends science, practice, and ethics, but is also influenced by relevant law. There are two important issues addressed in this chapter. First, forensic evaluations done with sexual offenders differ substantially from those performed for the purpose of diagnosis and treatment planning; the failure to recognize this distinction can lead to substantial problems in the forensic assessment process (Greenberg & Shuman, 1997). Second, a set of principles broadly applicable to FMHA (Heilbrun, 2001) exists that can be applied to the forensic evaluation of sexual offenders. In making this application, as I have in this chapter, two things become clearer: how well such broad principles fit the assessment of a specific population, and how much guidance they can provide in conducting FMHA with sexual offenders.

How well do these principles apply to FMHA with sexual offenders? I distinguished between *nonspecific FMHA* (performed with sexual offenders on issues not necessarily related to the nature of the offense) and *sexual offender–specific FMHA* (addressing questions that are raised specifically because of the nature of the offense). The principles seem to apply very well to nonspecific FMHA; for 23 of the 29 principles, I judged that there was no difference in their applicability generally and to nonspecific FMHA. There were more differences in the way these principles applied to sexual offender–specific FMHA—for 16 of the principles, some modification was necessary. These modifications reflected the difference in focus between evaluating the "clinical condition" of offenders generally and the particular aspects of functioning related to sexual offending, which are typically aspects of thinking, personality, arousal, and behavior rather than mental disorder. It was also important to modify the kinds of tools used, considering those validated for sexual offenders, and focusing particularly on the kind of forensic issues raised in such sexual offender–specific FMHA (reoffense risk and potential for risk reduction). However, these modifications were relatively minor, and fit comfortably within the domain of the larger principle.

This analysis suggests that a set of FMHA principles like this can offer substantial guidance in the forensic evaluation of sexual offenders. With relatively few modifications (for nonspecific FMHA) and adaptations that promote appropriate changes within the broader principles for a certain form of FMHA (with sexual offender–specific FMHA), these principles can provide a framework to guide the process of forensic evaluation with this population.

There are several implications for the adherence to such principles in conducting forensic assessment with sexual offenders, and other implications for the substantial failure to consider broad principles of FMHA. First, the use of such principles provides an important link between FMHA with sexual offenders and that performed with other populations. Certainly one reasonable way to consider the process of forensic assessment is to describe how different forms of FMHA—with differences defined by legal question and population—have indicated procedures that differ from other forms. This approach has been used successfully in leading works on forensic assessment (e.g., Melton et al., 1997; Poythress et al., 2002; Rogers & Shuman, 2000). However, it is also important to consider FMHA as a single field with unified guiding principles (Heilbrun, 2001; Heilbrun, Marczyk & DeMatteo, 2002). In the latter context, performing FMHA with sexual offenders in a fashion consistent with a set of unified principles yields a different way of considering the quality of the evaluation, and incorporates the support of law, ethics, science, and practice. More specifically, adherence to such principles should promote impartiality, thoroughness, communication, and validity, while maintaining respect for professional boundaries and ensuring that the appropriate informed consent or notification of purpose was incorporated.

By contrast, the failure to adhere to such principles may reflect an approach to FMHA with this population that is problematic. Such problems may be relatively isolated (e.g., the failure to obtain informed consent when conducting an evaluation requested by defense counsel), or they may be more pervasive and likely to affect the evaluation in a variety of ways (e.g., failure to achieve reasonable impartiality resulting from one's beliefs about the role of rehabilitation for sexual offenders). Applying a broad set of principles allows the identification of such problems, whether isolated or more pervasive, and the application of the appropriate remedy. In some instances, this might involve an attorney's challenging the findings of a poorly conducted evaluation. In other cases, it could allow the clinician to better identify strategies to enhance the quality of FMHA with sexual offenders in the broader context of such principles, making such evaluations more accurate, more difficult to challenge, and more informative for the court.

Applying such broad FMHA principles to forensic assessment with a specific population (sexual offenders), or with such a population to address a particular set of forensic issues, is one approach to enhancing the quality and usefulness of such evaluations. I do not suggest that it is the only approach, nor do I wish to overvalue the contributions that can be made by such principles. However, as the analysis in this chapter demonstrates, it is one viable way to address this goal. When this approach is combined with one that emphasizes the very specific aspects of any particular FMHA, the result should be a better forensic assessment for courts and attorneys.

REFERENCES

AMERICAN ACADEMY OF PSYCHIATRY AND THE LAW (1995). *Ethical guidelines for the practice of forensic psychiatry.* Bloomfield, CN: Author.

AMERICAN BAR ASSOCIATION (1989). *Criminal justice mental health standards.* Washington, DC: Author.

AMERICAN PSYCHIATRIC ASSOCIATION (1998). *The principles of medical ethics with annotation especially applicable to psychiatry.* Washington, DC: Author.

AMERICAN PSYCHOLOGICAL ASSOCIATION (1992). Ethical principles of psychologists and code of conduct. *American Psychologist, 47,* 1597–1611.

COMMITTEE ON ETHICAL GUIDELINES FOR FORENSIC PSYCHOLOGISTS (1991). Specialty guidelines for forensic psychologists. *Law and Human Behavior, 15,* 655–665.

GREENBERG, S. & SHUMAN, D. (1997). Irreconcilable conflict between therapeutic and forensic roles. *Professional Psychology: Research and Practice, 1,* 50–57.

GRISSO, T. (1986). *Evaluating competencies: Forensic assessments and instruments.* New York: Plenum Press.

HEILBRUN, K. (2001). *Principles of forensic mental health assessment.* New York: Kluwer Academic/Plenum Press.

HEILBRUN, K., MARCZYK, G. & DEMATTEO, D. (2002). *Forensic mental health assessment: A casebook.* New York: Oxford University Press.

Kansas v. Hendricks, 521 U.S. 346 (1997).

MELTON, G., PETRILA, J., POYTHRESS, N. & SLOBOGIN, C. (1997). *Psychological evaluations for the courts: A handbook for mental health professionals and lawyers* (2nd ed.). New York: Guilford.

MORSE, S. (1978). Crazy behavior, morals, and science: An analysis of mental health law. *Southern California Law Review, 51,* 527–654.

POYTHRESS, N., MONAHAN, J., BONNIE, R., OTTO, R.K., & HOGE, S. (2002). *Adjudicative competence: The MacArthur Studies.* New York: Kluwer Academic/Plenum.

Rogers, R., & Ewing, C.P. (1989). Ultimate opinion proscriptions: A cosmetic fix and a plea for empiricism. *Law and Human Behavior, 13*, 357–374.
Rogers, R., & Shuman, D. (2000). *Conducting insanity evaluations* (2nd ed.). New York: Guilford.
Slobogin, C. (1989). The ultimate issue issue. *Behavioral Sciences & the Law, 7,* 259–268.

Assessment of Sex Offenders

Lessons Learned from the Assessment of Non–Sex Offenders

RALPH C. SERIN AND DONNA L. MAILLOUX

Research Branch, Correctional Service of Canada, Kingston, Ontario K7L 5E6, Canada

ABSTRACT: Notwithstanding significant progress in the areas of risk appraisal and treatment of sex offenders, the contention is that further advancements could be realized through attention to research on non–sex offenders. Specifically, it is proposed that sex offenders share many characteristics of non–sex offenders and research with these populations should be integrated, not discrete. In particular, work in the area of multi-method offender assessment regarding criminogenic need is highlighted to suggest common treatment targets for sex offenders and non–sex offenders. As well, recent research in terms of treatment readiness is described and contrasted with the constructs of denial and minimization. Measurement strategies for cognitive schemas in use with violent offenders are also presented in order to expand the repertoire of approaches clinicians might consider as part of an assessment protocol. Further, performance-based measures of empathy and relapse prevention are described and compared with self-reports in terms of program participation and social desirability. Finally, a brief discussion of change scores and their application to post-treatment risk appraisal is provided, as is the requirement for a systematic decision model to inform post-treatment supervision.

KEYWORDS: sex offender, assessment; criminogenic need; performance-based measures; schemas

The purpose of this chapter is twofold. First, it is our contention that sex offenders are, for the most part, not unique from other groups of offenders. That is, they share many similarities regarding criminogenic[a] needs. As well, many components of sex offender assessment and programming are comparable to those for non–sex offenders. Second, we believe that more careful scrutiny of research in the general correctional literature may be instructive for researchers and practitioners who specialize in sex offenders. Indeed, failure to attend to innovations in such fields as corrections,

Address for correspondence: Ralph C. Serin, Director, Operations and Programs Research, Research Branch, Correctional Service Canada, c/o Frontenac Institution, 455 Bath Road, Kingston, Ontario K7L 5E6, Canada. Voice: 613-536-4169.

serinrc@csc-scc.gc.ca

[a]Criminogenic needs are dynamic attributes of the offender that, when changed, are associated with the changes in the probability of recidivism (Andrews & Bonta, 1998).

Ann. N.Y. Acad. Sci. 989: 185–197 (2003). © 2003 New York Academy of Sciences.

mental health, and addictions could well impede advances in the field of sex offender assessment, intervention, and supervision. Similar to other offenders, sex offenders often have co-occurring mental health and substance abuse needs. For some jurisdictions specialists provide interventions within these domains, making integration a key challenge. The focus of this chapter, however, will be primarily on assessment issues and the application of correctional issues to sex offenders.

The outline of the chapter is as follows: (1) an overview of the assessment methods used to determine criminogenic needs, and hence treatment targets or high-risk situations for offenders; (2) discussion of the construct and measurement of treatment readiness as an alternative to denial and minimization; (3) the assessment of schemas; (4) the utility of performance-based measures; (5) measurement of offender change; and (6) the need for a decision model to systematically integrate pretreatment risk appraisals and treatment-gain information.

CRIMINOGENIC NEED

For sex offenders in particular and offenders in general the task of determining the circumstances that contribute to an individual's criminality is not new. Although broad personality-based approaches have been and continue to be in use (for example, MMPI, MMPI-2), more recent efforts have been more specific. This specificity has been encouraged in part by the evidence that some offenders' criminal behavior is due to an inability to avoid high-risk situations (McGuire, 1995). The preliminary work in relapse prevention for substance abuse (Marlatt & George, 1984) has been transferred readily to the area of sex offending (Marshall & Barbaree, 1990). Three methods that have been employed to capture the frequency and severity of these antecedents are functional analyses, structured interview-based ratings, and self-report questionnaires. Rarely are these three approaches used concurrently to determine the relative strengths and limitations of each method.

Functional Analyses

Functional analyses typically include file and interview data. Efforts are made to determine the relationship among and importance of various antecedents to criminal behavior (McDougall, Clark & Fisher, 1994). Sometimes this analysis is used to determine treatment needs and severity. It is also used over time to determine whether similar risk behaviors are present, albeit with a different expression, such as sex offenders' writing letters to children from prison. Structured ratings (Level of Service Inventory–Revised, LSI-R: Andrews & Bonta, 1995) are increasingly being used within a risk appraisal strategy to determine risk levels and treatment needs for offenders, including sex offenders (Simourd & Malcolm, 1998). Some rating scales are actuarial instruments (e.g., LSI-R) with demonstrated predicted validity. Others such as the HCR-20 (Webster, Douglas, Eaves & Hart, 1997) are increasingly being used to structure appraisals and regulate clinical assessment given its limited predictive validity. The selection of approaches to measure criminogenic need, then, is related to risk appraisal, but is not exclusively a risk prediction enterprise. Regarding this latter point, for sex offender risk appraisal, not all risk scales appear equal (Barbaree, Seto, Langton & Peacock, 2001).

Interviews have also been used to determine antecedents in sex offenders with good success (Pithers, Kashima, Cummings, Beal & Buell, 1988). This work identified the distinct offence cycles of sex offenders and highlighted the importance of affective states as a cue to sexual assault. They further noted that such precursors could be predisposing (early), precipitating (immediate), and perpetuating (ongoing) risk factors. Such a viewpoint underscores the importance of their identification as treatment targets. Pithers et al. (1988) also presented data that confirmed differences between child molesters and rapists regarding antecedents or criminogenic needs. In particular, therapists were more likely to ascribe anger, personality disorder, alcohol abuse, and opportunity as important in understanding rapists' motivation relative to child molesters. There were minimal differences between rapists and child molesters regarding cognitive distortions, empathy deficits, or lack of sexual knowledge or social skills in terms of their contribution to their sexual assaults, but the prevalence of these antecedents was very high (ranging from 45–65%) for both groups. The single exception was *opportunity*; as a motive it was considered a relatively uncommon antecedent for child molesters (19%) compared to rapists (58%).

Almost a decade later Zamble and Quinsey (1997) published findings regarding the antecedents of criminal behavior for non–sexual offenders. Using confidential interviews conducted at intake to federal custody but retrospectively applied to the offenders' most recent crime, some similarities with sex offenders were noted. For instance, emotional difficulties were attributed as a contributor in 41% of the assaults, about half the rate reported by sex offenders. Offenders convicted of robbery frequently reported financial difficulties (54%), but not those convicted of assault (6%). Alcohol problems were comparable for both types of non–sex offenders (67% for assaulters, 51% for robbers), as were drug problems (26% for assaulters, 33% for robbers). Although there are clearly some differences between sex offenders and non–sex offenders, particularly in terms of the proportion of offenders reporting certain antecedents, it is clear that emotional difficulties and alcohol use are common precursors to crime for both groups.

More recently, the distinction between static and dynamic factors leading to sexual offending has been made more specific to include stable and acute dynamic factors (Hanson & Harris, 2000). Stable dynamic factors are changeable but typically have enduring features, while acute dynamic factors refer to offense timing issues. This had provided greater specificity regarding potential treatment targets (Hanson, 2000), but also the articulation of offense pathways (Ward & Hudson, 2000). The application of these pathways may be the identification of differential triggers and hence differential intervention and supervision of sex offenders.

Structured Interviews

Another method of determining criminogenic needs is to utilize semi-structured interviews and self-reference questions to inform global ratings. This is comparable to case-based functional analyses of the precursors to crime. Such work has been implemented at a systems level in the Correctional Service of Canada since 1994 (Motiuk, 1997). Completed at intake, this process model integrates information from multiple sources and provides global ratings for seven criminogenic need domains that are based on key indicators within each domain. Further, these domain ratings are related to programming requirements during the offender's sentence, from incarceration to completion of community supervision. These need domains are described elsewhere (Motiuk, 1997) and generally reflect research regarding the psychology of criminal conduct (Andrews & Bonta, 1998). Essentially, this body of research indicates that increased needs in the areas of employment, marital/family relationships, personal/emotional skills, substance abuse, criminal attitudes, associations, and community functioning all contribute to increased likelihood of recidivism. Using the previous example of static versus dynamic factors, these domains appear stable dynamic factors. Furthermore, assets (not just the absence of needs, but the demonstrated strength) in these areas are related to more successful community outcomes. In this manner, criminogenic needs can reflect both treatment targets and protective factors, with improvements being related to increased success and deterioration being related to increased failure (Motiuk & Brown, 1993; Motiuk, 1997).

Of interest, these intake indicators were employed to create an index to identify a group of high-risk violent non–sex offenders (Serin & Preston, 2001a). Items relating to violence and criminal risk were rationally a priori identified and aggregated as an index for a sample of 12,093 offenders. Using a cutpoint of 1 standard deviation above and below the mean, three groups were identified (low, moderate and high risk of repetitive violence). Not surprisingly, analyses with a sample of 764 of these offenders indicated that the high-risk group had a significantly higher rate of recidivism (Serin & Preston, 2001b) relative to the low group (50.5% versus 15.4%). What was striking was not the extent of their needs in these seven domains (employment, marital/family relationships, personal/emotional skills, substance abuse, criminal attitudes, associations, and community functioning). They were clearly a high-need group, with considerable needs ranging from 23.7% for community functioning to 88.7% for personal/emotional stability. This is perhaps not surprising, but the absence of assets or strengths with respect to criminogenic needs was striking. This high-risk group had no discernible assets with respect to those factors that are related to criminality. Assets were assessed for less than 3.3% for any of the seven need domains. In comparison, for the low-risk group using this index, they had prevalence rates for assets ranging from 21.1% to 32.2% for the seven need domains. It would appear that standardized assessment protocols could be used to profile offenders, determine treatment needs, and inform risk management strategies.

Similar data are available for sex offenders, who currently represent approximately 19% of all admissions to federal corrections in Canada (Correctional Service Canada, 2000), although sexual crimes represent only 2% of all federal statute charges (Solicitor General Canada, 2000). Comparing a large cohort of successive admissions of sex offenders ($n = 2,275$) and non–sex offenders ($n = 9,993$) to the federal correctional system according to these seven needs domains is instructive. In this example, sex offenders are defined as cases with an index sexual conviction. As noted earlier, few offenders have assets in any need domains. Similar to the other work on antecedents, substance abuse is similar (45.0% problem for sex offenders, 54.0% for non–sex offenders). Perhaps surprisingly, the proportion with employment needs and community functioning needs were similar for the two groups. Sex offenders had higher needs with respect to relationships (33.4% problem for sex offenders, 20.6% for non–sex offenders), but markedly lower with respect to personal/emotional needs (9.1% problem for sex offenders, 66.3% for non–sex offenders). Further, and importantly, criminal attitudes were comparable for both groups (32.5% problem for sex offenders, 35.5% for non–sex offenders).

Self-Report Questionnaires

A final method for determining precursors to crime is to utilize self-report questionnaires. One such example is the Antecedents to Crime Inventory (Serin & Mailloux, 2001). This scale measures offenders' awareness of criminal risk situations according to nine domains—impulsivity, social pressure, excitement, anger, social alienation, substance use, financial pressure, interpersonal conflict, and family conflict. The scale is organized such that offenders are asked to rate the frequency on a 4-point Likert scale with which certain situations preceded their current criminal behavior (e.g., "When I needed some excitement" on the excitement subscale). The original scale comprised 144 items, which was subsequently reduced to 54 items and 6 validity items through statistical analyses. The psychometric properties of the scale are reasonable (i.e., alpha > .83; good correlation with independent psychologists' ratings; inter-item $R > .39$). Of particular interest is that subscale scores differ (4 of 9 subscales) for recidivists and nonrecidivists, suggesting that self-reported precursors are relevant to clinical practice. Although speculative, it may be that increased understanding of risk situations may be a precursor to offenders managing their criminogenic needs. Further, application to a small sample of sex offenders revealed that rapist and incest offenders report higher anger scores than extrafamilial child molesters (Amos, 1992).

In a related area, it is of interest to note that recent research regarding the criminal attitudes of sex offenders shows these attitudes to be quite similar to those of non–sex offenders (Mills, Anderson & Kroner, 2002). Excluding incest offenders, sex offenders and non–sex offenders report similar proportions of criminal friends and associates and comparable criminal intent. Not surprisingly, rapists had stronger antisocial attitudes than did child molesters and incest offenders. Most importantly, criminal attitudes were more strongly related to criminal history in sex offenders than non–sex offenders. Further, other measure of offenders' views worth considering are the Criminal Sentiments Scale and Pride in Delinquency scale (Simourd & Van deVan, 1999).

In combination, these findings support the use of multi-method appraisals of criminogenic need in order to inform programming and supervision. Also, it would appear that while sex offenders may be specific regarding sexual deviance and perhaps intimacy deficits, they have many similarities to other offenders. Discounting such commonalities probably interferes with effective appraisals of risk and its management through treatment and supervision.

TREATMENT READINESS

A variety of self-report and rating scales have been developed for use with sex offenders (e.g., Denial & Minimization Checklist, Barbaree, 1991; Multiphasic Sex Inventory, Nichols & Molinder, 1984), but there appears to be little consensus regarding a preferred choice. Notably there is consensus regarding the high prevalence of denial and minimization in sentenced sex offenders and its impact on programming for juveniles (Hunter & Figueredo, 1999) and adults (Marshall, Thornton, Marshall, Fernandez & Mann, 2001). Given that the majority of sex offenders do not admit responsibility for their offenses and minimize them even after sentencing, there could be a concern about using denial to differentiate among sex offenders. Further, there is some debate regarding the interpretation of findings from meta-analyses regarding a lack of relationship between denial and risk (Hanson & Bussière, 1998; Lund, 2000). Perhaps somewhat alarmingly, from the perspective of treatment needs, as presently defined, denial is sometimes used to exclude sex offenders from treatment. Recently, denial has also actually been used as the primary treatment target for sex offenders as a prelude to inclusion in a regular treatment program (Marshall et al., 2001).

A perhaps broader construct that has been utilized with non–sex offenders which may have application to sex offender assessment is that of treatment readiness (Serin, 2001). This work has evolved from efforts to operationalize the concept of treatability in forensic applications (Heilbrun, Bennett, Evans, Offult, Reiff & White, 1992). In addition to including motivation, it also incorporates variables related to problem definition and supports for change. Emotional dissonance is also included and this has been related to the prediction of treatment-related change in antisocial individuals (Gerstely, McLellan, Alterman, Woody, Luborsky & Prout, 1989). Serin, Kennedy, and Mailloux (in preparation) have developed a behaviorally anchored rating scale for the assessment of treatment readiness with encouraging preliminary results. It is a continuous measure, not categorical; it is dynamic, with changes over time evident; and is related to program performance measures. With respect to sex offenders, treatment readiness is significantly correlated with denial ($R = .45, P < .001$) and somewhat less so with criminal risk as measured by the Level of Service Inventory–Revised ($R = -.27, P < .01$) (Mailloux, Serin, & Malcolm, in press). Pilot data indicate that rapists and incest offenders have low readiness scores before treatment relative to non–sex offenders. Further, there is a main effect for denial status, but not type of child molester.

In combination, these data are encouraging and suggest that research on treatment readiness developed on non–sex offenders may well merit application to sex offenders. Equally importantly, the construct of treatment readiness can be used to identify offenders in need of a "primer." Given the relation between readiness and program performance, it would be possible to empirically identify readiness items that predict either poor performance or program attrition. These items would then represent treatment targets for a pretreatment intervention that would occur prior to the offender's entering a standardized sex offender program. Notably, some research on non–sex offenders suggests that reaching a threshold of readiness is a better predictor of posttreatment gain than change scores (Williamson, Day, Howells, Bubner & Jauncey, 2002). This suggests that efforts to embed motivational interviewing and other strategies to address readiness throughout a program may not yield the same results as targeting low readiness and determining some minimal threshold of satisfactory motivation prior to treatment participation.

SCHEMAS

Schemas are internal scripts that are related to behavior. The scripts are central to a social information–processing model to explain behavior and incorporate cognitive distortions that are evident in many sex offenders. The measurement of schemas is notable in many areas of psychological functioning (e.g., eating disorders, depression, spousal assault, violence, and sex offending). For violent offenders, cognitive style has been proposed as being useful in differentiating among violent offenders (Novaco & Welsh, 1989). More specifically, for hostile individuals there has been an effort to utilize hypothetical vignettes as the stimulus set for appraising cognitive schemas (Crick & Dodge, 1994). This work with juveniles has illustrated that behavioral expression of aggression is related to social information–processing biases. Vignettes have been employed in part because self-reports of dysfunctional behavior are often influenced by response set and social desirability. The methodology requires that the assessor provide a sufficient repertoire of salient situations to the offender in order for the vignettes to elicit responses.

The methodology entails the presentation of a situation (e.g., "You're at a party and someone walks by with a couple of drinks. They bump into you, spilling some drink in your lap. They continue to walk by and do not look your way."). Probing questions are then used to score or rate specific constructs such as hostile attributions, aggressive beliefs, problem definition, goal-selection, anger, and empathy. Very preliminary data from a violent offender program indicates moderate inter-rater reliability ($R = .81–.93$). Also, pilot research investigating the correlations with vignette-based constructs and psychological tests is encouraging. Vignette indices of anger correlated 0.38 with the Reactions to Provocation Scale (Novaco, 1994). Comparable results were found for indices of impulsivity and hostile attributions and the majority of vignette measures changed from pre- to posttreatment testing (Serin & Preston, 2003). While promising, vignette-based scores must be related to dependent variables such as recidivism before they should be applied clinically. Their inclusion in this overview is to illustrate the point that research on the assessment of cognitive distortions among offenders could be adapted for use with sex offenders, perhaps informing treatment planning and risk prediction. Certainly, excellent work in this area already exists for sex offenders, but the methodology is different (Bumby, 1996).

PERFORMANCE-BASED MEASURES

In addition to research regarding the applicability of vignettes to assessment of offenders, performance-based measures were developed to measure treatment gain for specific skills. Rather than use self-report approaches to knowledge gain, it was considered more important to attempt to assess skill acquisition. This same pilot research used performance-based measures of empathy and relapse prevention. The empathy measures incorporated work by Hanson and Scott (1995) regarding the specific skills expected to effectively demonstrate empathy. Three inter-related domains were represented—perspective-taking, presenting an affective response, and coping with the other individual's distress. A range of situations was created and an offender's response aggregated across these situations for a total empathy skills score. Preliminary results are available for a sample of seventy offenders who completed an intensive violent offender treatment program. Inter-rater reliability was modest (perspective-taking: .61; affect: .75; coping with distress: .64). This empathy skills score was not significantly related to self-reported empathy ($R = .03$) using the Interpersonal Reactivity Index (Davis, 1983) or impression management ($R = .08$) as measured by the Paulhus Deception Scale (1998). More importantly the empathy skills score was significantly correlated with independent ratings of program performance

($R = .25$, $P < .05$). In contrast, self-reported empathy using the IRI yielded significant correlations with impression management ($R = .30$, $P < .0001$) and reduced correlations with ratings of program performance ($R = .22$, ns). Such findings complement research with sex offenders that describes generalized versus offense-specific empathy deficits among sex offenders (Marshall & Fernandez, in press; Fernandez, Marshall, Lightbody & O'Sullivan, 1999).

Similarly, competency measures of relapse prevention skills have been developed for sex offenders (Minor, Day & Nafpaktitis, 1989). Adaptation to nonsexual high-risk situations and preliminary application to high-risk violent offenders ($n = 70$) yields some evidence regarding their potential utility. Notwithstanding modest to weak inter-rater reliability, this performance-based measure was related to independent ratings of program performance. Inter-rater reliability varied according to the domain. For instance, problem recognition ($R = .27$) was noticeably poorer than hierarchy ($R = .68$), effectiveness ($R = .60$), and number of responses generated ($R = .69$). Correlation with impression management was not statistically significant ($R = .14$). Relapse prevention skills, however, were significantly related to independent ratings of group performance ($R = .57$, $P < .001$). For both of these performance-based measures the reliability ratings were determined from audiotaped interviews and the raters ($n = 20$) were blind to the offenders' criminal history and treatment status.

In a related theme, there has been interest in discerning the role of coping in offenders' ability to desist from crime (Zamble & Porporino, 1988). Research in the area of coping has considered personal coping style (Parker & Endler, 1996) and situational coping skills (Lazarus & Folkman, 1984). This work has been successfully applied to sex offenders (Cortoni & Marshall, 2001) and most recently, the distinction between intra and inter-individual coping deficits has been made to more specifically identify treatment targets in sex offenders (Cortoni, Anderson & Bright, in press).

It is clear that competency measures are not a panacea, but they may form a legitimate part of an assessment protocol for offenders. Research indicates they are less related to social desirability than self-reports, they have face validity, and are related to important dependent variables such as independent ratings of group performance and participation. While encouraging, it is also clear that improvements are required in terms of reliability. Further, evidence of discriminant and predictive validity is required. Other performance-based assessment approaches in the form of cognitive tasks have also been used in applied research with offenders (Blair, 2000; Fishbein, 2000; Newman, 1998), principally to identify executive functioning deficits, although to date these have not been incorporated into clinical practice. Nonetheless, computerized tasks appear to discriminate among offenders regarding processes underlying such important antecedents to criminality such as self-regulation. These processes are therefore important to understand in determining treatment gains. It is hoped that application of such strategies to offender assessment will proceed to inform both theory and practice.

MEASUREMENT OF OFFENDER CHANGE

The general consensus is that change scores for self-report scales (for stable dynamic factors) are often not predictive of outcome. For sex offenders, similar findings have also been noted for phallometric assessments (Quinsey, Rice, Harris & Lalumière, 1993). What is less clear is the extent to which baseline (pretreatment), threshold (posttreatment) or change scores are most predictive of outcome. Even where change scores are significant for groups of offenders, for those offenders who begin treatment with a moderate level of knowledge and/or skill, ceiling effects result in limited range of scores. Threshold scores are the most proximal and in other risk appraisals, proximity has enhanced predictive validity (Motiuk, 1997). The work on acute dynamic factors is consistent with this research on non–sex offenders.

Recently the application of the transtheoretical model of change (Prochaska & DiClemente, 1992) to offenders has resulted in usage of various stage-based measures of change. The stages of change proceed from precontemplation (the person is not thinking about change), to contemplation (the person is thinking about change), to preparation (the person is getting reading to change), to action (the person is actively involved in changing the behavior), to maintenance (the person is maintaining the change), to relapse (a normal part of the change process in which the person returns to the problem behavior), and finally to termination (a permanent exit from the stages of change). It is understood that people move through these stages at different rates and more in an incremental and cyclical than linear manner. The transtheoretical model has been used in appetitive disorders (addictions, smoking cessation, weight loss) with good success. More recently the University of Rhode Island Change Assessment scale has been adapted for use with spousal assaulters (Levesque, Gelles & Velicer, 2000). Briefly, it has been demonstrated that individuals proceed through discernible stages and that tailoring intervention to offenders' "readiness" may reduce attrition and improve program performance.

While such a model is appealing and has been applied to offenders, complementing motivational interviewing strategies, some authors have been disappointed regarding the reliability of stages-of-change measures. Two concerns are the transparency of scale items, resulting in a high correlation with social desirability and possible insensitivity to subtle changes in offenders. The latter may in part be due to the use of the word "problem" as a generic target to change and offenders' tendency to be quite black-and-white in their perceptions. Also, many institution-based programs do not provide much opportunity for offenders to practice new knowledge and skills in situations that were previously high-risk. Self-reports of gains could then be exaggerated.

Further, for offenders, there is an applied literature that describes major factors contributing to criminality (Andrews & Bonta, 1998). There is also an increasing literature that describes factors that contribute to offenders' termination of criminal behavior (Maruna, 2001; Uggen & Piliavin, 1998). Although desistence is not a new concept, the research to date has simply identified protective and coping factors. It is quite likely that protective factors are not simply the absence of risk factors and that the offender's resiliency is as important as the identification of risk factors. Measurement strategies must consider both risk and desistence factors and the extent to which their presence or absence is related to reductions in recidivism. The transtheoretical model does not specifically attend to this correctional research and as such may be somewhat limited to explain changes in offenders' criminal behavior. For these reasons, efforts to develop self-report measures that are grounded in theory about offender change are proceeding. Serin and Mailloux (in preparation) have developed a self-report scale that measures proximal or antecedent risk factors, treatment readiness, and desistence factors. The first two domains are reflected in existing self-report and rating scales, while the latter domain is modeled from work by Hubert and Hundelby (1993) and Brown (2002). Research regarding coping style and sex as a coping strategy may also be appropriate to incorporate into the domain of desistence (Cortoni *et al.*, in press). In a related theme, it is of interest to ascertain whether such offender-specific change scales are related to various correctional outcomes such as institutional adjustment, program attrition, and recidivism. The identification of factors that influence sex offenders' program completion is important given that at least some research has noted that deniers and rapists are less likely to complete sex offender programs (Mailloux & Serin, 2001). In research on non–sex offenders, program attrition is related to poorer outcomes (Dowden & Serin, 2003). Similar findings have been reported for sex offenders (Hanson & Bussière, 1998; Hanson, Gordon, Harris, Marques, Murphy, Quinsey & Seto, 2002).

DECISION MODEL

Notwithstanding gains with respect to correctional program design and delivery (McGuire, 1995), it remains problematic to systematically incorporate individual program performance information with pretreatment risk appraisals (Serin, 1998). In the area of sex offenders there is a variety of highly regarded actuarial risk scales that may be used to anchor an appraisal of an individual offender's likelihood of future sexual reoffending. Further, notwithstanding the issue of uninterpretable pretreatment measures of sexual preference, using phallometric procedures appears most predictive of sexual recidivism (Quinsey, Rice, Harris & Lalumière, 1993). Caution, then, appears warranted in using change scores or posttreatment indices in risk management. With such information available to the clinician, it remains obscure at best what additional dynamic or treatment information might be most salient in determining revisions to initial estimates of risk. Heuristics are now available regarding dynamic risk appraisals (Hanson & Harris, 2000), but these do not yet provide structured decision rules for individual cases. Serin (2001) has suggested a decision model that incorporates pretreatment risk, motivation, and treatment performance. Guidelines are provided to explicitly limit the extent to which risk estimates can be over-ridden because of treatment information, an apparently prudent practice (Seto & Barbaree, 1999). Presently this remains an untested theoretical model, but improved guidelines are required in order that the field might make advances regarding the incorporation of effective programming into risk management strategies.

SUMMARY

From this abbreviated review of various aspects of offender assessment, it should be clear that correctional assessment strategies could inform sex offender assessment. Evidence has been presented that confirms that more often than not, sex offenders share similarities with other offender groups. This is notable with respect to criminogenic needs, antecedents to their crimes, and criminal attitudes. Further, sex offenders, like non–sex offenders, have significant difficulties in the areas of addictions and mental health. While it was not the primary purpose of this chapter to address these areas specifically, it is clear that advances in these areas should also be considered in order to enhance research and clinical practice with sex offenders. Accordingly, research from corrections, addictions and mental health fields should be incorporated into the mainstream of sex offender assessment. Notwithstanding some specificity with respect to type of sex offender, to focus almost exclusively on sexual deviance issues and to discount commonalties with non–sex offenders could greatly impede progress with respect to the assessment and management of sex offenders.

REFERENCES

AMOS, N.L. (1992). *Antecedents to crime for sex offenders.* Unpublished honour's thesis, Queen's University, Kingston.

ANDREWS, D.A. & BONTA, J. (1998). *The psychology of criminal conduct* (2nd ed.). Cincinnati: Anderson Publishing.

ANDREWS, D.A. & BONTA, J. (1995). *The Level of Service Inventory–Revised.* Toronto, Canada: Multi-Health Systems.

BARBAREE, H.E. (1991). Denial and minimization among sex offenders: Assessment and treatment outcome. *Forum on Corrections Research, 3*, 300–333.

BLAIR, J. (2000). Neurocognitive explanations of the antisocial personality disorders. *Criminal Behaviour & Mental Health, 10*, 66–81.

BROWN, S.B. (2002). *The dynamic prediction of criminal recidivism: A three-wave prospective study.* Unpublished doctoral thesis.

BUMBY, K.M. (1996). Assessing the cognitive distortions in child molesters and rapists: Development and validation of the MOLEST and RAPE scales. *Sexual Abuse: A Journal of Research and Treatment, 8*, 37–54.

CORRECTIONAL SERVICE OF CANADA (2000). Homicide, sex, robbery and drug offenders in federal corrections: An end-of-1999 review. *Research Branch, No. B-24*, p. 2–14.

CORTONI, F., & MARSHALL, W.L. (2001). Sex as a coping strategy and its relationship to juvenile sexual history and intimacy in sexual offenders. *Sexual Abuse: A Journal of Research and Treatment, 13*, pp. 27–44.

CORTONI, F., ANDERSON, D. & BRIGHT, D. (in press). Locus of control, coping and sexual offenders. In Schwartz, B.A. & Cellini, C. (Eds.), *The Sex Offender, Volume 4.*

CRICK, N. R. & DODGE, K.A. (1994). A review and reformulation of social information-processing mechanisms in children's social adjustment. *Psychological Bulletin, 1*, 74–101.

DAVIS, M.H. (1983). Measuring individual differences in empathy: Evidence for a multidimensional approach. *Journal of Personality and Social Psychology, 44*, 113–126.

DOWDEN, C. & SERIN, R.C. (2003). Anger management programming for federal offenders: The impact of dropouts and other program performance variables on recidivism *(Research Report R-106)*. Ottawa: Correctional Service of Canada.

FERNANDEZ, Y.M., & MARSHALL, W.L. (in press). Violence, empathy, social self-esteem and psychopathy in rapists. *Sexual Abuse: A Journal of Research and Treatment.*

FERNANDEZ, Y.M., MARSHALL, W.L., LIGHTBODY, S., & O'SULLIVAN, C. (1999). The Child Molester Empathy Measure: Description and examination of its reliability and validity. *Sexual Abuse: A Journal of Research and Treatment, 11*, 17–32.

FISHBEIN, D.H. (2000). Neuropsychological dysfunction, drug abuse and violence; Conceptual framework and preliminary findings. *Criminal Justice & Behavior, 27*, 139–159.

GERSTLEY, L., MCLELLAN, T., ALTERMAN, A., WOODY, G., LUBORSKY, L. & PROUT, M. (1989). Ability to form an alliance with the therapist: A possible marker of prognosis for patients with antisocial personality disorder. *American Journal of Psychiatry, 146*, 508–512.

HANSON, R.K. & BUSSIÈRE, M.T. (1998). Predicting relapse: A meta-analysis of sexual offender recidivism studies. *Journal of Consulting and Clinical Psychology, 66*, 348–362.

HANSON, R.K. & SCOTT, H. (1995). Assessing perspective-taking among sexual offenders, nonsexual criminals, and non-offenders. *Sexual Abuse: A Journal of Research and Treatment, 7(4)*, 259–277.

HANSON, R.K. & HARRIS, A.J.R. (2000). Where should we intervene? Dynamic predictors of sexual offense recidivism. *Criminal Justice and Behavior, 27*, 6–35.

HEILBRUN, K.S., BENNETT, W.S.. EVANS, J.H. OFFULT, R.A., REIFF H.J., & WHITE, A.J. (1992). Assessing Treatability in Mentally Disordered Offenders: Strategies for Improving Reliability. *Forensic Reports, 5*, 85–96.

HUBERT, R.P. & HUNDELBY, J.P. (1993). Pathways to desistence: How does criminal activity stop? *Forum on Corrections Research, 5*, 13–18.

HUNTER, J.A., & FIGUEREDO, A.J. (1999). Factors associated with treatment compliance in a population of juvenile sexual offenders. *Sexual Abuse: A Journal of Research and Treatment, 11*, 49–68.

LAZARUS, R.S., & FOLKMAN, S. (1984). *Stress, appraisal, and coping.* New York: Springer Publishing Company.

LEVESQUE, D.A., GELLES, R.J. & VELICER, W.F. (2000). Development and validation of a stages of change measure for men in batterer treatment. *Cognitive Therapy and Research, 24(2)*, 175–199.

LUND, C.A. (2000). Predictors of sexual recidivism: Did meta-analyses clarify the role and relevance of denial? *Sexual Abuse: A Journal of Research and Treatment, 12*, 275–288.

MAILLOUX, D.L., & SERIN, R.C. (2001). *Issues impacting on programming for sex offenders* (Research Report). Ottawa: Correctional Service of Canada.

MAILLOUX, D.L., SERIN, R.C. & MALCOLM, P.B. (in press). *Denial and minimization in the management of sex offenders* (Research Report). Ottawa: Correctional Service of Canada.

MARLATT, G.A. & GEORGE, W.H. (184). Relapse prevention: Introduction and overview of the model. *British Journal of Addiction, 79*, 261–273.

MARSHALL, W.L. & BARBAREE, H.E. (1990). *Handbook of sexual assault: Issues, theories, and treatment of the offender.* New York: Plenum Press.

MARSHALL, W.L., THORNTON, D., MARSHALL, L.E., FERNANDEZ, Y.M. & MANN, R. (2001). Treatment of sexual offenders who are in categorical denial: A pilot project. *Sexual Abuse: A Journal of Research and Treatment, 13*, 205–216

MARUNA, S. (2001). *Making good.* Washington, DC: American Psychological Association.

McGUIRE, J. (Ed.). (1995). *What works: Reducing reoffending: Guidelines from research and practice.* Chichester: John Wiley & Sons.

MILLS, J.F., ANDERSON, D. & KRONER, D.G. (2002). *The antisocial attitudes and associates of sex offenders.* Submitted for publication.

MINER, M.H., DAY, D.M. & NAFPAKTITIS, M.K. (1989). Assessment of coping skills: Development of a Situational Competency Test. In D.R. Laws (Ed.). *Relapse prevention with sex offenders* (pp. 127–136). New York: Guilford.

MOTIUK, L.L. (1997). Classification for correctional programming: The Offender Intake Assessment (OIA) process. *Forum on Corrections Research, 9, (1)*, 18–22.

MOTIUK, L.L. & BROWN, S.L. (1993). *The validity of offender needs identification and analysis in community corrections.* (Research Report, R–34). Ottawa: Correctional Service of Canada.

NEWMAN, J.P. (1998). Psychopathic behavior: An information processing perspective. In D.J. Cooke, R.D. Hare, & A. Forth (eds.), *Psychopathy: Theory, research, and implications for society* (pp. 81–104). the Netherlands: Kluwer Academic Publishers.

NICHOLS, H.R. & MOLINDER, I. (1984). *Multiphasic Sex Inventory.* (Available from Nichols & Molinder, 437 Bowes Drive, Tacoma, WA 98466).

NOVACO, R.W. (1994). Anger as a risk factor for violence among the mentally disordered. In J. Monahan and H.J. Steadman (Eds.), *Violence and mental disorder: Developments in risk assessment,* (pp. 21–59). Chicago: University of Chicago Press.

NOVACO, R.W. & WELSH, W.N. (1989). Anger disturbances: Cognitive mediation and clinical prescriptions. In K. Howells and C.R. Hollin (Eds.), *Clinical approaches to violence* (pp. 39–60). London: John Wiley & Sons Ltd.

PARKER, J.D.A. & ENDLER, N.S. (1996). Coping and defense: A historical overview. In M. Zeidner & N.S. Endler (Eds.), *Handbook of Coping: Theory, Research, Applications* (pp. 3–23). New York: John Wiley & Sons.

PAULHUS, D.L. (1998). *Paulhus Deception Scales (PDS): The Balanced Inventory of Desirable Responding -7.* Toronto, Ontario: Multi-Health Systems, Inc.

PITHERS, W.D., KASHIMA, K.M., CUMMINGS, G.F., BEAL, L.S. & BUELL, M.M. (1988). Relapse prevention in sexual aggression. In R.A. Prentky & V.L. Quinsey (Eds.), *Human sexual aggression; Current perspectives* (pp. 244–260). New York: Annals of the New York Academy of Sciences.

PITHERS, W.D. (1990). Relapse prevention with sexual aggressors: A method for maintaining therapeutic gain and enhancing external supervision. In W. L. Marshall, D. R. Laws, & H. E. Barbaree (Eds.), *Handbook of sexual assault: Issues, theories, and treatment of the offender* (pp. 343–362). New York: Plenum Press.

PROCHASKA, J.O., DiCLEMENTE, C.C. & NORCROSS, J.C. (1992) In search of how people change: Applications to addictive behaviors. *American Psychologist, 47,* 1102–1114.

QUINSEY, V.L., RICE, M.E., HARRIS, G.T. & LALUMIÈRE, M.L. (1993). Assessing treatment efficacy in outcome studies of sex offenders. *Journal of Interpersonal Violence, 8,* 512–523.

SERIN, R.C. (2001). Treatability, treatment responsivity, and risk management. In K.S. Douglas, C.D Webster, S.D. Hart, D. Eaves, & J.P. Ogloff (Eds.), *HCR–20 Violence Risk Management Companion Guide,* (pp. 109–118). Simon Fraser University: Mental Health, Law and Policy Institute.

SERIN, R.C. (1998). Treatment responsivity, intervention and reintegration: A conceptual model. *Forum on Corrections Research, 10 (1),* 29–32.

SERIN, R.C., KENNEDY, S. & MAILLOUX, D.L. (in preparation). *The measurement of treatment readiness with offenders.*

SERIN, R.C. & PRESTON, D.L. (2001a). Managing and treating violent offenders. In J.B. Ashford, B.D. Sales, and W. Reid (Eds.), *Treating adult and juvenile offenders with special needs,* (pp. 249–272). Washington, DC: American Psychological Association.

SERIN, R.C. & PRESTON, D.L. (2001b). Violent offender programming. In L.L. Motiuk & R.C. Serin (Eds.), *Compendium 2000,* (pp. 146–157). Ottawa: Correctional Service of Canada.

SERIN, R.C. & PRESTON, D.L. (2003). Measurement of treatment change in a high intensity violent offender program. Manuscript in preparation.

SERIN, R.C. & MAILLOUX, D.L. (2001). *Development of a reliable self-report instrument for the assessment of criminogenic need* (Research Report, R-96). Ottawa: Correctional Service of Canada.

SERIN, R.C. & MAILLOUX, D.L. (in preparation). *Offender Change Scale.* (Research Report). Ottawa: Correctional Service of Canada.

SETO, M.C. & BARBAREE, H.E. (1999). Psychopathy, treatment behavior, and sex offender recidivism. *Journal of Interpersonal Violence, 14,* 1235–1248.

SIMOURD, D.J. & MALCOLM, P.B. (1998). Reliability and validity of the Level of Service Inventory with incarcerated sex offenders. *Journal of Interpersonal Violence, 13,* 23–28.

SIMOURD, D.J. & VAN DEVEN, J. (1999). Assessment of criminal attitudes: Criterion-related validity of the Criminal Sentiments Scale–Modified and Pride in Delinquency. *Criminal Justice and Behavior, 26,* 90–106.

SOLICITOR GENERAL OF CANADA (2000*). Corrections and conditional release statistical overview.*

UGGEN, C. & PILAVIN, I. (1998). *Asymmetrical causation and criminal desistance. National Institute of Justice Journal.* US Department of Justice.

WARD, T. & HUDSON, S.M. (2000). A self-regulation model of the relapse prevention. In D.R. Laws, S.M. Hudson & T. Ward (Eds.), *Remaking relapse prevention with sex offenders: A sourcebook* (pp. 219–235). Thousand Oaks: Sage.

WILLAMSON, P., DAY, A., HOWELLS, K., BUBNER, S. & JAUNCEY, S. (2002). *Assessing offender readiness to change problems with anger.* Unpublished manuscript.

ZAMBLE, E. & QUINSEY, V.L. (1997). *The criminal recidivism process.* New York: Cambridge University Press.

Actuarial Assessment of Risk among Sex Offenders

GRANT T. HARRIS AND MARNIE E. RICE

Research Department, Mental Health Centre Penetanguishene,
Penetanguishene, Ontario L9M 1G3, Canada

ABSTRACT: The appraisal of risk among sex offenders has seen recent advances through the advent of actuarial assessments. Statistics derived from Relative Operating Characteristics (ROCs) permit the comparison of predictive accuracies achieved by different instruments even among samples that exhibit different base rates of recidivism. Such statistics cannot, however, solve problems introduced when items from actuarial tools are omitted, when reliability is low, or when there is high between-subject variability in the duration of the follow-up. We present empirical evidence suggesting that when comprehensive actuarial tools (VRAG and SORAG) are scored with high reliability, without missing items, and when samples of offenders have fixed and equal opportunity for recidivism, predictive accuracies are maximized near ROC areas of 0.90. Although the term "dynamic" has not been consistently defined, such accuracies leave little room for further improvement in long-term prediction by dynamic risk factors. We address the mistaken idea that long-term, static risk levels have little relevance for clinical intervention with sex offenders. We conclude that highly accurate prediction of violent criminal recidivism can be achieved by means of highly reliable and thorough scoring of comprehensive multi-item actuarial tools using historical items (at least until potent therapies are identified). The role of current moods, attitudes, insights, and physiological states in causing contemporaneous behavior notwithstanding, accurate prediction about which sex offenders will commit at least one subsequent violent offense can be accomplished using complete information about past conduct.

KEYWORDS: sex offenders; actuarial; risk assessment; prediction; static versus dynamic

The past decade has seen a remarkable increase in empirical work on risk assessment among child molesters and rapists. Up to 1992 or so, researchers had identified reliable predictors of recidivism among sex offenders (Quinsey, 1984; 1986). However, this work would not have permitted decision makers to make statements about the risk posed by individual sex offenders. An assessor would have been able to comment on where a particular offender stood on some known risk factors (age, general criminal history, sex offense history, marital status, etc.), but a quantified

Address for correspondence: Grant Harris, Ph.D., Research Department, Mental Health Centre Penetanguishene, 500 Church Street, Penetanguishene, Ontario L9M 1G3, Canada. Voice: 705-549-3181, ext. 2613; fax: 705-549-3652.

gharris@mhcp.on.ca

Ann. N.Y. Acad. Sci. 989: 198–210 (2003). © 2003 New York Academy of Sciences.

summary statement would have been impossible. Dramatic change occurred upon the advent of actuarial tools developed by testing the selection and combination of risk factors.

It is revealing that this change has been based on a surprisingly small amount of empirical work. As far as we know, only five actuarial instruments for risk assessment among sex offenders have been published in the peer-reviewed literature. The *Violence Risk Appraisal Guide* (VRAG; Harris, Rice & Quinsey, 1993) was developed on a sample of 618 violent offenders, approximately 20% of whom were sex offenders. The instrument has subsequently been tested on several samples of sex offenders (see <www.mhcp-research.com/ragreps.htm>). A modification of the VRAG called the *Sex Offender Risk Appraisal Guide* (SORAG; also see <www.mhcp-research.com> for replications), designed to predict violent recidivism among sex offenders, was first mentioned by Rice and Harris (1997) and more fully described the next year (Quinsey, Harris, Rice & Cormier, 1998). Similarly, a four-item actuarial instrument called the *Rapid Risk Assessment for Sexual Offense Recidivism* (RRASOR) was described in an unpublished report (Hanson, 1997) that led to an expanded and improved instrument, the *Static-99* (Hanson & Thornton, 2000), itself partly based on an influential meta-analysis of sex offender recidivism (Hanson & Bussière, 1998). Both were designed to predict known sexual recidivism and both have been tested in peer-reviewed publications (e.g., Barbaree, Seto, Langton & Peacock, 2001). We are also aware of a fifth actuarial tool, the *Minnesota Sex Offender Screening Tool* (revised) or Mn-SOST-R (Epperson, Kaul & Hesselton, 1998), which has been tested in at least one peer-reviewed publication (Barbaree et al., 2001).

Other non-actuarial systems relying on structured clinical judgment have been promoted (e.g., the SVR-20; Boer, Hart, Kropp & Webster, 1998), but promulgation has usually preceded the presentation of data on predictive validity with the result that the method has, for the most part, not fared well when later tested against actuarial methods (e.g., Barbaree et al., 2001; Ducro, Claix & Pham, 2002; Dempster, Hart & Boer, 2001; Sjöstedt & Langström, 2002), resulting in modification and re-release (e.g., RSVP; Kropp, 2002). This chapter will concentrate on actuarial risk assessment of sex offenders. We address three topics: First we review the accuracy so far achieved and its realistic "ceiling." Second, we discuss prospects for increasing the accuracy with which actuarial systems can identify which sex offenders will commit subsequent offenses and the assertion that improvements in accuracy depend on the incorporation of "dynamic" variables. Finally, we discuss the suggestion (e.g., Heilbrun, 1997) that risk "prediction" (in contrast to "management") has minimal implications for intervention.

THE ACCURACY OF EXISTING ACTUARIAL METHODS

A discussion of the accuracy of any method for the prediction of anything requires some numerical means to evaluate and compare accuracies. The percentage of occasions a prediction is correct might seem the obvious choice. For example, weather forecasters might be thought to show high accuracy if they were correct 85% of the time. Unfortunately, whether 85% correct implies any acumen depends a lot on the base rate: a completely inexpert forecaster in the Sahara could achieve at least 85% correct by always predicting tomorrow's weather will be hot and dry. This is because the base rate (proportion of rainy days) is so low there. What is required is a statistic that captures accuracy that is unaffected by the base rate of the event predicted, permitting comparisons among predictions made in situations where base rates differ.

As we and others have explained elsewhere (Rice & Harris, 1995; Swets, Dawes & Monahan, 2000), many statistics familiar to psychologists and social scientists (e.g., correlation coefficients, chi-squares, odds ratios) are also affected by the base rate. The best available statistic to express the true accuracy of a test comes from the Relative Operating Characteristic or ROC, which is a plot of the hit rate (or sensitivity) as a function of the test's false alarm rate (1 – specificity). ROCs illustrate a test universal—there is always a trade-off between sensitivity and specificity. Unless the test is modified to increase its accuracy, sensitivity cannot be improved without worsening specificity (and vice versa). The area subtended by the ROC is a good overall index of the test's accuracy; several studies have shown that this area statistic is independent of the base rate and serves as a good way to summarize and compare predictive accuracies. Generally, the ROC area is equivalent to the Common Language Effect Size (McGraw & Wong, 1992). For the rest of this chapter, we present data on predictive accuracy in terms of ROC areas.

ROCs have limitations, however. Most clearly, ROC statistics can only be applied to binary outcomes (e.g., predicting which of a group of sex offenders will be arrested for at least one subsequent violent offense). ROC statistics could not, for example, be applied to a continuous scale reflecting the severity (ranging from zero for non-recidivists to a very large number for those who commit multiple homicides) of the outcome, or to the speed (measured in days since release, for example) with which recidivism occurs. Continuous outcomes present such statistical challenges as range restriction, extreme skewness, and differential sample censoring, so that newer statistical methods (e.g., maximum likelihood survival analyses) have been developed in response. However, it is presently unclear whether the newer techniques permit the comparison across studies with differing base rates afforded by ROC statistics. Fortunately, it appears that these different outcomes are sufficiently closely related (i.e., those offenders most likely to commit at least one reoffense also commit the most severe offenses and relatively quickly) that conclusions based on binary compared to continuous outcomes are very similar (Harris, Rice & Cormier, 2002; Quinsey et al., 1998; Rice & Harris, 1997).

ROC methods cannot compensate for changes in the instruments evaluated. That is, in evaluating a particular test, ROC statistics would not remedy problems caused by omitting or changing test items. It would be unwise to discuss the predictive accuracy of a commonly used IQ test in a study where researchers unilaterally omitted several subscales, and changed a digit-symbol substitution task to a test of juggling skill and a general knowledge task to a test of baseball trivia. Whatever else such a study might be, it would not be a test of the original instrument. Nevertheless, some studies of the accuracy of actuarial risk assessment instruments have altered or even omitted items completely (e.g., Tengstrom, 2001). Thus, it is reasonable to ask what the effect is of omitting items on the accuracy of an actuarial instrument.

Another limitation of ROC statistics is that they cannot compensate for other ways in which the measurement of a particular predictive test is poorly effected. That is, if the individual items of a predictive test were measured with low reliability and there was low reliability of the overall score, the test could not be expected to make accurate predictions. It is axiomatic that a test's reliability places an upper bound on its predictive validity. Some researchers have reported very high reliability in the independent measurement of individual items and the total scores of actuarial instruments. On the other hand, other authors have reported testing the accuracy of actuarial instruments despite achieving unacceptably low reliabilities for individual items (Grann, Belfrage & Tengstrom, 2000). It is reasonable to ask what the effect is of ensuring that individual items and the entire test are measured with high reliability.

Finally, ROC statistics cannot compensate for differences in the variability of the duration of the follow-up. Contrast two imaginary studies: 100 sex offenders released from prison on the same day and monitored for exactly two years of opportunity (i.e., there is no subject-to-subject variation in the follow-up duration). Those who are arrested for committing a subsequent violent offense are scored as failures and the rest are counted as successful. Any offender who spends time in prison for a nonviolent offense is considered to have had no opportunity to commit a violent offense during that subsequent imprisonment, and thus is followed for an additional amount of time to make exactly two years of opportunity. Compare that study to one in which 100 sex offenders are released over the course of ten years from a prison and then follow-up data are collected two years after the last release. Some subjects have had very lengthy opportunity for recidivism, as much as 12 years. Others have a very short opportunity—they were released near the end of the decade but then, during the subsequent two years, served time for a nonviolent offense (thus, had no opportunity to commit a violent offense while in prison). The prediction task seems easier in the former, exact follow-up case than in the latter. What is the effect of a constant and identical duration of follow-up for every subject?

TABLES 1 through 4 attempt to answer these three questions. The tables give ROC areas for four actuarial instruments (VRAG, SORAG, RRASOR, Static-99), predicting that outcome for which each was designed (violent recidivism for VRAG and SORAG; violent recidivism known to be sexually motivated for RRASOR and Static-99). ROC areas are presented as a function of the number of scale items that could not be scored (due to insufficiency of historical information) for each subject. As well, ROC areas are presented for different constant follow-up periods. For example, for a constant follow-up of two years, subjects who "recidivated" within two years of opportunity were coded as recidivists; subjects with less than two years of follow-up who had not recidivated were dropped; and those who recidivated after two years of opportunity were considered to have not recidivated. This simulates the outcome for a group of sex offenders with exactly two years of follow-up each. Finally, ROC areas are also presented for two groups of sex offenders (described fully in Harris, Rice, Quinsey, Lalumière, Boer & Lang, in press). The first group came from our own Sexual Behaviour Laboratory, where we were able to evaluate the reliability of the coding of the individual actuarial items (r's and kappas > 0.80) and the interrater reliability of each of the four actuarial instruments (all r's > 0.93). The second group came from two Canadian prisons and were coded by research assistants with less experience and training than the first group; there were no data on the interrater reliability for these sex offenders.

Although there is some noise in the results (25% of cell n's were less than 30), we contend that TABLES 1 and 2 show that ROC areas are optimized when actuarial instruments are comprehensive (VRAG or SORAG), follow-up is constant, no items

TABLE 1. Area under the ROC for VRAG predictions of violent recidivism as a function of duration of fixed follow-up, number of missing items, and sample

Fixed Follow-up (yr)	Number of Missing Items				
	0	1 or 2	3 or 4	5+	Overall
2	0.81 0.91	0.77 0.64	0.81 0.68	0.75 0.68	0.80 0.77
5	0.86 0.81	0.87 0.62	0.69 0.62	0.59 0.52	0.78 0.70
8	0.83 0.81	0.76 0.55	0.74 0.47	0.60 0.33	0.78 0.64
11	—	0.82 0.54	—	0.55 0.60	0.78 0.70

NOTE: Entries in the upper left corner of each cell are from the Penetanguishene samples in which interrater reliability was assessed; numbers in the lower right corners are from the Kingston and Pacific samples where interrater reliability was unknown. Exclusive of the "Overall" column, mean cell $n = 46$ (SD = 25).

TABLE 2. Area under the ROC for SORAG predictions of violent recidivism as a function of duration of fixed follow-up, number of missing items, and sample

Fixed Follow-up (yr)	Number of Missing Items				
	0	1 or 2	3 or 4	5+	Overall
2	0.85 0.90	0.75 0.74	0.83 0.70	0.83 0.50	0.81 0.76
5	0.95 0.83	0.86 0.63	0.92 0.66	0.66 0.50	0.81 0.70
8	1.0 0.88	0.81 0.60	0.73 0.51	0.60 0.37	0.78 0.64
11	—	0.79 0.57	0.85 0.63	0.49 0.58	0.76 0.71

NOTE: Entries in the upper left corner of each cell are from the Penetanguishene samples in which interrater reliability was assessed; numbers in the lower right corners are from the Kingston and Pacific samples where interrater reliability was unknown. Exclusive of the "Overall" column, mean cell $n = 51$ (SD = 28).

are omitted, and the reliability of measurement is known to be high. Indeed, under optimum conditions, ROC areas clearly exceed 0.85, and perhaps 0.90, values considerably higher than the ROC areas around 0.75 reported under more typical research conditions.

Although a ROC area of 0.90 might seem impressive, many diagnostic tests do better and values above 0.95 are not unheard of (Swets et al., 2000). Two points are relevant here. First, ROC areas over 0.90 are usually obtained in diagnostic, rather than in prediction studies. Usually, areas over 0.90 are obtained when the ability of one diagnostic test (e.g., CT scans for the detection of breast cancer) is compared to the ability of another, gold-standard method (e.g., histology), and the two tests are

TABLE 3. Area under the ROC for Static-99 predictions of sexual recidivism as a function of duration of fixed follow-up, number of missing items, and sample

Fixed Follow-up (yr)	Number of Missing Items							
	0		1		2		Overall	
2	0.71		0.85		0.90		0.80	
		0.84		0.80		0.55		0.72
5	0.69		0.73		0.86		0.64	
		0.89		0.70		0.46		0.59
8	0.67		0.60		0.86		0.64	
		0.86		0.58		0.49		0.59
11	0.59		0.56		0.72		0.59	
		0.64		0.64		—		0.59

NOTE: Entries in the upper left corner of each cell are from the Penetanguishene samples in which interrater reliability was assessed; numbers in the lower right corners are from the Kingston and Pacific samples where interrater reliability was unknown. Exclusive of the "Overall" column, mean cell $n = 37$ (SD = 27).

TABLE 4. Area under the ROC for RRASOR predictions of sexual recidivism as a function of duration of fixed follow-up, number of missing items, and sample

Fixed Follow-up (yr)	Number of Missing Items					
	0		1		Overall	
2	0.71		0.74		0.71	
		0.79		0.54		0.70
5	0.66		0.68		0.64	
		0.66		0.38		0.58
8	0.63		0.35		0.56	
		0.61		0.42		0.54
11	0.61		0.40		0.60	
		0.58		—		0.55

NOTE: Entries in the upper left corner of each cell are from the Penetanguishene samples in which interrater reliability was assessed; numbers in the lower right corners are from the Kingston and Pacific samples where interrater reliability was unknown. Exclusive of the "Overall" column, mean cell $n = 55$ (SD = 39).

conducted nearly contemporaneously. This is much different than trying to make a prediction about behavior several years in the future. Second, diagnostic tests achieving such high ROC values do so under conditions in which there is essentially no measurement error in the event to be diagnosed. In violence prediction, the situation is different.

We can score our dependent variable (arrest for a subsequent violent offense, for example) with very high reliability from official records, but that outcome is itself a crude operationalization of the actual outcome of interest—the commission of subsequent criminally violent behavior. It is well known that many crimes are not reported, are unsolved by the police, or do not result in criminal charges even when the perpetrator is known. As well, official records fail to associate crimes and offenders when offenders use aliases or move outside the jurisdiction, and some offenders are inappropriately counted as successes when they are actually deceased (i.e., they would have recidivated but never got the chance because, unbeknownst to the researchers, they died first). These are all sources of error in measuring the true outcome that do not plague researchers who evaluate most diagnostic tests (and report ROC areas above 0.90). We believe expecting an actuarial instrument for the prediction of criminal recidivism to achieve areas greater than 0.90 would demand the instrument predict the vagaries of the criminal justice system mentioned above. On these grounds, we contend that ROC areas of about 0.90 represent an effective upper bound in the prediction of violent criminal behavior as indexed by official records, or such other current methods of measuring recidivism as self-report or the combination of self-report, report by others, and criminal justice data (e.g., Monahan et al., 2002).

PROSPECTS FOR IMPROVING ACTUARIAL PREDICTION

Although firm conclusions are premature, consider the implications of the ROC areas obtained under optimal conditions shown in TABLES 1 and 2. Subject to replication in other studies, it appears that the VRAG/SORAG instruments can achieve ROC areas approaching or even exceeding 0.90. Again, if borne out by subsequent research, what are the implications of this finding for the idea that accurate risk assessment demands the incorporation of "dynamic" variables? First, let us clarify some confusion about the term "dynamic."

The assessment of anything at just one point in time is a static variable. The use of personal data available at or before release to predict which offenders will recidivate means that all predictors are static. Most of the variables other investigators have called "dynamic" have only been measured once (e.g., Beech, Friendship, Erikson & Hanson, 2002; Thornton, 2002). Showing that one-time assessments are related to recidivism says nothing about whether there is anything *dynamic* about such a relationship. For that to be shown, a "dynamic" variable must be shown to change over time, and, moreover, such changes (measured over at least two occasions) must be shown to add to the prediction of outcome after the initial score on the variable is included. Although there have been attempts at such demonstrations, we are aware of very few that have been successful (c.f., Quinsey, Coleman, Jones & Altrows, 1997).

Everything assessed before the opportunity to reoffend competes for variance in the outcome (e.g., whether the offender will be arrested for at least one violent offense). Predictive accuracy achieved by already-identified static, historical variables places a limit on the amount of remaining variance available for assessments (one-time or change scores) of such putatively dynamic variables as changes in mood, insight, or procriminal attitudes. We conclude that in predicting long-term violent recidivism, there is very little outcome variance left over for "dynamic" variables. This does not mean that such things as moods, insight, prosocial values, intimacy skills, motivation, and various other attitudes and values cannot be related to outcome. Indeed, there is recent evidence that such things are related to recidivism among sex offenders (Beech et al., 2002), and even that some prerelease change scores might be related to recidivism (Hudson, Wales, Bakker & Ward, 2002). As yet, there have been no demonstrations that change scores add anything to initial scores in predicting recidivism among sex offenders. The predictive accuracies achieved under optimal conditions by a comprehensive set of such static, historical predictors as PCL-R score, childhood conduct, and criminal history imply that such dynamic attitudinal and intrapsychic variables (assessed one or more times before release) cannot make an *incremental* contribution to the prediction of recidivism.

This question of the incremental validity afforded by hypothetically dynamic predictors is relevant to the idea that various moods, attitudes, values, and intentions must be evaluated for valid prerelease risk assessment. In fact, some studies have shown that the prerelease addition of purportedly dynamic variables to historical variables would actually decrease predictive accuracy for violent or sexual recidivism (e.g., Barbaree et al., 2001). Assessing sex offenders' attitudes, values, sentiments, and motivations is probably essential for some purposes (e.g., suitability for programs, identification of treatment targets), but the available data indicate that the assessment of such constructs is unnecessary (and probably insufficient) for the accurate prediction of recidivism once the appropriate static, historical variables have been measured.

Clearly, truly dynamic predictors (assessed prerelease) that undergo later unobserved changes during the follow-up period would be expected to lose their predictive ability. By definition, this cannot happen to truly static, historical predictors. Changes in dynamic variables that *are* observed during the follow-up do not compete with measures (static or "dynamic") obtained entirely before release. The two prediction issues are not commensurate—one relevant to release decisions and long-term supervision; and the other to short-term adjustments in disposition and supervision. Whether the associations between violence and changes in dynamic variables (observed during follow-up) vary as a function of long-term, static risk level is unknown. Some postrelease changes in the offender or environment must influence reoffending—behavior has contemporaneous causes and offenders' recidivistic behavior shows day-to-day variability—but research on the interplay between these domains is just beginning. It is unknown, for example, how well prerelease, static, historical variables alone predict postrelease circumstances: Are psychopaths most likely to select antisocial peers and procriminal environments after release? If prerelease measures of psychopathy strongly predicted postrelease context, postrelease context (and changes in context), though related to recidivism, might not make an incremental contribution to the prediction of recidivism after the effects of psychopathy had been included.

What of the role of treatment completion as a possible variable in the prediction of violent recidivism among sex offenders? The reduction in risk that may be accomplished by sex offender treatment is of particular relevance. Unfortunately, when tested incrementally, existing treatments (or progress in treatment) have not been shown to lower the risk of recidivism (Barbaree et al., 2001; Quinsey, Khanna & Malcolm, 1998; Seto & Barbaree, 1999). The most parsimonious explanation is that the effects of treatment completion are subsumed by other prerelease, static variables (e.g., offense history, antisocial personality/psychopathy): The most antisocial offenders are both more likely to recidivate and less likely to complete treatment.

It is expected that the discovery of truly effective treatments will eventually destroy or weaken the predictive accuracies achieved by the static, historical variables already identified. It is to be expected that knowledge of sex offenders' PCL-R scores, offense histories, childhood conduct, and so on will not be sufficient to achieve the best accuracies shown in TABLES 1 and 2; it will also be necessary to know about changes in risk-related variables induced by treatment. There exist no convincing data, for adult sex offenders, that such an effective treatment has yet been identified (Rice & Harris, 2002, 2003 [this volume]; Rice, Harris & Quinsey, 2001).

PREDICTION VERSUS MANAGEMENT

What is the role of long-term risk assessment (based on static, historical pre-release variables) in clinical practice, especially intervention, with sex offenders? Let us examine this question in some detail. It is clear that long-term risk (based on static historical variables) is relevant to many criminal justice interventions—suitability for bail, custodial versus community disposition, sentence length, the applicability of preventive detention statutes, and appropriateness for early conditional release. Clearly, such issues form an important part of the practice of some forensic clinicians, but what of intervention more usually thought of as clinical?

For many clinicians, ongoing therapeutic management with sex offenders is the crucial task. In the absence of effective specific treatments (or treatments that can be assumed to be effective), clinicians' only hope of affecting recidivism lies in day-to-day monitoring of sex offenders and the adjustment of clinical services and supervision conditions in response to fluctuations in those measures related to the likelihood that an offense is in the offing. Some preliminary research has identified a few measures that appear promising in this task (Quinsey et al., 1997; Hanson & Harris, 2000). Nevertheless, the task cannot begin without some way to determine which sex offenders will be candidates for ongoing supervision, and cannot proceed without some means to determine, for each candidate, how intensive supervision shall be.

In our view, the first task—that of determining which sex offenders are candidates for ongoing supervision—clearly depends on long-term, static risk assessment. The available evidence indicates that subjecting very low-risk offenders to such a regime could only alter risk by increasing the likelihood of recidivism (Andrews et al., 1990). Simultaneously, there are sex offenders whose risk of recidivism is so great that, if the option is available, incapacitation through indefinite incarceration is the only responsible course of action, and community management should not be considered. It is a nonscientific question of values where this level of intolerable risk is, but wherever the threshold is set, there will be some sex offenders who exceed it. Throughout this paragraph the term "risk" can only mean long-term risk of violent recidivism as assessed by static variables because it would be impossible to make such decisions based on fluctuating characteristics.

In our opinion, the second task pertaining to adjusting the intensity of supervision for an individual sex offender must partly depend on long-term risk. Certainly, adjustments in intensity of supervision would depend on fluctuations in dynamic risk indicators, but we advise that this occur within limits set by long-term static, historical risk assessment. Thus, sex offenders under community supervision at the high end of a long-term risk scale would have to demonstrate longer periods of greater stability and compliance (and perhaps higher levels of achievement in programs) before supervision conditions would be relaxed (compared to sex offenders from the low end of the risk scale). Similarly, clinicians' "tolerance" for noncompliance, supervision failures, or clinical regress would (at least partly) be inversely associated with long-term, static, historical risk. Finally, long-term, static risk would presumably set limits on how far supervision would ever be relaxed—for example, actuarially high-risk sex offenders, no matter how compliant, would never be permitted to receive unannounced supervision visits less often than, say, monthly. It seems to us, therefore, inescapable that clinical intervention with sex offenders must strongly depend on long-term risk indexed by static, historical variables (cf., Heilbrun, 1997). As well, it is clearly this long-term sense of risk that Andrews and colleagues (1990) propounded as the first of their three fundamental principles of effective correctional practice.

CONCLUSIONS

The use of actuarial methods for the prediction of violent recidivism among sex offenders routinely achieves ROC areas in the range from 0.74 to 0.79 with heterogeneous groups of sex offenders followed for highly variable lengths of opportunity. This is especially true when the actuarial instruments are employed without modification or deletion of items. Some previous studies have reported ROC areas as high as 0.88 (Dempster, Hart & Boer, 2001). The available data suggest that the use of fixed and constant follow-up leads to higher ROC areas and that higher ROC areas are also obtained if enough accurate historical information were gathered on each subject to permit the scoring of every actuarial item. Finally, ROC areas are maximized when the scoring of items and scales can be performed with high reliability. If all these conditions are met, the accuracy of comprehensive actuarial instruments based on static, historical variables appears to approach or even exceed 0.90 (expressed as ROC area) for violent recidivism among sex offenders. Given the error inherent in the measurement of the outcome for recidivism studies, these analyses imply that there is no additional outcome variance available to be captured by such dynamic factors as moods, attitudes, insight, motivation, and so on.

Such constructs might be of value in anticipating the timing of a reoffense, but the available data indicate that measuring such constructs is unnecessary for anticipating who will recidivate within a given time period (spanning more than a few months). Stated another way, whatever the role of evolutionary history, internal conditions (attitudes, moods, insight, neurological anomalies), and other aspects of the situation (intoxication, antisocial peers, bad neighborhoods) in causing violent crime, very accurate statements about the likelihood of another violent offense can be based on thorough knowledge of individuals' lifetime conduct.

Although we expect that effective treatments will eventually be demonstrated, the most parsimonious account of the available data on the prediction of recidivism is that no studies of sex offender recidivism yet published have included treatments with substantial ability to lower recidivism. When effective therapies are found, prediction based only on pretreatment, static, historical variables will be insufficient for accurate risk assessment; knowledge of treatment progress will also be necessary. With or without demonstrably effective treatments, management of sex offenders in the community requires clinicians to attend to changes in dynamic risk factors hypothesized to predict recidivism, but such clinical practice cannot proceed without consideration of long-term risk (indicated by static, historical factors).

Finally, although this chapter addresses very practical questions concerning the most accurate ways to assess risk among sex offenders, the findings have theoretical implications. Alhough sexually aggressive criminal behavior is potentially modifiable with therapy based on the principles of social learning theory, it is clear that there has been no adequate demonstration of such modification. Continued failures along these lines might weaken support for standard social learning accounts of sexual aggression. Similarly, the expression of sexually aggressive behavior is certainly influenced by the social environment, but, in our view, the best available evidence suggests that most sexual deviance and paraphilia is caused by very early biomedical events leading to neurodevelopmental disruption (Lalumière, Harris, Rice & Quinsey, 1997, in press; Quinsey, 2003, this volume).

Similarly, the preponderance of scientific evidence supports the idea that the majority of variance in violent criminal conduct (including sexual aggression) can be attributed to genetically and physiologically based enduring traits that, once initiated, exhibit life-long persistence under conditions so far observed (Harris, Skilling & Rice, 2001). This set of enduring characteristics is often manifest in aggressive and criminal behavior, the expression of selfish and procriminal attitudes, attraction to risky and antisocial circumstances, and a superficial, insensitive, and dishonest approach to oneself and others. These psychological characteristics are, however, best understood as the result, not the cause, of this phenomenon of life-course persistent antisociality. The available evidence implies that the therapies most clinicians are presently trained to deliver cannot make enduring changes in the outcome of this persistent antisociality under conditions currently typical of the institutional or community supervision of sex offenders. Until treatment efficacy is demonstrated, the best that clinicians can do is to carefully assess risk and manage offenders accordingly, while continuing the search for effective interventions.

REFERENCES

ANDREWS, D.A., ZINGER, I., HOGE, R.D., BONTA, J., GENDREAU, P. & CULLEN, F.T. (1990). Does correctional treatment work? A clinically relevant and psychologically informed meta-analysis. *Criminology, 28,* 369–404.

BARBAREE, H.E., SETO, M.C., LANGTON, C.M. & PEACOCK, E.J. (2001). Evaluating the predictive accuracy of six risk assessment instruments for adult sex offenders. *Criminal Justice and Behavior, 28,* 490–521.

BEECH, A., FRIENDSHIP, C., ERIKSON, M. & HANSON, R.K. (2002). The relationship between static and dynamic risk factors and reconviction in a sample of U.K. child abusers. *Sexual Abuse: A Journal of Research and Treatment, 14,* 155–167.

BOER, D.P., HART, S.D., KROPP, P.R. & WEBSTER, C.D. (1998). *Manual for the Sexual Violence Risk - 20 Professional Guidelines for Assessing Risk of Sexual Violence.* A joint publication of The British Columbia Institute Against Family Violence and the Mental Health, Law, and Policy Institute.

DEMPSTER, R.J., HART, S.D. & BOER, D.P. (2001). *Prediction of sexually violent recidivism: A comparison of risk assessment instruments.* Manuscript in preparation.

DUCRO, C., CLAIX, A. & PHAM, T.H. (2002, September). *Assessment of the Static-99 in a Belgian sex offenders forensic population.* Presented at the European Conference on Psychology and Law, Leuven, Belgium.

EPPERSON, D.L., KAUL, J.D. & HESSELTON, D. (1998). *Final report on the development of the Minnesota Sex Offender Screening Tool (MnSOST).* Paper presented at the Annual Conference of the Association for the Treatment of Sexual Abusers. Vancouver, BC.

GRANN, M., BELFRAGE, H. & TENGSTROM, A. (2000). Actuarial assessment of risk for violence: Predictive validity of the VRAG and historical part of the HCR-20. *Criminal Justice and Behavior, 27,* 97–114.

HANSON, K. (1997). *The development of a brief actuarial risk scale for sexual offense recidivism.* Anonymous. Ottawa: Department of the Solicitor General.

HANSON, R.K. & BUSSIÈRE, M.T. (1998). Predicting relapse: A meta-analysis of sexual offender recidivism studies. *Journal of Consulting and Clinical Psychology, 66,* 348–362.

HANSON, R.K. & HARRIS, A.J.R. (2000). Where should we intervene: Dynamic predictors of sexual assault recidivism. *Criminal Justice and Behavior, 27,* 6–35.

HANSON, R.K. & THORNTON, D. (2000). Improving risk assessments for sex offenders: A comparison of three actuarial scales. *Law and Human Behavior, 24,* 119–136.

HARRIS, G.T., RICE, M.E. & CORMIER, C.A. (2002). Prospective replication of the Violence Risk Appraisal Guide in predicting violent recidivism among forensic patients. *Law and Human Behavior, 26,* 377–395.

HARRIS, G.T., RICE, M.E. & QUINSEY, V.L. (1993). Violent recidivism of mentally disordered offenders: The development of a statistical prediction instrument. *Criminal Justice and Behavior, 20,* 315–335.

HARRIS, G.T., RICE, M.E., QUINSEY, V.L., LALUMIÈRE, M.L., BOER, D. & LANG, C. (in press). A multi-site comparison of actuarial risk instruments for sex offenders. *Psychological Assessment.*

HARRIS, G.T., SKILLING, T.A. & RICE, M.E. (2001). The construct of psychopathy. In M. Tonry & N. Morris (Eds.), *Crime and Justice: An annual review of research* (pp. 197–264). Chicago: University of Chicago Press.

HEILBRUN, K. (1997). Prediction versus management models relevant to risk assessment. *Law and Human Behavior, 21,* 347–359.

HUDSON, S.M., WALES, D.S., BAKKER, L. & WARD, T. (2002). Dynamic risk factors: The Kia Marama evaluation. *Sexual Abuse: A Journal of Research and Treatment, 14,* 103–119.

KROPP, R. (2002, May). *The RSVP.* Invited symposium at the Annual Convention of the Canadian Psychological Association, University of British Columbia, Vancouver.

LALUMIÈRE, M.L., HARRIS, G.T., RICE, M.E. & QUINSEY, V.L. (in press). *The nature of rape.* Washington, DC: American Psychological Association.

MCGRAW, K.O. & WONG, S.P. (1992). A common language effect size statistic. *Psychological Bulletin, 111,* 361–365.

MONAHAN, J., STEADMAN, H.J., SILVER, E., APPELBAUM, P.S., CLARK ROBBINS, P., MULVEY, E.P., et al. (2001). *Rethinking risk assessment: The MacArthur study of mental disorder and violence.* New York: Oxford University Press.

QUINSEY, V.L. (1984). Sexual aggression: Studies of offenders against women. In D. Weisstub (Ed.), *Law and mental health: International perspectives* (pp. 84–121). New York: Pergamon Press.

QUINSEY, V.L. (1986). Men who have sex with children. In D.N. Weisstub (Ed.), *Law and mental health: International perspectives* (pp. 140–172). New York: Pergamon Press.

QUINSEY, V.L., COLEMAN, G., JONES, B. & ALTROWS, I. (1997). Proximal antecedents of eloping and reoffending among mentally disordered offenders. *Journal of Interpersonal Violence, 12,* 794–813.

QUINSEY, V.L., HARRIS, G.T., RICE, M.E. & CORMIER, C.A. (1998). *Violent offenders: Appraising and managing risk.* Washington, DC: American Psychological Association.

QUINSEY, V. L., KHANNA, A. & MALCOLM, P. B. (1998). A retrospective evaluation of the regional treatment centre sex offender treatment program. *Journal of Interpersonal Violence, 13,* 621–644.

RICE, M.E. & HARRIS, G.T. (1995). Violent recidivism: Assessing predictive validity. *Journal of Consulting and Clinical Psychology, 63,* 737–748.

RICE, M.E. & HARRIS, G.T. (1997). Cross-validation and extension of violence risk appraisal guide for child molesters and rapists. *Law and Human Behavior, 21,* 231–241.

RICE, M.E. & HARRIS, G.T. (2002). Sexual aggressors: Scientific status. In D.L. Faigman, D.H. Kaye, M.J. Saks and J. Sanders (Eds.), *Modern scientific evidence: The law and science of expert testimony Vol 1.* (2nd ed., pp. 471–504). St. Paul, MN: West.

RICE, M.E., HARRIS, G.T. & QUINSEY, V.L. (2001). Treating the adult sex offender. In J.B. Ashford, B.D. Sales, & W. Reid (Eds.), *Treating offenders with special needs* (pp. 291–312). Washington, DC: American Psychological Association.

SETO, M.C. & BARBAREE, H.E. (1999). Psychopathy, treatment behavior and sex offender recidivism. *Journal of Interpersonal Violence, 14,* 1235–1248.

SJÖSTEDT, G. & LANGSTRÖM, N. (2002). Assessment of risk for criminal recidivism among rapists: A comparison of four different measures. *Psychology, Crime and Law, 8,* 25–40.

SWETS, J.A., DAWES, R.M. & MONAHAN, J. (2000). Psychological science can improve diagnostic decisions. *Psychological Science in the Public Interest: A Journal of the American Psychological Society, 1,* 1–26.

TENGSTROM, A. (2001). Long-term predictive validity of historical factors in two risk assessment instruments in a group of violent offenders with schizophrenia. *Nordic Journal of Psychiatry, 55,* 243–249.

THORNTON, D. (2002). Constructing and testing a framework for dynamic risk assessment. *Sexual Abuse: A Journal of Research and Treatment, 14,* 139–153.

Are Rapists Differentially Aroused by Coercive Sex in Phallometric Assessments?

MARTIN L. LALUMIÈRE,^{a} VERNON L. QUINSEY,^{b} GRANT T. HARRIS,^{c}
MARNIE E. RICE,^{c} AND CAROLINE TRAUTRIMAS^d

^{a}Centre for Addiction and Mental Health, Toronto, Ontario, Canada, M6J 1H4

^{b}Queen's University, Kingston, Ontario, Canada K7L 3N6

^{c}Mental Health Centre Penetanguishene, Penetanguishene, Ontario, Canada, L9M 1G3

^{d}York University, Toronto, Ontario, Canada, M3J 1P3

ABSTRACT: In this chapter we examine whether rapists are sexually aroused by coercive, nonconsensual sex. This question is theoretically important because it speaks to a potential sexual motivation underlying rape. It is also clinically important in that it may reveal an important assessment and treatment target. We first revisit and update quantitative reviews of studies that examined the phallometric responses of rapists and other men. We then present new data on the discriminative and diagnostic validity of a phallometric test for rapists. Finally, we discuss methodological and conceptual issues in phallometric assessment and the nature of rapists' sexual interests.

KEYWORDS: coercive sex; phallometric assessments; non–sex offenders; biastophilia; sadism

INTRODUCTION

Explanations of rape should be consistent with what is known about individual differences in men's propensity to commit sexually coercive acts, as well as with other empirical findings about rape, but sometimes the findings appear unclear. In this article we attempt to clarify what is known about individual differences in men's sexual arousal to coercive sex and whether these differences are related to the propensity to commit rape.

A common method to assess men's sexual arousal to coercive sex is to measure changes in erectile responses (phallometry) during the presentation of different types of sexual stimuli—most often recorded narratives depicting coercive and noncoercive sexual interactions. By manipulating characteristics of the stimuli, penile responses of men known to have committed rape can be compared to the responses of men who are not known to have committed sexually coercive acts. If there is a rela-

Address for correspondence: M.L. Lalumière, Law and Mental Health Program, Centre for Addiction and Mental Health, Unit 3 (4th Floor), 1001 Queen Street West, Toronto, Ontario, Canada, M6J 1H4. Voice: 416-535-8501 ext. 2969; fax: 416-583-4327.

Martin_Lalumiere@camh.net.

Ann. N.Y. Acad. Sci. 989: 211–224 (2003). © 2003 New York Academy of Sciences.

tionship between men's responses to sexually coercive and noncoercive material and their propensity to commit rape, the most straightforward expectation is that rapists will show greater relative arousal to sexually coercive material than other men. There are other ways to assess the link between interest in coercive sex and propensity for sexually coercive acts (e.g., Malamuth, 1981). In this chapter, however, we focus principally on the ability of current phallometric procedures to detect differences between rapists and other men, and whether these differences have explanatory and clinical utility.

Many authors have addressed this general question and have arrived at contradictory conclusions. The failure to arrive at a valid, agreed-upon conclusion has limited our progress in understanding the causes of rape, and in particular the sexual motivations for rape. In the following, we briefly revisit the phallometric literature and then provide new data on the discriminative and diagnostic value of a phallometric test for rapists. We then discuss some methodological and conceptual issues associated with the phallometric assessment of rapists, and identify important research needs.

PREVIOUS REVIEWS OF PHALLOMETRIC STUDIES

Narrative reviews of studies comparing rapists with other men have led to conflicting conclusions (e.g. Launay, 1999; Marshall & Fernandez, 2000). Quantitative review methods are sometimes able to resolve issues that narrative reviews cannot because of their greater statistical power and superior ability to deal with sampling error and methodological variations among studies. One can conceive of quantitative reviews, or meta-analyses, as reviews in which all studies are jointly analyzed with special statistical techniques. The superiority of quantitative reviews over narrative or qualitative reviews in producing valid and consistent conclusions is reminiscent of the superiority of actuarial methods over clinical or intuitive judgment in many spheres of life. Two quantitative reviews, using somewhat different methods, of phallometric studies of rapists appeared in the early 1990s. Both meta-analyses yielded very similar results.

Hall, Shondrick, and Hirschman (1993) examined nine published studies that compared officially detected or self-identified rapists with other men, either nonoffenders or other sex offenders. Lalumière and Quinsey (1994) examined 16 published and unpublished studies (one study produced two findings) that compared officially detected rapists with non–sex offenders (either other offenders or men recruited from the general community). The *rape index,* a ratio of responses to stimuli depicting rape to responses to stimuli depicting consenting sex, was a dependent variable in both meta-analyses. The size of the group difference on the rape index for each study was captured by Cohen's effect size d, the difference between the means of the two groups divided by the pooled standard deviation.

The overall average d was 0.71 in Hall et al. and 0.82 in Lalumière and Quinsey (after deleting one positive outlier). These are generally considered medium to large effect sizes (Cohen, 1992). These results indicate that rapists, on average, responded relatively much more to scenarios describing a man raping a woman than did other men. Note that the rape index is a relative measure; the difference between rapists

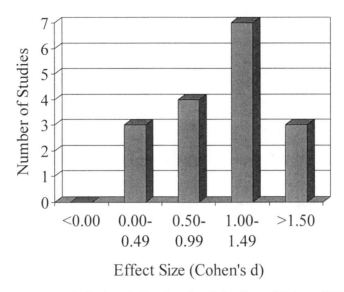

FIGURE 1. Distribution of effect sizes from Lalumière and Quinsey (1994).

and other men occurred even though rapists did not always prefer rape to consensual stimuli. FIGURE 1 shows the distribution of individual study effect sizes from Lalumière and Quinsey.

FIGURE 1 reveals that all studies produced a positive effect size—rapists always had a higher rape index than the comparison group. Because it is very unlikely that chance factors could have produced such a distribution of effect sizes (binomial test $P < .00001$), it is incontestable that rapists differed from nonrapists in their responses to sexually coercive stimuli (relative to consensual stimuli) in the laboratory studies reviewed. One reason why some narrative reviews failed to reach conclusions consistent with such clear data is that some individual studies did not reach statistical significance. These studies either had a small sample size, produced a small group difference, or both.

FIGURE 1 also shows a wide variation in effect sizes. Both meta-analyses revealed that some study characteristics significantly increased, and others decreased, the size of the group difference. For example, studies using more brutal and graphic rape scenarios produced larger effect sizes. Also, studies comparing rapists to other sex offenders produced smaller effect sizes, probably because some of these comparison sex offenders were, in fact, also rapists or because many sex offenders have multiple paraphilic interests (Abel & Rouleau, 1990).

NEWER PHALLOMETRIC STUDIES COMPARING RAPISTS AND NON–SEX OFFENDERS

A few studies have been published since 1994. Eccles, Marshall, and Barbaree (1994) published new data from subjects already included in Lalumière and Quinsey's (1994) meta-analysis using new stimuli and reported no difference between 19 rapists and 19 community men. Howes (1998) assessed 40 rapists and 50 non–sex offenders using stimuli presented in the form of slides, audiotapes, and videotapes. Rapists had significantly larger responses to rape stimuli than controls. Unfortunately, rape index effect sizes cannot be computed for these two studies from the information presented in the papers.

Three studies produced data that could be converted into a rape index effect size. Rice, Chaplin, Harris, and Coutts (1994) assessed 14 rapists and 14 nonrapists (10 men from the community and 4 men from the same institution as the rapists). A preliminary version of this study (the positive outlier) was included in Lalumière and Quinsey's (1994) meta-analysis but included fewer subjects. The effect size, based on the rape index calculated as a difference score, was $d = 5.51$. Seto and Barbaree (1993) compared the rape indices of 18 rapists and 18 men recruited from the community and obtained the first and only negative effect size in this literature, $d = -0.46$. Seto and Kuban (1996) assessed 21 rapists and 20 men recruited from the community and obtained a positive effect size, $d = 0.51$ to 0.85, depending on the type of stimuli used.

In sum, three of the five "new" studies showed greater responding to coercive sex by rapists compared to non–sex offenders, one showed no difference, and one showed greater responding among non–sex offenders. These results do not change the general conclusion that rapists tend to be much more aroused by scenarios describing coercive sex, relative to scenarios describing consensual sex, than men who are not known to have committed sex offenses. Some studies produced small differences, but all but one obtained differences in the same direction.

The study by Rice et al. (1994) produced the largest effect size. On the basis of the meta-analyses of moderator variables and results from other studies (e.g., Harris, Rice, Quinsey, Chaplin & Earls, 1992; Proulx, Aubut, McKibben & Côté, 1994; Quinsey, Chaplin & Upfold, 1984), we can identify probable reasons for this large effect. Rice et al. used extremely violent and graphic stimuli, used a large number of stimuli per category, and used scoring methods that maximize discriminative validity.

STUDIES OF SELF-IDENTIFIED RAPISTS

Phallometric procedures can detect sexual arousal to coercive sex in adjudicated rapists. Could such procedures detect similar patterns among men who report being rapists? In other words, do self-identified rapists differ sexually from men who do not report having been sexually coercive? A small number of studies suggest that they do. In these studies, large groups of men, (usually college undergraduates), filled out questionnaires about sexual behavior, and a proportion were invited to participate in a phallometric study. Some men reported they had been sexually coercive and some reported they had not. Most of the sexually coercive men reported engaging in coercive behavior that would not meet most legal definitions of rape.

Malamuth (1986) found that a rape index was the strongest correlate (among a large number of variables) of self-reported sexual coercion. Bernat, Calhoun, and Adams (1999) and Lohr, Adams, and Davis (1997) found that sexually coercive men were more aroused to rape scenarios than noncoercive men. Lalumière and Quinsey (1996), however, found no difference between coercive and noncoercive men.

Another way to look at this question is to study men who report an interest in rape or report that they often fantasize about it. Malamuth (1981) and Malamuth and Check (1983) found that men who said they might engage in rape if there were no adverse consequences to themselves showed higher arousal to rape scenarios than men who denied any such tendencies. Seto and Kuban (1996) examined the responses of eight men who admitted to sadistic sexual fantasies but who denied acting on these fantasies. These men produced a rape index that was not only higher than community controls, but also higher than men who had actually committed rape but who denied such fantasies. Altogether, these findings are consistent with the expectation that individual differences in men's propensity to rape (or sexual coercion) are associated with sexual arousal to depictions of such activities.

THE NATURE OF THE COMPARISON GROUP

Many studies of adjudicated rapists used a comparison group of young university students, some of young men recruited from the community, and very few of non–sex offenders recruited from the same institution as the rapists. Sometimes control subjects have been asked about previous sexual coercion, but often are not. In general, the nature of the control group has had little impact on the ability to detect group differences between rapists and comparison subjects. One comparison group not yet examined, however, are men who have been aggressive towards women but in nonsexual ways.

In the following section we present results from a new study of adjudicated rapists using two comparison groups—one of men recruited from the community who denied sexual coercion, and another of men from the same institution as the rapists who had committed at least one violent crime against a women, but who had not—based on official records and their self-report—been sexually coercive.

A NEW STUDY

Participants

Participants were 24 heterosexual men who had been charged with a sexual assault (or with a more serious offense, like murder, with a sexual nature) involving an adult woman, 11 heterosexual offenders who had been nonsexually assaultive against at least one woman (ranging from simple assault to murder), and 19 men from the local community. Rapists were recruited from the Sexual Behavior Laboratory of the Mental Health Centre Penetanguishene, a maximum-security psychiatric hospital in Ontario. Most rapists were assessed and then transferred to another institution (either another hospital or a prison). Nonsexual assaulters were recruited from among inpatients at the same institution. Community men were recruited through advertisements in newspapers and employment agencies. Comparison subjects were paid for their participation.

All 54 men were self-declared heterosexual on the Kinsey scale, and all produced phallometric responses that were readily interpretable (i.e., they produced an average response to the neutral stimulus category that was lower than the average response to at least one other category). Assaulters had no record of sexual assault and, like the community men, did not report having engaged in sexually coercive behavior on the Sexual Experiences Survey (Koss & Oros, 1982) or on another brief self-report questionnaire of coercive sexual behavior (available from the first author).

Four other men participated in the study but were excluded from the analyses for one of three reasons. One assaulter admitted having been sexually coercive toward a woman, two rapists reported a homosexual gender orientation, and one assaulter did not produce an interpretable phallometric profile. Of note, there was no minimum absolute penile response criterion in this study.

Rapists were on average 36 years old (SD = 11.1), 26% had been married or had lived in a common-law relationship, and 35% had completed high school. Assaulters were on average 37 years old (SD = 9.8), 9% had been married or had lived in a common-law relationship, and 27% had completed high school. Community men were on average 26 years old (SD = 5.8), 28% had been married or lived in a common-law relationship, and 90% had completed high school.

Apparatus

Participants were seated in a reclining chair located in a sound-attenuated and electrically shielded room equipped with a one-way mirror and intercom. Skin resistance was measured but not scored. Penile responses were measured using a mercury-in-rubber strain gauge that the participants fitted on the midsection of their penises. The leads from the gauge were connected to a Parks Electronic Model 270 Plethysmograph. Penile responses were recorded continuously for 120 seconds, starting at 2 seconds after the onset of each narrative, and stored on a computer. The narratives were presented via a tape recorder through headphones. All recording equipment was located outside of the participants' room. A wood panel with two buttons was laid across the participants' chair during the testing session.

Stimuli

Participants listened to 14 audiotaped narratives while their penile responses were recorded. The narratives were taken from Rice et al. (1994), who used a larger set of 32 narratives. We selected, from these 32 narratives, two neutral social interactions, four consenting sexual interactions, four nonconsenting violent sexual interactions in which the rape victim was described as experiencing intense pain and suffering, and four nonsexual but violent interactions in which a woman was physically beaten by a man. Half of the narratives were described from the female point of view in her voice, and half from the male point of view in his voice. The same male and female voices were heard in all the stories, and the tone of the voices was neutral. Two additional narratives (one neutral, one consenting) were presented before the test session as warm-ups to familiarize the participants to the procedure. All narratives contained approximately 200 words and lasted about 90 seconds. Details of the structure and format of the stories can be found in Rice et al. (1994).

Procedure

Upon arrival at the laboratory, participants received an explanation of the procedure and were asked to install the gauge in private. Participants were instructed to listen carefully to each story and to respond as if they were alone at home. They were also asked to press the left button on the wood panel lying across their chair when they heard sexual material, and the right button when they heard violent material, and both when they heard sexually violent material. This was done to ensure that participants attended to the content of the stimuli. This semantic-tracking task has been shown to limit attempts at voluntary control of the penile response (e.g., Harris, Rice, Chaplin & Quinsey, 1999; Proulx, Côté & Achille, 1993; Quinsey & Chaplin, 1988). The ability of participants to complete this task was monitored during the presentation of the warm-up stimuli, and feedback was given. Each narrative was presented a minimum of 30 seconds after the end of the prior narrative (i.e., at the end of the recording interval for the prior narrative), and after they had returned to baseline circumferential level. The test session lasted approximately one hour.

Treatment of the Data

The peak response occurring during the recording interval (120 seconds) minus the baseline was calculated for each trial, and then peak scores were transformed into z-scores for each participant. Thus, each participant had an average peak response (for the whole session) of zero with a standard deviation of one. An average response was then calculated for each of the following seven stimulus categories: neutral, consenting female point of view, consenting male point of view, rape female point of view, rape male point of view, nonsexual violence female point of view, and nonsexual violence male point of view. A rape index was then calculated by subtracting the average response to both consenting categories from the average response to both rape categories. A positive rape index indicates a higher response to rape stimuli.[a]

Results and Discussion

Examination of Response Profiles

FIGURE 2 shows the average responses of the three groups to the seven stimulus categories. Despite differences in age, education, marital status, and offender status, the two comparison groups showed very similar profiles; they both responded more to consenting scenarios (especially when described from the female point of view) than to any other categories. Rapists responded similarly to both rape categories and to consenting scenarios described from the female point of view, and less to consenting scenarios described from the male point of view. Average responses to nonsexual violence were low for all three groups and similar to responses to neutral scenarios.

---

[a]Rape index = mean (rape female point of view, rape male point of view) minus mean (consenting female point of view, consenting male point of view). We also calculated a rape index based on maximum category scores (replace mean by maximum in the formula) and observed nearly identical results. Rape indices calculated as difference scores produce slightly greater group discrimination than those calculated as ratio scores (Harris et al., 1992).

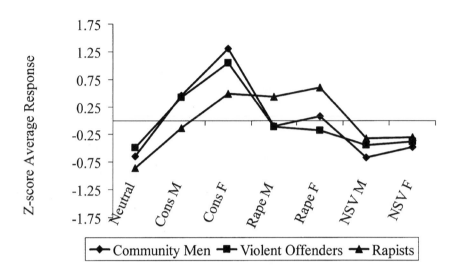

FIGURE 2. Phallometric profiles of rapists and two comparison groups.

In sum, comparison participants showed a preference for consenting scenarios, whereas rapists showed little discrimination between rape and consenting scenarios, and perhaps a slight preference for rape. The profiles shown in FIGURE 2 are very similar to the profiles reported in Rice et al. (1994). Very similar phallometric and recruiting procedures were used in both studies.

Rape Index

FIGURE 3 shows the group-average rape index, the statistic of most interest. The two comparison groups produced nearly identical and negative rape indices. Rapists produced much higher and positive rape indices. There was no overlap between the 95% confidence intervals of rapists and each of the two comparison groups. Consistent with the response profiles shown in FIGURE 2, rapists, as a group, almost showed a statistically significant absolute preference for rape stimuli over consenting stimuli (the lower bound of the confidence interval was –0.04), whereas nonrapists showed a clear average absolute preference for consenting stimuli.

Cohen's effect size for rapists versus community men was $d = 1.36$, and versus assaulters was $d = 1.50$. These values are large and higher than the average values reported in the meta-analyses, but are lower than the effect size obtained in the original study of Rice et al. (1994). One difference between the current study and Rice et al. is that the present study used a smaller number of rape scenarios; number of stimuli per category was identified in Lalumière and Quinsey's (1994) meta-analysis as a significant moderator of effect sizes (smaller number = smaller effect size).

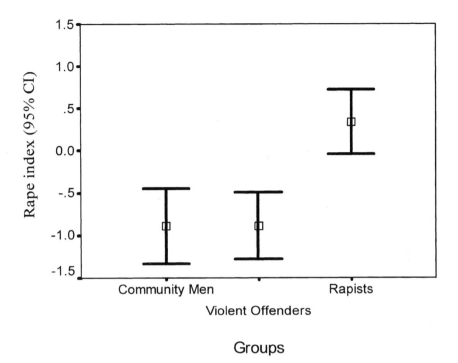

FIGURE 3. Average rape index for rapists and two comparison groups.

Sensitivity and Specificity

Let us assume for this analysis that all rapists prefer rape to consenting sex, and that all nonrapists prefer consenting sex to rape. If the phallometric test in this study is valid, most rapists would show a rape index greater than zero, and most nonrapists would show a rape index smaller than zero under that assumption. How well can the methods used in this study correctly detect the sexual preference for rape among rapists (sensitivity), and the absence of such a preference among nonrapists (specificity)?

The performance of the rape index as a diagnostic tool under the assumption that group membership is the same as sexual preference status is shown in FIGURE 4, a plot of the rape index's sensitivity as a function of all possible levels of specificity (the receiver operator characteristic or ROC). This ROC indicates a large effect size, with an area under the curve of 0.85 (0.50 represents chance level, 1.00 represents perfect accuracy). Sixty-three percent of rapists and 13% of nonrapists had a rape index larger than zero; thus, sensitivity of the rape index at zero was 0.63, and specificity was $1.0–0.13 = 0.87$ (0.84 and 0.91 based on community men and assaulters, respectively). These values are similar to the values obtained by Lalumière and Quinsey (1993) in their analysis of sensitivities and specificities of rape indices equal to one (because they used a ratio score rather than a difference score) in 14 data sets (13 studies). Studies using violent and graphic rape scenarios had moderate specificity and high sensitivity.

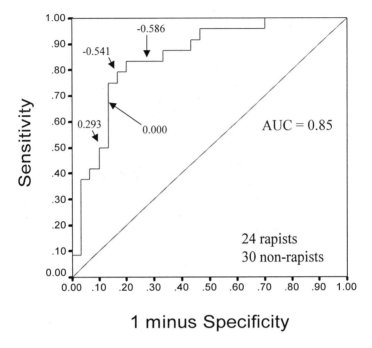

FIGURE 4. Receiver operating characteristic of the rape index (inset values are rape index cut-offs).

Of course, most scholars would argue that some men commit rape for reasons other than a sexual preference for rape, some have such a preference without acting on it, and some engage in sexually coercive acts without getting caught or admitting it. For these reasons, no one would expect perfect between-group discrimination by phallometry. Unfortunately, there are no empirical data that would permit correcting obtained sensitivities and specificities for these sources of contamination. The discrimination obtained here can be considered a minimum.

THE 60/90 BENCHMARK

Many laboratories assessing rapists have reported that about 60% of rapists show rape indices that are larger than the rape indices of about 90% of nonrapists. It turns out that the cut-point that produces these numbers is a score that determines preference (i.e., a rape index greater than zero when using a difference score, or one when using a ratio score; see Lalumière & Quinsey, 1993, for an early review). Clinicians who operate phallometric laboratories and who obtain results that deviate substantially from this 60/90 benchmark (especially in the direction of lower sensitivity and specificity) must determine how their procedures or the offenders they assess differ from the procedures or samples used in validation studies.

There are several procedures that have been found to maximize discriminative validity in phallometric assessment (see Harris et al., 1992), and others that have not been formally studied but that are used regularly in validation studies. These include methods to prevent or inhibit faking (semantic-tracking task), the stimulus media (audiotapes rather than videotapes or still pictures), the nature of rape scenarios (violent and graphic), the number of scenarios per category (preferably four or more), the use of a recording interval that exceeds the length of the scenario, baseline capture for each stimulus presentation (instead of determining a single baseline at the start of the session), the use of standard scores calculated within subjects (to eliminate between-subject differences in overall response magnitude and penis size), and the use of deviance indices to further capture relative responding.

Sample characteristics may also lead to variation in between-group discrimination, although much less is known in this regard. Despite suggestions that there exist valid rapist typologies and the standard—if not hackneyed—comment that rapists are heterogeneous, very little is known about whether there are identifiable and theoretically meaningful subgroups of rapists who have a sexual preference for rape and other subgroups that do not (for a step in that direction see Barbaree, Seto, Serin, Amos & Preston, 1994). In our recent work we found that rapists who score high on a measure of psychopathy (the Psychopathy Checklist-Revised) have higher than average rape indices (Harris, 1998; see also Firestone, Bradford, Greenberg & Serran, 2000). We might expect that rapists who have more victims (Abel, Becker, Blanchard & Djenderedjian, 1978) have inflicted greater injury to their victims (Quinsey & Chaplin, 1982), or who had committed their first rape at an earlier age would have higher rape indices, but little work has been done in this area. Among the rapists in the present study, rape index scores were positively related to Psychopathy Checklist-Revised scores (Spearman's rho = .23, n = 11), number of victims (.26, n = 18), but inversely to victim injury scores (−.24, n = 18). One might also expect that rapists assessed pretrial would yield less deviant results compared to rapists assessed posttrial (because pretrial assessees have greater incentives for dissimulation), and between naïve (first-time) versus experienced assessees (because deviance scores tend to decrease as a function of the number of assessments).

BIASTOPHILIA, SADISM, OR ANTISOCIALITY

One interesting question for future research is to distinguish among three theoretically distinct sexual arousal patterns as they apply to rapists' phallometric responses. The first hypothetically possible profile reflects *biastophilia*—sexual arousal to sexual activities involving a nonconsenting, struggling, resisting, but not necessarily injured or physically suffering, victim. The second possibility is *sadism*—sexual arousal to pain, suffering, and injury. In theory at least, sadism includes sexual arousal to the suffering experienced by someone who seeks pain (a masochist). The third possibility is simply general *antisociality*—indifference, including sexual indifference, to the interests, feelings, and desires of others.

The most consistent difference between consenting and rape scenarios in phallometric studies has to do with whether the "partner/victim" consents to sex (i.e., engages eagerly or forcefully says no and physically resists). The rape index is usually calculated by comparing all consenting scenarios on the one hand, and all rape scenarios on the other hand, regardless of other variations in content. The fact that good group discrimination is thereby achieved suggests that biastophilia is being detected. However, many phallometric studies of rapists and other men who have a proclivity to rape have shown that group discrimination is enhanced by the description of pain, injury, and humiliation by victims in rape scenarios. This suggests that sadism is being detected. Finally, the finding that psychopathy scores are positively related to phallometric rape indices suggests that rape also reflects a very general (not specifically sexual) indifference to the experience of the victim portrayed (Barbaree, Marshall & Lanthier, 1979; Quinsey & Chaplin, 1984). Further teasing apart of these theoretical possibilities might reveal some key motivational factors associated with rape.

CHALLENGES FOR RESEARCHERS

The study of phallometric assessment of rapists has gone on for decades, but many important questions are as yet unanswered. As discussed above, the theoretical distinctions among biastophilia, sadism, and antisociality (and their various possible combinations) represent important empirical questions. In addition to theoretical questions there are several procedural and clinical questions. What phallometric procedures, in addition to those already elucidated, maximize the detection of sexual arousal to rape among rapists? What is the best way to assess the reliability of phallometric responses in general, and of the rape index in particular, and how can we reconcile the fact that some assessments of reliability for phallometry are low yet at the same time indices of validity are high? How well should the rape index discriminate among different types of sex offenders, considering that different indices of sexual deviance correlate with one another (see Côté, Earls & Lalumière, 2002) and that many sex offenders are generalists? When the best methods are employed, how well do phallometric responses predict recidivism among rapists (e.g., Quinsey, Lalumière, Rice & Harris, 1995)? What are the behavioral and psychological correlates of the rape index and the sexual preference that it represents (e.g., Côté et al., 2002; Lalumière, Harris, Quinsey & Rice, 1998)? Are the sexual preferences associated with rape modifiable or at least manageable? Finally and crucially, how can the sexual preferences characteristic of adjudicated and self-identified rapists inform current theories of rape? Very few theories, if any, explicitly address the role of this important individual difference factor. Could it be that many theoreticians and clinicians are reluctant to consider the idea that many rapists do what they do because it is sexually arousing or gratifying?

ACKNOWLEDGMENTS

We are grateful to Ray Blanchard, Jessica Bristowe, Daniel Krupp, Michael Seto, and Scott Woodside for their comments on an earlier version of this paper; to Terry Chaplin, Garth Coleman, Tina Smith-Krans, and Michel Larose for their help with data collection; and to the Social Sciences and Humanities Research Council for financial support. The second author was partially supported by a Senior Research Fellowship from the Ontario Mental Health Foundation.

REFERENCES

ABEL, G.G., BECKER, D.H., BLANCHARD, E.B. & DJENDEREDJIAN, D.A. (1978). Differentiating sexual aggressives with penile measures. *Criminal Justice and Behavior, 5,* 315–332.

ABEL, G.G. & ROULEAU, J.L. (1990). The nature and extent of sexual assault. In W.L. Marshall, D. R. Laws & H. E. Barbaree (Eds.), *Handbook of sexual assault: Issues, theories, and treatment of the offender* (pp. 9–21). New York: Plenum Press.

BARBAREE, H.E., MARSHALL, W.L. & LANTHIER, R.D. (1979). Deviant sexual arousal in rapists. *Behaviour Research and Therapy, 17,* 215–222.

BARBAREE, H.E., SETO, M.C., SERIN, R.C., AMOS, N.L. & PRESTON, D.L. (1994). Comparisons between sexual and nonsexual rapist subtypes: Sexual arousal to rape, offense precursors, and offense characteristics. *Criminal Justice and Behavior, 21,* 95–114.

BERNAT, J.A., CALHOUN, K.S. & ADAMS, H.E. (1999). Sexually aggressive and nonaggressive men: Sexual arousal and judgments in response to acquaintance rape and consensual analogues. *Journal of Abnormal Psychology, 108,* 662–673.

COHEN, J. (1992). A power primer. *Psychological Bulletin, 112,* 155–159.

CÔTÉ, K., EARLS, C.M. & LALUMIÈRE, M.L. (2002). Birth order, birth interval, and deviant sexual preferences among sex offenders. *Sexual Abuse, 14,* 67–81.

ECCLES, A., MARSHALL, W.L. & BARBAREE, H.E. (1994). Differentiating rapists and nonoffenders using the rape index. *Behaviour Research and Therapy, 32,* 539–546.

FIRESTONE, P., BRADFORD, J.M., GREENBERG, D.M. & SERRAN, G.A. (2000). The relationship of deviant sexual arousal and psychopathy in incest offenders, extrafamilial child molesters, and rapists. *Journal of the American Academy of Psychiatry and the Law, 28,* 303–308.

HALL, G.C.N., SHONDRICK, D.D. & HIRSCHMAN, R. (1993). The role of sexual arousal in sexually aggressive behavior: A meta-analysis. *Journal of Consulting and Clinical Psychology, 61,* 1091–1095.

HARRIS, G.T. (1998, October). *Psychopathy and sexual deviance.* Paper presented at the 17th Annual Research and Treatment Conference of the Association for the Treatment of Sexual Abusers, Vancouver, BC, Canada.

HARRIS, G.T., RICE, M.E., CHAPLIN, T.C. & QUINSEY, V.L. (1999). Dissimulation in phallometric testing of rapists' sexual preferences. *Archives of Sexual Behavior, 28,* 223–232.

HARRIS, G.T., RICE, M.E., QUINSEY, V.L., CHAPLIN, T.C. & EARLS, C.M. (1992). Maximizing the discriminant validity of phallometric assessment. *Psychological Assessment, 4,* 502–511.

HOWES, R.J. (1998). Plethysmographic assessment of incarcerated nonsexual offenders: A comparison with rapists. *Sexual Abuse, 10,* 183–194.

KOSS, M.P. & OROS, C.J. (1982). Sexual Experiences Survey: A research instrument investigating sexual aggression and victimization. *Journal of Consulting and Clinical Psychology, 50,* 455–457.

LALUMIÈRE, M.L., HARRIS, G.T., QUINSEY, V.L. & RICE, M.E. (1998). Sexual deviance and number of older brothers among sexual offenders. *Sexual Abuse, 10,* 5–15.

LALUMIÈRE, M.L. & QUINSEY, V.L. (1993). The sensitivity of phallometric measures with rapists. *Annals of Sex Research, 6,* 123–138.

LALUMIÈRE, M.L. & QUINSEY, V.L. (1994). The discriminability of rapists from non-sex offenders using phallometric measures: A meta-analysis. *Criminal Justice and Behavior, 21,* 150–175.

LALUMIÈRE, M.L. & QUINSEY, V.L. (1996). Sexual deviance, antisociality, mating effort, and the use of sexually coercive behaviors. *Personality and Individual Differences, 21,* 33–48.

LAUNAY, G. (1999). The phallometric assessment of sex offenders: An update. *Criminal Behaviour and Mental Health, 9,* 254–274.

LOHR, B.A., ADAMS, H.E. & DAVIS, J.M. (1997). Sexual arousal to erotic and aggressive stimuli in sexually coercive and noncoercive men. *Journal of Abnormal Psychology, 106,* 230–242.

MALAMUTH, N.M. (1981). Rape proclivity among males. *Journal of Social Issues, 37,* 138–157.

MALAMUTH, N.M. (1986). Predictors of naturalistic sexual aggression. *Journal of Personality and Social Psychology, 50,* 953–962.

MALAMUTH, N.M. & CHECK, J.V. (1983). Sexual arousal to rape depictions: Individual differences. *Journal of Abnormal Psychology, 92,* 55–67.

MARSHALL, W.L. & FERNANDEZ, Y.M. (2000). Phallometric testing with sexual offenders: Limits to its validity. *Clinical Psychology Review, 20,* 807–822.

PROULX, J., AUBUT, J., MCKIBBEN, A. & CÔTÉ, M. (1994). Penile response of rapists and nonrapists to rape stimuli involving physical violence or humiliation. *Archives of Sexual Behavior, 23,* 295–310.

PROULX, J., CÔTÉ, G. & ACHILLE, P.A. (1993). Prevention of voluntary control of penile response in homosexual pedophiles during phallometric testing. *Journal of Sex Research, 30,* 140–147.

QUINSEY, V.L. & CHAPLIN, T.C. (1982). Penile responses to nonsexual violence among rapists. *Criminal Justice and Behavior, 9,* 312–324.

QUINSEY, V.L. & CHAPLIN, T.C. (1984). Stimulus control of rapists' and non-sex offenders' sexual arousal. *Behavioral Assessment, 6,* 169–176.

QUINSEY, V.L. & CHAPLIN, T.C. (1988). Preventing faking in phallometric assessments of sexual preference. In R.A. Prentky & V.L. Quinsey (Eds.), *Human sexual aggression: Current perspectives* (pp. 49–58). New York: Annals of New York Academy of Sciences.

QUINSEY, V.L., CHAPLIN, T.C. & UPFOLD, D. (1984). Sexual arousal to nonsexual violence and sadomasochistic themes among rapists and non-sex-offenders. *Journal of Consulting and Clinical Psychology, 52,* 651–657,

QUINSEY, V.L., LALUMIÈRE, M.L., RICE, M.E. & HARRIS, G.T. (1995). Predicting sexual offenses. In J.C. Campbell (Ed.), *Assessing dangerousness: Violence by sexual offenders, batterers, and child abusers* (pp. 114–137). Newbury Park: Sage Publications.

RICE, M.E., CHAPLIN, T.C., HARRIS, G.T. & COUTTS, J. (1994). Empathy for the victim and sexual arousal among rapists and nonrapists. *Journal of Interpersonal Violence, 9,* 435–449.

SETO, M.C. & BARBAREE, H.E. (1993). Victim blame and sexual arousal to rape cues in rapists and nonoffenders. *Annals of Sex Research, 6,* 167–183.

SETO, M.C. & KUBAN, M. (1996). Criterion-related validity of a phallometric test for paraphilic rape and sadism. *Behaviour Research and Therapy, 34,* 175–183.

Distinguishing and Combining Risks for Sexual and Violent Recidivism

DAVID THORNTON,[a] RUTH MANN,[b] STEVE WEBSTER,[b] LINDA BLUD,[b] ROSIE TRAVERS,[b] CAROLINE FRIENDSHIP,[b] AND MATT ERIKSON[b]

[a]Sand Ridge Secure Treatment Center, Mauston, Wisconsin 53948, USA

[b]Her Majesty's Prison Service, Abell House, John Islip Street, London SW1P 4LN, United Kingdom

ABSTRACT: A two-dimensional risk assessment system for sexual offenders was created that can classify them for risk of sexual recidivism, risk of nonsexual violent recidivism, and the composite risk of reconviction for sexual or nonsexual assaults. Receiver operating characteristic (ROC) analyses of separate follow-up samples were used for cross-validation. The system is easier to score than Static-99, and substantially easier to score than the VRAG or SORAG, while yielding comparable predictive accuracy in cross-validation samples with follow-ups from 2 years to 19 years. ROC AUC coefficients between .74 and .81 were found for the different scales and samples.

KEYWORDS: receiver prediction; sexual offender; sexual recidivism

INTRODUCTION

Thornton and Travers (1991) in a 10-year follow-up of a national sample of sexual offenders discharged from prison in England and Wales found that about a fifth were reconvicted for sexual offenses, and another fifth were reconvicted for nonsexual violence. The combined rate of recidivism for either kind of offense was 36%. Thus, sexual offenders present two distinct and equal kinds of risk: risk for sexual recidivism and risk for nonsexual assault. The two-dimensional nature of the risk presented by sexual offenders has not been represented in the structure of existing actuarial instruments for sexual offender risk assessment.

Examples of statistical instruments that now exist to assist clinicians in assessing the risk presented by sexual offenders include the Sex Offender Risk Appraisal Guide (SORAG), the Violence Risk Appraisal Guide (VRAG) (Quinsey, Harris, Rice & Cormier, 1998); the Minnesota Sex Offender Screening Tool: Revised (MnSOST-R: Epperson, Kaul & Hesselton, 1998); the Rapid Risk Assessment for Sex Offence Recidivism (RRASOR: Hanson, 1997); Structured Anchored Clinical Judgment (SACJ: Hanson & Thornton, 2000); and Static-99 (Hanson & Thornton, 2000).

Address for correspondence: David Thornton, Ph.D., Sand Ridge Secure Treatment Center, P.O. Box 700, Mauston, WI 53948. Voice: 608-847-4438, ext. 1744; fax: 608-847-1790.
david17thornton@aol.com

Ann. N.Y. Acad. Sci. 989: 225–235 (2003). © 2003 New York Academy of Sciences.

These instruments classify sexual offenders either by risk of sexual recidivism (MnSOST-R, RRASOR, SACJ, and Static-99) or by risk of overall violent (sexual plus other violent) recidivism (SORAG, VRAG, Static-99). None of them allow sexual offenders to be classified according to the risk they present of specifically non-sexual violent recidivism. Inevitably, then, none allow their relative risk of sexual versus nonsexual violence to be profiled. This limitation is potentially significant, since different risk management strategies may be appropriate for sexual offenders who present different combinations of these two kinds of risk. One goal of the present research was to create an instrument that could assess risk of sexual and non-sexual violent recidivism separately, allowing a risk profile to be expressed, as well as allowing the risk for the composite outcome—sexual or non-sexual assault—to be evaluated.

A further limitation of existing statistical instruments intended for evaluating sexual offenders is that to varying degrees they require significant time and clinical resources to gather and score the data. This limits their use by agencies for which the relevant clinical resources are scarce. The SORAG and VRAG both require complex and time-consuming clinical assessments like the PCL-R (Hare, 1991) or psychiatric diagnoses. The MnSOST-R contains complex and hard to identify items of criminal history (e.g., location of sexual offenses; number of distinct sexual acts committed during a single offense). RRASOR and Static-99 require a complete review of arrests, charges, and convictions for sexual offenses. This information can be difficult to retrieve and may simply not be available in some jurisdictions. For example, in the United Kingdom records of arrests/charges are deleted from the Police National Computer database if they do not result in a conviction. As a consequence, in some contexts, cost-effective use of these scales requires them to be approximated rather than fully applied. Further, the rules for scoring sexual priors in these scales are complex, and consequently they are time-consuming to apply and potentially vulnerable to scorer error. This is particularly true where there is some ambiguity over the identification of the index sexual offense. Different decisions here can make a major difference to the risk score assigned. The present research aimed to create a scale that could be scored from information that was more easily available, using simpler coding rules, but without loss of predictive accuracy.

STEPS IN DEVELOPING AND VALIDATING
A PREDICTION SCALE

The development of a statistical instrument for predicting sexual (or other) recidivism is normally seen as involving two distinct phases: scale construction and cross-validation. Scale construction is sometimes seen simply as the application of statistical procedures like regression analysis to a "construction sample." However, unless the construction sample is very large, such a process may well produce a prediction equation that is overfitted to the data and that will consequently predict less efficiently in future samples. The magnitude (rather than sign) of regression weights seems particularly vulnerable to this process. Weights estimated through regression analysis commonly turn out on cross-validation to be no more predictive than unitary weights. In general, simple weights work as well as more complex systems (Silver, Smith & Banks, 2000). An alternative to relying so heavily on regression analysis of a particular sample is to draw on reviews of previous research, especially meta-analyses, and also on theory, to select items for the scale and to define rules for scoring and combining them. Clearly, some allowance must then be made for correlations between predictors and for gross differences in the predictive value of items, and analyses of construction samples have a place here. However, in this alternative approach, simple weights are used in the place of precise regression weights, and some redundancy of items may be accepted so long as this doesn't reduce the predictive accuracy of the scale. This redundancy can be seen as a potential advantage, giving the resulting scale greater robustness when the predictive value of different indicators of the same construct fluctuate between data sets (reflecting either sampling error or real variation in the meaning of indicators between jurisdictions).

Cross-validation involves testing the prediction scale on data that was not used in its construction. A number of stages in cross-validation can be distinguished. Has there been any cross-validation? Has there been cross-validation on more than one sample? Have there been cross-validation studies carried out by authors not involved in the scale's construction? Have a sufficiently large and diverse range of cross-validation samples been studied that (a) the scale's predictive accuracy can be estimated with precision, and, (b) the degree to which its predictive accuracy varies from setting to setting to setting and type of offender to type of offender, can be assessed?

Cross-validation studies depend on some consistent index of predictive accuracy. The area under the Receiver Operating Characteristics (ROC) curve was used here as the measure of predictive accuracy (Hanley & McNeil, 1982; Swets, 1986; Mossman, 1994; Rice & Harris, 1995). The area under the ROC curve can range from 0.50 to 1.0, with 1.0 indicating perfect prediction and 0.5 indicating prediction no better than chance. The area under the ROC curve can be interpreted as the probability that a randomly selected recidivist would have a higher score than a randomly selected nonrecidivist. The area under the ROC curve has the advantage over other commonly used measures of predictive accuracy (e.g., percent agreement, the correlation coefficient) that it is not constrained by base rates or selection ratios (Swets, 1986).

ROC statistics were computed using ROCKIT version 0.9.1 (Metz, 1998). This software implements procedures based on Dorfman and Alf (1969) for estimating ROC statistics from discrete data.

Development of norms involves the large-scale application of the scale to samples representative of those to which it is to be applied. Norms are less significant for prediction scales than they are for ordinary psychometric scales. The latter typically characterize an individual in relation to the mean and standard deviation of representative samples. Prediction scales characterize individuals relative to the outcome (recidivism rate) typical of the risk category to which the individual has been assigned. Nevertheless, knowing what proportion of a population falls into particular risk categories can have implications for the use of a scale.

Determination of interrater reliability is often a surprisingly late part in scale development. This is because initial validation studies commonly involve computer programs applying scoring rules to databases, so there is in effect perfect interrater reliability (anyone applying the same program to the same data set will get the same results). Of course, the predictive accuracy they can obtain is constrained by the inter-rater reliability of the variables that entered the data set. Interrater reliability becomes more significant when the scale is in routine use. Here it becomes possible to ask how the reliability varies depending on levels of training, conditions of scoring, and so forth, and what level of reliability is attained under different conditions.

The present paper briefly describes earlier work constructing the new prediction scales and then reports studies cross-validating the scales.

CONSTRUCTING THE NEW SCALES

Constructing the Predictor for Sexual Recidivism: RM2000/S

The new scales being tested here were constructed by the first author (D.T.) in 2000, and are collectively referred to as the Risk Matrix 2000. The predictor for sexual recidivism was intended to be an updated version of the SACJ-Min scale (the latter was developed by the first author in the early 1990s and is described in Hanson & Thornton, 2000). SACJ-Min was based on a combination of the published literature on correlates of sexual recidivism and regression analyses carried out by Thornton and Travers (1991). The two steps in SACJ-Min are depicted in Appendix A.

In making the revision, the Hanson and Bussière (1998) meta-analysis was taken as a more complete guide to the literature, containing more precise and representative estimates of the predictive accuracy of individual factors than would be obtained from any individual study. This highlighted two deficiencies of the SACJ-Min scale: first, age is not represented in the scale, despite having an average r with sexual recidivism that was equivalent to items that were included; second, the scale weights prior sexual convictions equally with a number of other items, while the meta-analysis found the average r of recorded prior sexual offending with sexual recidivism to be about twice that of the other items used in SACJ-Min. On this basis, it was decided that the first step in RM2000/S should include age as a predictor and should differentiate recorded prior sexual offenses more finely.

A number of methods have been employed to differentiate levels of prior sexual offending, including number of charges, number of victims, and number of convictions. There are difficulties with each of these indicators. Friendship, Thornton, Erikson, and Beech (2001) found that, in England, the number of sentencing occasions and the kinds of convictions at these occasions, were reliably available, but that specific counts of convictions (of different kinds) were not reliably recorded. It was decided therefore to use as an item, a count of prior sentencing occasions that involved a sexual offence.

Considering age as a risk indicator, it was decided to follow the RRASOR scale (and Static-99) in giving most weight to the youngest age group (18 to 24), but other scales (SORAG, MnSOST-R) make differentiations at later ages as well, so it seemed worth following them by making an additional differentiation at age 34.

A construction data set was then obtained consisting of 1910 untreated sexual offenders discharged from prisons in England and Wales during the early 1990s and followed for two years. Some 54 of these offenders were reconvicted for sexual offenses within 2 years of release, while 116 of them were reconvicted for nonsexual assaults. Only limited information is available about the basic characteristics of this sample, but about a fifth had previous convictions for sexual offenses, a third for nonsexual violence, and a little under half had been sentenced on five or more occasions. It is thought that the group contained fewer "sexual specialists" and more general offenders whose repertoire occasionally includes sexual offending, than would normally be found in a treatment sample. They should also have been lower risk for sexual offending since selection processes at that time prioritized higher risk offenders for treatment. This sample was used to test various schemes for weighting these two variables. In addition, the added value of total sentencing occasions (for any offence) and of sentencing occasion for violence was assessed (these being factors included in step one of SACJ). This led to a decision to retain the former factor, but to drop nonsexual violence as a predictor, as its relation to future sexual offending appeared to be less consistent. Aggravating factors were left as in the original model.

A final modification was to abolish the distinction between index and prior sexual offences. The rationale for this was our experience with Static-99, where difficulty in defining the index offence has been found to be a common source of discrepancies in scoring. Appendix B shows the portion of the revised system that is concerned with sexual recidivism.

Constructing the Predictor for Nonsexual Violent Recidivism: RM2000/V

Two variables were selected on *a priori* grounds for inclusion in this scale: age upon release and amount of prior violence. Following Friendship et al.'s (2001) finding it was decided to use Number of Sentencing Occasions involving convictions for nonsexual assault as the indicator of prior violence. Violent offending, like most other kinds of crime, declines sharply with age, so it was decided to weight age heavily by differentiating several levels.

The same construction sample was used to explore the effect of different ways of coding these two factors on how well they predicted nonsexual violent recidivism. Then analyses were carried out to test whether number of sentencing occasions for each of a wide range of different kinds of offense enabled better prediction than just age and sentencing occasions for nonsexual assault. Sentencing Occasions for Burglary emerged as the best additional predictor. Once this variable was included in the regression equation, other offense-types (theft, damage to property, fraud, etc.) did not allow prediction to be improved to a useful extent. Further, coding sentencing occasions for Burglary as Any vs. None worked as well as using more categories. Exploratory analyses were used to determine the relative weights for these three factors. Simplified weights were chosen so as to reduce the likelihood of overfitting to the construction sample. The results of this process are shown in Appendix C.

Constructing the Predictor for Combined Sexual and Nonsexual Violent Recidivism: RM2000/C

Both RM2000/S and RM2000/V were constructed so as to yield four summary risk categories, labeled I (Low Risk), II (Medium Risk), III (High Risk), and IV (Very High Risk). To produce a combined scale these categories were weighted 0, 1, 2, or 3 and added together, giving a Combined scale with scores running from 0 to 6 points.

CROSS-VALIDATING THE NEW SCALES

Samples Used for Cross-Validation

Sample 1 consisted of male sexual offenders identified from a central database as having participated during the early 1990s in the national sexual offender treatment program operating in prisons in England and Wales and having subsequently been released and at risk for at least 2 years. The treatment program was a fairly circumscribed cognitive–behavioral approach, focused on cognitive distortions, victim empathy, and relapse prevention (Thornton and Hogue, 1993). The follow-up procedure involved tracing the sample on a national database (called the Offenders Index) that holds all criminal convictions incurred in courts in England and Wales from 1963 onwards. The sample consisted of 647 discharged prisoners who had been at risk in the community for at least 2 years and who were successfully matched on the Offenders Index so that their convictions (prior and subsequent) could be traced. Alternatively an average follow-up of 3.7 years was available for this sample. The mean age at discharge for this sample was 41.3 years (SD = 12.0). A third (33%) had been sentenced on five or more occasions for a criminal offence. About a quarter (28%) had a conviction for incest, and roughly four-fifths (84%) had at least one conviction for an offence against a person under 18.

Sample 2 was based on all male offenders discharged from prisons in England and Wales in 1979 following a sentence imposed for a sexual offence conviction. The sample consisted of all of these discharged prisoners who were successfully traced on the Offenders Index (19-year follow-up) and police records at New Scotland Yard's National Identification Service (formerly Criminal Records Office), where the follow-up time was 16 years. For sample 2, 429 cases were matched on both these databases, and therefore had follow-up data available. Convictions were considered as present if they were shown on either database. The mean age at discharge for this sample was 34.2 years (SD = 12.9). About one in eight had been convicted for incest (12%), 62% had a conviction for a sexual offence against a victim aged under 18, and 41% had been sentenced for a criminal offence on five or more occasions.

Sample 3 consisted of 311 adult males discharged from a prison in England and Wales in 1980 following a sentence of at least 4 years imposed for a sexual offense. This sample was followed up for 10 years on central police records. Note that for this sample the variable "Any Burglaries" was approximated by the highly correlated variable "Any Burglaries or Non-Motor Thefts." The variables required to score the S and C scales were not available for this sample.

Testing RM2000/S

Samples 1 and 2 were used to cross-validate the scale intended to predict sexual recidivism. TABLE 1 shows the observed two-year sexual reconviction rates for RM2000/S in Sample 1 and the 19-year sexual reconviction rates for Sample 2. The

TABLE 1. Sexual reconviction rates by Risk Matrix 2000 category

Caregory	Sample 1 (2-year follow-up)	Sample 2 (19-year follow-up)
I	0.9% (2 of 215)	8.0% (7 of 87)
II	1.3% (4 of 298)	18.1% (30 of 166)
III	5.7% (6 0f 105)	40.5% (49 of 121)
IV	17.2% (5 of 29)	60% (33 of 55)

TABLE 2. Violent reconviction rates by Risk Matrix 2000 category

Category	Sample 1 (2-year follow-up)	Sample 2 (19-year follow-up)	Sample 3 (10-year follow-up)
I	0% (0 of 297)	5% (8 of 151)	5% (3 of 62)
II	2.8% (6 of 218)	19% (25 of 130)	6.7% (8 of 119)
III	3.0% (3 of 100)	41% (39 of 96)	34% (35 of 104)
IV	18.8% (6 of 32)	63% (29 of 46)	50% (13 of 26)

TABLE 3. Combined violent reconviction rate by RM2000/C

RM2000/ C categories	Violent reconviction rate for Sample 1	Violent reconviction rate for Sample 2
0	0% (0 of 7)	12% (7 of 60)
1	0% (0 of 35)	27% (15 of 56)
2	1% (1 of 74)	39% (35 of 91)
3	10% (6 of 61)	46% (38 of 83)
4	16% (8 of 51)	66% (55 of 84)
5	24% (9 of 37)	78% (21 of 27)
6	46% (5 of 11)	100% (5 of 5)

table shows a monotonic trend with sexual reconviction rates rising in the expected way across the four risk categories in both samples. The ROC Area under the Curve statistic was 0.77 for Sample 1 and 0.75 for Sample 2.

Testing RM2000/V

The results for Samples 1, 2, and 3 are shown in TABLE 2. Each sample shows a monotonic increase in nonsexual violent recidivism rates across the four RM2000/V categories. As might be expected, rates are higher for the sample with the longer follow up. The ROC Area Statistics are 0.85, 0.80, and 0.78, respectively.

Testing RM2000/C

Samples 1 and 2 were used to test RM2000/C. TABLE 3 shows the combined violent (sexual plus nonsexual) reconviction rates for an average 3.7 year follow-up (all of Sample 1 were at risk for at least 2 years) and a 19-year follow-up (Sample 2). The ROC area under the curve statistic was 0.81 for Sample 1 and 0.74 for Sample 2.

NORMS FOR RM2000

Norms for a scale allow one to judge both what proportion of a population would fall into the different categories and how a particular person scores on the scale relative to others (e.g., are they above or below average). This is central to the interpre-

TABLE 4. Percentage of a national prison sample of sexual offenders falling into different RM2000 S and V categories

Risk category on RM2000	Percent falling in RM2000/S categories (%)	Percent falling in RM2000/V categories (%)
I	20	36
II	39	31
III	28	23
IV	13	11

TABLE 5. Percentage of a national prison sample of sexual offenders falling into different RM2000 C scores

Score	Percentage (%)
0	15
1	14
2	22
3	20
4	21
5	7
6	1

tation of many psychometric tests, but is less significant for prediction scales where the recidivism rate associated with a risk category is more important. Nevertheless, knowing the proportion falling in each risk category can be important information for planning resource allocation. TABLE 4 shows the percentage of Sample 2 falling in the different categories of RM2000's S and V scales. This sample was chosen because it is representative of all those serving sentences for sexual offenses in a national prison system.

TABLE 5 shows the percentage falling at each RM2000/C score for the same sample. In considering these norms, it is important to remember that they relate to one particular jurisdiction (England and Wales) in one particular era (late 1970s). The proportion of offenders falling in the different categories may be different for different time periods, for different jurisdictions, and for particular facilities within a jurisdiction. Thus administrators using the system will want to establish their own local norms to guide their resource planning processes.

DISCUSSION

The studies reported here suggest that RM2000 achieves the purposes for which it was designed, at least for convicted sexual offenders in England and Wales. The ROC Area statistics for RM2000 are comparable to those obtained for other actuarial instruments used to predict sexual or violent offending, despite the fact that it only uses simple and easily available components. Scales such as Static-99, the MnSOST-

R or the VRAG/SORAG family have typically reported AUC coefficients in the 0.70s (see Harris & Rice, this volume, on ways in which AUCs can be enhanced). It will only be possible to say how the scales compare in a more precise way when they have been tried out in a wider range of samples with all scales being scored on the same cases. For example, in Sample 2, RRASOR has an AUC coefficient of 0.70 and Static-99 has an AUC of 0.73, compared to RM2000/S's AUC of 0.75 for the same data. Results will inevitably vary from one sample to another simply because of sampling error. More fundamentally, the components of prediction scales may genuinely vary in their predictive value from one jurisdiction to another or even not exist in a comparable form in different settings. Ideally, a prediction scale would only use components that were robustly predictive across settings. RM2000 has deliberately been tested with treated and untreated samples, and with samples drawn from different eras (1979/1980 vs. 1990s). The fact that similar AUC coefficients were obtained gives some confidence as to its robustness, but further research testing it in diverse samples drawn from other jurisdictions is highly desirable.

There are some theoretical grounds that suggest circumstances in which some scales will do better than RM2000. RM2000 deliberately does not use direct assessment of complex psychological risk factors. Since such factors do allow predictive accuracy to be improved over and above simple static variables (Thornton, 2002), scales that include this kind of variable may be expected to do better than RM2000 in populations where these psychological risk factors are prevalent and only weakly correlated with the kind of static factors that RM2000 employs. The SORAG and VRAG include psychopathy and other mental health diagnoses as items, and the SORAG includes phallometric assessment of sexual interest. These scales may therefore possess particular advantages for some populations. On the other hand, they are much more resource intensive to apply and can only be appropriately used by qualified mental health professionals who have specialized in risk assessment. RM2000, in contrast, can appropriately be used by probation officers, police officers, and correctional personnel, so long as they are given specific training. Further, the data it employs are of a kind that can easily be routinely collected and computerized. This means that it can potentially be used to screen and categorize large populations of offenders.

REFERENCES

DORFMAN, D.D. & ALF, E. (1969). Maximum likelihood estimation of parameters of signal detection theory and determination of confidence intervals—Rating method data. *Journal of Mathmatical Psychology, 6,* 487.

EPPERSON, D.L., KAUL, J.D. & HESSELTON, D. (1998). *Final report of the Development of the Minnesota Sex Offender Screening Tool—Revised (MnSOST-R).* Presented at the Annual Research and Treatment Conference of the Association for the Treatment of Sexual Abusers, Vancouver, B.C., Canada.

FRIENDSHIP, C., THORNTON, D., ERIKSON, M. & BEECH, A. (2001). Reconviction: A critique and comparison of two main data sources in England and Wales. *Law and Criminological Psychology, 6,* 121–129.

HANLEY, J.A. & MCNEIL, B.J. (1982). The meaning and use of the area under a Receiver Operating Characteristic (ROC) curve. *Radiology, 143,* 29–36.

HANSON, R. K. (1997). *The development of a brief actuarial risk scale for sexual offense recidivism.* (User Report 97-04). Ottawa, Ont., Canada: Department of the Solicitor General of Canada.

HANSON, R.K. & BUSSIÈRE, M.T. (1998). Predicting relapse: A meta-analysis of sexual offender recidivism studies. *Journal of Consulting and Clinical Psychology, 66*, 348–362.

HANSON, R.K. & THORNTON, D.M. (2000). Static-99: Improving actuarial risk assessments for sex offenders. *Law and Human Behaviour, 24*, 119–136.

HARE, R.D. (1991). *The Hare Psychopathy Checklist—Revised.* Toronto, Ont., Canada: Multi-Health Systems.

HARRIS, G.T. & RICE, M.E. (2003). Actuarial assessment of risk among sexual offenders. This issue.

METZ, C.E. (1998). ROCKIT (Version 0.9.1) [Computer software]. Chicago, IL: University of Chicago.

MOSSMAN, D. (1994). Assessing predictions of violence: Being accurate about accuracy. *Journal of Consulting and Clinical Psychology, 62*, 783–792.

QUINSEY, V.L., HARRIS, G.T., RICE, M.E. & CORMIER, C.A. (1998). *Violent offenders: Risk appraisal and management.* Washington, DC: American Psychological Association.

RICE, M.E. & HARRIS, G.T. (1995). Violent recidivism: Assessing predictive validity. *Journal of Consulting and Clinical Psychology, 63*, 737–748.

SILVER, E., SMITH, W.R. & BANKS, S. (2000). Constructing actuarial devices for predicting recidivism: A comparison of methods. *Criminal Justice and Behavior, 27*, 733–764.

SWETS, J.A. (1986). Indices of discrimination or diagnostic accuracy: Their ROCs and implied models. *Psychological Bulletin, 99*, 100–117.

THORNTON, D. & TRAVERS, R. (1991). A longitudinal study of the criminal behavior of convicted sexual offenders. *Proceedings of the 1991 Prison Psychologist's Conference in Scarborough, England.* Her Majesty's Prison Service.

THORNTON, D. & HOGUE, T. (1993) The large-scale provision of programmes for imprisoned sex offenders: Issues, dilemmas and progress. *Criminal Behaviour and Mental Health, 3*, 371–380.

THORNTON, D. (2002). Constructing and testing a framework for dynamic risk assessment. *Sexual Abuse: A Journal of Research and Treatment, 14*, 139–153.

Appendix A: The SACJ-Min classification algorithm

Step 1[a]

Most recent sentencing occasion includes a sex offense?	Yes/No
Any prior sentencing occasions include a sex offense?	Yes/No
Most recent sentencing occasion includes a conviction for nonsexual violence?	Yes/No
Any prior sentencing occasions include a conviction for nonsexual violence?	Yes/No
More than four sentencing occasions (including the current occasion)?	Yes/No

Step 2: Aggravating Factors

Any convictions for a sex offense against a male?	Yes/No
Single (i.e., never married)?	Yes/No
Any convictions for a noncontact offense?	Yes/No
Any convictions for a sex offense against a stranger?	Yes/No
Put up one level for each two aggravating factors present.	

[a]Score one point for each yes; 0–1 point, level I; 2–3 points, level II ; 4+ points, level III.

Appendix B: RM2000/S classification algorithm

Step 1	Points[a]
Sexual appearances—the number of sentencing occasions that included a sex offense	1 = 0 points
	2 = 1 point
	3–4 = 2 points
	5+ = 3 points
Criminal appearances—the number of sentencing occasions for any kind of criminal offense	4 or fewer = 0 points
	5+ = 1 point
Age at next opportunity to offend	Under 18 = 0 points
	18 to 24 = 2 points
	25 to 34 = 1 point
	35 and older = 0 points

Step 2: Aggravating Factors		
Any conviction for a sex offense against a male?	Yes/No	Put up one level for each two aggravating factors present
Any conviction for a sex offense against a stranger?	Yes/No	
Single (i.e., never married)	Yes/No	
Any conviction for a noncontact sex offense?	Yes/No	

[a]Total score: 0, level I; 1–2, level II; 3–4, level III; 5+, level IV.

Appendix C: RM2000/V classification algorithm

Factor	Score[a]
Age on release	18–24 = 3
	25–34 = 2
	35–44 = 1
	Older = 0
Violent appearances	0 = 0
	1 = 1
	2–3 = 2
	4+ = 3
Any convictions for burglary?	No = 0
	Yes = 2

[a]Total score and risk category: 0–1 point, I; 2–3 points, II; 4–5 points, III; 6+, IV.

Risk Assessment: Discussion of the Section

THOMAS GRISSO, *Moderator*

*Department of Psychiatry, University of Massachusetts Medical School,
Worcester, Massachusetts 01655, USA*

NEIL M. MALAMUTH, HOWARD BARBAREE, VERNON QUINSEY,
AND RAYMOND KNIGHT, *Discussants*

Commentary on the preceding papers is provided by four eminent scholars—Drs. Malamuth, Barbaree, Knight, and Quinsey—who have contributed much to the research literature on assessment of sex offender recidivism. Although each of the commentators focuses on a number of issues, four primary questions that they raised generated the greatest amount of discussion at the conference:

- How do the sex offender recidivism instruments work, and how do they compare to each other?

- Why do we have trouble identifying dynamic factors that make a difference in risk assessment, and what research approaches might further our efforts?

- How much can we trust the available measures of sex offender recidivism? Are they as valuable as they claim to be? And how predictive do they have to be in order to meet the requirements of legal decision making?

- Is there room for clinical adjustments of actuarially achieved conclusions, and if so, how could one guide clinical adjustments?

Comments by Dr. Malamuth

The ability to longitudinally predict criminal recidivism is an impressive feature of the studies presented in this session. Also praiseworthy is the researchers' careful attention to important psychometric issues and the emphasis on systematic replications.

Strength of the Actuarial Predictors

I'd like to comment on the magnitude of the prediction of recidivism, which some appear to suggest is strong. As elaborated later in my comments, this is an important question when examined in the context of the application of this research to legal decision-making.

Compared to the general use of clinical prediction, as Karl Hanson and others have shown, the actuarial approach is a major improvement. Indeed, if comparisons are made among individuals falling in different major categories, particularly at dis-

Address for correspondence: Thomas Grisso, Ph.D., Department of Psychiatry, University of Massachusetts Medical School, 55 Lake Avenue North, Worcester, MA 01655. Voice: 508-856-3625; fax: 508-856-2725.

Thomas.Grisso@umassmed.edu

Ann. N.Y. Acad. Sci. 989: 236–246 (2003). © 2003 New York Academy of Sciences.

tribution extremes, recidivism differences are dramatic, as documented by David Thornton. Therefore, conclusions regarding the relative likelihood of offender recidivism based on such comparisons seem well founded. Nevertheless, conclusions regarding the overall predictive utility of the actuarial scales and their application to more subtle distinctions merit further consideration.

Some in the audience who are accustomed to relying on correlational rather than ROC (Receiver Operating Characteristic) curve statistics might examine both, as suggested earlier by Hanson and Thornton (2000). The ROC values for predicting sexual recidivism were about 0.70, similar to those presented today. These corresponded to correlations of about 0.30. As the authors recognize, such prediction is moderate.

Correlations provide an easy means of computing the amount of shared variance by simply squaring the values obtained. Therefore, using these correlations, the overall amount of shared variance between the predictors and the outcomes (i.e., either sexual or violent recidivism) is about 9%. Depending on the standards used, that degree of association may or may not be considered sufficiently high. If one suggests that the strength of a prediction is very good, it is important to clarify what standards are being used to judge this prediction.

While a correlation indicates degree of association between two variables rather than prediction *per se,* the related statistical tool of multiple regression, which is a measure of prediction, can be used for similar purposes as ROC analyses (Altman, 1999). The correlation values reported above give us a good indication of the likely multiple regression results since the strength of the correlations reflects a composite of the various predictors that would have been used in the regression analyses.

It would be helpful for the authors of these papers to clarify why they appear to prefer the use of ROC statistics to correlational and/or multiple regression analyses. Regression may be more useful in identifying the relative strength of the contributing components of the equation and in enabling assessment of interactions among these components. This would enable consideration of the degree to which prediction is based primarily on the severity of previous antisocial behavior, a typically powerful predictor, as compared to the additional prediction achieved by the inclusion of other factors. However, justification for the ROC approach might be based on other considerations, such as Altman's (1999) emphasis that "The ROC method is perhaps most useful when comparing two or more competing methods." (p. 418) Although such comparisons have been made in this literature, this does not appear to be a primary focus here. Generally the comparisons that have been made seem to reveal considerable similarity among the results yielded by the various actuarial scales, suggesting that common underlying constructs are being assessed in different ways.

If one considers the overall strength of the predictions rather than applications that involve comparisons among extreme groups, it may be instructive to consider other areas of the psychological literature to see what values are judged as strong prediction based on ROC statistics. Using this standard, the ROC values obtained in the papers presented here might not be judged sufficiently strong for some applications.

Political Considerations when Judging the Strength of Predictive Equations

When predictive equations are applied to cases involving critical legal decisions, such as incarceration of a person for a crime they might commit, it is vital to appraise whether the predictive validity is sufficiently strong to be the foundation for such a decision. One the one hand, since clinical judgments may be used as the alternative, despite their lack of scientific validation, it may be argued that at least now we have a stronger tool with actuarial predictive equations.

On the other hand, as scientists we must be cognizant of the political and cultural values that affect decisions regarding sexual offenses in our society. We must consider whether there may be a political bias to overestimate the degree of accurate prediction achieved in order to justify keeping some offenders imprisoned. In other words, are these actuarial scales being misused by some who have already made up their minds to keep an offender incarcerated for crimes they have not yet committed? Although this may be justified by certain considerations, the political climate requires a very rigorous analysis of the actual strength of the prediction. This critical analysis should be made separately from the value judgments that will inevitably affect how the predictive scales will be used. In this context, it is particularly important to explicitly weigh the consequences of making different errors: a false positive (i.e., incarcerating someone who will not "recidivate") vs. a false negative (i.e., releasing someone who will repeat the crime). As Altman (1999) notes, such decisions regarding what is the "best" cut-off in balancing the two types of errors are not really a statistical matter. It reflects the values of the society in ascribing differing "costs" to each type of error.

Clinical Adjustments of Actuarial Predictions

I'd like to briefly comment on a related issue discussed here, namely, whether or not some causes warrant the adjustment of actuarial predictions by clinicians' judgments. It seems contradictory to conclude, on the one hand, that clinical prediction lacks accuracy, but on the other hand, to enable some clinicians to adjust the actuarial scales in some cases. I understand that it may be argued in support of such recommendations that there may be some unusual cases not fully encompassed by the actuarial approach and/or certain clinicians who may have special abilities or knowledge not typical of most clinicians. The lack of any systematic way of determining when that is the case would appear to potentially undermine the actuarial approach altogether. However, there may be better justification in very unusual cases for concluding that the actuarial scales are irrelevant to these cases because they do not reflect the population used to develop and test the actuarial scales. If some systematic process is developed for determining such cases, it may be appropriate in such exceptional cases not to use the actuarial scales at all. For example, some very extreme cases mentioned earlier (e.g., Jeffrey Dahmer) might justify such an approach. Also, if there are clinicians with knowledge that gives them particularly good predictive ability, it is hoped that we may find a way to apply their knowledge and criteria to develop better actuarial predictive scales.

Comments by Dr. Barbaree

I will focus my remarks on the presentations on actuarial risk assessment methodologies. I am a consumer of actuarial instruments, not a developer, but a discerning consumer: We have done some research that I will describe that compares the various instruments.

In my role as clinical director at the Law and Mental Health Program at the Center for Addiction and Mental Health, I am responsible for the quality of assessment reports that are made by our staff. Many of these are forensic evaluations of sex offenders. I read many of the current reports, and, on occasion, for legal purposes, I read those that were completed some time ago, sometimes going back into the 1950s. As a consequence, I have a good perspective on the way these reports have developed over the past few decades. Their quality has improved substantially, and the most pronounced increase in quality occurred with the recent availability of actuarial instruments. I would like to express a debt of gratitude to the people who have been instrumental in developing those instruments, including Karl Hanson, Vern Quinsey, Marnie Rice, Grant Harris, and David Thornton.

Comparative Value of the Instruments

Two presentations make comparisons among actuarial instruments. Marnie Rice found that the VRAG and SORAG were superior to others, and Karl Hanson reported that the RRASOR and Static-99 were superior to others. It is often the case, perhaps not surprisingly, that the developers of instruments report that their particular instrument is superior. We published a paper in August 2001 in *Behavioral Sciences and the Law,* in which we compared the predictive accuracy of five actuarial instruments. We found that the RRASOR, Static-99, the VRAG, and the SORAG were essentially equal in their ability to predict most recidivism outcomes, including sexual recidivism. David Thornton spoke of the importance of independent cross validation: Independent cross validations are accumulating in the peer-reviewed literature, attesting to the ability of these four instruments to accurately predict recidivism.

This morning, Kirk Heilbrun recommended using multiple sources of information to strengthen forensic reports, looking for convergence from various sources. If we now have four actuarial instruments that have been found to be equally predictive in independent cross validation, then it might be reasonable to recommend that forensic evaluations of sex offenders include a few or all of them depending on the information available.

One of the actuarial instruments we evaluated in our comparison was the Mn-SOST-R. Among the actuarial instruments that have been described in the literature, there is not as much obvious support for the MnSOST-R. I know of only two reports of cross validations—Karl Hanson made reference to them this morning, ours being one of them. We found that the MnSOST-R was not a significant predictor, though the AUC statistic was near the level of statistical significance. Moreover, when you compare the MnSOST-R with the other instruments in terms of independent cross validations, the MnSOST-R is not accumulating independent cross validations compared with the other instruments, and yet it is used quite frequently in sexually violent predator evaluations throughout the United States.

Static and Dynamic Risk Factors

I will end by commenting on the static versus dynamic risk issue. The research that has led to the development of the actuarial instruments has identified static variables as being helpful in making these predictions. These studies have involved long-term follow-up studies. It seems to me, from a statistical point of view, that the only variables that possibly could be predictive are static ones because the dynamic ones will have changed several times during the follow-up period. In using long-term follow-up designs, it is not surprising that the static variables turn up as being predictive, while the dynamic ones do not turn out to be particularly helpful.

Vern Quinsey will be talking about a different research design that he has used with his colleague Brian Jones in a study of mentally disordered offenders. Karl Hanson and his colleague Andrew Harris have conducted a similar study with sex offenders. In their design individuals are followed on a daily basis, and changes in dynamic variables are examined to see whether there is a predictive relationship with re-offense.

It seems to me that static and dynamic factors are entirely different. Actuarial instruments using static factors tell you *who* in a sample of offenders are more likely to offend than others. Dynamic factors are quite different. They tell you *when* an individual is more likely to re-offend. Static factors are a between-subject kind of variable and dynamic factors are a within-subject variable.

Comments by Dr. Quinsey

I have one specific comment to make and then I am going to discuss some of the issues that are common to many of the presentations. The specific comment concerns the issue of rapists responding to nonsexual violent scenarios in phallometric assessments. Heterosexual rapists respond to nonsexual violence in phallometric assessments only if the victim is a woman. They do not respond to violence *per se*. If the identical acts are done to a man they show absolutely nothing.

Measuring Recidivism Risk: A Single Underlying Super-Factor?

There are many actuarial instruments in use. Most of these have performed very well in cross validation. They predict a variety of different kinds of antisocial outcomes and they are all correlated with each other. In the psychometric literature on intelligence, the phrase, "the indifference of the indicator" describes the repeated finding that a wide variety of measures, such as vocabulary tests, maze performance, reaction time, discerning embedded figures, and so forth, all tap "g," the super-factor that underlies their relationship to intelligence. David Rowe has proposed exactly the same thing in the area of individual differences in criminality. Rowe proposes that a super-factor, called "d," underlies all of the disparate correlates of criminal propensity. A large number of actuarial instruments could thus be constructed out of non-overlapping items; all of these instruments would correlate with each other and predict antisocial outcomes.

But these instruments don't necessarily inform us about theory. Why do they work the way they do? And what is the nature of d? In the area of intelligence, we now know that g is a biological variable reflecting some aspect of neural processing speed. It is much less clear what the nature of d is. I do not think we will find out from prediction research. That research is an applied enterprise—important, but suboptimal for theory construction. The studies that are going to inform us about the nature of d will cut across genes, development, and the brain, the domains known to be important in understanding individual differences in behavior.

Static and Dynamic Risk Factors

Dr. Barbaree distinguished between dynamic and static variables. The development of prediction instruments using dynamic variables has lagged behind the development of prediction instruments using static variables. One of the reasons for this is that the term *dynamic* is confusingly applied to classes of predictors that are conceptually and methodologically different from each other. Whether dynamic or not, all factors that are measured before the opportunity to reoffend are historical. In contrast, variables that change during the time a person has the opportunity to reoffend can be used to adjust supervision and treatment.

Actuarial instruments are commonly criticized for containing only static predictors. This criticism is misguided for two reasons. First, many prerelease dynamic variables were used in the development of many actuarial instruments but did not win the competition with the static variables that remain in these instruments. Second, dynamic predictors measured in the follow-up period cannot compete with prerelease historical predictors for variance in outcome. Variables measured before the opportunity to reoffend are suitable for estimating the probability that an offender will commit at least one crime of a particular type over a specified (and generally lengthy) period of opportunity, whereas within-offender differences in variables measured during the follow-up period reflect variations in imminence over short time frames. Actuarial instruments tell us who to worry about in the long-term and post-release dynamic variables tell us when to worry.

So where do we go from here? Because actuarial instruments are already fairly accurate in estimating the likelihood of at least one occurrence of an antisocial event over a long time interval for a particular offender, they are going to be very difficult to improve. The greatest improvement in accuracy will likely come from working on the outcome measures rather than on the predictors. Although I don't think we are going to get very far trying to improve the accuracy of actuarial instruments, we do need to simplify them where possible, and we saw a good example of that with David Thornton's approach. In my view, future progress in the applied area is going to come from the study of post-release dynamic predictors—the antecedents of criminal acts. There has already been a great deal of work in this area that has not informed much of the discussion at this meeting.

For example, there is a large literature on institutional violence where enough is known about the antecedents of violent behavior to be useful in training staff to avoid getting physically attacked. However, the dynamic variables likely to be of interest to people working with sex offenders are not things that occur in the five minutes before an antisocial event, but things that change over days or weeks. These dynamic variables can guide supervision. In yet unpublished research, we have identified dynamic variables that are related to the imminence of violent and sexual offenses. These variables change slowly enough that clinicians could actually use them to intervene before the antisocial acts occur.

Comments by Dr. Knight

The presentations on assessment that we have heard are united by the common goal of striving to improve the dispositional and diagnostic decisions that are faced daily by the clinical and legal professionals who work to reduce the incidence of sexual aggression. These presentations consistently emphasized one way of improving such decision-making—increasing the accuracy of judgments by developing and testing actuarial risk assessments. We must not, however, let the increased accuracy afforded by these instruments blind us to potential misuses of these instruments in particular practical situations. The consideration of the application of these risk assessment scales to one decision process, the civil commitment for sexual dangerousness, provides a cautionary example and gives us a touchstone to judge both what we have achieved and what work remains.

Utility theory (Swets, Dawes & Monahan, 2000) provides a theoretical and practical context in which to evaluate this application. The utility of a decision encompasses not only the accuracy of the decision, but also its payoff, or the consequences of a given decision—the costs of incorrect decisions and the benefits of correct decisions (Cronbach & Gleser, 1964). In this theory the extant actuarial techniques for assessing risk are simply *statistical prediction rules* [SPRs; Swets et al., 2000]). Their incremental accuracies can be examined against the backdrop of the accuracy of simply using the base rates for decisions. Because the consequences of misses can be identified in the commitment process, we can propose a quantification of the values of both false positive and false negative misses so that the utility of the current SPRs can also be examined. After considering the consequences of a decision process that mechanically applies the SPRs, I will also discuss the consequences of the *de facto* manner in which SRPs are clinically and legally applied. Finally, I will argue for a process-oriented, performance-based strategy to guide future assessment research in this area.

Evaluation of Extant SPRs for Risk Assessment

Accuracy: Lloyd and Grove (2002) have provided a detailed analysis of the Minnesota Sex Offender Screening Tool—Revised (the MnSOST-R; Epperson, Kaul & Hesselton, 1997), applying Bayes' theorem to determine the accuracy of this SPR compared to decisions from base rates. The accuracy rates yielded by the MnSOST-R for the analyses calculated by Lloyd and Grove (2002) are comparable with the best rates for current sexual offender SPRs (Barbaree, Seto, Langton, & Peacock, 2001). A base rate decision would simply predict the most frequent outcome for all offenders. So, for example, in their meta-analysis involving 61 studies and 23,393 offenders Hanson and Bussière (1998) calculated an aggregated sexual recidivism rate across studies of 13.4%. The base rate prediction for this recidivism rate would yield an accuracy of 86.6% by predicting that no offender would recidivate.

Using the recommended cutoff of +13 on the MnSOST-R, Lloyd and George found that the gain in prediction over base rate was at best very small across the range of possible base rates. There was no gain using Hanson and Bussière's (1998) recidivism rate, and using the highest base rate reported in the literature, 41% (e.g., see Hanson et al., this volume, and Harris and Rice, this volume), there was a trivial gain (0.65 and 0.59, respectively for the MnSOST-R, and the base rate decision). Because the higher recidivism rates identified in the literature appear to be found among samples at higher risk, which have already had dispositional decisions determine their status, it could be argued that the more general Hanson and Bussière (1998) estimate should constitute the best base rate comparison for determining the accuracy of SPRs in civil commitment decisions. One would have to conclude from Lloyd and Grove's analysis that using SPRs for risk assessment is at best trivially better than using a base rate prediction.

The recommended MnSOST-R cutoff was not designed to maximize overall hit rate because of the unacceptably high rate of false positives that would result. Base rate selection can never outstrip selection with a test that has a validity that is greater than zero, if the cutoff is set to minimize the overall misses (e.g., Wiggins, 1973). Lloyd and Grove's calculations are an indictment of the current *application* of SPRs to commitment decisions and not of the SPRs themselves.

Utility: Accuracy constitutes only one part of decision theory. One must consider the cost of errors and the benefit of correct decisions. It is possible to have an assessment tool whose overall hit rate equals the base rate prediction, but the tool is still valuable because it allows us to reduce a more serious error, even if it is at the cost of increasing frequency of a less serious error. In their analysis of utility of the Mn-SOST-R, Lloyd and Grove (2002) employ a formula that weighs the relative value of false positive and false negative errors. A false positive error involves convicting an innocent person of a crime, detaining that person, perhaps indefinitely, denying him his civil liberties, and paying the costs of incarcerating and treating that offender. Since the recent reintroduction of sexual predator commitment laws in the 1990s, 1200 individuals have been committed, and only 61 have been released (see Prentky, this volume). Thus, the likely length of incarceration in a false positive error is substantial. According to the criteria used to generate the outcomes for the SPRs, the false negative error is defined as preventing a single sexual offense that could range in severity from fondling to a brutal sexual assault (Doren, 2002). Given the low probability of high or extreme sexual violence, even among sexual offenders civilly committed as sexually dangerous (Bard et al., 1987), it is more likely that a false negative error would involve a less serious physically damaging offense.

It is obviously the prerogative of society and its representatives to determine the weights assigned to each error. Citing a comprehensive review of the legal scholarship on the controversial topic of the relative value of the misses in legal judgments (Volokh, 1997), Lloyd and Grove suggest Blackstone's famous assertion, "Better that ten guilty persons escape, that that one innocent suffer" represents a reasonable compromise weighting. Their utility calculations indicate that for this relative weighting of the value of errors, both recidivism base rates (i.e., 41% and 13.4%) would yield higher utility than using the MnSOST-R.

Clinical Adjustments to Actuarial Scores

When evaluating the benefit of actuarial methods, we must not only consider their abstract, pristine efficacy in well-controlled research studies, where SPRs are applied mechanically and reliably, but we must also examine their *de facto* application in practical clinical and legal contexts. These instruments are commonly incorporated into the recommendations for civil commitment, yet they are rarely, if ever, applied in an unadulterated actuarial fashion, following the prescribed mechanical procedures (Doren, 2002). Instead, clinicians adjust the SPR ratings in light of unstandardized clinical impressions and clinical judgments, justifying their modification with arguments that information relevant to assessing recidivism has been neglected.

A substantive literature comparing clinical and actuarial prediction indicates the likely consequences of such clinical judgment adjustments (Grove & Meehl, 1996; Grove, Zald, Lebow, Snitz & Nelson, 2000). What happens when clinicians make judgments using the same or more data than a strictly mechanical combining of the information? In a meta-analysis of all of the studies published in English from the

1920s to the early 1990s, comparing clinical with statistical prediction of health-related phenomena or human behavior, Grove et al. (2000) found that mechanical prediction was equal to or notably better than clinical prediction in 94% of the studies assessed, despite the fact that in many of the studies the clinicians had more data available to them. In only 6% of the 136 studies in the analysis was clinical judgment superior, whereas actuarial prediction was superior in 47% of the studies. These results held across all content domains assessed. The inferiority of clinical judgments to mechanical prediction was exacerbated when clinicians had interviews as part of their assessment. The amount of other kinds of information available to the clinicians did not affect the superiority of mechanical over clinical prediction.

Consequently, there is a high probability that the practical, real-life, clinically adjusted incorporations of SPRs for risk assessment will be less reliable and accurate than the purely mechanical actuarial techniques that they incorporate and modify. If the ideal, mechanical application of pure SPRs yields decisions that are of questionable incremental accuracy and utility in comparison to straightforward base rate judgments, it is likely that the clinically adjusted judgments will be a cut below these. Such data would argue strongly that the best strategy currently available is simply to predict the base rates.

Future Directions for Assessment Research

Different types of risk factors are relevant for different types of risk decisions. Static, fixed or historical factors (such as age at first offense, prior criminal history) have been used to assess long-term recidivism potential (e.g., Barbaree et al., 2001). The evaluation of change in offender risk level, however, requires the consideration of *dynamic* (changeable) risk factors, which can be further divided into stable dynamic and acute dynamic factors. Stable dynamic factors, such as impulsivity, emotional detachment, or deviant sexual preferences, may also be used for long-term risk assessments, but they are crucial for assessing enduring changes (e.g., treatment outcome, parole release). Because of the development of integrated theoretical models of sexual aggression (Knight, in press; Knight & Sims-Knight, in press; this volume; Knight & Sims-Knight, Malamuth, 1998), we are now at the point that a process-oriented approach to the assessment of stable dynamic factors can be undertaken. This strategy uses well-established models from personality, psychopathology, and cognitive neuroscience to generate and test specific theory-driven hypotheses about the core processes (i.e., dynamic traits) leading to and maintaining sexual aggression. To accomplish this goal we must shore up our self-report assessments by solving the duplicitous responding problem with the new technology available (Holden, 1995; Paulhus, 1991; Zickar & Drasgow, 1996). Moreover, cognitive neuroscience is replete with performance-based tasks that can be adapted for testing theory-driven hypotheses about these underlying processes (e.g., Levenston, Patrick, Bradley & Lang, 2000; Logan, Schachar & Tannock, 1997; McFall, Treat & Viken, 1998). The identification of the underlying processes contributing to sexual aggression and the development of performance-based and duplicity-free assessments of these processes should be a central focus of future research. Such research holds the promise not only of increasing predictive accuracy, but also of enhancing decision utility by providing the metrics to assess and improve treatment efficacy and increase the benefits of dispositional decisions (Swets et al., 2000).

Additional Comment by Dr. Quinsey

A few additional comments: First, correlations and percent variance accounted for are not measures of predictive accuracy; they are measures of association. Second, no one is proposing to use actuarial methods in the determination of guilt. Third, it is very important to treat violent and sexual recidivism together because both are undesirable from a societal perspective and their combination boosts the base rate of undesirable but predictable outcomes, thus making the utilities of these predictions very much better. Fourth, explicit cutoffs can be chosen with any actuarial instrument to reflect any societal objective, such as identifying only the most dangerous at the cost of missing some truly dangerous offenders. Lastly, the accuracy of prediction is constrained by the reliability of the outcome measure. The accuracy of a particular instrument is underestimated in follow-up research by the unreliability of the outcome measure.

REFERENCES

ALTMAN, D.G. (1999). *Practical statistics for medical research.* CRC.

BARBAREE, H.E., SETO, M.C., LANGTON, C.M. & PEACOCK, E. J. (2001). Evaluating the predictive accuracy of six risk assessment instruments for adult sex offenders. *Criminal Justice and Behavior, 28,* 490–521.

BARD, L.A., CARTER, D.L., CERCE, D.D., KNIGHT, R.A., ROSENBERG, R. & SCHNEIDER, B. (1987). A descriptive study of rapists and child molesters: Developmental, clinical, and criminal characteristics. *Behavioral Sciences and the Law, 5,* 203–220.

CRONBACH, L.J., & GLESER, G.C. (1964). *Psychological tests and personnel decision* (2nd ed.). Urbana: University of Illinois Press.

DOREN, D. M. (2002). *Evaluating sex offenders: A manual for civil commitments and beyond.* Thousand Oaks, CA: US Sage Publications, Inc.

EPPERSON, D.L., KAUL, J.D. & HESSELTON, D. (1997). *Final report on the development of the Minnesota Sex Offender Screening Tool—Revised (MnSOST-R).* St. Paul, MN: Minnesota Department of Corrections.

GROVE, W.M. & MEEHL, P.E. (1996). Comparative efficiency of informal (subjective, impressionistic) and formal (mechanical, algorithmic) prediction procedures: The clinical-statistical controversy. *Psychology, Public Policy, and Law, 2,* 293–323.

GROVE, W.M., ZALD, D.H., LEBOW, B.S., SNITZ, B.E. & NELSON, C. (2000). Clinical versus mechanical prediction: A meta-analysis. *Psychological Assessment, 12,* 19–30.

HANSON, R.K., & BUSSIÈRE, M.T. (1998). Predicting relapse: A meta-analysis of sexual offender recidivism studies. *Journal of Consulting and Clinical Psychology, 66,* 348–362.

HANSON, R.K. & THORNTON, D. (2000). Improving risk assessments for sex offenders: A comparison of three actuarial scales. *Law & Human Behavior, 24,* 119–136.

HOLDEN, R.R. (1995). Response latency detection of fakers on personnel tests. *Canadian Journal of Behavioural Science, 27,* 343–355.

KNIGHT, R. A. (in press). Typologies/profiles of rapists. In J. R. Conte, (Ed.), *Handbook of trauma and abuse.* New York: Sage Publications.

KNIGHT, R.A. & SIMS-KNIGHT, J.E. (in press). The developmental antecedents of sexual coercion against women in adolescents. In R. Geffner & K. Franey (Eds.) *Sex Offenders: Assessment and Treatment.* New York: Haworth Press.

LEVENSTON, G.K., PATRICK, C.J., BRADLEY, M.M. & LANG, P.J. (2000). The psychopath as observer: Emotion and attention in picture processing. *Journal of Abnormal Psychology. 109,* 373-385.

LLOYD, M.D. & GROVE, W.M. (2002). *The uselessness of the Minnesota Sex Offender Screening Tool-Revised (MnSOST-R) in commitment decisions.* Manuscript submitted for publication.

LOGAN, G., SCHACHAR, R.J. & TANNOCK, R. (1997). Impulsivity and inhibitory control. *Psychological Science, 8,* 60–64.

MALAMUTH, N.M. (1998). An evolutionary-based model integrating research on the characteristics of sexually coercive men. In J. Adair, K. Dion, & D. Belanger, D. (Eds.). *Advances in psychological science: Vol. 1. Social, personal, and developmental aspects.* (pp. 151–184). Hove, England UK: Psychology Press/Erlbaum.

MCFALL, R.M., TREAT, T.A. & VIKEN, R.J. (1998). Contemporary cognitive approaches to studying clinical problems. In D. K. Routh & R. J. DeRubeis (Eds.), *The science of clinical psychology: Accomplishments and future directions* (pp. 163–197). Washington, DC: American Psychological Association.

PAULHUS, D. . (1991). Measurement and control of response bias. In J. P. Robinson, P. R. Shaver, & L. S. Wrightsman (Eds.), *Measures of personality and social psychological attitudes* (pp. 17–59). San Diego, CA: Academic Press.

SWETS, J.A., DAWES, R.M. & MONAHAN, J. (2000). Psychological science can improve diagnostic decisions. *Psychological Science in the Public Interest, 1,* 1–26.

VOLOKH, A. (1997). n guilty men. *University of Pennsylvania Law Review, 146,* 173–216.

WIGGINS, J. S. (1973). *Personality and prediction: Principles of personality assessment.* Reading, MA: Addison-Wesley Publishing Company.

ZICKAR, M.J. & DRASGOW, F. (1996). Detecting faking on a personality instrument using appropriateness measurement. *Applied Psychological Measurement, 20,* 71–87.

Legislative Responses to Sexual Violence

An Overview

ERIC S. JANUS

William Mitchell College of Law, St. Paul, Minnesota 55105, USA

ABSTRACT: In the past three decades, the legislative response to sexual violence has undergone two sets of reforms. The feminist reforms, beginning in the 1970s, sought to modify legal forms and practices to reflect new theories of the nature of sexual violence. The "regulatory" reforms of the 1990s were atheoretical, and adopted a "preventive" strategy to close perceived gaps in the system of social control. This article examines the second wave of reform, with special emphasis on Sexually Violent Predator (SVP) laws. It summarizes the current legal controversies generated by these laws, and suggests that the underlying assumptions and forms adopted by the 1990s reforms may undercut some of the advances achieved by the feminist reforms in understanding and addressing sexual violence.

KEYWORDS: sexual violence; legislative responses; rape reform; regulatory intervention; mental disorder; sexually violent predator laws

INTRODUCTION

Over the past 35 years, the legal framework for addressing sexual aggression has taken two qualitative leaps. The first set of reforms, arising in the 1970s with the feminist movement, sought to change legal forms to reflect a new, theory-driven conception of sexual violence. The second set of reforms, beginning in the early 1990s, were reactive and atheoretical, opportunistically making use of existing legal forms for innovative purposes. In this overview, by examining the more recent legal innovations (especially Sexually Violent Predator Laws), I have two goals. First, I seek to provide a straightforward summary of legal developments arising from these reforms. Second, I speculate about changes these legal developments might portend for our understanding of sexual violence. I argue that the innovations, and the legal concepts they have spawned, may undercut the earlier advances in addressing sexual violence.

Address for correspondence: Eric S. Janus. Professor of Law, William Mitchell College of Law, 875 Summit Avenue, St. Paul, MN 55105. Voice: 651-290-6345; fax: 651-290-6406.
ejanus@wmitchell.edu

The author has served as co-counsel in extensive litigation challenging the constitutionality of Minnesota's Sexually Dangerous Person Law.

Ann. N.Y. Acad. Sci. 989: 247–264 (2003). © 2003 New York Academy of Sciences.

EARLY REFORMS: "RAPE REFORM"

"Rape reform" arose in the 1970s from the feminist movement and sought fundamental shifts in the criminal law and the criminal justice system. These reforms were based on the theory that rape arises from a gendered distribution of power in society. The existing structure and practice of rape law invisibly incorporated this power differential as "normal," and in this way supported and reproduced the power imbalance.[1]

Reformers sought to expose, and then change, the unequal power relationships by adjusting key legal forms and practices. Rape law reform and rape shield laws incorporated the underlying theory by changing legal definitions of consent and force,[2] seeking to address widespread attitudes that women often bore responsibility for being raped. Reformers sought to construct legislation around the new realization that sexual violence was ubiquitous rather than aberrational, perpetrated more often by acquaintances and family members than stranger-psychopaths.[3] This, together with new knowledge about the damage caused by sexual violence, led to lengthening criminal sentences and supervision, and increased rates of incarceration, reflecting an enhanced calibration of seriousness, particularly in the newly important areas of child and acquaintance sexual abuse.[4] In short, by "domesticating" sexual violence, the reformers sought to place responsibility squarely with perpetrators and with the society at large, whose prevailing values and attitudes about gender relations provided the conditions in which sexual aggression could thrive.[5]

"REGULATORY" REFORM OF THE 1990s

The innovations of the 1990s represent the second leap. These reforms make use of legal forms that are "regulatory" rather than criminal, imposing controls on sex offenders not as punishment, but as a means of preventing future dangerous behavior. Registration laws oblige convicted sex offenders to register with law enforcement agencies periodically. Community notification laws place an obligation on the state to notify the public, in a variety of ways, when sex offenders are released from custody.[6] Sexually Violent Person (SVP) laws allow the state to use "civil commitment" to confine dangerous, mentally disordered sex offenders. These laws were conceived in state task forces convened in the late 1980s in response to the perception—fueled by heinous sex crimes committed by paroled rapists—that the criminal justice system had serious gaps in its ability to control sexual violence.[7]

The reforms of the 1990s share their predecessors' determination to take sexual violence seriously. But there are salient differences. The new laws adopt civil, "regulatory" legal forms, whose primary justification is prevention, rather than modifications of criminal laws and practices, whose primary justification is punishment. The role of government is more explicitly active. The new laws deploy risk assessment and risk reduction, rather than crime-solving and criminal apprehension, as their central strategies.

Finally, unlike the earlier reforms, the recent innovations were "atheoretical." They did not reflect a new understanding of sexual violence, making visible, and thereby reshaping, the hidden assumptions and attitudes that propped up sexual violence. Rather, they were very practical, grass-roots solutions to the most visible, iconic instances of sexual violence, the violent stranger rapist.

This essay suggests that the new reforms to some extent undercut the theory-driven advances of the first generation reforms. The new reforms tend to portray sexual violence as aberrational rather than domestic, as psychologically pathological rather than the fruit of misogynist attitudes and practices, and as the product of uncontrollable "predispositions" rather than as the product of choices for which the individual is responsible.

ARTICULATING THE LEGAL FRAMEWORK FOR REGULATORY INTERVENTION

The innovations of the 1990s claim to be civil regulation rather than criminal punishment. To the extent that this civil claim is valid, these interventions are exempt from the strict constitutional protections that constrain criminal loss of liberty, most importantly the protections against self-incrimination, double jeopardy, and *ex post facto* laws.

The constitutional litigation generated by the reforms has been aimed at testing the claim to the "civil" classification, and working out its implications. There have been four stages in this development. First, in the 1940s through the '60s, courts examined the early "sex psychopath" laws. Courts understood these laws as benign dispositional alternatives for sex offenders too sick to deserve punishment, and satisfied themselves that legislatures could expand the notions of "insanity" or "incompetence" beyond their traditional meanings. But the implicit premise was that the new forms of "insanity"—what the courts called "moral insanity"—bore a family resemblance to the traditional forms, at least in the sense that they impaired the ability of the detained individual to control his actions.[8]

The second development arose from several Supreme Court cases decided in the '70s and '80s. Some advocates and scholars read into these cases a broad "jurisprudence of prevention": the notion was that states could civilly deprive a person's liberty to protect the public against dangers, and that the source of the danger—whether disease, mental disorder, or simply some other form of "dangerousness"—was immaterial.[9]

Third, the courts rebuffed this jurisprudence of prevention, articulating in its stead the principle that the criminal law must remain the state's primary vehicle for addressing antisocial violence and that civil commitment must be exceptional.[10] Thus, dangerousness alone will not support civil commitment, without some additional factor such as mental disorder.[11] Relatedly, the Supreme Court's opinions suggest that incapacitation alone is an insufficient purpose for civil commitment, without an additional purpose such as treatment.[12] SVP laws are, on their faces, constitutional because they address dangerousness that is coupled with "mental disorder" and provide for some form of treatment in nonpenal secure institutions.

In the fourth and current stage of litigation, the courts are working out the details of these principles: what kind of "mental disorder" suffices; what are the legal standards regarding dangerousness; what "treatment" does the Constitution mandate? It is to these issues that this paper now turns.

MENTAL DISORDER

Legal Developments

While the courts have been quite clear in holding that SVP commitments constitutionally require proof of a "mental disorder," they have been manifestly confused about what kinds of mental disorders will suffice. Initially, challengers argued that the Constitution was violated by the SVP laws' failure to require proof of a "medically valid" disorder. The courts' responses were confusing, holding that the mental disorder predicate was a legal, rather than medical concept, and simultaneously ascribing constitutional significance to the fact that the actual diagnoses of the individual litigants (as opposed to the statutorily defined terms) *were* medically valid.[13] It seems probable, now that the dust has settled, that the "mental disorder" predicate for civil commitment must have both medical validity and normative validity. Medical validity helps bestow legitimacy on SVP laws in at least two ways. Its boundaries for civil commitment are arguably "real," as opposed to socially constructed. This is important because socially constructed boundaries could be expanded arbitrarily, allowing civil commitment to swallow up the social control function of the criminal law. Further, persons with true mental disorders are arguably proper subjects for "treatment," a necessary (if secondary) state goal in civil commitment.

Both of these claims about mental disorder can be seriously challenged.[14] Nonetheless, they offer the most cogent explanation for the courts' reliance on medical validity in upholding SVP commitments.

Secondly, the mental disorder predicate in civil commitment must serve to justify the distinction between persons eligible for SVP commitments, and the great bulk of dangerous persons who are not.[15] In order to "justify" the distinction, the existence of the mental disorder needs to do more than provide a factual difference between the two groups. Justification requires relevant reasons, and it is in reference to these that the constitutional mental disorder predicate must have a form of "normative" validity.[16]

In *Crane*, the Supreme Court explained that "proof of serious difficulty in controlling behavior ... must be sufficient to distinguish the dangerous sexual offender whose serious mental illness, abnormality, or disorder subjects him to civil commitment from the dangerous but typical recidivist convicted in an ordinary criminal case."[17] The *Crane* decision has currently split state courts, some of whom have held that *Crane* requires an explicit finding of "serious difficulty controlling" behavior,[18] while others hold that the required element of control-dysfunction is implicit in other statutorily required findings, such as "predisposition" to commit further offenses.[19]

The holding in *Crane* should prompt lower courts to give additional definition to the concept of "inability to control" behavior. The concept is notoriously opaque and ambiguous. Without further definition, its operation will be highly arbitrary and it will not accomplish its constitutional justification purpose.[20]

A full exposition of the control issue is well beyond the scope of this essay.[21] I would propose that there are three key points that are necessary if there is to be any clarity in the legal use of the concept. First, the concept must "distinguish the dangerous sexual offender [subject to SVP commitment] ... from the dangerous but typical recidivist convicted in an ordinary criminal case."[22] At a minimum, this requires that the concept apply only to a small group of offenders.

Second, the "inability to control" concept must have a normative as well as psychological component. In general, "unable" expresses the normative judgment that the individual tried as hard as we would expect anyone to try—and nonetheless did not accomplish the task at hand.[23] Further, it must perform the normative function of justifying the selection of the small group for different (and adverse) legal status (eligibility for postprison "civil" confinement).

Third, the ability-to-control concept should be transparent and logical, rather than so opaque and paradoxical that its application is indeterminate and broadly expandable. Conceptual transparency requires avoidance of terms like "volition" which have multiple meanings, and no clear operational application. Lack of clarity in the relationship between terms like "choice," "voluntariness," "predisposed" and "intentional," on the one hand, and inability-to-control, on the other, produces nonsensical semantic acrobatics.[24]

The path out of the mess requires an approach that is more nuanced, empirically based, conceptually sound, and phenomenological. Courts might begin by drawing on the literature on self-regulation, which posits that human action operates via parallel, and often conflicting, processes.[25] Self-regulation posits an implicit hierarchy of those processes, and the imposition of the "higher" process to control the lower. The imposition of the higher process on the lower involves an identifiable and observable set of abilities, such as setting standards for behavior and self-monitoring. As well, self-regulation takes effort—physical effort and also something called willpower—and people might lack sufficient strength to sustain effective self-regulation, or can simply give up that effort if it is too arduous.[26]

Ward and Hudson make use of this self-regulation model to examine sex offender behavior, identifying concretely the ways in which some sex offenders have impaired self-regulation.[27] Their approach allows experts and courts to tie their discussions of inability-to-control to observable facts, exposing quite clearly the normative questions underlying the concept such as how much "willpower" the law expects a person to exert before his "giving in" to sexual violence is labeled "inability" to control rather than unwillingness.

In the end, courts will not be able to offer truly coherent definitions of "inability to control" until they understand why the concept is being used in this legal context. On this question, the court opinions are entirely unhelpful. We can only speculate about the deeper justifications that "inability to control" might bring to SVP commitments. Two come to mind. Lack of control over behavior often is associated with criminal irresponsibility. Since this mental state excludes an individual from the reach of the criminal law, the state would have a clear and heightened interest in a noncriminal form of social control. Alternatively, lack of ability to control might be emblematic of "diminished personhood." Free will is the lynchpin of personhood, and "lack of ability to control" behavior suggests its absence.[28] One might posit that diminished personhood entails diminished interest in freedom and correspondingly lowered legal protections.

Though no courts have explicitly endorsed either of these "deep meanings,"[29] I suggest they are implicitly present if the notion of "inability to control" is to make any sense.

Consequences of the Mental Disorder Requirement

SVP laws account for only a small proportion of sexual violence, but they can attain symbolic importance as the "flagship" in the public's armamentarium in the battle against sexual violence. Although the civil commitment form was chosen as an expediency, it necessarily brings along a particular psychological explanation for sexual violence that may reshape our collective understanding of sexual violence in two ways. First, by implicitly demanding "medically valid" diagnoses that distinguish persons subject to commitment from other criminals, SVP laws may put pressure on mental health professionals to expand the definitions of "mental disorder" as they apply to sexual violence. There is some evidence that this "medicalization" of sexual violence is occurring, particularly in the expansion of the "paraphilia" diagnosis and its application.

Consider two sets of simple, descriptive statistics. In a study of all 116 men committed in Minnesota's sex offender commitment scheme during the period 1975 through 1996, Dr. Nancy Walbeck and I examined treatment records and found that only 46% of the men had been diagnosed with at least one paraphilia, while fully 54% had no such diagnosis. When examined by year of admission, the proportion of paraphilia diagnoses increased from about 25% in 1993 to more than 90% in 1996. As of May 2001, the proportion in the total population had increased to 97%.[30]

Second, I examined all SVP appellate cases reported on Westlaw through March 2002. I counted the proportion of those cases that mentioned a diagnosis of paraphilia (rape) or paraphilia NOS. The former diagnosis is controversial,[31] and the use of the NOS ("not otherwise specified") classification might be an indication that examiners and courts are stretching the boundaries of the paraphilia diagnosis to include patterns that are not traditionally included. I checked seven states, each of which had more than ten cases in Westlaw. The paraphilia (rape) diagnosis was mentioned in 21% of the Washington cases, 8% of the California cases, and in none of the cases from Florida, Illinois, Iowa or Minnesota. The NOS diagnosis occurred in 17% of the Washington cases and 10% of the California cases, and either not at all or substantially less in the other states.

These patterns are some evidence that SVP laws, at least as interpreted in certain states, are exerting pressure on diagnosticians to expand sexual deviancy categories and to apply sexual deviancy, as a diagnosis, more broadly. Yet it is clear that sexual violence is a "complex amalgam of factors" that only sometimes includes deviant sexuality, and often includes antisocial behaviors and distorted attitudes about women and sexuality.[32] The proper understanding and classification of sexual violence is an ongoing project that ought to be informed by both science and social policy. But the accidental adoption of the civil commitment format may be exerting extraneous pressure to elevate the medicalized, sexual deviancy explanation above others.

A second influence may arise by the adoption, as a central motif, of the notion of "inability to control." Ascribing sexual violence to a diminished ability to control behavior reframes sexual violence in the "causal" language of psychology rather than the language of choice and freewill inherent in the law and morality. This choice of paradigm ironically supports the rationalizations that many offenders use to minimize their own responsibility,[33] and reinforces societal views that tolerate sexual violence.[34]

RISK ASSESSMENT

Legal Developments

The assessment of risk forms a centerpiece of SVP laws, providing one of the key justifications for these schemes. I will describe the legal context in which this assessment of risk takes place, and then make several observations about the potential social consequences of this central focus on risk assessment.

Advocates and courts uniformly seek to justify commitment laws by characterizing them as highly selective processes, confining only the most dangerous.[35] Indeed, in view of the extreme expense of SVP laws, this claim is also central to any social policy justification for these laws.[88]

There are grounds for doubting that this central justification describes the actual implementation of these laws. The traditional critique argues that mental health experts are not skilled at risk assessment, and their unavoidable inaccuracy leads to the commitment of the nondangerous and the release of the dangerous. But recent advances in actuarial risk assessment[36] suggest that some reasonable degree of accuracy may be attainable.[37] Even so, the continued reliance on clinical or clinically adjusted assessment in many cases[38] suggests that the old critique may still have some force.[39]

Further, neither the SVP statutes nor the courts have established clear thresholds for judging that the risk of a particular individual is high enough to justify deprivation of liberty. As a result, the process leaves wide discretion to experts, trial judges, and juries, with almost no reason to think that applied risk thresholds are either particularly high or uniform.[40]

As originally formulated by Brooks, dangerousness, or risk, may be analyzed into four separate components: likelihood, severity, imminence, and frequency.[41] Courts have given the most intense scrutiny[42] to the first element, likelihood.

All SVP laws set some threshold for this element, generally making use of words like "likely" or "probable" to define the degree of likelihood required to justify the deprivation of liberty. A review of the case law allows two conclusions about this legal standard. First, there is large variability in how courts interpret the statutory likelihood standard. Several courts interpret "likely" to mean "highly likely" or "highly probable."[43] A second set of courts interpret "likely" to mean "more likely than not."[44] A third set of courts refuses to define the term any further.[45] Finally, at least one court has held that "likely" means "substantial danger—that is, a serious and well-founded risk," and clarifies that such a risk could include probabilities that are smaller than 50%.[46]

The variability of language used to set the risk threshold is exacerbated by the courts' refusal to translate the qualitative threshold standards into numerical probability equivalents. As a result, commitment hinges on the application of qualitative terms ("serious risk," "highly likely," etc.) that will be interpreted by experts, judges and juries in variable ways,[47] involving substantial implicit definition of the legal terms.

Early challenges urged courts to find that SVP laws violated constitutional protections because risk assessments were simply too inaccurate to satisfy due process requirements. This is the most fundamental due process challenge, at bottom arguing that the deprivation of liberty, based on necessarily flawed predictions of future violence, is simply arbitrary. Courts quickly rejected these arguments, essentially holding that prediction is a central—and traditionally accepted—part of many legal processes.[48] These decisions do not purport to give an unconditional imprimatur to risk assessment. Rather, they place reliance on the adversary system to sort out adequate from inadequate instances of risk assessment.[49]

The legal system provides three points at which the adequacy of risk assessment might be checked: admissibility, legal sufficiency, and credibility. In the admissibility determination, judges must determine that expert risk assessment testimony is sufficiently reliable and relevant, but not misleading (prejudicial).[50] If there is conflict among the admitted risk assessment opinions, fact finders (juries or judges) must make credibility determinations to choose among them. Finally, judges decide whether the state's evidence, if deemed credible by the jury, would be sufficient to surpass the legal threshold for risk.

Judgments of legal sufficiency offer the best prospect of policing the risk assessment process, because courts must articulate a legal standard for risk with sufficient clarity to judge actual case-specific assessments. These judgments then form a body of precedent that facilitates uniform application of the standard. However, to date, appellate courts have not established specific standards, and therefore, no appellate court has reversed a commitment on grounds of the insufficiency of risk assessment testimony.[51]

A key reason for the failure of courts to develop more careful risk thresholds is the ubiquity in SVP cases of clinical—as opposed to actuarial—judgments of risk. Since clinicians have no reliable way to quantify their qualitative risk judgments, specific numerical standards would add at best illusory precision to the assessment process.

To a degree that is not clear, examiners use actuarial methods as part of the risk assessment process in commitment cases.[52] Opponents have challenged the admissibility of this testimony on the grounds that it does not satisfy the standards for expert testimony under the prevailing standards of *Frye* and *Daubert*.[53] Using somewhat different phraseology, these two cases impose standards designed to insure the reliability of the testimony offered by experts.[54] Four central challenges have been leveled at actuarially based risk assessment testimony. First, critics complain that actuarial instruments have been inadequately developed: that they lack user manuals, have not been sufficiently cross-validated, do not conform to professional testing standards, and have not been subjected to peer review publication. Second, critics point out that the actuarial method is too inflexible, that actuarial instruments rely on limited and fixed lists of factors—often "static" factors that do not reflect changeable circumstances such as response to treatment—and are therefore insufficiently individuated. Third, opponents argue that some actuarial tools lack sufficient relevancy because they were developed on samples from other countries and on populations that differ in age, community supervision, and treatment status from the prison populations now being released. Finally, critics worry that triers of fact will be unduly swayed by the veneer of science, the aura of statistics, and the apparent precision of numerically expressed results.[55]

The central measure for admissibility—reliability—is inherently indeterminate. Since no scientific or expert method is perfectly reliable, of necessity courts must make judgments about how much reliability is required.[56] This judgment, in turn, will rest on two bases: first, given the nature of the decision, how much reliability is required; second, how well can the trier of fact evaluate the testimony, or, in legal parlance, how "prejudicial" or prone to misinterpretation is the testimony.

As of this date, most of the appellate courts that have addressed the issue have ruled that actuarially based evidence is admissible in SVP trials.[57] Three courts have addressed directly the level of validation achieved by actuarial tools and have split on its adequacy.[58] The courts' disagreement about the sufficiency of the validation highlights the logical priority of establishing how much reliability is required. Two courts have walked around the problem by characterizing actuarial methods as just one aspect of the clinical judgment courts are accustomed to admitting. These courts emphasize that actuarial results must be interpreted by clinicians, and the actuarial numbers are therefore "supplemented" by clinical observations.[59] The most sophisticated judicial approach, in my view, was taken by a New Jersey appellate court. In a crucial passage, the court noted that "actuarial instruments are at least as reliable, if not more so, than clinical interviews." It continued:

> Since expert testimony concerning future dangerousness based on clinical judgment alone has been found sufficiently reliable for admission into evidence at criminal trials, we find it logical that testimony based upon a combination of clinical judgment and actuarial instruments is also reliable. Not only does actuarial evidence provide the court with additional relevant information, in the view of some, it may even provide a more reliable prediction of recidivism.[60]

Reflections and Implications

The centrality of risk in the legal innovations of the 1990s provides an incentive for the development and improvement of technologies—particularly actuarial risk assessment instruments—for measuring and communicating risk. This is a positive development for both public safety and individual rights. In addition to bringing increased accuracy, the development and use of actuarial tools may help increase accountability, and therefore legitimacy, of the new regulatory interventions. Actuarial methods make the process of risk assessment transparent, thereby exposing both its strengths and weaknesses. In contrast, clinical assessments are often based, in the end, on the opaque *ipse dixit* of the expert. Further, actuarial assessments can be reported as numerical probabilities with estimates of likely error. The quantification of risk facilitates, and perhaps demands, legal standards of sufficient clarity to allow for appellate review and the consequent uniformity and accountability. These will uniformly be seen as positive developments.

But the centrality of risk, and the quantification and actuarialization of risk, may have serious unintended and undesired consequences. First, risk is a term that is neutral as to responsibility and blame. A person can be a risk in the same sense that nuclear waste, a lawnmower, or a bear can be a risk. "Risk" has no implication of moral agency. Second, making risk the currency for policy and law naturally raises the question of who will bear the risk. In a way, the community notification and commitment schemes represent different instincts: notification encourages individuals to protect themselves from risk, whereas commitment in a sense takes the burden on the society to protect potential victims. But both also clearly shift to the offender a burden corresponding to the risk (as opposed to guilt or blameworthiness) he poses.

Third, the increased availability of risk information will demand action to protect the public from known—as well as knowable—risks. The specter of an individual being "allowed" to commit a crime despite a risk that could have been known may be too much for public officials to bear. The improvements in risk assessment technologies for sex offenders will surely migrate to other forms of violence, and perhaps other forms of antisocial behavior. Will the availability of the scientific tools to predict undesirable and harmful behavior create the need for legal tools to contain that behavior?

Finally, the currency of risk—particularly when it is actuarially measured and reported in stark numerical probabilities—may affect our fundamental conceptualization of sexual violence, and violence more generally. Risk assessment discounts the future to the present, crystallizing and reducing an unknown and unknowable set of complex contingencies into a probability—a present risk. That risk then becomes a characteristic, a descriptor, of the person, something *dangerous* that he "is."[61] Probabilities are inherently group-based: risk assessment seeks to strip away what is accidental, and discover that which is "essential," for it is only through essential similarities that group-based statistics have proper relevance.[62] This reductionist and essentialist characterization of sex offenders undercuts fundamental notions of personal accountability and control. After all, if the "essence" of a person is "risk," how can we expect that person to act or become otherwise? If prediction of risk is valid, what has happened to free choice and personal accountability?

TREATMENT AND CONDITIONS OF CONFINEMENT: EFFICACY AND REMEDIES

Legal Developments

Persons confined under civil commitment have constitutional rights to treatment and nonpunitive conditions of confinement. But the Supreme Court has spoken only minimally on these two issues, and many questions remain unanswered.

The questions have important practical consequences. State of the art treatment, provided in a humane, therapeutic environment is much more expensive than the standard punitive conditions of correctional institutions or even intensive supervision in the community.[63] If states are required to adhere to these expensive standards, the *quid pro quo* for the public protection offered by SVP laws will be viewed as prohibitive by many states.[64] Further, if treatment is ineffective and conditions punitive, SVP programs will face the unhappy choice of discharging inadequately treated, unhappy inmates, or housing ever-growing populations of hopeless patients.

The constitutional right to nonpunitive conditions of confinement, and the constitutional right to treatment, have somewhat different contours. The constitutional "conditions" analysis arises from the foundational principle that civil commitment may not be "punitive." As the Supreme Court held in *Youngberg*, "persons who have been involuntarily committed are entitled to more considerate treatment and conditions of confinement than criminals whose conditions of confinement are designed to punish,"[65] and *Allen* suggests that individuals may not be "confined under conditions incompatible with the state's asserted interest in treatment."[66] The complication is that all deprivation of liberty is inherently punitive, at least when viewed from the confined person's perspective.[67] The Court has articulated two standards for measuring conditions to determine whether they are punitive in the constitutional sense. First, restrictions must be "reasonably related to legitimate therapeutic and institutional interests."[68] Second, conditions will be judged with deference to the professional judgments of state officials who operate the institution.[69]

The right to treatment analysis is a bit more complex.[70] In the recent SVP litigation, the Supreme Court appears to say that a state must have "treatment" as a purpose if its SVP law is to pass constitutional muster.[71] Without treatment, the sole remaining purpose—incapacitation—is impossible to distinguish from punitive criminal sanctions. States must follow through on this "purpose" because due process requires that "the nature and duration of commitment [must] bear some reasonable relation to the purpose for which the individual is committed."[72]

At least three aspects of the right to treatment remain clouded. First, what treatment objective is constitutionally required? In *Youngberg*, a case involving severely retarded persons who were assumed to be incapable of living outside of the institution, the Supreme Court held that treatment needed to be adequate to facilitate physical safety and freedom from bodily restraint.[73] Analogous reasoning might suggest that treatment for SVPs, who are able to live outside of the institution, must be aimed at enabling them to do so.[74]

The second unresolved issue concerns enforcement. Though courts can award damages and issue injunctions to correct unconstitutional conditions,[75] it is unclear whether these violations ever require the release of SVPs. In *Seling v. Young*, the Supreme Court considered a petition for release on grounds of persistent failure of the State of Washington to remedy unconstitutional conditions and lack of treatment at its SVP facility.[76] The Court did not question the persistence of the conditions or their unconstitutionality, but dismissed the petition on legal grounds. It is possible to explain the *Young* dismissal as a consequence of the particular legal theories advanced (*ex post facto* and double jeopardy). This leaves open the possibility that a challenge on substantive due process grounds might support an order to release.[77] But there remains great uncertainty on this point.

This leads us to the final unresolved question: does the Constitution require treatment that is efficacious, or, to ask the question in a slightly different way, may states confine forever individuals who prove unamenable to treatment and therefore remain dangerous? When the Court has spoken on this question, it is always with a carefully hedged negative, pointing out that it has "never held that the Constitution prevents a State from civilly detaining those for whom no treatment is available, but who nevertheless pose a danger to others."[78] In a contrary vein, some Supreme Court cases hold that the due process clause of the Constitution places a strict durational limit on nontreatment civil confinement,[79] and permits the state a "reasonable" period to accomplish its commitment purpose.[80] This line of precedent might require release of sex offenders for whom it has become clear there is no reasonable likelihood of successful treatment.[81]

The practical importance of the law in this area becomes apparent from an examination of the meager success rates, so far, of SVP treatment programs. Lieb and Nelson report as of June 2000 that fewer than 2% of SVPs under detention had been released even conditionally. Removing Arizona, which had a rate of release substantially greater than that of the other states (15%, compared to the next most successful state, Washington, with a 4% rate), the overall rate of release was 1%.[82] As of Fall 2002 in Minnesota, only one of the 183 committed men had been provisionally released, and about 7% of the men had reached the highest two stages of the six-phase treatment program.[83]

The consequences are serious. As commitments continue, institutional population size will increase without short-term limits. The resources devoted to SVP institutions will correspondingly increase, both as an absolute level, and, most likely, as a proportion of the prevention and treatment resources generally available for sex offenders. A Minnesota Task Force estimated that the annual cost of "current practice" will increase by 450% (from $17 million to $76.9 million) in the twelve years from 1998 to 2010,[84] even though SVP costs already account for a large percentage of the state's treatment and prevention resources.[83]

Of course, the high cost and minimal discharge rates for SVP programs might be viewed as positives. Strict discharge criteria and high expenditures might reflect the high value of protecting the public from the "most dangerous" sex offenders.[86] Still, in times of limited public resources, expenditures inevitably involve choices among competing needs,[87] and alternate approaches to the problem of sexual violence go unfunded because of sex offender commitment programs.

CONCLUSIONS

The regulatory interventions of the 1990s arose, in part, from the same heightened awareness of sexual violence that characterized the feminist movement and the reforms it inspired in the 1970s and '80s. But while the earlier reforms proceeded quite intentionally from a particular theory about the nature of sexual violence, the later innovations were atheoretical, practical responses to perceived shortcomings in the criminal justice system.

SVP laws claim two purposes: incapacitation and treatment of the "most dangerous" sex offenders. At best, they are accomplishing the first of these purposes by confining about 1200 people who are at higher risk of sexual reoffending than the average sex offender.

This protection, however, comes at a substantial cost. At the most obvious level, the cost is measured in dollars and in missed opportunities to address sexual violence in other ways. At a more fundamental level, the SVP laws adopt and give official and symbolic importance to a conception of sexual violence that is largely at odds with the feminist view underlying the rape reforms of the 1970s and '80s. SVP laws change the "architecture" of sexual violence in three strong ways.

First, SVP laws frame the policy question underlying the societal response to sexual violence in a specific way: SVP laws are the answer to the question: "How can we prevent the highest risk of sexual violence?" There is an alternate framing of the question that would yield very different policy choices: "How can we prevent the most sexual violence?" The latter framing of the question is consistent with the feminist view that sexual violence is widespread and domesticated. The new paradigm paints sexual violence as a small and exceptional aberration.

Second, the legal structure of SVP laws—civil commitment—contributes to this alternate framing of sexual violence. To fit SVP laws into the civil commitment mold, sex offenders have to be portrayed as so "mentally disordered" that they lack control of their violent behavior, and are in that way distinguishable from "ordinary" dangerous criminals. These characterizations support the view that sexual violence —or at least that portion of it that deserves the most attention and public resources— is "different in kind" and aberrational. Community notification laws support the same paradigm shift by representing sexual violence as assault by unknown strangers whose identities can be known only via notification, as opposed to family members and acquaintances, whose histories are more likely available to potential victims.

Third, the centrality of risk assessment, and the development of more refined methods of measuring and communicating risk of sexual violence, may also contribute to this paradigm shift. By focusing on individuals, risk assessment ineluctably calls for an individual response commensurate with individual risk. Accurate risk assessment makes it easier to identify, and isolate, the "most dangerous," and thereby diverts attention from identifying and preventing the "most danger." On the positive side, actuarial risk assessment adds accuracy and transparency to the process. By exposing the group-based foundations of all prediction, however, and by reducing the prediction to a single measure of probability, actuarial methods contribute to the characterization of sex offenders as different in kind. The future becomes embedded in the present; group-predication implies that the individual shares the group's "essence;" freewill and individual responsibility disappear as the seemingly immutable probabilities of violence emerge from the actuarial computations and are reified as "dangerousness."

The reforms of the past three decades share a compelling purpose: the prevention of sexual violence. It is now time to begin serious assessment of the recent reforms to determine whether they represent the optimal approaches to sexual violence.

NOTES

1. *See, generally*, John D'Emilio & Estelle B. Freedman, INTIMATE MATTERS: A HISTORY OF SEXUALITY IN AMERICA (University of Chicago Press, 2^d ed., 1997).
2. *See, e.g.*, Stephen J. Schulhofer, *Rape: Legal Aspects, in* ENCYCLOPEDIA OF CRIME & JUSTICE 1306 (Joshua Dressler, ed., 2002).
3. *See*, Eric S. Janus, *Civil Commitment as Social Control: Managing the Risk of Sexual Violence, in* DANGEROUS OFFENDERS: PUNISHMENT AND SOCIAL ORDER (Mark Brown and John Pratt, eds., 2000).
4. *See, generally,* Paula M. Ditton & Doris James Wilson, *Truth in Sentencing in State Prisons*, U.S. DEP'T OF JUST., BUREAU OF JUST. STAT. (1999); Darrell K. Gilliard & Allen J. Beck, *Bulletin: Prisoners in 1997*, BUREAU OF JUST. STAT. (Aug. 1998).
5. *See* Janus, *Civil Commitment as Social Control, supra* note 3.
6. *See, generally,* Wayne A. Logan, *Sex Offender Registration and Community Notification: Emerging Legal and Research Issues* (2003; this volume).
7. Governor's Task Force on Community Protection, *Task Force on Community Protection: Final Report to Booth Gardner Governor State of Washington*, (Nov. 28, 1989); Office of the Attorney General, State of Minnesota *Attorney General's Task Force on the Prevention of Sexual Violence Against Women* (1989).
8. State *ex rel.* Pearson v. Probate Court of Ramsey County, 205 Minn. 545, 549, 287 N.W. 297, 300 (Minn. 1939).
9. *See generally* Edward P. Richards, *The Jurisprudence of Prevention: The Right of Societal Self-Defense Against Dangerous Individuals*, 16 HASTINGS CONST. L.Q. 329 (1989).
10. *See, e.g.*, Matter of Linehan, 518 N.W.2d 609 (Minn. 1994); see also, e.g., Kansas v. Crane, 122 S. Ct. 867, 151 L. Ed. 856 (2002).
11. *See* Foucha v. Louisiana, 504 U.S. 71, 86, 112 S. Ct. 1780, 1788 (1992); Kansas v. Hendricks, 521 U.S. 346, 358, 117 S. Ct. 2072, 2080 (1997).
12. See *id.* at 369; Seling v. Young, 531 U.S. 250, 121 S. Ct. 727 (2001).
13. "In this action, the mental abnormality—pedophilia—is at least described in the *DSM-IV. American Psychiatric Association, Diagnostic and Statistical Manual of Mental Disorders* 524–525, 527–528 (4th ed. 1994)." Hendricks, 521 U.S. at 372 (Kennedy, J., concurring). See, e.g., *In re* Commitment of Pletz, 239 Wis. 2d 49, 58-59, 619 N.W.2d 97, 101 (Wis. Ct. App. 2000).
14. *See*, Eric S. Janus, *Foreshadowing the Future of* Kansas v. Hendricks, 92 Nw. U. L. REV. 1279, 1291 (1998) (enumerating and critiquing various roles for the "mental disorder" predicate in civil commitment).

15. *See* Robert F. Schopp & Barbara J. Sturgis, *Sexual Predators and Legal Mental Illness for Civil Commitment*, 13 BEHAV. SCI. & L. 437, 449 (1995) (legislative use of "mental disorder" must justify differential treatment).
16. *Id.*
17. Kansas v. Crane, 112 S.Ct. 867, 870 (2002).
18. *In re* Spink, 48 P.3d 381 (Ct. App.Wash. 2002); Converse v. Dept. of Children and Families, 823 So.2d 295 (Ct. App. Fla. 2002); *In re* Thomas, 74 S .W.3d 789 (Mo. 2002).
19. *See, e.g., In re* Varner, 198 Ill. 2d 78, 759 N.E.2d 560 (Ill. 2001); *In re* Leon G., 200 Ariz. 298, 26 P.3d 481 (Ariz. 2002), *judgment vacated*, 122 S. Ct. 1535 (2002); People v. Hubbart, 88 Cal. App. 4th 1202, 106 Cal. Rptr. 2d 490 (Cal. Dist. Ct. App. 2001).
20. *See, e.g.,* People v. Hicks, No. D037117, 2002 WL 139718, at *3 (Cal. Dist. Ct. App. Jan. 29, 2002) (offering the circular explanation that "When such a person cannot control those emotions or urges, they demonstrate a volitional impairment—an inability to control those emotions.")
21. *See* Eric S. Janus, *Sex Offeder Commitments and the "Inability to Control": Developing Legal Standards and a Behavioral Vocabulary for an Elusive Concept, in* THE SEXUAL PREDATOR: LEGAL ISSUES, CLINICAL ISSUES, SPECIAL SITUATIONS (Anita Schlank, 2001).
22. *Crane,* 122 S. Ct. at 870.
23. *See* Stephen J. Morse, *Culpability and Control,* 142 U. PA. L. REV. 1587, 1588 (1994) (framing the question as how much pain we expect a person to endure before we judge their "giving in" as beyond their control.).
24. Several examples of such acrobatics can be cited. The court in People v. Hatfield, 80 Cal. Rptr. 2d 268, 282 (Cal. Dist. Ct. App. 1998), *ordered not published, previously published at:* 68 Cal. App. 4th 594 (Cal. Dist. Ct. App. 1999) drew a distinction between "inability to control" and "compelled choice to so act." The court equated inability to control with being "predisposed" to act. An expert in *In re* Det. of Brooks, 94 Wash. App. 716, 730, 973 P.2d 486, 493 (Wash. Ct. App. 1999) distinguished between disorders, such as schizophrenia, that are "biochemical abnormalities over which a person has limited control," and paraphilias, which are "under voluntary muscular control."
25. ROY F. BAUMEISTER *et al.*, LOSING CONTROL: HOW AND WHY PEOPLE FAIL AT SELF-REGULATION 6 (1994).
26. *Id.* at 7–9.
27. *See* Tony Ward & Stephen M. Hudson, *Future Directions in the Assessment and Treatment of Sex Offenders*, 14 BEH. CHANGE 215 (1997).
28. *See* Andreas Eshete, *Character, Virtue and Freedom,* 57 PHILOSOPHY 495, 497 (1982).
29. *But see Linehan*, 518 N.W.2d at 615 (Gardebring, J. dissenting) ("Either appellant has the capacity to intend his vicious acts, in which case he is properly held accountable in the criminal justice system, or he suffers from the "utter lack of *power* to control [his] sexual impulses," and is therefore subject to commitment as a psychopathic personality.").
30. Personal communication from Minnesota Department of Human Services, May 11, 2001. Since most of the 1996 population remained committed as of 2001, the recent figures reflect a re-diagnosis of a substantial portion of the non-paraphilia-diagnosed pre-1996 group. In the 1996 study, most of those in the non-paraphilia group had a personality disorder diagnosis and/or chemical abuse or dependency. *See* Eric S. Janus & Nancy H. Walbek, *Sex Offender Commitments in Minnesota: A Descriptive Study of Second Generation Commitments*, 18 BEHAV. SCI. & L. 343 (2000).
31. *See, e.g.*, Gene G. Abel & Joanne L. Rouleau, *The Nature and Extent of Sexual Assault, in* HANDBOOK OF SEXUAL ASSAULT 9, 18 (W. L. Marshall *et al.*, 1990) (arguing for the creation of a category of "paraphilia" called "rape as paraphilia," despite the fact that the DSM rejects such a category.).
32. Robert Prentky, *Rape: Behavioral Aspects, in* ENCYCLOPEDIA OF CRIME & JUSTICE 1301, (Joshua Dressler, ed., 2002)

33. *See,* Diana Scully & Joseph Marolla, *Convicted Rapists' Vocabulary of Motive: Excuses and Justifications,* 31 SOCIAL PROBLEMS 530, 530 (1984) (criticizing the characterization, since 1925, of "irresistible impulse" and "disease of the mind" as the causes of rape, on the grounds, in part, of their finding that more than 50% of rapists "explained themselves and their acts by appealing to forces beyond their control, forces which reduced their capacity to act rationally and thus compelled them to rape.").

34. *See generally* SHARON LAMB, THE TROUBLE WITH BLAME: VICTIMS, PERPETRATORS & RESPONSIBILITY 76 (Harvard University Press 1996) (arguing that "men's lack of control over their sex drive" is "the dominant discourse of sexuality widely believed and accepted in our culture.... This vision of male sexuality makes it appear as if choice is overwhelmed by urge.").

35. *See, e.g.,* Kelly A. McCaffrey, Comment, *The Civil Commitment of Sexually Violent Predators in Kansas: A Modern Law for Modern Times,* 42 U. KAN. L. REV. 887, 905 (1994) (arguing that SVP laws are "necessary" laws that are "narrowly focused" on only the "most dangerous"); State v. Post, 541 N.W.2d 115, 122 (Wis. 1995), *cert. denied,* Post v. Wisconsin, 521 U.S. 1118, 117 S. Ct. 2507 (1997).

36. Researchers classify risk assessments as "clinical" and "actuarial," distinguished by Litwack as follows: [A]ctuarial assessments are assessments based on supposedly validated relationships between measurable predictor and outcome variables and ultimately determined by fixed, or mechanical, and explicit rules.... Conversely, clinical assessments are viewed here as assessments ultimately determined by human judgment (beyond a human judgment to rely solely on a particular actuarial instrument)... Thomas R. Litwack, *Actuarial Versus Clinical Assessments of Dangerousness,* 7 PSYCHOL. PUB. POL'Y & L. 409, 412 (2001).

37. *See, e.g.,* Howard E. Barbaree *et al., Evaluating the Predictive Accuracy of Six Risk Assessment Instruments for Adult Sex Offenders,* 28 CRIM. JUST. AND BEHAV. 490, 492 (2000).

38. *See, generally,* John Petrila & Randy K. Otto, *The Admissibility of Expert Testimony in Sexually Violent Predator Proceedings,* in THE SEXUAL PREDATOR: LEGAL ISSUES, CLINICAL ISSUES, SPECIAL POPULATIONS 3–20 (Anita Schlank, ed., 2001).

39. *See id.* (asserting there is "no basis to claim that one's opinions based on an adjusted actuarial approach are as valid as judgments based on an actuarial approach. Yet examiners routinely use such an [adjusted] approach ...").

40. *See* Janus & Walbek, *supra* note 30 (finding wide variation among Minnesota commitments in risk-relevant factors such as number of prior sex offenses); Janus, *infra,* note 88 (describing factors contributing to variable dangerousness among commitment detainees).

41. *See* Eric S. Janus & P. E. Meehl, *Assessing the Legal Standard for Predictions of Dangerousness in Sex Offender Commitment Proceedings,* 3 PSYCHOL., PUB. POL'Y, & L. 33, 37 (1997).

42. Some courts and laws narrow "severity" by requiring a focus on "violent" offending. *See, e.g., In re* Commitment of Marberry, 231 Wis. 2d 581, 584, 605 N.W.2d 612, 615 (Wis. Ct. App. 1999). Most courts set no imminence requirement, allowing multi-year horizons on risk assessment, and refusing to require a "recent overt act" as a predicate. *See, e.g., Hubbart v. Superior Court,* 19 Cal.4th 1138, 81 Cal.Rptr.2d 492, 969 P.2d 584, 600 (Cal.1999). *Contra In re* Reese, 13 Mass.L.Rptr. 195, 2001 WL 359954 (Mass. Super. Apr 05, 2001 (holding "likely to engage in sexual offenses" means "a substantial likelihood, at least more likely than not, that the respondent will commit a new sexual offense within the immediate future, understood generally to be within the next five years but with a longer time horizon if the anticipated future harm is extremely serious"). Finally, most laws require some form of "habitual" or "repeated" offending as a predicate for commitment, thus defining the "frequency" prong. *See, e.g.,* MINN. STAT. ANN. § 253B.02 (West 2002) (stating that one factor the State must prove is that the defendant has evidenced a habitual course of misconduct in sexual matters).

43. *See, e.g.,* Matter of Linehan ("Linehan II"), 557 N.W.2d 171 (Minn. 1996) ("likely" means "highly likely"); *In re* Leon G., 200 Ariz. at 305–306 ("likely" means "highly

probable"); *cf. In re* Commitment of Curiel, 227 Wis. 2d 389, 401, 597 N.W.2d 697, 702 (Wis. 1999) (affirming that the statutory term "substantial probability" means "much more likely than not.").
44. Westerheide v. State, 767 So. 2d 637, 652–653 (Fla. Dist. Ct. App. 2000). ("likely" means "having a better chance of existing or occurring than not"); Commonwealth v. Reese, No. CIV .A 00-0181B, 2001 WL 359954, at *15 (Mass. Sup. Ct. Apr. 5, 2001) ("likely to engage in sexual offenses" means "a substantial likelihood, at least more likely than not.").
45. Commitment of Curiel, 221 Wis. 2d 596 (Wis. Ct. App. 1998), *aff'd on other grounds,* 27 Wis. 2d 389 (Wis. 1999).
46. Cooley v. Superior Court, 29 Cal.4th, 228, 57 P.3d 654, 127 Cal.Rptr.2d 177, *opinion modified,* Cooley v. Superior Court, 2003 WL 122554 (Cal. Jan. 15, 2003).
47. *See, e.g., In re* Curiel, 227 Wis. 2d at 396 ("Both witnesses for the State testified that, to a reasonable degree of psychological certainty, it was substantially probable that Curiel would engage in future acts of sexual violence. The one witness for the defense testified that it was not. None of the witnesses, however, used the same working definition of 'substantially probable' in reaching their conclusions.").
48. *See, e.g.,* People v. Buffington, 74 Cal. App. 4th 1149, 1155 (Cal. Dist. Ct. App. 1999) ("The compelling interest in protecting society against sexually motivated injury and in providing beneficial treatment for such disordered persons should not be sacrificed by requiring a certainty of prediction which is currently impossible to attain."); *Westerheide,* 767 So. 2d at 658 (stating that prediction of the likelihood of reoffense under such Acts may be made by qualified experts with a sufficient degree of accuracy).
49. *See* Barefoot v. Estelle, 463 U.S. 880, 103 S. Ct. 3383 (1983).
50. *See generally* Petrila & Otto, *supra* note 38.
51. *But see In re* Commitment of Kienitz, 227 Wis. 2d 423, 432, 597 N.W.2d 712, 716 (Wis. 1999) (trial court considered, but rejected contention that risk assessment testimony was insufficient to satisfy legal standard.).
52. Petrila & Otto, *supra* note 38, suggest that the extent of use is unknown. Dr. Dennis Doren, testifying in an adversarial proceeding, testified that "most" examiners in SVP cases employ the "clinically-adjusted actuarial assessment." *In re* Commitment of R.S., 339 N.J. Super. 507, 521, 773 A.2d 72, 80 (N.J. Super. Ct. App. Div. 2001).
53. *See* Petrila & Otto, *supra* note 38.
54. *See generally* D. L. Faigman *et al., How Good is Good Enough?: Expert Evidence Under* Daubert *and* Kumho, 50 CASE W. RES. L. REV. 645–667 (2000).
55. *See* Eric S. Janus & Robert A. Prentky, *The Forensic Use of Actuarial Risk Assessment with Sex Offenders: Accuracy, Admissibility and Accountability,* 40 AM. CRIM. L. REV. (forthcoming 2003).
56. Faigman, *supra* note 54.
57. For a more detailed discussion, *see* Janus & Prentky, *supra* note 55.
58. *See In re* Holtz, 653 N.W. 2d 613 (Iowa App. 2002); People v. Taylor, 335 Ill.App.3d 965, 270 Ill.Dec. 361, 782 N.E. 2d 920 (2002); *In re* R.S., 801 A.2d 219, 173 N.J. 134.
59. *See* State *ex rel.* Romley v. Fields, 201 Ariz. 321, 35 P.3d 82 (Ariz. Ct. App. 2001); Garcetti v. Superior Court, 102 Cal. Rptr. 2d 214, 239 (Cal. Ct. App. 2000).
60. *In re* R.S., 339 N.J.Super 507, 537–538, 773 A.2d 72 (2001), *aff'd per curium* 801 A.2d 219, 173 N.J. 134 (NJ 2002).
61. Marie A. Bochnewich, *Prediction of Dangerousness and Washington's Sexually Violent Predator Statute,* 29 CAL. W. L. REV. 277, 296 (1992) (prediction of dangerousness is actually a statement of a "condition" of the individual).
62. *See* Michael Tonry, *Prediction and Classification: Legal and Ethical Issues,* 9 CRIME & JUST. 367 (1987).
63. *See* John Q. La Fond, *The Costs of Enacting a Sexual Predator Law,* 4 PSYCHOL., PUB. POL'Y & L. 468, 478 (1998) (estimating that in Washington in 1998, the cost per resident for one year of commitment was approximately $91,969). The per diem cost of SVP commitment in Minnesota is $310, Minnesota Department of Human Services, Bulletin #02-77-01 (June 24, 2002), while the most intensive level of parole supervi-

sion for sex offenders costs $17 per day per offender. E-mail to Eric Janus from Steven Huot, 11/25/02 (on file with author).

64. *See* W. Lawrence Fitch, *NASHMPD Update: Civil Commitment of Sex Offenders in the U.S. (A Quick and Dirty Survey)* (October 1, 1998) (manuscript on file with author).

65. Youngberg v. Romeo, 457 U.S. 307, 321-322 (1982).

66. *In re* Det. of Campbell, 139 Wash.2d 341, 349 (Wash. 1999) (quoting Allen v. Illinois, 419 U.S. 364, 373).

67. Bell v. Wolfish, 441 U.S. 520, 536, 99 S.Ct. 1861, 1872 (1979).

68. West v. Macht, 237 Wis.2d 265, 276-277, 614 N.W.2d 34, 40 (Wis. Ct. App. 2000), *review denied by*, 237 Wis.2d 260, 618 N.W.2d 750 (Wis. 2000) (citing *Youngberg*, 457 U.S. at 322).

69. *West*, 237 Wis.2d at 276-277; *see also Youngberg,* 457 U.S. 307; *Bell,* 441 U.S. 520.

70. *See, generally,* Eric S. Janus & Wayne A. Logan, *Substantive Due Process and the Involuntary Confinement of Sexually Dangerous Predators*, 31 CONN. L. REV. (forthcoming 2003).

71. *See* Kansas v. Hendricks, 521 U.S. 346, 366 (1997) (attaching importance to fact that treatment was "ancillary goal" or "purpose" of Kansas SVP law and noting "obligation to provide treatment for committed persons"). *See also id.* at 371 (Kennedy, J., concurring) (denominating the absence of treatment as an "indication of the forbidden purpose to punish."); *id.* at 382 (Breyer, J., dissenting) (asserting that a "statutory scheme that provides confinement that does not reasonably fit a practically available, medically oriented treatment objective, more likely reflects a primarily punitive legislative purpose.").

72. Jackson v. Indiana, 406 U.S. 715, 738, 92 S. Ct. 1845, 1858 (1972); *See also*, Seling v. Young, 529 U.S. 1017 (2000).

73. Romeo's "primary needs are bodily safety and a minimum of physical restraint"—which it has recognized as "constitutionally protected liberty interest[s]"—and "training may be necessary to avoid unconstitutional infringement of those rights." 457 U.S. 307, 318.

74. *See, e.g.,* Alexander S. v. Boyd, 113 F.3d 1373 (4th Cir. 1997) ("The court finds that, under the Constitution, a minimally adequate level of programming is required in order to provide juveniles with a reasonable opportunity to accomplish the purpose of their confinement, to protect the safety of the juveniles and the staff, and to ensure the safety of the community once the juveniles are ultimately released.").

75. *See* Seling v. Young, 531 U.S. 250; *see, e.g.*, Turay v. Seling, 108 F. Supp. 2d 1148 (W.D. Wash. 2000).

76. *See Seling*, 531 U.S. 250.

77. *See, generally,* Janus & Logan, *supra* note 70.

78. *Hendricks*, 521 U.S. at 366.

79. *See* U.S. v. Salerno, 481 U.S. 739, 107 S.Ct. 2095 (1987).

80. Zadvydas v. Davis, 533 U.S. 678, 682, 121 S. Ct. 2491, 2495 (2001); *Salerno*, 481 U.S. 739; *Jackson*, 406 U.S. at 738.

81. *See* Janus & Logan, *supra* note 70, for a full development of this argument.

82. Roxanne Lieb & Craig Nelson, *Treatment Programs for Sexually Violent Predators—A Review of States*, in 2 THE SEXUAL PREDATOR: LEGAL ISSUES, CLINICAL ISSUES, SPECIAL POPULATIONS (Anita Schlank ed., 2001).

83. E-mail communication to Eric S. Janus from Anita Schlank, Ph.D., November 24, 2002 (correspondence on file with author).

84. MINNESOTA DEPARTMENT OF CORRECTIONS, CIVIL COMMITMENT STUDY GROUP 1998 REPORT TO LEGISLATURE 2–3 (1998).

85. In 2002, the State of Minnesota, for example, spent about $3.2 million on sex offender treatment in correctional settings (community and prison), compared to about $20 million, which is the annual budget for the SVP program. *See* Minnesota Department of Human Services, Bulletin #02-77-01 (June 24, 2002); Janus, *infra* note 88.

86. *See, e.g.,* Paul Demko, *Throwing Away the Key*, CITY PAGES (Minneapolis-St. Paul, Minn.), March 13, 2002, at 15 (quoting Ramsey County Attorney Susan Gaertner, who characterized the absence of SVP discharges as a sign that the system is working properly).

87. National Association of State Mental Health Program Directors, *Policy Statement on Laws Providing for the Civil Commitment of Sexually Violent Criminal Offenders* (1997) (SVP programs "divert scarce resources away from people who have been diagnosed with a mental illness and who both need and desire treatment"); Janus, *infra* note 88.

88. Eric S. Janus, *Minnesota's Sex Offender Commitment Program: Would an Empirically-Based Policy be More Effective?*, 29 WM. MITCHELL L. REV. 1083 (2003).

A Sex Equality Approach to Sexual Assault

CATHARINE A. MacKINNON[a]

University of Michigan Law School, Ann Arbor, Michigan 48109, USA

ABSTRACT: Sexual assault is a practice of sex inequality. It is not generally addressed as such by law, including criminal law, and should be.

KEYWORDS: sexual assault; rape; sex; gender; sexuality; power; consent; hierarchy; inequality; equality; forced sex; criminal law; male dominance

Sexual assault is a sex-based violation. This analysis is supported by the data and experience on sexual assault that have emerged since 1970.[1] Among humans, sexual abuse is systematically inflicted by and on people who are socially gendered unequal to one another. The gendered inferiority attributed to sexual victims, and used to target them, and the gendered superiority attached to sexual prowess, along with the erotization of subordination and dominance, are socially imbricated with established and inculcated notions and roles of masculinity and femininity respectively. A prominent observable regularity is that men more often perpetrate, women are more often victimized. Even more of the variance is explained by the observation that sexual atrocities are inflicted on those who have less social power by those who have more, among whom gender is the most significant cleavage of stratification.

In light of the evidence, human sexual aggression is best understood as social—attitudinal and ideological, role-bound and identity-defined—not natural. Causally speaking, nothing makes inevitable its high prevalence and incidence in everyday life,[2] or in wars or genocides, except social-rank orderings, advantage-seeking, inculcation, imitation, and conformity (to peer behavior and pressure, standards of prior generations, orders, media representations, and the like). These forces plainly make sexually aggressive behavior attractive and possible by some people against certain others, producing social incentives for perpetrators to attack and pressures for victims to be ignored under many different conditions.[3] Sexual perpetrators and victims are largely socially constructed males and females, respectively—gendered in part by societies that impel and excuse both their relative hierarchical positions and the violative acts that express and define those positions by attributing both to men's and women's natures or physical bodies.

Address for correspondence: Catharine MacKinnon, University of Michigan Law School, 625 South State Street, Ann Arbor, MI 48109-1215.

smrenier@umich.edu

[a]Elizabeth A. Long Professor of Law, University of Michigan, and long-term visitor, University of Chicago School of Law.

Ann. N.Y. Acad. Sci. 989: 265–275 (2003). © 2003 New York Academy of Sciences.

In this light, as explanation for sexual aggression, appeals to biology are revealed to prove both too little and too much. In the first place, not all women are victims and not all men are aggressors, and not only women are victims and not only men are aggressors. That sexual assault is propelled, indeed motivated, by social hierarchy rather than factors or forces of nature is evidenced by the fact of biologically female sexual aggressors[4] (if few, showing how powerful socialization is), as well as by the many biologically male victims and the child victims of both sexes,[5] not to mention postmenopausal women victims and same-sex victims of both sexes,[6] against all of whom sexual assault is a reproductive and, one suspects, evolutionary dead end.

Further evidence for a social over a biological explanation is the numbers of men who do not sexually aggress who have nothing wrong with them physically and the participation of race and class hierarchy in designating "appropriate" victims of sexual assault.[7] In genocides, in which women of the group to be destroyed are systematically raped by men of the group intending to destroy them, nothing biological has changed from a prior nongenocidal era. What has changed is that a political decision is made to destroy another racial or ethnic or religious group and the realization that rape is a highly effective tool to that end.[8] Nor do wars change men's biology; they do change the conditions of access, permission, and motivation for raping both women and men. In other words, sexual assault is based on social and political inequality not on biological distinction.

Embodied in the ideology of the naturalness of sexual assault (whether it takes the form of religious fundamentalism, fascism, or sociobiology) is necessarily the view that gender hierarchy—male supremacy and female inferiority—of which sexual aggression is a cardinal manifestation, is also natural. If the sexes are biologically different but not biologically superior and subordinate, sexual aggression is socially not biologically impelled, an act not of difference but of dominance, not of sexual dimorphism but of gender hierarchy. Put another way, because women are not men's sexual inferiors in nature, but are so ranked in societies in which sexual abuse of women in particular flourishes with social support, enforcing and expressing that inferiority, and because the sex roles and stereotypes that become realities gender sexual assault unequally and indelibly, and because gender is the social form sex takes, sexual abuse is properly analyzed as an act of sex inequality.

This realization is increasingly reflected by diverse legal authorities. The Supreme Court of Canada recognized in a 1993 rape case that "Sexual assault is in the vast majority of cases gender based. It ... constitutes a denial of any concept of equality for women."[9] International authorities including the General Assembly of the United Nations, the Committee on the Elimination of All Forms of Discrimination Against Women, the Organization of American States, the Beijing Conference, and the Council of Europe have all defined and condemned sexual violence as a gender-based function of unequal social power between the sexes.[10] The law against sexual harassment in the United States, which makes sexual incursions in employment and education civilly actionable as sex discrimination, construes sexual assault in certain settings as gender-based inequality.[11] The U.S. Supreme Court once found that women are raped because they are women, calling the capacity to be raped a result of the victim's "very womanhood."[12] In the Violence Against Women Act (VAWA), rape was made civilly actionable as sex discrimination when the violence was "because of" or "on the basis of gender," including "animus based on the victim's gender."[13] Presumably, Congress was not making a natural fact into a federal case, nor standing against nature when it legislated the United States' first zero tolerance standard for sex-based violence. Even the Supreme Court that invalidated the VAWA on other grounds did not question the legislative conclusion that sexual assault is generally describable as a practice of discrimination on the basis of sex.[14]

The growing consciousness of this reality is reflected virtually not at all in the criminal law of rape in the United States. Although sexual assault is always sexual and often physically violent, the awareness that rape is not so much an act of violence or sex as it is an act of sex inequality—specifically of sex eroticized by the dominance that inequality embodies and permits, of which physical violence is only one expression—is barely traceable in U.S. criminal law. Remarkably, given that criminal statutes are mostly state law, the equalization of which the Fourteenth Amendment was passed to guarantee, the well-documented sex inequalities in the criminal law of rape, from its design to most aspects of its state administration,[15] have remained almost entirely free of Equal Protection scrutiny, except for those rare rape statutes that differentiate between men and women on their face.[16] Surely the legal tolerance of sexual assault[17] is not a fact of nature. It is a fact of sex inequality in human societies, supported by ideologies that explain and exonerate systemic abuses of women by appeals to biological fiat. And, if the U.S. criminal law of rape does not meet a sex equality standard, as contended here, it must also be said that it has not been legally subjected to one.

In fundamental aspects of its doctrine, the U.S. rape laws can be seen to presuppose and enforce inequality between women and men in sex. A central instance is the legal standard for consent to sex, which does not hold contested sexual interactions to a standard of sexual equality. That is, when the law of rape finds consent to sex, it does not look to see whether the parties were social equals in any sense, nor does it require mutuality or positive choice in sex,[18] far less simultaneity of desire. The doctrine of consent in the law of forcible rape envisions instead unilateral initiation (the stereotyped acted/acted-upon model of male-dominant sex[19]) followed by accession or not by persons tacitly presumed equal. Consent is usually proven by the acted-upon not saying no; it can, however, even famously include saying no.[20]

A lot of not-yes-saying passes for consent to sex.[21] The accession to proceeding known as legal consent that makes sex not rape can, in addition to an express *no* that becomes a legal *yes*, include resigned, silent, passive, dissociated acquiescence in acts one despairs at stopping; fraud or pretense producing compliance in intercourse for false reasons[22] or with persons who are not who they say they are; multiplicity triggered by terror or programming (so that the person who accedes to the sex is just one inhabitant of the body with whom sex is had)[23]; and fear of abuse short of death or maiming or severe bodily injury (such as loss of one's job or not being able to graduate from high school, and including jurisdictions that do not consider rape itself a form of severe bodily injury) resulting in letting sex happen.[24]

Outside settings of war and genocide, little to no legal attention is paid to whether the parties enter sexual intercourse as social equals. Not even known hierarchies of boss-worker, teacher-student, doctor-patient, priest-penitent, or lawyer-client formally register in the doctrine of the criminal law of rape. This law is indifferent to whether the sexual transactions in which assault is claimed occurred at (what contract law calls) arm's length. People who could not sign a binding contract, under conditions of overreaching under which it would not be enforced, can have sex and the law is none the wiser. In popular culture, where no one (man or women) describes a magical moment of sexual intimacy or connection or eroticism as "consensual," the term consent is nonetheless used as if it actually means choice, mutuality, and desire. This is a fiction. Within its legal ambit, consent can include sex that is wanted, but it can also include sex that is not at all wanted and is forced by inequality.

Usually, consent is a club used as a defense by a man at the point a woman says he raped her, or, in what amounts to the same thing, when she says that her prostitution was not freely chosen. Consent is more attributed than exercised. As is by now well known, if sexual intercourse took place, particularly if the woman had had sex before, if the parties knew each other, or lived together, or if the man paid, consent tends to be presumed or found.[25] Whether receipt of money makes sex wanted, or knowing a man or living in the same household with him means one wants to have sex with him, is not asked because whether a person wants to have sex is not the full legal meaning of consent. Whether she or he tolerated it, or could have appeared to the defendant to have gone along with it, is included.

This is to say one simple thing: consent to sex is not the same as wanting it. That a woman has reasons for giving up and letting sex happen that have nothing whatever to do with desire to have sex and everything to do with social gender hierarchy —all the way from saving one's job or future to placating a physically or emotionally abusive man—is irrelevant to the criminal law. No doubt many people think it should be. It fails to meet an equality standard, however. An equality standard, such as the one applied in the civil law that recognizes sexual harassment is sex discrimination, requires that sex be welcome.[26] For the criminal law to change to this standard would require that sex be wanted for it not to be assaultive.

Awareness of social hierarchy is absent in the criminal law of rape's treatment of force as well. In this area of law, forms of force typically correlated with male sex and gender—such as the economic dominion of employers, dominance in the patriarchal family, authority of teachers and religious leaders, state office of police officers and prison guards, and the credibility any man has (some much more than others based on race and class and age), not to mention the clout of male approval and the masculine ability to affirm and confirm feminine identity—are not regarded as forms of force at all. But they are. Whether or not men occupy these roles, these forms of power are socially male in that they are not equally available for women to assert over men, socially speaking, because women in general are neither socialized to these forms of power nor, as women, are they commonly authorized, entitled, socially positioned, or permitted to exercise them. That there are exceptions confirms the rule as well as further highlights its social determinants.

Of all the forms that power can take, the criminal law of rape's doctrine of force similarly registers only physical overpowering.[27] Some courts have begun to consider that a variety of factors can constitute force, such as Pennsylvania's embodiment of "moral, psychological or intellectual force used to compel a person to engage in sexual intercourse against that person's will" in its definition of "forcible compulsion." It also includes "the extent to which the accused may have been in a position of authority, domination or custodial control over the victim," together with age, mental and physical conditions, and the atmosphere and physical setting.[28] What even this standard, which is not the norm, does not expressly include is attention to inequalities including sex and race (as is well known, racism targets women of spe-

cific racial groups for sexual incursions and in the United States often accords greater credibility to white people than to African-Americans), and other major social
inequalities. Even consideration of physical force under standard approaches typically shows little sensitivity to the physical factors of height and weight, which on
average stack the deck in favor of men over women.[29]

Only extreme physical force, preferably including weapons not the penis, is usually credible enough to meet the criminal law's standard for enough force for sex to
look like rape. Depending on how well the parties know each other, the amount and
type of force required to prove that the sex was physically forced escalates.[30] While
resistance requirements have been largely modified or abolished, it is as if they have
not, if a woman's calculation not to fight because she would rather be raped than
dead, for example, an assessment some women make every day, means that the sexual acts are legally determined not to have been forced.

Typically, the only vulnerability recognized by the rape law as tantamount to an
inequality is age,[31] in most places for underage girls only (in some for boys as well).
The law of statutory rape makes all sex rape below an age line. While simplifying
the administration of justice, this rule (along with a similar result of strict prohibitions on sex between teachers and students) confuses people by defining as rape
some sex that some people want to have. It also presumptively authorizes all sex
above the age line whether it was wanted or not, unless proven nonconsensual by
standards that take no inequalities into account. Other inequalities, such as disparities of access and trust, that often go with age but do not end with the age of majority,
are also neglected above and below the line.

If the rape law worked, there would be no need for statutory rape laws. Abuse of
power, access, trust, and exploitation of vulnerabilities to pressure people into sex
that is not wanted for its own sake would be illegal. Age would be one powerful
inequality to be taken into account. Instead, the only inequality the law will counte-
nance is youth, whether statutory rape laws are justified as making consent
irrelevant or force unnecessary or both (the law is oddly indifferent to its actual
rationale). Young age or age differential below a certain age is thus ossified into an
absolute rule. This segregates some of the most sympathetic cases for relative structural powerlessness in sexual interactions and leaves the rest of the victims—including, in most states, underage boys who have sex with women over the age of
majority—unprotected, their inequalities uncounted. By cushioning its excesses,
this helps keep male dominance as a social system in place. One also suspects that
debates over shifting the age of consent are driven more by what legislators (mainly
men) want in a female sex object than by what sex women want in their lives and
when they want it.

Sex is relational; so is sexual assault. In unequal societies, what makes sexual assault sexual as well as possible is the hierarchy of relation between the parties. Rape
is thus a crime of sexualized dominance on the basis of sex (which often includes sex
and age, sex and race, sex and class variously combined and pyramided) that is
legally unrecognized as such. Inequality, its central dynamic, is flat-out ignored by
the criminal law. Far from promoting equality between women and men, the criminal
law tacitly assumes that such equality already exists. More accurately still, it shows
total lack of interest in whether it exists or not.[32] In other words, exactly what this
crime *is*, the law has refused to make criminal about it. This misfit between the law's
concept of sexual assault and its reality produces legal standards that cannot see

abuse in the real world and encourages neglect or worse by legal actors of the dynamics that make the abuse happen. This in turn serves as state collaboration in sexual assault and accordingly in the inequality of the sexes.

In this view, until inequality is directly addressed by the law of sexual assault, nothing adequate will be done about it. You cannot solve a problem you do not name. For the same reason, legal reform through consent alone or force alone, while improvements, will intrinsically fall short unless the concepts are fundamentally recast in terms of inequality. Requiring affirmative consent, as some states do,[33] for example, is an improvement over existing law, but can be polluted by inequality. No means no is an improvement over no meaning yes, but until equality exists, not even yes can reliably mean yes. Yes can be coerced. It can be the outcome of forced choices, precluded options, constrained alternatives, as well as adaptive preferences conditioned by inequalities. This may be why states that require affirmative consent also require that it be freely chosen. But whether the experiences of inequalities that make choice unfree—say, for instance, having been sexually abused in childhood, as are a third to a half of girls in the United States,[34] not to mention first sexual intercourse being forced, as it is documented to be for up to a third of all girls in the world[35]—are adequately included in the evaluations of the facts of individual cases remains to be seen.

The problem with consent-only approaches to criminal law reform is that sex under conditions of inequality can look consensual when it is not wanted, at times because women know that sex that women want is the sex men want from women. Men in positions of power over women can thus secure sex that looks, even is, consensual without that sex ever being freely chosen, far less desired. Consent, in other words, has never legally been equivalent to free choice. Even if it did in law, if the conditions for the exercise of freedom in life are not ensured—meaning actual conditions of equality, or a standard sensitive to inequalities between the parties so long as conditions of inequality exist—an autonomy approach to consent will not alone solve this problem in real life. Autonomy in sex cannot exist without sex equality. Similarly, force-alone approaches cannot address the problem of sexual assault in real life unless forms of force other than the physical, including all of those that enforce inequalities, are expressly recognized.

The question therefore framed is: what would a rape law look like that understood sexual assault as a practice of inequality? In brief, it would recognize that rape is a physical attack of a sexual nature under coercive conditions,[36] and that inequalities are coercive conditions. The law of sexual assault could make it a crime to take advantage of a relation of inequality (including access or trust) to force sex on a person who does not want it. If force were defined to include inequalities of power, meaning social hierarchies, and consent were replaced with a welcomeness standard, the law of rape would begin to approximate the reality of forced and unwanted sex. Force could be defined so that it is sensitive to the vulnerabilities social hierarchies concretely create: age (middle over young and old), family (husband over wife, parents over children, older children over younger children), race (in the United States, white over people of color), authority (educational, medical, legal, spiritual among them); law (police and prison guards over citizens and inmates), as well as illegal statuses such as those created by the law of immigration , homosexuality, and prostitution; and economics (poverty, and employers over employees).

Gender too is a social hierarchy (masculine over feminine), ringed with stereotype, enforced by socialization to subordinate and superordinate identification as well as by physical force. Socially, it is largely fused with sex (male and female). The idea here is not to prohibit sexual contact between hierarchical unequals *per se*, but to legally interpret sex that a hierarchical subordinate says was unwanted in light of the forms of force that animate the hierarchy between the parties. To counter a claim that sex was forced by inequality, a defendant could (among other defenses) prove the sex was wanted—affirmatively and freely wanted—despite the inequality, and was not forced by the socially entrenched forms of power that distinguish the parties.[37] The assumption that money provides or shows consent to sex would be replaced by the assumption that money is a form of force in sex. On a social level, inequalities could also be reduced, of course. A recognition in law that sex is made an inequality in society through gender hierarchy, and sexual assault is a central practice and expression of that inequality, would go a long way toward ending its considerable social and legal impunity and toward making sexual assault obsolete.

If society is structured to promote, and even encourage, sexual assault, and the law against it evades the forces driving it so that there is nothing effective to stop it, no wonder sexual assault happens. An approach designed to rectify this situation could underlie new statutes, provide a set of common law rules for interpreting existing statutes, or sketch a set of equality standards for assessing the Fourteenth Amendment constitutionality of existing state practices or conformity of national laws and practices with international obligations. As a priority, new civil rights laws—sex equality laws—could be passed for all victims of sexual assault to use. Civil laws potentially offer accountability to survivors, a forum with dignity and control by them, the stigma of bigotry for perpetrators, a possibility of reparations, and the potential for social transformation by empowering survivors. This is not to say that perpetrators do not deserve incarceration, but rather to say that jail has not tended to change their behavior, and indeed has often entrenched and escalated it. Civil rights laws offer the prospect of redistributing power, altering the inequalities that give rise to the abuse.

This framework for analysis has been described as principles of direction in order to be adaptable to diverse cultural settings and varying structures of existing law. Should anyone act on it, the approach offers the chance to embody in law the sexual equality that people often say they want in their laws and in their relationships.

ACKNOWLEDGMENTS

The thoughts and research help of Lisa Cardyn and Candice Aloisi are gratefully acknowledged.

NOTES AND REFERENCES

1. Data are summarized in Catharine A. MacKinnon, *Sex Equality* [hereinafter, *Sex Equality*] 776–778 (Foundation Press, 2001).
2. See Mary P. Koss *et al.*, *No Safe Haven: Male Violence Against Women at Home, at Work, and in the Community* 167–71 (1994) (analyzing major studies on rape prevalence done as of 1994, many showing approximately 20 percent of women subject to

completed rape, some numbers lower, some higher); Diana E.H. Russell, *Sexual Exploitation: Rape, Child Sexual Abuse, and Workplace Harassment* 31, 35 (1984) (finding 9.5 percent of rapes reported and 24 percent of women experiencing rape in lifetime in large probability sample).

3. The work of Diana E.H. Russell, David Finkelhor, Peggy Reeves Sanday, Diana Scully, and many others converges on this conclusion.

4. Andrea J. Sedlak & Diane D. Broadhurst, U.S. Department of Health & Human Services, *Executive Summary of the Third National Incidence Study of Child Abuse and Neglect* 14 (1996) found that 12 percent of all sexually abused children are abused by a female.

5. Before they reach the age of majority, 38 percent of girls report having been sexually abused, most by men close to them or in authority over them. The average age of first abuse is around ten. Diana E.H. Russell, "The Incidence and Prevalence of Intrafamilial and Extrafamilial Sexual Abuse of Female Children," in Handbook on *Sexual Abuse of Children* 19, 24 (Lenore E. Walker ed., 1986); Diana E.H. Russell, *The Secret Trauma* 99–100 (1986); Gail E. Wyatt, "The Sexual Abuse of Afro-American and White American Women in Childhood," 9 *Child Abuse & Neglect* 507 (1985) (finding 57 percent of sample of African American women and 67 percent of white American women report at least one incident of sexual abuse before age eighteen).

6. Data on sexually assaulted men includes documentation showing that 6 percent of the rapes reported to a survey of victims age 12 and over in 1996 were rapes of men by men. See Bureau of Justice Statistics, 2001 National Crime Victimization Survey, *Bureau of Justice Statistics Bulletin* Tbl 2, Tbl 38 (2001). Sexual abuse of boys has been found to be "common, underreported, underrecognized, and undertreated." William C. Holmes & Gail B. Slap, "Sexual Abuse of Boys: Definition, Prevalence, Correlates, Sequelae, and Management," 280 *JAMA* 1855, 1855 (1998).

7. African American women are generally considered to be subjected to a higher incidence of rape than white women in the American population. See Diana E.H. Russell, *Sexual Exploitation* 82 (1984) (reporting all studies to date). Professor Russell's study found that the highest percentage of women to be subjected to at least one rape or attempted rape were Native American women (55 percent), followed by Jewish women (50 percent), white non-Jewish women (45 percent), African American women (44 percent), Latinas (30 percent), Asian women (17 percent), Filipinas (17 percent), and other ethnicities (28 percent). See id. at 83–84. Note that these are figures for women ever raped or victimzed by attempted rape, not the number of rapes. According to recent statistics, persons from households with low incomes experienced higher violent crime victimization rates than persons from wealthier households. For instance, persons from households with annual incomes below $7,500 were 26 times as likely as those from households with incomes of $75,000 to be rape and sexual assault victims, and have significantly higher rates of rape, sexual assault, and aggravated assault compared with persons in all other income groups. See *Bureau of Justice Statistics, Criminal Victimization in the United States 2000*, Table 14 (2000).

8. See, for example, Binaifer Nowrojee, *Shattered Lives: Sexual Violence During the Rwandan_Genocide and its Aftermath* 1–2 (1996)

9. *R. v. Osolin* [1993] 4 S.C.R. 595, 669 (Cory, J.).

10. The General Assembly of the United Nations in 1994 adopted a resolution condemning sexual violence that defined it as gender-based violence, G.A. Res. 48/104, U.N. GAOR, 48th Sess., at art. 4, U.N. Doc. A/48/49 (1994); 33 I.L.M. 1049. General Recommendation No. 19, Committee on the Elimination of Discrimination Against Women, 11th Sess., U.N. Doc. CEDAW/C/1992/L.1/Add. 15 (1992). The most far-reaching international convention to date, the Convention of Belem do Para adopted by the Organization of American States in 1994, recognized in its preamble that violence against women "is…a manifestation of the historically unequal power relations between women and men." Convention of Belem do Para, 33 I.L.M. 1994. It declares that "every woman has the right to be free from violence in both the public and private spheres" Id. at art. 3, and required in detail that states parties and societies take action "to protect the right of every woman to be free from violence." Id. at

art. 10. The Beijing Declaration and Platform of Action in 1995 expressly embraced the right of women "to have control over and decide freely and responsibly on matters related to their sexuality" as a human right, Beijing Declaration and Platform for Action of the United Nations Fourth World Conference on Women, U.N. Doc. A/CONF.177/20 (1995) at ¶ 96, and condemned violence against women as "a manifestation of the historically unequal power relations between men and women, which have led to domination over and discrimination against women by men," all expressly analyzed as social realities. Id. at ¶ 118. The Committee of Ministers of the Council of Europe recently "reaffirm[ed] that violence towards women is the result of an imbalance of power between men and women and is leading to serious discrimination against the female sex, both within society and within the family." Council of Europe, Committee of Ministers, Recommendation Rec(2002)5 of the Committee of Ministers to member states on the protection of women against violence (30 April 2002).

11. See *Meritor Sav. Bank v. Vinson*, 477 U.S. 57 (1986) (recognizing hostile environment sexual harassment on facts of repeated rape as sex discrimination in employment); *Alexander v. Yale University*, 631 F.2d 178 (2d Cir. 1980) (recognizing sexual harassment in education as prohibited under Title IX prohibition on sex discrimination); *Franklin v. Gwinnet County Public Schools*, 503 U.S. 50 (1992) (permitting damages for Title IX sexual harassment).

12. *Dothard v. Rawlinson*, 433 U.S. 321, 336 (1977) (permitting women to be excluded from contact positions in high security prison employment on the basis of sex because of capacity to be raped). The Court may have been thinking of sexual biology, but the sexed reality was nonetheless observed.

13. 42 U.S.C. § 13981 (1994).

14. See *United States v. Morrison*, 529 U.S. 598, 635-36 (2000).

15. Most sexual assaults remain unreported, unprosecuted, and unremedied. See, for example, National Victim Center, Crime Victims Research and Treatment Center, *Rape in America* 5 (1992) (finding that 16 percent of rapes are reported); Staff of Senate Comm. on the Judiciary, 103rd Cong., *The Response to Rape: Detours on the Road to Equal Justice* iii (Comm. Print 1993) (drawing on data from several jurisdictions, concluding that 98 percent of rape victims "never see their attacker caught, tried and imprisoned.")

16. An example is *Michael M. v. Superior Court of Sonoma County*, 450 U.S. 464 (1981).

17. The manifest ineffectiveness of existing laws against sexual assault was amply demonstrated before the Congress that passed the Violence Against Women Act. See *Women and Violence: Hearings Before the Senate Comm. on the Judiciary*, 101 Cong. (1990). Estimates are that the likelihood of a rape complaint ending in conviction is 2 to 5 percent of rapes. See Joan McGregor, "Introduction to Symposium on Philosophical Issues in Rape Law," 11 *Law & Phil.* 1, 2 (1992).

18. The Antioch College Sexual Offense Prevention Policy (June 8, 1996), reproduced in *Sex Equality* 836–837, does.

19. The model was recently pungently described by a female-to-male transsexed person and long-time advocate of S/M (sadism and masochism) in sex, when asked why he transsexed: "[r]unning the fuck is an integral part of maleness in our society." Patrick Califia, Transman Seeks Sex Life: T 4 U, *Village Voice*, June 26–July 2, 2002

20. See, e.g., *Commonwealth v. Berkowitz*, 609 A.2d 1338 (Pa. Super. Ct.), aff'd 641 A.2d 1161 (Pa. 1994). The Pennsylvania legislature attempted to address the problem after public outcry, see, e.g., 18 Pa. Cons. Stat.. Ann. § 3124.1, but it is unclear if they did. One better approach can be seen in *R. v. Ewanchuk*, [1999] 169 D.L.R. 4th 193 (Can.) (holding that consent is a purely subjective fact to be determined by trial judge by ascertaining complainant's state of mind toward sexual touching when it occurred and that consent out of fear is not freely given, hence ineffective).

21. Women are not alone in this. See, e.g., *R. v. R.J.S.* [1994] 123 Nfld & P.E.I.R. 317 (finding that erection may be sufficient evidence of consent to sex).

22. Examples are *Boro v. Superior Court*, 163 Cal. App. 3d 1224, 210 Cal. Rptr. 122 (1985) and *People v. Ogunmola*, 238 Cal. Rptr. 300 (Cal. Ct. App. 2d Dist. 1987) involving doctors and patients. In *Boro*, the patient, who had permitted sex in the

guise of treatment, was found to have consented. In *Ogunmola*, two patients who consented to an examination but were penetrated by the doctor's penis instead were found not to have consented. California partially addressed the *Boro* situation by statute prohibiting sexual intercourse "procured by false or fraudulent representation or pretense that is made with the intent to create fear, and which does induce fear" with a spousal exception. Cal. Penal Code §266C. (The spousal exceptional was removed by amendment in 1994, see Cal. Penal Code §266C.) Recent developments in the law of rape by fraud are discussed in Patricia J. Falk, "Rape by Fraud and Rape by Coercion," 64 *Brook. L. Rev.* 39, 89-131 (1998). See also Jane E. Larson, "Women Understand So Little, They Call My Good Nature "Deceit": A Feminist Rethinking of Seduction, 93 *Colum. L. Rev.* 374 (1993).

23. For general discussion of multiplicity, see Daniel Brown, Alan W. Scheflin, & D. Corydon Hammond *et al.*, *Memory, Trauma Treatment, and the Law* (1998); for a brilliant treatment of the subject, see Harvey Schwartz, *Dialogues with Forgotten Voices* (2000). See also Carole Goettman, George B. Greaves & Philip M. Coons, *Multiple Personality and Dissociation, 1791–1992, A Complete Bibliography* (1994) and Sabra Owens, *Criminal Responsibility and Multiple Personality Defendants* (American Bar Association, 1997).

24. See, for example, *State v. Thompson*, 792 P.2d 1103 (Mont. 1990) (defendant high school principal allegedly forced student to submit to sexual intercourse by threatening to prevent her from graduating from high school; court affirmed dismissal of sexual assault charges because of lack of physical force). The Supreme Court of Canada found a rape threat to be a threat of severe bodily harm in *R. v. McCraw*, [1991] 3 S.C.R. 72, a conclusion far from obvious to many courts in the world.

25. See Morrison Torrey, "When Will We Be Believed?", 24 *U.C. Davis Law Review* 1013; Robin West, "Equality Theory, Marital Rape, and the Promise of the Fourteenth Amendment," 42 *Univ. Fla. L. Rev.* 45, 66–70 (1990). See also Jaye Sitton, Comment, "Old Wine in New Bottles: The 'Marital' Rape Allowance," 72 *N.C.L. Rev.* 261, 280–281 (1993) (describing extension of traditional marital rape law's doctrine of implied consent to cohabitants and "voluntary social companions.")

26. For the standard's initial articulation, see *Meritor Savings Bank v. Vinson*, 477 U.S. 57, 69 (1986), a sexual harassment case distinguishing between the criminal law standard of "voluntary" sex and the civil equality standard of "unwelcome" sex. For further discussion, see *Sex Equality* 977–989.

27. An excellent examination of this topic is Stephen Schulhofer, *Unwanted Sex: The Culture of Intimidation and the Failure of Law* (Harvard University Press, 1998).

28. *Commonwealth v. Rhodes*, 510 A.2d 1217, 1226 (Pa. 1986).

29. See *People v. Warren*, 446 N.E.2d 591 (Ill. App. Ct. 1983) (finding of stranger rape allegations that 6'3" 185-pound defendant, "apart from picking up [5'2" 100-pound woman] complainant and carrying her into and out of the woods" where he had sex with her, insufficient force, and faulting complainant for failing to resist). Analysis of the role of women's and men's different average height and weight in the context of potential rape can be found in *Dothard v. Rawlinson*, 433 U.S. 321 (1977) (holding that a particular minimum height/weight standard for prison guards at male-only prisons discriminated against women on the basis of sex).

30. My impression of marital rape cases where they are prosecuted is that the amount of force required for a conviction is often extreme, compared with what is required in stranger rape cases in the same jurisdictions.

31. Some states have prohibitions similar to statutory rape for prison guards, e.g. Conn. Penal Code § 53a–71.

32. One of the few legal discussions of this question took place in the *Michael M.* case, *Michael M. v. Superior Court of Sonoma County*, 450 U.S. 464 (1981), the Supreme Court justices, majority and dissenting alike, falling all over each other not to question whether women and men were equal in sex in the name of sexual egalitarianism.

33. See, for example, *State in the Interest of M.T.S.*, 609 A.2d 1266 (N.J. 1992).

34. Before they reach the age of majority, 38 percent of girls report having been sexually abused, most by men close to them or in authority over them. See Diana E. H. Russell, "The Incidence and prevalence of intrafamilial and Extrafamilial Sexual Abuse

of Female Children," in *Handbook on Sexual Abuse of Children* 19, 24 (Lenore E. Walker ed., 1998) (also finding 16 percent of girls abused by a family member); Diana E.H. Russell, *The Secret Trauma* 99–100 (1986).

35. World Health Organization, *World Report on Violence and Health* 149 (Etienne G. Krug *et al.*, eds, Geneva 2002) (finding "up to one-third of adolescent girls report their first sexual experience as being forced.").

36. This is a variant on the test in *Prosecutor v. Akayesu*, Case No. ICTR 96 4 T (1998) addressing rape in the Rwandan genocide. There, the coercive conditions were provided by the other jurisdictional requisites under the Tribunal's statute, which include crimes against humanity and genocide. It is also enacted at Cal. Civ. Code 52.4 (c) (2) as a civil claim for gender-based discrimination.

37. This arrangement could make a reconstructed definition of consent into an affirmative defense.

Rape-Law Reform circa June 2002

Has the Pendulum Swung Too Far?

STEPHEN SCHULHOFER

*Robert B. McKay Professor of Law, New York University Law School,
New York, New York 10012, USA*

ABSTRACT: This paper reviews court decisions determining the scope of liability for rape over the period 1998–2002. It finds many troubling signs that some courts, under some circumstances, are still wedded to the traditional (very strict) view of the kind of force necessary to support a charge of rape. There are, however, signs of encouraging progress: convictions in circumstances where even a decision to prosecute would have been unthinkable 20 years ago, and holdings that accept power, authority, or indirect intimidation as sufficient "force." Is it possible to go *too far* in this direction? And is there any reason to worry that this could actually happen in reality? The research identifies several areas in which this surprising possibility may be about to materialize, for example on the normatively and practically difficult question of the degree of intoxication or alcohol-induced willingness sufficient to invalidate consent.

KEYWORDS: rape; sexual coercion; rape-law reform; intoxication; proof of physical violence

INTRODUCTION

In a symposium entitled "Understanding and Managing Sexually Coercive Behavior," most of the discussion and the papers focus, quite properly, on egregious, unambiguously harmful behavior that is universally condemned. Because such behavior can be hard to predict, hard to deter, and hard to treat, there are many tough problems for which we still lack adequate answers. But there is no doubt whatever that such behavior should be considered illegal.

My own work has focused primarily on what might look like a problem of much lower priority—that is, forms of sexual coercion that are not physically violent. Such behavior encompasses a diverse conglomeration of abuses, from physical intimidation and implied threats of violence through coercion by threats of economic retaliation, interference with job security and professional advancement, exploitation of the teacher–student relationship, and nonviolent abuses of authority by professionals such as doctors, lawyers, psychologists, marital counselors, and clergy.

Address for correspondence: Stephen Schulhofer, Robert B. McKay, Professor of Law, New York University Law School, 40 Washington Square South, New York, NY 10012. Voice: 212-998-6260; fax: 212-995-4692.

schulhos@juris.law.nyu.edu

Ann. N.Y. Acad. Sci. 989: 276–287 (2003). © 2003 New York Academy of Sciences.

When the target of nonviolent coercion is an adult, behavior of that sort is not clearly illegal and is not universally considered wrong. But behavior of that sort is orders of magnitude more common than the physically violent abuses that justifiably have the first claim on our attention. Moreover, although the harms of sexual coercion are much less obvious and much less dramatic when the coercion takes a nonviolent form, those harms are significant nonetheless; sometimes they can be devastating. The woman or man who is the target of nonviolent sexual coercion may suffer lasting emotional injury and damage to her ability to trust those who are close to her. If the person coercing her is a teacher or her boss, she may suffer permanent damage to her career and to her self-image as a professional. Yet the great majority of American states still refuse to consider nonviolent coercion of this sort a criminal offense.[1]

In a 1998 study, I documented the nature and prevalence of these nonviolent sexual abuses, and I examined the legal doctrines that generally stand in the way of efforts to prosecute them.[2] I argued that what was missing from the law was recognition of the importance of *sexual autonomy.* In countless other areas of life, the law protects the individual's freedom of action—to vote (or not vote), to sell property (or not sell it), to accept medical treatment (or not accept it)—unless the individual decides to do otherwise in a fully autonomous, freely chosen act. Our sexual independence, the freedom to choose whether and when to have a sexual encounter, is at least as important as these other sorts of autonomy, and is probably far more important than most of them. Yet, alone among our most fundamental interests, sexual autonomy is not comprehensively recognized and protected by the law. The 1998 study documents the halting, incomplete, and inadequate attempts that had been made to expand criminal law and regulatory prohibitions to cover nonviolent sexual abuse.

In recent research, I revisited this problem to see what courts have done with the problem of nonviolent sexual coercion over the past four years. When I began that project, I never dreamed that I might end it with the concern that is stated as the subtitle of this article—namely, whether the movement to protect fully autonomous sexual choice (a movement I consider myself a part of) might, in the brief space of a few years, have achieved too much success. Yet in some jurisdictions, courts have moved so far, so fast, that the concern about too much success now needs to be taken seriously.

As I stressed throughout the 1998 study, sexual autonomy is two sided, consisting of both the freedom *from* unwanted sex and the freedom *to have* a wanted intimate relationship with another person who is also willing. Indeed, the need for intimacy is fundamental, and the search for that special companion and partner is for most of us one of life's most important goals. Were that not the case, the protection of sexual autonomy would be a simple matter, for we could simply prohibit all sexual encounters in the absence of a fully informed, freely chosen agreement between parties who are in every sense social and economic equals. But a rule of that sort, vigorously protecting us from any risk of impairing our negative sexual autonomy (the freedom from unwanted sex), would have a devastating impact on our positive sexual autonomy (the freedom to pursue a sexual relationship that is mutually desired).

The challenge is both cultural and legal—to achieve genuine social understanding of the importance of both facets of sexual autonomy to human well-being, and to design laws and regulations that protect negative sexual autonomy effectively without impairing positive sexual autonomy in unnecessary or inappropriate ways. How well are the courts responding to the legal component of this challenge? Many courts now are beginning to take sexual autonomy seriously. Some courts, at least some of the time, impose rules that vigorously protect against the risk of injury to negative sexual autonomy. Some occasionally go so far in that direction that positive sexual autonomy is endangered, and the imperative to treat criminal defendants fairly is sacrificed in the process.

More specifically, this paper will present four findings. First, in some respects the pendulum clearly has *not* swung too far; and too many courts still fail to appreciate the harm from, and lack of justification for, coercive (though nonviolent) sexual exploitation. Second, there are many encouraging signs of progress toward a regime of appropriate protection for sexual autonomy. Third, some of the recent judicial steps extend the criminal prohibition in ways that are at best quite troubling and debatable even for those like myself who support the project of extensive reform. Finally, several of these ostensibly progressive steps represent serious mistakes, not only for principles of just punishment but also for the reform movement itself.

It is of course obvious, and for lawyers not a matter that needs defending, that all these points, and the discussion explaining them, will be saturated with normative judgments. Nonetheless, for the sake of social and biological scientists whose tastes and research preferences run in more objective factual directions, I will endeavor to spotlight the empirical issues underlying these normative judgments, issues on which social science research remains crucial for framing the structure of appropriate and effective laws.

PERSISTENT EMPHASIS ON PROOF OF PHYSICAL VIOLENCE

Numerous recent decisions continue to insist that the "force" requirement for conviction in a rape case cannot be met unless the defendant has caused or threatened some sort of physical injury, a measure of violence beyond that involved in physical penetration itself. For example, *Sabol v. Commonwealth*,[3] a Virginia case, involved two instances of alleged rape. In one, the defendant had pushed the unwilling, resisting victim (who was his 22-year-old step-daughter) down a hall and into a bedroom, where he penetrated her; the court held that those actions were sufficient to prove the force required for conviction of rape. But in the other instance, where the step-daughter had submitted only in response to the defendant's threats to withhold financial support and other privileges, the court reversed the conviction, stating that coercion is sufficient to prove rape only when the prosecution can prove "an intention to do bodily harm."[4]

A recent decision of the Montana Supreme Court stresses the same point and reverses a conviction on much more troubling facts.[5] The defendant, Haser, operated a photography studio and had arranged to take photographs of two women who wished to pursue modeling careers. In each instance, while adjusting the woman's pose, Haser moved his hands to her genital area and, without warning, digitally penetrated her. He was convicted of two counts of "sexual intercourse without consent," but the court reversed the convictions and held that penetration by surprise was not sufficient to meet the statutory requirements. The court rejected the State's argument that "the victims were not afforded the opportunity to consent and therefore the use of force may be implied by the act of penetration itself."[6] Instead, the court held, intercourse (penetration) is "without consent" under the Montana statutory scheme only when the victim is "compelled to submit by force," and such "'force' must be related somehow to bodily injury [or] the attempted infliction of bodily injury."[7]

Worse yet is the decision of a Virginia appellate court in *Bower v. Commonwealth*.[8] Bower entered the bedroom where his 13-year-old daughter slept and lay down beside her in bed. He began to fondle her breasts, inserted his finger into her vagina, and remained in that position, penetrating her, for approximately 20 minutes, while she lay motionless, facing away from him, pretending to be asleep. He was convicted of penetrating her by "force, threat or intimidation," but the appellate court reversed the conviction. Like the Montana Supreme Court, the Virginia court held that penetration by surprise was not a crime and that its statute required "putting the victim in fear of bodily harm."[9]

Whether the problem in these cases was attributable more to the statutory wording or to staggering judicial insensitivity, it is clear that in jurisdictions like these, much work remains to be done to secure adequate protection for sexual autonomy.

SIGNS OF PROGRESS

In other jurisdictions there are encouraging signs of progress. In *State v. McKnight*,[10] the Ohio appellate court held that the superior power and authority of a police officer was sufficient to meet the statutory element of force necessary for a rape conviction, and several states have held that indirect forms of intimidation can be sufficient to establish "force." Such steps, while important, remain conceptually close to the traditional paradigm centered on physical violence, since the facts of these cases implied the possibility of physical injury if the victims had resisted.

Similar, but a further step away from the narrowest conceptions of force, is *People v. Alford*.[11] The victim testified that when the defendant began to take off her shirt, she told him to stop, but he did not. Instead, he shoved her on to the bed and sexually penetrated her. She repeatedly told him to stop but made no effort to struggle or to escape through the unlocked bedroom door, because she "froze" and feared for her safety. And she did not cry out because she thought that no one would hear her. Though some courts in the 1980s would have found an absence of force or an implication of consent on such facts,[12] the New York appellate court found the facts sufficient to prove forcible compulsion and upheld the conviction.

Another, more telling, indication of progress in protecting sexual autonomy, even in the absence of physical threats, can be found in the treatment of cases involving some degree of impairment in the victim's capacity to consent. In *State v. Chaney*,[13] the 18-year-old defendant offered the 14-year-old victim several beers, which she drank through a straw because he told her that if she did so "she would get drunk quicker."[14] The victim became intoxicated, had slurred speech, and had difficulty walking. But when the defendant asked her for sex, she firmly said no, and he allowed her to leave to go to her bedroom. Sometime later, she apparently invited him in, and he lay down on her bed; she left to use the bathroom and then returned to the bedroom and joined Chaney in bed. The jury found Chaney guilty of rape under instructions that permitted a conviction, even if the jury believed that the victim had expressly consented, if the jury concluded that because of intoxication, she was "incapable of giving consent because of... the effect of any alcoholic liquor."[15] An intermediate appellate court reversed on the ground that the victim's actions in refusing consent at one point showed that she was not too drunk to give valid consent later. But the Kansas Supreme Court reinstated the conviction, holding that the question whether the victim had the capacity to give valid consent was a factual question for the jury to decide under all the circumstances. As a result, the court held, Chaney's rape conviction could be sustained even if the jury believed that the young woman had given affirmative consent both in her words and in her actions.

In effect, on this view, intoxication can invalidate consent because of its capacity to alter inhibitions and sound judgment, even when the intoxication is self-induced and even when it does not impair a woman's ability to offer verbal and physical resistance. Even among the more progressive contemporary courts, not all would agree with this approach,[16] and, as discussed below, it is not free of difficulty on its merits. Nonetheless, the court's opinion reflects a willingness to consider autonomous choice as a value in its own right, independent of any concern about threats of bodily harm or the exploitation of physical strength.

Another, quite different way to measure progress is simply to observe the kinds of cases in which prosecutors are now willing to press charges. A precise study of this question would have to be grounded in close examination of charging and bargaining decisions in cases that never reach the appellate level. But there are suggestions of significant change in what we can see at the tip of this iceberg, in the reported appellate decisions. We can all remember the days when many police, prosecutors, and jurors felt that agreeing to a date, or inviting a man up to an apartment, was considered tantamount to giving consent to sex. In some instances even accepting a drink or permitting a man to pay for dinner were seen as indications of consent.

Those days are emphatically over. Several recent cases involve women who not only accepted dates and agreed to necking and sexual foreplay, but also voluntarily undressed, voluntarily joined their date in bed and voluntarily agreed to sexual intercourse. The difficulty was that at some point during intercourse the women demanded that their partners stop, and the men refused to do so. At that point the men are engaging in intercourse by force and without consent, they were convicted of rape, and the appellate courts properly upheld the convictions.[17] There is nothing conceptually problematic about such cases (assuming that juries can be persuaded of the facts beyond a reasonable doubt), but it is noteworthy that such cases are now being filed and that juries are now convicting. We are certainly a long way from the days when merely accepting a date or inviting a man up to the apartment were actions sufficient to render any claim of rape inherently implausible and unsustainable.

The Chaney case, mentioned earlier,[18] illustrates another aspect of this shift. Despite the four-year age difference between the offender and victim, the case nonetheless involved two teenagers experimenting with alcohol and sex, with both of them freely choosing to get drunk, and no evidence of physical brutality or threats. A classic example of the kind of case police and prosecutors once would have marked "unfounded" or dismissed before trial, Chaney instead resulted in prosecution, conviction by a jury, and affirmance on appeal.

Similarly, in *People v. Giardino*,[19] a 16-year-old victim voluntarily drank several glasses of bourbon, became "woozy" and "tipsy," but was not too drunk to participate very vigorously in numerous acts of intercourse and oral copulation. Unlike the Kansas Supreme Court, the California Supreme Court reversed the defendant's conviction, on the ground that the trial judge had failed to give adequate instructions concerning the level of intoxication that would be necessary to invalidate consent. In *Giardino*, the bottom line is perhaps little different from what it would have been 20 years ago, but it nonetheless marks a sea change in culture and in the institutional resistance of the criminal justice system that such a case was prosecuted at all and that the jury was willing to convict.

It is worth noting, moreover, that the California court was entirely in agreement with its Kansas counterpart that intoxication can invalidate consent even when it is self-induced and even when it stops well short of impairing the victim's ability to offer physical or verbal signs of her unwillingness. The emphasis, the California court said, is on "the effect of the intoxicants on the victim's powers of judgment rather than on the victim's powers of resistance" and therefore the test is simply whether alcohol has rendered the victim "unable to make a reasonable judgment as to the nature or harmfulness of the conduct."[20] This may even mean, as the court indicated in summarizing an earlier decision, that it is sufficient for the prosecution to show that the victim "would not have engaged in intercourse with [the offender] had she not been under the influence of the [intoxicants]."[21]

Even more striking as an indication of change in what is now considered "prosecutable" is a recent Florida case, *State v. Soukup*.[22] The alleged victim had just turned sixteen, and for her birthday party she and her friends hired Soukup, a male stripper, to dance for them. While he performed, she and her friends were drinking heavily, and she decided to take off her clothes and join him on the small stage. Soon she was performing oral sex on him. The young woman was over Florida's age of consent, but she claimed afterwards that she hadn't really consented because she was "numb" and "not thinking straight."[23] On that basis Soukup was prosecuted, and a jury convicted him of sexual assault on the theory that the young woman was incapable of giving consent because she had been incapacitated by alcohol. The Florida appellate court reversed the conviction, but the very fact of prosecution on these facts, and the jury's willingness to convict, marks a dramatic change in criminal justice attitudes about consent (not to mention the change it indicates in aspirations for the contemporary "sweet sixteen" party).

TOO MUCH PROGRESS?

In several important senses, the law now may be going *too far* in its willingness to uphold convictions in rape and sexual assault cases. I want to make this point very cautiously, because there undoubtedly remain many important jurisdictions and doctrinal areas in which the law still has not gone nearly far enough. (The second section of this article mentions several disturbing examples.) Nonetheless, there is serious potential for injustice in the other direction as well.

The law relating to intoxication and incapacity, illustrated in several cases already discussed, is a significant example. What does "incapacity" mean in cases in which the alleged victim actively participated, with apparent pleasure and enthusiasm, in the sexual conduct? When does alcohol's effect on inhibition and good judgment become sufficient to render consent to sex invalid? One luckless defendant asked his trial judge for an instruction giving the jury some standard, any standard, by which to decide when alcohol would invalidate consent. The judge refused, the jury convicted, and the appellate court affirmed. There was no need, the court said, to explain the standard to a jury because everyone knows what it means to be incapable of giving consent.[24]

A recent California decision at least acknowledges that the jury must be given some standard, but the test it impliedly approved—that the alleged victim "would not have engaged in intercourse with [the defendant] had she not been under the influence of the [intoxicants]"[25]—cannot be right. By that standard, many married couples and happily cohabiting long-term partners are raping each other every night. Such a standard simply gives the jury a license to convict either party (or both?) any time alcohol has mixed with sex, which is to say, for a substantial proportion of Americans, virtually any time at all. A recent Washington decision seems to delegate the matter to the experts, and it allowed an expert to testify that a blood-alcohol level of 0.15 was sufficient to render an alleged victim incapable of meaningful consent because individuals in that condition cannot "appreciate the consequences of their actions."[26] This is more definite and considerably more limited, but far from sufficient.

Boundaries in this area are sure to be tested more and more often. The need for good research exploring the impact of alcohol on judgment is clear, as are the needs for similar research on the impact of youth and immaturity on judgment (along with research on the interactive effects of youth and alcohol).

A second area in which the law may have broadened too much concerns the culpability requirement in prosecutions for rape and sexual assault. Very few American jurisdictions require a showing of subjective culpability (knowing that, or being reckless about whether, consent was absent); the prevailing view permits conviction on a showing of negligence, ordinary civil negligence at that.[27] And in many of these jurisdictions, a claim of reasonable belief in consent is a defense only in theory, not in practice. This is so because many jurisdictions, perhaps most, deny the defense of mistake when the alleged victim claims unambiguous acts of resistance and the defendant testifies to victim behavior indicating unambiguous consent. In such cases, the courts say, the only question for the jury is to decide which party is telling the truth.[28] In order to be granted a jury instruction on the mistake defense, a defendant in these jurisdictions must testify (or proffer evidence) that the victim's behavior was equivocal. But as soon as he does so, he convicts himself because he has in effect conceded his negligence (indeed recklessness) with respect to the victim's possible unwillingness to have sex.

Of course, there is nothing wrong in principle with a rule that bars a defendant from presenting inconsistent defenses. It would be perfectly fair to bar a defendant from simultaneously claiming that he had affirmative consent and that he was nowhere near the scene at the time of the offense. The problem with the common restriction on the mistake-of-fact defense in rape is that a claim of mistake is not inherently inconsistent with testimony that the defendant thought he had clear signals of affirmative willingness.

When two parties tell diametrically opposed stories, it is not inevitably true that only one is lying. Often a reasonable jury can conclude that both parties are exaggerating, that the truth lies somewhere in between. Or a jury might conclude that the defendant honestly believed (and that a reasonable person might also believe) he was being given clear signals of willingness, even though the victim's behavior in reality was ambivalent and equivocal.[29] The proper question is not whether the defendant can prove a defense of "mistake." Rather, it is whether the jury concludes that the defendant honestly and reasonably believed that the complainant was consenting. (More precisely, the proper question is whether the jury concludes beyond a reasonable doubt that a reasonable person would have known that the complainant was not, or might not be, consenting.) A defendant's testimony describing unequivocal indications of consent is not in itself an affirmative claim that he made a mistake, but it surely is not inconsistent with the perfectly appropriate claim that the prosecution has failed to prove the necessary *mens rea* beyond a reasonable doubt.[30]

Thus, the common restriction on a defendant's ability to claim absence of *mens rea* is illogical and amounts to a back door method of converting rape into a strict liability offense. In fact, several jurisdictions have decided to do so explicitly. In at least three states, Maine, Massachusetts, and Pennsylvania, a defendant cannot get mistake-of-fact instructions under any circumstances and the jury will be told that a mistake of fact about consent is not a defense even if it is both honest and reasonable.[31]

Is strict liability something we should be worried about? In one recent Massachusetts case,[32] the court reasoned that there is no need to prove a *mens rea* with respect to the absence of consent, because the prosecution is required in any event to prove beyond a reasonable doubt that the defendant used force. As a result, subjective culpability is inherent in his actions, whenever the jury is convinced that he did use force to commit the act.

There are several serious flaws in that reasoning. First, as in cases where defendant and complainant both describe unambiguous facts relating to consent, the jury need not accept the entirety of a witness's testimony. Just as the jury may believe that both parties are exaggerating in their descriptions of consent or nonconsent, it may find sufficient force without necessarily believing that the defendant's actions were unambiguously threatening in the way the complainant describes. In such cases, the required element of force is met, but it does not follow that the defendant will have realized or should have realized that his actions were perceived as forcible by the victim and by the jury. Very often that will be the case, but it will not always or inevitably be the case.

Thus, whether the required *mens rea* ought to be subjective recklessness or only negligence, its presence in a given case is a question separate from the question whether the facts establish the *actus reus* element of force. There is no justification, therefore, for withdrawing the separate *mens rea* issue from the jury, unless we simply are untroubled by convicting an entirely innocent person (one whose has taken all appropriate precautions and has an entirely reasonable belief in consent) or unless we think that the moral cost of doing so is outweighed by the additional deterrence gained by imposing strict liability instead of requiring proof of negligence. Neither claim has much intuitive plausibility; elsewhere I have developed in detail the more precise reasons for rejecting those views.[33]

There are practical difficulties with the strict liability position as well. If the force requirement is to be relaxed, as I, in common with other reformers, emphatically believe it must be, then there is all the more reason for concern that a defendant may not realize that his actions are perceived as intimidating. If we extend the definition of force without preserving a *mens rea* requirement, we may achieve progress in promoting more sensitive male behavior, but at the cost of risking conviction of the blameless in order to do so. Worse yet, if courts are serious about relying on the force requirement to insure that defendants are culpable, they (and jurors thinking in the same terms) will be pushed to limit conviction to cases involving clear-cut physical violence, thus stifling the very reform movement these strict liability advocates seek to promote. We can achieve substantial progress in condemning and preventing non-violent sexual abuse, without risking conviction of the morally blameless, simply by coupling a greatly expanded conception of force or coercion with rules that preserve a significant *mens rea* requirement.

Far more prevalent than strict liability is the approach that acknowledges the need for a minimum culpability of at least negligence. Should we worry about possible unfairness in convicting defendants on that basis? The answer depends in part on the conceptual structure of "consent." Most fundamentally, consent can be an internal matter, a state of mind (candidates here could be desire for sex, willingness to accept sex, or absence of an abhorrence for sex), or consent can be an external matter, an act that grants permission (or the absence of an act that withholds permission).

Culpability concerns are least acute if consent and nonconsent are conceived as external acts rather than internal attitudes. For example, if nonconsent *means* the externally observable action of emphatic physical resistance, the defendant will inevitably be aware that "nonconsent" is present. He will be convicted under a negligence standard, of course, but he would also be convicted under a standard requiring recklessness or knowledge, because he would be fully aware of the existence of the facts (emphatic physical resistance) that the law defines as sufficient to constitute the offense. There is no unfairness in convicting such a defendant, regardless of one's position on culpability for mistakes of fact, because negligence and subjective awareness are coextensive under this conception of nonconsent.

A similar analysis holds for most other definitions of consent that are conceptualized as external rather than internal: that is, acts rather than attitudes. Thus, if nonconsent means saying "no," then whenever the *actus reas* of nonconsent exists, nearly all defendants (all those with unimpaired hearing and proficiency in the language) will know that there was (external) nonconsent. Such defendants will be convicted under a negligence standard, but they would likewise be convicted under a standard requiring recklessness or knowledge, because they would be fully aware of the existence of the facts (a verbal "no") that the law defines as sufficient to constitute the offense. Again, there is no unfairness in convicting such defendants, regardless of one's position on culpability for mistakes of fact, because negligence and subjective awareness are coextensive under this conception of nonconsent.

There are two qualifications to this analysis. First, one might argue that there is a potential for unfairness to the defendant who makes a mistake of law, for example the defendant who was unaware that the law (on the preceding assumptions) had defined nonconsent as the external act of saying "no." This is a legitimate concern, but mistake-of-law unfairness is inherent in any law reform measures that are to be enforced in a transition period of imperfect public awareness.

Second, a defendant who is not proficient in the language might make a reasonable or unreasonable mistake of *fact*. He might think that the word meaning "yes" had been said, when in fact the complainant had said the word meaning "no." There is at least one such case reported: a soldier stationed in Japan during the Occupation accosted a woman he thought was a prostitute and had sex with her after she said words that he claimed to have misunderstood.[34] Even if his testimony was truthful, a jury probably could have found conscious recklessness, given his apparently limited familiarity with the language, but a negligence standard might convict a few defendants who would be acquitted if conscious recklessness were required. But such cases are no doubt very rare. We might prefer a negligence standard, as it would at least impose an affirmative duty of care. Or we might think it preferable to preserve the requirement of subjective culpability, since it would rarely if ever pose a real obstacle to effective enforecment. Either way, there is no significant risk of unfairness (or of ineffective enforcement), so long as we insist that consent be understood as an observable act that grants affirmative permission.

The scope of the unfairness problem changes, however, if consent is understood as an internal attitude rather than an external act. Many rape statutes define the crime as intercourse by force "against the will" of the woman. Language like that suggests that consent is legally understood to be a subjective state of desire or willingness. If that is the right way to understand the content of consent, then many more sorts of mistakes become possible, and the tension between fairness and effective enforcement becomes much more acute. Courts rarely get very far in sorting out this question concerning the conceptual structure of consent, but if there is a dominant tendency, it is probably to treat consent as a matter of the complainant's internal attitude. Whether that approach is right or wrong should not be a question of ontology —of what consent *is*. Rather the problem is to choose the conception of consent that works best for legal purposes, including such concerns as the need for fair warning, ease of administration, and minimization of total costs of type one and type two errors. From that perspective, there is a clear case for treating consent as an external act signaling unambiguous affirmative permission.[35] But so long as courts continue to treat consent as a matter of the internal subjective preferences of each partner, good faith mistakes will occur, and convictions based on negligence, especially ordinary civil negligence, risk imposing severe felony sanctions disproportionate to the degree of the defendant's fault.

The problem of potential unfairness is compounded when we move to setting the appropriate *mens rea* with respect to the complainant's *capacity* to give consent. As discussed above, capacity issues are an emerging flashpoint in the law of sexual assault. Increasingly, courts are willing to find that voluntary, self-induced intoxication can render a woman's consent invalid, and extraordinarily vague standards govern the determination at trial of what counts as an incapacitating level of intoxication. Even if it is not considered unfair to convict on the basis of negligence, rather than subjective culpability, with respect to actual consent, problems arise if we apply the same *mens rea* requirement with respect to *capacity* to consent.

Those who want to give short shrift to defendants claiming a mistake of fact about consent are usually thinking about the kind of case in which a defendant claims to have thought that *no* really meant *yes*, or that silence and passivity (often a product of fright) meant willingness. Men in that situation should know better, and these days most of them do. Similarly, those who want to give short shrift to defendants claiming a mistake of fact about capacity to consent are usually thinking about the kind of case in which the complainant is too drunk to stand up or fight back, barely conscious but too drunk even to say *no*. There is little reason to sympathize with the defendant who equates silence or passivity in that situation with consent and then claims unawareness of the complainant's incapacity.

But many of the newer intoxication cases discussed above involve very different scenarios; the complainants had clearly said yes and actively participated in the sexual acts.[36] It is much less clear in these settings that we should be so dismissive of a defendant's claim that he accepted the complainant's enthusiastic participation at face value and was unaware that she was "too drunk," especially when the standard for excessive intoxication remains only dimly articulated.

The *mens rea* problem with respect to capacity to consent poses another difficulty as well. In cases like *Chaney* and *Giardino*,[37] both the male and female parties were drinking heavily. The woman actively participated, and because the man was so drunk, he may not have realized how drunk his partner was. If he had been sober, he presumably would have realized that her capacity to consent was impaired. If so, his mistake of fact concerning her capacity to consent must be considered unreasonable, and under a negligence standard, he is clearly guilty of rape. But by the same reasoning, his level of intoxication may well impair *his* capacity, his consent would be invalid, her belief that he was validly consenting would be mistaken, and that mistake, a product of her drunkenness, would also be unreasonable. Thus, under a negligence standard, she too would be guilty of rape.

That result—that each of them was guilty of raping the other—can't be right. But the main reason for concern about that result is not simply the apparent logical paradox. The reason why it seems so obviously wrong to consider the intoxicated young woman guilty of rape is that however unwise she was to drink so heavily, she did not exploit or abuse her male partner, who enthusiastically participated, and her poor judgment does not entail criminal culpability—at least it need not inevitably entail criminal culpability if she did not trick him into getting drunk, take advantage of his situation, or realize how badly his judgment was impaired. By the same token, it is wrong in a roughly similar way, though perhaps less obviously, to consider the intoxicated young man guilty of rape: However unwise he was to drink so heavily, he did not exploit or abuse his female partner, who enthusiastically participated, and his poor judgment does not entail criminal culpability—at least it need not inevitably entail criminal culpability if he did not trick her into getting drunk, take advantage of her situation, or realize how badly her judgment was impaired. The potential unfairness of convicting for rape on the basis of negligence becomes especially acute when the mistake of fact relates to capacity to consent, particularly when so much drinking and sexual experimentation is voluntary at the outset and when so much immaturity and poor judgment exists on both sides of the sexual partnership.

For those interested in law reform, and especially for those interested in the project of reducing the various forms of nonviolent sexual abuse, the unfairness of convictions based on negligence must be assessed in relation to the goal of enacting laws that can be effectively enforced. And subjective culpability requirements—especially in the area of capacity to consent—can pose a barrier to effective enforcement. But if we want effective laws against sexual abuse, it becomes crucial to consider why people obey the law. This, of course, is an empirical question, and the assumption that obedience results primarily from the credible threat to impose severe punishment is only that: an assumption. Despite the power of that prevalent cost–benefit perspective, recent research suggests that people's willingness to obey the law may depend primarily on the perceived legitimacy of the legal system, including in particular its apparatus for imposing blame and criminal sanctions.[38] And that research also suggests that perceived legitimacy, in turn, may depend primarily on insuring that severe criminal punishment is reserved for individuals who really deserve it.[39] If so, and if we want modern, more sensitive conceptions of consent and coercion to be socially accepted, enforced, and complied with, we may need to rediscover the older, more traditional conception of culpability in matters of mistakes of fact. If instead the pendulum of reform continues to move in the direction of simultaneously extending substantive conceptions of coercion and diluting *mens rea* prerequisites for criminal conviction, we may find that we have sacrificed both the fairness and the effectiveness of our laws against sexual abuse.

REFERENCES

1. *See* Stephen J. Schulhofer, *Unwanted Sex* (1998).
2. *Id.*
3. 553 S.E.2d 533 (Va. App. 2001).
4. *Id.*, at 537.
5. *State v. Haser,* 20 P.3d 100 (Mont. 2001).
6. *Id.*, at 109.
7. *Id.*
8. 551 S.E. 2d 1 (Va. App. 2001).
9. *Id.*, at 10.
10. 749 N.E.2d 761 (Ohio App. 2000).
11. 731 N.Y.S. 2d 563 (App. Div. 2001).
12. *E.g., People v. Warren,* 446 N.E. 2d 591 (Ill. App. 1983).
13. 5 P.3d 492 (Kan. 2000).
14. *Id.*, at 493.
15. *Id.*, at 495.
16. *Compare People v. Giardino,* 82 Cal. App. 4th 454 (2000).
17. *People v. Roundtree,* 91 Cal. Rptr.2d 921 (Cal. App. 2000); *In re John Z,* 2001 Cal. App. Lexis 2729 (2001); *McGill v. State,* 18 P.3d 77 (Alaska, 2001).
18. *See* text at note 5, supra.
19. 82 Cal. App. 4th 454 (2000).
20. *Id.*, at 462.
21. *Id.*, at 463.
22. 760 So. 2d 1072 (Fla. App. 2000).
23. *Id.*, at 1073.
24. *State v. Chaney,* 5 P.3d 492 (Kan. 2000).
25. *People v. Giardino,* 82 Cal. App. 4th 454, 463 (2000).
26. *State v. Al-Hamdani,* 2001 WL 1645773 (Wash. App. 2001).
27. *See* Sanford H. Kadish & Stephen J. Schulhofer, *Criminal Law and Its Processes* 358 (7th ed., 2001).
28. *Id.*, at 360.
29. *Id.*
30. *See* Rosanna Cavallaro, *A Big Mistake: Eroding the Defense of Mistake of Fact About Consent in Rape,* 86 J. Crim. L. & Criminology 815 (1996).
31. *See* Kadish & Schulhofer, *supra* note 27, at 354–58.
32. *Commonwealth v. Lopez,* 745 N.E.2d 961 (Mass. 2001).
33. Schulhofer, *supra* note 1, at 257–59.
34. *United States v. Short,* 16 C.M.R. 11 (1954).
35. Schulhofer, *supra* note 1, at 264-73.
36. *E.g., State v. Chaney,* 5 P.3d 492 (Kan. 2000); *People v. Giardino,* 82 Cal. App. 4th 454, 463 (2000).
37. *Id.*
38. See Tom R. Tyler, *Why People Obey the Law* (1990); Paul H. Robinson & John M. Darley, *The Utility of Desert,* 91 Nw. U. L. Rev. 453 (1997).
39. *Id.*

Asking What Before We Ask Why: Taxonomy, Etiology, and Rape

KATHARINE K. BAKER

Chicago-Kent College of Law, Chicago, Illinois 60661, USA

ABSTRACT: This article presents a spectrum of sexual coersion. By looking at the social meaning of the different acts of coercion along the spectrum, the author suggests that most acts of sexual coercion can be classified as either rape (a sexual act with intent to do harm to the victim) or sex (a sexual act engaged in without any intent to harm the victim). Ironically, though, the author suggests that the most and least egregious acts of sexual aggression, that is, the acts we most readily identify as rape and the acts we are most reluctant to label rape are the ones that most easily evade explanation as either rape or sex.

KEYWORDS: taxonomy; etiology; rape; sexual coercion; prostitution; social meaning; impersonal sex

Much of this volume is devoted to the scientific study of etiology. This article looks at etiological questions through a different lens, the lens of social meaning. To do that, the article lays out a taxonomy of rape, putting six different categories of sexual coercion along a spectrum from most to least severe. The taxonomy is not meant to be complete; it is instead trying to offer some ideal types from which we can draw inferences. I will draw those inferences by examining the social meaning of different acts of sexual coercion. By examining the social meaning, we also examine etiology, that is, the communicative content of many acts of sexual coercion helps explain why men rape. Social meaning may not be able to explain all acts of sexual coercion, however. Indeed, I will argue that it is those coercive acts at the most severe and least severe ends of the spectrum that evade social explanation.

This article first lays out a sexual coercion spectrum and a brief explanation of each category along that spectrum. It then proceeds to divide the spectrum into two different categories, rape and sex, explaining how all the acts of sexual coercion on the spectrum are socially understood as either rape or sex. The fact that we are able to discern the social meaning of many of these acts of sexual coercion should help us understand why men commit these acts and help us articulate strategies for prevention. Finally, the article looks at the forms of sexual coercion at the far ends of spectrum, "rape" and "sex," and argues that in order to deal effectively with these

Address for correspondence: Katharine K. Baker, Professor of Law and Associate Dean for Faculty Development, Chicago-Kent College of Law, 565 West Adams, Chicago, IL 60661. Voice: 312-906-5391; fax: 312-906-5280.
    kbaker@kentlaw.edu

Ann. N.Y. Acad. Sci. 989: 288–299 (2003). © 2003 New York Academy of Sciences.

Sexual Coercion

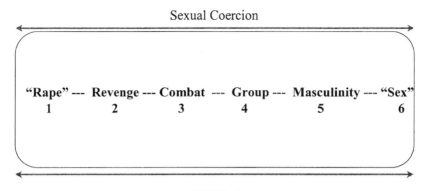

FIGURE 1.

acts we must change the social understanding of sex. In short, to prevent and justly punish *rape*, we must come to view the term *impersonal sex* as an oxymoron.

FIGURE 1 shows six categories of sexual coercion. Each category represents a different kind of sexual assault.

Category #1: Rape. Category one is exemplified by a single rapist who uses physical force or threat of force to overpower his victim. Often, though not always, the physical injury (aside from the rape itself) is limited to that which is necessary in order to get the victim to stop fighting. The rapist in this category is probably the man with whom most of the contributors to this volume have the most experience. I say that because of the rapists presented here, he is the one most likely to be punished for his acts. As further discussion will show, the other acts of sexual coercion on the spectrum either do not get reported,[1] or get "unfounded" by the police,[2] or get excused by the jury.[3]

Category #2: Revenge. The man in this category rapes as a form of revenge against a woman whom he sees as having inappropriate control over him. This control is perceived as sexual. Men react with anger at women who are, in the men's view, flaunting their sexuality, thereby making men want something they cannot necessarily have. Timothy Beneke describes this as men seeing women's "appearance as a weapon."[4] Men fight back, using sex as a weapon. One of Beneke's subjects put it this way, "If a guy's not all there to begin with and then he gets fucked over by a couple of girls, he may just have something building up and something will just tick him off about what a girl says and he'll just follow her through the night and rape her."[5] Professor Schulhofer quotes a man demonstrating this kind of attitude as well, "Women knew when I was attracted to them. ... I definitely felt played with, used, manipulated, like women were testing their power over me. I hated it with a passion. ... I wanted to slam someone's head up against a wall."[6]

Category #3: Combat. Whether in official or unofficial wars, men rape their opponents' women as a way getting back at those men. One rather famous example of this is the massacre at My Lai, during the Vietnam war. American soldiers systematically raped and then murdered much of the female population in My Lai. A helicopter pilot flying over the scene several days later saw a body in the field below. "It was a woman ... She was spread-eagled, as if on display. She had an 11th Brigade patch between her legs—as if it were some type of ... badge of honor."[7] Eldridge

Cleaver talks about the use of rape for this purpose also, though the war he was fighting, the race war, did not involve organized armies and brigades. Nonetheless, rape played a role. "Rape is an insurrectionary act. It delighted me that I was defiling the white man's women."[8] The numerous accounts of rapes in the former Yugoslavia, rapes designed to poison enemy women so that the enemy men could no longer love them, are also examples of this.[9]

Category #4: Group. Group rapes, fraternity rapes, "trains" in the lingo of some young men, are examples of a different kind of rape. These rapes usually involve one woman and many men. The woman, if she does not start out drunk or comatose, often ends of up that way because she needs to turn off so as to numb herself to what is happening to her. One man after another usually takes turns penetrating the woman or sodomizing her or, in one case involving St. John's University lacrosse players, banging their erect penises against her head.[10] It appears that men in these situations perform these acts as a way of bonding with each other.[11] In the words of Nathan McCall, who at 13 was part of a group rape of a neighborhood girl, the "train marked our real coming together as a gang."[12] Another rather famous example of this kind of behavior is the rape at the Big Dan Tavern in New Bedford Massachusetts, the story retold in the movie *The Accused.*[13] There, the men in a bar stood around and cheered each other on as the men took turns penetrating the victim who was splayed on a pool table.

Category #5: Masculinity. This category includes a great many of what are also known as acquaintance rapes. I am not designating an "acquaintance rape" category generally because it would be too broad and overlap too significantly with some of the other categories. Category #5 involves rapes committed by mostly young[14] men eager to assert their masculinity by asserting their sexual prowess as heterosexual beings. The studies done with college population males suggests that most of them use rape as a way of getting sex and they want sex so badly because sexual performance is critically constitutive of their sense of their own masculinity.[15] Men demonstrate their masculinity in order to enhance their status with their male peers, and they demonstrate their masculinity by performing sexually.[16] A perfectly explicit example of this was the Spurr Posse Gang's point system.[17] It is an entirely recognizable dynamic to anyone familiar with locker-room banter, however. When men "score" they get "points" from their friends. The idea for this category is thus not only that rape is instrumental to getting sex, sex is instrumental to getting respect or status within the male community.

Category #6: Sex. Category #6 involves those acts of sexual coercion in which the woman actually says "yes," but her yes is a function of her very limited options. Because she says yes, I have labeled this category "sex." The kind of stories that make up this category come directly from the pages of Professor Schulhofer's book.[18] They include the high school principal who demands sex from a high school senior, threatening to block her graduation if she refuses,[19] the divorce lawyer who initiates sexual contact from a client he knows is resistant, extremely fragile emotionally, and under psychiatric care,[20] and the therapist who initiates sex with a patient after leading her to believe that sex is an important part of the therapeutic process.[21] Into this category we might also put, if one reads the paper these days, literally hundreds of clergymen and probably many incest cases.

What motivates these men in Category #6? That is an important question. It has a very different answer than the same question posed for Categories #4 and #5, because the Category #6 rapists are not engaging in sex in order to garner the esteem that comes with sexual activity. These men cannot make their actions public. Getting sex in the manner these men have has, for years, subjected them to severe sanction from their governing boards, superiors, ethics panels, or school boards. These men have not been subject to legal sanction because the victims involved consented in a physical sense. There is no force or threat of force; there is just a power dynamic that effectively destroys any ability the victim might have to meaningfully exercise an autonomous choice to say no. The professional organizations, aware of that power dynamic, make these acts sanctionable. Thus, these men cannot brag about their exploits, so their sexual encounters stay private, and they stay private because they are condemned socially. What motivates these men to do it despite the social condemnation?

This article will not answer that question fully, but it will suggest that what motivates these men, at the far right of the spectrum, may not be very different than what motivates the rapists in Category #1, at the far left of the spectrum. Thus, it is the acts that have not been illegal at all, Category #6, that may share the most with the acts that have always been illegal, Category #1. Moreover, this article will suggest that the motivation common to categories #1 and #6 is very different than what is motivating the men in between.

To explain why, let us examine the social meaning of the different acts on the spectrum. As a matter of social meaning, if not law, one can divide the spectrum into two groups, with all of the left hand categories falling into a definition of rape, and all of the right hand categories falling into a definition of sex.[22] By dividing it as FIGURE 2 does, it is easier to unpack what the acts are really about.[23]

What do these broad labels of rape and sex mean? By rape, I mean, "intent to do harm through sexual activity." By sex, I mean "intent to engage in sexual activity without necessarily doing harm." These are not, lest anyone wonder, legal definitions. The legal definition of rape is far more complicated,[24] and to my knowledge,

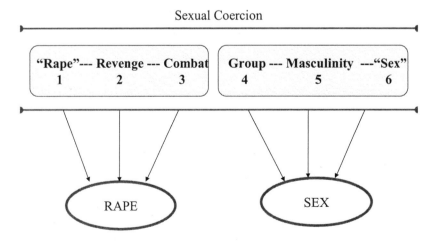

FIGURE 2.

there is no legal definition of sex. The definitions that I have given to the terms rape and sex are social definitions. We know what I am talking about because the term "rape" has social meaning, as does the term "sex." The social meaning implicit in the term rape incorporates a notion of harm toward the victim. When one rapes the land, for instance, one harms the land, one takes from the land its ability to give life and nourishment.[49] The social meaning implicit in the term sex involves no such notion of harm. Thus one can have sex without meaning to do harm, but one cannot rape without meaning to do harm.

What the men in Categories #2 and #3 are doing is using sex and sexual acts as weapons to do harm, and everyone knows it. The communicative content of the act is purposefully degrading. In Category #2 they are trying to hurt the victim because they perceive her as hurting them. In Category #3 they are trying to hurt the victim because by hurting her they will be inflicting injury on other men with whom she is associated.[25]

The acts in Categories #4 and #5 are actually quite different. Pathetic as it is, the victim in these cases rarely seems to be the focus of the perpetrator's acts. The victim is secondary to the sex itself. Men perform these acts because the sexual act will send a message, not to the woman whom they are raping, but to other men. The status of the woman, whether she is completely drunk, unconscious, or petrified into paralysis, is inconsequential to these men.[26] In one of his projects Eugene Kanin found five cases of women who were actually so immobilized by fear that they could not communicate nonconsent.[27] One might take just a moment to think about what sex would be like in that instance. What is it that motivates a man to have sex with a woman who is too paralyzed to say no. What can that sex be about?

The empirical and theoretical work done with these populations suggests that the sex is about neither harming nor expressing affection for the victim.[28] These men want sex, not rape, and while they might be okay with something like lovemaking, for the most part they cannot be bothered. What they are interested is not a relationship with the woman with whom they are engaging; they are interested in the accomplishment of having engaged. It is that accomplishment that gives them masculinity points with their peers.

There is a partial analogy to commodification that can be helpful here. A man in Category #4 or #5 rapes to get something. Because he gets it without the woman's consent, it is akin to stealing. But it is not stealing, because what he gets is not what she loses. He may not even want her to lose at all and, according to his world view, it would be possible for him to gain without her losing. This illustrates an important difference between the rape and sex categories. With rape, the gain that the perpetrator is able to get, the sense of satisfaction with his act, is directly tied to how hurt the victim is. With the sex crimes, her pain or lack thereof is irrelevant to what he is able to take from the experience.

Where does this breakdown into rape and sex get us? For one thing, it helps us understand how and why the law has treated these acts as it has. The crimes on the right have not been prosecuted because they are not seen as crimes of violence, as crimes in which there was *mens rea*[50]—or intent to do harm.[29] In contrast, the crimes on the left are seen as crimes of violence, crimes in which there was intent to do harm, but for Categories #2 and #3, that crime has been excused because the intent to do harm was legitimate in the circumstances. Thus, we have a jury foreman who judged a case in which a man was charged with knifing, beating with a rock, and twice raping a woman dressed in a lace miniskirt and wearing no underwear, saying "We felt she ... asked for it the way she was dressed ... [W]ith that skirt, you could see everything she had."[30] The jury acquitted, but the foreman did not suggest that the woman was not raped. He suggested that the rape was justified. Comparably, the behavior of soldiers in wartime is seen as inevitable, the sexual byproduct of an intrinsically violent situation.[31]

I think that the fact that we can unpack what is going on in Categories #2–#5 both socially and legally is good news. It is good news because once we unpack the social meaning, we can actually start trying to alter the social conditions and messages from which the social meaning emanates. Thus, for Categories #2 and #3, we can work to make clear that there is no such thing as asking for rape. It is absurd that people think it is somehow legitimate for men to avenge any feeling of frustration they might have when a woman makes them feel needy. It is as absurd for men to feel offended by women's dress as it was 40 years ago for whites in the South to feel offended when African-Americans looked them in the eye. What is wrong is our still current social structure in which men presume that it is somehow unfair for any woman to have the power to affect them. As far as attempts to remedy the extent to which the legal system has excused these acts, the following simple jury instruction could help: "frustration, sexual attraction, flirtation, or anger, however understandable, can never be a legitimizing reason for coercing sex."

In a world of equality, the combat rapes in Category #3 would drop out also. If women were not seen as the property of men, it would make little sense to rape women as a way of aggressing against men. Anecdotal evidence, from the North Vietnamese, who used women soldiers in combat, lends credence to this hypothesis. The ban on raping women, even the enemy's women, was enforced by the North Vietnamese because they could not afford for their men to view their comrades as "rapable."[32]

As for the right-hand side of the spectrum, there is clearly a need to change the social meaning of sex. As I have argued elsewhere, if we were to try to alter the social understanding of sex, by teaching our young and forcing ourselves to reject the patterned behavior that allows us to avoid awkward and difficult conversations about sex, we could emerge with an understanding of sex as about creating, enriching, and/ or solidifying a relationship.[33] Having sex could be seen socially, like having children is, an act of love and sacrifice—one whose benefits exist almost exclusively in the unique relationship created by the act. The purpose of having sex, like the purpose of having children, could be to create a relationship of mutual understanding, and maybe even love, a relationship that has no currency to anyone other than those in it.

This is not easy work. It is extraordinarily difficult work, but it is work that we can begin to conceptualize. Once sex is seen as something that cannot be separated from the person with whom one experiences it, her loss cannot be irrelevant to him. Her loss is his loss. In such a world it seems unlikely that men would tie the number of their sexual encounters to accomplishment. We simply do not think of relationships in such ordinal terms.[34] The need for masculine competition, if indeed it is innate, can work itself out on the football field and in automobile ownership—areas far less likely to have as byproducts the number of sexual assault victims we see today. Legal reform must emphasize that the intent to do harm is not the defining characteristic of rape. The defining characteristic of rape is coercion. The jury must be instructed that "intent to have sex regardless of consent" is a self-contradictory phrase.

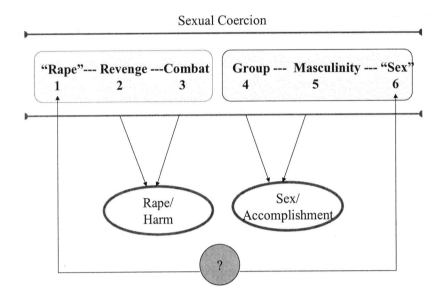

FIGURE 3.

This then leaves us with Categories #1 and #6 (FIG. 3). Category #6 is like Categories #4 and #5 in the extent to which the women's enjoyment or lack thereof is irrelevant, but it is unlike Category #4 and #5 in that the men in Category #6 are not using sex as a way to get the esteem of others. If we change the meaning of sex such that everyone understands sex to be more about relationship than accomplishment, then maybe the men in Category #6 will stop because they will understand that what they are getting is not sex as that term will come to be culturally understood. I am not particularly confident of that, though. My lack of confidence stems from our confusion over what motivates these men in the first place. We can help eliminate the acts in Categories #4 and #5 by making sex not equal masculinity anymore, but are we as sure that this will help the men in Category #6, who do not seem to be getting masculinity points out of their currently coercive practices? Nor are the Category #6 men getting what we can see the men in Categories #2 and #3 getting. They do not necessarily intend to cause their victims pain. Instead, what these men seem to be getting is what the men in Category #1 get, which I take to be the satisfaction of some kind of physical urge, a pathological demand to satisfy a sexual need regardless of the mutual desire of the participant.

Some might explain this male desire for sex devoid of relationship and communication in evolutionary terms.[35] Others might explain it as a function of hormonal differences in men and women.[36] Still others would suggest that male sexual demands are primarily a socially constructed aspect of patriarchy that helps routinize male dominance.[37] Whatever explains the origins of men's "appetites" for impersonal sex, our task must be to teach men to overcome them, to make a desire for sex devoid of relationship as pathological as is raping someone at gunpoint. People see Category #1 as pathological because for most people the idea of using a gun or a knife to force a woman to have sex is abhorrent. From where does the horror emanate, though, the gun or the forced sex? It is critical that we understand the origins of our horror, because from the woman's perspective, the use of a knife, gun, or fist may not be that different than the threat of losing your therapist, your lawyer, or your high school diploma. Various studies of women's reactions suggest that violent, stranger rapes and rapes by someone to whom the victim is emotionally close have comparable negative impacts on victims.[38]

If we conclude that the difference between Categories #1 and #6 is merely the kind of weapon, it should refine our etiological inquiries and our strategies for prevention. We have let the presence of the gun imply an intent to do harm and therefore harm. In doing so, we have pathologized the gun, not the coercion, and we have ignored the fact that harm comes even when there is no intent. We have also ignored the fact that the motivating factor for the man in Category #1 may be nothing other than the "sex" that motivates the men on the right side of the spectrum. If the motivating factor is the same, it seems odd to label Category #1 as pathological "rape" and Category #6 as understandable "sex." Some people might read this as a conclusion that the man in Category #1 is therefore not pathological. I think the inverse conclusion is more appropriate. It is our willingness to condone the behavior on the right-hand side of the spectrum, to accept as legitimate a desire for impersonal sex, that we must come to view as pathological.

A world in which sex devoid of relationship was seen as pathological need not be a world in which sexual experimentation and one-week flings cease to exist. It need only be a world in which the two parties have communicated enough with each other to understand that their consensual sex is a mutually desired aspect of a consensual relationship. One-night stands and temporary relationships are acceptable as long as neither party thinks about sex as a goal independent of the thinking, feeling, communicating person who shares the experience. It is the disregard for the other person that we must see as abhorrent.

A world in which sex devoid of relationship was seen as pathological would be a world without legal prostitution. The fact that we have labeled what prostitutes sell as "sex" shows just how impoverished our understanding of sex is. As others have cogently observed, what a prostitute really sells is rape.[39] It is rape because, as the accounts written by prostitutes or those who work with them clearly demonstrate, prostitutes do not want the sex.[40] A prostitute's job is to "project" back his fantasy."[41] To survive at all, prostitutes numb themselves and fake their pleasure at a client's demand.[42] Prostitution belongs in Category #6. The commodification question that surrounds the issue of prostitution is thus not whether sex should be bought and sold, but whether rape should be.

Various different writers, across many decades, have argued that regardless of whether prostitution is best conceptualized as rape, it is most honestly evaluated as an alternative form of marriage, that is, male payment for access to female sexuality.[43] There is an important difference, though, between marriage (even if seen in the crassest of market terms) and prostitution. Marriage involves a relationship that is composed of more than just the sex itself, whereas prostitution institutionalizes sex devoid of relationship. Institutionalizing impersonal sex in this manner perpetuates a culture that condones sexual coercion because it legitimates male desire for impersonal sex. It is that male desire for impersonal sex that we must work to make pathological.

It is far from clear that the appropriate way to delegitimate prostitution is to punish the prostitutes, however. First, it seems remarkably strange to punish rape victims, even if they did receive compensation for the rape. Second, as many have documented, the great majority of prostitutes "enter" the profession under conditions that are themselves coercive. Prostitutes start at a very young age.[44] Sex with many of these women is a violation of statutory rape laws.[45] Most prostitutes, somewhere between 60 and 70%, were victims of childhood sexual abuse.[46] Punishing women for "choosing" prostitution when for most of the girls involved the choice first came when they were not even old enough to enter into a legal contract and when their understanding of sexuality had already been horribly polluted by past abuse seems gravely unjust. Third, what is pathological is not a young and traumatized women's "choice" to make money given the male demand for impersonal sex, but that so many men want impersonal sex. It is the estimated 60% of American men who have used prostitutes,[47] most of whom have not been subject to childhood abuse, most of whom are not children themselves, most of whom are not desperately poor, and many of whom live perfectly respectable middle and upper middle class lives, whose behavior is so problematic. As Kathleen Barry writes, "Women are in prostitution because men buy them for sex. ... Prostitution is a male consumer market. The intense public focus on women's will, her choice or her 'right to prostitute' deflects attention from the primary fact that prostitution exists first because of male customer demand."[48] If demand is the problem, then the solution must address the problem of that demand. One way to address that problem is to get serious about arresting and punishing the john (with a felony conviction perhaps), not the hooker.

CONCLUSION

Male demand for impersonal sex, and the perceived legitimacy of that demand, explains not only prostitution, but a tremendous amount of rape. If we are serious about trying to prevent rape, we must shun, shame, and ban the male demand for impersonal sex. It is no answer to say that the male demand for impersonal sex is natural or biological or innate. We do not accept such answers for other forms of physical violence (battery, assault, or murder, for instance) and there is no reason to accept such answers for rape. Only by making the demand for impersonal sex itself strange, pathological, and "other" can the law deal effectively with rape.

The law is made up of decision makers—police, prosecutors, judges, jurors, and victims. When male demand for impersonal sex is understood as normal, those decision makers condone coercive sex because they do not see intent to do harm. Once we collectively see impersonal sex itself as harmful, wrong, and other, we not only eliminate the motivations of many men who currently rape, we move into a world in which we can finally punish those who still rape.

NOTES AND REFERENCES

1. Many acquaintance rapes do not get reported. For a discussion, see KATHARINE K. BAKER *Sex, Rape and Shame*, 79 B.U. L. REV. 663, 683 (1999).
2. When police and prosecutors determine that a victim's rape allegations are unverifiable or highly likely to result in acquittal, they "unfound" the allegation. See LYNN HECHT

SCHAFRAN, *Writing and Reading about Rape: A Primer*, 66 ST. JOHN'S L. REV., 979, 1010–1011 (1993).

3. *See infra* text accompanying note 30.
4. BENEKE, T. (1982). *Men on rape*(p. 20). St. Martin's Press. New York.
5. *Id.* at 37.
6. SCHULHOFER, S.J. (1998). *Unwanted sex: The culture of intimidation and the failure of law* (p. 48). Harvard University Press. Cambridge.
7. Susan Brownmiller recounts this description in her book *Against our will: Men, women and rape* (p. 105). (1974). Fawcett Columbine. New York.
8. CLEAVER, E. (1968). *Soul on ice* (p. 14). Dell Publications. New York.
9. LABER, J. (1993, March 25). Bosnia—Questions of rape. *New York Review of Books*, pp. 3,4 (discussing the prevalence of rape as an aggressive tool in Bosnia).
10. The story of this rape is told in KAREN KRAMER, *Rule by Myth: The Social and Legal Dynamics Governing Alcohol-related Acquaintance Rapes.* 47 STAN. L. REV. 115, 136–138 (1994).
11. It is worth reiterating that each category represents a type. It is perfectly possible for the types to overlap, so that during one rape, men could be both trying to inflict injury on a common enemy (Category #3) and trying to bond with each other (Category #4).
12. MCCALL, N. (1994). *Makes me wanna holler* (p. 47). Random House. New York.
13. For an account of the actual rape, *see* LYNN S. CHANCER, *New Bedford, Massachusetts, March 6 1983–March 22, 1984: The "Before" and "After" of Group Rape.* 1 GENDER & SOC. 239, 244–245 (1987).
14. Somewhat arbitrarily, I will define "young" as under age 25.
15. *See* BAKER, *supra* note 1 at 673–679.
16. *Id.* at 675–676.
17. For a discussion of this incident in which boys literally kept score of their number of sexual encounters and compared their scores with each other, *see* Michelle Oberman *Turning Girls into Women: Re-evaluating Modern Statutory Rape Law.* 85 J. CRIM. L. & CRIMINOL. 15–18 (1994).
18. See SCHULHOFER, *supra* note 6.
19. *Id.* at 2.
20. *Id.* at 239.
21. *Id.* at 206.
22. I think it not coincidental that the two categories of social meaning that I have chosen, "rape" and "sex" track quite closely the two main predictive factors, "hostile masculinity" and "impersonal sex" that Neil Malamuth highlights in his study of etiology. See *supra* this volume. The attitudes that we can identify as "causing" sexual coercion are developed in a social setting that may promote and/or condone the byproducts of those attitudes.
23. The caveats here are Categories #1 and #6. For reasons explained *infra*, it is not clear that Category #1 belongs exclusively in the rape category or that Category #6 does not.
24. Each state has its own definition of "rape" or "sexual assault," and the definitions vary widely. For a brief discussion of this variety, *see* KATHARINE K. BAKER, *Once a Rapist? Motivational Evidence and Relevancy in Rape Law*, 110 HARV. L. REV. 563, 575 n. 56 (1997).
25. There are those, particularly in the biological fields, who dismiss these arguments, suggesting that whatever violence may or may not be involved, what motivates rapists is biological and essentially sexual in origin. The violence or harm involved is instrumental to the sex. *See*, for instance, CRAIG T. PALMER et al., *Is it Sex Yet? Theoretical and Practical Implications of the Debate over Rapists' Motives.* 39 JURIMETRICS 271 (1999) (making fun of those that argue rape is more about violence than sex). There are both long and short responses to the biological characterization. The short response I will offer here is the simple facts from Oncale v. Sundowner Offshore Services, Inc., 523 U.S. 75 (1998), as reported by the Court of Appeals for the Fifth Circuit, 83 F.3d 118, 118-19 (1996). Oncale did not involve any form of intercourse, or even ejaculation, and it did not involve any kind of male on female violence. Both the victim and the perpetrators were men. The acts that were held to

constitute sexual harassment included "restraining Oncale while [a co-worker] placed his penis on Oncale's neck on one occasion and on Oncale's arm, on another occasion," and "push[ing] a bar of soap into Oncale's anus. ..." Under my definition, Mr. Oncale was raped. The perpetrators used sexual acts to inflict injury, mostly emotional, on their victim. If we can agree that sex can be used as a weapon to harm Mr. Oncale, then it seems perfectly self-evident that sex can be used as weapon to harm women also—even though that harm or violence against women may also have reproductive consequences.

26. The men from the St. John's incident communicated with their victim only once. When she screamed, they slapped her and told her screaming was not allowed. Otherwise, they let her drift in and out of consciousness, more interested in watching each other's performances than in her. *See* KRAMER, *supra* note 10.

27. KANIN, E. (1984). Date rape: Unofficial criminals & victims. *Victimology, 9*, 95, 97.

28. *See* BAKER, *supra* note 1 at 666–667 (citing studies).

29. An observer of a gang rape trial in Michigan explained the acquittal this way, "I don't believe she was raped ... I believe they ran a train on her." CHRIS O'SULLIVAN, *Acquaintance Gang Rape on Campus, in* ACQUAINTANCE RAPE: THE HIDDEN CRIME (Andrea Parrot & Laurie Bechhofer, eds., 1991) at 140. A juror interviewed after the acquittal of the St. John's University lacrosse team explained the jury did not "want to ruin the boys' lives." JOSEPH FRIED, *St. John's Juror Tells of Doubts in Assault Case: He Went Along with Vote to Acquit*, N.Y. TIMES, Sept. 14, 1991, at 24.

30. *Jury: Woman in Rape Case "Asked For It,"* CHI. TRIB. Oct. 6, 1989 at 11.

31. *See* BROWNMILLEr, *supra* note 7 at 31–34. For a comprehensive analysis of the prevalence of rape by soldiers and an argument challenging the inevitability of sexual violence by soldiers, *see* MADELINE MORRIS, *By Force of Arms: Rape: War and Military Culture*, 45 DUKE L. J. 651 (1996).

32. BROWNMILLER, *supra* note 7 at 90–91.

33. BAKER, K.K. (1999). Unwanted supply, unwanted demand. *Green Bag, 2*, 103, 110–112.

34. For instance, we no longer (if we ever did) think the man who sires twelve children is somehow more masculine or in any way more accomplished than the man who sires two. We look at the quality of his relationships with his children, not the number of children.

35. THORNHILL, R. & PALMER, C.T. (2000). *A natural history of rape: Biological bases of sexual coercion*. MIT Press. Cambridge, MA.

36. KAFKA, M. (2003). The monoamine hypothesis for the pathophsiology of paraphilic disorders: An update, this volume.

37. HENDERSON, L. (1992). Rape and responsibility. *Law and Philosophy, 11*, 127.

38. RUSSELL, D. (1975). *The politics of rape: the victim's perspective*.

39. As Carter and Giobbe write, prostitution is "rape that is bought and paid for." VEDNITA CARTER AND EVELINA GIOBBE, *Duet: Prostitution, Racism and Feminist Discourse*, 10 HASTINGS WOMEN'S L. J. 37, 46 (1999).

40. "[W]hat they're buying, in a way, is power ... They can tell you what to do and you're supposed to please them, follow orders. Even in the case of masochists, who like to follow order themselves, you're still following his orders. Prostitution not only puts down women, but it puts down sex—it really puts down sex." "J" *in* THE PROSTITUTION PAPERS 25, 33 (Millett ed., 1975)(emphasis supplied). St. Albans, UK, Paladin.

41. LEIDHOLDT, D. (1993). Prostitution: A violation of women's rights, *Cardozo Women's Law Journal, 1*, 133, 135 (emphasis supplied).

42. "I close my eyes and ears. I cut out everything to do with feelings." CECILE HOIGARD & LIV FINSTAD, BACKSTREETS: PROSTITUTION, MONEY AND LOVE 65-66 (1992). Penn State Press, University Park, PA; "I was so numb I felt nothing." "J," *supra* note at 43. "You were the lowest of the low if you allowed yourself to feel anything with a trick ... The way you maintain your integrity is by acting all the way through." ROBERTA VICTOR *in* STUDS TERKEL, WORKING 91, 94 (1974). Pantheon. New York.

43. MACKINNON, C. (2001). *Sex equality* (pp. 1422–1423).

44. From the studies done, it appears that the average age of entry into the profession is somewhere between thirteen in San Francisco, MIMI SILBERT & AYALA PINES, *Occupations Hazards of Street Prostitutes*, 8 CRIM. JUST. BEHAV. 395, 397 (1981), and 15 and a half in Norway. *See* HOIGARD AND FINSTAD, *supra* note 42 at 76.

45. For a sample of statutory rape laws, *see* BAKER, *supra* note 23 at 575, n. 58.
46. *See* LEIDHOLDT, *supra* note 40 at n. 4.
47. ERBE, N. (1984). Prostitutes: Victims of men's exploitation and abuse. *Law & Inequality Journal, 2,* 609, 624 n. 117 (citing JENNIFER JAMES, *Prostitutes and Prostitution, in* DEVIANTS: VOLUNTARY ACTORS IN A HOSTILE WORLD 398, 402 (Edward Sagarin and Fred Monanima eds., 1977). General Learning Press. Morristown, NJ.
48. BARRY, K. (1995). *The prostitution of sexuality* (p. 39). NYU Press. New York.
49. This observation was first made by Robin West. See Robin West, *Legitimating the illegitimate: A comment on 'Beyond Rape,'* 93 Colum. L. Rev. 1442, 1449 (1993).
50. *Mens rea* is a legal term used to describe criminal intent.

Sex Offender Reentry Courts

A Cost Effective Proposal for Managing Sex Offender Risk in the Community

JOHN Q. LA FOND[a] AND BRUCE J. WINICK[b]

[a]University of Missouri–Kansas City School of Law,
Kansas City, Missouri 64110-2499, USA

[b]University of Miami School of Law, Coral Gables, Florida 33146, USA

ABSTRACT: Recently enacted legal strategies to protect society from dangerous sex offenders generally use two very different approaches: Long-term incapacitation or outright release. The first strategy relies on harsh criminal sentences or indeterminate sexual predator commitment laws. The second relies primarily on registration and notification laws. Both strategies rely on prediction models of dangerousness. Authorities determine at a single moment the likelihood that an offender will sexually "recidivate" and then choose the appropriate type of control for an extended period. This paper reviews the problems of predicting sexual recidivism in the context of both strategies. It then proposes special sex offender reentry courts to manage the risk that sexual offenders will reoffend. Risk management allows decision makers to adjust calculations of individual risk on an ongoing basis in light of new information and to adjust the level of control. Drawing on Therapeutic Jurisprudence—a belief that legal rules, procedures, and legal roles can have positive or negative psychological impact on participants in the legal system—these courts can impose, and then adjust control over sex ofenders in the community. In a sex offender reentry court, the judge is a member of an interdisciplinary team that uses a community containment approach; the offender, as a condition for release, enters into a behavioral contract to engage in treatment and submit to periodic polygraph testing. This therapeutic jurisprudence approach creates incentives for offenders to change their behavior and attitudes, thereby reducing their recidivism risk and earning more freedom. It can also monitor compliance and manage risk more effectively.

KEYWORDS: therapeutic jurisprudence; sex offenders; public safety; risk management approach; sex offender reentry courts

Addresses for correspondence: John Q. La Fond, Edward A. Smith/Missouri Chair in Law, the Constitution and Society, University of Missouri–Kansas City School of Law, 5100 Rockhill Road, Kansas City, MO 64110-2499. Voice: 816-235-5818; fax: 816-235-5276.
  lafondj@umkc.edu
  Bruce J. Winick, Professor of Law, University of Miami School of Law, 1311 Miller Drive, Room 476, Coral Gables, FL 33146. Voice: 305-284-3031; fax: 305-284- 6619.
  bwinick@law.miami.edu

Ann. N.Y. Acad. Sci. 989: 300–323 (2003). © 2003 New York Academy of Sciences.

Several new legal strategies have been enacted in the U.S. since about 1990 to protect society from dangerous sex offenders. These strategies assume that sex offenders are especially dangerous and that many of them pose a high risk of committing
repeated sex crimes. To counter this perceived ongoing threat, legislatures have developed two very different approaches to prevent sexual recidivism: long-term and
indefinite incapacitation or release into the community subject to a mandatory
registration requirement and potential community notification.

These strategies assume that public safety requires public officials to predict
whether a convicted sex offender is likely to commit another sex crime if released
into the community. These strategies also require public authorities to choose
between confining sex offenders for a very long time or simply releasing them with
minimal supervision into the community.

This article will review the problems of predicting sexual recidivism in the context of these strategies. It will then argue that a risk-management approach implemented through sex offender reentry courts is a more cost-effective strategy both for
protecting the community and for rehabilitating sex offenders. These courts, which
are based on Therapeutic Jurisprudence principles, can provide more intensive community supervision for a much larger group of sex offenders, while at the same time,
create powerful incentives for sex offenders to change their attitudes and behavior.

LIMITED CHOICES

Long-Term or Indeterminate Incapacitation

Longer Criminal Sentences

Many states have relied on the criminal justice system for protection against sexual recidivism. State legislators lengthened sentences for sex offenses, enacted harsh
mandatory minimum sentences for repeat offenders, including sex offenders, and
passed life-time sentences under "one, two, or three strike(s)" laws. Between 1993
and 1995 twenty-four states and the federal government enacted "three-strike" statutes that enhanced sentences for repeat offenders, including serious sex crimes.
Some of these laws require mandatory life sentences for specified repeat offenders
(Clark, Austin & Henry, 1997).

From 1980 to 1994 the prison population in the United States increased by 206%,
while the number of imprisoned sex offenders increased by 330%. Between 1985 and
1993 the average time served by convicted rapists in state prisons increased from about
3 years to 5 years, an increase in percentage of sentence served from 38% to 50%. Put
differently, for sex offenders released from prison from 1985 to 1993 there has been a
significant increase in the average length of stay in prison and in the percentage of sentence served before release. Since 1980 the number of prisoners sentenced for violent
sexual assault other than rape increased by nearly 15%—faster than any other category
of crime except drug trafficking (Greenfield, L., 1997).

Critiques of Criminal Sentencing

Mandatory minimum and lifetime sentences are overinclusive. Because they use
only criminal history and use it incorrectly to determine the risk of sexual recidivism

(Hanson, 1998), many sex offenders who do not pose a serious risk of reoffending will be confined. These sentences can also be underinclusive because they will not result in the confinement of many sex offenders who would be considered much more dangerous if the best risk assessment techniques were used. Because mandatory minimum sentences will also confine sex offenders for a much longer period than is necessary to prevent them from reoffending, they are also excessive. It is not surprising that sex offenders are an incredible "growth industry" for our prisons and jails.

Indeterminate Civil Commitment

At least 15 states have passed sexually violent predator (SVP) laws that invoke the state's civil commitment authority to hospitalize mentally ill persons who are dangerous. SVP laws authorize the indefinite commitment for control and treatment of sex offenders who are about to be released from prison or have been released from prison and suffer from a "mental abnormality" or a "personality disorder" that makes them likely to reoffend. These laws are intended to confine disturbed and dangerous sex offenders who have served their full criminal sentence and can no longer be held in the criminal justice system. Except in California, where the initial commitment is for two years, sexually violent predators are committed for an indeterminate period and cannot be released until they are "safe" to live in the community (Fitch & Hammen, 2003).

Critiques of SVP Commitment

SVP laws do protect the community against some of the most dangerous sex offenders. These offenders cannot commit new sex crimes against the community while they are in secure mental health facilities.

Though much narrower than the criminal sentencing approach, these laws are still overinclusive. They can be used against any offender convicted of a *single* qualifying sex crime. Although these laws provide generous due process protection, states still win an extremely high percentage of cases that are filed, ranging from about 75% to just under 100%. While the government's incredible success rate may reflect careful case screening, more likely explanations include the inability to initially place a sex offender in a community release program subject to intensive control and the inexorable urge for juries to err on the side of safety rather than risk (La Fond, 1998). Thus, some sex offenders who would not reoffend if released from prison or placed in closely supervised community release programs will be confined indefinitely.

To the extent that SVP commitment can only be used in a relatively small number of cases due to statutory and constitutional elements of proof and the extreme cost of these commitments, SVP laws are underinclusive; that is, dangerous sex offenders must be released at the end of their prison sentence into the community.

Resorting to this unique civil commitment scheme that can be used only after an offender has served his full prison term blurs the line between criminal punishment based on personal responsibility for past crimes and involuntary hospitalization to treat mental illness and prevent possible future harm. It is also a misuse of the psychiatric hospital that threatens basic justice, *bona fide* therapy, and constitutional values (Morse, 2003). Moreover, these laws provide disincentives for sex offenders

facing criminal charges to accept criminal responsibility for their behavior by pleading guilty and for convicted offenders to engage in treatment while in prison or, if
they do participate, to do so in earnest (Winick, 2003c). Consequently, these laws
may actually undermine prison treatment, which has much greater potential for success because it is offered closer in time to the offense, thereby discouraging denial
and minimization by the offender (Wettstein, 1992).

Offender Information Collection and Dissemination

The second basic strategy relies primarily on sex offender registration and community notification laws, which provide some information about the offender to law
enforcement agencies and, to a lesser extent, to the community (Winick & Wexler,
2003; Winick, 2003a).

Registration Laws

All 50 states have enacted a sex offender registration law that requires most convicted sex offenders to register with the police where they live and to provide information about their residence, employment, and criminal history to law enforcement
agencies. Offenders may also have to furnish identifying information such as pictures, fingerprints, and DNA samples. Registration laws are intended to deter registered offenders from committing another sex crime and to aid police investigation of
sexual offenses.

Notification Laws

All 50 states also have enacted community notification laws since 1990 (Logan,
2003). These laws authorize or require the police to disseminate or make available
information about dangerous sex offenders to various members of the community
where the offender lives. They were passed because legislators believed that registration laws alone would not protect the community adequately. In theory, organizations, like schools and day care centers, and individual citizens would act on this
information and take necessary steps to protect themselves from the risk posed by a
dangerous offender living in the neighborhood. Other than requiring sex offenders
to register and, in some cases, providing information to the public, these laws do not
control dangerous sex offenders living in the community.

Critiques of Registration and Notification Laws

Most registration laws are rigid, requiring most sex offenders to register for at least
ten years and often longer. Most statutes provide no incentive for sex offenders to engage in community treatment or to demonstrate by their law-abiding behavior that they
pose little risk of reoffending and should no longer have to register. While one would
think that providing this information should make citizens more confident of their ability to control risk in their environment, studies have shown that notification laws actually *increase* community anxiety (Zevits & Farkas, 2000). These laws may also spawn
intense guilt should the offender commit a sex crime against the child of a parent who
was notified of the offender's presence but failed to protect his child (Winick, 1998).

No research establishes that either type of law prevents sexual recidivism (Finn,
1997). Moreover, these laws do not explicitly require the state to exercise any direct

control over released sex offenders designed to prevent them from reoffending. Indeed, a good case can be made that notification laws are an attempt by the state to absolve itself of any duty to prevent sexual recidivism (La Fond, 2004).

Summary

Harsh criminal sentences may keep a number of dangerous sex offenders from returning to the community for a long time, thereby preventing them from committing another sex crime. However, these laws overconfine, locking up large numbers of offenders who could live safely in the community if released or, if necessary, subject to appropriate community supervision. Once sex offenders are released from prison and parole—and most of them will be sooner or later—the state is extremely limited in what it can do to protect the community from ongoing danger. Currently available options include indefinite commitment under an SVP law or releasing offenders subject to information compilation and, in some cases, dissemination to the community. These are rather stark choices: indeterminate confinement or release with no supervision.

THE PREDICTION MODEL OF DANGEROUSNESS

Both strategies rely on prediction models of dangerousness, which requires a determination of sexual risk—whether an offender will commit another sex crime if released to the community—at some point in time. This judgment is based on information about the offender that is known at that moment of prediction. New information learned about the offender after the prediction is made cannot be taken into account and, unless the offender is still on probation or parole, it is very difficult to adjust the degree of control exercised over the offender in light of that information.

Mandatory minimum sentencing laws use a categorical approach of prediction based exclusively on the offender's past criminal offense history. SVP laws designate officials who have discretionary authority to initiate commitment based on their one-time prediction of risk. Registration laws are fairly inclusive and effectively predict that most sex offenders may reoffend over a long time period. They require almost all sex offenders to register for at least ten years and often much longer, while notification laws generally (but not always) confer limited discretion on authorities as to which offenders will be subjects of notification and the extent thereof.

Prediction Method

Three methods have generally been used to predict sexual dangerousness whenever discretion is involved: clinical, actuarial, and guided-clinical. The clinical method relies primarily on the expert's individual assessment of the offender; it is subjective. The actuarial method relies on instruments derived from studying groups of repeat sex offenders to determine their common characteristics; it is objective. Guided clinical evaluation begins with the actuarial approach and then adjusts in light of individual characteristics (Hanson, 1998). It is both objective and subjective. Today actuarial methods are the primary basis for predicting sexual dangerousness.

Duration

These predictions of sexual dangerousness generally apply to an extended period of time. Criminal sentences protect the community from the risk of sexual reoffending during the term the offender is actually incarcerated and, to a lesser extent, on parole or probation. SVP laws protect the community during the period of institutional commitment, and to a lesser extent, on community release. Registration law protection, minimal at best, lasts during the required registration period; that is usually a minimum of ten years and may last a lifetime. It is not clear how long notification protection lasts in each case since notification is usually a one-time event.

Criticisms of Actuarial Predictions of Sexual Dangerousness

Actuarial prediction can only identify a range of risk for a group of sex offenders. It cannot identify which individual(s) among the group will reoffend. Nor can it specify where within the range any individual falls; the individual's risk may be lower or higher than the group range. If so, the individual may be more or less dangerous than the group. An actuarial prediction cannot provide any psychological insight into an individual's sexual behavior.

Actuarial predictions also make judgments about an individual based on group characteristics. This approach has been criticized for not making judgments based solely on the individual and, instead, relying on his similarity to a group. However, a great deal of public health information concerning risk is based on this same approach.

In any event, some experts are confident that actuarial risk assessment can identify a group of sex offenders who will sexually reoffend at a rate that can "conservatively be estimated at 50% and could reasonably be estimated at 70% to 80%" (Hanson, 1998). Even assuming this high level of accuracy, predictions will have a false positive rate of from 20% to 50%. These predictions also assume that no control is exercised over the sex offender during the period of risk. Actual risk can be lowered significantly if aggressive control is exercised over the individual.

Predictions about less dangerous sex offenders are less accurate because they have a lower base rate of offending. These predictions will result in more erroneous predictions, including predictions of danger (an offender predicted to reoffend will not) and of safety (an offender predicted not to reoffend will). As a result, it is not clear whether these offenders should be confined for a long period or released.

The Problem of Accurately Determining Sexual Recidivism

Sexual recidivism (the commission of another sex crime) is generally measured by studying official records to determine whether convicted sex offenders are subsequently arrested, charged, or convicted with another sex crime. This general approach of relying on official records, which is typically used in measuring all criminal recidivism, indicates that, as a group, sex offenders have a relatively low risk of sexual recidivism when compared to many other types of violent criminals. Hanson and Bussiere (Hanson and Bussiere, 1998) conducted a meta-analysis of 61 sex offender recidivism studies involving 23,393 sex offenders. They found that overall, 13.4% of those offenders committed a new sex crime in the 4–5-year followup period. In this same study, 18.9% of rapists committed another sex crime during this period, as did 12.7% of child molesters. Other studies indicate that burglars (31.9%), larcenists (33.5%), and drug offenders (24.8%) have higher recidivism rates than sex offenders (Recidivism of Prisoners Released in 1983).

On the other hand, many sex crimes are never reported to the police; consequently, they would not be "counted" in recidivism studies. Even if reported, the perpetrator is not always arrested. If arrested, the case may not go to trial. If it goes to trial, the defendant may plead guilty to a non-sex crime or be acquitted. Thus, recidivism studies invariably underreport sex crimes and, therefore, underreport sexual recidivism.

Victim surveys in which women and children are asked whether they have ever been the victim of a sex crime corroborate this undercounting. The surveys indicate that the number of sex crimes committed in the United States is far higher than official statistics indicate. Self-reporting by sex offenders also supports this conclusion (La Fond, 2004).

Given the apparent disagreement between sex offender recidivism research, on the one hand, and victim surveys and offender self-reports, on the other hand, sex offenders as a group *may* be more dangerous than official records and recidivism research indicate. If they *are* more dangerous, then current methods of predicting sexual recidivism may grossly underpredict sexual dangerousness. There may also be a significant number of sex offenders who have committed more sex crimes than disclosed by official records. If so, these offenders may be much more dangerous than actuarial instruments would indicate. Because the true rate of sexual recidivism is problematic, the use of risk-management strategies for preventing sex offenders living in the community from committing more sex crimes is imperative.

TREATMENT EFFICACY

In the late 1980s public policy clearly assumed that sex offenders were not sick and that treatment did not reduce sexual recidivism. Recently, many experts have expressed renewed confidence that they can effectively treat sex offenders, thereby reducing the risk of sexual recidivism. New treatment approaches using cognitive restructuring, relapse prevention, other cognitive–behavioral techniques, and—in appropriate cases—pharmacological agents that reduce testosterone are now being used in a variety of settings to treat sex offenders. These techniques do not require a conception of sex offending as illness. But does treatment, in fact, reduce sexual reoffending?

After reviewing the available literature two eminent researchers concluded that there is simply not enough high-quality research to answer that question (Rice & Harris, 2003). In their view, there were not enough well-designed studies to establish that treatment does reduce sexual reoffending. Consequently, they remain agnostic about whether treatment reduces sexual reoffending (Rice & Harris, 2003).

Other researchers, however, believe there is some empirical basis for modest optimism that treatment does reduce sexual recidivism. An international committee of experts reviewed the available research on the effectiveness of psychological treatment in reducing sexual reoffending. (Hanson et al., 2002). They conducted a meta-analysis of 43 studies with a combined sample of 9,454 sex offenders. Most of the studies examined rapists and child-molesters and had an average follow-up period of 4 to 5 years. They found that, on average, adult sex offenders who received cognitive–behavioral treatment and adolescent sex offenders who received systemic treatments that address family needs and other social systems that influence young offenders were less likely to reoffend than sex offenders who did not receive treatment. Specifically, they found that contemporary treatments were associated with a "significant reduction in both sexual recidivism (17% to 10%) and general recidivism (51% to 32%)." (Hanson et al., 2002). The Committee also found that community treatment appeared to be as effective as institutional treatment. In addition, sex offenders who failed treatment were at higher risk of reoffending than sex offenders who completed treatment.

Despite this guarded optimism, the Committee stressed that its findings should be interpreted cautiously because there were few high-quality research studies, the treatment effects were not large in absolute terms (7%), and its findings provide little direction on how to improve treatment for sex offenders. It also noted that not all treatment programs are effective; consequently, public officials should not assume that any treatment is better than no treatment. In addition, no treatment program can assure a complete cessation of offending (Solicitor General of Canada, 2002).

It seem fair to conclude that there may be some basis for supposing that treatment can reduce sexual reoffending, but that a more definitive answer to that question awaits further research. Given this uncertainty, a prudent approach to many sex offenders living in the community would be to provide incentives for them to participate in treatment, while still monitoring them for a reasonable period of time to prevent them from committing new sex crimes.

PREDICTING SAFETY

Although experts have made significant progress in predicting sexual dangerousness, they have not made nearly as much progress in predicting sexual safety. That is, experts do not know when sex offenders can be released into the community with little danger of sexually reoffending (Hanson, 1998).

Though it is complicated, predictions of risk are based primarily on past, fixed, or static factors that do not change, although some dynamic factors, such as failing in prison treatment programs, can predict a greater likelihood of sexual recidivism. Predictions of safety are based primarily on dynamic factors that change over time. These might include empathy for victims, changed attitudes toward women, and successful mastery of relapse-prevention techniques. To date, however, experts have not managed to identify those factors that indicate reduced risk sufficiently to determine whether sex offenders once considered at high risk of sexual recidivism can be safely released into the community. Nor have they developed the functional equivalent of actuarial instruments to identify a group of sex offenders who have a lowered risk of reoffending, arguably justifying their conditional release from confinement.

The problem of identifying which SVPs can be conditionally released is proving particularly troublesome for states that enacted SVP laws. Many more sex offenders are being committed than are being conditionally released and very few SVPs have been released completely from state control (La Fond, 1998).

Most experts agree that realistic risk assessment for sex offenders cannot be conducted in a secure institution. Instead, it requires ongoing monitoring and assessment of how the offender behaves in a real world environment to see how he applies what he has learned about sex offending in that context (La Fond, 2003a; Schlank, 1999). Even then, errors are inevitable. Some sex offenders will be released who will reoffend.

THE RISK MANAGEMENT APPROACH TO SEXUAL RECIDIVISM

Clearly, risk management as a strategy for protecting the community from sexual recidivism is far superior to a prediction strategy (Heilbrun et al., 1998; Winick, 1998). Under a risk management model, an initial risk assessment for each sex offender, using state-of-the-art actuarial instruments and other techniques, would be conducted at the time of sentencing. Sentencing would be imposed and the release of the offender into the community would be managed using this model. Control both within the institution and in the community can be increased or decreased over time in light of ongoing assessments.

Criminal Sentencing

Risk assessment would be used in imposing the initial sentence on a convicted sex offender. Offenders determined to be at high risk of reoffending would have an additional increment added to their normal prison sentence. If indicated by subsequent risk assessments, this additional increment could be served on intensive parole in which a community containment approach could be used to monitor the offender's behavior in the community.

Washington State uses a different approach, sometimes called "determinate plus" sentencing, which is based on the crime of conviction and offender history. It requires that *nonpersistent* offenders who have committed one of the enumerated sex crimes or sexually motivated crimes *must* be given the maximum sentence. The court can then sentence the offender to serve some portion of the sentence after he is released from confinement in community custody under the supervision of the Department of Corrections (Wash. Rev. Code §§9.94A.712; 713., 2002).

Under a risk management approach, offenders considered at low risk for reoffending could have their sentence reduced. In carefully selected cases, offenders would be diverted into an intensive community supervision and treatment program (Wash. Rev. Code §§9.94A.670 2002).

Treatment would be made available to all sex offenders in confinement in order to reduce risk.

Sexual Predators

A risk management approach should also be used to commit SVPs initially to an LRA (community placement) or to release them from institutional commitment. This approach would be especially useful in determining and managing the release to the community of sex offenders committed under SVP laws. (La Fond, 2003a).

Advantages

A risk management strategy has several distinct advantages over long-term or indefinite confinement, on the one hand, and release into the community subject to mandatory registration and possible community notification, on the other.

Risk management can be used to control many more sex offenders as they are released from criminal confinement. Thus, more sex offenders can be monitored and controlled in the community. The level of control can be adjusted up or down, depending on periodic risk assessments. This creates strong incentives for offenders to change their attitudes and behavior in order to earn more freedom. It also assures the community that increased control, including reincarceration, will be imposed on the offender if necessary to protect the community.

Risk management should be much less costly than confinement under either a state SVP law or a criminal sentencing law (La Fond, 1998). It will surely be more effective than merely compiling relatively useless information about the offender under registration laws or in warning the community to watch out for itself. In sum, this approach provides the best of both worlds: stronger community protection measures combined with strong incentives for sex offender rehabilitation.

THE REENTRY PROCESS FOR SEX OFFENDERS

An essential goal of any sensible correctional process is the successful reentry of the offender into the community (Travis, 2000). Success in this context means not merely lack of recidivism, but also community reintegration. It is hoped that the returning offender has been rehabilitated and has undergone attitudinal and behavioral change in ways that avoid future offending. In addition, the returning offender will become a productive member of society, an asset to the community rather than a liability.

As discussed earlier, predictions of safety or of danger are difficult to make in an institutional environment. Unsupervised release to the community of an offender accustomed to the controls of total institutionalization with little more than community notification significantly increases risk to the community. Instead, there should be a graduated release process in which offenders are subjected to close monitoring and supervision until they can demonstrate their successful adjustment to community life. Supervised release should also be accompanied by services in the community designed to help them to achieve this goal.

This graduated release strategy has reduced general recidivism; it also should reduce sexual recidivism. A comprehensive study of Colorado's community corrections system (25 half-way houses throughout the state that serve both probation and parolee populations) found that offenders who were not placed on postrelease supervision (Woodburn & English, 2002) after release from the community corrections system were almost twice as likely to reoffend when compared with offenders released from the community corrections system who were placed on postrelease supervision. Moreover, among those offenders released from prison through the community corrections system who did reoffend (measured by a new criminal charge), those who were not subject to postrelease supervision tended to reoffend more quickly.

Any sensible reentry process for sex offenders must focus both on community protection and on offender rehabilitation. Reentry should be graduated. The individual should gradually move from more restrictive to less restrictive supervision based upon changes in dynamic risk factors that suggest a decreasing risk of reoffending. Risk should be closely and continually monitored through periodic risk assessment.

The individual should move gradually from the total institutionalization of the prison or hospital to partial release and, eventually, to total discharge. For example, an offender might start on work release from a prison, then move to a half-way house in the community with structured restrictions, then to living at home subject to partial home confinement or electronic monitoring. Gradually these restrictions would be eased, but with continued monitoring and supervision. The offender must earn these graduated reductions in the restrictions to which he is subjected through behavior that demonstrates a reduction in risk in the face of increasing exposure to opportunities in the community for reoffending. This process requires close monitoring and supervision of the individual by probation or parole professionals, periodic reassessment of risk, and participation by the offender in sex offender treatment designed to teach him how to avoid reoffending.

THE COMMUNITY CONTAINMENT APPROACH

Multidisciplinary Case Management Teams

How can such a sex offender reentry process be best structured? An innovative model is the community containment approach developed in Colorado (English, Jones & Patrick, 2003). The community containment approach involves a specially trained, multidisciplinary case management team composed of a probation or parole officer, a treatment provider, and a polygraph examiner acting together to reduce the offender's privacy, access to past or potential victims, and opportunities to reoffend. Limiting opportunities to reoffend requires accurate information about the offender's past and potential victims and high-risk behavior patterns. This information is solicited and verified through use of periodic polygraph testing. Such testing or its potential has been found to increase the scope and accuracy of sexual history information, provides a basis for verifying whether the offender is currently engaging in high-risk or assaultive behavior, and helps to break down the denial that perpetuates much sexual violence, enabling cognitive restructuring and other treatment interventions to be more successful (English, Jones & Patrick, 2003).

Extensive Use of Polygraph

The community containment approach is a risk management/treatment model which uses polygraph examinations extensively. Polygraph testing assists both the risk management and treatment process by producing much needed and otherwise largely unavailable information about the offender's sexual history and *modus operandi*, his preferred victim types and offending patterns, the frequency and extent of deviant sexual arousal and behaviors, and the events and emotional states that are precursors or triggers to reoffense (English, Jones & Patrick, 2003). Assembling this more detailed information concerning the offender provides a superior foundation for supervision and surveillance plans tailored to the offender and designed to reduce risk by limiting his access to victims and to opportunities to reoffend. The individual typically is subjected to significant restrictions as conditions of probation or parole, such as restrictions on contact with children or being in locations where children are likely to be present, random home visits, urine testing, and electronic monitoring.

Failure to comply with these conditions is both deterred by and detected by polygraph examination.

Effect on Treatment

This information also assists in the treatment process by providing opportunities to confront and break down the offender's denial. In addition, it facilitates the design and implementation of more effective relapse-prevention plans customized to the individual. The answers provided by the offender in periodic polygraph examination significantly assist the monitoring and supervision process. Polygraph examination functions as a deterrent to the offender's engaging in high-risk behavior.

Violations and Sanctions

If violations of an offender's conditions of release are discovered, a variety of sanctions can be imposed by the probation or parole officer, including increased surveillance, house arrest, electronic monitoring, home visits by the officer, requirements that the offender provide location information to the officer, additional mandated treatment, required community services, short-term jail sentences, placement in a half-way house for sex offenders, or even revocation of probation or parole. These sanctions are an essential condition for successful sex offender treatment. In sum, polygraph examination increases the offender's candor in treatment, helps to break down denial, and provides the external pressures that may be needed to keep the offender from reoffending.

Necessary Resources

The community containment model has much to offer. For it to work effectively, however, probation or parole officers should have caseloads limited to 20 or 25 sex offenders (English, Jones & Patrick, 2003). Unfortunately, in recent years many jurisdictions have eliminated parole or significantly reduced the extent of parole supervision. Moreover, in most jurisdictions probation officers have enormous caseloads, which can significantly undermine the effectiveness of the containment approach. Unless the probation or parole officer can closely monitor compliance with the conditions of release and enforce them through the court's authority, the likelihood of offender noncompliance is greatly increased.

The Judiciary

We propose an expansion of the containment approach that adds a more active role by the judiciary, one that starts at the beginning of a criminal prosecution and ends with final discharge of the offender. It begins with plea-bargaining and continues with a sentencing process that plans from the very outset for eventual release of the offender. Judges, applying a risk management approach and principles of therapeutic jurisprudence, can strengthen the containment approach and provide even stronger incentives for offender rehabilitation and risk reduction. This proposal builds on some very promising developments occurring in the past dozen years in which a variety of specialized treatment courts (or "problem solving courts," as they increasingly are becoming known) have been utilized to deal with a whole range of psychosocial problems.

REENTRY COURTS AND OTHER PROBLEM SOLVING COURTS

In recent years, a variety of specialized problem-solving courts have been established to deal with various offender populations (Winick, 2003a). The modern antecedents of this model can be traced to drug treatment court, founded in the late 1980s in Miami (Hora, Schma & Rosenthal, 1999; Hora, 2002; Winick & Wexler, 2002). In order to avoid the revolving-door effect that traditional criminal-prison approaches to drug possession have failed to deal with effectively, drug treatment court emphasizes offender rehabilitation and casts the judge as a central member of the rehabilitative team. Offenders electing to participate in drug treatment court agree to remain drug-free, to participate in a prescribed course of drug treatment, to submit to periodic urinalysis to monitor their compliance with the treatment plan, and to report periodically to court for judicial supervision of their progress.

Other specialized treatment courts, or problem-solving courts (Conference of Chief Justices and Conference of State Court Administrators, 2000) have been based on the very promising success of the drug treatment model. These include domestic violence court (Fritzler & Simon, 2000; Winick, 2000), and mental health court (Lurigio et al., 2001; Goldkamp & Irons-Guynn, 2000; Winick, 2003b).

These new judicial models involve a collaborative, interdisciplinary approach to rehabilitation and problem solving in which the judge plays a leading role. They all involve the explicit use of judicial authority to motivate offenders to accept needed treatment services and to monitor their compliance and progress (Winick & Wexler, 2003; Winick, 2003a).

The Role of the Judge

The judge–offender interaction is an essential ingredient in the effectiveness of these new judicial models. Not only does the judge supervise and monitor treatment and adherence, but also the judge serves as a behavioral motivator, shaping successful performance in treatment through praise and other types of positive reinforcement, and punishing lack of required participation in treatment or instances of relapse through the application of agreed-upon sanctions, ranging from sitting in the jury box for several hours to brief periods of jail detention to revocation of probation. Anecdotal reports and preliminary research suggests that there is a kind of "magic" in the judicial robe, that is, that the judge's direct participation and interaction with the offender makes an important difference in offender compliance and rehabilitation.

A new application of these special judicial models is reentry court, designed to assist offenders released from prison on parole to effect a successful reintegration into the community (Travis, 2000; Petersilia, 2000; Saunders, 2002). These courts manage the return to the community of prisoners, using the authority of the court to apply positive reinforcement and graduated sanctions, and to marshal treatment and other resources in the community designed to help the offender make a successful adjustment to community life. They combine supervision with counseling and treatment, attempting to produce both rehabilitation and the protection of public safety.

Behavioral Contracts

Reentry courts were first proposed by former National Institute of Justice Director Jeremy Travis (Travis, 2000) and were based explicitly on the drug treatment court model. As with drug treatment court, offenders who agree to participate in reentry court enter into an explicit behavioral contract (Travis, 2000; Winick & Wexler, 2003; Winick, 2003a; *see* Winick, 1991, pp. 772–788, pp. 793–797 [describing behavioral contracting or contingency management, analyzing the psychological principles on which it is based, and illustrating its application by government to achieve various social and individual goals]). The contract sets forth specific intermediate and long-term goals. Motivation to achieve the goals is facilitated through contract terms providing for agreed-upon rewards or positive reinforcers for success or sanctions or aversive conditioners for failure. The behavioral contract harnesses a number of principles of psychology to help to bring about compliance and goal achievement, including the goal-setting effect, intrinsic motivation, commitment, cognitive dissonance, and the psychological value of choice.

The court closely monitors and supervises the released offender's progress in the community. This involves compliance with contract provisions, including participation in treatment, employment, and desistance from the use of drugs or alcohol. The court closely monitors whether the offender has remained law-abiding. Through the application of judicial praise or other forms of positive reinforcement, including the gradual lessening of restrictions, and graduated sanctions, including home confinement, electronic monitoring, more restrictive conditions, and ultimately revocation of parole, the reentry court judge helps the offender to achieve a successful reintegration into society, fosters his or her rehabilitation, and protects community safety. If the offender does commit another sex crime during his supervised release, he has broken his contract with the court. In most cases the offender will be immediately returned to custody and the prosecutor will be notified.

Therapeutic Jurisprudence

Like the other problem-solving courts, reentry court can be seen as applying principles of therapeutic jurisprudence (Winick, 2003a; Simon, 2003a). Therapeutic jurisprudence is an interdisciplinary approach to legal scholarship and law reform that sees legal rules and the way they are applied as social forces that produce inevitable consequences for the psychological well-being of those affected (*see generally* Wexler & Winick, 1996). Therapeutic jurisprudence calls upon scholars to study these consequences with the tools of the behavioral sciences, and upon legislators, judges, and policymakers to reshape law in ways designed to minimize law's antitherapeutic effects, and when consistent with other legal goals, to increase law's therapeutic potential.

Problem-solving courts often use principles of therapeutic jurisprudence to enhance their functioning (Conference of Chief Justices and Conference of State Court Administrators, 2000; Winick, 2003a; Simon, in press). These principles include ongoing judicial intervention, close monitoring of and immediate response to behavior, integration of treatment services with case processing, multidisciplinary involvement, and collaboration with community-based and governmental organizations (Conference of Chief Justices and Conference of state Court Administrators, 2000). These courts can be seen as taking a therapeutic jurisprudence approach to the processing of cases inasmuch as their goal is the rehabilitation of the offender, and they use the legal process and the role of the judge in particular to accomplish this goal. Through their supervision and monitoring of the offender's treatment progress, these judges themselves function as therapeutic agents (Winick & Wexler, 2003; Winick, 2003a). Moreover, these courts apply principles of therapeutic jurisprudence to spark motivation for treatment, to reinforce treatment success, and to increase treatment compliance (Winick, 2003a; Casey & Rottman, 2000; Fritzler & Simon, 2000; Hora, Schma & Rosenthal et al, 1999; Petrucci, 2002; Winick, 2000; Winick & Wexler, 2002; Simon, 2003a).

A SEX OFFENDER REENTRY COURT

We propose an adaptation of the problem-solving court model for sex offenders —a sex offender reentry court. As with other problem-solving courts, these proposed courts would apply principles of therapeutic jurisprudence to motivate sex offenders to deal with their underlying problems and to monitor their compliance with and progress in treatment, within both the prison or psychiatric facility and the community, once they have been released. As with these other courts, the judge in reentry court would function as a member of an interdisciplinary team, in this case serving as a "reentry manager" for sex offenders (Travis, 2000).

Reentry as a Process

The reentry process can be seen as beginning at the offender's initial sentencing. As with most criminal offenders, the overwhelming majority of sex offenders plead guilty to their charges. The plea colloquy at which such a plea is accepted can provide an important opportunity for the judge to assist the offender to accept responsibility for his offense. Because denial, minimization, and rationalization are common in sex offenders and help to perpetuate their reoffending, the sentencing judge should not accept pleas of *nolo contendere* or *Alford* pleas, both of which allow the offender to avoid acceptance of responsibility (Wexler & Winick, 1991). The plea colloquy can become an important opportunity for the offender to acknowledge his wrongdoing and recount the facts of his crime and the impact it had upon the victim. These discussions held in open court and on the record can help the process of breaking down the offender's cognitive distortions that may facilitate repetitive offending, paving the way for a positive cognitive restructuring in treatment.

Treatment Incentives

There is an inevitable gap in time between acceptance of the plea or a verdict of guilty and the imposition of sentence, and this period can be an important one during which to spark the offender's motivation to accept treatment. Courts increasingly have been recognizing postoffense rehabilitation as a ground for a reduction in sentence or a basis for probation (Winick, 1999a). When a thorough risk assessment concludes that the risk of reoffending appears to be low, perhaps in a case involving a first-time nonviolent sex offender, the court, in considering the setting of bail, can require the offender to accept treatment as a condition of release on bail. This condition often is applied in the context of domestic violence court (Winick, 2000), and in appropriate low-risk cases, this same approach can be used by the sex offender reentry court. In cases in which the offender appears to be making substantial progress in treatment, the court may consider a deferral of sentencing to permit the treatment process to proceed (Winick, 1999a; Edwards & Hensley, 2001).

The offender's knowledge that the court will take his progress in treatment into account in imposing sentence and that a deferred sentence is possible can serve as powerful motivators for the offender to participate meaningfully in treatment and to gain significant benefits from it. If the defendant has been given a deferred sentence conditioned on his successful participation in treatment in the community, the court can hold periodic hearings to monitor the offender's ongoing treatment, similar to how drug treatment courts monitor treatment compliance and progress for drug offenders.

Sentencing

Assuming that the judge decides to impose a sentence involving imprisonment, the judge, in pronouncing sentence, can discuss future reentry with the offender. The judge can motivate the offender to accept whatever treatment might be available within the prison, noting that participation in prison treatment (or a continuation within the prison of treatment that the offender began within the community) will be taken into account positively when consideration is given to the offender's release. When authorized, the court can impose a sentence involving a period of incarceration followed by a period of community release under the court's supervision (Travis, 2000).

The court can advise the offender that the ultimate goal is his release into the community once he has paid his debt to society and has demonstrated his ability to be law-abiding (Travis, 2000). The court can further inform the offender that, starting at that very moment, the court and offender together will begin a process of developing a plan for attaining that goal. The plan will involve treatment in prison as well as in the community, and hopefully will include the participation of the offender's family, friends, and other support networks. The court can monitor the offender's prison adjustment and participation in prison programs designed to prepare him for community release.

Under this proposal, the court would retain sentencing discretion to permit early release when appropriate. In imposing sentence, the court will use risk assessment instruments and clinical assessment to develop an appropriate sentence and release plan. At appropriate intervals, the offender's risk of reoffending can be reassessed in light of his behavior in prison, including participation in prison treatment programs.

Community Release

The judge should advise the offender that the extent of risk he presents will be all-important in determining when and if partial release to the community will be authorized. The offender should be told that while many of the factors taken into account in performing the risk assessment are fixed, involving historic facts that will remain unchangeable, many are dynamic, subject to change through his behavior in prison and in the community, including participation in treatment, compliance with conditions of release, and the like. This knowledge can help the offender to understand the instrumental value of engaging in appropriate behavior, including participation in prison rehabilitative programs and, in due course, those in the community. In short, it can motivate the offender to participate meaningfully in treatment and help to bring about positive treatment results (Winick, 1998). In this way, the court will be applying a risk management model, calibrating its release decision in light of the offender's risk as it may change over time (Winick, 1998).

Offender Support Network

The judge also could involve in the sentencing process the stakeholders who ultimately will be responsible for the offender's reentry. The offender's family members, friends, and other members of whatever support network he might have would be requested to help to develop the reentry plan, and asked what kind of support they would provide to help to prepare him for a successful reentry. A parole or probation officer, or similar official who ultimately will be involved in the offender's supervision in the community, also should participate in the planning process.

ADAPTATION OF THE COMMUNITY CONTAINMENT APPROACH FOR USE IN SEX OFFENDER REENTRY COURT

Our proposal contemplates a system of graduated release, either from prison or from SVP commitment, correlated to the extent of risk the offender presents over time. Once institutional release is contemplated, we suggest the use of the community containment model developed and researched in Colorado and implemented there by the Colorado Sex Offender Management Board (English, Jones & Patrick, 2003). In this model, polygraph testing is used to increase information about the offender and his offending patterns in order to increase the efficacy of judicial supervision and monitoring in the community.

A key ingredient in the drug treatment court model is periodic drug testing, the results of which are quickly made known to the judge and become the basis for judicial response—the application of positive reinforcement or sanctions. There is no parallel test to detect sex offending or engagement in risky behavior that might increase its likelihood. However, polygraph testing, although lacking the objectivity and precision of urinalysis, seems to be sufficiently reliable, when performed by trained polygraph examiners, to fulfill this function.

Polygraph Testing

Polygraph testing has been deemed insufficiently reliable to be introduced as evidence in a criminal case, either by the state or the defendant (*United States v. Scheffer*, 1998, pp. 309–312; Faigman et al., 1997, p. 565; Giannelli & Imwinkelried (1993), pp. 225–227). The sex offender reentry court, however, would not use the results of polygraph testing for purposes of proving guilt concerning any past sex offenses. Indeed, we think that, to the extent polygraph examination probes into the existence of past criminal activity, the offender should be given a form of use-immunity with regard to the information revealed in the offender's responses and to other information gathered from links or leads provided by his responses (*Kastigar v. United States*, 1972). Otherwise, such use of the offender's responses would raise serious Fifth Amendment and due process problems (*Casamassima v. State, 1995*).

The reentry court's use of this information would be restricted to its risk management functions. Although the offender's responses to polygraph examination, together with other evidence, might lead to the imposition of sanctions by the reentry court judge, including revocation of parole for a released prisoner or of conditional release for an offender committed as an SVP, this use would not violate the Fifth Amendment ban on compulsory self-incrimination as long as the responses themselves were not admitted into evidence (*Cassamasima v. State*, 1995). These answers would also alert the community containment team that further investigation is warranted.

The Fifth Amendment Privilege against Self-Incrimination

If in response to polygraph testing that suggests the offender has been deceptive in answering questions asked in the examination, the offender admits wrongdoing, can his admission be admitted into evidence consistent with the Fifth Amendment for purposes of determining whether probation or parole should be revoked? As long as the offender has agreed as part of the behavioral contract to respond truthfully to polygraph questioning, the answer would appear to be "yes." In *Minnesota v. Murphy* (1984) the U.S. Supreme Court held that a state may compel answers to incriminating questions without violating the Fifth Amendment as long as the probationer had agreed to do so as a condition of probation and provided that the answers may not be used in a criminal proceeding. The Court noted that a probation revocation proceeding is not itself a criminal trial; therefore, the Fifth Amendment does not apply when the probationer accepts this requirement as a probation condition.

Although *Murphy* involved a requirement that the probationer answer truthfully to questions asked by his probation officer, and did not involve polygraph testing, the court's analysis would appear to apply equally in the polygraph context provided the offender had agreed to submit to polygraph testing as a condition of release on probation, parole, or conditional release from SVP commitment. Because these release programs serve a "vital penological purpose," the "minimal incentives to participate" offered offenders would not amount to compulsory self-incrimination when they agree to participate in a treatment program that includes polygraph examination (*McKune v. Lile*, 2002). Thus, while polygraph results suggesting that the offender lied would not themselves be admissible at a probation or parole revocation hearing, an offender's refusal to respond to the polygraph examiner's questioning when he agreed to do so as a condition of release, or any admission that he might make that he violated a condition of release, would be admissible in a hearing to determine whether release should be revoked. While the offender could invoke his Fifth Amendment privilege to refuse to answer a particular question in polygraph examination, if his refusal to respond is itself a violation of an agreed-upon condition of his release, his invocation of the privilege can serve as a basis for revoking his probation or parole.

The increased information provided by the use of polygraph examination by the reentry court as a component of a multidisciplinary containment approach can considerably improve the court's ability to manage the risk of reoffending, protect the safety of the community, and facilitate the offender's rehabilitation and reintegration into the community.

Impact on Sex Crimes against Familiars

The reentry court model proposed here also can do much to address the largely neglected problem of sex crimes committed by intimates or others familiar to the victim. The SVP laws and registration and community notification laws overemphasize the problem of sex crimes committed by strangers, neglecting the well-established fact that the overwhelming majority of sex offenses are committed by family members and others known to the victim (Simon, 2003b). The new strategies developed in the 1990s to deal with sexual violence have distracted us from dealing effectively with the more extensive problem of preventing sexual violence by offenders who know their victims.

Reentry courts can help meet this neglected need. Collecting sex offense histories and offender patterns for each offender through clinical interviews and polygraph examination can identify the offender's previous victims in the community, allowing development of customized restrictions on contact with past victims and on the ability of the offender to visit places where he will be tempted to reoffend. Intense supervision and polygraph examination can also help assure that these restrictions are followed. When the offender has abused a child or other intimate within the household to which he will be returning, the threat of polygraph examination can significantly deter future abusive conduct, much of which might otherwise go undetected because family members are often reluctant to report crimes of intimate violence. The containment approach is most appropriate for use with perpetrators who know their victims. It acknowledges that 80% to 90% of sex crimes occur between those who know each other. The reentry court model thus can do considerably more than sex offender registration and community notification to protect prior victims.

Impact on Notification Laws

The reentry court model can considerably improve the functioning of notification laws generally. While a majority of states using these notification laws base the degree of notification required on the offender's placement in one of several tiers of risk, 13 states only use one tier of risk and many others, in practice, rarely if ever consider a change in tier risk level (Winick, 2003d). As a result, many of these community notification schemes can be seen as reflecting a prediction model because they are static, basing notification requirements on historic facts existing at the point of discharge. In contrast, states using several tiers of risk can be seen as applying a risk management model, at least to the extent that individuals are capable of being moved between tiers as new information develops over time. Those jurisdictions that use only one tier of risk or that rarely permit reconsideration of risk level can be criticized as antitherapeutic inasmuch as they provide no incentive to the offender to change (Winick, 2003d). It would be more therapeutic to have three or more tiers of risk and to allow periodic reassessment of the extent of risk based on changing circumstances and to permit changes to risk classification as a result.

For jurisdictions that convert their community notification statutory schemes from prediction to risk management models, the reentry court model proposed here can facilitate their functioning by providing constantly updated information about the offender and his functioning in the community. The reentry court should be in close contact with the prosecutor or local sheriff charged with administering these notification laws, funneling them updated information that can be used to reclassify offenders as new information emerges concerning their extent of risk. The reentry court, in the process of doing this, can further help to motivate offenders to obtain treatment and to act in ways that reduce risk. Indeed, consideration might be given to having the reentry court judge take over the function of risk classification for community notification law purposes.

In any event, whether administered by the reentry court or by the prosecutor or sheriff, restructuring notification laws to convert them into instruments of risk management can allow the reentry court judge to use an additional tool of motivation in the risk management process. By informing offenders that there will be a payoff for controlling their behavior, engaging in treatment, and complying with conditions of release, the court can provide an additional incentive for prosocial behavior and disincentive for antisocial behavior. Moreover, by taking into account the additional information that the reentry court process will generate, such restructured notification law schemes will further increase the accuracy of risk assessment, thereby allowing them better to achieve the community protection purposes they are designed to serve.

Impact on Sex Offenders

By requiring the released offender periodically to report to court in a manner similar to the way drug treatment courts function, the reentry judge can come to know the offender better and have an ongoing dialogue with him. By treating the offender with dignity and respect and demonstrating concern for his well-being, the reentry court judge can forge a personal relationship with the offender that can itself be therapeutic (Winick, 2003a; Winick & Wexler, 2003; Petrucci, 2002). To perform this function effectively, the reentry court judge must develop enhanced interpersonal skills and use some basic principles derived from psychology and social work. The judge playing this role is functioning as a therapeutic agent. The emerging therapeutic jurisprudence literature on problem-solving courts provides a number of instrumental prescriptions for judges playing these new roles (Winick, 2003a), and these insights will be particularly helpful for sex offender reentry court judges.

Moreover, affording offenders the opportunity to participate in decision making concerning the conditions of their reentry can have significant therapeutic value (Winick, 2003a; Winick, 2003b; Winick, 1999). A body of research on the psychology of procedural justice demonstrates the psychological value of affording people an opportunity to participate in hearings that they regard as fair (Lind & Tyler, 1988; Tyler, 1990; Cascardi et al., 2000). People given a sense of "voice," the opportunity to tell their story, and "validation," the feeling that what they have said is taken seriously by the judge, and who feel that they have been treated fairly, with respect for their dignity, will likely experience greater satisfaction with the hearing process and a greater willingness to comply with the results of it, even if unfavorable. The periodic provision of hearings that will characterize reentry sex offender court can thus have a therapeutic value for the offender.

These hearings will have the added benefit of placing offenders in the position of advocating to the court that they have gained from treatment and rehabilitative efforts, and that their present risk of reoffending is significantly reduced. Affording them this opportunity can further assist to facilitate their acceptance of wrongdoing, the breakdown of denial and cognitive distortions about it, and their willingness to accept rehabilitative efforts (Winick, 2003c).

CONCLUSION

After criticizing the two major new legal approaches to dealing with sex offenders, mandatory minimum sentencing laws and sexually violent predator laws as well as registration and community notification laws, we propose the use of special sex offender reentry courts to manage the risk that sexual offenders will reoffend. Risk management practices will allow the court to readjust calculations of individual risk on an ongoing basis in light of new information about the offender, much of it generated through the judge's use of the containment model, which includes periodic polygraph examination, and to adjust and readjust the conditions of control that are imposed.

In recent years, a variety of specialized problem-solving courts have been established to deal with special offender populations. These courts apply principles of therapeutic jurisprudence to motivate offenders to deal with their underlying problems, to engage in behavioral contracting in which they formally agree to achieve certain rehabilitative and risk reduction goals, and to facilitate the court's monitoring of their compliance with conditions and progress in treatment.

Our proposal adapts these approaches to the sex offender context, positing for the judge a leading role as a member of an interdisciplinary risk management and treatment team that uses the community containment approach. The offender must, as a condition for gaining his release from prison or SVP commitment, agree to enter into a behavioral contract with the court to engage in sex offender treatment and to undergo periodic polygraph examination to allow the court better to monitor compliance and manage risk. This model provides incentives for offenders to change their behavior and attitudes, thereby decreasing the degree of risk of recidivism and earning greater freedom. It also monitors compliance and manages risk in a more effective manner. In addition, this model can impose greater controls on offenders who manifest increased risk of sexual recidivism, thereby providing the appropriate level of protection for the community in light of the offender's current recidivism risk.

In sum, we propose a viable solution to the serious problem of sexual recidivism that is both smart and tough. It strikes an appropriate balance between enhancing community safety by aggressively monitoring more sex offenders in the community, while also creating and managing powerful incentives for sex offenders to invest in rehabilitation, thereby reducing sexual recidivism and increasing community protection.

REFERENCES

CASCARDI, M., POYTHRESS, N.G. & HALL, A. (2000). Procedural justice in the context of civil commitment: An analogy study. *Behavioral Science and the Law, 18,* 731–740.
CASEY, P. & ROTTMAN, D.B. (2000). Therapeutic jurisprudence in the courts. *Behavioral Sciences & the Law, 18,* 445–457
Cassamassima v. State, 657 So.2d 906 (Fla. 5th DCA 1995) (en banc).
CLARK, J., AUSTIN, J. & HENRY, D.A. (1997). Three strikes and you're out: A review of state legislation. *National Institute of Justice Research in Brief, September 1997.* Washington, DC: National Institute of Justice.
CONFERENCE OF CHIEF JUSTICES & CONFERENCE OF STATE COURT ADMINISTRATORS (2000). CCJ Resolution 22 & COSCA Resolution 4, *In support of problem-solving courts.*

EDWARDS, W. & HENSLEY, C. (2001). Restructuring sex offender sentencing: A therapeutic jurisprudence approach to the criminal justice process, *International Journal of Offender Therapy and Comparative Criminology, 45,* 646– 662.

ENGLISH, K., JONES, L. & PATRICK, D. (2003). Community containment of sex offender risk: A promising approach. In Bruce J. Winick & John Q. La Fond, (Eds). *Protecting society from sexually dangerous offenders: Law, justice, and therapy,* Washington, DC: American Psychological Association,

FAIGMAN, D., KAYE, D., SAKS, M. & SANDERS, J. (1997). *Modern scientific evidence.* St. Paul, MN: West Publishing Co.

FINN, P. (1992). *Sex offender community notification; research in action.* Washington, DC: National Institute of Justice.

FITCH, W.L. & HAMMEN, D.A. (2003). The new generation of sex offender commitment laws: Which states have them and how do they work? In Bruce J. Winick & John Q. La Fond, (Eds). *Protecting society from sexually dangerous offenders: Law, justice, and therapy.* Washington, DC: American Psychological Association.

FRITZLER, R.B. & SIMON, L.M.J. (2000). The development of a specialized domestic violence court in Vancouver, Washington utilizing innovative judicial paradigms. *University of Missouri–Kansas City Law Review, 69,* 139–177.

GIANNELLI, P. & IMWINKELRIED, E. (1993). *Scientific evidence,* 2nd ed. Charlottesville, VA: Mitchie Co.

GOLDKAMP, J.S. & IRONS-GUYNN, C. (2000). *Emerging judicial strategies for the mentally ill in the criminal caseload: Mental health courts in Ft. Lauderdale, Seattle, San Bernardino, and Anchorage.* Washington, DC: U. S. Department of Justice, Office of Justice Programs, Bureau of Justice Assistance.

GREENFELD, LAWRENCE A. (1997). *Sex offenses and offenders, an analysis of data on rape and sexual assault.* Washington, DC: Bureau of Justice Statistics .

HANSON, R.K. (1998). What do we know about sex offender risk assessment? *Psychology, Public Policy, and Law, 4,* 50–72.

HANSON, R.K. & BUSSIERE (1998). Predicting relapse: A meta-analysis of sexual offender recidivism studies. *Journal of Consulting and Clinical Psychology 66,* 348–362.

HANSON, R.K., GORDON, A., HARRIS, A.J.R., MARQUES, J.K., MURPHY, W., QUINSEY, V.L. & SETO, M.C. (2002). First report of the collaborative outcome data on the effectiveness of psychological treatment of sex offenders. *Sexual Abuse: A Journal of Research and Treatment, 14,* 169–194.

HANSON, R.K. (2003). Who is dangerous and when are they safe? Risk assessment with sexual offenders. In Bruce J. Winick & John Q. La Fond (Eds.), *Protecting society from sexually dangerous offenders: Law, justice, and therapy,* Washington, DC: American Psychological Association.

HEILBRUN, K., NEZU, C., MAGUTH, K.M., CHUNG, S. & WASSERMAN, A.L. (1998). Sexual offending: Linking assessment, intervention, and decision making, *Psychology, Public Policy, and Law, 4,* 138–174.

HORA, P.F. (2002). A dozen years of drug treatment courts: Uncovering our theoretical foundation and the construction of a mainstream paradigm. *Substance Use & Misuse, 37,* 1469–1488.

HORA, P.F., SCHMA, W.G. & ROSENTHAL, J.T.A. (1999). Therapeutic jurisprudence and the drug treatment court movement: Revolutionizing the criminal justice system's response to drug abuse and crime in America. *Notre Dame Law Review 74,* 439–537.

Kansas v. Crane, 122 S. Ct. 867 (2002).

Kansas v. Hendricks, 521 U.S. 346 (1997).

Kastigar v. United States, 406 U.S. 441 (1972)

LA FOND, J.Q. (1998). The costs of enacting a sexual predator law. *Psychology, Public Policy, and Law, 4,* 468–504.

LA FOND, J.Q. (2003a). Outpatient's new frontier: sexually violent predators. *Psychology, Public Policy, and Law, 9,* 159–182.

LA FOND, J.Q. (forthcoming, 2004). *Preventing sexual violence: How society should cope with sex offenders.* Washington, DC: American Psychological Association.

LIND, E.A. & TYLER, T.R. (1988). The social psychology of procedural justice. New York: Plenum Press.

LOGAN, W. (2003). Registration and community notification: emerging legal and research issues. *Annals of the New York Academy of Sciences, 989,* (this volume).
LURIGIO, A.J., WATSON, A., LUCHINS, D.J. & HANRAHAN, P. (2001). Therapeutic jurisprudence in action: Specialized courts for the mentally ill. *Judicature, 84,* 184.
McKune v. Lile, WL 1270605 (U.S.) (2002)
Minnesota v. Murphy, 465 U.S. 420 (1984).
MORSE, S.J. (2003). Bad or mad? Sex offenders and social control. In Bruce J. Winick & John Q. La Fond (Eds.), *Protecting society from sexually dangerous offenders: Law, justice, and therapy* (pp. 165–182). Washington, DC: American Psychological Association.
PETERSILIA, J. (November, 2000), *When Prisoners Return to Communities: Political, Economic, and Social Consequences, Sentencing & Corrections: Issues for the 21st Century,* Washington, DC: U.S. Department of Justice, National Institute of Justice, NCJ 184253.
PETRUCCI, C.J. (2002). Respect as a component in the judge-defendant interaction in a specialized domestic violence court that utilizes therapeutic jurisprudence, *Criminal. Law Bulletin, 38,* 263–277.
Recidivism of prisoners released in 1983. (1989). Washington, DC: Bureau of Justice Statistics.
RICE, M.E. & HARRIS, G.T. (2003). What we know and don't know about treating adult sex offenders. In Bruce J. Winick & John Q. La Fond (Eds.), *Protecting society from sexually dangerous offenders: Law, justice, and therapy* (pp. 101–117). Washington, DC; American Psychological Association.
ROTTMAN, D.B. (2000). Does effective therapeutic jurisprudence require specialized courts (and do specialized courts imply specialist judges)? *Court Review, 37,* 22–27
SAUNDERS, T. (Winter 2002). Staying home: Effective reintegration strategies for parolees. *The Judges' Journal, 41,* 34–36.
SCHLANK, A. (1999). Guidelines for the development of new programs, *in* Anita Schlank & Fred Cohen (Eds.), *The sexual predator: Law, policy, evaluation and treatment,* pp. 12–5 & 12–6. Kingston, NJ: Civic Research Institute, Inc.
SIMON, L.M.J. (2003a). Proactive judges: Solving problems and transforming communities. In David Carson & Ray Bull (Eds.), *The Handbook of Psychology in Legal Contexts,* 2nd ed. (pp. 449–472). West Sussex, England: John Wiley & Sons Ltd.
SIMON. L.M.J. (2003b). Matching legal policies with known offenders. In Bruce J. Winick & John Q. La Fond (Eds.), *Protecting society from sexually dangerous offenders: Law, justice, and therapy* (pp. 149–163). Washington, DC: American Psychological Association.
SOLICITOR GENERAL OF CANADA. (2002). *Research summary: The effectiveness of treatment for sexual offenders.*
TRAVIS, J. (2000). *But they all come back: Rethinking prisoner reentry.* Washington, DC: U.S. Department of Justice.
TYLER, T.R. (1990). *Why people obey the law.* New Haven, CT: Yale University Press.
United States v. Scheffer, 523 U.S. 303 (1998).
WASH. REV. CODE §§9.94A.712. 713 (West, 2002).
WASH. REV. CODE §9.94A.670 (2002).
WETTSTEIN, R.M. (1992). A psychiatric perspective on Washington's sexually violent predator law. *University of Puget Sound Law Review, 15,* 597–633.
WEXLER, D.B. & WINICK, B.J. (1992). Therapeutic jurisprudence and criminal justice mental health issues, *Mental & Physical Disability Law Reporter, 16,* 225–231
WEXLER, D.B. & WINICK, B.J. (Eds.) (1996). *Law in a therapeutic key: Developments in Therapeutic jurisprudence.* Durham, NC: Carolina Academic Press.
WINICK, B.J. (2003a). Therapeutic jurisprudence and problem solving courts. *Fordham Urban Law Journal, 30,* 1055–1090.
WINICK, B.J. (2003b). Outpatient commitment: A therapeutic jurisprudence analysis. *Psychology, Public Policy & Law, 9,* 107–144.
WINICK, B.J. (2003c). A therapeutic jurisprudence assessment of sexually violent predator laws. In Bruce J. Winick & John Q. La Fond (Eds.) *Protecting society from sexually dangerous offenders: Law, justice, and therapy* (pp. 213–229). Washington, DC: American Psychological Association.

WINICK, B.J. (2003d). A therapeutic jurisprudence analysis of sex offender registration and community notification laws. In Winick, B.J. & La Fond, J.Q. (Eds.) *Protecting society from sexually dangerous offenders: Law, justice, and therapy.* Washington, DC: American Psychological Association.

WINICK, B.J. (1999a). Redefining the role of the criminal defense lawyer at plea bargaining and sentencing: A therapeutic jurisprudence/preventive law model. *Psychology, Public Policy & Law, 5,* 1034–1083.

WINICK, B.J. (1999b). Therapeutic jurisprudence and the civil commitment hearing, *Journal of Contemporary Legal Issues, 10,* 7–60.

WINICK, B.J. (1998) Sex offender law in the 1990s: A therapeutic jurisprudence analysis, *Psychology , Public Policy & Law, 4,* 505–572

WINICK, B.J. (1991). Harnessing the power of the bet: Wagering with the government as a mechanism for social and individual change, *University of Miami Law Review, 45,* 737–813.

WINICK, B.J. & WEXLER, D.B. (2002). Drug treatment court: Therapeutic jurisprudence applied. *Touro Law Review, 18,* 479–485.

WINICK, B.J. & LA FOND, J.Q. (Eds.) (2003). *Protecting society from sexually dangerous offenders: Law, justice, and therapy.* Washington, DC: American Psychological Association.

WINICK, B.J. & WEXLER, D.B. (Eds.) (2003). *Judging in a therapeutic key: Therapeutic jurisprudence and the courts.* Durham, NC: Carolina Academic Press.

WOODBURN, S.G. & ENGLISH, K. (2002). *Community corrections in Colorado: A report of the findings.* Office of Research and Statistics, Division of Criminal Justice. Denver, CO. Colorado Department of Public Safety.

ZEVITS, R.G. & FARKAS, M. (2000). *Sex offender community notification: Assessing the impact in Wisconsin: Research in brief.* Washington, DC: National Institute of Justice.

Sexual Aggression

Mad, Bad, and Mad

ROBERT F. SCHOPP

University of Nebraska, College of Law, Lincoln, Nebraska 68583-0902, USA

ABSTRACT: Legal institutions in the Western liberal tradition ordinarily rely primarily on the criminal justice system to address conduct by some individuals that deliberately harms other individuals. The mental health system provides an alternative institutional structure through which societies can address such harmful behavior. Those who deliberately engage in conduct that causes harm to others are traditionally addressed through either the criminal justice or mental health systems on the basis of their being categorized as either "bad or mad." This paper examines some of the relevant reasons for categorizing sexual aggression as bad or mad. It emphasizes the significance of such categorization for the broader set of legal institutions of coercive social control and for the manner in which we respond to persons within those institutions.

KEYWORDS: sexual aggression; coercive social control; criminal justice system; mental health system; sexual offender; criminal punishment; civil commitment

INTRODUCTION

Societies frequently attempt to prevent and respond to violent assaults by some individuals against others through two distinct but related bodies of substantive law and two corresponding sets of legal institutions. The criminal justice system addresses assailants who meet systemic standards of criminal competence and responsibility. The mental health system addresses those who suffer major psychological impairment that has resulted in past assaults or that renders these individuals likely to engage in future attacks. Stated colloquially, the criminal justice system addresses assailants who are bad, and the mental health system addresses those who are mad. Sexual offenders have been addressed within both systems under various provisions.[1]

Contemporary sexually violent predator statutes are controversial, partially because they apply confinement represented as civil commitment to offenders who have been criminally convicted and completed their criminal sentences. These commitments are frequently based upon the determination that the individual suffers a mental abnormality that renders him likely to engage in further sexual violence, and this determination is frequently based primarily upon the past criminal behavior.[2]

Address for correspondence: Robert F. Schopp, Robert K. Kutak Professor of Law and Professor of Psychology, University of Nebraska, College of Law, Lincoln, NE 68583-0902. Voice: 402-472-1204 ; fax 402-472-5185.
rschopp@unl.edu

Ann. N.Y. Acad. Sci. 989: 324–336 (2003). © 2003 New York Academy of Sciences.

These provisions, convictions, and commitments apparently represent the conclusions that these offenders are bad and mad.

I have argued elsewhere that these statutes and commitments are objectionable partially because they undermine the conceptual and justificatory foundations of the criminal justice and mental health systems of coercive behavior control.[3] In this paper, I consider a separate but related concern regarding the manner in which these provisions and commitments might distort our emotional responsiveness to sexual offenses and offenders, and perhaps by extension, to crimes and criminals more generally. This paper presents an initial exploration of three violent episodes and of common emotional responses to these events and perpetrators, discusses the significance of these cases and emotional responses for our understanding of the relationship between the criminal justice and mental health systems as institutions of coercive behavior control, and examines the nature and functions of the retributive emotions.

INITIAL CASES AND RESPONSES

Initial Cases[4]

The *Smiths* are the parents of a child who is abducted on the way home from school, sexually assaulted, and killed. The police arrest a suspect who is convicted of kidnapping, sexual assault, and murder. The Smiths confer with the prosecuting attorney's office throughout the guilt and sentencing phases of the trial. They steadfastly support the prosecutor in seeking the death penalty. When the jury returns a sentence of death, the Smiths wait outside the court room and thank the jurors as they leave, telling the jurors that they made the right decision. They explain to the jurors that nothing will end the pain or bring closure, but the death sentence is a very important resolution—it helps. Throughout the process, they struggle to contain their sadness and grief at the loss of the child and at each other's grief. They continue participating in the process despite a deep sense of helplessness and resignation that they can never recover from this loss. Throughout the process, they struggle to contain and direct their intense anger and resentment toward the killer for the harm he has done to their child, their spouses, and themselves. The police, prosecutor, jurors, and others find it difficult to interact with the Smiths without sharing in that sense of sadness and anger.

Brown is a forest ranger whose responsibilities include monitoring and managing the interaction between people and bears in some of the campgrounds bordering a wilderness area. One problem bear becomes more aggressive in seeking food in campgrounds and approaching humans. Before the rangers can capture and relocate the bear to a remote area, the bear kills a child who startles the bear while it feeds. Brown tracks and shoots the bear in order to prevent any further harm to humans. The parents of the child are overcome with overwhelming sadness, grief, and loss. Brown and others regret having to kill the bear and do so with a sense of sadness, regret, and failure at not having prevented the incident. Brown also experiences empathy for the parents and guilt that he did not prevent their loss. Finally, he experiences sadness for the bear and a sense of responsibility to all for failing to prevent the incident. Brown experiences no anger or resentment toward the bear, but he does become angry when he thinks about other campers who have deliberately left food out for bears or failed to maintain clean camps.

Common Emotional Responses

The Smiths respond to the loss of their child with grief, sadness, and hopelessness. They respond to the killer with anger, resentment, and a powerful urge to retaliate. The police, prosecutor, jurors, and others who interact with the Smiths share in these emotional reactions. Their responses are not limited to sympathy for the Smiths. Rather, they experience empathic grief, sadness, anger, resentment, and the inclination to retaliate. The more closely these others interact with the Smiths, the more strongly they experience empathic emotions in the form of feeling something similar to the emotions experienced by the Smiths. Many readers will experience similar responsiveness. To the extent that we can realistically imagine these events, we experience sadness for the child and the Smiths, as well as empathic sadness, grief, anger, and the inclination to retaliate with the Smiths.

Brown's emotional responses share common features with those of the Smiths, but there are important differences. Sadness represents a strong common experience for the Smiths and for Brown. Brown also experiences strong emotions of regret, failure, and responsibility regarding the child's death, and he experiences anger at the human beings who have previously fed bears. The child's parents react with sadness, grief, and guilt at having failed to prevent the incident. They may also experience anger and inclination to retaliate, but they are at a loss regarding where to direct that anger and resentment. They may experience an initial inclination to hate the bear, but to the extent that they are able to reflect on their reactions, they probably have some understanding that this is misguided. Many readers will experience pervasive sadness for the child, the family, Brown, and the bear. Many of us will experience sadness and regret over the incident and empathy with the family's sadness, loss, grief. We will also experience empathic sadness with Brown and empathic anger toward campers who contributed to this tragedy.

We experience sadness, grief, loss for the victims and survivors in both cases. Anger and the inclination to retaliate differentiate the responses of the survivors and of many readers to the two cases. We experience a strong sense of anger and inclination to retaliate toward the Smith offender, but not toward the bear. Brown's sense of responsibility and guilt regarding his failure to prevent the incident and his anger at the careless campers suggests the tendency to respond with anger toward accountable agents who are responsible for the loss. Might these examples and apparent attributions of responsibility simply reflect our differential responses to humans who cause harm and animals who cause harm?

A Third Case and an Underlying Question

Consider a third case involving Black, who while driving a car runs a red light and hits children in the crosswalk. Black is unable to stand upright when the police remove him from the car and arrest him for DUI and motor-vehicle homicide. The dominant immediate reaction of witnesses, the victims' parents, and the community is extreme anger, resentment, and calls for severe punishment—"string the drunk up." Two days later, however, a newspaper reports that the prosecutor will not pursue charges against Black because drug and alcohol tests were negative. Black suffered a stroke while driving, paralyzing the right side of his body and rendering him unable to move his right foot from the accelerator to the brake or to steer the car. The harm is unabated, but our anger dissipates, sadness becomes the dominant response— sadness for the children, the families, and Black.

Notice that our emotional responses to Black are not identical to those we experience toward the Smith perpetrator or toward the bear. Initially, our responses to Black resembled those directed toward the Smith perpetrator. After we learn of the negative tests and the stroke, however, our reactions resemble our response to the bear in that the dominant response is sadness rather than anger. Black's stroke negates our initial attributions of responsibility and blame, removing the basis for our anger. We might sympathize with the bear and with Black, feeling sorry for both because they must suffer through no fault of their own. We can also empathize with Black, however, in that we can imagine ourselves in that position and feel something similar to what we believe he feels—"How will he live with this?" What, if anything, do these responses to these cases suggest about the significance of emotional responsiveness, including sadness, empathy, anger, and resentment, for our understanding of the appropriate application of coercive behavior control through criminal punishment or civil commitment?

CRIMINAL PUNISHMENT AND CIVIL COMMITMENT

Instrumental and Expressive Functions

The purpose and justification of criminal punishment have been subject to extensive debate, and I do not attempt to resolve or summarize these issues here. It seems clear that societies maintain institutions of criminal punishment at least partially for the purpose of reducing crime through a variety of processes, including incapacitation and deterrence. According to one widely recognized conception of criminal punishment, that institution differs from civil or regulatory institutions designed to shape and direct behavior in that criminal punishment expresses condemnation. Condemnation includes reprobation as a stern message of disapproval and resentment as emotionally laden attitudes including anger and vengefulness.[5] The expression of condemnation inherent in criminal punishment communicates the judgment that the criminal behavior is not merely counterproductive, it is wrongful by the standards of public morality embodied in law. Criminal punishment expresses condemnation of the criminal conduct as wrongful and of the offender as one who culpably performed that wrong.[6]

This expression of condemnation serves several functions. Some of these expressive functions are instrumental in that they are intended to reduce crime by reinforcing widely accepted standards of public morality embodied in law, and thus promoting voluntary compliance with those standards. The expression of condemnation also serves some deontic functions in that recognizing and repudiating wrongs and injustice is a good independent preventive of consequences.[7] By expressing condemnation of criminal conduct and of the culpable criminal for committing that crime, punishment vindicates the law and the standing of the victim. This vindication can serve instrumental purposes in that it might promote voluntary acceptance of and compliance with the law. Similarly, it might promote instrumental purposes by supporting recovery by the victim or by discouraging further crimes against that victim or against other potential victims. Vindicating the law and the standing of the victim can also carry deontic value, however, in that repudiating injustice, vindicating standards of justice embodied in law, and expressing respect for the standing of victims and for the general category of persons may be seen as right in principle, independent of any positive instrumental effects. Thus, the expressive functions of criminal punishment can have instrumental and deontic value, and these values can interact such that they are distinct but related.

I have argued elsewhere that criminal punishment and civil commitment provide two complementary institutions through which the state exercises the police power. Criminal punishment serves as the primary institution of coercive behavior control for those who possess the minimally adequate capacities of practical reasoning that enable them to function as accountable participants in the public jurisdiction of a liberal society. Criminal punishment of those who commit crimes while possessing these capacities expresses condemnation of wrongs and of culpable wrong doers such as the Smith perpetrator. Police power civil commitment provides an alternative institution of coercive behavior control for those who harm or endanger others while suffering impairment that renders them incapable of functioning as accountable participants in the public jurisdiction and thus, as subject to the criminal justice system. These individuals cause harm, but they do not qualify for condemnation as culpable wrongdoers. To the extent that we are persuaded that they do not qualify for condemnation, we respond instrumentally with treatment and behavior management, rather than with punishment.[8]

Understood in this manner, criminal punishment and civil commitment are complementary in that both are designed to pursue the preventive purpose by reducing the rate at which some individuals engage in conduct that is harmful to others. These institutions differ in that criminal punishment addresses behavior performed under conditions of culpability, and it expresses condemnation of the criminal wrongs as well as of the culpable wrongdoers. Police-power civil commitment, in contrast, addresses harmful or dangerous conduct performed by those who lack the capacities that render them culpable for their harmful conduct, and thus, who do not qualify for the condemnation inherent in criminal punishment.[9]

Sexual Offender Commitment

According to this interpretation, sexually violent predator statutes, and some applications of general civil commitment statutes to sexual offenders who have completed their sentences, are misguided precisely because they undermine the structure of these complementary legal institutions of coercive behavior control. Such commitments undermine the conceptual and justificatory foundations that define the limits of each institution and the boundaries between the two. Thus, they weaken the constraints these institutions place on the exercise of coercive force by the state. These "commitments" of offenders who have been convicted and served criminal sentences for their offenses distort the expressive functions of criminal punishment and of commitment. Such commitments apparently express the contradictory judgments that these offenders qualify as culpable subjects of the criminal justice system because they possess the capacities of accountable agency and that they are subject to civil commitment in the alternative police power institution because they do not possess these capacities. Thus, they are appropriate subjects of the condemnation inherent in criminal punishment and they are not appropriate subjects of that condemnation.

Consider, for example, the perpetrator in the Smith case. Assume that he was evaluated psychologically and was diagnosed as manifesting pedophilia and antisocial personality disorder. Pedophilia was diagnosed on the basis of an ongoing pattern of sexual urges, fantasies, and conduct involving prepubescent children, and antisocial personality disorder was diagnosed on the basis of an extended pattern of irresponsible and antisocial behavior accompanied by a lack of remorse for that behavior or empathy with those injured by it.[10] Although the offender in the Smith case was sentenced to death, other sexual offenders with similar diagnoses who commit noncapital crimes are sentenced to prison terms and subject to commitment under sexual predator statutes at the end of their sentences.[11] The Smith offender elicits anger and resentment as well as expressions of condemnation from the family, prosecutor, and from many readers. Does the application of civil commitment to offenders with similar disorders suggest that we should repudiate the inclination to respond with anger and resentment toward these offenders and toward the Smith perpetrator? Does it suggest that we should abandon criminal punishment with its expression of condemnation in favor of an instrumental approach such as civil commitment that is designed to address harmful or dangerous conduct by those who lack the capacities that would qualify them for condemnation? Should we take such evidence as good reason to repudiate our anger and to address this offender in a purely instrumental manner similar to that with which we address the bear?

Consider one more case. White has been diagnosed with chronic paranoid schizophrenia. He receives orders from a voice that he understands to be the voice of God. During one prior period, this voice told him he was Joseph, returned to earth to reconcile with his brothers. White wore a homemade coat of many colors and accosted strangers on the street, attempting to "make up" with them. During a different period, the voice told him he was John the Baptist, returned to earth because he had failed in his mission to baptize the Jewish population. White stood outside synagogues and sprinkled water on the members as they left. During the most recent period, the voice told him that he was Abraham, returned to earth because the need for sacrifice was greater now than ever. White went to the local playground with a knife and killed a young child he called Isaac. The police found him kneeling next to the child's body on the picnic table on which he "sacrificed" the child. He was praying over the child's body, addressing God in fragmented, idiosyncratic language the police could not comprehend.[12]

Are your initial emotional responses to White more similar to those you experience toward the Smith perpetrator or to those you experience toward the bear? Are there good reasons why we should respond (emotionally and institutionally) to White as we do to the Smith perpetrator, as we do to the bear, as we do to Black, or in some alternative manner?

Many of us, if we are persuaded that these descriptions of these perpetrators are accurate, will find that our emotional responses to the perpetrators are similar for Black, White, and the bear. These include sadness and regret for all three and for those who they harmed; empathy with Black and with White to the extent that we can recognize shared experience with him. Many of us will find that our responses differ for the Smith perpetrator toward whom we will experience anger, resentment, the inclination to retaliate.

The application of ostensibly civil commitment to offenders such as the Smith perpetrator distorts the expressive functions of these institutions. These commitments mislead us regarding the appropriate expression of condemnation and regarding the appropriate subjects of our anger. Such commitments distort the institutional representation of the appropriate bases for our retributive emotions of anger, resentment, and the inclination to retaliate. By convicting and sentencing culpable offenders, we identify them as appropriate subjects of retributive anger. By then subjecting them to civil commitment, ostensibly on the basis of serious impairment in their ability to control their sexual behavior, or some similar impairment, we identify them as appropriate subjects of our sadness, concern, or sympathy, rather than of our anger.[13] These convictions and commitments appear to express the judgments that these offenders are and are not culpable, that they are and are not appropriate subjects of condemnation, and that we should and should not respond to them with anger, resentment, and the urge to retaliate. Thus, these convictions and commitments undermine our legal institutions of coercive behavior control and our emotional responsiveness that these institutions reflect.

A critic might respond that this is a strength of these commitments, because they accurately reveal the lack of any defensible role for retributive emotions or for legal institutions that reflect them. Such a critic might suggest that retributive emotions represent an atavistic or misguided response that we should repudiate in favor of a more civilized, purely instrumental approach to coercive behavior control. According to such a critic, we should abandon the distinction between criminal punishment and civil commitment as institutions that express condemnation and refrain from doing so, respectively. Rather, we should purge ourselves and our institutions of retributive emotions and expressions of condemnation in favor of purely instrumental interventions designed to minimize the frequency and severity of harmful behavior.

Such a critic raises important questions regarding the legitimacy of our emotional responses and of the legal institutions that embody these responses. Are our emotional responses to the Smith perpetrator, including anger, resentment, and the inclination to retaliate, ones that we should repudiate and attempt to purge from our emotional life, or are they responses that we should embrace, cultivate, and discipline? Should we design our legal institutions to embody, discipline, and apply such emotions, or should we design our institutions to repudiate such responsiveness in favor of a more "civilized" instrumental approach to offenses and offenders?

THE DEVELOPMENT AND FUNCTIONS
OF RETRIBUTIVE EMOTIONS

Development and Function

Consider some work in developmental psychology regarding the circumstances that tend to elicit anger and the nature of anger responses. Some researchers characterize the tendency to respond to certain circumstances with anger as a universal characteristic of human beings with an innate, evolutionary basis. These writers contend that anger is an adaptive response to some circumstances, in that expression of anger can provide important social communication.[14] It is not entirely clear whether the claim of universality is intended to apply across individuals, cultures, or some alternative domain. A modest interpretation of this claim would take it as asserting at least that the tendency is very common across individuals and cultures.

The experience and expression of anger becomes more specific and refined as cognitive capacities and social awareness develop. Very young children frequently respond to frustration or deprivation with diffuse generalized indications of distress.[15] This pattern shifts in early childhood, however, as anger becomes differentiated from diffuse distress, and the circumstances that elicit anger shift from deprivation or frustration to perceptions of unfairness or injustice. At a relatively early age, children begin to direct responsive anger toward injuries that they perceive as deliberate, directed, or avoidable.[16] In contrast to passive emotions such as sadness or regret, anger is an active emotion that generates active interventions or retaliation for perceived injustice.[17] Thus, children of an early age appear to distinguish between wrongs and mere harms and to direct their anger toward wrongs. This tendency to respond actively with anger to deliberate or avoidable harms appears to reflect attribution of culpability or blameworthiness that resembles a rudimentary version of the criminal law doctrines of culpability or *mens rea*.

Empathy involves a process of "feeling with" another as compared to sympathy as "feeling for" another. An individual responds empathically when that individual experiences emotional responsiveness appropriate to another's experience. The empathetic individual may not experience exactly what the other is experiencing, but he or she experiences emotional responsiveness reflective of the experience of the other. This emotional responsiveness tends to promote active responses to the other's situation.[18] In infancy these responses take the form of generalized expressions of empathic distress such as crying when the other cries. As the child becomes older, however, empathy promotes socially adaptive behavior such as attempting to comfort the child in distress or seeking assistance for that child. Children tend to express empathic distress for other children when they do not attribute cause or blame for the other child's distress to that child. Child development researchers interpret the development of empathy as critical to moral motivation, action, and development.[19]

Empathic anger occurs when X becomes angry at Y in response to Y's unfair or wrongful conduct toward Z. Children who are more empathic with other children are more likely to respond with anger when third parties treat those other children unfairly. As they develop the cognitive capacities needed to understand principles of fairness, they become more able to make relatively accurate and impartial judgments of fairness and unfairness. The combination of cognitive development and empathy enables children to make reasonable judgments regarding justice and injustice, to respond to injustice to others with empathic anger, and to exercise that anger in the form of corrective action.[20]

As children learn to participate in social interaction, they develop an understanding of reciprocal cooperation. As they appreciate reciprocity and develop the capacity for empathy, they begin to respond with anger toward those who fail to reciprocate, and they direct that anger toward those who engage in perceived injustice against themselves or against others. By participating in reciprocal cooperation, they develop shared values and adopt moral principles represented by these systems of social cooperation.[21] This pattern of responsiveness is thought to have evolutionary roots and adaptive value for individuals and for communities that develop shared standards and expectations.[22]

These sources reveal a general picture of anger as an active emotional response to perceived injustice against oneself or others. The tendency to respond to injustice with anger promotes active intervention to rectify that perceived injustice, and the tendency to respond to failures of reciprocity with anger maintains systems of reciprocal cooperation. As children develop the cognitive capacities needed to recognize standards of justice and of reciprocal cooperation, they learn to adopt shared social values. The tendency to recognize and respond to the difference between mere harms and injustices or wrongs reflects the abilities to identify avoidable injuries caused by culpable conduct and to respond differently to these than one responds to accidental or unavoidable injuries.

Adult responses to harm or loss are consistent with this developmental pattern in that adults respond to such injuries with a variety of negative emotions, including anxiety, guilt, shame, sadness, and anger. Attributions of blame play an important role in identifying instances in which harm or loss leads to anger. When an individual suffers harm or loss and attributes blame for that injury to another person, the injured individual is likely to respond with anger at the other. When the injured individual blames himself for the harm or loss, that individual is likely to respond with anger directed toward self or with the related emotions of guilt or shame.[23] Those who suffer harm, loss, or insult blame the agents who cause that harm, loss, or insult when they perceive those agents as accountable or responsible because they caused the injuries intentionally or in some appropriate sense had control over them.[24] According to this interpretation, anger is a response to a wrong as a harm, loss, or insult for which the responding individual believes the agent who caused the harm is accountable in a manner that renders that agent blameworthy. Thus, the tendency to respond to injury with anger is closely associated with the recognition that some agents who cause injury are accountable in a sense that justifies holding them blameworthy.

"Civilizing" Criminal Punishment

Given this picture of the circumstances that elicit anger and the tendency to retaliate for perceived injustice, repudiation of that responsiveness and of the accompanying tendency to retaliate suggests three strategies. Individuals who wish to purge this tendency from their characters, or societies that decide to "civilize" their institutions of criminal punishment by purging them of anger in favor of purely instrumental approaches might pursue these goals by implementing these strategies. First, an individual or society might seek to purge responsive anger and the inclination to retaliate by learning to cease recognizing or caring about wrongs, injustice, unfairness, or failures of reciprocation. If people tend to respond with anger and the urge to retaliate when they perceive deliberate wrongs, injustice, unfairness, or the failure to reciprocate in circumstances of social cooperation, then one strategy to reduce or eliminate these tendencies would involve ceasing to recognize the distinction between these culpable wrongs and mere harms. Insofar as anger reflects the special significance that persons attribute to these wrongful injuries, rejecting this special significance or ceasing to care about it might reasonably be expected to reduce the tendency to experience responsive anger.

Similarly, removing the requirements of *mens rea* or culpability from an institution of criminal law might reflect a related strategy on an institutional level. Eliminating the culpability requirements that separate criminal wrongdoing from mere harms and render the criminal conduct appropriate for coercive social control through the criminal law would remove an institutionally reinforced recognition of the distinction between wrongs and mere harms. If individuals in a particular society learned to address wrongs or injustice as simply another form of counterproductive behavior, they might adopt a purely instrumental approach to such conduct. Similarly, if legal institutions abandoned the distinction between culpable crimes and civil injuries, they might decrease the tendency to experience anger and express condemnation in response to crimes. In short, ceasing to recognize, care about, or respond to the distinction between mere harms and wrongs on either the individual or institutional level represents one plausible strategy for reducing the tendency toward responsive anger.

Alternately, individuals might learn to respond to wrongs or injustice with passive emotions such as sadness or regret, rather than with active anger and the inclination toward aggression. Those who continued to recognize and care about wrongs, injustice, unfairness, or failure to reciprocate, but did so in a passive rather than an active manner, might be less inclined to engage in excessive or misdirected retaliation than those who respond with anger. Insofar as the decreased risk of excessive or misdirected retaliation reflected a shift from active to passive emotional responsiveness, however, one should expect a general decrease in active intervention. Thus, the decreased risk of misguided retaliation might reasonably be expected to reflect a decreased tendency toward corrective action generally.

Finally, a society might substantially decrease the tendency toward anger that occurs among its citizens and in its social institutions by decreasing the degree to which the members of that society experienced empathy with others. Because empathy promotes the tendency to feel with others and to respond in a manner consistent with their experience, it promotes the tendency to respond with anger to the infliction of wrongs or injustice on others. Insofar as participation in social structures or situations involving reciprocal cooperation promotes empathic anger in response to wrongful injuries to others, one plausible strategy for reducing the tendency toward anger and aggression would involve reducing the tendency to respond empathically to the unfairness suffered by others. This might require reduced participation in such cooperative interactions or participation with a detached attitude of disengagement from others.

According to one account of the psychological processes involved in adopting and applying moral principles, this process fuses cognition and affect. Those who adopt moral principles endorse impartial standards of moral behavior, and they respond with anger when they are treated in a manner that violates these standards as well as with empathic anger when others are subject to such treatment. The responsive anger reflects the recognition of such treatment as wrong, and the empathic anger at wrongful treatment of others reflects the impartiality of the cognitive judgment as well as the capacity to feel with others.[25] If this account is roughly accurate, reducing anger and vengefulness in response to wrongs or injustice perpetrated against oneself or others might require repudiation of shared principles of social morality in favor of purely instrumental rules of social coordination.

All three of these strategies for eliminating or reducing the tendency to respond to wrongs with anger or aggression seem to undermine the uniquely human moral sensibility. The human capacities to recognize the distinction between mere harms and culpable wrongs and to care about this distinction are central to the human abilities to recognize and apply moral principles, to subject action to moral evaluation, and to guide our conduct in a manner consistent with that evaluation. The ability to participate empathically in reciprocal cooperation with others enables humans to develop communities with common understanding of social morality. Insofar as the tendency to respond with anger and the inclination toward aggression reflects these abilities and sensitivities, this tendency serves a valuable function in the development of moral agency, relationships, and communities.

The association between anger and the recognition that some agents who cause injury are blameworthy for that injury reflects our ability to recognize and respond to the special standing of moral agents as those who possess the capacities needed to participate in morally relevant relationships and institutions as accountable agents.[26] This tendency to respond with anger to culpable injuries by blameworthy agents represents the recognition that they possess the capacities of moral agency, and it constitutes a component in the process of holding them accountable as such agents. Thus, judgments of blameworthiness and the accompanying emotional response of anger are components in the process that recognizes the significance of moral agency and responds to those who possess the capacities of moral agency by holding them accountable for the manner in which they exercise those capacities. Insofar as anger in response to wrongful injury reflects our recognition of the significance of moral agency, attempts to "civilize" our responses to such wrongs by repudiating responsive anger may require that we reduce the degree to which we recognize the significance of moral agency for personal accountability and standing.

Insofar as our tendency to respond with anger toward ourselves for blameworthy wrongs reflects this recognition that we posses the capacities of accountable agency, repudiation of responsive anger as a reaction to wrongs may undermine our inclination to hold ourselves accountable to standards of moral agency. Thus, repudiation of responsive anger may undermine the process of self-discipline as well as respect for moral agency in others.

CONCLUSION

I make no claim that anger is an unqualifiedly reliable measure of injustice or that conduct motivated by retributive anger is invariably adaptive or prosocial. Rather, I contend only that retributive emotions are intimately associated with uniquely human moral sensibilities reflected in individual morality, moral relationships, and shared community values. These retributive emotions can fulfill positive functions when disciplined and directed. These positive functions apply to individuals and to social institutions that embody the shared moral principles of the community. Legal institutions that ignore these retributive emotions or that mislead us regarding the appropriate experience, direction, and exercise of these emotions undermine our individual and collective senses of moral agency and of justice. When criminal punishment and civil commitment are designed and applied as complementary institutions for the application of coercive behavior control to those who possess or lack the capacities of accountable agency, respectively, they reinforce shared community values and the standing of responsible persons in the public jurisdiction. Commitment under sexual predator statutes, or similar application of civil commitment statutes to those who have been adjudicated culpable for their criminal behavior, distorts the principles of public morality underlying these legal institutions. By confusing us regarding the appropriate experience, expression, and application of our retributive emotions, these provisions and practices undermine our ability to pursue principled approaches to individual and community morality.

NOTES AND REFERENCES

1. *See* Eric Janus, *Legislative Responses to Sexual Violence: An Overview,* this volume.
2. Robert F. Schopp, COMPETENCE, CONDEMNATION, AND COMMITMENT 14–16 (2001).
3. *Id.* at 159–187.
4. Robert F. Schopp, *"Even a Dog...": Culpability, Condemnation, and Respect for Persons, in* PROTECTING SOCIETY FROM SEXUALLY DANGEROUS OFFENDERS 183 (Buce J. Winick & John Q. La Fond, eds. 2003).
5. Joel Feinberg, DOING AND DESERVING 98–101 (1970); SCHOPP, *supra* note 2, at 145.
6. Feinberg, *id.*; SCHOPP, *supra* note 2, at 146.
7. THE CAMBRIDGE DICTIONARY OF PHILOSOPHY 176 (Robert Audi ed., 2nd ed. 1995).
8. Schopp, *supra* note 2, at 144–148.
9. I contend only that this is the manner in which these institutions would function if they were designed and implemented to instantiate their underlying justifications, not that they always operate this way in practice.
10. AMERICAN PSYCHIATRIC ASSOCIATION, DIAGNOSTIC AND STATISTICAL MANUAL OF MENTAL DISORDERS 701-06 (antisocial personality disorder), 566-576 (paraphilias) (4th ed. TR 2000) (both diagnoses can be derived primarily from the pattern of criminal conduct).
11. *Kansas v. Crane,* 534 U.S. [3] (2002); *Kansas v. Hendricks,* 521 U.S. 346, 360 (1997); SCHOPP, *supra* note 2, at 51–53.
12. An earlier version of White appears as Peter in SCHOPP, *supra* note 2, at 159–160.
13. *Crane,* 534 U.S. at [4-8]; *Hendricks,* 521 U.S. at 358-360.
14. John D. Coie & Kenneth A. Dodge, *Aggression and Antisocial Behavior, in* HANDBOOK OF CHILD PSYCHOLOGY 786–787, 795 (William Damon ed., 5th ed. 1998); William R. Charlesworth, *The Child's Development of a Sense of Justice, in* THE SENSE OF JUSTICE 261–264 (Roger D. Masters & Margaret Gruter eds., 1992).
15. Coie & Dodge, *id.* at 787–789; Charlesworth, *id.* at 261–264.
16. Coie & Dodge, *id.* at 787–789, 795; Charlesworth, *id.* at 267–273.
17. Coie & Dodge, *id.* at 787; Joseph R. Campos, Rosemary G. Campos & Karen Caplovitz Barrett, *Emergent Themes in the Study of Emotional Development and Emotion Regulation,* 25 DEVELOPMENTAL PSYCHOLOGY 394, 395–397 (1989).
18. Elliot Turiel, *The Development of Morality, in* HANDBOOK OF CHILD PSYCHOLOGY, *supra* note 14, at 863, 875–878.
19. Martin L. Hoffman, *Empathy, Social Cognition, and Moral Action, in* I HANDBOOK OF MORAL BEHAVIOR AND DEVELOPMENT 275, 278–282 (William M. Kurtines & Jacob L. Gewirtz eds., 1991) [hereinafter Hoffman 1991A]; Carolyn Sarni, Donna L. Mumme & Joseph J. Campos, *Emotional Development: Action, Communication, and Understanding, in* HANDBOOK OF CHILD PSYCHOLOGY, *supra* note 14, at 274–278; TURIEL, *supra* note 18, at 875–878.
20. Hoffman 1991A, *id.* at 282–284, 290–291; MARTIN L. HOFFMAN, *Commentary* 34 HUMAN DEVELOPMENT, 105, 106–108 (1991) [hereinafter 1991B]; Martin L. Hoffman, *Moral Development, in* DEVELOPMENTAL PSYCHOLOGY: AN ADVANCED TEXTBOOK 497, 512–515, 524 (1988) [hereinafter Hoffman 1988].
21. Charlesworth, *supra* note 14, at 267–273; Hoffman 1991A, *supra* note 19, at 289–297; Hoffman 1991B, *supra* note 20, at 106–108; Hoffman 1988, *supra* note 20, at 512–15, 524; Turiel, *supra* note 18, at 875–879.

22. Frans B.M. de Waal, *The Chimpanzee's Sense of Social Regularity and Its Relation to the Human Sense of Justice, in* SENSE OF JUSTICE, *supra* note 14 at 241–255; Herbert Helmrich, *An Ethological Interpretation of the Sense of Justice on the Basis of German Law, in* SENSE OF JUSTICE, *supra* note 14, at 211–238 (both describing similar patterns in primate colonies).
23. Lazarus, R.S., EMOTION AND ADAPTATION 218, 223 (1991).
24. *Id.* at 218, 223–224.
25. Hoffman 1991A, *supra* note 19; HOFFMAN 1991B, *supra* note 20.
26. Lazarus, *supra* note 23, at 218, 223–224.

Sex Offender Registration and Community Notification: Emerging Legal and Research Issues

WAYNE A. LOGAN

William Mitchell College of Law, St. Paul, Minnesota 55105, USA

ABSTRACT: Sex offender registration and community notification laws, now in effect nationwide, have inspired considerable controversy. This article examines the variety of legal challenges brought against the laws since the mid-1990s and surveys issues likely to receive judicial attention in the immediate future. The article also provides an overview of the limited empirical work done to date on registration and notification, and the major areas that warrant additional research, including, most notably, inquiry into efficacy, costs, and consequences.

KEYWORDS: sex offender registration; community notification; sex offender; Megan's laws

INTRODUCTION

Although often merged in the public consciousness, sex offender registration and community notification laws in actuality differ in their origins, histories, and purposes. Registration laws in particular date back to 1947, when California initiated the nation's first registry dedicated exclusively to sex offenders.[1] Like "sexual psychopath" laws, also decades old,[2] however, registration provisions existed in relative desuetude until the 1990s, when a series of high-profile victimizations of women and children inspired a torrent of state legislative activity.[3] Today, under pressure from Congress, all U.S. jurisdictions have registration laws,[4] which require that sex offenders provide authorities with an array of personal information prior to community release, and threaten criminal prosecution for failure to comply with registration requirements, on an ongoing basis, for a minimum of ten years. For its part, the federal government has initiated a national registry,[5] which, in President Clinton's words, is designed to "keep track of [sexual offenders]—not just in a single state, but wherever they go...Deadly criminals don't stay within state lines, so neither should law enforcement's tools to stop them."[6]

Washington State initiated the nation's first community notification law in 1990, after a local police chief anxious about the release of a convicted child sex offender

Address for correspondence: Wayne A. Logan, Associate Professor of Law, William Mitchell College of Law, 875 Summit Ave., St. Paul, MN 55105. Voice: 651-290-6433; fax: 651-290-6427.

wlogan@wmitchell.edu

Ann. N.Y. Acad. Sci. 989: 337–351 (2003). © 2003 New York Academy of Sciences.

took it upon himself to notify community members.[7] Today, notification laws exist in all U.S. jurisdictions, again under threat of losing federal funding.[8] Jurisdictions disseminate registrants' information by various means, including active efforts such as door-to-door visits by police, leaflets or mailings, media notices, and community meetings, and more passive strategies, such as telephone "hot lines" and Internet Web sites.[9] The particular information disseminated varies among jurisdictions, but typically includes, in addition to registrants' names and offense histories, photos and general (and at times quite specific) community location information. Jurisdictions also vary in terms of the registrants subject to notification and the duration of registration, as well as the community members entitled to receive information. In roughly half of the states these outcomes are driven by discretionary, individualized risk assessments of registrants; elsewhere the outcomes are nondiscretionary, mandated by set criteria specified in statutory law.[10]

Registration and notification are premised on the idea that the collection and dissemination of information on sexual offenders promotes community safety, involving to varying degrees the efforts of police, community members, and registrants themselves. With respect to police, it is hoped that providing them ready access to registrants' information will facilitate the detection and apprehension of recidivists. With respect to communities, it is hoped that the information provided will better enable them to guard against victimization and help police monitor suspicious activity. Finally, with respect to registrants, it is hoped that their prospects for living crime-free will be enhanced as a result of the increased regimentation and visibility associated with the laws.

To date the laws have proven enormously popular with the public and legislators, yet their effects remain largely unexplored and untested. Moreover, although now in effect nationwide, questions remain over the legality of registration and notification laws. This paper provides an overview of the evolution of the pertinent jurisprudence, and surveys the limited empirical work done to date, with added attention to the major areas that still warrant research attention, including most notably inquiry into efficacy, costs, and consequences.

PAST, PRESENT, AND FUTURE LEGAL CHALLENGES

Registration and notification laws, while uniformly seen as a valid exercise of police power in principle,[11] have nonetheless been the subject of frequent legal challenge. Most commonly, the laws have been challenged on the ground that they constitute "punishment," and hence violate the Double Jeopardy, Ex Post Facto, Bill of Attainder, and Cruel or Unusual Punishment bans contained in state and federal constitutions. In March 2003, the U.S. Supreme Court at last definately resolved this question, holding that Alaska's Internet-based notification regime was punitive in neither design nor effect for ex post facto purposes, a conclusion that will likely foreclose similar claims under the above-noted constitutional provisions.[12] Challenges sounding in privacy,[13] the right to travel[14] or associate,[15] and unlawful search and seizure[16] have proved equally unavailing within the lower courts. Nor have petitioners had much success arguing that the laws violate due process, in the absence of advance advisement at the time of a guilty plea, on the rationale that the laws are a "collateral consequence" of criminal conviction.[17]

In another case decided in its 2003 term, *Connecticut Dep't of Public Safety v. Doe*,[18] the Supreme Court entertained a procedural due process challenge, a variety of constitutional claim that has enjoyed comparative success.[19] In proceedings below,[20] the Second Circuit held that Connecticut's registration and notification law jeopardized a protectible "liberty interest," triggering a Fourteenth Amendment due process right to notice and an opportunity to be heard on whether such an infringement is warranted. The Court reached its result by applying the "stigma-plus" test articulated by the Supreme Court in *Paul v. Davis*,[21] and used by courts to assess whether governmental stigmatization implicates a due process right. Because Connecticut mandated that *all* statutorily eligible exoffenders register and be subject to community notification, via a State-sponsored Internet Web site, without any individualized hearing to gauge risk, the Court concluded that the law risked false stigmatization. This, despite the fact that the site contained a disclaimer relating that the State has "made no determination that any individual included in the registry is currently dangerous." According to the Second Circuit:

> The sexual offender registry conveys the message that *some* of the persons listed on the registry are currently dangerous...But the list is undifferentiated; it does not say which registrants are or may be currently dangerous and which are not. We think it follows that publication of the registry implies that each person listed is more likely than the average person to be currently dangerous. That implication seems to us necessarily to flow from the State's choice of these particular individuals about whom to disseminate information, a record as to their sexual offenses, and information as to their current whereabouts. This information stigmatizes every person listed on the registry.[22]

The Second Circuit also concluded that the "plus" factor was satisfied, focusing on the State's "extensive and onerous" requirements, including the requirement that individuals verify their registration information annually for a minimum period of 10 years (with some registrants being required to do so every 90 days for their lifetimes); notify authorities of "regular" travel into another state, or any change in their name or address; supply a blood sample for DNA analysis; provide a photo at least once every five years; and be subject to prosecution for a felony if the conditions were violated.[23] Taken together, the Court concluded, the requirements amounted to a "new set of legal duties" sufficient to trigger a due process right to notice and a hearing before notification could legally occur.[24]

The Supreme Court, by a 9–0 vote, however, adopted a different view of Connecticut's law. The *Doe* Court altogether avoided answering the threshold question of whether the regime implicated a liberty interest, as the Second Circuit had affirmatively held.[25] Assuming *arguendo* that such an interest was at stake, the Court held, no hearing was called for because "the fact that respondent seeks to prove—that he is not currently dangerous—is of no consequence under Connecticut's Megan's Law."[26] This was because, as explained on the State's Web site, eligibility for notification was triggered by "an offender's conviction alone—a fact that a convicted offender has already had a procedurally safeguarded opportunity to contest."[27] Moreover, the disclaimer on the site explicitly communicated that the respondent's "alleged non-dangerousness simply does not matter."[28] While expressly reserving opinion on whether Connecticut's law violated substantive due process,[29] the Court concluded that any procedures designed to determine whether the respondent was in fact dangerous would be a "bootless exercise." [30]

Given the difference of opinion among lower courts on the availability of a procedural due process claim, the *Doe* Court's rather cursory opinion comes as a disappointment. Rather than addressing the key question of whether notification implicates a liberty interest, the Court in effect satisfied itself with the teleological inquiry into whether a hearing would preclude an individual being subject to coverage under Connecticut's law, which mandated notification solely on the basis of the individual being convicted of a statutorily enumerated offense. Manifestly, a hearing into dangerousness under such a regime would serve no purpose; this conclusion, however, left unanswered whether the acknowledged adverse consequences of notification jeopardize a protectible liberty interest such that due process should be afforded before notification can be lawfully effectuated.[31]

In the wake of *Doe*, it appears that jurisdictions need not engage in individualized risk assessments, at least when a disclaimer accompanies notification. At this time, roughly twenty states employ a compulsory approach similar to that of Connecticut,[32] and *Doe* permits them to avoid adoption of the more onerous, rights-based regimes employed by the balance of states. Whether these latter states resort to a compulsory approach in the coming years remains to be seen, an evolution that likely will be influenced by ever increasing resource concerns,[33] as well as the dictates of indigenous state (as opposed to federal) constitutional doctrine.[34]

Taken together, the pair of decisions rendered by the Court in Spring 2003 swept away much of the constitutional uncertainty hindering full application of the laws. As noted, however, the *Doe* majority reserved opinion on the basic question of whether the legislative decision to subject specified offenders to registration and notification might be amenable to substantive due process challenge. In a concurring opinion, Justices Souter and Ginsburg offered that a claim possibly might also be brought under the Fourteenth Amendment's Equal Protection Clause, insofar as Connecticut specified that certain offenders can be exempted by courts from registration or subject to some limited form of notification.[35] Both equal protection and substantive due process, however, are notoriously difficult to sustain in the absence of a court applying strict scrutiny to the challenged law. Because registration and notification laws do not single out individuals based on a suspect classification, such as race, national origin, or gender, it is very likely that reviewing courts will apply highly deferential rational basis analysis in any equal protection challenge.[36] Similarly, the other basis to trigger heightened judicial scrutiny, whether the law at issue implicates a fundamental constitutional right—also a precondition in substantive due process analysis[37]—would appear to be lacking. Conceivably, intrusions on registrants' rights to travel and privacy might qualify, but courts have been largely unreceptive to such claims. [38]

Consistent with these observations, equal protection claims have heretofore proved largely unsuccessful,[39] with winning claims arising in only quite narrow circumstances.[40] Future, possibly successful litigation, however, might arise on the basis of the ever-expanding range of registration-eligible offenses, many of which are nonviolent or nonsexual in nature, calling into question the public safety motivations behind the laws. There is also the possibility that courts, even when applying rational basis scrutiny for substantive due process purposes, will more closely scrutinize the laws. Research already casts significant doubt on the purported disparately high recidivism rates of sex offenders,[41] now codified in dire "legislative findings" of predicted high recidivism and predatory abuse.[42] If, as discussed later, research calls into question the basic utility and rationality of the laws, even greater judicial scrutiny might be in store, with courts perhaps viewing the intrusive consequences of the laws as being outweighed by their avowed benefits.[43]

Other than equal protection and substantive due process there appears to be little remaining room for constitutional challenge. One possible basis, however, involves separation of powers. Appellate courts in Arizona,[44] Florida,[45] Kentucky,[46] and Ohio[47] have rejected such claims, on the rationale that the judiciary's traditional adjudicative authority is not impaired by legislative directives contained in registration and notification laws. Recently, however, the Hawaii Supreme Court took issue with an effort by its state legislature to limit judicial review of registration and notification provisions. Noting that statutory law expressly provided that "a sex offender shall have a diminished expectation of privacy in [registration] information," the Court in *State v. Bani* emphasized that the legislature's effort to immunize the law from constitutional scrutiny violated separation of powers.[48] The *Bani* Court went on to state that "[a]ccordingly, it is this court, at the appropriate time, and not the legislature, that will determine whether...a sex offender has a 'diminished' expectation of privacy in statutorily enumerated 'relevant information.'"[49] Numerous other states have similar provisions, proclaiming that registrants' privacy expectations are diminished or outweighed by public safety concerns.[50] These provisions will likely attract continued attention, especially if state courts, in response to federal courts' reluctance to find protective rights in the U.S. Constitution, are asked to invoke their respective state constitutions,[51] famously referred to by Justice Brennan collectively as a "font of individual liberties."[52]

Litigation will likely also continue to be generated by the criteria used by states to trigger eligibility for registration and notification. Among the most common species of challenge relates to whether potentially eligible offenders satisfy particular statutory criteria, narrow claims that have achieved some measure of success.[53] Another challenge enjoying some success concerns whether a conviction for a crime committed elsewhere warrants registration anew upon the individual relocating in a new jurisdiction, or, in the case of federal crimes, requires registration within one's current state of residence.[54] In one recent case, for instance, an individual successfully contended that his federal conviction for trafficking in child pornography did not require registration in New York because the elements under the applicable state and federal laws were not sufficiently alike.[55] The eligibility of juvenile sex offenders will also likely continue to be a major source of controversy.[56]

Finally, the broad statutory language used by many states will also likely be challenged.[57] Kansas, for instance, imposes registration and notification upon persons convicted of "sexually motivated" crimes, meaning that "one of the purposes for which the defendant committed the crime was for the purpose of a defendant's sexual gratification."[58] Construing this language in *State v. Patterson*,[59] the Kansas Court of Appeals upheld a lower court's decision to require registration of a petitioner who pled guilty to burglary and misdemeanor theft in relation to his taking several pieces of female underwear from his neighbor's apartment. The court, however, expressed "some concern over the possibility that this statute could be extended beyond reason. For instance, would a defendant fall under the provisions of the [registration law] if he or she stole contraceptives or engaged in disorderly conduct by shouting sexually explicit words?"[60]

BEHIND THE CURVE: RESEARCH CONCLUSIONS AND GAPS

Although most of the major legal issues have now been addressed, basic empirical questions persist over the consequences of registration and notification. Like "three strikes" laws and other punitive outgrowths of the 1990s, also codified in a rapid-fire fashion, often without debate, the effects of registration and notification are only now being assessed. The following discussion provides an overview of the scant research thus far carried out, and identifies important work that yet needs to be done, touching on four basic areas: crime control effectiveness (including recidivism and registration compliance rates); effects on registrants; effects on community members; and costs.

Crime Control Effectiveness

Remarkably, given the ostensible public safety premise of registration and notification, it largely remains an untested article of faith that the laws tangibly contribute to community safety. To date, only two studies on registrant recidivism, one potential measure, have been conducted. In Washington State[61] and Iowa[62] researchers tracked registrant and control groups for over four years. Neither study found a statistically significant difference in recidivism.[63] The Washington study did find, however, that individuals subject to registration and notification were arrested for new crimes more quickly than those who were not.[64]

If specific deterrence is to continue as a supporting rationale of the laws, it is imperative that additional research focus on whether they discourage recidivism, or as found in Washington, merely facilitate rearrest. The authors of the Washington study were unsure of the reason for this latter outcome, speculating that high-risk registrants might be "watched more closely," and that the "increased attention results in earlier detection."[65] Future work must focus on *how* such rearrests come about. If they result solely from ready access by police to registrants' information, and not input from enlightened community members, policymakers might have reason to question the value of community notification.

With respect to future work on recidivism, researchers must be mindful of how recidivism is measured, with particular attention paid to the seriousness of the new offenses; whether they are sexual in nature; whether victims and offenders are acquainted; and where the new offenses are committed.[66] Work must also focus on the extent to which compliance violations of registration requirements, as with an earlier generation of registration laws,[67] serve as a significant basis for rearrest,[68] and the nature of the violations.

In conducting recidivism work, it often will prove difficult to secure comparative cohorts, given that application of the laws can date back many years. However, noncomparative work itself can be instrumental in addressing one of the most troubling concerns regarding notification: that notifying residents in the immediate proximity of registrants is of little use if registrants victimize persons outside the notification zone. The limited work done to date—a study looking at the offense characteristics of thirty-six incarcerated offenders who would have been subject to notification, but were not, due to the law's implementation date—suggests that victims in only four instances would have had a "good" chance of potentially benefitting from advance warning that a stranger with an offending history was living nearby.[69] Research in this regard, coupled with the reality that the vast majority of sex offenders are known to their victims,[70] will prove invaluable in future efforts to calibrate and optimize application of community notification efforts.[71]

Research must also continue to assess whether the laws target those offenders most worthy of attention: culling "false positives"—offenders who pose risks not worthy of notification and perhaps even registration—and "false negatives"—offenders who assuredly do warrant such attention. Although considerable work has been done on sex offense risk prediction,[72] more needs to be done, especially as applied to registration and notification.[73] This work will help resolve the basic public policy divide now evidenced in the jurisdictions' approaches to registration and notification. In almost half the states, an actuarial approach, driven by a predominant fear of false negatives, mandates that statutorily specified offender groups be subject to registration and notification; in others, more individualized, clinical decisions determine outcomes. Under the actuarial approach in particular, reliable data will be invaluable in assessing whether the criteria now used reflect risk to the best extent possible. Such ongoing recalibration is necessary to ensure prudent use of limited resources, and to minimize the social and economic costs associated with overbroad laws.[74]

Finally, basic work yet needs to be done on whether registries contain accurate and complete data, the lynchpin of the information-is-empowerment premise of the laws.[75] While jurisdictions have reported high initial registration "compliance rates,"[76] studies make clear that the systems notably fail to ensure ongoing compliance.[77] It must be recognized that initial compliance rates, and indeed conviction rates for those the authorities somehow come to realize are not in compliance, are inadequate measures of success. Without ongoing verification of registry information, jurisdictions have no way of knowing whether the laws are fulfilling their idealized educational and surveillance functions. Work must also assess which verification methods are most cost-effective and how they can be improved, as well as which offenders are most likely to not comply, and why this is so. Equally important, evaluative work must focus on the compliance of eligible registrantsemigrating from other jurisdictions, a major concern only now coming to be recognized.[78]

Effects on Registrants

To date, little work has focused on the tangible consequences of the laws on registrants. While to be sure recidivism data will shed some much-needed light on whether the laws correlate with deterrence and prevention, work still needs to be done on the practical, individualized effects of the laws. On the positive side, one can postulate that the laws possibly afford registrants a greater sense of accountability and awareness that they are being monitored; increase registrants' appreciation of the harms they have caused; and encourage rehabilitative efforts among registrants, not the subject of notification, who wish to avoid its burdens.[79]

However, the more common concern is that the laws actually have significant antitherapeutic effects. In one of the few published studies to date, focusing on 30 highest risk-level registrants in Wisconsin, researchers found that employment problems, harassment, ostracization, residential exclusion, and negative impacts on family and friends were all common consequences of notification.[80] Most registrants believed that notification would have no deterrent effect,[81] and some made clear that the social isolation, pressures, and difficulties they experienced actually increased the likelihood of recidivism,[82] a view with significant support in the literature.[83] It was also apparent that the subjects viewed their high-risk designation as unjust and arbitrary,[84] a sentiment research has shown to undercut individuals' willingness to cooperate and comply with societal rules.[85] Efforts must be directed at replicating the foregoing findings elsewhere and within larger subject groups. Other important research questions involve asking whether the laws:

- foster negative self-attributional views among registrants, leading to a hopeless sense that they are immutably a sex offender, which might encourage recidivism;

- encourage registrants to commit crimes outside the geographic area of notification; and/or

- negatively affect offenders' *prerelease* rehabilitative efforts, if they fear that the information provided will be used by authorities to heighten registration and notification burdens.

In the end, while it is tempting to ignore the views and experiences of those subject to registration and notification, this would be short-sighted. The information they provide can assist in increasing the capacity of the laws to serve more as a boon, and not a barrier, to law-abiding behavior.

Effects on Community Members

Despite enjoying enormous popular support, little is known about the actual effects of notification on community members. Basic research needs to be done on whether residents, in the wake of notification, are actually aware of the presence of registrants, and the information they come to possess. Although there is a great temptation for jurisdictions to use the cheapest method available, as evidenced in the current rush to create Internet Web sites, it remains unclear whether such mass-dissemination techniques work. As an initial matter, not all residents have access to the Internet, a matter of particular concern in poorer communities (the "tech have nots"), areas where registrants tend to cluster given the greater availability of affordable housing. Other similarly passive approaches run equal risk of informing only those residents who are proactively inclined, not necessarily those perhaps most in need of information. More active strategies, such as door-to-door visits by police, community meetings, or leafleting, are more expensive, yet also largely untested in their effectiveness.[86]

Similarly, more needs to be known about the consequences of notification on community members who actually receive the information. Although to this day it remains a subject of debate whether Megan Kanka's parents were aware that a recidivist sex offender lived nearby,[87] it is expected that notification at once enables/encourages self-protective measures and increases the surveillance capacity of residents. It is critically important to test whether in fact these hoped-for benefits exist, and if so, how they manifest. At the same time, research must assess whether notification has the unhealthy effect of instilling in some residents a debilitating paranoia, or perhaps has a "fatigue effect" when subject to repeated warnings (a particular problem in poor areas, which, as noted, often accommodate a disproportionate number of registrants).[88] Relatedly, research must examine whether there is a "lulling effect" in communities outside the scope of notification, insofar as such individuals perhaps feel safer and hence less inclined to be vigilant in exercising care.

Finally, research must be done on whether the significant burdens the laws impose on registrants might have the perverse effect of discouraging the reporting of sex crimes. This concern would appear especially justified in cases of nonstranger victimizations, incest in particular. To date, the little evidence we have, in anecdotal form, supports this concern.[89] If further substantiated, jurisdictions might be wise to modify the scope of notification in particular instances.

Costs

As jurisdictions have painfully become aware, registration and notification, whatever their benefits, are far from cost-free.[90] Fiscal impacts can be expected to vary in terms of the methods used to execute the laws. It can be expected, for instance, that costs will be higher in states that employ an individual risk assessment approach for offender classification decisions; undertake rigorous registration verification efforts; and implement notification by active means. It can also be expected that with the advent of technological efficiencies, some of the most resource-intensive aspects of both verifying registrants and carrying out notification can be lessened.[91]

However, it is clear that there is no escaping the basic fiscal and resource impacts associated with implementing and maintaining the laws. Increasingly, glaring shortcomings detected in registration and notification systems are being blamed on inadequate funding.[92] With a stream of eligible offenders reentering society daily, adding to already burgeoning registration rolls, these complaints can only be expected to multiply. So too will complaints from state officials faced with what they contend is an unfunded federal mandate,[93] and from local officials upset at their states for not adequately funding operation of the laws.[94] Meanwhile, politicians of all stripes, wrestling with budget demands and competing constituent concerns, will be obliged to ask not just whether current expenditures are warranted, but also whether, presuming a reliable system is attainable, its cost is simply too great to absorb.

Finally, beyond fixed costs, research must also focus on several collateral ramifications of the laws that are now becoming apparent. One is that defendants, fearful of being subject to registration and notification, are passing up guilty pleas and demanding trials, with attendant burdens to the justice system.[95]Another is that prosecutors, disturbed at the prospect of triggering potentially life-long registration for juvenile offenders in particular, are modifying their charging decisions to avoid required registration, which is troubling if for no other reason than it possibly deprives young offenders of rehabilitative attention.[96]

CONCLUSION

In the 1990s, sex offender registration and notification laws were enacted nationwide, usually without meaningful debate or consideration.[97] Only now, a decade later, are the ramifications of the nation's massive experiment in social control coming into focus. While many of the basic constitutional uncertainties besetting the laws have been resolved, litigation doubtless will continue in the years to come. Meanwhile, basic research regarding registration and notification remains to be done. Only with such findings will it be possible to answer whether the laws enjoy anything more than symbolic value, and even if they do, whether their benefits outweigh their costs and consequences.

NOTES AND REFERENCES

1. *See* Elizabeth A. Pearson, *Status and Latest Developments in Sex Offender Registration and Notification Laws*, *in* NATIONAL CONFERENCE ON SEX OFFENDER REGISTRIES 45 (U.S. Bureau of Justice Statistics ed., 1998). Roughly a decade earlier, in 1936, Philadelphia required registration of all criminal offenders, not merely sex offenders. *See* Note, *Criminal Registration Law*, 27 J. CRIM. L. & CRIMINOL. 295, 295 (1936-1937). In the ensuing decades the laws were repeatedly challenged; with the exception of *Lambert v. California*, 355 U.S. 225 (1957), the claims achieved little success. *See* Wayne A. Logan, *Federal Habeas in the Information Age*, 85 MINN. L. REV. 147, 169 (2000) (discussing *Lambert*, where the Court invalidated a general criminal registration law on notice grounds, and other court challenges).
2. *See generally* Samuel J. Brackel & James L. Cavenaugh, *Of Psychopaths and Pendulums: Legal and Psychiatric Treatment of Sex Offenders in the United States*, 30 N.M. L. REV. 69 (2000).
3. The most prominent of these were the abduction by a masked gunman of 11-year-old Jacob Wetterling in Minnesota, in October1989; the brutal assault of Texas real estate agent Pam Lyncher, in August 1990; and most notably, the rape and murder of 7-year-old Megan Kanka by a recidivist sex offender who lived nearby, in July 1994.
4. *See* The Jacob Wetterling Crimes Against Children and Sexually Violent Offenders Registration Act, Pub. L. No.103-322, 108 Stat. 2038 (1994) (codified as amended at 42 U.S.C. §14071 (1994 & Supp. IV. 1998).
5. *See* The Pam Lyncher Sexual Offender Tracking and Identification Act of 1996, Pub. L. No. 104-236, 110 Stat. 3093 (codified as amended at 42 U.S.C. § 14072 (Supp. IV 1998).
6. BRIAN MCGORY, *Clinton Sets Tracking of Sex Offenders*, BOSTON GLOBE, Aug. 25, 1996, at A1.
7. Center for Sexual Offender Management, *Community Notification and Education* 2 (April 2001).
8. *See* Megan's Law, Pub. L. No. 104-115, 110 Stat. 1345 (1996) (amending 42 U.S.C. § 14071(d) (1994) (threatening loss of federal law enforcement funds unless states "release relevant information that is necessary to protect the public concerning a specific person required to register under [the Act]"). *See also Final Guidelines for the Jacob Wetterling Crimes Against Children and Sexually Violent Offender Registration Act*, 64 Fed. Reg. 572, 581-82 (Jan. 5, 1999) [hereinafter *Guidelines*].
9. *See* Devon B. Adams, *Summary of State Sex Offender Registries, 2001* (Bureau of Justice Statistics, March 2002).
10. *See* Wayne A. Logan, *A Study in "Actuarial Justice": Sex Offender Classification Practice and Procedure*, 3 BUFF. CRIM. L. REV. 593, 602-19 (2000).
11. *See, e.g.,* Roe v. Office of Adult Probation, 938 F. Supp. 1080, 1092 (D. Conn. 1996) (stating that the laws seek "to protect the public from devastating crimes. This goal certainly is one within the traditionally broad police powers of the State.").
12. *Smith v. Doe,* 123 S. Ct. 1140 (2003).
13. *See, e.g.,* Russell v. Gregoire, 124 F.3d 1079 (9th Cir. 1997); Akella v. Mich. Dep't of State Police, 67 F. Supp. 2d 716 (E.D. Mich. 1999); People v. Malchow, 739 N.E.2d 433 (Ill. 2000).
14. *See, e.g.,* State v. Cameron, 916 P.2d 1183 (Az. Ct. App. 1996); In re Registrant J.G., 2001 WL 799557 (N.J. 2001).
15. *See, e.g.,* Miller v. Taft, 151 F. Supp. 2d 922 (N.D. Ohio W. Div. 2001).
16. *See*, e.g., Rise v. Oregon, 59 F.3d 1556 (9th Cir. 1995); Rowe v. Burton, 884 F. Supp. 1372 (D. Alaska 1994); Doe v. Poritz, 662 A.2d 367 (N.J. 1995).
17. *See* Wayne A. Logan, *Liberty Interests in the Preventive State: Procedural Due Process and Sex Offender Community Notification Laws*, 89 J. CRIM. L. & CRIMINOLOGY 1167, 1210 (1999) (citing cases). The courts have also rejected due process challenges to laws making it a felony to violate registration requirements, on the ratio-

nale that the heavy penalty is rationally related to the important goals and purposes of registration. *See, e.g.,* People v. Marsh, 768 N.E.2d 108 (Ill. Ct. App. 2002).

18. 123 S. Ct. 1160 (2003).

19. *See, e.g.,* Cutshall v. Sundquist, 193 F.3d 466 (6th Cir. 1999) (denying claim); Russell v. Gregoire, 124 F.3d 1079 (9th Cir,. 1997) (denying claim); E.B. v. Verniero, 119 F.3d 1077 (3d Cir. 1997) (granting claim); Doe v. Williams, 167 F. Supp. 2d 45 (D.D.C. 2001) (granting claim); Doe v. Pryor, 61 F. Supp. 2d 1224 (M.D. Ala. 1999) (granting claim); Helman v. State, 784 A.2d 1058 (Del. 2001) (denying claim); Noble v. Bd. of Parole and Post-Prison Supervision, 964 P.2d 990 (Or. 1998) (granting claim).; State v. Bani, 36 P.3d 1255 (Haw. 2001) (granting claim).

20. 271 F.3d 38 (2d Cir. 2001).

21. 424 U.S. 693 (1976).

22. *Doe,* 271 F.3d at 49.

23. *Id.* at 57.

24. Id.

25. *Doe,* 123 S. Ct. at 1164.

26. *Id.*

27. *Id.*

28. *Id.*

29. *Id.*

30. *Id.*

31. The Court's approach, while unfortunate, is not unprecedented. See Lanni v. Engler, 961 F. Supp. 1105 (W.D. Mich. 1997); Patterson v. State, 985 P. 2d 1007 (Alaska Ct. App. 1999); People v. Logan, 705 N.E.2d 152 (Ill. Ct. App. 1998); State v. Wilkinson, 9 P.3d 1 (Kan. 2000).

32. *See* Brief for the United States as Amicus Curiae Supporting Petitioner, at 2, Connecticut Dep't of Public Safety v. Doe, 123 S. Ct. 1160 (2003). In addition, as of October 2002, pursuant to the Campus Sex Crimes Prevention Act of 2000, all U.S. jurisdictioons are required to use a similar compulsory approach with respect to eligible sex offenders on college campuses. *Id.*

33. However, this immediate cost impact might yield longer-term dividends insofar as individualized assessments might decrease the overall number of persons targeted by the laws, lessening administrative costs proportionately. This should be of particular concern in those jurisdictions that employ "active" (as opposed to "passive") notification methods. Costs aside, moreover, there is reason to believe that targeting the laws with greater selectivity will maximize the chance that the community will remain alert to risk. *See* In Re Registrant E.I., 693 A.2d 505, 508 (N.J. Super Ct. App. Div. 1997) ("[I]f Megan's Law is applied literally and mechanically to virtually all sexual offenders, the beneficial purpose of this law will be impeded.") *Cf.* New York Times v. Sullivan, 403 U.S. 713, 729 (1971) (Stewart, J. concurring) "[W]hen everything is classified, then nothing is classified, and the system becomes one to be disregarded by the cynical or the careless.").

34. *See, e.g.,* Doe v. Attorney General, 686 N.E.2d 1007, 1013 n.8 (Mass. 1997) (finding liberty interest under Massachusetts Constitution); Doe v. Poritz, 662 A.2d 367, 419 (N.J. 1995) (finding liberty interest under New Jersey Constitution).

35. Doe, 123 S. Ct. at 1166 (Souter, J., concurring).

36. *See, generally,* ERWIN CHEMERINSKY, CONSTITUTIONAL LAW: PRINCIPLES AND POLICIES, §§ 9.1.1–9.1.2, at 643–48 (2d ed. 2002).

37. *Id.* §§10.1.1–10.1.2, at 762–66. See also JOHN E. NOWAK & RONALD D. ROTUNDA, CONSTITUTIONAL LAW §11.4, at 423–24 (6th ed. 2000).

38. *See supra* notes 13 and 14 and accompanying text.

39. *See, e.g.,* Cutshall V. Sundquist, 193 F.3d 466 (6th Cir. 1999); Artway V. Att'y Gen., 81 F.3d 1235 (3d Cir. 1996); Helman v. State, 784 A.2d 1058 (Del. 2001).

40. See, e.g., State v. C.M., 746 So. 2d 410 (Ala. Crim. App. 1999) (invalidating law because it permitted adult but not juvenile registrants to return to a home where a minor resides); People v. Felarca, 88 Cal. Rptr. 2d 587 (1999) (invalidating required registration of person convicted of oral copulation with a minor but not those convicted of sexual intercourse with a minor).

41. *See* R. Karl Hanson & Monique T. Bussiere, *Predicting Relapse: A Meta-Analysis of Sexual Offender Recidivism Studies*, 66 J. CONSULTING & CLINICAL PSYCHOL. 348 (1998) (concluding based on meta-analysis of 61 follow-up studies that only 13% of subjects committed new sex offenses within 4–5 year follow-up period).
42. *See, e.g.*, Fla. Stat. Ann. §775.21 (3) (a) (2002) ("Sexual offenders are extremely likely to use physical violence and repeat their offenses ..."); Tenn. Code Ann. sect. 40–39–101 (b) (1) (2002) ("sexual offenders pose a high risk of engaging in further offenses after release ... and protection of the public from these offenders is a paramount public interest.").
43. *See, e.g.*, Paul P. v. Verniero, 170 F.3d 396 (3d Cir. 1999) (finding that home addresses of registrants are entitled to some privacy protection but intrusion outweighed by purported public saftey benefits of notification); Doe. v. Poritz, 662 A.2d 367 (N.J. 1995) (holding that assembled information disseminated implicates privacy interest but that purported benefits of notification outweighed interest).
44. Martin v. Reinstein, 987 P.2d 779 (Az. Ct. App. 1999).
45. Kelly v. State, 795 So. 2d 135 (Fla. Ct. App. 2001).
46. Hyatt v. Comm., 72 S.W.3d 566 (Ky. 2002).
47. State v. Thompson, 752 N.E.2d 276 (Ohio 2001).
48. 36 P.3d 1255, 1261 n.4 (2001) (citing Haw. Stat. § 846E-3(c)).
49. *Id.*
50. *See, e.g.*, Ala. Code § 15-20-20.1 (2002); Fla. Stat. Ann. § 944-606(2) (West 2002); Okla. Stat. Ann. tit. 57, § 581(b) (West Supp. 2002). According to the Florida Legislature, Florida courts have a "duty" to uphold the laws, and that any contrary judicial action "unlawfully encroaches on the Legislature's exclusive power to make laws and places at risk significant public interests of the state." Fla. Stat. Ann. § 775.24(1) (West 2002).
51. *See, e.g.*, note 34 and accompanying text.
52. WILLIAM J. BRENNAN, JR., *State Constitutions and the Protection of Individual Rights*, 90 HARV. L. REV. 489, 491 (1977).
53. *See, e.g.*, State v. Thibodeaux, 680 So. 2d 50 (La. Ct. App. 1996) (because defendant not convicted of enumerated offense, registration not required); State v. McPherson, 758 N.E.2d 1198 (Ohio Ct. App. 2001) (same).
54. *See, e.g.*, 42 Pa. Cons. Stat. § 9795.2(b)(1) (2002) (requiring registration if conviction elsewhere constitutes an "equivalent offense" for which registration is required under Pennsylvania law).
55. *In re* Nadel, 724 N.Y.S.2d 262 (N.Y. Sup. Ct. 2001). *See also* Radney v. State, 840 So. 2d 190 (Ala. Crim. App. 2002) (denying required registration because defendant convicted of federal not state offense; Alabama law required that conviction occur in state or municipal court); Graves v. State, 772 A.2d 1225 (Md. 2001) (denying use of nonstate conviction in "sexually violent predator" classification because state law did not expressly permit consideration of such convictions).
56. *See generally* Michael L. Skoglund, Note, *Private Threats, Public Stigma? Avoiding False Dichotomies in the Application of Megan's Law to the Juvenile Justice System*, 84 MINN. L. REV.1805 (2000). For an overview of the varied approaches taken by states, see In re J.G., 2001 WL 799557 (N.J. 2001).
57. *See, e.g.*, Cal. Penal Code § 290(a)(2)(E) (West 2002) (crimes committed "as a result of sexual compulsion or for the purpose of sexual gratification"); Conn. Gen. Stat. § 54-254(a) (2002) (crimes "committed for a sexual purpose.").
58. Kan. Stat. Ann. § 22-4902(c)(14) (2001).
59. 963 P.2d 436 (Kan. 1998).
60. *Id.* at 440. *See also, e.g.*, People v. Meidinger, 987 P.2d 937 (Colo. Ct. App. 1999) (upholding registration of offender who pled guilty to contributing to the delinquency of a minor, a nonenumerated offense, because of the "underlying circumstances of the offense."); Sequeira v. State, 534 S.E.2d 166 (Ga. Ct. App. 2001) (invalidating registration because law did not specify that it could be based on "conduct underlying a criminal conviction," even if conduct was sexual in nature); State v. Halstien, 857 P.2d 270 (Wash.1993) (upholding registration of a paperboy who broke into home and stole a box of condoms and vibrator sex toy); Andrews v. State

40 P.3d 708 (Wyo. 2002) (invalidating registration for burglary involving women's clothing because not an enumerated offense).
61. Donna D. Schram & Cheryl D. Milloy, *Community Notification: A Study of Offender Characteristics and Recidivism* 3 (1995).
62. Geneva Adkins et al., *The Iowa Sex Offender Registry and Recidivism* (2000).
63. Of note, in Washington, the authors found that among juvenile registrants, as to which there was no comparative cohort, the recidivism rate was very high (79%). *See* Schram & Milloy, *supra* note 61, at 19.
64. *Id.* at 18.
65. *Id.* at 19. Work recently done in Britain suggests that registrant information is used by police to intervene in and prevent potential criminal activity in high-risk situations, yet that it enjoys only limited use in investigations and prosecutions. *See* Joyce Plotnikoff & Richard Woolfson, *Where are They Now?: An Evaluation of Sex Offender Registration in England and Wales*, Police Research Series Paper 126, at 41–42 (2000).
66. In the Washington study, for instance, only 14% of registrants in the State's highest risk category were arrested for new sexual offenses. Schram & Milloy, *supra* note 61, at 3.
67. *See* Note, *Criminal Registration Ordinances: Police Control Over Potential Recidivists*, 103 U. PA. L. REV. 60, 62–63 (1954) (identifying the rearrest of those who failed to comply with registration requirements as a "principal" objective of circa 1950s registration laws).
68. *See* David Chanen, *A Decade Later, It's Imperfect*, STAR-TRIBUNE (Minneapolis-St. Paul), Feb. 10, 2001, at A1 (noting that in Illinois 3000 of 16,200 sex offenders were returned to prison for registration violations).
69. ANTHONY J. PETROSINO & CAROLYN PETROSINO, *The Public Safety Potential of Megan's Law in Massachusetts: An Assessment From a Sample of Criminal Sexual Psychopaths*, 45 CRIME & DELINQUENCY 140 (1999). The study's authors hastened to add a caveat: "It is important to note that even if a potential victim was notified and took preventive steps, it does not mean that the specific offender would have stopped committing offenses. The crime or crimes might simply have been displaced toward other more vulnerable targets." *Id.* at 152.
70. *See* Lawrence Greenfield, *Sex Offenses and Offenders: An Analysis of Data on Rape and Sexual Assault* (U.S. Dep't of Justice, 1997) (reporting that 90% of sexual assault victims knew their assailants).
71. This is especially so with respect to intrafamilial victimizations where notification of the wider community has dubious educational value, in the absence of an established likelihood of future victimizations of nonfamily members, and might actually prove counterproductive. *See infra* note 89 and accompanying text.
72. *See, e.g.*, Grant T. Harris et al., *Appraisal and Management of Risk in Sexual Aggressors: Implications for Criminal Justice Policy*, 4 J. PSYCHOL. PUB. POL'Y & LAW 73 (1998).
73. *See, e.g.*, Nathaniel J. Pallone, *Identifying Pedophiles "Eligible" for Community Notification Under Megan's Law: A Multivariate Model for Actuarially Anchored Decisions*, 28 J. OF OFF. REHAB. 41 (1998).
74. So too must work be done to ensure that the laws are being applied consistently *within* jurisdictions. *See, e.g.*, Jeffrey T. Walker & Gwen Ervin-McLarty, *Sex Offenders in Arkansas: Characteristics of Offenders and Enforcement of Sex Offender Laws* (Ark. Crime Information Center 1999) (noting "alarming" discrepancies among local approaches to assessing registrants' risk for purposes of notification).
75. This is especially so with respect to the thousands of registrants who are not under parole or probation supervision; for them, authorities must rely solely on the good faith of registrants and any compliance mechanism used. Moreover, experience has shown that registry inaccuracies can result in stigmatization and harassment of persons wrongly thought to be registrants. With the increasing use of the Internet, and its greater capacity for mass communication, the accuracy and completeness of registration becomes all the more important.
76. *See, e.g.*, Washington State Institute for Public Policy, *Sex Offenses in Washington State: An Update* 40 (1998) (reporting compliance rate of 84%). *Cf.* Joyce Plotnikoff

& Richard Woolfson, *Where are They Now?: An Evaluation of Sex Offender Registration in England and Wales*, Police Research Series Paper 126, 6–7 (2000) (reporting a compliance rate of 94.7%, but noting that the rate is "misleading").

77. *See, e.g.,* Karl J. Karlson, *Study Finds Many Sex Offenders Not Properly Registered*, ST. PAUL PIONEER PRESS, Jan. 2, 1998, at 1B (reporting that 70% of registrants were not living at their reported address).

78. *See* Lawrence Sussman, *Sex Offender List Leaves Some Out; Out-of-State Man's Visit to Sheriff's Office Sparks Awareness in Grafton*, MILWAUKEE JOURNAL SENTINEL, Dec. 14, 2001, at 1A

79. *See* Peter Finn, *Sex Offender Community Notification* 12 (Nat'l Inst. of Justice 1997) (discussing impact in Washington and New Jersey).

80. Richard G. Zevitz & Mary Ann Farkas, *Sex Offender Notification: Managing High Risk Criminals or Exacting Further Vengeance?*, 18 BEHAV. SCI. & THE LAW 375, 381–84 (2000).

81. *Id.* at 387.

82. *Id.* at 387–88. Housing difficulties experienced by registrants, in particular, can have major collateral consequences, insofar as they serve to concentrate offenders in particular locales, possibly further impeding community reintegration. *See* Kevin Blocker, *High-Risk Offenders Housed in Hotels, Motels*, SPOKESMAN-REVIEW (Spokane, Wash.), March 2, 2002 (noting that 40 of 53 of one apartment building's residents were registrants, with 13 of them classified as highest risk offenders). Moreover, by forcing registrants into transience it becomes more difficult to ensure compliance with registration requirements.

83. *See, e.g.,* Candace Kruttschnitt et al., *Predictors of Desistance Among Sex Offenders: The Interaction of Formal and Informal Social Controls*, 17 JUSTICE QTLY. 61 (2000).

84. Zevitz & Farkas, *supra* note 80, at 389.

85. *See* Tom R. Tyler, *Trust and Law Abidingness: A Proactive Model of Social Regulation*, 81 B.U. L. REV. 361 (2001); Tom R. Tyler, *What is Procedural Justice? Criteria Used By Citizens to Assess the Fairness of Legal Procedures*, 22 LAW & SOC'Y REV. 103 (1998).

86. For a recent study of the role of community meetings, *see* Richard G. Zevitz & Marry Ann Farkas, *Sex Offender Community Notification: Examining the Importance of Neighborhood Meetings*, 18 BEHAV. SCI. & LAW 393 (2000).

87. *See* Daniel M. Filler, *Making the Case for Megan's Law: A Study in Legislative Rhetoric*, 76 IND. L.J. 315, 351 (2001) (citing conflicting news accounts based on interviews with neighbors).

88. *See, e.g.,* David Chanen, *An Unwelcome Mat for Sex Offenders*, STAR-TRIBUNE (Minneapolis-St. Paul), May 13, 1999, at 1B (noting same); Mary H. Gottfried, *Sex Offenders Live in Poorer Areas*, PIONEER PRESS (St. Paul), Mar. 8, 2002, at A1 (same).

89. *See, e.g.,* Nat'l Criminal Justice Assoc., Policy Report, *Sex Offender Community Notification* 29 (Oct. 1997) (citing experiences in Louisiana where teen-age girls were molested by their stepfathers but were "fearful of being identified when their stepfather's picture is published in the local newspaper.").

90. *See, e.g.,* Kathleen Ingley, *A Fearful Eye: Keeping Watch on the Valley's Sex Offenders; Monitoring Procedures Get Tougher*, ARIZ. REPUBLIC, May 2, 1999, at A1; Kay Lazar, *States Lack Money, Manpower to Do the Job*, BOSTON HERALD, July 19, 1998, at 9.

91. *See* Logan, *supra*, note 1, at 200-01 (discussing innovations such as "Megan's Mapper"); Ronnie L. Paynter, *Getting the Word Out*, 26 LAW ENF. TECH. 76 (June 1999) (describing notification technologies).

92. *See, e.g.,* Denise M. Bonilla & Joy L. Woodson, *Continuing Debate over Megan's Law; Some Question Whether Sex Offender List Curbs Crime*, LOS ANGELES TIMES, Feb. 14, 2003, at 2; Dave Morantz, *Sex Offenders' Risk Often Slow to Be Assessed*, OMAHA WORLD-HERALD, Oct. 28, 2001, at 1A.

93. *See* Cong. Rec. H4456, May 7, 1996 (remarks of Rep. Melvin Watt) (noting that while unfunded mandates have become politically unpopular, "in this area, somehow or another we cannot seem to justify allowing states to make their own decisions...All of a sudden, the Big Brother Government must direct the States to do something that is not even necessarily a Federal issue.").

94. *See, e.g.,* News Service, *Compliance Money Sought,* SEATTLE TIMES, Jan. 10, 1999, at B3 (reporting effort by county to obtain reimbursement from state for money spent as a result of state-mandated registration compliance measures).

95. *See, e.g.,* Alison Bass, *Suspects Battle to Stay Off Sex Offender Registry,* BOSTON GLOBE, Aug. 16, 1999, at A1.

96. *See* H.J. Cummings, *Courts Shield Young Sex Offenders; Judges Keeping Some Juveniles Off Registry,* STAR-TRIBUNE (Minneaspolis-St. Paul), Oct. 6, 2002, at 1A.

97. *See* LORD WINDLESHAM, POLITICS, PUNISHMENT AND POPULISM 177–188 (1998); Jonathan Simon, *Megan's Law: Crime and Democracy in Late Modern America,* 25 LAW AND SOC. INQUIRY 1111 (2000).

Legislative Responses

Summary of Presentations

JOHN KIP CORNWELL

Seton Hall University School of Law, Newark, New Jersey 07102, USA

The legislative responses session of this symposium addresses two distinct aspects of sexual coercion: the conceptualization and prosecution of the crime of sexual assault by the criminal justice system and the society's use of the mental health system to control sexual aggression. Professor Eric Janus began the session by providing an overview of legislative responses to sexual aggression, highlighting the "qualitative shift" that has occurred over the last 35 years, first in the criminal justice system's broadening of the scope of criminal sexual conduct and, more recently, in the shift from punishment to prevention through laws providing for community notification and the civil commitment of sexually violent predators. Professor Janus explored the structure of the law underlying these shifts and the larger consequences of these new legal paradigms. For example, if we are to move from a punishment to a prevention model, what are the types and thresholds of risk for intervention and how are they assessed? What, in addition, are the treatment rights of civilly detained sex offenders and how will these rights be enforced?

Next, Professors Catherine MacKinnon, Stephen Schulhofer, and Katherine Baker spoke on different aspects of the crime of rape. Professor MacKinnon advocated a sex equality approach to sexual assault. Her proposal would restructure laws pertaining to sexual assault to reflect her belief that sex is made an inequality in society through gender hierarchy, and sexual assault is a central practice and expression of that inequality. Accordingly, Professor MacKinnon suggests a redefinition of the element of "force" and "consent" to include social hierarchies founded upon a number of factors, including age, race, and gender. Sex forced by these inequalities would constitute rape, subject to proof by the defendant that it was freely and affirmatively wanted. Professor MacKinnon also calls for the passage of new civil rights laws to offer accountability to victims, the stigma of bigotry for perpetrators, the possibility of reparations, and the potential for social transformation by empowering survivors.

In contrast to Professor MacKinnon, Professor Schulhofer highlighted the tremendous progress made over the past 20 years in prosecuting sexual assault as evidenced, for example, by states' recognition of power or indirect intimidation as sufficient for force and "frozen fright" as sufficient for proof of nonconsent. By the same token, he wonders whether the pendulum has swung too far in the past few years. That is, is it possible that we have made *too much* progress in prosecuting the

Address for correspondence: John Kip Cornwell, J.D., Professor of Law, Seton Hall University School of Law, One Newark Center, Newark, NJ 07102. Voice: 973-642-8882.
cornweki@shu.edu

Ann. N.Y. Acad. Sci. 989: 352–354 (2003). © 2003 New York Academy of Sciences.

crime of rape? He offers a number of potentially troubling developments in this regard. For example, does requiring the defendant to carry the burden of proof on consent improperly dilute the culpability requirement? Does, moreover, the defense of reasonable belief as to consent exist in theory only? And when and to what degree, normatively speaking, should intoxication or drug/alcohol consumption render consent legally ineffective?

Professor Baker focuses on the taxonomy and etiology of sexual coercion. She begins by dividing sexual coercion into six categories, from the most to least severe. She then collapses the six categories into two, rape and sex, which are differentiated by the presence or absence of an intent to do harm. She opines that our ability to discern the social meaning of many of these acts of sexual coercion should help us understand why men commit these acts and thereby help us articulate strategies for prevention. Because coercive acts at the most and the least severe ends of the spectrum evade social explanation, Professor Baker argues that, to deal effectively with them, we must change the social understanding of sex by viewing the term "impersonal sex" as an oxymoron.

The remaining speakers focused on the role of mental health law in controlling harmful sexual behavior, specifically through sexually violent predator statutes. Professor Robert Schopp argued that sexual predator commitment statutes undermine the justifications for criminal punishment and civil commitment. Whereas criminal punishment expresses condemnation for culpable wrongdoers, those subjected to civil commitment do not qualify for condemnation, because they have an impairment that renders them incapable of functioning as "minimally competent practical reasoners." Accordingly, we respond not with punishment, but with treatment and behavior management, reflective of societal sadness, concern, and sympathy for their position. Professor Schopp believes, however, that this framework breaks down in the context of sexual predator commitment, where the public reaction is not one of sadness and sympathy, but rather anger and resentment toward the subject. At the same time, responding with anger and retributive emotions in such situations is important, Schopp notes, since doing so fulfills significant social functions, such as culpability, vindication for the victim, and reaffirmation of collective values.

In order to minimize the excesses of such emotions, and to restore to a certain degree the boundaries between criminal punishment and civil commitment, Professor Schopp suggests two strategies. The first advocates the development of institutional structures designed to provide disciplined, proportionate, and consistent application of retributive emotions. The second attempts to "civilize" criminal punishment by, *inter alia*, learning to react with sadness or regret instead or anger and aggression and decreasing the extent to which society empathizes with others. He acknowledges, however, that both strategies undermine principles of public morality.

Professors John La Fond and Bruce Winick completed the legislative responses session by introducing their proposal for "sex offender reentry courts." These courts would utilize a risk management approach in releasing sex offenders into the community and would serve as an alternative to current practices that address community risk through long-term criminal sentencing, indeterminate civil commitment, and mandatory registration. In determining eligibility for release, sex offenders would undergo risk assessments conducted at regular intervals, beginning at the time of sentencing, that would continually reassess the threat they pose to the community based on behavior in or outside of prison and participation in treatment programs.

Judges, acting as "reentry managers," would retain broad discretion to order and monitor release. All reintegration into the community would occur gradually, subject to close monitoring by a case management team and repeated polygraph examinations designed to provide important information such as victim types, offending patterns, and frequency.

La Fond and Winick posit that sex offender reentry courts would better serve both the community and the offender. Continual reevaluation of an offender's public safety risk provides a more accurate picture of how well an offender is behaving in a real-world environment, which guides officials' determination of the appropriate placement of the offender within the community. In addition, the proposal's emphasis on treatment ultimately benefits the offender by providing the best opportunity for long-term recovery from the mental disorders that will otherwise keep them locked away indefinitely in prison or in a secure psychiatric hospital.

Legislative Responses

Panel Critique

JOHN KIP CORNWELL[a] AND THOMAS GRISSO[b]

[a]Seton Hall University School of Law, Newark, New Jersey 07102, USA
[b]Department of Psychiatry, University of Massachusetts Medical School,
Worcester, Massachusetts 01655, USA

The legislative responses session of this symposium addresses two distinct aspects of sexual coercion: first, how the criminal justice system conceptualizes and prosecutes the crime of sexual assault and, second, how the mental health system has been used as an alternative institutional structure through which society can control sexual aggression. The discussion that follows groups the presentations accordingly.

Professors Baker, MacKinnon, and Schulhofer addressed different, though related, aspects of the crime of sexual assault. Professor Baker focused on the taxonomy and etiology of rape, outlining a spectrum of sexual coercion ranging from "traditional" rape, where a perpetrator acts alone in using physical force or the threat of physical force to overpower his victim, to situations typically labeled "sex," where the victim consents to intercourse only because she feels that she has no choice but to do so. Between these two extremes, Professor Baker identifies four additional categories of sexual coercion, two of which she labels "rape," by virtue of the perpetrator's intent to do harm, and two of which she labels "sex," due to the absence of an intent to do harm. She thus unpacks the social meaning of rape to promote the identification and articulation of strategies for the prevention of sexual assault.

Included within these two intermediate categories of sex are group rapes, such as the incident dramatized in the movie *The Accused*, and so-called "acquaintance" rapes, whereby young men assert their masculinity by flaunting their sexual prowess as heterosexual beings. Professor Baker believes that to curb this sort of antisocial behavior, society must teach boys and young men that sex is not so much about accomplishment and bonding with each other as it is about relationships. Males must view the desire for impersonal sex as illegitimate and pathological.

This interesting idea begs several questions. First, what exactly is "impersonal sex?" Professor Baker does not, for example, believe that "temporary relationships" or "one-night stands" are unacceptably impersonal, provided "the two parties have communicated enough with each other to understand that their consensual sex is a mutually desired aspect of a consensual relationship." It appears, therefore, that it is the parties' mutuality of understanding that it is critical, not its personal or impersonal nature. That is, if a man and a woman who have just met agree to get together once a week for sex and nothing more, Professor Baker's proposal would be satis-

Address for correspondence: John Kip Cornwell, J.D., Professor of Law, Seton Hall University School of Law, One Newark Center, Newark, NJ 07102. Voice: 973-642-8882.
cornweki@shu.edu

Ann. N.Y. Acad. Sci. 989: 355–359 (2003). © 2003 New York Academy of Sciences.

fied, even though one could not truly characterize the sexual experience as "personal." If, as she suggests, it is one party's disregard for the other that is abhorrent, a mutual decision to engage in impersonal sex would not appear to be problematic.

If, therefore, we want to teach men not to engage in sex in the absence of mutuality of feeling or understanding, how are we to go about this? This would be a daunting task, a reality that Professor Baker herself acknowledges. While education both at home and in the schools would no doubt prove useful, its ultimate efficacy is somewhat speculative in light of the implicit promotion—if not glorification—of male sexual conquest in popular culture.

Professor Baker also refers to the role that inequality between men and women in American social structure serves in promoting sexual assault. She is particularly persuaded as to the centrality of social inequality with respect to two categories of rape: men who sexually assault women as revenge for the women's assertion of what the men regard as inappropriate control over them and men who rape their opponents' women as a way of getting back at those men. With regard to the former, Professor Baker discusses a 1989 rape case where, following the defendant's acquittal, the jury foreman stated that the complainant "asked for it the way she was dressed. [W]ith that skirt, you could see everything she had."

To remedy this sort of miscarriage of justice, Professor Baker advocates the incorporation of a jury instruction stating that "frustration, sexual attraction, flirtation, or anger, however understandable, can never be a legitimizing reason for coercing sex." While adding this instruction may be beneficial, its utility seems dubious where acquittals are based, in large part, on jury nullification. Put differently, if jurors acquit defendants who are technically guilty because they feel that the defendants' actions are justified by the complainants' conduct, it is unclear to what extent the result will differ by simply reminding jurors not to do what they knew they were not supposed to do in the first place.

Professor Catherine MacKinnon advocates a fundamentally different approach. Like Professor Baker, Professor MacKinnon recognizes gender inequality as a cause —or, more accurately, *the* cause—of male sexual assault of women. Unlike Professor Baker, however, Professor MacKinnon calls for fundamental structural changes in the criminal law to incorporate awareness of social hierarchy in defining the crime of sexual assault. For example, because she believes that gender inequality leads some women to consent to sex even though they do not desire it, Professor MacKinnon finds "consent" a misleading and inappropriate standard by which to gauge the presence or absence of sexual assault. She recommends, instead, that the criminal law adopt the "welcomeness" standard used in Title VII sexual harassment claims; sex, that is, would need to be wanted for it not to be assaultive. She likewise advocates a redefinition of the element of "force" to include inequalities of power founded upon social hierarchies such as gender, age, family association, and race. Accordingly, to successfully defend against a charge of rape brought by a woman (of the same race), a man would need to demonstrate both that sex was affirmatively and freely wanted *and* was not forced by "the socially entrenched forms of power" that distinguish men from women.

This proposal is appealing inasmuch as it shifts the trial's focus from the conduct of the complainant—which has long been a problem in the context of rape—to that of the defendant. In so doing, however, it raises several other concerns worthy of consideration. First, as explained by Professor MacKinnon, the substitution of welcomeness for consent means that sex that "looks, even is, consensual" could be rape because social hierarchy precluded meaningful freedom of choice. Thus, a man who had sex with a woman who reasonably appeared to be a willing partner would be labeled a rapist based not on his own culpable *mens rea* but rather on general societal conditions that disadvantage one gender *vis-à-vis* the other; in short, he must pay for evolutionary injustice with his own freedom and the life-long stigmatization that will accompany his conviction. Holding a man responsible without a truly "guilty" state of mind would square more closely with traditional criminal law principles if Professor MacKinnon believed that sexual assault should be a strict liability crime. Her allowance of affirmative defenses, however, belies such an understanding.

Professor Stephen Schulhofer also questions whether this apparent dilution of culpability in prosecuting sexual assault is problematic. He focuses, in particular, on the element of consent and he wonders whether such reforms as requiring the defendant to carry the burden of proof on consent and/or making reasonable belief as to consent a defense more in theory than in fact have pushed the proverbial envelope too far. The issue of reasonable belief as to consent seems an especially difficult one. For example, Professor Schulhofer queries whether mistake about consent is ever possible, given proof of force, and whether an unreasonable mistake can ever be honest.

These situations seem possible, at least in theory. Imagine the following: A celebrity invites a fan up to his room for sex. Five minutes later, she arrives and tells him how excited she is to be there. He begins immediately to caress and undress her. Shocked, she "goes along" with this, saying nothing. He ultimately pushes her onto the bed and has intercourse with her. As he penetrates her, she begins to cry. Surprised, he withdraws immediately and apologizes as she hurriedly dresses and leaves. She later explains that she never intended to have sex with him and went up to his room only for a picture and autograph.

Prosecuted for rape, the celebrity may plausibly argue that, while his conduct was sufficient to demonstrate force, he honestly and reasonably believed she had consented based on her apparent acceptance of his explicit invitation to come to his room for sex and the absence of evidence indicating any contrary intention on her part. Even if the defendant's conduct were considered unreasonable, it is not necessarily dishonest (i.e., reckless) since nothing in the complainant's conduct would have clearly made him aware that she had not come to his room for the stated purpose of his invitation.

Of course, the fact that honest and reasonable mistakes are possible does not mean that they are common or likely. Still, to disallow defenses based on them altogether threatens compounding injustice. Instead, and in light of the risk inherent in excusing coercive sexual conduct, it may be better to allow the defense in very limited circumstances subject to an exacting burden of persuasion applied to the defendant.

While we have thus far focused on the criminal law, it is the civil law that is perhaps the proper forum for reforms designed to reduce or eliminate criminal conduct founded upon gender-based inequality. Professor MacKinnon acknowledges as much, commenting that while rapists may deserve to be jailed, incarceration has tended not to change their behavior but "has often entrenched and escalated it." Accordingly, her call for the passage of new civil rights laws seems an excellent idea. Unlike criminal statutes, civil rights laws "offer the prospect of redistributing power" and reducing inequality "by putting state power in the hands of victims."

There is also much merit in Professor Baker's call for greater communication between parents and children about the role of intimacy in sexual relations. Indeed, any serious effort to redefine the social understanding of sex requires early intervention in the lives of male children before their attitudes are saturated with contrary imagery promoted by the media and popular culture.

The remaining presentations by Professors Janus, Schopp, LaFond, and Winick raise issues about clinical concepts and procedures associated with sex offender commitment laws. State statutes typically have two criteria about which mental health professionals are likely to have to testify: (*a*) the presence of a mental illness that impairs volitional control and predisposes the person to future sex offending, and (*b*) the likelihood that the individual will engage in future sex offenses.

The presenters identified some troubling consequences of mental illness and impaired volitional control as criteria for sex offender commitment laws. First, as Professor Schopp clearly points out, the approach in most sex offender commitment laws is duplicitous, requiring the legal system to live with an illogical process and a tortured conclusion. Imagine that a court has held a sex offender fully responsible for his behavior by having tried, convicted, and sentenced him years ago. Now, at the end of his lengthy prison term, the court commits him because of a mental illness that impairs his ability to control his sexual behavior. In effect, the court is saying that the original decision to hold him responsible was wrong. Figuratively, we tell the victim that we held the rapist responsible, but now we see that "he couldn't help it—it wasn't his fault." Perhaps the victim wouldn't care, as long as this illogical conclusion keeps the individual locked up longer. But history is not kind to systems —legal or otherwise—that tolerate internally inconsistent means to achieve convenient ends.

Second, linking mental illness and volitional incapacity dehumanizes people with mental illnesses, thus impeding rehabilitation. There is no surer way to reduce the capacity of persons with mental illnesses to exercise responsibility than to deny that they can. LaFond and Winick's therapeutic jurisprudence approach may meet some difficult practical hurdles, but at least it does not play into this trap. It holds the individual responsible and uses that to motivate rehabilitation.

Third, requiring volitional incapacity for sex offender civil commitment perpetuates the myth that anybody can reliably judge whether an individual's act arose because of an impulse that he was incapable of resisting or an impulse that he did not care to resist. In the annals of American psychiatry, there is not a single scrap of evidence that mental health professionals have any meaningful basis for judging whether or not a person was capable of resisting an impulse (with or without mental illness). Nearly 20 years ago, the U.S. Congress adopted a definition of insanity in criminal cases (18 U.S.C. § 402, 1984) that eliminated the "volitional prong" for the insanity defense (inability to conform one's conduct to the requirements of law). This arose in part because the American Psychiatric Association acknowledged the inability of mental health professionals to judge volitional capacity at the time of the offense. On what basis do sex offender commitment laws presume that mental health professionals can do what they admit they cannot, especially when other areas of modern criminal law agree with the professionals?

These papers also point up several issues in the use of instruments and tools designed to estimate the likelihood of sex offense recidivism. Their comments are focused less on the validity of the instruments (which is debated in other sections of this volume) and more on the role they play in legal proceedings regarding sex offender commitment. The issues are several: (*a*) sometimes the courts do not allow clinicians to do as well as they can; (*b*) other times they require that clinicians do more than they should; and (*c*) sometimes they listen to clinicians but don't understand what they are saying.

Concerning the first of these, courts sometimes exclude clinicians' testimony about the likelihood of future sex offending when it is based on scores from sex offender recidivism instruments (applying the criteria from *Daubert v. Merrell Dow Pharmaceuticals, Inc.,* 113 S.Ct. 2786, 1993). Evidence presented elsewhere in this volume suggests that the empirical value of at least some of these instruments exceeds that of many other traditional psychological tests that courts routinely do not question. Moreover, courts almost always allow clinicians to testify to future risk of recidivism on the basis of nothing more than an unstructured clinical interview for which no validity at all can be demonstrated. To be sure, clinicians sometimes misuse results of sex offender recidivism instruments by testifying about likelihood of recidivism based *solely* on the score. But, since the law admits clinical opinion without any empirical methods, it is difficult to understand its exclusion of testimony based on an assessment process, including many sources of data and "anchored" with a score from one of the better sex offender recidivism instruments.

Second, courts sometimes require that clinicians do more than they should. For example, clinicians are sometimes asked to testify whether—"yes" or "no"—the individual is "likely to engage in future sexual violence." As Professor Janus pointed out, how is a clinician to know what the law means by "likely"? It is not defined anywhere in statutes or case law. Certainly individuals in a 40% probability group are more likely than most other sex offenders to recidivate, even if it is more likely that they won't than that they will. Persons in a 50–60% probability group might be said to be in a "more likely than not" category, but whether or not they will recidivate is still pretty much a flip of the coin rather than "likely." Courts should be asking clinicians for estimates of likelihood, not dichotomous opinions as to whether they are "likely." The field must take a proactive stance to educate judges and clinicians about ways to deal with these circumstances in which the courts ask more of clinicians than they can provide.

Finally, many courts misinterpret testimony about sex offense recidivism even when clinicians testify well. When a clinician says that a person is in a group with a 50% probability of reoffending, some judges will hear this as "a pretty high risk" (not a bad translation), but others will hear it as "total uncertainty" (the clinician doesn't know, as in "50–50"), and a few judges will presume that it means "the person will be dangerous half the time." There is a need for the field to begin to "manualize" the manner in which clinicians can testify to best avoid misinterpretations by the courts.

Overview of Rehabilitative Efforts in Understanding and Managing Sexually Coercive Behaviors

BARBARA K. SCHWARTZ

Justice Resource Institute,
Bridgewater, Massachusetts 02324, USA

ABSTRACT: In reviewing approaches to rehabilitative efforts in understanding and managing sexually coercive behaviors within the past two decades, one is struck by the development of two totally divergent paths. In 1971, there were a few civil commitment programs operated by mental health departments— most notably were the Sexual Psychopath Program at Western State Hospital in Fort Steilacoom, Washington, and the Massachusetts Treatment Center for Sexually Dangerous Persons. There were a few programs in prisons started by therapists who were interested in this population but given little recognition and even fewer resources. Additionally there were a handful of community-based programs including the J.J. Peters Institute in Philadelphia and PASO (Positive Approaches to Sex Offenders) in Albuquerque, New Mexico. Today there are thousands of specialized sexual offender treatment programs treating sexual abusers of every age, gender, ethnicity, and with a wide range of comorbid conditions. They are treated in the community, prisons, mental hospitals, residential facilities, and private practices. There is an international organization, a specialized research journal, and a specialized branch of the Department of Justice, the Center for Sex Offender Management. This chapter will provide an overview of the developments in the field, primarily covering the last 25 years. It will look at the evolution of theoretical approaches, the development of specialized approaches for subpopulations, significant landmarks, and possible future trends.

KEYWORDS: rehabilitative efforts; sexual offender treatment programs; Center for Sex Offender Management; cognitive behavioral theories; adolescent sexual offenders; mentally ill sexual offenders

THE EVOLUTION OF THEORETICAL APPROACHES

The treatment of sexual offenders has largely emulated the treatment approaches that were popular for the general population at that specific time. Consequently it is not surprising that the first reports of therapy with individuals experiencing paraphilias was individualized, long-term psychoanalysis and is now currently focused on cognitive-behavioral approaches supplemented by treatments developed by behav-

Address for correspondence: Barbara K. Schwartz, Ph.D., Justice Resource Institute, 63 Main Street, Suite 6, Bridgewater, MA 02324. Voice: 508-697-2452; fax: 508-697-2738.
bschwartz@jri.org

Ann. N.Y. Acad. Sci. 989: 360–383 (2003). © 2003 New York Academy of Sciences.

iorists and by those working with traumatized individuals. Many of the techniques originally developed in the substance abuse field such as relapse prevention and motivational interviewing have been adapted for use in the treatment of inappropriate sexual behavior.

Early Psychodynamic Theories

Very early theorists included Krafft-Ebing (1892) who devised a very reasonable typology and Schrenck-Notzing (1895) who prescribed a variety of treatment approaches including hypnosis and "severe mountain walks extending over months" (p. 205). Freud and his followers explored human sexuality and theorized that perversions were based on fixations at various psychosexual stages (1938). Concepts such as castration anxiety, reaction to the seductive mother, inadequate ego/ superego, confusion of aggression and libidinal drives, and the narcissistic representation of self as a child contributed to the first comprehensive theories of human sexuality and the impact of trauma on sexual deviance.

Early ego psychologists were actually the first to look at the impact of cognitions on sexually inappropriate behavior. Hammel (1968) and Ostrow (1974) discussed the role of primitive thought processes, including disorganization, tolerance of ambiguity, and emotionality on the maintenance of deviant behavior. These writers pointed out how an inability to use organized abstract thought processes might relate to an inability to substitute fantasy for action, thus leading to acting-out behavior. Ego psychologists also contributed the basic theory of object relation and how the inability to attach to others may contribute to an inability to empathize with others and neutralize aggressive impulses. Relational concepts in psychoanalysis as explored by Sullivan, Klein, and Lichtenstein (Mitchell, 1988) stressed the human as part of a social network. Current interest in attachment disorders and their relation to sexual disorders has renewed attention to these theories.

Groth (1979) in his book, *Men Who Rape*, became a pioneer of modern day sexual offender treatment. Through his work with institutionalized sexual offenders and the influence of psychoanalysts, such as Murray Cohen and Theo Seghorn, with whom he worked at the Massachusetts Treatment Center for Sexual Dangerous Persons, he developed a typology of rapists and child molesters and discussed the role of sexual victimization in the development of sexual deviance.

This interest in psychodynamic approaches centered on the East Coast, while the West Coast developed highly confrontive group approaches that focused on accepting responsibility for one's behavior and steered clear of the exploration of early dynamics. Subsequently sexual offender treatment looked quite different depending on the region of the country one was in. These differences continued up to the 1990s.

Behavioral Theories

In the late 1960s there was an ongoing debate concerning the mechanisms by which deviant sexual arousal might be conditioned and consequently could be counterconditioned. Is this behavior developed through operant conditioning or classical conditioning? Obviously one would not want to resolve this debate by conditioning college freshmen to have deviant sexual arousal. However, one could study which techniques could reduce deviant arousal by treating sexual offenders who already manifested this aberration. Cautela (1967) developed covert sensitization in which deviant arousal is paired with an aversive fantasy. He postulated that this was a form of imagery-based or instrumental punishment. However, Rachman and Teasdale (1969) argued that these stimuli function as conditioned stimuli that decrease arousal. Dougher and associates (1987) demonstrated that "covert sensitization is a classical counterconditioning procedure by which means deviant sexual stimuli simply lose their capacity to reinforce sexual behavior" (p. 15-2).

Behavioral theories have led to the development of a variety of techniques in addition to covert sensitization, including assisted covert sensitization (Maletzky, 1974), olfactory conditioning (Laws, Meyer & Holmen, 1978), masturbatory satiation (Abel & Anon, 1982), and verbal satiation (Laws & Osborn, 1982).

Cognitive Behavioral Theories

Cognitive behavioral treatment of sexual offenders originates from two unrelated sources. Yockelson and Samenow (1984) theorized that "criminals" show distinct thinking patterns that help them to justify, rationalize, and minimize their antisocial behavior. Thus a burglar might blame a home owner for not installing an expensive home security system and thus making it easy for someone to break into his home. sexual offenders have a wide variety of excuses for victimizing others. A rapist may insist that his victim was wearing provocative clothing, while a child molester might claim that the six-year-old that he molested had seduced him. Thus much of what goes on in a sexual offender treatment group is the confronting of these distortions, hoping that the offender will truly change his beliefs.

The other root of cognitive behavioral treatment emerged from the experience of William Pithers and Janice Marques (Pithers, Marques, Gibat & Marlatt, 1983), who, while interning at Atascadero State Hospital, began to adapt the work of Marlatt and Gordon (1985) in relapse prevention. This technique was originally developed to treat substance abusers who might relapse and then proceed to totally abandon themselves to their alcohol or drug abuse, feeling their abstinence was a fluke. In relapse prevention offenders are taught that any dysfunctional behavior does not "just happen." It is preceded by an identifiable chain of thoughts, feelings, and behavior. Relapse prevention is the most commonly used technique for treating sexual offenders.

Integrative Theories

A number of different theorists have hypothesized that sexual deviance is a highly complex phenomenon containing many different variables. Murphy and associates (1979) presented a prescription for rape that not only explained why men sexually assault women but also explains why they do not. They identified four general groups of individuals with numerous gradations between them. The first group includes highly psychopathic individuals who harbor intense hostility toward women, show an inability to express anger appropriately, fear rejection, accept rape myths, misperceive female behavior, and are sexually aroused to aggressive sexual cues. These individuals are at high risk to commit a rape. Other groups showing different combinations of the above characteristics might be sexually coercive or engage in antisocial behaviors, but men who show none of the above dynamics would be highly unlikely to engage in sexual assault.

Finkelhor (1984) developed a four-factor theory of child abuse that included basic motivation, disinhibitors, the environment, and the victim's behavior. It provided suggestions for strengthening precautions in the environment and teaching children protective behaviors.

A dynamic theory of sexual assault was developed by Schwartz (1989) based on the model of a dam. The motivational reservoir includes a complex network of beliefs, values, thoughts, feelings, and behavior that set the stage for a variety of deviant sexual behaviors, which would explain why an individual would be attracted to sexually abusive behavior. The motivational reservoir is held in check by floodgates that represent disinhibitors, including stress, substance abuse, psychoses, cognitive impairments, cognitive distortions, and lack of empathy. An individual who is motivated to commit a sexual assault and whose behavior has been disinhibited, then needs to find the appropriate environment. For some of these individuals, the environment must be very specific, and for others almost any environment will suffice. Then into that environment must be brought (or spontaneously appear) a victim who fits the offender's mental template of "a victim." For some individuals this may be a boy between 6 and 8, for others a young woman who appears to be vulnerable, and for a few almost any age, gender, or appearance fits the template.

Schwartz and Masters (1993) combined psychodynamic and trauma-based theory with cognitive behavioral and addictive approaches to formulate an integrated approach to sexual deviance and a multimodel treatment approach. Sexually abusive behavior, according to these theorists, has its roots in early childhood trauma and is maintained by cognitive distortions. Clients are trained in relapse prevention to control their behaviors.

Ellis (1993) was one of the first to present a biosocial approach to rape, claiming that the behavior can be understood through evolutionary theories that point out that (1) there are two basic drives related to rape: the sex drive and the drive for power and control, (2) males have a stronger sex drive than women, and (3) rape is reinforced because it has proven to be a successful way to implant one's genes in the gene pool.

This volume contains two empirically based models of sexually aggressive behavior, both of which strive to integrate various dynamic factors. Malamuth, Heavey, and Linz (1993) have researched the antecedents to the development of (1) compulsive/deviant/impersonal sexuality, and (2) hostile/dominance antisociality. Challenging Malamuth, Knight (in press) suggests a three-path model that includes (1) physical and verbal abuse of the child, which leads to callousness and inhibited emotionality, which disinhibits sexual drive and fantasies, (2) sexual abuse, which leads to hostile sexual fantasies, and (3) early antisocial behavior.

CONTRASTING TREATMENT STYLES FROM COAST TO COAST

The East Coast

Because until the 1980s there was no formal mechanism for professionals interested in this population to communicate with each other, the field grew in very different ways depending on physical location. In the 1950s and 1960s universities on the East Coast, such as Boston University, trained their psychologists in a psychoanalytic model. Graduates with this orientation obtained positions at the Massachusetts Treatment Center and began to train interns from these doctoral programs. Thus the treatment of involuntarily committed sexually dangerous persons evolved into a program that stressed individual therapy with an analytic orientation. In the early 1970s Nicolas Groth, Ph.D., wrote *Men Who Rape* (1979), which to this day is probably the only book to attempt to offer an explanation of the psychology of sexual offenders to a popular audience. Coming from a psychodynamic model, it focused on the sexual abuse that many sexual offenders have experienced in their childhood.

Another program that stressed resolving early trauma in the lives of adult male sexual offenders was ROARE (Prendergast, 1991) that was conducted at the Adult Diagnostic and Treatment Center by William Prendergast, Ph.D. This intensive approach used group therapy, often conducted in a large television studio within the institution, with numerous groups being conducted simultaneously and visually recorded. This treatment was featured in a popular television movie entitled *Rage*.

Another innovation found on the East Coast was the early establishment of outpatient sexual offender treatment groups for probationers in Philadelphia. This program continues to offer these groups. Another early community-based program on the East Coast was Drs. Gene Abel and Judith Becker's practice in New York City. This program made use of the phallometric assessment and behavioral treatment and was probably best known for its research into the range and scope of the deviant behavior of their patients.

The West Coast

Because the Massachusetts Treatment Center and the Adult Diagnostic and Treatment Center were established exclusively for the treatment of sexual offenders, the professionals in these facilities had to come up with treatment for their problems. However, the individuals committed under the Sexual Psychopath Statute in Washington State were sent to a generic mental hospital. The psychiatrist in charge of their treatment had little idea about what would help them and certainly did not have the resources to offer individual long-term psychodynamic therapy. However, he was candid enough to admit this to his charges. These individuals then proposed the establishment of groups that they would run themselves. Known as Structured Self-Help, these groups continued to be operated by the patients with therapists monitoring the sessions through videotapes or notes taken by a group member. Perhaps due to the power issues that these men manifested or perhaps due to the highly confrontational style developed by substance abuse programs of that era, a highly "in your face" approach developed and became associated with the therapeutic style of that region. A great number of professionals were trained in that program, and many continue to treat and teach in that area.

At Oregon State Hospital a program was established for sexual offenders from the Department of Corrections who would volunteer to transfer to this intensive treatment program. Director Rob Freeman-Longo and his associates pioneered the use of a variety of approaches. In addition to groups and psychoeducational approaches, the staff built a penile plethysmograph and used behavioral techniques. They also made use of antiandrogens. Men in the program were allowed to slowly transition from the program, living in the surrounding area, and returning to the hospital for outpatient treatment.

Professionals in the Northwest were some of the first to establish collaborative networks with parole, probation, and community supervision agents. Parole officers in some areas assisted with therapy groups. To this cooperative team were added polygraphers who help to monitor offenders. This approach was dubbed the *containment model* and will be discussed later.

Institutional versus Community-Based Treatment

Institutional and community-based treatment may have either developed independently of each other or as a by-product of each other. For example, in Washington State, and to a lesser degree in Massachusetts, staff trained in programs for involuntarily committed sexual offenders established private practices and later on were available to provide services to individuals on probation or parole. On the other hand, Texas had a substantial number of community providers before it had a large institution-based program. Since all incarcerated sexual offenders in Texas receive their treatment in one geographic locale, it is unlikely that staff leaving that program would be able to provide services across the entire state. New York and California have neither large programs in their prisons nor community-based providers commensurate with the size of their populations. When one program is the offspring of another, there is likely to be philosophical compatibility between the two programs. When they develop independently, there may be widely diverse approaches. To ensure some uniformity and thus a smooth transition between institutional-based programming and outpatient treatment, states, and in some cases groups of providers, have taken different approaches. In Washington the state certifies sexual offender treatment providers. These individuals must be a licensed mental health provider, have at least a year of supervised experience, take a written test, and pay a substantial licensing fee. Colorado has a Sex Offender Management Board that oversees treatment in the state and oversees private practitioners. Massachusetts at one time maintained a list of "network providers" who contracted with the Commonwealth to offer services at a substantially reduced rate in exchange for referrals. Some states, such as California, pay for outpatient sexual offender treatment services and contract with vendors to provide this, while other jurisdictions expect the offender to pay.

Institutional and community-based programs may differ from each other in the amount of time available for treatment. Outpatient groups typically run for 90 minutes once a week. With up to 12 individuals in a group, there is little time for anything other than monitoring how the participants have coped with risky situations during the past week. If one individual is in crisis, other members may have trouble finding any time to comment on their adjustment. There is also little time for formal skills training or for teaching new members how to prepare a relapse prevention plan. Most community-based programs describe themselves using the cognitive-behavioral model, indicating that they use relapse prevention and focus on dealing with cognitive distortions.

Comprehensive institutional-based programs may devote much more time to treatment. Some programs such as those located in Massachusetts, New Jersey, Missouri, and Washington offer between 6–10 hours of direct treatment supplemented by a variety of other therapeutic activities. They are able to offer skill-building courses, substance abuse treatment, and family work. These programs have a cognitive behavioral base but may be able to add supplemental approaches.

Programs for involuntarily committed sexual offenders are meant to be long term. One could argue that they are meant to institutionalize the individual for life while providing him with meaningful treatment during that entire time. This is a significant challenge to the staff who constantly have to come up with ways to challenge and motivate these patients. Having a clear set of treatment goals that can be individualized and finding meaningful ways to use the talents of individuals in the latter stages of treatment are two ways to deal with this problem. Civil commitment programs, being mental health programs, are ethically bound to offer treatment in the "least restrictive environment." This suggests that each of these programs must have some type of transition facility for residents who have finished the bulk of the treatment program. This is a major challenge for some programs, such as Washington's Special Commitment Center that is under a consent decree to establish such a program.

In order to provide an adequate amount of treatment and a smooth transition between institutional and community treatment, several types of programs need to be implemented. There should be residential treatment programs for nonincarcerated sexual offenders, just as there are for substance abusers. A program that runs for 28 days would be able to provide meaningful evaluation and treatment services to newly arrested sexual offenders or serve as a diversion program for prison. There also need to be halfway houses for men being released from prison. There is substantial funding from the federal government to support transitional services for violent offenders, but most states exclude sexual offenders from these services.

Cognitive Behavioral versus Addiction Model

These two approaches have been perceived as diametrically opposed approaches to treating sexual deviance. Sexual addiction is most associated with the work of Patrick Carnes (1983) who has proposed that inappropriate sexual behavior of all types can be conceptualized as one of many addictive behaviors. This approach has its own organization, the Association of Sexual Addiction and Compulsivity, with its own journal. Several self-help groups, including Sexaholics Anonymous and Sexual Addicts Anonymous, have developed, which follow a 12-step model.

Although viewed by many as incompatible, the addiction model addresses cognitive distortions, relapse prevention, and the physiological basis of inappropriate sexual behavior. Its attention to past trauma has been adopted by many cognitive behaviorists who have expanded their approach. Within this camp are found therapists who treat Level 1 (Carnes, 1983) patients, whose behavior is maladaptive but not illegal. The addiction model has also embraced physicians specializing in the new field of Addiction Medicine. Those few residential programs for adults with inappropriate sexual behavior have been established by proponents of the addiction model. Communities seem to be much more tolerant of treating individuals labeled as "sexual addicts" rather than "sexual abusers," even if their behavior is identical.

Special Populations

Sexual offender treatment started with the worst cases, those who were involuntarily committed, and has steadily progressed to include programs from a widely diverse population. As previously referenced, the initial programs were for individuals labeled as "sexual psychopaths," "sexually dangerous persons," or "mentally disordered sexual offenders." Then prison-based or community-based programs for males in the criminal justice system were instituted. Currently there are programs for the following groups.

Adolescent Sexual Offenders

In 1980 there was one specialized program for adolescent sexual offenders. Today there are over 1000 programs that identify themselves as offering specialized services to this population. There are a substantial number of these programs that offer long-term residential care. Why the sudden growth? Certainly there is a need for programs that can handle violent youth who act out sexually. However, it can be argued that many of these programs grew out of fear and finances, and the interplay between the two. The common assumption regarding juvenile sexual offenders was that they were budding adult sexual offenders and therefore highly dangerous. School systems certainly did not want the responsibility of maintaining these students in regular public school settings. Therefore they were often willing to provide funds for residential care. Many judges were interested in seeing that these young people received early intervention and were willing to require states to pay for specialized treatment. Residential facilities established to treat other types of adolescent problems (e.g., conduct disorders and substance abuse) saw this population as a way to insure long-term funding of their patients. There was nothing wrong with this. However, it may have resulted in juveniles with sexual behavior problems being perceived as more pathological than they actually were. In some cases separating these youths from their homes and families, sometimes for years, and labeling them a "sexual offenders" may have done significant harm.

Many early basic assumptions about young people with sexual behavior problems need to be questioned. Which individuals are actually suffering from impulse disorders of which their sexual behavior is only a symptom? Which ones are engaging in sexual exploration that would be amenable to an educational program versus those who have deep-rooted deviance in need of long-term specialized care? What does early labeling do to these children? And, perhaps most significantly, which ones (if any) should be considered adults to be incarcerated in adult prisons?

Additionally the form that therapy takes for this population should be questioned. Multisystemic approaches that focus on intensive work with the families of sexually abusive youth have shown success (Henggler, Schoenwald & Pickrel, 1995). Helping a young person develop healthy self-esteem, social skills, and appropriate interests by focusing on the four domains (mind, body, emotions, and spiritual self) may be more useful than focusing on deviance (Longo, 2002). Only appropriate research can tell us which is the most effective.

Female Sexual Offenders

Many lay persons are not aware that there are female sexual offenders—unless, of course, they have been the victim of one. Small children may be unable to distinguish sexual abuse by females from routine caregiving, and in this culture an adolescent male may be told that he is "lucky" if he is molested by an older female. Consequently few women are incarcerated on these charges, and there are few programs available to them. Those who do end up in prison are often codefendants with male sexual offenders.

Incarcerated female sexual offenders represent a fraction of the overall sexual offender population, and furthermore they differ in many significant ways. There are female sexual offenders who suffer from paraphilias with accompanying deviant sexual arousal and share many dynamics with their male counterparts. However, there are also female sexual offenders who are coerced into this behavior by male sexual offenders who have often selected these women because they share many of the characteristics of the children that these men sexually desire. They may be small in stature and easily controlled because they may be disabled in some way (mentally ill, developmentally disabled, extremely passive), or they may be immigrants who do not speak English. Their vulnerability makes them easy to control. These women need a treatment program that can distinguish the different types of offenders and offer modified services to those who are as much victims as perpetrators. While they must also take responsibility for their behavior, they need to learn how to assert their rights as autonomous beings and to stay out of these types of dysfunctional relationships.

Sexually Reactive Children

Another population that has been recently identified as in need of specialized services are prepubescent children who act out sexually. Kikuchi (1995) found that 20% of all rapes and 30–50% of child molestations are committed by children or young adolescents. Sibling incest is the most common type of child sexual aggression (Carter & Van Dalen, 1998). It may, however, be difficult to distinguish normal childhood sexual curiosity from sexual assault. Gray, Busconi, Houchens, and Pithers (1997) have offered five criteria to help distinguish the difference: (1) the repetitiveness of the sexually aggressive acts, (2) the unresponsiveness to adult intervention, (3) the criminal nature of the behavior if it were committed by an adult, (4) the occurrence of the behavior across time, and (5) the variety and sophistication of the sexual acts exhibited.

Miranda and Davis (2002) suggest that comorbid conditions, including attention deficit hyperactivity disorder, conduct disorders, and obsessive compulsive disorder must be carefully evaluated in devising a treatment plan for the young offender. Of course, the family will play a crucial role in understanding and helping to control sexually inappropriate behavior. In addition, many of the techniques used with adult offenders, such as dealing with cognitive distortions and accepting responsibility, can be adapted for youngsters.

Developmentally Disabled Sexual Offenders

There is a great need for specialized programs for this population, and while some are available, there are not nearly enough to meet the demand. Seriously developmentally disabled individuals who act out sexually were once held in large state institutions for the mentally retarded. However, with the move toward deinstitutionalization, they may be quite difficult to place. The staff in group homes may not be able to supervise them adequately. They may be found incompetent to stand trial, and thus will not be imprisoned. Because they may not have a criminal record, they will be exempt from involuntary commitment in most states. Some organizations have established creative programs to serve this population. Justice Resource Institute, a Boston-based nonprofit, has responded to this need by establishing both an outpatient and a residential program, both of which are in Rhode Island. Integrative Services provides outpatient treatment groups for these individuals but also provides around-the-clock consultation to the group homes where these individuals live. This type of intense support has enabled developmentally disabled sexual offenders to remain in the community.

Mentally Ill Sexual Offenders

Mentally ill individuals who have committed sexual assaults are possibly the last of the major subpopulations to receive specialized sexual offender services. It has been a widespread assumption that the sexually inappropriate acts committed by seriously mentally ill individuals are a by-product of their mental illness and not a co-morbid condition. It was assumed that treatment of the primary psychiatric disorder would bring sexual behavior under control. With the continuing closure of mental hospitals, mentally ill sexual offenders have been some of the few remaining residents not qualified for release. In order to eventually be able to reintegrate these individuals into community settings, some individuals are being offered specialized sexual offender treatment, adapted so that it does not aggravate their other conditions. Although inappropriate sexual behavior is occasionally secondary to major mental illness, such as when it is a response to command hallucinations or dementia, it often is a separate and distinct problem that needs its own specialized treatment.

MODERN LANDMARKS IN SEXUAL OFFENDER TREATMENT

Passage of Original Sexual Predator Laws

As often happens in the history of sexual offender treatment, in 1937 a horrendous crime galvanized the public into trying to find a solution to these atrocities. The answer was Sexual Psychopath Laws. That year Michigan passed the first law that was quickly declared unconstitutional. Shortly thereafter Illinois framed legislation that did pass constitutional muster. The Minnesota law became the model, and between 1937 and 1976, 30 states passed variants of this law. This public policy was based on the assumption that the behavior of some sexual offenders was rooted in mental illness; the condition was specifically the "utter lack of power to control their sexual impulses." Between 1975 and 1981 half of all these states repealed their legislation for a variety of reasons. By 1985 only six states used these laws, and by 1989 only Minnesota occasionally committed individuals to their program. A number of factors contributed to this demise (Prentky & Burgess, 2000). The feminist movement dismissed the idea that men who commit sexual assault are mentally ill. These men, they maintained, represented the result of male socialization. They did not deserve to be placed in a mental health facility. They should be held accountable for their actions. Society should make a statement to these men by imprisoning them. Additionally professional organizations made statements against these laws, considering them to be an abuse of psychiatry (1959). Concerns about constitutional rights of committed men were raised. Finally there were some highly publicized crimes committed by men on work release from these programs. By 1988 two of the largest programs (Washington and Massachusetts) were closed to further admissions.

Founding of Safer Society

In 1964 a Quaker activist named Fay Honey Knopp, who had fought for civil rights and prison reform, established the Prison Research Education Action Project, devoted to advocating for the study and treatment of the most detested group in this county, sexual offenders. In 1984 she published the first review of sexual offender treatment programs (Knopp, 1984). In 1985 the organization changed its name to the Safer Society, and in 1995 it became the Safer Foundation. Over a 30-year period this courageous elderly woman traveled the country, documenting efforts to treat this population. She published books on the treatment of adult and juvenile sexual offenders, relapse prevention, prison rape and numerous other documents to aid in the rehabilitation of these difficult individuals. However, more than that she served as the personal support system of the professionals struggling to establish this field and to many sexual offenders striving for recovery. Her death in 1995 touched the lives of thousands who relied on her inspiration.

Founding of the Association for the Treatment of Sexual Abusers

In 1983 Rob Longo convened a series of brown bag lunches attended primarily by employees of the Oregon State Hospital and primarily devoted to exploring the ethics and methods of administering behavioral treatment to sexual offenders. This group eventually incorporated and was named the Association for the Behavioral Treatment of Sexual Abusers (ABTSA), eventually to be renamed the Association for the Treatment of Sexual Abusers (ATSA). Meanwhile funds from the National Institute of Mental Health allowed Gene Abel and Judith Becker to organize a series of conferences to treat sexual offenders, which began in 1977 in Memphis, Tennessee. ABTSA was able to pick up this endeavor and sponsored their first conference in Newport, Oregon in 1987.

ATSA now has a fully staffed office and is active in attempting to shape public policy. It sponsors research and encourages students interested in the field. It issues position papers that are accessible through its Web site, and it publishes a newsletter and peer-reviewed research journal that disseminates the latest research.

National Academy of Corrections Trains States in Systems Approach to Sexual Offenders

In 1984 Dr. Hank Cellini, a program specialist at the National Academy of Corrections in Boulder, Colorado, proposed a series of training programs on the management of sexual offenders. The suggestion was greeted with skepticism and the typical bureaucratic reluctance to take up a controversial issue. (There remain fewer less popular and more controversial issues than sexual offender treatment.) However, John Moore of the Washington office agreed to pursue the suggestion. Drs. Roger Smith and Randy Green of the Oregon State Hospital, Dr. Michael Dougher from the University of New Mexico, and Barbara Schwartz from the New Mexico Department of Corrections, as well as Fred Cohen, Esq., a lawyer with expertise in correctional mental health issues, designed a week-long training meeting to be delivered to five-member teams of highly positioned officials in the criminal justice system from different states.

The emphasis of this training was on a systems approach that would integrate, for example, the apprehension, conviction, sentencing, disposition, and supervision of sexual offenders. Collaboration was the key. Additionally a specific treatment model was fashioned, combining group therapy, behavioral treatment, and psychoeducational classes in a cognitive behavioral framework, emphasizing relapse prevention.

Over 30 states were trained in the initial series, which was then followed regularly by additional training for seven years. A volume, *A Practitioner's Guide to Treating the Incarcerated Male Sex Offender* (Schwartz & Cellini, 1989) was published. Numerous technical assistance grants were awarded to Illinois, Wisconsin, Arizona, Washington, Hawaii, Texas, Georgia, Arizona, and Kansas, to name only a few, which supported the establishment or remodeling of prison-based sexual offender programs. A few of the programs have lost their funding, but the vast majority of the programs are actively involved in treating thousands of offenders nationwide.

The Center for Sexual Offender Management Established

In 1996 the Office of Justice Programs gathered 180 experts in Washington, DC for The National Summit: Promoting Public Safety through Effective Management of Sex Offenders in the Community. In response to their recommendations, the Center for Sex Offender Management (CSOM) operated by the Center for Effective Public Policy was established. The goals of this agency include (1) provision of information for managing sexual offenders in the community by synthesizing and disseminating the latest knowledge and practices, (2) identifying the lessons on managing sexual offenders from communities that have developed effective systems through collaboration, and disseminating this knowledge to others, and (3) providing a variety of training and technical assistance to agencies and jurisdictions.

These goals are achieved by providing information through a Web site, through a list serve, that responds to inquiries and collects and disseminates relevant information. The CSOM provides technical assistance, periodic training sessions, and has developed a training curriculum accessible through their Web site. Nineteen resource sites have been identified that exemplify the effective use of collaboration in devising effective management techniques for both adult and juvenile offenders. These sites range from the state of Vermont, to local counties, to Indian tribes. A number of sites have been selected to receive research grants. Monies available from this federal agency have encouraged the implementation of the containment approach by assisting jurisdictions to train polygraphers; add victim advocates to supervision teams; train lawyers, judges, probation, and parole officers; and encourage public education.

Public Policy Changes

In 1990 a heinous crime in Washington State against a young boy by a recently released sexual offender who had threatened to harm children upon his release brought about an immediate reaction from public officials. A special blue-ribbon panel was assembled and made a number of recommendations. Some were rational, such as the certification of sexual offender treatment specialists. However, in an attempt to avoid discussion regarding sentence structuring, which had changed the length of sexual offender sentences from indeterminate to determinate sentences, in which a first degree rapist would serve a standard five years, the state unanimously adopted a variant of the old Sexual Psychopath legislation. Instead of being committed for treatment in lieu of imprisonment, sexual offenders could be institutionalized at the end of their criminal sentence for a day to life. This model of dealing with perceived dangerous sexual offenders was adopted by another 15 states in the next nine years, despite vehement opposition by several professional groups (American Psychiatric Association, 1999; National Association of State Mental Health Program Directors, 1999).

This same panel also recommended the registration of all sexual offenders as well as a procedure for informing the public of their whereabouts. In 1994 Megan Kanka, a young New Jersey girl, was murdered by her neighbor, a previously incarcerated sexual offender. This resulted in federal legislation known as Megan's Law that mandated all states to pass public notification laws or lose substantial amounts of federal anti-crime block grants. The ramification of these policies will be discussed at length in other chapters of this volume.

Development of Risk Assessment Instruments

In response to a sudden need to identify candidates for involuntary commitment as well as to ascertain risk levels for the purpose of public identification, researchers have rushed to develop actuarial assessment instruments. A number of instruments have emerged. Most of these instruments concentrate on static variables such as past criminal history, victim characteristics, and demographic characteristics. However, some scales measuring dynamic features are being developed. There remains considerable controversy over how these scales should be used. Should a single instrument be used, or should the tools be used as a baseline from which to add aggravating or mitigating factors? Should clinical judgment play any part in these assessments? What should one do with a high-scoring individual who has recently become a double amputee or a low-scoring individual who assures the assessor that he intends to attack a child when released?

Treatment Efficacy

Any discussion of sexual assault eventually comes around to the issue of whether sexual offenders can be effectively treated. The study of sexual offender treatment, like the study of all psychotherapeutic interventions, has problems with research design, including establishing appropriate control groups (randomly assigned or matched samples), number of subjects, length of follow-up, and base rates for the untreated population. However, a number of studies have been reported, and the quality of the research is improving. There are a number of studies that report that treated sexual offenders show lower recidivism rates than untreated ones (Becker & Hunter, 1992; Berlin, Hunt, Malin, Dyer, Lahne & Dean, 1991; Huot, 1999; Mander, Atrops, Barnes & Munafo, 1996; Marshall & Barbaree, 1988; Pithers & Cunningham, 1989; Scott, 1997).

There have been three meta-analyses studying sexual offender treatment programs. In 1993 Alexander (1993) examined 424 studies of this issue, eliminating 356 of them due to methodological problems. The remaining 68 studies showed a significant reduction in recidivism. Hall (1993) found an overall reduction in recidivism of 30% for treated sexual offenders. A study sponsored by the Association for the Treatment of Sexual Abusers found that through the use of cognitive behavioral treatment and systematic approaches sexual recidivism was reduced from 17.4% to 9.9%, and that general recidivism was reduced from 51% to 32% (Hanson, Gordon, Harris, Marques, Murphy, Quinsey & Seto, 2002).

In 1999, Grossman, Martis, and Fitchner concluded that "although treatment does not eliminate sex crime, research supports the view that treatment can decrease sex offenses and protect potential victims" (1999, p. 349). On April 7, 1998 the American Psychological Association stated in a press release that "Sex offenders are not as likely to relapse as thought, according to a study of 23,393 sex offender cases: Staying in treatment is a big factor."

RECENT INNOVATIONS

Containment Model

In 1996, English, Pullen, and Jones published the results of their study of supervision models of sexual offenders, concluding that one approach seemed to be particularly effective. They dubbed this the Containment Model. It emphasizes collaborative networking in the community among a sexual offender's supervising agent (probation or parole officer), the therapist, and a polygrapher. This was first used in the Pacific Northwest but has now been adapted in many jurisdictions and is actively promoted by the Center for Sex Offender Management. This approach demands close communication and collaboration with a number of governmental agencies, including the courts, probation, corrections, the parole board, parole officers, the polygrapher, and the community-based therapist. It is critical that all of these players subscribe to the same treatment approach and are committed to the concept of supervised community reintegration.

Technological Advances

As mentioned above, polygraphy, which has long been controversial, is receiving increased acceptance in its use in the management of sexual offenders. Often the mere idea of being polygraphed is enough to keep an offender from engaging in high-risk behaviors. While some parole boards may be reluctant to mandate polygraphy, they may order that a parolee comply with the conditions of treatment, and the therapist may have the discretion to demand that the sexual offender agree to polygraphs as part of therapy. Usually this technology is used in three different ways: (1) full disclosure in which the offender must disclose all past deviance to the therapist, (2) routine monitoring to insure that the offender is avoiding or intervening in high-risk situations, and (3) specific issue tests to assess specific past or present behaviors. Initiating the use of the polygraph may require different branches of the government to come to agreement on some very sensitive issues. If passing a full disclosure polygraph is required, can the individual be prosecuted for the revelation of new crimes? If a specific issue test suggests that the offender's story, rather than the victim's version or the police report, is true, how will that be handled in treatment? Can failure to pass a polygraph alone result in a probation or parole violation? These issues should be settled among all parties before this technology is adapted.

Another technology that has enhanced monitoring of sexual offenders is electronic monitoring. This allows the supervising agent to maintain constant tracking of the location of a supervisee. Some systems even allow for alcohol blood level measures.

Global positioning and radio frequency monitoring allows for very close tracking of an offender in the community. The Florida Department of Corrections has monitored a variety of offenders using both radio frequency and global positioning systems with significant success. The department compared the total number of revocations between traditional community control and the above technology. With community control, 31.6% of offenders had their supervision revoked compared to 12.1% for radio frequency monitoring and 20% for global positioning (Florida Department of Corrections, 2001). Sexual offenders (14%) were revoked less than other offenders (26.8%).

EMERGING TRENDS

Therapeutic Style

Much of sexual offender treatment has been modeled on substance abuse counseling. Relapse prevention was adapted from the treatment of drug and alcohol abuse. Therapeutic communities in corrections were developed for the treatment of drug abusers and have since been used with sexual offenders. The therapeutic style of treating involuntary patients, including anyone who is court ordered into treatment, has in the past stressed heavy-duty, "in-your-face" confrontation. This was designed to break down denial and resistive personality dynamics and rebuild the individual in a more prosocial mold. However, this approach has been questioned. A new approach based on motivational interviewing is being used with sexual abusers (Miller & Rollnick, 1991). This model stresses the expression of empathy for the client, help in developing discrepancy between where the client is and where he needs to be in the therapeutic process, avoiding argumentation and the development of shame, supporting self-efficacy, and reinforcing successive approximation.

Research done by Fernandez and Serran (2002) on therapy style supports motivational interviewing as the most effective therapeutic style. Reviewing videos of treatment sessions, the researcher found that there were three basic approaches—confrontive, unchallenging, and motivational. Confrontation was shown to be ineffective and possibly even dangerous, as this approach evoked aggressive responses in clients with high self-confidence. The motivational approach proved to be the most effective.

Psychopharmocology

As reviewed in other chapters in this volume, there is a variety of evidence that physiological influences may play a role in the development of aberrant sexual behavior. Psychopharmaceutical approaches for treating sexual offenders are well established and indeed are one of the earliest approaches that go back to the 1960s (Lerner, 1964; Money, 1968, 1970).

Berlin (1983, 1989) has reported significant reduction in recidivism with the use of medroxyprogesterone acetate (MPA: Provera, Upjohn) at The Biosexual Psychohormonal Clinic at Johns Hopkins University in Baltimore. In Canada cyproterone acetate is available to treat paraphilias, but this has not been approved for use in the United States.

Some research (Rosler & Witztum, 1998; Thibaut, Cordier & Kuhn, 1993) reported on the gonadotropin-releasing hormone (Gn-RH), which acts as an antiandrogen, has shown promising results. However, the number of subjects has been small, and some patients were also being treated with other antiandrogens.

More recently the selective serotonin uptake inhibitors (SSRIs) have been used. The rationale behind the use of these drugs is that paraphilias are often associated with affective symptoms and mood disorders as well as obsessive-compulsive disorders and substance abuse disorders. Successful clinical responses were noted in several studies (Kafka, 1994b; Kafka & Hennen, 2000).

Response to Internet Sex

Our culture has been profoundly influenced by the internet. Communication patterns, shopping habits, and the acquisition of knowledge have all been revolutionized by this technological revolution. Cooper (1998) and Freeman-Longo and Blanchard (1998) report that pornography is the internet's most frequently accessed topic. In accessing adult erotica it is not difficult to come upon child pornography, a subject that might have been of little interest to an individual if it had required much effort to acquire. Whether individuals who are apprehended for downloading child pornography are pedophiles or not is a topic of much contention in the field. Foley (2002) has presented an interesting typology that categorizes those individuals who access this material. These types are (1) the mastery type, which is characterized by individuals who are attempting to master their own experience of sexual victimization by finding an image that matches their own assault, (2) the rebellious/angry type who is attracted by the idea of violating the taboo associated with child pornography, (3) the disorganized type who downloads vast amounts of pornography with little distinction between type, and (4) the pedophilic/child molester/traveler type who has had a long-time preferential interest in having sex with children. Law enforcement officials tend to assume that anyone in possession of child pornography belongs to the latter category. However, Foley (2002) has found that only 33.3% of individuals charged with possession of internet-acquired child pornography showed a sexual interest in children based on their response on the Abel Screen.

Whether sexually deviant or not, individuals who become "addicted" to internet pornography can ruin their careers and marriages, even if their behavior is not considered illegal. Sexual offender treatment providers have therapeutic skills that can be helpful to these individuals.

Triaging

Currently a number of studies show recidivism rates of under 10% or under for treated offenders (Grossman, Martis & Fitchner, 1999). It is doubtful that it would cost beneficial to continue to reduce this rate in the heterogeneous populations currently being treated in institutionally based programs. The most responsible way to use scarce resources would be to begin to triage offenders, spending fewer resources on those with low risk to reoffend, and saving the more intensive treatment for high-risk offenders. Actuarial tools have made it increasingly possible to make these distinctions. Researchers assessing effective correctional programming have been recommending for years that prison-based programs should target high-risk offenders (Gendreau & Goggin, 1996). This policy may run headlong into the controversy regarding treating those offenders with psychopathic characteristics.

In instituting triaging with sexual offender populations, a systems approach that involves cooperation between a number of different agencies will be most effective. Attorneys and judges will need to be educated on how to interpret and use actuarial assessments. Low-risk offenders may then be sentenced to programs similar to Washington State's Special Offender Sentencing Alternative, in which low-risk offenders must seek treatment and avoid risky situations. This works best with specially trained probation officers who work closely with specially trained sexual offender treatment specialists. Currently many sexual offenders are placed on probation, but this may or may not be handled in a systematic manner, depending on the jurisdiction. Rather than using consistent, scientifically grounded criteria, a person may be placed on probation based on a number of subjective factors.

Higher-risk offenders would serve prison sentences where they would again be screened into subgroups, depending on the resources and philosophical approach of the particular jurisdiction. Some states may have the resources to offer treatment to all willing offenders, while others with more limited resources may choose to treat only those with a moderate risk to reoffend. These individuals might have the best chance to be paroled into a specialized sexual offender supervision unit based on the containment model.

Different states handle the highest risk offenders in a variety of ways. Some states sentence these individuals to extremely long prison terms, which may or may not offer the possibility of parole. Others have instituted involuntary commitment, which purports to target the most dangerous individuals. Others simply allow those who are viewed as too dangerous to be paroled or who reside in states with determinate sentences to complete their sentences and to leave prison with no supervision at all.

Texas has instituted a creative way of dealing with their high-risk sexual offenders that is designed to combine intensive supervision with involuntary commitment. However, sexually violent predators in this state are sentenced to mandatory treatment in the community rather than in an institution. This could also be accomplished with the use of lifetime parole. Under either circumstance high-risk sexual offenders could be closely monitored using the above-mentioned technology. Violation of the strict criteria for release should result in reinstitutionalization for prolonged periods.

Sex courts, similar to drug courts, have been proposed that could coordinate the triage process. This would save having to enlist the cooperation of every defense and prosecuting attorney as well as every judge in the state.

Methods are now available to effectively manage sexual offenders without violating basic human rights or expending vast sums of money. Effectively networking all components of the criminal justice system can result in scientifically based triaging and offering specifically designed treatment and monitoring to sexual offenders in at least three different risk levels.

FUTURE RESPONSES

Restorative Justice

Restorative justice is a new paradigm that stands in contrast to our current system of retributive justice. While the latter seeks to assign guilt and exact punishment, restorative justice seeks to heal the victim, the community, and the perpetrator. When justice belongs to lawyers and judges in an adversarial system, the process is focused on who wins regardless of what the truth is. Restorative justice is grounded in principles espoused by indigenous peoples whose system of justice strives toward resolving conflicts so that the community is maintained. Within the last decade a number of processes associated with restorative justice have been adopted, including victim-offender mediation, family group processing, and community support systems.

In victim-offender mediation, such as that sponsored by the Terrance County District Attorney's office in Austin, Texas, trained mediators counsel victims and offenders, eventually arranging meetings between the two. This has been done in the past with nonviolent crimes, but the Texas project works with individuals who have committed violent crimes, including rape and murder.

Family group counseling seeks to involve the victim, the perpetrator, their support systems, and representatives of the community to heal the harm that has been done to all parties by the commission of a crime. An example of this is the recently established program, RESTORE, founded in Tucson by Dr. Mary Koss, a well-known researcher on victim's issues. This program works with date rape situations in an attempt to bring justice and healing into this painful situation without resorting to the use of the criminal justice system.

An example of community support systems is the public notification of sexual offenders in King and Snohomish Counties in Washington State. Instead of placing an offender's name on a list or his picture on an internet site, police officers hold community meetings to personally introduce the offender to his community—not to subject the offender to public ridicule, but to allow the offender to present himself as an individual, to inform the public of his relapse prevention plan, and, we hope, enlist the community in assisting him in his reintegration. Members of the public have been known to help these persons obtain work or housing.

Restorative justice offers ways for sexual offenders who are currently branded with the mark of cain through policies, such as public notification, to be either retrained in, or reunited with, their communities. If the hope is for the offender to refrain from reoffending, then assisting them with being able to find housing, work, and a social network aids in achieving that goal.

Elimination of Involuntary Commitment and Public Notification

Both public notification and involuntary commitment were passed with no thought to researching the effectiveness of such measures. While registration had been in place for a number of years in some states, such as California, it was combined with public notification in Washington in 1990. Immediately there were a number of vigilante acts, including the burning of homes. However, it was not until with the murder of Megan Kanka that the U.S. Congress enacted legislation that would force every state to adopt public notification.

No hearings were ever held on this issue. Enactment of public notification has cost states significant funds to establish a process to track and label every sexual offender in their jurisdiction. An agency must be established. Some states have established boards that determine the level of notification, composed of an average of five professionals as well as the bureaucracy to sustain the system. A more hidden expense would be the cost of creating a roadblock to employment, housing, and community acceptance for exoffenders who may turn back to crime or otherwise become dependent upon the public for their support. This is counterproductive to the rehabilitation of sexual offenders. Furthermore the system may not actually inform the public in a way that prevents crimes.

As previously discussed, involuntary commitment was resurrected in Washington State in 1990 for largely political reasons. Currently in 16 states these programs are phenomenally expensive, with little research to show that they have effectively reduced the rate of violent sex offenses. In Minnesota, for example, in 1998 it cost the state $16,995,600 to maintain 126 patients. (Minnesota Department of Corrections, 1999). This cost grows each year as few of these offenders are released from any of these programs.

Certainly there are more productive ways to spend these public funds. Even simply incarcerating dangerous individuals for longer periods of time would be less expensive than having to maintain special institutions for the provision of treatment. It is hoped that the trend to adopting this public policy is over and that more productive ways of dealing with these individuals will be devised.

PUBLIC HEALTH MODEL

Sexual assault is not just a crime that involves a perpetrator and his or her victim(s). It is a societal tragedy that involves individuals, families, and communities. The only way to decrease its prevalence is to mobilize all of these units in primary, secondary, and tertiary prevention. Using a public health model seeks to mobilize the average citizen so that this individual is vested in combating this behavior, just as this model has been used to raise awareness of the dangers of smoking, drunk driving, and not wearing automobile seatbelts. All of these risky behaviors were once tolerated by our culture until individuals whose lives had been affected by them united to bring these issues to the public. When citizens began to recognize how these behaviors influenced the health of their peers, they ceased to passively tolerate them and have succeeded in changing attitudes that were subtly reinforcing.

Taking a public health approach to the problem of sexual abuse would stress public awareness of the prevalence and consequences of this behavior. It would look at societal attitudes that reinforce sexual aggression. For example, research conducted with male college students has shown alarmingly large numbers reporting that they "forced someone to engage in sexual intercourse against their will." Such a large percentage of students endorse this behavior that one must question whether our society condones this conduct. A public health approach might use television ads to stress that "No means no" and that failure to heed this is a crime that results in long prison sentences. Child sexual abuse receives less obvious societal reinforcement, but the media has been guilty of sexualizing small children. Advertisers should be made aware that they may be reinforcing deviant sexual arousal in some individuals.

One public health approach that deals with child sexual abuse is STOP IT NOW founded by Fran Henry. It seeks to mobilize the community by enhancing awareness of this problem and by assisting adults who may be tempted to engage in this behavior or who may be aware of situations where abuse is occurring to report it to a hotline. Self-reporting abusers are offered an anonymous evaluation and assistance in negotiating with the district attorney to seek treatment in lieu of prosecution as long as their behavior meets certain criteria. In this way the burden of reporting and thus controlling child sexual abuse does not become the responsibility of child victims. So far 20 adults and 98 adolescents have sought our treatment through this process, and 15 adults and 10 adolescents have turned themselves in to the legal system (Henry & Tabachnick, 2002).

The STOP IT NOW public education campaign has significantly raised public awareness on a variety of issues related to this topic. Adult awareness of child sexual abuse was tracked over the four years that a campaign was operated in Vermont. The percentage of Vermonters who could explain child sexual abuse has increased from 44% in 1995 to 84.8% in 1999 (Henry & Tabachnick, 2002). This program continues to identify and address misconceptions regarding this issue.

FULL CONTINUUM OF SERVICES

The Center for Sex Offender Management has encouraged the networking of all parts of the criminal justice system involved with sexual offenders. Collaboration is the key to effectively containing these individuals. This must begin with the arrest, continue with thorough presentence evaluations, proceed with a court process conducted by educated judges knowledgeable in risk assessment and support for the victim, include the best treatment in both the community and within the institution, and continue with specialized probation and parole supervision. This has been achieved in some jurisdictions. However, one crucial component has proven universally difficult to establish. Residential programs for adults are desperately needed to handle (1) less serious offenders who might participate in such a program as a deferred sentence, (2) programs for sexual offenders on probation who may have been ordered to move out of their homes, and (3) paroled offenders who need a structured reentry program. Due to the difficulty in siting these programs, few of them exist. Generic programs for criminal offenders often exclude sexual offenders due to fear that public notification laws will reveal the presence of sexual offenders to neighbors and result in harassment or closure of these programs. It will take some very creative approaches to enable these programs to be established in local communities. Some suggestions, however, are (1) renovating warehouses into housing in industrial areas, (2) taking over buildings on the grounds of an abandoned mental hospital, (3) using housing on closed military bases, and (4) using camps in isolated areas, or motels in the off-season for intensive short-term treatment programs. These alternatives, however, all have limitations. The real solution will be public education and involvement with the rehabilitation of these persons. This approach will increase the community's willingness to accept sexual offenders back into the community.

CONCLUSION

The problem of sexual abuse touches every citizen, either directly or indirectly. Fortunately it is a problem that has attracted the interest of a number of professionals who today are coordinating their efforts to supervise these offenders. However, public policy has not, in many instances, been based on the knowledge gained by experts working with this population. Thus at least two major policies, involuntary commitment and public notification, became law in response to heinous crimes, and were based on emotionality, as opposed to careful deliberation. As a result they are immensely costly and in many cases counterproductive. This chapter has reviewed many approaches that are proving to be productive as well as pioneering efforts that offer hope for the future.

REFERENCES

ABEL, G.G. & ANON, J.S. (1982, April). *Reducing deviant sexual arousal through satiation.* Workshop presented at the 4th Annual Conference on Sexual Aggression. Denver, CO.

AMERICAN PSYCHIATRIC ASSOCIATION. (1999). Task Force on Sexually Dangerous Offenders. Washington, DC: American Psychiatric Association.

ALEXANDER, M. (1993). *Treatment efficacy with sex offenders: A meta-analysis.* Presented at the International Conference of the Association of the Treatment of Sexual Abusers. Boston, MA, October.

BECKER, J.V. & HUNTER, J.A. (1992). Evaluation of treatment outcome for adult perpetrators of child sexual abuse. *Criminal Justice and Behavior, 19,* 74–92.

BERLIN, F.S. (1983). Sex offenders: A biomedical perspective and a status report on biomedical treatment. In J.G.Geer & I.R. Stuart (Eds.), *The sexual aggressor: Current perspectives on treatment.* New York: Van Nostrand Reinhold.

BERLIN, F.S. (1989). The paraphilias and depo-Provera: Some medical, ethical and legal considerations. *Bulletin of the American Academy of Psychiatry and the Law, 17,* 233–239.

BERLIN, F.S., HUNT, W.P., MALIN, H.M., DYER, A., LAHNE, G.K. & DEAN, S. (1991). A five-year plus follow-up study of criminal recidivism within a treated cohort of 406 pedophiles, 111 exhibitionist and 109 sexual aggressives: Issues and outcome. *American Journal of Forensic Psychiatry, 12,* 5–27.

CAUTELA, J.R. (1967). Covert sensitization. *Psychological Record, 20,* 459–468.

CARTER, G.S. & VAN DALEN, A. (1998). Sibling incest: Time limited group as an assessment and treatment planning tool. *Journal of Child and Adolescent Group Therapy, 8*(2), 233–238.

COOPER, A. (1998). Sexuality and the internet: Surfing into the new millennium. *CyberPsychology and Behavior, 1,* 181–187.

DOUGHER, M.J., CROSSENM J.R., FERRARO, D.P & GARLAND, R.J. (1987). Covert sensitization and sexual preference: A preliminary analogue experiment. *Journal of Behavioral Therapy and Experimental Psychiatry, 18,* 231–242.

DOUGHER, M.I. (1995). Behavioral techniques to alter sexual arousal. In B.K. Schwartz and H.R. Cellini (Eds.). *The sex offender: Corrections, treatment and legal practice* (pp. 15-1–15-7). Kingston, NJ: Civic Research Institute.

ELLIS, L. (1993). Rape as a biosocial phenomenon. In G. Nagayama Hall, R. Hirschman, J.R. Graham & M.S. Zaragozee (Eds.), *Sexual aggression: Issues in etiology, assessment and treatment.* Bristol, PA: Taylor and Francis.

ENGLISH, K., PULLEN, S. & JONES, L. (1996). *Managing adult sex offenders: A containment approach.* Lexington, KY: American Probation and Parole Association.

FERNANDEZ, Y.M. & SERRAN, G. (2002). Characteristics of an effective sex offender therapist. In B.K. Schwartz (Ed.), *The sex offender: Current treatment modalities and systems issues* (Vol. 4, pp. 9-1–9-17). Kingston, NJ: Civic Research Institute.

FINKELHOR, D. (1984). *Child sexual abuse: New theory and research.* New York: The Free Press.

FOLEY, T.P. (2002). Current forensic assessment of internet child pornography offenders. In B.K. Schwartz (Ed.), *The sex offender: Current treatment modalities and systems issues.* (pp. 26-1–26-18) Kingston, NJ: Civic Research Institute.

FREEMAN-LONGO, R.E. & BLANCHARD, G.T. (1998). *Sexual abuse in North America: Epidemic of the 21st century.* Brandon, VT: Safer Society Press.

FREUD, S. (1919). A child is being beaten: A contribution to the study of the origin of sexual perversions. In S. Freud (Ed.) *Collected papers* (Vol. 2). London: International Universities Press.

GENDREAU, P. & GOGGIN, C. (1996). Principles of effective correctional programming. *Forum on Correctional Research, 8*(3), 26–43.

GRAY, A.S., BUSCONI, A., HOUCHENS, P. & PITHERS, W.D. (1997). Children with sexual behavior problems and their caregivers: Demographics, functioning and clinical patterns. *Sexual Abuse: A Journal of Research and Treatment, 9*(4), 267–290.

GROSSMAN, I.S., MARTIS, B. & FITCHNER, C.G. (1999). Are sex offenders treatable? A research overview. *Psychiatric Services, 50,* 349–360.

GROTH, A.N. (1979). *Men who rape: The psychology of an offender.* New York: Plenum Press.

GROUP ON FORENSIC PSYCHIATRY OF THE GROUP FOR THE ADVANCEMENT OF PSYCHIATRY (1950). *Psychiatrically deviated sex offenders.*

HAMMER, E. (1968). Symptoms of sexual deviance: Dynamics and etiology. *Psychoanalytic Review, 55*(1), 5–27.

HANSON, R.K., GORDON, A., HARRIS, A.J.R., MARQUES, J.K., MURPHY, W., et al. (2002). First report of the collaborative date project on the effectiveness of psychological treatment for sex offenders. *Sexual Abuse: A Journal of Research and Treatment, 114* (2), 169–194.

HENGGLER, S., SCHOENWALD, S. & PICKREL, S. (1995). Multisystemic theapy: Bridging the gap between university- and community-based treatment. *Journal of Counseling and Clinical Psychology, 63*(5), 709–717.

HENRY, F. & TABACHNICK, J. (2002). STOP IT NOW! The campaign to prevent child sexual abuse. In B.K. Schwartz (Ed.), *The sex offender: Current treatment modalities and systems issues* (Vol. 4, pp. 8-1–8-9). Kingston, NJ: Civic Research Institute.

HUOT, S. (1999). *Sex offender treatment and recidivism: A research summary.* Minnesota Department of Corrections.

KAFKA, M.P. (1994b). Sertraline pharmacotherapy for paraphilias and paraphilia-related disorders: An open trial. *Annals of Clinical Psychology, 6,* 189–195.

KAFKA, M.P. & HENNEN, J. (2000). Psychostimulant augmentation during treatment with selective serotonin reuptake inhibitors in men with paraphilias and paraphilia-related disorders: A case series. *Journal of Clinical Psychiatry, 61,* 664–70.

KIKUCHI, J.J. (1995). When the offender is a child: Identifying and responding to juvenile sexual abuse offenders. In M. Hunter (Ed.), *Child survivors and perpetrators of sexual abuse: Treatment innovations* (pp. 108–124). Thousand Oaks, CA: Sage.

KNIGHT, R.A. & SIMS-KNIGHT, J.E. (in press). The developmental antecedents of sexual coercion against women in adolescents. In R. Geffner & K. Franey. (Eds.) Sex offenders: Assessment and treatment. New York: Haworth Press.

KNOPP, F.H. (1984). *Retrai.ning adult sex offenders: Methods and models.* Orwell, VT: Safer Society.

KRAFFT-EBING, R. (1892). *Psychopathia sexualis.* New York Pioneer Publications, Inc., 281–285.

LAWS D.R., MEYER, J. & HOLMEN, M.I. (1978). Reduction of sadistic sexual arousal by olfactory aversion: A case study. *Behavioral Research and Therapy, 16,* 281–285.

LAWS, D.R. & OSBORN, C.A. (1982). A procedure to assess incest offenders. Proposal submitted to research committee. Atascadero State Hospital.

LERNER, L.J. (1964). Hormone antagonists: Inhibitors of specific activities of estrogen and androgen. *Recent Progress in Hormone Research* (Vol. 20, pp. 454–490). New York: Academic Press.

LONGO, R.E. (2002). A holistic/integrated approach to treating sexual offenders. In B.K. Schwartz (Ed.), *The sex offender: Current treatment modalities and systems issues* (Vol. 4, pp. 2.1–2.19). Kingston, NJ: Civic Research Institute.

MALAMUTH, N.M., HEAVEY, C.L. & LINZ, D. (1993). Predicting man's antisocial behavior
    against women: The interactional model of sexual aggression. (pp. 63–69) In G.
    Nagayama Hall, R. Hirschman, J.R. Graham & M.S. Zaragozee (Eds.), *Sexual
    aggression: Issues in etiology, assessment and treatment.* Bristol, PA: Taylor and
    Francis.
MANDER, A.M., ATROPS, M.E., BARNES, A.R. & MUNAFO, R. (1996). Sex offender treat-
    ment program: Initial recidivism study. *Alaska Legal Forum, 13*(2), 25–36.
MARLATT, G.A. & GORDON, J. (1985). Determinants of relapse: Implications for the main-
    tenance of change. In P.O. Davidson & S.M. Davidson (Eds.), *Behavioral medicine:
    Changing health lifestyles.* New York: Brunner/Mazel.
MALETZKY, B.M. (1974). "Booster" sessions in aversion therapy: The permanency of treat-
    ment. *Behavior Therapy, 8,* 460–463.
MARSHALL, W. & BARBAREE, H. (1988). The long-term evaluation of a behavioral treatment
    program for child molesters. *Behavior Research and Therapy, 26,* 499–511.
MILLER, W.R. & ROLLNICK, S. (1991). *Motivational interviewing: Preparing people to
    change addictive behavior.* New York: Guilford Press.
MINNESOTA DEPARTMENT OF CORRECTIONS. (1999). Civil commitment study group. 1998
    report to the legislature. Unpublished report.
MIRANDA, A.O. & DAVIS, K. (2002). Sexually abusive children-etiological and treatment
    considerations. In B.K. Schwartz (Ed.), *The sex offender: Current treatment modali-
    ties and systems issues* (Vol. 4, pp. 8-1–8-9). Kingston, NJ: Civic Research Institute.
MITCHELL, S.A. (1988). *Relational concepts in psychoanalysis: An integration.* Cambridge,
    MA: Harvard University Press.
MONEY, J. (1968). Discussion on hormonal inhibition of libido in male sex offenders. In
    R.P. Michael (Ed.), *Endocrinology and human behavior.* London: Oxford University
    Press.
MONEY, J. (1970). Use of an androgen-depleting hormone in the treatment of male sex
    offender. *Journal of Sex Research, 6,* 165–172.
MURPHY, W.D., COLEMAN, E.M., HAYNES, M.R. & STALGARTIS, S. (1979). *Etiological theo-
    ries of coercive sexual behavior and their relationship to prevention.* Unpublished
    manuscript.
NATIONAL ASSOCIATION OF STATE MENTAL PROGRAM DIRECTORS MEDICAL DIRECTORS
    COUNCIL. (1999). *Issues pertaining to the development and implementation of pro-
    grams for persons civilly committed for treatment under sexually violent predator
    statutes,* from http://www. nasmhpd.org/sexpred.htm
OSTROW, M. (1974). *Sexual deviation: Psychoanalytic insights*: New York: New York
    Times Book Co.
PITHERS, W.D. & CUNNINGHAM, G.F. (1989). Can relapse be prevented? Initial outcome
    data from the Vermont treatment program for sexual aggressors. In D.R. Laws (Ed.),
    Relapse prevention with sex offenders. New York: Guilford Press.
PITHERS, W.D., MARQUES, J.K., GIBAT, C.C. & MARLATT, G.A. (1983). Relapse prevention
    with sexual aggressives: A self-control model of treatment and maintenance of
    change. In J.G. Greer and I.R. Stuart (Eds.), *The sexual aggressor: Current perspec-
    tives on treatment.* New York: Van Nostrand Reinhold.
PRENDERGAST, W.E. (1991). *Treating sex offenders in correctional institutions and outpa-
    tient clinics: A guide to clinical practice.* Binghamton, NY: Haworth Press.
PRENTKY, R.A. & BURGESS, A.W. (2000). *Forensic management of sexual offenders.* New
    York: Plenum.
RACHMAN, S. & TEASDALE, J. (1969). *Aversion therapy and behavior disorders: An analy-
    sis.* Coral Gables, FL: Univeristy of Miami Press.
ROSLER, A. & WITZTUM, E. (1998). Treatment of men with paraphilia with a long-acting
    analogue of gonadotrophin-releasing hormone. *New England Journal of Medicine,
    338,* 416–422.
SCHRENCK-NOTZING, A. (1895). *The use of hypnosis in psychopathia sexualis.* New York:
    Institute for Research in Hypnosis Publication and Julian Press.
SCHWARTZ, B.K. & CELLINI, H.R. (1988). *Treatment of the incarcerated male sex offender.*
    Washington, DC: United States Department of Justice.

SCHWARTZ, M.F. & MASTERS, W.H. (1993). Integration of trauma-based, cognitive behavioral, systematic and addiction approaches for treatment of hypersexual pair-bonding disorder. In P.J. Carnes (Ed.), *Sexual addiction and compulsivity* (Vol. I). New York: Brunner/Mazel.

SCOTT, L.K. (1997). Community management of sex offenders. In B.K. Schwartz (Ed.), *The sex offender: New insights, treatment innovations and legal developments* (Vol. 2, pp. 16.1–16.12). Kingston, NJ: Civic Research Institute.

THIBAUT, F., CORDIER, B. & KUHN, J.M. (1993). Effect of a long-lasting gonadotrophin hormone-releasing agonist in six cases of severe male paraphilia. *Acta Psychiatrica Scandinavica, 87,* 445–450.

YOCKELSON, S. & SAMENOW, S. (1984). *The criminal personality. Vol. 1: A profile for change.* New York: Jason Aronson.

Restorative Justice for Sexual Violence

Repairing Victims, Building Community, and Holding Offenders Accountable

MARY P. KOSS, KAREN J. BACHAR, AND C. QUINCE HOPKINS

University of Arizona, Tucson, Arizona 85719, USA

Washington and Lee University, Lexington, Virginia 24450

ABSTRACT: Problems in criminal justice system response to date and acquaintance rape, and the nonpenetration sexual offenses are identified: (1) these crimes are often markers of a career of sexual offense, yet they are widely viewed as minor; (2) perpetrators of these crimes are now held accountable in ways that reduce their future threat of sex offending; and (3) current criminal justice response to these crimes disappoints and traumatizes victims and families. In response to these identified problems, we are implementing and evaluating RESTORE, an innovative victim-driven, community-based restorative justice program. Restorative justice views crime as harm for which the person responsible must be held accountable in meaningful ways. RESTORE uses a community conference to involve the victim, offender, and both parties' family and friends in a face-to-face dialogue directed at identifying the harm, and developing a plan for repair, rehabilitation, and reintegration into the community.

KEYWORDS: restorative justice; community conferencing; RESTORE

Our collaborative group (Pima County Attorney's Office, Southern Arizona Center against Sexual Assault, and College of Public Health, University of Arizona) has identified problems in the handling of date and acquaintance rape, and nonpenetration sexual offenses. Following a brief review of the problems, we describe the solution that we are implementing. The offenses we have targeted are common. The National Violence against Women Survey (Tjaden & Thoennes, 1998) documented that 18% of women in the United States have been raped. Six out of every seven rapes involve people who know each other. Nonpenetration offenses are even more prevalent; almost half of women in the United States have encountered an indecent exposer in their lifetime (Riordan, 1999). Recent data projects that between 20–25% of the more than 8 million women students will be raped while attending university, and *within the past seven months*, 5% (approximately 400,000 women) had someone expose their sexual organs to them, 5% received obscene telephone calls, and anoth-

Address for correspondence: Mary P. Koss, 1632 E. Lester Street, Tucson, Arizona 85719. Voice: 520-626-9502; fax: 520-626-9515.

mpk@email.arizona.edu

Ann. N.Y. Acad. Sci. 989: 384–396 (2003). © 2003 New York Academy of Sciences.

er 2.5% were observed naked without their permission (Fisher, Cullen & Turner, 2000). Because these crimes reinforce women's fear of crime and restrict spatial and social freedom, it is paramount for the justice system to act affirmatively. However, we have identified three serious problems in the current response.

PROBLEMS DOCUMENTED

"Minor" Sex Offenses Are Markers of a Sex-Offending Career, but Most Perpetrators Exit the System with No Preventive Measures in Place

Gene Abel (2001) presented data from a very large data set on rapists he has accumulated from sexual offender treatment centers across the United States. Rapists self-reported, either voluntarily or under polygraph, multiple past acts of sexual deviance for which they might or might not have been caught: 40% had watched people naked or having sex without their permission, 20% had exposed themselves, another 23% had masturbated in public, and 22% had made obscene telephone calls. Likewise, 14% of college student rapists admitted other sexual assaults (Lisak and Miller 2002; also see English, 2002 for evidence from polygraph examination of convicted sexual offenders). Experts conclude that most perpetrators are involved in multiple acts of sexual deviance, with multiple victim types (male/female; family/nonfamily; child/adult) (Abel, Becker, Cunningham-Rathner & Mittelman, 1988; Abel, & Osborn, 1992; Burdon & Gallagher, 2002; English, Pullen & Jones, 1996; Knapp, 1996; Burdon & Gallagher, 2002; Strate, Jones, Pullen & English, 1996; English 2002).

The processing of the crimes that we target is out of step with what the "minor" sexual offenses signal. Arizona law, like that of many states in the United States, classifies nonpenetration offenses at the lowest level of criminal culpability, punishable by a fine. In practice, these cases are usually settled with no fine, one year unsupervised probation, and no mandated treatment (personal communication, Kathleen Mayer, Assistant Pima County Attorney, February 8, 2002). By statute Arizona requires mandatory sexual offender registration only upon a third repeated offense of indecent exposure or exhibitionism. Acts of individual perpetrators are unlikely to be interrupted by laws, which wrongly assume they repeat the same type of offense. Additionally, the low level of sanction impairs general deterrence by communicating to the public that these offenses are less serious than a traffic offense, such as drag racing, which in Arizona carries a higher penalty than nonpenetration sexual offenses.

On paper, rapes are subject to greater sanctions, including incarceration, mandatory sexual offender registration, and sexual offender treatment. Yet, in practice, most alleged rapists exit the system with none of these preventive measures in place. Of 1198 reported rapes in Philadelphia between June 30, 1974 and June 30, 1975, only 163 (13%) led to a guilty verdict, a finding that is explained both by the high attrition rate of rape cases from the system prior to trial and by the outcome of trials (McCahill, Meyer & Fischman, 1979). Twenty years later, the situation was just as dismal in Minneapolis, where only 25% of reported rapes were accepted for prosecution and just 12% of the cases actually tried resulted in a guilty finding (Frazier & Haney, 1996; also see Frohman, 1991; 1997; 1998). Even when rape victims brought a legal advocate with them to interact with prosecutors, two of three rape victims had their cases turned down for prosecution, and 8 of 10 turndowns were against the victim's expressed wishes (Campbell, Sefl, Barnes, Ahrens, Wasco & Zaragosa-Diestfeld, 1999). Less than 1% of the intimate rapes, involving boyfriends, girl-friends, cohabiters, spouses, and exes of these types of relationships (including both reported and nonreported crimes), disclosed on a recent national survey, resulted in incarceration (Tjaden & Thoennes, 2000).

The Effectiveness of Criminal Justice Prevention of Sexual Violence Is Not Established

In the fraction of cases where sanctions are applied, the criminal justice system attempts to deter individuals from future offenses with incarceration and civil com-mitment, mandatory sexual offender registration (sometimes with and sometimes without neighborhood notification), and court-ordered treatment. Clearly incarcera-tion/commitment is effective in preventing sex offending in the community during the period of detention; however, more to the point is its effectiveness upon release. Prentky and colleagues report a 25-year recidivism rate for rapists of 39% (Prentky, Lee, Knight & Cerce, 1997; also see Looman, Abracen & Nicholaichuk, 2000). This rate is lower than the rates for nonsexual criminals (61–83%), but it must be inter-preted with caution because many sexual offenses are never reported to police and those that are reported frequently are not adjudicated or are downgraded to nonsex-ual offenses (Hanson, Scott & Steffy, 1995). The efficacy of sexual offender regis-tration is not well documented, but preliminary evidence suggests that rearrest rates are higher in the notification group (Schram, Miller & Milloy, 1995; Burdon & Gallagher, 2002). Although this difference could reflect the community's success in reporting law violations, it points out that neither notification nor nonnotification lowers the rate of reoffense. And, it may have unintended negative effects on reha-bilitation. Over 90% of sexual offenders stated that notification severely affected their ability to reintegrate into the community, leading to ostracism, harassment, loss of employment, eviction from housing, and breakup of relationships.

As for sexual offender treatment, there are approximately 710 sexual offender treatment programs in the United States, only 90 of which are prison based, suggest-ing that little treatment occurs in prisons. A recent quantitative review (Gallagher, Wilson, Hirschfield, Coggeshall & MacKenzie, 1999; also see also see Hall, 1995) compared outcomes for treated and untreated perpetrators. The evidence suggests that treated perpetrators do better than untreated perpetrators overall and that treat-ment provided in outpatient settings, as opposed to prisons, is more effective. There are multiple methodological problems in this area of research that are very difficult to solve within practical limitation, among them the sizable number of offenders who drop out of treatment (Harris & Rice, 2002). When perpetrators are mandated to seek treatment, they may enter at earlier stages of change (e.g., prior to recogniz-ing that they have a serious problem). Thus, they are less motivated to participate and will drop out if permitted (Cosyns, 1999). Completing treatment is one of the best predictors for successfully controlled sex offending (Anglin & Hser, 1991). Better outcomes are expected from treatment if treatment is initiated early in the course of an offending career and where policies are in place that help ensure retention (Burdon & Gallagher, 2002).

Criminal Justice Response Often Disappoints and Traumatizes Victims

Extensive reviews have documented that rape is traumatic and has long-lasting health consequences for victims (e.g., Crowell & Burgess, 1996; Koss, Goodman, Browne, Fitzgerald, Keita & Russo, 1994). Even the "minor" sexual offenses are upsetting to women (Cox, 1988; Smith & Morra, 1994; Riordan, 1999). Yet, women perceive that these crimes are trivialized. Disbelief and unsupportive comments by medical providers and law enforcement officers were most severe for victims of date and acquaintance rape as opposed to stranger rape (Campbell et al. 1999). Victims who participate in a civil or criminal trial learn that their role in the justice process is to serve as "evidentiary cannon fodder for the defense attorney" (Braithwaite & Daly, 1998, p. 154). The term *critogenic harms* denotes law-caused harms to litigants (Gutheil, Bursztajn, Brodsky & Strasburger, 2000; also see Des Rosiers, Feldthusen, Hankivsky, 1998; Frazier & Haney, 1996). Problematic features of the courtroom experience for sexual crime victims include the public nature of the procedure combined with the demand to retell intimate details of the offense, the sequestering of witnesses who may also be the victim's family and supporters, and defense attorney questioning that exacerbates self-blame. As these features are inherent to defendants' constitutional due process guarantees, there is little that can be done to mitigate them, short of a constitutional amendment. Data from 990 criminal trials for rape showed that most victims believed that rapists had more rights, thought the system was unfair, felt victims' rights were not protected, and expressed concerns that they were deprived of information about, and control over the handling of, their case (Frazier & Haney, 1996). Most bothersome to victims is the perpetrator's unmovable stance that he is not guilty of a crime (Holmstrom & Burgess, 1975, 1978; Madigan & Gamble, 1989; Martin & Powell, 1994; Matosian, 1993; Sanday, 1996). Although this denial of guilt again derives from defendants' constitutional rights, namely the presumption of innocence and the privilege against self-incrimination, failure to acknowledge intentional harm done to others has been shown in experimental studies to cause subjects to aggress against those who have intentionally harmed them. This effect is inhibited when the harm doer apologizes (Ohbuchi, Kameda & Agarie, 1989).

Many antiviolence advocates have poured energy over the past 20 years into lobbying for incremental reforms in law and retributive justice processing. These initiatives have increased the sentences for rape, removed spousal exclusions in rape laws, changed requirements that victims resist, removed corroboration requirements, added partial shields against revealing victim's sexual and social history, created civil commitment options for sexual offenders, and established mandatory sexual offender registration and notification. However, what is often unrecognized is that evaluations of these initiatives have revealed very limited to no effect on rates of reporting, charging, prosecuting, and convicting (Horney & Spohn, 1991; Matosian, 1993).

The Association for the Treatment of Sexual Abusers (ATSA, 2000) has concluded, on the basis of a review of the scientific evidence, that it is unlikely that even the most psychotic individuals lack control of their sexual behavior. They argue that sexual offenders *intend* to commit sexual crimes. Multiple factors constitute the origins of the deviant arousal patterns that characterize sexual offenders (see Malamuth; Barbaree, Blanchard & Langton; Knight & Sims-Knight; and Friedrich et al., this volume). But in the moments immediately proximal to committing an offense, control is possible if conditions are not conducive, and behavior is driven by a calculated assessment of the risks versus the perceived personal benefit according to the perspective of exchange theory (Homans, 1967). When the perceived costs of sexual offenses against women fail to outweigh the rewards, continued intentional injury and abuse of women is predicted. Moreover, the negative impact of the low accountability goes beyond individual wounds to the victim or reinforcement of sexual offending in perpetrators. Ultimately citizen acceptance supports and maintains sexual offending (Koss, 2000). Laws cannot successfully compete with norms that encourage and condone sexual violence. A more ideal approach to reducing perpetration of these classes of sexual offenses would intervene both at the level of holding perpetrators more accountable and at the level of reducing public acceptance.

IDENTIFIED SOLUTION

Restorative Justice and Community Conferencing

Restorative justice is a philosophy that places emphasis on repairing harm by empowering a victim-driven process. It emphasizes offender accountability through reparations and rehabilitation rather than punishment and aims to transform the community's role in addressing crime. Recent literature reveals numerous and escalating calls for application of restorative justice to crimes against women (Braithwaite & Daly, 1998; Bazemore, in press; Coker, 1999; Dignan & Cavadino, 1996; Hudson, 1998; Koss, 2000; Peled, Eiskovitz, Enosh & Winstok, 2000; Snider, 1998). Restorative justice models include (a) civil proceedings, (b) victim-offender reparation through mediation, and (c) community conference approaches. Civil justice for sexual offenses is a positive option, especially when responsible parties have substantial financial assets. When both parties lack resources, attorneys may sometimes takes these cases, permitting victims to pursue their case for expressive and symbolic purposes. However, representation often cannot be obtained, and our combined experienced with thousands of cases suggests that few women want litigation (Hopkins, in press). Also, civil justice like criminal justice is an adversarial process, with the attendant traumatizing features, and additionally involves comparative fault doctrine, which promotes victim blame (Bublick, 1999). Mediation's conceptual foundation is *inappropriate* for application to crimes against women because it fails to acknowledge the structural inequalities between the victim and offender (for a procedural critique, see Brown, 1994; Zellerer, 1996).

Many experts believe community conferencing comes the closest to achieving restorative justice ideals (Dignan & Cavadino, 1996). Community conferencing brings together victims, offenders, and their supporters for a face-to-face meeting in the presence of a facilitator, where they are encouraged to discuss the effects of the incident on them and to make a plan to repair the damage done and minimize the likelihood of further harm (Moore, as quoted in Stubbs, 1997, p. 110; also see Umbreit, 2000). The community conferencing approach to accountability places emphasis on accepting responsibility, making things right, fixing what is broken, and earning redemption. Community conferencing has been applied to juvenile justice and drunk driving worldwide, to juvenile justice in many U.S. jurisdictions, and to domestic violence, and child, sexual, and physical abuse in First Nation settings (e.g., Braithwaite & Daly, 1998, Coker, 1999; Nader, 1990; Pennell & Buford, 2000). Most outcome evaluations have involved applications to juvenile justice (for a review, see Umbreit & Coates, 1998). A number of performance indicators have been examined, including rate of restitution completion. Data from North American and Canadian programs (over 300 total) reveal that over 90% of restitution agreements are completed in one year compared to the typical 20–30% compliance achieved by court-ordered restitution following conviction (see Umbreit, 1996). Also relevant in the present context is the quasiexperimental evaluation of family group conferencing for families of sexually and physically abused children by Pennell and Burford (2000). Their data demonstrated that 8 of 10 conference plans had been carried out completely or in some measure, that two-thirds of participants felt their family was better off, and that substantiated reports of physical and sexual abuse of children were halved in the conference group, while they doubled in the comparison cases.

The following material is a brief overview of RESTORE (Responsibility and Equity for Sexual Transgressions Offering a Restorative Experience), a restorative justice–based, community conference approach to selected sexual offenses that our collaboration is implementing in Pima County, Arizona.

Design of the RESTORE Program

Candidate crimes are first known nonpenetration sexual offenses and sexual assaults involving perpetrators that used minimal force, have no prior arrests, and no record of domestic violence calls. There are four stages.

Referral Stage

Although victims report crimes to law enforcement, there are insufficient resources in the U.S. justice system to investigate and prosecute every case. In Pima County, law enforcement makes decisions about their response to reported crimes on the basis of criteria provided by prosecution. These criteria aim to identify that fraction of cases that is destined for trial. For example, 709 adult sexual assaults were reported to law enforcement in 2000. Of these, 361 (51%) were assigned for investigation, and only 18% were authorized for arrests (data collected by Pima County Interagency Council, 2001). One of the major policy changes brought about by RESTORE is implementation of new issuing criteria to guide law enforcement so that greater numbers of the kind of cases it addresses can flow through the system.

When a case meeting RESTORE's eligibility criteria is presented to prosecution by law enforcement, the Sex Crimes Unit schedules appointments with the victim and perpetrator (separately). A prosecutor explains what crime is being charged, what the options are, and what participation would entail. The victim meeting is first. As RESTORE is voluntary, if the victim does not want adjudication by restorative justice, it cannot be offered to the perpetrator. Given the numerous constitutional protections afforded defendants under the retributive system, why would a defense attorney advise a client to participate? Defense attorneys are ethically bound to give their clients choice. Offenders understand that it is important to avoid mandatory registration. RESTORE is a way to get some help for an offender while at the same time taking off the table the risk of incarceration and the risk of mandatory sexual offender registration, while offering no criminal record if the perpetrator completes the program and confidentiality unless the participant reoffends. There is a sliding scale fee assessed of the offender to participate, and he must acknowledge that the sexual act occurred.

Preparatory Stage

Preparation is a key to success in community conferencing. A case manager meets with the victim to complete the intake assessment, including a safety assessment; to decide who will be attending the conference with the victim; to prepare her to describe the injury she has experienced, and to formulate appropriate reparation expectations. Arrangements are made to identify someone trusted to step in for the victim should she be unable to speak for herself once in the conference. Family members may accompany the victim, and, in addition, a separate preparation meeting may be held with them if they are willing to attend. Items that victims or family members could suggest as reparation include payment of direct expenses, including lost time from work, medical and counseling expenses for the victim, service to surrogate victims, "stay-away" agreements, community service, formal apology, and answers to victim's questions, such as "Why did you choose to do this?" or "Was there something about me that caused you to choose me?" All redress plans contain the stipulation that the offender be evaluated by a state licensed sexual offender treatment provider and, if indicated, undergo treatment targeting deviant arousal patterns, alcohol/drug use, and anger. These forms of reparation may reduce the victim's future vulnerability to revictimization, and holding a face-to-face meeting may reduce fear of the offender. Involving the closest family and friends in the conference provides them all with societal validation of the victimization, which may translate into less negative emotional support during the victim's recovery. Research shows that it is the presence of negative support, not the quantity of positive support, that adversely affects recovery outcomes (Davis, Brickman & Baker, 1991).

A different (male) case manager meets with the perpetrator. The perpetrator signs a consent form that gives him confidentiality within the limits of mandatory reporting and informs him that he will have no record of conviction if he completes the program, but that he will be re-referred to prosecution if he fails. Then the coordinator completes an intake assessment, including a threat assessment to ensure that he poses no imminent danger of reoffending, despite the stringent eligibility criteria focusing on minimal risk perpetrators. RESTORE also works with an experienced sex offender evaluator to provide psychological assessment (and polygraphs for felonies) prior to the conference. At this time individual differences that could predict program outcome are assessed. The case coordinator also helps the perpetrator identify who will attend the conference from his family and friends, briefs him on expected conduct, and reviews the terms and conditions of supervision as well as the potential forms of redress that may be expected of him.

Conferencing Stage

The conference is held in a secure location (i.e., with weapons screening and availability of armed response to err on the side of caution). A pair of conference facilitators is appointed who have no prior contact with victim or offender. All participants sign confidentiality agreements, which are enforceable contracts. No written record is kept except of the redress plan. No attorneys are involved in the conference in an official capacity (some conference attendees could be attorneys by profession). The conference begins with the offender telling what he has done. Next, the victim describes the impact of his actions on her, followed by family and friends on both sides describing what they experienced. The perpetrator acknowledges and responds to what he hears. Then the facilitator turns conference participants toward developing the redress plan, which is primarily victim-driven, but which also benefits from input from other conference attendees and incorporates the recommendations for treatment made by the psychologist–evaluator (De Haan, 1990). The redress plan is written, signed by victim and offender, and specifies what will be done, the dates by which it will be completed, and how fulfillment will be documented.

The RESTORE conference also offers a unique approach to cultural competence. The conference brings together community members and family of the victim and perpetrator. Since most crime occurs within ethnic groups, conference participants are most often members of the same ethnic/cultural community. For example, 72.4% of the rapes of white women are by white men, and 83.5% of the rapes of African-American women are by African-American men (U.S. Department of Justice, 1997; figures on other ethnicities were not provided). The result is that their shared language, religion, economic status, race, and/or sexual orientation becomes the dominant culture of the conference. The RESTORE conference can be conducted entirely in Spanish when that is the preferred language of participants. Or, the redress plan can reflect culturally specific methods of healing, such as Native-American ceremonies or church involvement. The conference also allows offenders to air issues of adverse childhood, substance abuse, racial oppression, and economic disadvantage without framing these issues as exculpatory. It invites the community to express their solidarity while also repudiating violence against women. The conference format may help mitigate the racism and unequal access to justice that is perceived to permeate the U.S. criminal justice system by its nonincarceration focus and its use of a process that is shaped through the participation of other members of the victim's and offender's cultural groups.

Accountability/Supervision Stage

Case managers assigned to perpetrators will be responsible for supervising them for 12 months following the conference. They will have weekly telephone and monthly face-to-face contact, receive the documentation from perpetrators as stipulated in their redress plans, and track it against their timelines. In addition, they will apply standard conditions for supervision used by the Adult Probation Department. These conditions require that the offender will not possess or have contact with sexually stimulating or sexually oriented materials; will not pick up hitchhikers; will abide by any stay-away agreement he has made; and will be responsible for personal appearance and wear appropriate clothing, including undergarments, both at home and in public places. Standard conditions also include consenting to polygraph examination if the supervisor suspects that the perpetrator is not fully disclosing information. These conditions have been selected to be conservative in approaching victim and community safety and with the goal of producing demonstrable impact.

A community accountability board made up of volunteers with specialized knowledge in sexual assault meets monthly to receive supervision reports from case managers. Supervisees who falling behind are identified and counseled privately by the board up to three times to assist them in getting back on their plan. Those who fail are re-referred to prosecution for reconsideration of their case by the issuing attorney. Perpetrators who complete their plan appear personally before the board, with the victim and her community attending, if desired, for closure and reintegration into the community. Both the community conference and the community accountability board are designed to promote reintegration, by preserving relationships, involving an extended community circle, and providing the perpetrator with the means to make amends and reach an end point where he has earned the privilege of placing the offense behind him. The processes follow LaFond and Winnick's (this volume) outline for the therapeutic justice-based reentry court, except that RESTORE is preconviction, involves social service professionals in supervision, instead of limiting participation to judges, and expands therapeutic justice ideals beyond just offenders to everyone who has been affected.

Expected Benefits

A process and outcome evaluation plan has been developed to document program implementation, measure system and individual level outcomes, and facilitate replication by others. Our intentions in designing the program were to deliver justice that both heals (secondary prevention) and increases public safety (primary prevention) by:

- offering victims choice about how their violation is addressed and empowering them in the context of a nonadversarial process;
- responding decisively to first arrests for nonpenetration sexual offenses and date and acquaintance rape, thereby raising the ratio of costs to benefits and accomplishing both individual and general deterrence;
- maximizing the effectiveness of community-based sexual offender treatment by ordering and monitoring participation starting at the first known offense;
- multiplying the community's social control resources by providing a process to respond to the violation;
- maximizing reintegration by maintaining the perpetrator in the community and offering a way to make amends and a concrete duty-paid end point at which they are no longer stigmatized;
- improving recovery outcomes and reducing revictimization by providing victims with social validation and increasing access to services;
- accomplishing targeted prevention by aiming antiviolence communications to family and peer group of known perpetrators; and by
- contributing to general deterrence by disseminating RESTORE's activities through the public media, undercutting societal supports for gender-linked abuse, and increasing victim willingness to report crime.

REFERENCES

ABEL, G.G. (2001, November). *What We Have Learned ... Where We are Going.* Paper presented at the 1st Statewide Sexual Assault Conference Sponsored by the Arizona Attorney General's Office, Phoenix, AZ.

ABEL, G.G., BECKER, J.V., CUNNINGHAM-RATHER, J. & MITTLEMAN, M., et al. (1988). Multiple paraphilic diagnoses among sex offenders. *Bulletin of the American Academy of Psychiatry & the Law, 16(2),* 153–168.

ABEL, G.G. & OSBORN, C.A. (1992). The paraphilias: The extent and nature of sexually deviant and criminal behavior. In J.M.W. Bradford (Ed.), *Psychiatric Clinics of North America 15(3): 675–687.* Philadelphia, PA: W.B. Saunders Company.

ANGLIN, M.D. & HSER, Y. (1991). Criminal justice and the drug abusing offender: Policy issues of coerced treatment. *Behavioral Sciences and the Law, 9,* 243–267.

ATSA. (2000). Brief for the Association for the Treatment of Sexual Abusers as Amicus Curiae in support of petitioner. *Kansas vs. Crane.*

BARBAREE, H., BLANCHARD, R., LANGTON, C.M. (2003). The development of sexual aggression through the life span: Effects of age on sexual arousal and sexual recidivism in sex offenders. *Annal of the New York Academy of Sciences, 989.* This volume.

BAZEMORE, G. (2000). *Balance in the response to family violence: Challenging restorative principles.* Austin, TX: Communications Enterprises.

BRAITHWAITE, J. & DALY, K. (1998). Masculinities, violence, and communitarian control. In S.L. Miller (Ed.), *Crime control and women: Feminist implications of criminal justice policy* (pp. 151–172). Newbury Park, CA: Sage.

BROWN, J.G. (1994). The use of mediation to resolve criminal cases: A procedural critique. *Emory Law Journal, 43,* 1273–1279.

BUBLICK, E.M. (1999). Citizen no-duty rules: Rape victims and comparative fault. *Columbia Law Review, 99(6),* 1413–1419.

BURDON, W.M. & GALLAGHER, C.A. (2002). Coercion and sex offenders: Controlling sex-offending behavior through incapacitation and treatment. *Criminal Justice and Behavior, 2 (1),* 87–109.

CAMPBELL, R., SEFL, T., BARNES, H.E., AHRENS, C.E., WASCO, S.M. & ZARAGOZA-DIESFELD, Y. (1999). Community services for rape survivors: Enhancing psychological well-being or increasing trauma? *Journal of Consulting and Clinical Psychology, 67 (6),* 847–858.

COKER, D. (1999). Enhancing autonomy for battered women: Lessons from Navajo peacemaking. *UCLA Law Review, 47,* 1–111.

COSYNS, P. (1999). Treatment of sexual abusers in Belgium. *Journal of Interpersonal Violence, 14,* 396–410.

COX, D.J. (1988). Incidence and nature of male genital exposure behavior as reported by college women. *Journal of Sex Research, 24,* 227–234.

CROWELL, N.A. & BURGESS, A.W. (1996). *Understanding Violence Against Women.* Washington, DC: National Academy Press.

DAVIS, R.C., BRICKMAN, E. & BAKER, T. (1991). Supportive and unsupportive responses of others to rape victims: Effects on concurrent victim adjustment. *American Journal of Community Psychology, 19,* 443–451.

DE HAAN, W. (1990). *Politics of redress: Crime, punishment and penal abolition.* London: Academic Booksellers.

DES ROSIERS, N., FELDTHUSEN, B., HANKIVISKY, O.A.R. (1998). Legal compensation for sexual violence: Therapeutic Consequences for the judicial system. *Psychology, Public Policy, and Law, 4(1/2),* 433–451.

DIGNAN, J. & CAVADINO, M. (1996). Towards a framework for conceptualizing and evaluating models of criminal justice from a victim's perspective. *International Review of Victimology, 4,* 153–182.

ENGLISH, K. (2003). Sexual offender containment: Use of the postconviction polygraphy. *Annals of the New York Academy of Sciences, 989.* This volume.

ENGLISH, K., PULLEN, S. & JONES, L. (1996). *Managing adult sex offenders: A containment approach.* Lexington, KY: American Probation and Parole Association.

FISHER, B.S., CULLEN, F.T. & TURNER, M.G. (2000). The sexual victimization of college women. *Research Report (National Institute of Justice (U.S.).* Washington, DC: U.S. Dept. of Justice, Office of Justice Programs, National Institute of Justice.

FRAZIER, P.A. & HANEY, B. (1996). Sexual assault cases in the legal system: Police, prosecutor, and victim perspectives. *Law & Human Behavior, 20,* 607–628.

FROHMANN, L. (1991). Discrediting victims' allegations of sexual assault: Prosecutorial accounts of case rejections. *Social Problems, 38,* 213–226.

FROHMANN, L. (1997). Convictability and discordant locales: Reproducing race, class, and gender ideologies in prosecutorial decision-making. *Law and Society Review, 31,* 531–555.

FROHMANN, L. (1998). Constituting power in sexual assault cases: Prosecutorial strategies for victim management. *Social Problems, 45,* 393–407.

FRIEDRICH, W.N., DAVIES, W.H., FEHRER, E. & SRIGHT, J. (2003). Sexual behavior problems in preteen children: Developmental, ecological, and behavioral correlates. *Annals of the New York Academy of Sciences, 989.* This volume.

GALLAGHER, C.A., WILSON, D., HIRSCHFIELD, P., COGGESHALL, M.B. & MACKENZIE, D. (1999). A quantitative review of the effects of sex offender treatment on sexual reoffending. *Corrections Management Quarterly, 3,* 19–29.

GUTHEIL, T.G., BURSZTAJN, H., BRODSKY, A. & STRASBURGER, L.H. (2000). Preventing "critogenic" harms: Minimizing emotional injury from civil litigation. *Journal of Psychiatry & Law, 28,* 5–18.

HALL, N.G.C. (1995). Sexual offender recidivism revisited: A meta-analysis of recent treatment studies. *Journal of Consulting and Clinical Psychology, 63,* 802–809.

HANSON, R.K., SCOTT, H. & STEFFY, R.A. (1995). A comparison of child molesters and non-sexual criminals: Risk predictors and long-term recidivism. *Journal of Research in Crime and Delinquency, 32(3),* 325–337.

HOLMSTROM, L.L. & BURGESS, A.W. (1975). Rape: The victim and the criminal justice system. *International Journal of Criminology and Peneology, 3,* 101–110.

HOLMSTROM, L.L. & BURGESS, A.W. (1978). *The victim of rape: Institutional reactions.* New York: Wiley.

HOMANS, G.C. (1967). *The nature of social science.* New York: Harcourt, Brace & World.

HONEY, J. SPOHN, C. (1991). Rape law reform and instrumental change in six urban jurisdictions. *Law & Society Review, 25(1),* 117–153.

HOPKINS, C.Q. (2001). Rescripting relationships: Towards a Nuanced Theory of Intimate Violence as Sex Discrimination. *Virginia Journal of Social Policy and the Law,9,* 411–456.

Indecent exposure; classification (13-1402). Retrieved January 30, 2002, from http://www.azsexoffender.com/laws/1402/htm.

Intensive probation; evaluation; sentencing; criteria; limit; conditions (13-914). Retrieved January 30, 2002, from http://www.azleg.state.az.us/search/oop/qfullhit.asp?CiWebbHitsFil....

LONGO, R.E. & GROTH, A.N. (1983). Juvenile sexual offenses of adult rapists and child molesters. *International Journal of Offender Therapy and Comparative Criminology, 27 (2),* 150–155.

HUDSON, B. (1998). Restorative justice: The challenge of sexual and racial violence. *Journal of Law and Society, 25(2),* 237–256.

KNIGHT, R.A. (2003). The developmental antecedents of sexual coercion against women: Testing alternative hypotheses with structural equation modeling. *Annals of the New York Academy of Sciences, 989.* This volume.

KOSS, M.P. (2000). Blame, shame, and community justice responses to violence against women. *American Psychologist (Nov),* 1332–1343.

KOSS, M.P., GOODMAN, L.A., BROWNE, A., FITZGERALD, L.F., KEITA, G.P., RUSSO, N.F. (1994). *No safe haven: Male violence against women at home, at work, and in the community.* Washington, DC: American Psychological Association.

KNAPP, M. (1996). Treatment of sex offenders. In K. English, S. Pullen & L. Jones (Eds.), *Managing adult sex offenders: A containment approach* (pp. 13.2–13.16). Lexington, KY: American Probation and Parole Association.

LISAK, D. & MILLER, P.M. (2002). Repeated rape and multiple offending among undetected rapists. *Violence and Victims, 17(1),* 73–84.

LOOMAN J., ABRACEN J., NICHOLAICHUK, T.P. (2000). Recidivism among treated sexual offenders and matched control: data from the regional treatment centre. *Journal of Interpersonal Violence, 15(3),* 279–290.

MADIGAN, L. & GAMBLE, N.E. (1989). *The second rape: Society's continued betrayal of the victim.* Lanham, MD: Lexington Books.

MALAMUTH, N. (2003). Criminal and noncriminal sexual aggressors: Integrating psychopathy in a hierarchical–mediational confluence model. *Annals of the New York Academy of Sciences, 989.* This volume.

MARTIN, P.Y. & POWELL, M. (1994). Accounting for the second assault: Legal organizations' framing of rape victims. *Law and Social Inquiry, 14,* 853–890.

MATOSIAN, G. (1993). *Reproducing rape: Domination through talk in the courtroom.* Chicago: University of Chicago Press.

MCCAHILL, T.W., MEYER, L.C. & FISCHMAN, A.M. (1979). *The aftermath of rape.* Lexington, Mass: Lexington Books.

Misdemeanors and fines in Arizona according to statute 13-802. Retrieved January 30, 2002, from http://www.azleg.state.az.us/search/oop/qfullhit.asp? CiWebbHitsFil....

NADER, L. (1990). Origin of order and the dynamics of justice. In M.J. Lerner (Ed.), *New direction in the study of justice, law, and social control* (pp. 189–206). New York: Plenum Press.

OHBUCHI, K., KAMEDA, M. & AGARIE, N. (1989). Apology as aggression control: its role in mediating appraisal of and response to harm. *Journal of Personality and Social Psychology, 56(2),* 219–227.

PELED, E., EISKOVITZ, Z., ENOSH, G. & WINSTOK, Z. (2000). Choice and empowerment for battered women who stay: Toward a constructivist model. *Social Work, 45,* 9–21.

PENNELL, J. & BURFORD, G. (2000). Family group decision making: Protecting children and women. *Child Welfare, 79(2),* 131–158.

PIMA COUNTY INTERAGENCY COUNCIL. (2001). *Report Compiled by Pima County Attorney's Office for PCIC.* Tucson, AZ.

PRENTKY, R.A., LEE, A.F., KNIGHT, R.A. & CERCE, D. (1997). Recidivism rates among child molesters and rapists: a methodological analysis. *Law & Human Behavior, 21,* 635–659.

RICE, M.E. & HARRIS, G.T. (2003). The size and sign of treatment effects in sex offender therapy. *Annals of the New York Academy of Sciences, 989.* This volume.

RIORDAN, S. (1999). Indecent exposure: The impact upon the victim's fear of sexual crime. *Journal of Forensic Psychiatry, 10, (2),* 309–316.

SANDAY, P.R. (1996). *A woman scorned: Acquaintance rape on trial.* New York: Doubleday.

SCHRAM, L.B., MILLER, L.L. & MILLOY, C. (1995). A sentencing alternative for sex offenders: A study of decision making and recidivism. *Journal of Interpersonal Violence, 10 (4),* 487–502.

SMITH, M.D. & MORRA, N.N. (1994). Obscene and threatening telephone calls to women: Data from a Canadian National Survey. *Gender and Society, 8, (4),* 584–596.

SNIDER, L. (1998). Feminism, punishment, and the potential of empowerment. In K. Daly & L. Maher (Eds.), *Criminology at the crossroads: Feminist readings in crime and justice* (pp. 246–261). New York: Oxford University Press.

STRATE, D.C., JONES, I., PULLEN, S. & ENGLISH, K. (1996). Criminal justice policies and sex offender denial. In K. English, S. Pullen & L. Jones (Eds.), *Managing adult sex offenders: A containment approach* (pp. 4–9). Lexington, KY: American Probation and Parole Association.

STUBBS, J. (1997). Shame, defiance, and violence against women: A critical analysis of "communitarian" conferencing. In S. Cook & J. Bessant (Eds.), *Women's encounters with violence: Australian experiences* (pp. 109–126). Thousand Oaks, CA, US: Sage Publications.

TJADEN, P. & THOENNES, N. (1998). *Prevalence, incidence, and consequences of violence against women: Findings from the National Violence Against Women Survey* (National Institute of Justice Centers for Disease Control and Prevention Research in Brief, Report No. NCJ-172837). Washington, DC: U.S. Department of Justice, National Institute of Justice.

TJADEN, P. & THOENNES, N. (2000). *Extent, nature, and consequences of intimate partner violence: Findings from the National Violence against Women Survey* (Report No. NCJ-181867). Washington, DC: U.S. Department of Justice, Office of Justice Programs.

UMBREIT, M.S. (1996). Restorative justice through mediation: The impact of offenders facing their victims in Oakland. *The Journal of Law and Social Work, 5(1),* 1–13

UMBREIT, M.S. (2000). Homicide offenders meet the offender prior to execution: reply to Radelet and Borg. *Homicide Studies: An Interdisciplinary & International Journal, 4(1),* 93–97.

UMBREIT, M.S. & COATES, R.B. (1998). *Multi-cultural implications of restorative justice: potential pitfalls and dangers.* Washington, DC: Office of Victims of Crime, US Dept. of Justice.

ZELLERER, E. (1996). Community-based justice and violence against women: issues of gender and race. *International Journal of Comparative and Applied Criminal Justice, 20 (1,2),* 233–234.

Juvenile Sexual Offenders

Characteristics, Interventions, and Policy Issues

JUDITH V. BECKER AND SCOTIA J. HICKS

Department of Psychology, University of Arizona. Tucson, Arizona 85721, USA

ABSTRACT: The incidence and prevalence of sexual offenses committed by juveniles are examined and current policies regarding juvenile sexual offenders are evaluated by considering the relevant psychological literature. Characteristics of juvenile sex offenders are reviewed, noting the heterogeneity of this population. Recent research on developmental pathways and typologies is presented, intervention strategies are reviewed, and recommendations for research and policy are made.

KEYWORDS: juvenile sexual offenders; public policy; public health; mental health

INTRODUCTION

Although the problem of sexual abuse and assault has been systematically addressed by groups and organizations devoted to its study and prevention for the last 30-40 years, most of this research has been devoted to interventions at the tertiary level of health care. It is only very recently that mental health professionals, medical professionals, and policymakers have begun to consider sexual violence from a public health perspective. In 1995, the Centers for Disease Control and Prevention (CDC) declared violence to be a public health priority in the United States (Foege, Rosenberg & Mercy, 1995). Since then, there has been a perspective shift in sexual assault research, toward prioritizing the prevention of first occurrences of sexual violence (STOP IT NOW! 2002).

INCIDENCE, PREVALENCE, AND DETRIMENTAL EFFECTS OF SEXUAL VIOLENCE

The long-standing need for effective approaches to the problem of sexual violence is evidenced by its incidence, prevalence, and detrimental effects. According to the FBI's Uniform Crime Report, there were 90,186 forcible rapes in 2000 (UCR,

Address for correspondence: Judith V. Becker, Ph.D., Department of Psychology, Room 312, P.O. Box 210068, Tucson, AZ 85721. Voice: 520-621-7455.
JVBecker@u.arizona.edu

Ann. N.Y. Acad. Sci. 989: 397–410 (2003). © 2003 New York Academy of Sciences.

2001), and, although the complete statistics for 2001 are still unavailable, preliminary analyses indicate that the incidence of reported rapes has risen another 0.2%
(UCR Preliminary Report, 2002). These figures represent only "forcible rapes,"
which are somewhat narrowly defined by the FBI as "the carnal knowledge of a
female forcibly and against her will" (UCR, 1999). This narrow definition, coupled
with research findings indicating that most sexual assaults go unreported
(Kilpatrick, Edmunds & Seymour, 1992; Crowell & Burgess, 1996; Bureau of
Justice Statistics, 1996), suggests that the incidence of forcible rapes as reported in
the UCR is actually a significant underestimate of the true incidence of sexual
violence in the United States.

Studies on the prevalence of sexual violence reveal that rates vary from 13%–
30% for females (Kilpatrick, Edmunds & Seymour, 1992; Koss, 1993; Resnick,
Kilpatrick, Dansky, Saunders & Best, 1993; and Russell, 1986) and 5%–16% for
men (Finkelhor, Hotaling, Lewis & Smith, 1990; Finkelhor, 1994; and Berliner &
Elliott, 1996). As with the incidence of sexual violence, however, underreporting
likely results in an underestimate of the prevalence of sexual assault.

Part of the rationale for conceptualizing sexual violence as a public health issue
also stems from its association with negative effects on the health of its victims.
Victimization through sexual violence has been associated with a variety of mental
health problems, including depression, anxiety, posttraumatic stress disorder, and increased risk for suicide (Friedrich, Beilke & Urquiza, 1988; Gidyz & Koss, 1989;
Holmes & Slap, 1999; McLeer, Deblinger, Atkins, Ralphe & Foa, 1988). It has also
been associated with problems that affect physical health, such as sexually transmitted diseases (Lindegren, Hanson, Hammett, Beil, Fleming & Ward, 1998) and
substance abuse (Crowell & Burgess, 1996).

Taken together, these research findings on the incidence, prevalence, and detrimental effects of sexual assault indicate the need to identify sexual violence as a public health priority. Because of underreporting, the problem of sexual violence is
likely even more widespread than national figures indicate.

JUVENILE SEXUAL OFFENDERS

A significant portion of sexual violence in the United States is perpetrated by
juveniles. According to the FBI's Uniform Crime Report (2001), in 2000, 16.4% of
arrests for forcible rape and 18.6% of arrests for other sex offenses (defined as
offenses other than forcible rape and prostitution) were of individuals under the age
of 18. Furthermore, 6.4% of arrests for forcible rape and 9.7% of arrests for other
sexual offenses were of individuals under the age of 15, including individuals as
young as 10 years of age. These figures are comparable to those of previous years,
indicating that despite fluctuating rates of sexual violence, juveniles consistently account for almost 20% of arrests for rape and other sex offenses. Because the UCR
contains only information on juveniles who have been apprehended and arrested, it
is likely that the number of juvenile sexual offenders is actually higher than is
reflected in these reports. Other research supports this hypothesis, indicating that
almost half of all cases of child molestation are committed each year by juveniles
(Barbaree, Hudson & Seto, 1993).

RESEARCH FINDINGS ON JUVENILE SEXUAL OFFENDERS

There have been many misconceptions regarding juveniles with sexual behavior problems and juveniles who commit sexual offenses, including the beliefs that juvenile sexual offenders will become adult sexual offenders and that juvenile sexual offenders are similar in most ways to adult sexual offenders. The National Center on Sexual Behavior of Youth recently (2002) published a fact sheet in which they describe common misperceptions and current evidence related to them. This section will focus on what is known regarding the characteristics, developmental pathways, and typologies of juvenile sexual offenders and the intervention strategies that can be used with young offenders.

Characteristics of Juvenile Sexual Offenders

In reviewing the literature on juvenile sexual offenders, the majority of published studies focus on characteristics of male juvenile sexual offenders, as opposed to female sexual offenders and young children who have sexual behavior problems. Juveniles who commit sexual offenses show many of the same types of sexually abusive behaviors as do adults. Behaviors can range from voyeurism and exhibitionism to behaviors involving penetration. As with adults, juveniles have molested both male and female children. The age range of their victims may also vary (Becker & Hunter, 1997).

Fehrenbach, Smith, Monastersky & Deisher (1986) reported on sexual offense behaviors for a sample of 305 juvenile sexual offenders. In this study, the most common sexual offenses found to have been committed by juveniles were fondling (59%), followed by rape (23%), exhibitionism (11%), and other noncontact offenses (7%). Similarly, Miranda & Corcoran (2000) compared the perpetration characteristics of male juvenile and adult sexual offenders. Results indicated that juveniles engaged in intrafamilial sexual abuse more frequently (67%) than adults (21%), and used force more frequently than adults. In contrast, juveniles were less likely to engage in sexual behaviors involving penetration (13%) than did adults (41%), and adult offenders had committed more sexually abusive incidents as compared to juveniles.

Several literature reviews have provided characteristics of a juvenile sexual offender population (Davis & Leitenberg, 1987; Becker et al., 1993; and Righthand & Welch, 2001). Davis & Leitenberg (1987) reviewed the available literature up to that point in time on juvenile sexual offenders. They reported that 90% of sex offenses committed by juveniles were committed by males. They also reported that male juvenile sexual offenders appeared to have higher frequencies of maltreatment in their backgrounds than nonoffenders, as well as frequent behavioral and/or school disturbances. Becker, Harris & Sales (1993) reviewed 73 articles that appeared in the professional literature and published a critical review of the research up to that point in time. This review concluded that juvenile sexual offenders are a heterogeneous group of individuals and noted that an empirically derived and validated classification system describing the heterogeneity had not been developed. In summarizing the available literature to date, Becker et al. (1993) reported that the following personality characteristics were frequently reported among juvenile sexual offenders: a lack of social interactional skills, a history of conduct-disordered behavior, serious learning problems, lack of impulse control, and depressive symptomatology.

Graves, Openshaw, Ascione & Ericksen (1996) used meta-analysis to evaluate empirical data relating to demographic characteristics of juvenile sexual offenders. These authors reported that three categories of juvenile sexual offender emerged based on demographic characteristics: *pedophilic offender, sexual assault offender,* and *mixed offense offender.* Pedophilic offenders were described as lacking confidence in their ability to engage in social interactions and being socially isolated from their peers. Sexual assault offenders were characterized as juveniles whose first offenses were reported between the ages of 13 and 15, who tended to victimize more females than males, and offended against victims of varying age groups. Those classified as mixed offense offenders had committed a variety of offenses involving children much younger than themselves. Their offenses also included exhibitionism, voyeurism, frotteurism, and other forms of sexual behavior. Graves et al. described this mixed offense offenders category as having the most widespread and severe social and psychological problems.

Becker (1998) reported on literature reflecting on the assessment of comorbid psychological and/or psychiatric problems in a juvenile sexual offender population. Kavoussi, Kaplan & Becker (1998), reported that of the juvenile sexual offenders interviewed, conduct disorder was the most common (48%) diagnosis. Becker, Kaplan, Tenke & Tarthelini (1991) assessed depressive symptomatology in a sample of youthful sexual offenders using the Beck Depression Inventory, and found high rates of depressive symptomatology. Becker & Stein (1991) reported that 61% of a sample of juvenile sexual offenders seen at an outpatient clinic admitted to alcohol consumption and 39% reported illegal drug usage.

Righthand & Welch (2001), in reviewing the literature, also observed that juvenile sexual offenders are a heterogeneous group. They noted that juvenile sexual offenders frequently engage in nonsexual criminal and antisocial behavior as well as sexual offending behavior. In a number of cases, juvenile sexual offenders were also found to have had childhood experiences of being physically abused, neglected, and witnessing family violence.

Developmental Pathways and Typologies

Although a number of theories have been proposed to explain the etiology of sexually inappropriate behavior on the part of adults, there is no generally accepted theory regarding juvenile sexual offending. A number of factors, however, have received empirical and clinical attention in the literature. These factors include history of maltreatment, exposure to pornography, substance abuse, and exposure to aggressive role models (Becker & Hunter, 1997). Ryan, Lane, Davis & Isaac (1987) describe a sexual abuse cycle. This model begins with the juvenile's having a negative self-image, resulting in increased probability of maladaptive coping strategies when confronted with negative responses. This negative self-image leads the juvenile to predict a negative reaction from others. In an effort to protect against anticipated rejection, the juvenile becomes socially isolated, withdrawn, and fantasizes to compensate for his lack of control and powerlessness. The sexual offense occurs, leading to more negative self-image and thoughts of rejection, and then becomes a repetitive cycle.

Becker & Kaplan (1988) propose a model in which the first sexual offense results from a combination of individual characteristics, including lack of social skills, history of nonsexual deviance, family variables, and social environment variables such as social isolation and antisocial behavior. Following the commission of the first sexual offense, three possible paths may ensue: a dead-end path, in which the juvenile commits no further crimes; a delinquency path, in which the juvenile not only commits other sexual offenses but also engages in general nonsex offenses and deviant behaviors; and a sexual interest path, in which the juvenile continues to commit sexual offenses and often develops a paraphilic arousal pattern. It is important to note that none of the above-mentioned models has been empirically validated.

Kobayashi, Sales, Becker, Figueredo & Kaplan (1995), using structural equations modeling, tested a theoretical model of the etiology of deviant sexual aggression in male juvenile sexual offenders. This model included several family factors, including perceived parental deviance, child physical and sexual abuse history, and child bonding with parents. Results indicated that physical abuse by fathers and sexual abuse by males increased sexual aggression by juveniles. Bonding to mothers was found to decrease sexual aggression.

Johnson & Knight (2000) explored developmental pathways among childhood abuse, juvenile delinquency, and personality dimensions leading to juvenile sexual coercion. Those authors used a retrospective self-report inventory and assessed the extent to which juveniles reported experiencing childhood trauma, engaged in delinquent behavior, and exhibited cognitive biases. Subjects consisted of 122 juvenile sexual offenders with a mean age of 15.9 years who were given the computer and written versions of the Multidimensional Assessment of Sex and Aggression (MASA). Path analysis was used and results indicated that sexually coercive behavior patterns in juvenile offenders were predicted by multiple developmental antecedents. Two paths emerged, one labeled Sexual Compulsivity and the other Hypermasculinity. These paths, through the use of misogynistic fantasies, significantly discriminated those juvenile sexual offenders who were verbally and physically coercive from those juvenile offenders who did not report using force in their offenses. The authors also suggested that alcohol abuse may play a more prominent role in the expression of sexually aggressive behavior in juveniles than has previously been noted.

Attempts have been made to develop typologies of juvenile male sexual offenders. O'Brien & Bera (1986) developed a classification system based on such factors as victim age, general delinquency, family functioning, sexual history, and personality. They identified seven subgroups: Naïve Experimenter, Undersocialized Child Exploiter, Pseudosocialized Child Exploiter, Sexual Aggressive, Sexual Compulsive, Disturbed Impulsive, and Group Influenced. To date, there do not appear to be any empirical data evaluating this classification system.

Smith, Monastersky & Deisher (1987) evaluated MMPI data from juvenile male sexual offenders. Utilizing a cluster analysis, four groups emerged. Group I was described as shy, emotionally overcontrolled, and isolated. Group II was found to be narcissistic, insecure, argumentative, and disturbed. Group III was prone to violent outbursts, outgoing, and honest, and Group IV was described as mistrustful, impulsive, and undersocialized. More recently, Worling (2001) utilizing California Personality Inventory scores from 112 juvenile male sexual offenders, attempted to define personality-based subgroups of juvenile male offenders. Worling also examined whether there was any relationship between group assignment and sexual or nonsexual recidivism. A cluster analysis of factor-derived scores indicated four personality-based subgroups: Antisocial/Impulsive, Unusual/Isolated, Overcontrolled/ Reserved and Confident/Aggressive. Juvenile subgroup membership was unrelated to victim age, victim gender, and offender history of sexual victimization. Worling reported that the four-group typology derived from the CPI based on personality functioning was "remarkably similar" to that found by Smith et al. (1987).

Recidivism data had been collected on these youth for a period of 2–4 years. Those offenders in the more pathological groups (Antisocial/Impulsive and Unusual/Isolated) were more likely to be charged with subsequent violent (both sexual and nonsexual) or nonviolent offenses. Thirty-three percent of the offenders in the Overcontrolled/Reserved and Confident/Aggressive groups had subsequent criminal charges for any type of criminal offense after an average of 6 years. Fifty-five percent of the offenders from the Antisocial/Impulsive and Unusual/Isolated groups had further charges. Regarding subsequent charges for sexual offending, 11% of the juveniles received subsequent charges for a sexual offense and there was no difference across the four personality groups. Worling notes that this study lends support to the fact that juvenile sexual offenders are not a homogeneous group and that assessing for significant differences in personality functioning has clinical importance in regard to both etiology and treatment.

Hunter, Figueredo, Malamuth & Becker (in press) have undertaken a series of research studies in an attempt to identify developmental pathways and, ultimately, a typology for juvenile male sexual offenders. Male juvenile sexual offenders who offended against prepubescent children were contrasted with male juvenile offenders who targeted pubescent and postpubescent females. Path analyses revealed that those juveniles who targeted prepubescent children had greater deficits in psychosocial functioning and used less force in the commission of the sexual offense, and that their victims were more likely to be relatives. Results indicated that childhood physical abuse by a father or stepfather and exposure to violence against females were associated with higher levels of anxiety and depression among the juvenile offenders. Those juveniles who had been sexually victimized by a nonrelative male were more likely to sexually offend against a male child. This study's authors note that the findings hold implications for prevention programming. The youths in this study had high levels of exposure to child maltreatment, abuse of females, and male-modeled antisocial behavior.

Intervention Strategies

Studies examining developmental pathways and the development of typologies have important implications for treatment of juvenile sexual offenders. Given the heterogeneity of juvenile sexual offenders, and the fact that typologies are emerging, treatment should be individualized to address the specific needs of the juvenile relative to personality and other characteristics. A "one size fits all" approach is not recommended, given the differing psychological needs of these youth.

Unfortunately, there is a paucity of research reports on treatment outcome. To date, there are only two controlled treatment outcome studies in the psychological literature. Borduin, Henggeler, Blaske & Stein (1990) conducted a controlled outcome study comparing the effectiveness of Multisystemic Therapy (MST) with individual therapy. MST is an ecologically focused treatment that addresses multiple determinants of behavior. Youth were randomly assigned to either treatment condition. Juveniles were followed for an average of 37 months. Seventy-five perecnt of youths who received individual therapy "recidivated," compared with 12.5% of those who received MST. This was a well-designed and executed study. The sample size, however, was very small, and the study has not as yet been replicated.

Lab, Shields & Schondel (1993) evaluated a court-based sexual offender outpatient treatment program. Youth were assigned either to the court-based program, which was 20 weeks in duration, or to a non–sexually specific treatment program in the community. Recidivism rates were low for both groups, and those who received the specialized treatment did not evidence better rates than those who received treatment that was regularly offered in the community. Although a comparison group was used, the juveniles were not randomly assigned to treatment groups. They were instead assigned to groups on the basis of their risk status.

There have been other treatment outcome reports in the empirical literature, although these studies were not controlled (Becker, Kaplan & Kavoussi, 1988; Hunter & Santos, 1990; Kaplan, Morales & Becker, 1993; Mazur & Michael, 1992). Treatments employed by Becker et al. and Kaplan et al. used outpatient cognitive–behavioral interventions. Hunter & Santos used cognitive–behavioral interventions and family therapy within a residential treatment center. Mazur and Michael used a family/sexual offender–specific outpatient treatment.

More recently, Worling and Curwen (2000) evaluated a specialized community-based treatment for juvenile sexual offenders. Fifty-eight juvenile offenders participated in treatment using a cognitive–behavioral and relapse prevention model. Youth received individual therapy, group therapy, and family therapy. Recidivism data were collected on sexual, violent nonsexual, and nonviolent offenses for all groups. Of those juveniles who received the treatment, 5.17% reoffended sexually, 18.9% engaged in violent nonsexual offenses, and 20.7% engaged in nonviolent offenses. The comparison group had higher rates of recidivism, with 17.8% reoffending sexually, 32.2% reoffending violent nonsexually, and 50% engaging in nonviolent recidivistic acts. In looking at facts that predicted recidivism, the authors reported that sexual recidivism was predicted by sexual interest in children, and nonsexual recidivism was predicted by factors commonly related to delinquency, including low self-esteem, history of previous offenses, and antisocial personality.

Schram, Milloy & Rowe (1991) examined service delivery in ten treatment programs for juvenile sexual offenders in the state of Washington. The rate of sexual recidivism at a one-year follow-up period for youth who had been in these programs was 10%.

A critique of existing treatment studies with juvenile sexual offenders and directions for service delivery and research are provided by Brown & Kolko (1998). These authors note that the treatment outcome literature is still developing, although initial reports indicate that juvenile sexual offenders and their family members appear responsive to treatment. They note, however, that the relationship between risk assessment, treatment, and recidivism warrants further investigation. These authors propose that our society needs to develop, implement, and evaluate services for juvenile sexual offenders on a systematic basis. The authors recommend that the first step is conducting controlled clinical trials and bridging the gap between clinical trials and services research for juvenile sexual offenders.

Furthermore, in order to more accurately identify those youth who are at risk for reoffending, it is imperative that empirically based risk assessment instruments be developed. At the present time, there are two empirically guided juvenile risk assessment instruments. Worling and Curwen (2001) have developed an empirically guided clinical judgment assessment to assist in predicting juvenile sexual recidivism. The authors note that it is designed to assist evaluators to estimate the risk of a sexual reoffense for individuals aged 12–18 who have previously committed a sexual assault. Twenty-five items are rated. These items are based on the sexual offender risk assessment literature. Prentky, Harris, Frizzell & Righthand (2000) describe the development and evaluation of an actuarial risk assessment protocol for use with juvenile sexual offenders. Twenty-three items are rated. These instruments are a first start in assisting clinicians in evaluating risk for juvenile sexual offenders. Cross-validation of these instruments is still needed.

JUVENILE JUSTICE APPROACH TO THE PROBLEM OF JUVENILE SEXUAL OFFENDING

While the mental health field has striven to improve the state of knowledge concerning characteristics, developmental pathways, and treatments for juvenile sexual offenders, in the absence of clear answers, and in response to the societal problem of sexual abuse and aggression, lawmakers have forged ahead with policies designed to address juvenile sex offending. One approach to the problem of juvenile sexual offenders has been to pass legislation that changes the way juvenile offenders are handled at various stages of the legal process. While the balance of interests is an important consideration in policymaking, the legislative changes regarding juvenile sexual offenders have focused primarily on the protection of society. Consequently, juveniles are being held legally accountable for their criminal actions, more so than in the past. Thus far, the reforms that have been used in addressing the problem of juvenile sexual offending include: waivers to adult court; sentencing guidelines; public access to juvenile offense records; community notification and registration; and mandated treatment.

Waivers to Adult Court

One way that the judicial system has attempted to deal with juvenile sexual offenders has been to waive their cases from juvenile courts to adult courts. The result of this process is that juveniles can be tried as adults for alleged sexual offenses. While courts may use their discretion to waive only cases that are deemed serious enough to warrant trial in an adult court, the trends indicate that even delinquency cases are increasingly waived to adult courts. In fact, during the period between 1985 and 1994, waivers of delinquency cases to adult courts increased by more than 70% (National Center for Juvenile Justice, 1998). Most states have increased the opportunity for such waivers by lowering the age at which juveniles may be tried as adults, and 20 states do not require juveniles to be a minimum age in order to be tried as adults (National Center for Juvenile Justice, 1998).

Sentencing Guidelines

Juveniles who are convicted of sexual offenses as adults are more likely to serve time than are juveniles who remain within the juvenile justice system. Part of the reason for this may be attributable to the difference in goals between the retributive-justice-oriented adult criminal system and the more rehabilitation-oriented juvenile court. However, it is also the case that public dissatisfaction with perceived "light" sentences for violent offenders has resulted in legislation that mandates minimum sentences for repeat offenders. Such "three strikes" laws may therefore be applied to juvenile offenders who recidivate and are waived to adult courts.

Public Access to Juvenile Offense Records

Another trend in juvenile justice legislation has been to permit public access to the kinds of juvenile criminal records that have traditionally been sealed and kept confidential. While there are various restrictions to such access, some states allow open juvenile hearings, and more than half of the states allow at least limited public access to juvenile court records (Center for Sex Offender Management, 1999).

Community Notification and Registration

Many states have extended the community notification and registration laws that apply to adult sexual offenders to juvenile offenders. As an application of "Megan's Law," which requires law enforcement agencies to disseminate information about sexual offenders necessary to public safety, states can now also require juveniles to register as sexual offenders. Almost 30 states (Center for Sex Offender Management, 1999) have enacted legislation explicitly requiring juvenile sexual offenders to register in this manner.

Mandated Treatment

A final legislative approach to juvenile sexual offending has been to offer adjudicated juveniles mandated treatment as an alternative to criminal punishment. Under this model, the juvenile receives treatment in the community from a mental health provider, and case management/supervision is provided by law enforcement in a parole or probation role. The treatment provider and supervisor submit reports to the court regarding compliance with treatment and supervision. Continued participation and cooperation is a condition of sentence suspension, and therefore juveniles who do not comply can be brought back to court for review (Center for Sex Offender Management, 1999).

CRITIQUE OF JUVENILE JUSTICE APPROACHES

It appears that the legislative trends described above were intended to shift the balance of interests in juvenile justice in such a way as to emphasize public safety and encourage individual responsibility of juvenile offenders for their actions. However, there does not currently appear to be any convincing evidence to support these policies in terms of their effect on public safety or on juvenile sexual offending. Although changes in legislation regarding juvenile offenders have been implemented in more than 90% of the states (Center for Sex Offender Management, 1999) the representation of juvenile sexual offenders in the criminal justice system has remained relatively constant over time.

Conceptually speaking, there are three main factors that may contribute to the ineffectiveness of current legislative trends. First, the policies being enacted assume that juvenile offenders are simply smaller, younger versions of adult sexual offenders. That is, it is assumed that they are on a singular trajectory to becoming adult sexual offenders (Chaffin & Bonner, 1998). This assumption in part underlies waivers of juvenile sexual offenders to adult courts. Accordingly, if juvenile sexual offenders are sufficiently similar to adult sexual offenders, they should be subjected to the same legal processes and interventions as adult sexual offenders. This assumption also underlies policies regarding juvenile sexual offender registration and community notification, public accessibility to juvenile court records, and sentencing guidelines. These policies all apply restrictions and penalties that have traditionally been within the realm of the adult criminal system to juvenile offenders. The assumption that juvenile sexual offenders inevitably become adult sexual offenders, however, is unsupported by the literature (e.g., Chaffin & Bonner, 1998). By treating juveniles as adults, courts may be failing to take advantage of the supervision, family involvement, and treatment that would be available through the juvenile system. In addition, by subjecting juveniles to incarceration and putting them in contact with serious adult offenders, these policies may even increase juveniles' likelihood of recidivating.

Second, despite the change in focus, from an emphasis on rehabilitation in juvenile justice to an emphasis on punishment and public safety, it is not clear that the legislative trends enacted are actually conducive to protecting the public. In the same way that traditional legal methods have not significantly reduced recidivism for adult sexual offenders, it seems unlikely that new policies for juveniles will prevent juvenile sexual offenders from reoffending or deter new offenders from committing their first offenses. Community notification, in particular, has suffered several challenges to implementation with adult sexual offenders, including concern about vigilantism, impediments to community reintegration of offenders, constitutionality issues, and unintended consequences such as increases in plea bargaining, lack of offender compliance with registration, and a reluctance to report and bring charges in certain kinds of cases (e.g., intrafamilial offenders) (Center for Sex Offender Management, 1997). It is likely that community notification and registration policies will face similar problems as applied to juveniles.

Third, although societal concern about sex offending behavior has motivated a shift toward retributive justice for juveniles, to the extent that rehabilitation is still a secondary goal, these legislative trends may prove to be antitherapeutic. First, incarceration removes juveniles from resources in their families, schools and communities. As discussed previously, the most promising interventions for juvenile sexual offenders incorporate these resources in treatment, rather than focusing solely on the juvenile. Second, contact with serious adult offenders in the correctional system, some of whom are likely to be antisocial, may contribute to the further socialization of juveniles as offenders. Such socialization would be at odds with the goal of reintegrating juvenile offenders into their communities. Third, imposing adult penalties for juvenile sexual offenders may provide motivation for them to deny crimes, an impediment to the goal of increasing accountability for criminal actions and also a hindrance to successful treatment.

RESEARCH AND POLICY RECOMMENDATIONS

Clearly, the problem of sexual violence in the United States warrants prioritization. The scope of the problem, as measured by its incidence, prevalence, and detrimental effects is vast and its personal costs to individual victims are immeasurable. Despite the attempt to address societal concerns about violent crime by creating more serious legal consequences for offenders, it is not clear that the legislative trends discussed above have produced their intended results.

In terms of mental health research, although there has been a growth of treatment programs since the late 1980s, there remains a paucity of empirical literature to guide intervention strategies for juvenile sexual offenders. Progress is being made as per the work of Johnson & Knight (2000) in examining developmental pathways as well as the work of Hunter & colleagues (as well as Worling, 2001) in developing typologies. Treatment reports to date indicate relatively low sexual recidivism rates for those juveniles who have received treatment.

From a clinical standpoint, Brown & Kolko (1998) provide comprehensive recommendations for research to be conducted on juvenile sexual offenders. These recommendations include identifying ecological factors potentially related to sexual offending (e.g., family, peer, school and community characteristics); examining the relationship of typologies to treatment outcome and long-term adjustment; matching case characteristics and treatment components; identifying needed changes in service delivery; evaluating the efficacy of alternative models and community-based treatments; and evaluating the cost-effectiveness and maintenance effects of existing treatments.

Furthermore, in order to effectively provide interventions to juvenile offenders, it is critical that comprehensive assessments be conducted and that evidence-based interventions be used. Research will help inform us ultimately as to which youth are at risk for engaging in sexually inappropriate behavior, how to best assess these youth and their family members, and how to best intervene.

From a policy perspective, it is recommended that, where possible, legislation concerning juvenile sexual offenders be informed by methodologically sound research findings. For example, as discussed in Trivits & Reppucci's (2002) analysis of Megan's Law, to the extent that registration and community notification legislation is based on offenders' risk of recidivism, the application of these policies to juveniles should be tempered by differences between the recidivism rates of juveniles and adults. By taking differences between adults and juveniles into account, the justice system could use a graded system, where juvenile justice policies would be applied to individual juveniles on the basis of their specific offense history and resulting risk.

In order to reconcile the issues of policy and mental health research for juvenile sexual offenders, a public health approach, focusing on the prevention of sexual offending, is recommended. Through improved research, the mental health field will ideally be able to offer accurate prevalence rates of sexual assault, risk factors, evaluation of current treatment programming, and information about what currently works (McMahon, 1997). By focusing on prevention and early intervention, a public health approach may provide a more optimistic alternative to the concept of rehabilitation, while at the same time limiting the need for punitive legislation for juveniles.

REFERENCES

BARBAREE, H.E., HUDSON, S.M. & SETO, M.C. (1993). Sexual assault in society: The role of the juvenile offender. In: H.E. Barbaree, W.L. Marshall & S.W. Hudson (Eds.), *The juvenile sex offender.* New York: Guilford.

BECKER, J.V. (1998). What we know about the characteristics and treatment of juveniles who have committed sexual offenses. *Child maltreatment, 3,* 317–329.

BECKER, J.V., HARRIS, C. & SALES, B.D. (1993). Juveniles who commit sexual offenses: A critical review of research. In: G.C. Nagayama-Hall, J. Hirschman, J.R. Graham, & N.S. Zaragoza (Eds.) *Sexual aggression: issues in etiology, assessment, treatment and policy.* PA: Taylor & Francis. pp. 215–228.

BECKER, J.V. & HUNTER, J.A. (1997). Understanding and treating child and juvenile sexual offenders. In: T. H. Ollendick & R. J. Prinz (Eds.) *Advances in Clinical Child Psychology, Vol. 19.* New York: Plenum Press. pp. 177–197.

BECKER, J.V., & KAPLAN, M.S. (1988). The assessment of juvenile sexual offenders. In: Prinz, R.J. (Ed.) *Advances in Behavioral Assessment in Children and Families, Vol. 4, JAI,* Greenwich, CT, pages 97–118.

BECKER, J.V., KAPLAN, M.S. & KAVOUSSI, R. (1988). Measuring the effectiveness of treatment for the aggressive juvenile sex offender. *Annals of the New York Academy of Sciences, 528,* 215–222.

BECKER, J.V., KAPLAN, M.S., TENKE, C.E. & TARTHELINI, A. (1991). The incidence of depressive symptomatology in juvenile sex offenders with a history of abuse. *Child Abuse and Neglect: The International Journal, 15,* 531–536.

BECKER, J.V. & STEIN, R. (1991). Is sexual erotica associated with sexual deviance in adolescent males? *International Journal of Offender Therapy and Comparative Criminology, 34*(2), 105–113.

BERLINER, L. & ELLIOTT, D.M. (1996). Sexual abuse of children. In J. Briere, L. Berliner, J.A. Bulkley, C. Jenny & T. Reid (Eds.), *The APSAC Handbook of Child Maltreatment* (pp. 51–71). Thousand Oaks, CA: Sage.

BORDUIN, C.M., HENGGELER, S.W., BLASKE, D.M. & STEIN, R.J. (1990). Multisystemic treatment of juvenile sex offenders. *International Journal of Offender Therapy and Comparative Criminology, 34,* 105–113.

BROWN, E.J. & KOLKO, D.G. (1998). Treatment efficacy and program evaluation with juvenile sexual abusers: A critique with directions for service delivery and research. *Child Maltreatment, 3*(4), 362–373.

BUREAU OF JUSTICE STATISTICS (1996). *National Crime Victimization Survey.* Washington, D.C.: Department of Justice.

CENTER FOR SEX OFFENDER MANAGEMENT (1999). Understanding juvenile sexual offending behavior: Emerging research, treatment approaches and management practices.

CENTER FOR SEX OFFENDER MANAGEMENT (1997). An overview of sex offender community notification practices: Policy implications and promising approaches.

CHAFFIN, M. & BONNER, B. (1998). Editors' introduction: "Don't shoot, we're your children": Have we gone too far in our response to adolescent sexual abusers and children with sexual behavior problems? *Child Maltreatment, 3*(4), 314–316.

CROWELL, N. & BURGESS, A.W. (1996). *Understanding Violence Against Women.* Washington, D.C.: National Academy of Sciences.

DAVIS, G.E. & LEITENBERG, H. (1987). Juvenile sexual offenders. *Psychological Bulletin, 101,* 417–427.

FEHRENBACH, P.A., SMITH, W., MONASTERSKY, C. & DEISHER, R.W. (1986). Adolescent sexual offenders: Offender and offense characteristics. *American Journal of Orthopsychiatry, 56*(2), 225–233.

FINKELHOR, D. (1994). Answers to important questions about the scope and nature of child abuse. *Future of Children, 4,* 112–116.

FINKELHOR, D., HOTALING, G., LEWIS, I.A. & SMITH, C. (1990). Sexual abuse in a national survey of adult men and women: Prevalence, characteristics and risk factors. *Child Abuse and Neglect, 14,* 19–28.

FOEGE, W.H., ROSENBERG, M.L. & MERCY, J.A. (1995). Public health and violence prevention. *Current Issues in Public Health, 1,* 2–9.

FRIEDRICH, W.N., BEILKE, R.L. & URQUIZA, A.J. (1988). Behavior problems in young sexu-
    ally abused boys: A comparison study. *Journal of Interpersonal Violence, 3*, 21–28.
GIDYZ, C.A. & KOSS, M.P. (1989). The impact of juvenile sexual victimization: Standard-
    ized measures of anxiety, depression and behavioral deviancy. *Violence and Victims,
    4*, 139–149.
GRAVES, R.B., OPENSHAW, D.K., ASCIONE, F.R. & ERICKSEN, S.L. (1996). Demographic and
    parental characteristics of youthful sexual offenders. *International Journal of
    Offender Therapy and Comparative Criminology, 40*, 300–317.
HOLMES, W.C. & SLAP, G.B. (1999). Sexual abuse of boys: Definition, prevalence, corre-
    lates, sequelae, and management. *Journal of the American Medical Association, 280*,
    1855–1862.
HUNTER, J.A. & SANTOS, D.R. (1990). The use of specialized cognitive behavior therapies
    in the treatment of juvenile sex offenders. *International Journal of Offender Therapy
    and Comparative Criminology, 34*, 239–247.
HUNTER, J.A., FIGUEREDO, A.J., MALAMUTH, N. & BECKER, J.V. (In press). Developmental
    pathways in youth sexual aggression and delinquency: Risk factors and mediators.
    Journal of Family Violence.
HUNTER, J.A., FIGUEREDO, A.J., MALAMUTH, N. & BECKER, J.V. (In press). Juvenile sex
    offenders: Toward the development of a typology. *Sexual Abuse: A Journal of
    Research and Treatment.*
JOHNSON, G.M. & KNIGHT, R.A. (2000). Developmental antecedents of sexual coercion in juve-
    nile sex offenders. *Sexual Abuse: A Journal of Research and Treatment, 12*(3), 165–178.
KAPLAN, M.S., MORALES, M. & BECKER, J.V. (1993). The impact of verbal satiation on juve-
    nile sex offenders: A preliminary report. *Journal of Child Sexual Abuse, 2*, 81–88.
KAVOUSSI, R.J., KAPLAN, M.S. & BECKER, J.V. (1988). Psychiatric diagnosis and juvenile
    sex offenders. *Journal of the American Academy of Child and Juvenile Psychiatry,
    27*, 241–243.
KILPATRICK, D.G., EDMUNDS, C.N. & SEYMOUR, A.K. (1992). *Rape in America: A Report to
    the Nation.* Arlington, VA: National Victim Center and Medical University of South
    Carolina.
KOBAYASHI, J., SALES, B.D., & BECKER, J.V., FIGUEREDO, A.J. & KAPLAN, M.S. (1995). Per-
    ceived parental deviance, parent-child bonding, child abuse, and child sexual aggres-
    sion. *Sexual Abuse: A Journal of Research and Treatment, 7*, 25–44.
KOSS, M.P. (1993). Detecting the scope of rape: A review of prevalence research methods.
    Journal of Interpersonal Violence, 8, 198–222.
LAB, S.P., SHIELDS, G.,& SCHONDEL, C. (1993). Research note: An evaluation of juvenile
    sex offender treatment. *Crime & Delinquency, 39*, 543–553.
LINDEGREN, M.L., HANSON, I.C., HAMMETT, T.A., BEIL, J., FLEMING, P.L. & WARD, J.W.
    (1998). Sexual abuse of children: Intersection with the HIV epidemic. *Pediatrics,
    102*, E46.
MAZUR, T. & MICHAEL, P.M. (1992). Outpatient treatment for juveniles with sexually inap-
    propriate behavior: Program description and 6-month follow-up. *Journal of Offender
    Rehabilitation, 18*, 191–203.
MCLEER, S.V., DEBLINGER, E., ATKINS, M.L., RALPHE, D.L. & FOA, E. (1988). Posttrau-
    matic stress disorder in sexually abused children. *Journal of the American Academy
    of Child and Juvenile Psychiatry, 27*, 650–654.
MCMAHON, P. (1997). *The public health approach to the prevention of sexual violence.*
    Paper presented at the Annual Conference of the Association for the Treatment of
    Sexual Abusers, Washington, DC, Oct.
MIRANDA, A.O., & CORCORAN, C.L. (2000). Comparison of perpetration characteristics
    between male juvenile and adult sexual offenders: Preliminary results. *Sexual Abuse:
    A Journal of Research and Treatment, 12*(3), 179–188.
NATIONAL CENTER FOR JUVENILE JUSTICE (1998). Frequent Questions and Answers. Pitts-
    burgh, PA: National Center for Juvenile Justice.
NATIONAL CENTER ON SEXUAL BEHAVIOR OF YOUTH. (2002). Fact Sheet. Center on Child
    Abuse and Neglect. University of Oklahoma Health Sciences Center.
O'BRIEN, M.J. & BERA, W.H. (1986). Juvenile sexual offenders: A descriptive typology.
    Preventing Sexual Abuse, 1, 1–4.

PRENTKY, R., HARRIS, B., FRIZZELL, K. & RIGHTHAND, S. (2000). An actuarial procedure for assessing risk with juvenile sex offenders. *Sexual Abuse: A Journal of Research and Treatment, 12*(2), 71–94.

RESNICK, H.S., KILPATRICK, D.G., DANSKY, B.S., SAUNDERS, B.E. & BEST, C.L. (1993). Prevalence of civilian trauma and PTSD in a representative national sample of women. *Journal of Consulting and Clinical Psychology, 61*, 984–991.

RIGHTHAND, S. & WELCH, C. (2001). Juveniles who have sexually offended: A review of the professional literature. Office of Juvenile Justice and Delinquency Prevention.

RYAN, G., LANE, S., DAVIS, J. & ISAAC, C. (1987). Juvenile sex offenders: Development 7 correction. *Child Abuse & Neglect, 11*, 385–395.

RUSSELL, D. (1986). *The Secret Trauma: Incest in the Lives of Girls and Women.* New York: Basic Books.

SCHRAM, D.D., MILLOY, C.D. & ROWE, W.E. (1991). Juvenile sex offenders: A follow-up study of reoffense behavior. Washington State Institute for Public Policy.

SMITH, MONASTERSKY, & DEISHER (1987). MMPI-based personality types among juvenile sex offenders. *Journal of Clinical Psychology, 43*, 422–430.

STOP IT NOW! (2002). Proceedings from the STOP IT NOW! Expert Panel Meeting, April 24–25, 2002. Washington D.C.

TRIVITS, L.C. & REPPUCCI, N.D. (2002). Application of Megan's Law to juveniles. *American Psychologist, 57*(9), 690–704.

UNITED STATES DEPARTMENT OF JUSTICE (2001). *Uniform crime report.*

UNITED STATES DEPARTMENT OF JUSTICE (2002). *Uniform crime report, preliminary.*

WORLING, J.R. (2001).

WORLING, J.R. & CURWEN, T. (2001). The "ERASOR": Estimate of Risk of Juvenile Sexual Offense Recidivism Version 2.0. SAFE-T Program, Thistletown Regional Center.

Sexual Offender Containment

Use of the Postconviction Polygraph

KIM ENGLISH, LINDA JONES, DIANE PATRICK, AND DIANE PASINI-HILL

Colorado Division of Criminal Justice, Denver, Colorado 80215-5865, USA

ABSTRACT: Victims of sexual assault are unlikely to report the crime. For many sexual offenders, then, their sexually deviant behavior remains largely unknown except for crimes that result in arrest or notification to social services. Little is known about the offender's past behavior and little will be known about the offender's future abusive behavior. It is within this context that the containment approach for managing sexual offenders becomes critical to protecting future victimization by known offenders. This paper describes the need to incorporate information learned from the postconviction polygraph examination into intense treatment and criminal justice supervision. Age of onset and frequency and variety of deviant behavior are known risk factors, probably because they reflect the extent to which deviancy is part of the offender's lifestyle. Treatment and supervision plans must incorporate this information, along with the risk presented by these offenders to very specific age and gender groups. This study of data collected on disclosures made by 180 convicted sexual offenders (most were convicted of crimes against children) during the course of four different treatment/polygraph programs found that 39% had a history of sexually assaulting adults, 31% had sexually assaulted both male and female victims, 36% had engaged in bestiality, and two-thirds of the incest offenders had assaulted victims outside the family. Complete information is necessary for treatment providers and supervising officers to develop meaningful and relevant treatment and supervision plans, and for imminent, situational risk factors to be managed and contained.

KEYWORDS: sexual offenders; containment approach; risk; polygraph; crossover; incest

INTRODUCTION

Offenders in the Neighborhood

Nine of ten convicted sexual offenders serving time in prison will return to the community (Greenfeld, 1997). In fact, the majority of convicted sexual offenders never see a prison cell, receiving sentences that instead call for supervision in the community. Notwithstanding public outcry concerning sexual offenders in our neighborhoods, somewhere between 78 and 86% of sexual assaults are committed by the victim's relatives and acquaintances (Kilpatrick, Edmunds, and Seymour,

Address for correspondence: Kim English, Colorado Division of Criminal Justice, 700 Kipling, Suite 3000, Denver, CO 80215-5865. Voice: 303-239-4442; fax: 303-239-4491.
kim.english@cdps.state.co.us

Ann. N.Y. Acad. Sci. 989: 411–427 (2003). © 2003 New York Academy of Sciences.

1992; Snyder, 2000, respectively).[1] Further analysis of the data analyzed by Kilpatrick et al. (1992) revealed that only 10% of child rapes were committed by strangers (Smith et al., 1992). It is not surprising, then, that 70% of reported sex crimes are committed in the home of the victim, increasing to more than 80% when the victim is under the age of 12 (Snyder, 2000). Despite public policies that focus on stranger crimes, the most common rapist is a person who occupies a place among the victim's circle of family and friends.

This familiarity gives sexual abusers incredible access to actual and potential victims. The National Violence Against Women Survey found that one of six American women reported experiencing a completed or attempted sexual assault in their lifetime (Tjaden and Thoennes, 1998). Only the context of the familiar and the private can explain the extremely high prevalence of a crime society abhors. Privacy and familiarity nurture the single most important aspect of the crime from the perpetrator's perspective: secrecy.

Secrecy

Secrecy allows access to the victim. Often, it allows continued access to the victim. More than half of the women in the *Rape in America* study reported being raped more than once (Kilpatrick et al., 1992). Lamb and Edgar-Smith (1994) studied 60 incest victims. One-fifth had been abused for more than 5 years, and half had been abused on a weekly basis. Resler and Wind's (1994) study of 228 incest victims reported an average duration of abuse of 7.8 years, usually beginning when the victim was six years old. The American Medical Association declared the following in a 1995 position paper: "Because many of these attacks occurring daily go unreported and unrecognized, sexual assault can be considered a silent-violent epidemic in the United States today."

The secrecy that surrounds crimes of sexual assault ensures that most perpetrators never come to the attention of authorities. Lawson and Chaffin (1992) studied 28 children between the ages of 3 and 12 who were not previously suspected of being sexually abused and were admitted to a hospital emergency room for having a sexually transmitted disease. Only 43% disclosed the abuse when interviewed by a skilled professional. In Sauzier's (1989) study of 156 children treated at a Boston program for the sexually abused, only 55% of the children disclosed the abuse. In this study, children were likely to "never" disclose when the perpetrator was a natural parent (53%) or a relative (40%). Likewise, another study found that disclosure of the sexual assault(s) was significantly less likely when something the researchers called "close proximity" occurred. Close proximity was measured as the existence of at least one of these: (1) a relationship with the perpetrator; (2) location of the abuse; and (3) effect of the abuse on the family (Wyatt and Newcomb, 1990). Smith et al. (2000) also found that delayed disclosure was tied to the victim's being a younger age at the time of the rape, having a family relationship with the perpetrator, and experiencing a series of assaults. In fact, disclosure was 3.69 times more likely to occur when the perpetrator was a stranger.

A survey of 930 female residents in San Francisco in the early 1980s found only 8% of rapes were reported to authorities. In this study, only 2% of incest crimes were reported (Russell, 1986). In Kilpatrick et al.'s (1992) national study of 4008 women, researchers from the Medical Center at the University of South Carolina found that only 16% of the women who had been the victim of a rape[2] reported the crime within 24 hours. Nearly half (47%) of the child rape victims did not tell anyone for at least five years. In fact, 28%—one in four rape victims—never told anyone till the researcher asked (Smith et al., 2000). This finding is consistent with Finkelhor et al.'s (1990) national sample of 511 adults that found that 33% of the women and 42% of the men first disclosed the rape to the researcher. Lamb and Edgar-Smith's (1994) sample of 60 victims of intrafamilial sexual abuse reported delaying disclosure, on average, for 10 years. Roseler and Wind (1994) found the average age of disclosure to be 25, nearly 20 years after the abuse started.

Official Detection

Official detection is rare. Once these crimes are reported to authorities, few result in arrest. Snyder (2000) analyzed sexual assault arrest data from 12 states and found that an arrest resulted in only 27% of reported sex crimes (prosecution was declined in 6% of these cases). The National Youth Survey, a 25-year old longitudinal self-reported data study of a general population sample of more than 1735 subjects, identified 72 males and 8 females who reported committing a serious sexual assault. Only two (1.1%) of these individuals were arrested for sexual assault (neither were convicted) (Grotpeter and Elliott, 2002). Ahlmeyer et al. (2000) used the postconviction polygraph to encourage disclosures of past victims from prisoners participating in treatment. This study revealed that only 1% of victims were identified using official record data. Only 0.8% of the perpetrators in the *Rape in America* study served time in prison for the crime.

The Containment Approach

Given the low likelihood that sexual offenders will enter the criminal justice system and serve sentences for the assault, the public should expect the criminal justice system to develop interventions that focus on preventing known offenders from harming *again*. When implemented comprehensively, this multidisciplinary, collaborative strategy makes it difficult for convicted sexual offenders under the supervision of the criminal justice system to reoffend (English, Pullen, and Jones, 1996). Labeled the *containment approach,* this model is being adopted in jurisdictions nationwide.[3]

This management strategy is designed to give offenders the opportunity to learn new skills and methods of internal controls from mandated participation in specialized treatment while monitoring the offender's behavior and interfering with any opportunity he or she may take to assault again. When fully implemented, it operates in the context of multiagency collaboration, explicit policies, and consistent practices that combine case evaluation, risk assessment, sexual offender treatment, behavioral monitoring, and intense community monitoring and surveillance. These activities are designed specifically to maximize public safety and protect past and potential victims. As described elsewhere (Colorado Sex Offender Management Board, 1999; English et al., 1996; English, 1998; English et al., 2000; English, Jones, and Patrick, 2003) the containment approach requires case decisions, individual case practices, and cross-agency policies to be based on methods that prevent harm toward current and potential victims by known sexual offenders. Understanding that victims rarely report this crime is the first step in managing sexual offenders. It means that obtaining detailed information about sexual offenders, and their offending patterns, must become a goal of the containment approach so that professionals are informed and empowered.

THE POSTCONVICTION POLYGRAPH EXAMINATION

The Need for Accurate Information

The use of the polygraph examination significantly increases the information disclosed by the offender in the context of treatment. The containment approach focuses on holding the offender accountable, so it includes an expectation of honesty and a commitment by the offender to actively engage in treatment. The polygraph exam plays a critical role in the containment strategy because of its obvious focus on deception. Using polygraphy with sexual offenders is akin to testing urine with drug offenders. It is a method of validating offenders' self-reports of treatment compliance and monitoring very specific behaviors.

The containment approach requires complete and accurate information to determine and manage the offender's risk to the public and to develop a relevant treatment and monitoring plan. Complete information about the scope and frequency of a sexual offender's deviant activities is available only from the offender, yet most sexual offenders have deceived many people, usually for many years. Sexual offenders report the time between their first sex crime and their first conviction to be, on average, 13 to 16 years (Freeman-Longo, in an unpublished study cited in Salter [1995], and Ahlmeyer et al. [2000], respectively). Deception by sexual offenders led the Association for the Treatment of Sexual Abusers to state, in its *Practitioner's Handbook* (ATSA, 1993), that therapists should not rely solely on offenders' self-reports. Rather, to determine compliance with treatment requirements, ATSA made recommendations for the use of the polygraph to validate the offender's self-report. In its *Practice Standards and Guidelines* (2001), ATSA includes a five-page appendix on the use of polygraphy.

Detailed information obtained from this integration of treatment, supervision, and polygraph monitoring allows for the development of meaningful treatment and supervision plans: "Therapists need valid, reliable information from the sexual offender. Without this, the treatment is less likely to identify the precise treatment needs and to quantify treatment's long term effects" (Abel and Rouleau, 1990, p. 10). The containment approach requires that these plans be tailored to the individual sexual offender and his or her deviant sexual patterns of behavior. It is, in fact, this individual focus that holds the promise that the treatment provider and the supervising officer will make the most relevant decisions for the offender while maintaining community safety. The intent of containment is to identify *precursor behaviors and at-risk situations* (see Pithers, Kashima, Cumming, and Beal, 1988; Pithers, 1990; Laws, Hudson, and Ward, 2000; Hudson, Ward, and McCormack, 1999). Monitoring risky behaviors makes it possible for treatment providers and supervising officers to actively address and contain problems *before* the offender commits a new sex crime.

Certainly there is much to learn about sexual offenders. Research on sexual offenders reveals an astonishing level of undetected sexual abuse. Freeman-Longo

(1985) studied 23 rapists in prison using anonymous surveys.The men reported committing 319 sexual assaults on children and 178 rapes of adult women. Abel and Rouleau (1990) found that half of their community sample of 561 men reported committing more than 300 sex crimes before their eighteenth birthday. Ahlmeyer et al. (2000) found in their sample of prisoners in treatment that each had committed, on average, 528 sex offenses in their lifetime against 184 victims.[4]

It seems logical, then, that the postconviction polygraph examination, used in the context of treatment and supervision, would be helpful in obtaining information about the offender that he or she would otherwise likely keep secret. Its use helps many offenders move through stages of denial, and when used consistently the exam can make treatment more meaningful, just as honesty with a physician about medical history and current symptoms can improve the effectiveness of the medical intervention. Failure to meet the expectation of honesty will become obvious during the polygraph examination, and the consequences that may be invoked for failure to cooperate are intended to hold the offender accountable for his or her participation in treatment. Such consequences are consistent with the sanctions that follow noncompliance with other supervision conditions.[5]

How is the Postconviction Polygraph Exam Used?

Preparation for the polygraph actually begins when the treatment provider and the supervising officer emphasize the need for complete honesty as a first step toward responsibility, accountability, and community safety. Offenders are encouraged to disclose complete and accurate information so that a viable treatment plan can be developed. Age of onset of sexually abusive behaviors, scope and frequency of deviant activity, recency of inappropriate behavior (especially during treatment), the offender's thinking and assault planning strategies—all these pieces of information are necessary to assess each individual's ongoing risk and treatment needs.

Three types of polygraph examination are most commonly used to obtain information on offender behaviors and verification of offender truthfulness. *Sexual history disclosure* polygraph examinations are used to verify the accuracy and completeness of the sexual history information a sexual offender provides during treatment. Just as a physician will require information regarding onset, frequency, intensity, and variety of a serious presenting symptom or illness, an offender's history of deviance is obtained using a very specific treatment tool: sexual history documentation. This treatment task involves the offender recalling and recording in a notebook the gender, age, and method of assault for every past victim.[6] The sex history document—to be completed within three to six months of commencing treatment—is then provided to the polygraph examiner who, after reading it carefully along with other case file information, asks the offender very specific questions about the accuracy of parts of his or her sex history. In most cases, the completed sex history document is long, with disclosures of many prior assaults and attempted assaults, and many different types of assaults as well. The clear expectation that the offender will be accurate and truthful on the sex history assignment, coupled with the ability to verify truthfulness through polygraph exams, increases the offender's incentive to disclose this potentially embarrassing and illegal information to the treatment provider.[7]

Specific-issue exams verify the details of the conviction offense. These tests are usually given when the offender's version of the crime varies from the victim's version, or the offender continues to deny committing the crime of conviction. Specific-issue exams are also used to address a single concern or suspicion that arises during an offender's probation or parole, such as suspected contact with children. Specific-issue tests are also recommended as a follow-up to deceptive results on previous exams to clarify the nature of the deception. *Maintenance and monitoring* exams are used to verify whether a probationer or parolee is complying with the conditions of community supervision and cooperating with treatment expectations. These exams require the polygraph examiner, the treatment provider, and the supervising officer to work together to identify questions that target high-risk behavior related to the assault patterns described in the offender's sexual history document.

The exam itself is a three-stage process, and usually takes between 90 and 120 minutes. The "pretest" portion of the exam is the longest, when the examiner explains the equipment and the consent form, calibrates the machine to the individual, reviews each of the 20-or-so questions and reviews the terminology in each of the questions. The next phase is the "in-test" when the examinee is asked the question sets at least three times so the examiner has multiple charts to score. The final phase of the exam is essentially a discussion of the exam findings. Inconsistencies are identified and the offender has an opportunity to explain or clarify issues that may have surfaced.

METHODS FOR THE CURRENT STUDY

Sample

Four containment programs in three states were selected to reflect different levels of postconviction polygraph implementation. In two programs (A and B, 57 and 62 cases, respectively) the postconviction polygraph had been implemented for a number of years as part of the sexual offender treatment program, but the programs varied in terms of the extent to which the polygraph exam was fully integrated into the treatment and supervision process. In the third state, polygraph testing was newly implemented. In C, 31 of the sexual offenders had received at least one postconviction polygraph examination, and in D, 30 were "under the threat" of the polygraph test; these offenders knew that polygraph exams would eventually be administered to them as part of their treatment and supervision programs. Because the polygraph was imminent and offenders in the sample were in group therapy with those who had taken the polygraph test and were completing the same homework and journaling assignments in preparation for the polygraph, these cases were also included in the analyses of the impact of the postconviction polygraph.[8] This sample of 180 adult sexual offenders included offenders who were serving probation or parole sentences in the community at the time of the study.[9] Sites C and D included misdemeanor and felony conviction crimes, whereas A and B were felony cases. For seven of the 180 the victim in the current crime was an adult, 10 were convicted of exhibitionism, and the remainder were convicted for crimes against children. Several of the crimes against children were brutal rapes.[10]

Active case files of offenders who had served at least 6 to 18 months of the community sentence were systematically selected (every *n*th case) from a total of 31 officer caseloads. Data sources were the criminal justice information in the officer's files, including police reports, presentence investigation reports, and chronological notes. From the therapist's files data were gathered from sex history questionnaires or journals, homework assignments related to the polygraph, case notes, and polygraph examination reports. Data were collected from a total of 426 polygraph exams, 35.2% of which were scored as "nondeceptive."

A complex data collection instrument was designed to gather demographics, criminal history, current crime, placements and sentencing information, victim information (number, age group, gender, and relationship to offender), type and frequency of paraphilia and/or risk behavior, a profile of the perpetrator's early behaviors, and information regarding polygraph tests. A "victim" was defined as someone who was sexually assaulted without their consent or knowledge (e.g., they were asleep). For minors, the definition of a victim required a four-year age difference between the age of the perpetrator and the victim, force, or that the perpetrator was an adult and the minor victim had not reached the age of consent in that state.[11] Data were coded to compare the amount of information available to the containment team before and after polygraph testing.[12]

Brief Description of the Sample

Across the sites, 4.3% were women; 79.4% were white, 10% were black, and 7.9% were Hispanic. Just over one-third (38.5%) of the sample was single, 37.5% were married or joined by common law, and 24.1% were divorced. Ten percent of the sample were between the ages of 19 and 25, 13.5% were between 26 and 30, 39.6% were 31 to 40, 27.1% were between 41 and 55, and 9.5% were over the age of 55. In terms of criminal history, 42.4% had an adult nonviolent arrest record and 38.3% had an adult nonviolent conviction. One-fifth (21.3%) had a prior arrest for a violent crime, and 15.5% had a prior conviction for a violent crime. Fourteen percent (14.1%) had a prior arrest for a sex crime, and 12.1% had a prior conviction for a sex crime.

Approach

Information known *before the treatment/polygraph process* was compared to all that was known *after the treatment/polygraph process* (data gathered on pages 1 through 4 of the data collection instrument). Although data were gathered separately for the juvenile and adult histories of offenders, these data were combined in the analyses presented here except where indicated. The original objective was to extract information from the self-report sex history and compare this to what was reported separately in the polygraph examinations. However, it was not always possible to ascertain whether information in the polygraph file was the first disclosure. A self-report sex history disclosure form or journal assignment, administered as part of the treatment process, was validated (or not) during a sex history polygraph exam. The offender prepared the sex history assignment with the knowledge that it is inextricably tied to the postconviction polygraph examination. The use of the term "treatment," however, does not imply that information from other aspects of treatment was included or identified for the analysis. For instance, information revealed through group treatment sessions was not included unless it was specifically related to infor-

TABLE 1. Comparison of hands-on offenses, hands-off offenses, and risk behaviors before and after treatment/polygraph process[a]

	Before (%)	After (%)
Hands-on offenses		
Vaginal penetration	56.7	72.8
Attempted penetration	5.6	15.0
Anal penetration	9.4	18.3
Oral sex	36.7	56.1
Fondling/frottage	66.7	85.6
Excess aggression	3.9	9.4
Assault (including domestic violence)	11.7	18.3
Hands-off offenses		
Exhibitionism	13.9	46.7
Voyeurism	8.9	53.9
Stalking	2.2	3.9
Risk behaviors		
Urination w/sex act	1.7	8.3
Bestiality	4.4	36.1
Pornography	13.3	38.3
Obscene Internet/phone	2.2	18.9
Masturbate to deviant fantasy	8.3	46.7
Excess masturbation	1.7	13.9
Specific preparation (e.g., driving around)	8.3	21.7
Other[b]	17.8	65.6

[a]Proportion reporting a history of these behaviors ($n = 180$).

[b]Other behaviors include such behaviors as the offender's use of drugs or alcohol during the assault; substance use while under supervision; specific grooming behaviors; engaging in prostitution; deviant fantasies; engaging in juvenile fire-setting; and toruture of animals.

mation also revealed through the treatment element of self-disclosure or through a polygraph examination. For these analyses we were interested in information gathered as a result of implementing the postconviction polygraph examination as a management tool.

RESULTS

More Information

Not surprisingly, more information was obtained after the treatment/polygraph process. The proportion admitting a history of assaulting male victims increased from 20% to 36%; the proportion admitting to sex crimes against both male and female victims increased from 10% to 29%; the proportion admitting to assaulting both child and adult victims increased from 10% to 33%; and the proportion of the

TABLE 2. Comparison of hands-on offenses, hands-off offenses, and risk behaviors before and after treatment/polygraph process[a]

Age and Gender of Victims	Before (%)	After (%)	Offender Was Adult[b] (%)
Males 0–5	4.4	12.8	80.5
Females 0–5	12.2	28.3	84.5
Males 6–9	8.3	15.6	67.9
Females 6–9	24.4	38.9	78.6
Males 10–13	5.6	15.6	74.0
Females 10–13	42.8	52.2	85.0
Males 14–17	5.0	12.8	96.7
Females 14–17	40.0	61.7	93.0
Males 18+	0.6	8.3	87.8
Females 18+	15.6	39.4	93.1
Males elderly/at risk	1.7	1.7	100
Females elderly/at risk	1.7	3.3	84.8

[a]Proportion reporting a history of these behaviors ($n = 180$).
[b]The proportion of offenders who disclosed assaulting this age group when the perpetrator was an adult.

sample known to be perpetrators of incest increased from 38% to 58% (data not presented).

An increase in the proportion of the sample reporting deviant behaviors occurred in every behavior category. Exhibitionism, voyeurism, and bestiality were significantly more prevalent in the sample than would have been known before the treatment/polygraph process. Approximately half of the sample reported a history of exhibitionism (46.7%)[13] and voyeurism (53.9%), and one-third (36.1%) of the sample reported a history of sex with animals (a ninefold increase from the 4.4% known to have engaged in bestiality) (TABLE 1).

Victims' Age and Gender

The information in TABLE 2 reflects the proportion of the sample that disclosed sexually assaulting victims in very specific age categories. Disclosures of assaults on certain age groups reflect activity on the part of a relatively small proportion of the sample (for example, only 12.8% reported assaulting males age 5 and younger). However, the size of that perpetrator group increased nearly threefold. The prevalence of this behavior in the sample increases from one in twenty to about one in eight, considerably changing the profile of the group.

Because the data collected combined disclosures of a lifetime of deviant behavior plus current information that surfaced in therapy and maintenance/monitoring polygraph exams, data were coded to identify activity that occurred when the offender was a juvenile versus an adult. It seemed likely that for some of the youngest categories the offender may have also been a child. To address this question, the victims assaulted when the offender was a juvenile were compared to assaults committed when the offender was an adult. The third column in TABLE 2 shows that approximately four out of five offenders assaulted these age groups when the perpetrator was an adult.[14]

Further analysis of these age groups (data not presented) determined that 56.5% of the 23 offenders who assaulted boys aged 5 years and younger also assaulted girls in the same age category; 52.2% assaulted boys between the ages of 6 and 9, and 26.0% assaulted women over the age of 18. Of the 28 who disclosed assaulting boys 6 to 9 years old, two-thirds (64.3%) disclosed assaulting girls in the same age grouping; 57.1% reported male victims aged 10–13, and 39.3% reported assaulting adult women. The most frequently identified victim group was females between the ages of 14 and 17 (111 offenders reported assaulting victims of this age and gender), and nearly one-third (31.5%) of this group reported victimizing girls aged 5 and younger; 41.4% victimized girls 6–9; 60% victimized girls 10–13; and 42.3% disclosed assaulting women in the 18+ age category. When analyzing assaults against boys by the 111 offenders, about 10% were "active" in *each* of the male age categories (excluding the elderly/at-risk men category). Age and gender crossover appears common for about one-third of this sample. Since the data presented here are likely to underestimate, overall, the scope of the sexually assaultive behavior,[15] crossover activity is probably even more common than once thought. Abel et al. (1988), in their study of 561 men voluntarily seeking evaluation or treatment for paraphilia and who completed confidential questionnaires, found 20% of the sample crossed-over gender, and 11.2% crossed-over three age groups.

Age of Onset

In a later paper, Abel and Rouleau (1990, p. 13) found that more than half of this group (53.6%) reported "the onset of at least one deviant sexual interest prior to age 18." In the current study of what is most certainly a more serious population,[16] 26% reported the onset of hands-on deviant behavior when they were between the ages of 5 and 8; 23% reported onset at ages 9–11; 21% reported hands-on onset at 12 or 13, and 27% reported onset between the ages of 14 and 20.

Incest Behavior

Incest was defined as being related to the victim (rather than an acquaintance, stranger, or person with whom the perpetrator was in a position of trust). Although there were 80 cases in which the subject was convicted of crimes involving incest, 104 offenders (58% of the sample) disclosed committing incest. Of this group of 104 offenders, 56.7% reported additional victims whom they had assaulted from a position of trust, 34.8% disclosed assaulting strangers, and two-thirds (64.4%) of this group disclosed assaulting victims in one or both of these relationship categories (data not presented). Two-thirds of the incest offenders in this group, then, "crossed over" relationship categories. Studies have found that incest offenders are reconvicted at a much lower rate compared to other sexual offenders (Firestone et al., 1999; see review by Marshall and Barbaree, 1990), so it is commonly believed that incest offenders are "specialists" and it would be a rare incest perpetrator who would harm victims outside the family, but these data do not support that idea.

Further, incest perpetrators were more likely to disclose hands-on deviant behavior at an earlier age of onset (median of 10 years old) compared to a median age of

TABLE 3. Information from treatment/polygraph: Comparison of relative-only[a] perpetrators with relative-plus[b] perpetrators (*n* = 104)

	Relative-Only Perpetrators (*n* = 37)	Relative-Plus Perpetrators (*n* = 67)
Hands-on offenses		
Vaginal penetration	64.9	79.1
Attempted penetration	8.1	28.4
Anal penetration	10.8	29.9
Oral sex	43.2	79.1
Fondling/frottage	83.8	98.5
Excess aggression	8.1	7.5
Assault (including domestic violence)	13.5	20.9
Hands-off offenses		
Exhibitionism	32.4	70.1
Voyeurism	37.8	77.6
Stalking	0	3.0
Risk behaviors		
Urination w/sex act	2.7	14.9
Bestiality	27.0	56.7
Alcohol/drugs to victim	13.5	4.5
Offender under influence	21.6	17.9
More than 1 unwilling participant in single incident	5.4	10.4
Pornography	24.3	47.8
Obscene Internet/phone	16.2	23.9
Masturbate to deviant fantasy	29.7	70.1
Excess masturbation	13.5	20.9
Specific preparation (e.g., driving around)	18.9	32.8

[a]Relative-only are those offenders not identified with victims outside the family; 44.5% of the polygraphs administered to this group were scored as deceptive.

[b]Relative-plus offenders are those who disclosed additional victims from outside the family. 31.2% of the polygraph exams administered to this group were scored as deceptive.

onset of 12 for the group of offenders with no known incest victims. Generally, incest offenders are not considered dangerous (for example, Hanson [2000]), perhaps because it is assumed that they do not offend outside the family. Yet many studies have reported the lack of "fidelity" by incest perpetrators. Faller (1990) studied 65 biological incest fathers in intact families and found one-third had molested outside the home, and approximately 80% molested more than one child. Weinrott and Saylor (1991) studied 99 incarcerated sexual offenders and reported that 50% admitted to abusing children outside the home (none of these incidents was detected). Becker and Coleman (1988) found 44% of the female-oriented incest offenders in their study assaulted girls outside the home (and 11% assaulted males outside the home). Becker et al. (1986) found that 9 of 22 sibling offenders assaulted nonsiblings. Abel and Rouleau (1990) reported that 23.3% of the interfamilial offenders assaulted victims outside the family.

We compared incest offenders who reported offenses only against family members ("relatives only") with a group of offenders that also reported committing incest and assaults against victims outside the family ("relatives plus") (TABLE 3.) The data indicate that a larger proportion of the "relatives plus" group engaged in the variety of behaviors documented. The "relatives-only" group may be more likely to under-report these behaviors, but it should also be noted (data not presented) that both of these groups of incest offenders had polygraph results that were deceptive *at some point*. (Nearly one-third of the "relatives plus" group and 44.5% of the "relatives only group" had at least one deceptive polygraph.) Thus, the results represent these groups of offenders only at a point in time. Some offenders who were once in the "relatives-only group" may, as treatment progresses, disclose more information about nonfamilial assaults.

DISCUSSION AND IMPLICATIONS

The containment approach is built around obtaining sufficient information about *individual* sexual offenders so that risk in the community can be managed and perhaps reduced. Papers in this volume that address actuarial risk describe characteristics of *groups* of offenders that increase the probability of *future* reconviction (or some other measure of crime documented in official records). Community containment focuses on imminent risk, managed through the development of treatment and supervision plans that are individualized according to each offender's specific offending pattern. Treatment plans can address the full scope of the offender's deviant behavior, once that behavior is disclosed and verified via the polygraph examination. When the containment approach is fully implemented, access to potential victims, including animals, is prohibited when the victims have characteristics (the least of which are age and gender) that reflect those the offender has abused in the past.

For 85% of the sample, the current crime represented the first arrest for a sex crime, so official record data are of limited value in determining risk. The unimportance of the crime of conviction as a description of the offender's sexual preference (since 39% of the child molesters in the study also raped an adult) becomes clear in the face of the additional information obtained from the treatment/polygraph process. Even for offenses traditionally viewed as "not dangerous," such as exhibitionism, more information is needed.[17]

In sum, the aggregate data presented here reflect a frequency and variety of behavior that is not captured in official records. Age of onset, frequency, and duration and variety of behavior are aspects that describe career offending (Blumstein, Cohen, Roth, and Visher, 1988). Early onset is one of the strongest predictors of "serious, long-term and frequent" (Piquero et al., 1999, p. 275) deviant behavior later in life (Blumstein, Farrington, and Moitra, 1985; Quinsey, Harris, and Rice, 1995; Marshall, Barbaree, and Eccles, 1991). Frequency of offending history, number of prior victims, and variety of deviant behavior are empirically linked to risk of reoffense (Hanson and Bussiere, 1998; Proulx et al., 1997; Serin et al., 2001). Only this level of information on *individual* offenders can empower therapists, supervising officers, and other decision makers to operate most effectively, outside the secrecy and deception that surrounds these crimes. Sufficient resources must be devoted to obtaining complete information about all sexual offenders to enhance the likelihood that the appropriate interventions can have the maximum impact—on both the offender and on community safety. Excessive containment when it is unnecessary and relaxed containment when there is danger are equally irresponsible reactions to a lack of complete information. In fact, the extent of victimization disclosed by the sample in this study begs the following question: Is it ethical and humane *not* to direct the necessary resources toward obtaining complete and accurate information about each offender's age of onset, prior assault history, variety of deviant behavior, and the age and gender of victims that were once harmed by the offender? Will we otherwise overcontrol some offenders and undercontrol others? Can our interventions be effective without this knowledge?

Study Limitations

These analyses, of course, did not include victims whom the offender never admitted or those who were never documented in the file. Because of this, the findings underestimate both the number of victims and the range of deviant behaviors for the sample.[18] Also, because before and after comparisons included agencies at different stages of implementing the postconviction treatment/polygraph process, among other variations discussed in the text, the findings are unlikely to represent the information that would be obtained from any single agency.

NOTES

1. Kilpatrick et al. (1992) conducted a health study of a national sample of 4008 women, and used the Uniform Crime Report (UCR) definition of rape: penetration or attempted penetration. Snyder (2000) studied law enforcement arrest data from 12 states.
2. In this study, the researchers used the FBI's definition of rape: penetration or attempted penetration.
3. We are grateful to officials from the Office of Justice Programs, in the U.S. Department of Justice, who have supported efforts to prevent sexual assault by known offenders. In particular, the leadership of former U.S. Assistant Attorney General Laurie Robinson, Esq., has been essential in the replication of the containment strategy in jurisdictions across the country.
4. Abel and Rouleau (1990) and Ahlmeyer et al. (2000) include both hands-on and hands-off offenses. Ahlmeyer et al. report a median of 95 sex offenses against a median of 26 victims.
5. The accuracy of the polygraph depends on many factors, including the skill of the examiner (who must receive special training in the area of sexual offender testing), question construction, and the "stake" the offender has in the outcome of the exam. Research in the last 20 years has decreased subjective aspects of the exam. Accuracy studies suffer from serious methodological problems, not the least of which is identification of available and appropriate criterion validity measures ("ground truth"). Its weaknesses are well understood by the U.S. Department of Defense (DOD), which conducts and funds most of the research on this tool. The DOD administers approximately 30,000 polygraph examinations annually, primarily in the context of crime investigations and espionage detection. The postconviction polygraph exam, when

well integrated with treatment, elicits information about past and current relevant behavior because offenders disclose information before and/or after the exam. The courts have allowed the use of polygraph findings in revocation hearings where there is a lesser standard of proof than the "beyond a reasonable doubt" required at trial. The courts have generally found that disclosures made during the exam are not compelled.See LaFond and Winick, this volume.

6. Sometimes questionnaires are used to obtain historical information. While this is a more efficient method of gathering and reviewing data, it has the significant disadvantage of not obtaining the patterns of behavior and emotions preceding each assault. Important information such as method of victim selection, extent and means of planning, and characteristics of each type of assault may remain secret, interfering with the ability of professionals to interrupt future assaults.

7. Although it is common for sexual offenders to disclose additional crimes while in treatment, important concerns must be addressed about whether the information disclosed during the polygraph examination is considered compelled. Agreements regarding prosecution for past crimes or instances of limited immunity must be discussed with the offender in advance. Most commonly, the prosecution makes the decision to prosecute past crimes on a case-by-case basis. Frequently there is insufficient information to prosecute. Sometimes prosecutors grant limited immunity for past crimes, agreeing not to pursue prosecution as long as the offender actively participates in treatment. Victims' organizations must make recommendations about the value of contacting past and recent child victims from whom there has been no outcry and offering services.

8. There were no identified sample differences between sites C and D in terms of the *number* of hands-on and hands-off crimes reported. Very little variation was found between the two samples in terms of age and gender of victims reported.

9. An empirical question was whether probation and parole cases were similar enough to be combined. Chi square analyses revealed few differences in the two groups. Probationers reported a higher number of total victims compared to parolees, but the difference was not significant. Not surprisingly, the parole group had a more extensive history recorded in official records. Compared to probationers, parolees were also more likely to have a documented arrest for domestic violence. Parolees were slightly older and less likely to be employed at the point of arrest for the current offense. No statistical differences were found in the analysis of postconviction polygraph disclosures, so the two groups were combined.

10. The variation in the sample design was intentional. Across the United States, there is substantial variation—across jurisdictions, across programs, across professionals—in efforts to treat and supervise the convicted sexual offender population, not to mention the variation in the offenders who are managed in these programs. The generalizability of the findings from studies of offenders is always suspect owing to variation at the state and local level in official and unofficial policies and the criminal history of offenders in a given sample.

11. The age of consent varied across the states. In five cases there was a minimal age difference between the offender and the victim for the conviction crime, and the documentation included a victim statement reporting consent. Nevertheless, a decision had been made to prosecute the case, and these cases were coded as victims.

12. The lengthy data collection instrument contained two major sections. The first section described offending information known to the criminal justice system *before* the treatment/polygraph process. It included all information regarding the offender's current crime, along with the sex offending history that was known to the criminal justice system prior to the beginning of treatment. Data sources for the first section included presentence investigation reports, police reports of the instant offense, and case notes of the supervising officer regarding information learned independently of the treatment/polygraph process. Information about the offender's juvenile sexual offense history was recorded separately from the offender's adult sexual offense history. The second section of the data collection instrument contained all information about the offender resulting from elements of treatment relating to preparation for the polygraph examination, as well as disclosures made during the exam itself. Sec-

ond section data sources were the self-reported sex history document, homework assignments relating to polygraph exam information, polygraph examination reports, and case management notes pertaining to the treatment/polygraph process. All files were extensively examined, and data were extracted to the collection form. Decisions on how to record data were made with a data collection supervisor available to develop consistent protocols. Every effort was made to separate data known to the criminal justice system without the postconviction/treatment polygraph process from that known as a result of this process. For instance, if a risk behavior was detected after sentencing through the normal supervision process, this information was not attributed to the polygraph/treatment process.

13. Ten offenders had a current conviction for exhibitionism.
14. The average age of onset for hands-on sex crimes was 12 years.
15. At least four reasons may lead to underestimates of activity: (1) data were collected only on victims that were disclosed by the offender and documented in the file; (2) data collectors made conservative decisions when recording victim information, so any error would be in the direction of underreporting victimizations; (3) some victimizations known to the therapist, polygraph examiner, and supervising officer may not have been documented in the files; and (4) only one-third of the polygraph examinations were scored as nondeceptive.
16. Only 5% of the 561 had ever been arrested for a sex crime.
17. Ten offenders were convicted of exhibitionism in the current sample. Four disclosed forcing vaginal penetration, 3 disclosed forcing oral sex, 4 disclosed bestiality, 8 had a history of fondling/frottage, 1 had forced anal penetration, and all reported prior exhibitionism and assault. Six had deceptive polygraph exam scores.
18. Ahlmeyer et al. (2000) found polygraph disclosures and the proportion of nondeceptive test results increased during subsequent exams when offenders were engaged in intense treatment.

REFERENCES

AMERICAN MEDICAL ASSOCIATION. (1995). "Sexual Assault in America." Position paper, November 6, 1995.

ABEL, G.G. & ROULEAU, J.-L. (1990). The nature and extent of sexual assault. In W.L. Marshall, D.R. Laws & H.E. Barbaree (Eds.), *Handbook of sexual assault: Issues, theories and treatment of the offender* (pp. 9–20). New York: Plenum Press.

ABEL, G.G., BECKER, J.V., CUNNINGHAM-RATHNER, J., MITTLEMAN, M. & ROULEAU, J.L. (1988). Multiple paraphilic diagnoses among sex offenders. *Bulletin of the American Academy of Psychiatry and the Law, 16,* 153–168.

AHLMEYER, S., HEIL, P., MCKEE, B. & ENGLISH, K. (2000). The impact of polygraphy on admissions of victims and offenses in adult sex offenders. *Sexual Abuse: A Journal of Research and Treatment, 12,* 123–138.

ASSOCIATION FOR THE TREATMENT OF SEXUAL ABUSERS. (1993). *Practitioner's handbook.* Beaverton, OR.

ASSOCIATION FOR THE TREATMENT OF SEXUAL ABUSERS. (2001). *Practice standards and guidelines for members.* Beaverton, OR.

BECKER J.V. & COLEMAN, E.M. (1988). Incest. In V.B. VanHassett, R.L. Morrison, A.S. Bellack & M. Hersen (Eds.), *Handbook of family violence* (pp. 197–205). New York: Plenum.

BECKER, J.V., KAPLAN, M.S., CUNINGHAM-RATHNER, J. & KAVOUSSI, R. (1986). Characteristics of adolescent incest sexual perpetrators: Preliminary findings. *Journal of Family Violence, 1,* 85–97.

BLUMSTEIN, A., FARRINGTON, D.P. & MOITRA, S.D. (1985). Specialization and seriousness during adult criminal careers. *Journal of Quantitative Criminology, 4,* 303–345.

BLUMSTEIN, A., COHEN, J., ROTH, J.A. & VISHER, C.A. (Eds.). (1988). *Criminal careers and career criminals* (Vols. 1 and 2). Washington, DC: National Academy Press.

COLORADO SEX OFFENDER MANAGEMENT BOARD (1999). *Standards and guidelines for the assessment, evaluation, treatment, and behavioral monitoring of adult sex offenders.* Denver: Colorado Division of Criminal Justice.

ENGLISH, K., JONES, L., PATRICK, D. & PASINI-HILL, D. (2000). *The value of the post-conviction polygraph.* National Institute of Justice. Washington, DC: U.S. Department of Justice.

ENGLISH, K., JONES, L. & PATRICK, D. (2003). Community containment of sex offender risk: A promising approach. In B.J. Winick & J.Q. La Fond (Eds.), *Protecting society from sexually dangerous offenders: Law, justice and therapy,* Washington, DC: American Psychological Association.

ENGLISH, K., PULLEN, S. & JONES, L. (Eds.). (1996). *Managing adult sex offenders: A containment approach.* Lexington, KY: American Probation and Parole Association.

ENGLISH, K. (1998). The Containment Approach: An aggressive strategy for the community management of adult sex offenders. *Psychology, Public Policy and Law, 14*(2/1).

FALLER, K.C. (1990). Sexual abuse by paternal caretakers: A comparison of abusers who are biological fathers in intact families, stepfathers, and non-custodial fathers. In A.L. Horton, B.L. Johnson, M. Roundy & D. Williams (Eds.), *The incest perpetrator: A family member no one wants to treat* (pp. 65–73), Newbury Park, CA: Sage.

FINKELHOR, D., HOTELING, G.T., LEWIS, I.A. & SMITH, C. (1990). Sexual abuse in a national survey of adult men and women: Prevalence, characteristics and risk factors. *Child Abuse and Neglect, 14,* 12–28.

FIRESTONE, P., BRADFORD, J.M., MCCOY, M., GREENBERG, D.M., LAROSE, M.R. & CURRY, S. (1999). Prediction of recidivism in incest offenders. *Journal of Interpersonal Violence, 14,* 511–532.

FREEMAN-LONGO, R.E. (1985). *Incidence of self-reported sex crimes among incarcerated rapists and child molesters.* Unpublished manuscript, as cited in Salter, A. (1985). *Transforming trauma: A guide to understanding and treatment of adult survivors of child sexual abuse.* Thousand Oaks, CA: Sage.

GREENFELD, L.A. (1997). *Sex offenders and offenses.* Bureau of Justice Statistics. Washington, DC: U.S. Department of Justice.

GROTPETER, J.K. & ELLIOTT, D.S. (2002). *Violent sexual offending.* Center for the Study and Prevention of Violence, University of Colorado, Boulder.

HANSON, R.F., RESNICK, H.S., SAUNDERS, B.E., KILPATRICK, D.G. & BEST, C. (1999). Factors related to the reporting of childhood rape. *Child Abuse and Neglect, 23,* 559–569.

HANSON, R.K. (2000). What is so special about relapse prevention? In D.R. Laws, S.M. Hudson & T. Ward (Eds.), *Remaking relapse prevention with sex offenders: A sourcebook.* Thousand Oaks, CA: Sage.

HANSON, R.K. & BUSSIERE, M.T. (1998). Predicting relapse: A meta-analysis of sexual offending recidivism studies. *Journal of Consulting and Clinical Psychology, 66,* 348–362.

HUDSON, S.M., WARD, T. & MCCORMACK, (1999). Offense pathways in sexual offenders, *Journal of Interpersonal Violence,14,* 779–798.

KILPATRICK, D.G., EDMUNDS, C.N. & SEYMOUR, A. (1992). *Rape in America: A report to the nation.* Charleston: Medical University of South Carolina, National Victim Center and Crime Victims Research and Treatment Center.

LAMB, S. & EDGAR-SMITH, S. (1994). Aspects of disclosure: Mediators of outcome in childhood sexual abuse. *Journal of Interpersonal Violence, 9,* 307–326.

LAWS, D.R., HUDSON, S.M. & WARD, T. (2000). *Remaking relapse prevention with sex offenders: A sourcebook.* Thousand Oaks, CA.: Sage.

LAWSON, L. & CHAFFIN, M. (1992). False negatives in sexual abuse disclosure interviews. *Journal of Interpersonal Violence, 7,* 532–542.

MARSHALL, W.L. & BARBAREE, H.E. (1990). Outcomes of comprehensive cognitive-behavioral treatment programs. In W.L. Marshall, D.R. Laws & H.E. Barbaree (Eds.), *Handbook of sexual assault: Issues, theories, and treatment of the offender* (pp. 363–385). New York: Plenum.

MARSHALL, W.L., BARBAREE, H.E. & ECCLES, T. (1991). Early onset and deviant sexuality in child molesters. *Journal of Interpersonal Violence, 6,* 323–335.

PIQUERO, A., PATERNOSTER, R., MAZEROLLE, P., BRAME, R. & DEAN, C.W. (1999). Onset age and offense specialization. *Journal of Research in Crime and Delinquency, 36,* 275–299.

PITHERS, W.D., KASHIMA, K.M., CUMMING, G.F. & BEAL, L.S. (1988). Relapse prevention: A method of enhancing maintenance of change in sex offenders. In A.C. Salter (Ed.), *Treating child sex offenders and victims: A practical guide* (pp. 131–170). Newbury Park, CA: Sage.

PITHERS, W.D. (1990). Relapse prevention with sexual aggressors: A method for maintaining therapeutic gain and enhancing external supervision. In W.L. Marshall, D.R. Laws & H.E. Barbaree (Eds.), *Handbook of sexual assault: Issues, theories, and treatment of the offender.* New York: Plenum Press.

PROULX, J., PELLERIN, B., PARADIS, Y., MCKIBBEN, A., AUBUT, J. & OUIMET, M. (1997). Static and dynamic predictors of recidivism in sexual aggressors. *Sexual Abuse: A Journal of Research and Treatment, 9,* 7–28.

QUINSEY, V.L. RICE, M.E. & HARRIS, G.T. (1995). Actuarial prediction of sexual recidivism. *Journal of Interpersonal Violence, 10,* 85–105.

RESLER, T.A. & WIND, W.T. (1994). Telling the secret: Adult women describe their disclosures of incest. *Journal of Interpersonal Violence, 9,* 307–326.

RUSSELL, D.E.H. (1986). *The secret trauma: Incest in the lives of girls and women.* New York: Basic Books.

SALTER, A. (1995). *Transforming trauma: A guide to understanding and treating adult survivors of child sexual abuse.* Thousand Oaks, CA: Sage.

SAUZIER, M. (1989). Disclosure of child sexual abuse: For better or for worse. *Psychiatric Clinics of North America, 12,* 455–469.

SERIN, R.C., MAILLOUX, D.L. & MALCOLM, P. (2001). Psychopathy, deviant sexual arousal and recidivism among sexual offenders. *Journal of Interpersonal Violence, 16,* 234–246.

SMITH, D.W., LETOURNEAU, E.J., SAUNDERS, B.E., KILPATRICK, D.G., RESNICK, H.S. & BEST, C. (2000). Delay in disclosure of childhood rape: Results from a national survey. *Child Abuse and Neglect, 24,* 273–287.

SNYDER, H. (2000). *Sexual assault of young children as reported to law enforcement: Victim, incident, and offender characteristics.* Bureau of Justice Statistics. Washington, DC: U.S. Department of Justice.

TJADEN, P. & THOENNES, N. (1998). *Prevalence, incidence and consequences of violence against women: Findings from the National Violence Against Women Survey.* National Institute of Justice. Centers for Disease Control and Prevention: Research in Brief. Washington, DC: U.S. Department of Justice.

WEINROTT, M.R. & SAYLOR, M. (1991). Self-report of crimes committed by sex offenders. *Journal of Interpersonal Violence, 6,* 286–300.

WYATT, G.E. & NEWCOMB, M. (1990). Internal and external mediators of women's sexual abuse in childhood. *Journal of Consulting and Clinical Psychology, 58,* 758–767.

WYATT, G.E. & POWELL, G.J. (Eds.). (1990). *Lasting Effects of Child Sexual Abuse,* Newbury Park, CA: Sage.

The Size and Sign of Treatment Effects in Sex Offender Therapy

MARNIE E. RICE AND GRANT T. HARRIS

Research Department, Mental Health Centre Penetanguishene,
Penetanguishene, Ontario L9M 1G3, Canada

ABSTRACT: We review scientific criteria for the minimally useful evaluation of psychosocial treatment for sex offenders. The Association for the Treatment of Sexual Abusers recently supported a meta-analysis (Hanson et al., 2002) of the effectiveness of psychological treatment for sex offenders. It was concluded that current treatments for sex offenders reduce recidivism. In this chapter, we reevaluate the evidence. Whereas the random assignment studies yielded results that provided no evidence of treatment effectiveness, Hanson et al. reviewed approximately a dozen others (called "incidental assignment" studies), which yielded substantial positive results for treatment. Upon close inspection, we conclude that such designs involve noncomparable groups and are too weak to be used to draw inferences about treatment effectiveness. In almost every case, the evidence was contaminated by the fact that comparison groups included higher-risk offenders who would have refused or quit treatment had it been offered to them. We conclude that the effectiveness of psychological treatment for sex offenders remains to be demonstrated. Furthermore, we outline solutions that we think will lead to progress in the field of sex offender treatment.

KEYWORDS: sex offenders; treatment; review

In its two most serious forms (child sexual molestation and coercive sexual acts by men against women), sex offenses are fairly common crimes. In addition, for at least the past three decades, the sexual exploitation and coercion by men of women and children has attracted a high degree of sociopolitical attention. There has been considerable pressure on all sides of the political spectrum to recognize these phenomena as worthy of much effort to achieve change. As well, of course, all parents are concerned about the risks of physical and emotional harm represented by sex offenders who target children. Entering this highly charged arena, mental health professionals have attempted to stake out legitimate turf by showing that sex offenders have psychological disorders that are amenable to assessment and treatment (e.g., Barrett & Marshall, 1990). Consequently, in North America, many sex offenders receive treatment aimed at reducing their propensity to commit such offenses, and

Address for correspondence: Marnie E. Rice, Research Department, Mental Health Centre Penetanguishene, 500 Church Street, Penetanguishene, Ontario L9M 1G3, Canada. Voice: 705-549-3181, ext. 2614; fax: 705-549-3652.
riceme@mcmaster.ca

Ann. N.Y. Acad. Sci. 989: 428–440 (2003). © 2003 New York Academy of Sciences.

many criminal justice systems are heavily invested in providing clinical services for sex offenders.

There are some generally agreed-upon standards for conducting research, in general, and treatment evaluation, in particular. Most commonly, evaluating treatment entails two stages (Streiner, 2002). The first stage, establishing efficacy, involves rigorous research designs (random assignment, double-blind placebo, and multiple outcome measures) and maximizing treatment effects (homogeneous groups, manualized therapy, and treatment process measures). The second stage, establishing effectiveness, involves studying the smaller treatment effects achieved in ordinary practice where such thorough control of therapeutic efforts is usually not possible. In the field of psychological treatment for sex offenders, the question of efficacy (can treatment work) has not been settled. Most investigators in the field have skipped to the effectiveness question (does treatment work), which has greater relevance to public policy.

Investigators generally agree that it is desirable to eliminate or control possible sources of measurement bias, and that useful evaluation comes from studies in which a treated group is contrasted with a comparable group that receives no treatment (or a clearly different treatment). Differences among experts arise in matters of degree. No study can be free from all threats to internal validity, and so the crucial question concerns how tightly designed a study must be before it can be informative. The gold standard is a random assignment study, but even random assignment to treatment does not guarantee that groups are comparable: random assignment merely guarantees that differences are randomly distributed. Most experts would agree that something can be learned from imperfect research (since no study is perfect). There is less agreement about how much can be learned from studies, the level of methodological quality, and the standards that should define minimally useful evaluation research.

Our own position tends to demand relatively high quality (closer to efficacy evaluation) before conclusions are warranted. In our view, advocating low standards entails two unacceptable risks. The first risk is the overly credulous acceptance of findings. A famous example is the Cambridge Somerville Youth Study (McCord, 1978). In this study, several hundred boys from disadvantaged neighborhoods were randomly assigned to either a treatment or control group. The families of boys in the treatment group received services for an average of five years, including family counseling, extra tutoring, summer camp, Boy Scouts, the YMCA, and other community programs. Thirty years later, weak inference, subjective evaluations of the program by those who received it suggested it had very positive effects. However, more rigorous evaluation comparing the treatment and control groups indicated that the program had adverse effects on criminal behavior, death, disease, occupational status, and job satisfaction.

Two other recent examples have been appeared in the popular press. Without a random assignment study, the health risks of hormone replacement therapy for menopausal women would have gone unnoticed (Anstett, 2002; Park, 2002; Writing Group for the Women's Health Initiative Investigators, 2002). Without a placebo-controlled random assignment trial, the futility of arthroscopic knee surgery would not have been revealed (Horowicz, 2002; Moseley et al., 2002). In short, the risks of weak inference evaluation, in doing harm and wasting resources, are simply too great. Weak inference evaluation leads to too many errors (in incorrectly accepting the existence of beneficial effects) and cannot be justified on epistemological grounds. A second risk of weak inference evaluation is that outsiders will perceive that weak inference is promoted in the evaluation of one's own clinical efforts while strong inference is demanded of the efforts of others. In our view as sex offender therapists, the best hope our specialty has for credibility lies in adherence to strong inference evaluation of clinical work.

THE DIFFICULTIES IN EVALUATING SEX
OFFENDER TREATMENT EXEMPLIFIED

Consider a particularly revealing example of the methodological problems that characterize this field. One Canadian prison-based treatment program for sex offenders has been the subject of three evaluation studies using overlapping samples from the same population but reporting contradictory results about treatment effectiveness. Davidson (1984) studied a behavioral treatment program for sex offenders by comparing the outcomes of 101 treated men with those of a matched control group of untreated men. Groups were followed for criminal recidivism (using police records) for up to five years after release. There was no difference between groups in the likelihood of a new conviction for a sex offense, although treated offenders were more likely to incur a new charge for a sex offense and significantly less likely to be convicted of any new violent (which included sexual) offense or any new offense.

The treated men were those prisoners who had prior sex offenses on their criminal records treated in the Regional Treatment Centre of the Kingston Penitentiary in Kingston Ontario between 1974 and 1982 and released prior to August 1982. The comparison subjects were drawn from men admitted to Ontario penitentiaries between 1966 and 1974, and released by 1977. The comparison sample was matched to the treated sample on age and sex of victim, and whether the offender was an incest offender. This practice of choosing comparison subjects from a different cohort has been common in treatment outcome studies for sex offenders.

In a second study, Quinsey, Khanna, and Malcolm (1998) studied the postrelease recidivism (average follow-up of 44 months) of 213 men who completed the treatment program at the same institution as the Davidson study. In addition, they studied 183 men who were assessed as not requiring treatment, 52 who refused to be assessed, 27 who were assessed but deemed to be unsuitable, and 9 who were considered to require treatment but who did not receive it for a variety of reasons. All participants were assessed or treated between 1976 and 1989, and released prior to 1992. Treated offenders were the most likely to be rearrested for sex offenses, and, even after statistically controlling for several variables that predicted reoffending, the treatment program was associated with more sexual rearrests, but not violent (including sexual) rearrests. Furthermore, therapists' ratings of progress and need for further treatment were unrelated to recidivism. The authors suggested that treatment might have increased sexual recidivism.

In contrast, the third study (Looman, Abracen & Nicholaichuk, 2000) concluded their investigation "clearly indicates that the RTC program was effective in terms of reducing the risk of future recidivism" (p. 288), reporting a significantly lower sexual recidivism rate (based on national police records) among the treated offenders. Similar to Davidson (1984), this study used matched offenders from a different cohort but drawn from a different region of the country. They were matched to treated subjects on age at index offense, date of index offence, and number of past criminal convictions. The treated participants (Looman et al., 2000) were a subset ($n = 89$) of the treated sample from Quinsey et al. (1998) that excluded men treated outside the residential program setting ($n = 27$), whose treatment format (group, individual, or outpatient) was unclear ($n = 36$), whose treatment occurred outside the period 1976 to 1989 ($n = 12$), who received treatment at another institution ($n = 9$), or could not be matched. The Looman et al. (2000) follow-up time was relatively long (nearly 8 years on average).

What could a disinterested reader make of these three studies from the same population? A generous interpretation is illustrated by a meta-analysis of sex offender therapy (Hanson et al., 2002), which dismissed the Quinsey et al. (1998) study as having a weaker design than the other two. The results of Davidson (1984) and Looman et al. (2000) were averaged to obtain an overall beneficial treatment effect: a sexual recidivism rate of 26% in the treated group and 32% in the comparison group (odds ratio = .78, indicating that for every 100 untreated offenders who recidivate, only 78 treated offenders would recidivate), a finding in line with the main general conclusion (overall mean odds ratio = .81) of the meta-analysis (Hanson et al., 2002).

On the other hand, we find the aggregate results of the three studies to be inconclusive regarding treatment effectiveness. Although the Quinsey et al. (1998) study used only statistical procedures to match groups, all subjects came from the same cohort and jurisdiction, and that study had strengths the others did not. It carefully monitored the outcomes for treatment refusers and offenders not offered treatment, and both groups were found to have lower rates of sexual recidivism than those who were treated. Quinsey et al. examined therapists' ratings about performance and gains made in treatment and showed that these ratings were unrelated to subsequent outcome. As well, Quinsey et al. examined pre- and posttreatment psychometric measures for the treatment group and related each to outcome. Almost invariably, pretreatment scores more strongly predicted outcome than did posttreatment scores. These results resemble those of a previous treatment evaluation at a different institution (Rice, Quinsey & Harris, 1991), showing that pretreatment phallometric deviance scores were more highly related to outcome than posttreatment scores. In our view, the most parsimonious interpretation of these analyses by Quinsey et al., as well as the other two reports, is that treatment did not reduce recidivism.

MINIMALLY INFORMATIVE EVALUATION

Elsewhere we have laid out our criteria for studies that, in our considered judgment, can provide useful scientific data on the effectiveness of treatment (Quinsey, Harris, Rice & Lalumière, 1993). Briefly, unless a study measures officially recorded recidivism from at least two distinct groups of sex offenders (at least one of which received treatment), and unless the groups are, except for treatment, comparable, that study has no scientific value in evaluating the treatment. Clearly, the best way of achieving group comparability is through random assignment. The only other acceptable way to achieve comparability is through matching on factors known to be related to recidivism. Matching can be achieved by pairwise direct matching or, less desirably, through statistical matching using static, historical risk factors as covariates. To be even minimally useful, the groups need to be comparable on (1) established static predictors of recidivism, (2) jurisdiction and cohort, and (3) volunteering for and completing treatment. Thus, matching on other characteristics notwithstanding, no useful scientific data on treatment efficacy can be derived from contrasting sex offenders who completed treatment with those who dropped out. This is because quitting treatment is a recidivism risk factor that is unlikely to be obviated by matching on historical variables. Of course, sex offenders who are not offered treatment cannot volunteer and cannot complete it. Samples of untreated sexual offenders will contain a substantial minority who would refuse treatment if offered, and another subset who, after beginning treatment, would quit or be ejected. In our opinion, few useful scientific data on effectiveness can come from studies contrasting treatment completers with sex offenders not offered treatment because such contrasts almost inevitably entail noncomparable groups.

Treatment Refusal

Experts clearly agree that the available data support the conclusion that quitting treatment (or being ejected) is a risk factor (e.g., Hanson et al., 2002). There is, however, less agreement about refusing treatment. Some empirical data were provided by a meta-analysis of sex offender treatment (Hanson et al., 2002) that reported that refusers had nonsignificantly lower rates of sexual recidivism than dropouts and, for general recidivism, treatment refusers were nonsignificantly more likely to fail than dropouts. Together, these results suggest that refusers are similar in risk to dropouts. Hanson et al. also compared recidivism rates of those who attended any treatment (i.e., completers plus dropouts) with those of treatment refusers and reported that those who refused treatment exhibited higher rates of general recidivism but did not exhibit greater sexual recidivism. The treatment groups for these latter comparisons included dropouts who are known to be of much higher risk than completers. Thus, it is highly probable that, irrespective of the effects of treatment, those who refuse represent greater risk than those who volunteer for and complete it.[a] Our criteria do not permit the evaluation of treatment by comparing sex offenders who complete treatment with a group not offered it. Any study that does not track both refusers and dropouts cannot provide scientifically useful data in support of treatment effectiveness because there are clear *a priori* reasons to expect differences between the groups in recidivism.[b]

---

[a]Hanson (personal communication, September 25, 2002) reported that direct comparisons between completers and refusers are reported in several studies; on average, there was no difference for sexual recidivism, but there was a difference for general recidivism. Although he did not regard the data as providing full support, Hanson concluded that, "[T]here are *a priori* reasons that treatment refusers should be [considered] high risk." We agree.

[b]Because dropping out and refusing treatment are risk factors, studies finding no effects of treatment, though not reporting outcomes for dropouts and refusers, do provide useful data about the *lack* of effectiveness of the treatment evaluated (cf. Rice, Harris & Cormier, 1992; Rice et al., 1991).

EVALUATING ALL REPORTS OF PSYCHOLOGICAL
TREATMENT FOR SEX OFFENDERS

The recent meta-analysis by leading experts in the sex offender field (Hanson et al., 2002, hereafter abbreviated Hanson et al.) and supported by the Association for the Treatment of Sexual Abusers (ATSA) concluded, "We believe that the balance of available evidence suggests that current treatments reduce recidivism, but that firm conclusions await more and better research" (p. 187). The Hanson et al. meta-analysis performed a great service to the field by including all (43) published and unpublished studies of psychological treatment (reporting sexual or general criminal recidivism and comparing treated sex offenders to others) that the authors could find. Although its conclusions are very similar to those of previous meta-analyses (Gallagher, Wilson, Hirschfield, Coggeshall & MacKenzie, 1999; Hall, 1995), the Hanson et al. study included more than twice as many individual studies. It is safe to conclude that the studies in the Hanson et al. meta-analysis represent just about all the evidence there is about the effectiveness of psychological treatment for sex offenders. Its comprehensiveness demands careful consideration.

Our judgment that the effectiveness of sex offender treatment has not been demonstrated does not technically contradict the conclusive statement by Hanson et al. in the previous paragraph, but it certainly carries a different emphasis. Our conservative emphasis in not accepting the existence of an effect until one is obliged by data is Occam's razor, a generally accepted epistomological principle (cf. Sagan, 1992). The Hanson et al. report has been widely disseminated, but the tentative tone of the major conclusion is often lost. For example, a recent publication (Solicitor General Canada, 2002; also see Tang, 2002) summarizes it as follows: "... current treatments were associated with a significant reduction in both sexual recidivism (from 17% to 10%) and general recidivism (51% to 32%)." With few exceptions, the studies included in this meta-analysis did not meet our criteria for minimally useful evaluation.

The Assignment to Research Design

Hanson et al. assigned studies to one of six research-design categories. The first category was the random assignment of subjects to either psychological treatment or no psychological treatment. This is clearly the strongest design and the one that best supports conclusive statements about treatment effects. Unfortunately, Hanson et al. found only four studies they could assign to this category. Two indicated deleterious effects of treatment. One of these (Romero & Williams, 1983) involved dynamically oriented psychotherapy that has not fared well for offenders in general (Andrews, Zinger, Hoge & Bonta, 1996). The other study (Marques, 1999; Marques, Day, Nelson & West, 1994) was the most well-designed and executed study the sex offender treatment field has ever seen or is likely to see for some time, and used a state-of-the-art intervention for a large number of adult sex offenders that included a follow-up component, and tracked refusers and dropouts as well as treated and control subjects. The only random assignment study that reported positive treatment results for sexual recidivism was Borduin, Henggeler, Blaske, and Stein (1990) that included eight treated and eight untreated adolescents (later expanded to 24 in each in an unpublished study; Borduin, Schaeffer & Heilblum, 2000). The treatment was "multisystemic therapy" that Hanson et al. admit would be difficult to apply to adult offenders. The fourth random-assignment study (Robinson, 1995) reported positive results in reducing general recidivism for sex offenders who participated in a cognitive-behavioral program run for a wide variety of offenders. For offenders as a whole, however, the treatment had no significant positive effect when dropouts were included. Moreover, treatment was most effective for the lowest risk offenders, a finding in contradiction to the general risk principle, which states that correctional treatment is most effective when directed at high-risk offenders (Andrews et al., 1996). We agree with Hanson et al. that no empirical support for treatment effectiveness can be drawn from the random assignment studies, and especially not for sex offender–specific treatment for adults.

The second and most crucial design category considered by Hanson et al. was called "incidental" assignment to treatment. In these studies, comparison groups were offenders drawn from criminal record archives but who were released before the implementation of the treatment or who came from different geographical areas, who received an earlier version of the treatment, or who received either no treatment or an alternate treatment due to such administrative reasons as too little time remaining in their sentence. Hanson et al. called these 17 studies incidental because they claimed there was no obvious, *a priori* reason that treated and untreated offenders would differ in risk. It was claimed that neither offenders nor therapists determined who would receive treatment, leaving no obvious biases in group assignment. A third design category was called "assignment based on need"—studies in which the treated subjects were assessed as requiring treatment while control subjects were assessed as not requiring it or being unsuitable. The other design categories were (1) comparisons of treatment completers with dropouts, (2) dropouts with refusers, and (3) those who received any treatment (including dropouts) with refusers. Hanson et al. (2002) considered random and incidental assignment to be informative.

We agree with Hanson et al. about random designs as strong enough, and about the designs they considered too weak. We disagree, however, about the incidental designs. Indeed, we do not agree that assignment based on need is inferior to their incidental assignment category. Assignment based on need studies yielded an overall odds ratio of 3.10 for sexual recidivism, indicating that those who were treated reoffended at over three times the rate of the untreated. Hanson et al., of course, dismissed these studies because they argued (without much empirical support) that the highest risk offenders would be most likely to be judged to "need" treatment and it would be unfair to evaluate treatment by comparing treated and untreated groups because they would differ in risk at the outset. However, we believe that statistical controls for such group differences can make this design more worthwhile than some incidental designs. Some of the assignment based on need studies, for example, statistically controlled for as many static factors as possible before examining whether the dichotomous variable "treated or not" added anything to the prediction of outcome. In our view, this statistical matching is preferable to almost all of the incidental designs. At least one of the six studies categorized as based on need used a matching design (Rice et al., 1991), as did the dismissed Quinsey et al. (1998) study. Interestingly, neither found a beneficial effect of treatment.

Reconsidering the Hanson et al. (2002) ATSA Meta-Analysis

Hanson et al. reported that, of the 38 studies of sexual recidivism, the treatment effect was much larger (and only significant) in the 17 unpublished studies (odds ratio = .65, 95% CI .52–.81) than in the 21 published studies (odds ratio = .95, 95% CI .79–1.15). The main reason that unpublished studies are included in the meta-analysis is the "file drawer" problem: studies that fail to find an effect are less likely to be published (Rosenthal, 1995; Streiner, 1991). Clearly this trouble does not plague the field of sex offender treatment. Could Hanson et al. have obtained a significant treatment effect without the unpublished studies? The answer depended on further sorting.

Hanson et al. further classified treatments as "current" or not. Current treatments were said to be those still being offered (thereby excluding all but those labeled cognitive-behavioral or multisystemic). Although no reason was provided, cognitive-behavioral treatment delivered before 1980 was also excluded, eliminating one study (Perkins, 1987) that reported a large adverse treatment effect (odds ratio = 3.38); curiously, the offenders were treated between 1974 and 1983, with the majority after 1980 (Perkins, 1987). The treatments categorized as noncurrent by Hanson et al. indicated no beneficial effect of treatment, but the twelve random and incidental studies of current treatment yielded an odds ratio for sexual recidivism of .60 (95% CI .48–.75), indicating a positive effect of treatment in which there was no significant difference between published and unpublished results. Similar results were obtained for general recidivism.

In the end, because the random assignment studies indicated no beneficial effect of treatment, the optimistic conclusions of the Hanson et al. meta-analysis rest on about a dozen incidental assignment studies of current treatments, and most ($n = 11$) reported a difference between treated and comparison groups that favored the treated offenders. Few of these incidental studies of current treatment meet our criteria for minimally informative evaluation. All but three (Lindsay & Smith, 1998; Marshall, Eccles & Barbaree, 1991; McGrath, Hoke & Vojtisek, 1998) clearly included men in the comparison group that were not offered treatment.

To be specific, the Allam (Allam, 1998; 1999); Bakker, Hudson, Wales, and Riley (1999); Clearwater (Hanson & Nicholaichuk, 2000; Nicholaichuk, Gordon, Gu & Wong, 2000); Proctor (1996); RTC Ontario (Davidson, 1984; Looman et al., 2000); and Worling and Curwen (1998) studies listed in Table 1 of Hanson et al. appear to have excluded refusers from the treated group, but included in the comparison group offenders who would have refused treatment had it been offered. In addition, the Bakker et al.; Clearwater; Guarino-Ghezzi, and Kimball (1998); La Macaza (Earls, 1997; Earls, Martin & Bélanger, 1999); and RTC Ontario studies listed in Table 1 of Hanson et al. appear to have excluded dropouts from the treated group, but included in the comparison group men who would have dropped out if treatment had been offered. As discussed earlier, sex offenders selected for having completed treatment are not comparable to sex offenders who are not offered treatment. Designs using such noncomparable groups are not informative about treatment effectiveness because refusal and dropping out are *a priori* risk factors.

Consider the three remaining incidental studies (Lindsay & Smith, 1998; Marshall et al., 1991; McGrath et al., 1998). Marshall et al., reported on two treatment regimens for exhibitionists from two different temporal cohorts with differences in the duration of follow-up. Hanson et al. used the original reports to equate follow-ups, but large documented decade-to-decade changes in overall crime statistics (Finkelhor, 2002) mean that contrasting a recent treatment with an earlier yields an apparent but spurious treatment effect. Thus, the Marshall et al. (1991) study does not meet our criteria for a useful evaluation of sex offender treatment.

The study that reported the largest treatment effect (comprising data from three publications: Lindsay, Marshall & Neilson, 1998; Lindsay, Neilson & Morrison, 1998; Lindsay & Smith, 1998) compared seven "treated" intellectually disabled sex offenders and seven intellectually disabled comparison men. The odds ratio reported for this study was .05, implying that for every 100 untreated offenders who reoffended, only five of the treated offenders would reoffend. Upon close inspection, we find many reasons to question this remarkable result. All offenders received the identical therapy, but the treated group received it for twice as long—two years of probation versus one. Therapy was conducted in groups of four (how there came to be seven offenders in each group is unclear) for 2.5 hours per week and consisted of a review of each offender's week and discussion of general events, with a focus on attitudes or behavior that was of concern, further discussion focusing on denial and minimization, and informal chatting. Follow-up data were gathered "at least two years after probation had finished." The authors did not discuss possible group differences in follow-up times and treatment dropout, but concluded, "In terms of reoffending, two [comparison] subjects ... have been charged with crimes similar to their previous offenses and two further subjects are strongly suspected of reoffending by those professionals still in contact with them." None of the treated group were suspected of reoffending. Hanson et al. incorporated this as a 0% recidivism rate for the treated group and a 57% recidivism rate for the comparison group.

In the third study (McGrath et al., 1998; odds ratio = .11), 71 probationers received specialized sex offender treatment, and a comparison group received non-specialized therapy from different clinicians. The original authors reported that some offenders received nonspecialized treatment because they chose, for a variety of reasons, not to receive the specialized treatment, including "a few" who "appeared to have consciously avoided the specialized program and enrolled in less-demanding treatment programs" (p. 207). Hanson et al. admit that calling the McGrath et al. study incidental (i.e., one in which "neither offenders nor programs determined who would receive treatment") was controversial; it was coded as incidental "because the offenders' choices appeared to be based primarily on administrative reasons (e.g., they were already involved with a therapist that they liked) p. 178." This strikes us as an odd use of the phrase "administrative reasons," and it was quite clear that the original authors suspected that higher-risk offenders were more likely to choose the nonspecialized, comparison treatment. McGrath et al. (1998) noted, for example, that incest offenders made up 35% of the treated group, but only 19% of the comparison group, and that the comparison group had a longer follow-up. These are clear "a priori reasons that treated and untreated offenders would differ in risk" and mean that the McGrath et al. (1998) study meets neither our criteria for a minimally useful evaluation nor the Hanson et al. definition of "incidental assignment."

In contrast to Hanson et al., we find six studies of sex offender treatment that meet our criteria for minimally useful evaluation (Borduin, Schaeffer & Heilblum 2000; Lindsay & Smith, 1998; Marques, 1999; Quinsey et al., 1998; Rice et al., 1991; Romero & Williams, 1983). Although highly variable, the mean effect of treatment on sexual recidivism indicated a trend toward treatment having been detrimental (odds ratio = 1.39, 95% CI .61–3.39), with a similar result for general recidivism. We conclude that the studies considered by Hanson et al. (especially the so-called "current incidental" category) cannot support even the tentative positive conclusions drawn. Indeed, the Hanson et al. analysis of incidental designs illustrates an important limitation of meta-analysis. The analysis of a set of uniformly weak designs cannot attribute variation in effect size to study quality. An overall effect size derived from studies of uniformly poor quality cannot obviate universal methodological weaknesses. Conclusions based on such a meta-analysis are no more justified than conclusions based on the individual studies.

In the end, we are obliged to conclude that the available data afford no convincing scientific evidence that psychosocial treatments have been effective for adult sex offenders. And, apart from suggesting that insight-oriented treatment may be harmful, the literature provides almost no information about which treatment would be most beneficial. Nor does it seem that sex offender therapists have any ability to say which offenders have profited from treatment. Seto and Barbaree (1999), for example, found that therapists' ratings of how well offenders had done in a comprehensive cognitive-behavioral program were actually inversely related to outcome. This is a troubling result for those who assume that such therapies are the treatment of choice for sex offenders. We conclude neither that treatment has been shown to be a waste of time nor that it has been demonstrated to be ineffective. However, it is abundantly clear that any conclusions about the effectiveness of psychological therapy await many more random assignment studies. The current empirical support suggesting beneficial effects of treatment rests on the use of noncomparable groups in which control subjects were of higher *a priori* risk.

STRONGER INFERENCE IN THE EVALUATION OF SEX OFFENDER TREATMENT

Whether readers agree with our conservative appraisal of the available evaluation research, we suspect all would agree that very little knowledge has accumulated about several crucial matters. Thus, there is no information about what aspects of treatment (teaching social skills, versus exploring the offense chain, versus practicing relapse prevention strategies) might produce reductions in recidivism. No one knows anything about which types of offenders (child molesters versus rapists, intra- versus extrafamilial offenders) are most responsive to treatment. Anyone attempting to start a treatment program would find little or no empirical foundation from the sex offender treatment literature. This dearth of knowledge about sex offender treatment contrasts sharply with the rapid expansion of knowledge in other areas.

Most obviously, the appraisal of recidivism risk among sex offenders has shown remarkable progress in less than a decade. In the early 1990s there was almost no basis for the empirical assessment of risk among sex offenders. Some reliable predictors of recidivism had been identified (e.g., Quinsey, 1984; 1986), but there was no means to make empirically valid statements about the risk posed by individual offenders. In only a few years, the field has seen the advent of several validated actuarial methods for risk assessment among sex offenders (see other chapters in this volume). Clearly, the reason behind this rapid advance has been the use of strong inference research methods—large representative samples of sex offenders with reliably measured predictor variables and for whom outcome data have been reliably and independently coded from national criminal justice data bases. Such data sets afford the opportunity for rigorous development and cross-validation testing of any proposed actuarial system. Rapid progress is almost guaranteed. In contrast, weak inference methods leave the field of sex offender treatment drawing conclusions that differ little (or not at all) from those that could be empirically supported 10 or 20 years ago.

Elsewhere in this volume are examples of innovative explanations for why human males engage in sexual coercion against women and children. Most of these, whether focusing on attitudes and values, personality, neurohormonal influences, or subtle forms of neurological deficit imply interventions that would reduce sex offending behavior. These implied interventions vary considerably: therapy to alter deviant, sex offense–supportive attitudes; behavioral programs to increase the likelihood of detection and reduce the payoff of sexual aggression; pharmacological treatments aimed at the remediation of neurohormonal anomalies; and possibly intensive super-vision of sex offenders targeting those personal characteristics and behaviors empir-ically or theoretically related to sexual aggression. Strong inference evaluation research in the comparison of these or other interventions has the greatest chance of producing real progress in intervention technologies and in understanding the etiol-ogy of sex offending in the first place. Weak inference methods (as exemplified by almost all of the studies reviewed by Hanson et al., 2002) ensure that the field of sex offender treatment will continue to exhibit change without progress.

This in turn runs the unnecessary risk that the following statement (consistent with the Hanson et al. conclusion) will apply for many years to come. "The balance of available evidence suggests that various well-known threats to validity and the re-liance on noncomparable groups are responsible for apparent beneficial treatment effects, but that firm conclusions await better research."

ACKNOWLEDGMENTS

The authors are grateful to Karl Hanson, Zoe Hilton, Martin Lalumière, Shari McKee, and Vern Quinsey for helpful comments on earlier drafts.

REFERENCES

ALLAM, J. (1998). *Community-based treatment for sex offenders: An evaluation*. Birming-ham, U.K.: University of Birmingham.

ALLAM, J. (1999). *Effective practice in work with sex offenders: A re-conviction study com-paring treated and untreated offenders*. West Midlands Probation Service Sex Offender Unit (Available from Jayne Allam WMPS SOU, 826 Bristol Road, Selly Oak, Birmingham, West Midlands, B29 6NA).

ANDREWS. D.A., ZINGER, I., HOGE, R.D. & BONTA, J. (1996). Does correctional treatment work? A clinically relevant and psychologically informed meta-analysis. In D.F. Greenbert & F. David (Eds.), *Criminal careers, Vol 2. The International Library of Criminology, Criminal Justice, and Penology* (pp. 437–472). Dartmouth Publishing Company Limited: Brookfield, VT.

ANSTETT, P. (2002, July 9). Study raises alarm on use of hormones. *Toronto Star.*

BAKKER, L., HUDSON, S., WALES, D. & RILEY, D. (1999). *"And there was light": An evaluation of the Kia Marama Treatment Programme for New Zealand sex offenders against children.* Unpublished report. New Zealand.

BARRETT, S. & MARSHALL, W.L. (1990). *Criminal neglect: Why sex offenders go free.* Doubleday: Toronto, ON.

BORDUIN, C.M., SCHAEFFER, C.M. & HEILBLUM, N. (2000, May). *Multi-systemic treatment of juvenile sexual offenders: A progress report.* Paper presented at the 6th International Conference on the Treatment of Sexual Offenders, Toronto.

Borduin, C.M., Henggeler, S.W., Blaske, D.M. & Stein, R.J. (1990). Multisystemic treatment of adolescent sexual offenders. *International Journal of Offender Therapy and Comparative Criminology, 34,* 105–113.

DAVIDSON, P.R. (1984, January). *Behavioural treatment for incarcerated sex offenders: Post-release outcome.* Paper presented at the Sex Offender Assessment and Treatment Conference, Kingston, ON.

EARLS, C.M. (1997). Étude sur la récidive. *Clinique La Macaza Bulletin d'information, 2,* 1–2.

EARLS, C.M., MARTIN, I. & BÉLANGER, H. (October, 18, 1999). *La Macaza outcome study.* Unpublished raw data.

FINKELHOR, D. (2002, October). *Decline in child sexual abuse: What's going on?* Paper presented at the 21st Annual Research and Treatment Conference of the Association for the Treatment of Abusers, Montreal.

GALLAGHER, C.A., WILSON, D.B., HIRSCHFIELD, P., COGGESHALL, M.B. & MACKENZIE, D.L. (1999). A quantitative review of the effects of sex offender treatment on sexual reoffending. *Corrections Management Quarterly, 3,* 19–29.

GUARINO-GHEZZI, S. & KIMBALL, L.M. (1998). Juvenile sex offenders in treatment. *Corrections Management Quarterly, 2,* 45–54.

HALL, G.C. (1995). Sexual offender recidivism revisited: A meta-analysis of recent treatment studies. *Journal of Consulting and Clinical Psychology, 63,* 802–809.

HANSON, R.K., GORDON, A., HARRIS, A.J.R., MARQUES, J.K., MURPHY, W., et al. (2002). First report of the collaborative outcome data project on the effectiveness of psychological treatment for sex offenders. *Sexual Abuse: A Journal of Research and Treatment, 14,* 169–194.

HANSON, R.K. & NICHOLAICHUK, T. (2000). A cautionary note regarding Nicholaichuk et al. (2000). *Sexual Abuse: A Journal of Research and Treatment, 12,* 289–293.

HARRIS, G.T., RICE, M.E. & CORMIER, C.A. (1994). Psychopaths: Is a therapeutic community therapeutic? *Therapeutic Communities, 15,* 283–300.

HOROWICZ, J.M. (2002, July 22). What the knees really need. *Time,* 32.

LINDSAY, W.R., MARSHALL, I. & NEILSON, C. (1998). The treatment of men with a learning disability convicted of exhibitionism. *Research in Developmental Disabilities, 19,* 295–316.

LINDSAY, W.R., NEILSON, C.Q. & MORRISON, F. (1998). The treatment of six men with a learning disability convicted of sex offences with children. *British Journal of Clinical Psychology, 37,* 83–89.

LINDSAY, W.R. & SMITH, A.H.W. (1998). Response to treatment for sex offenders with intellectual disability: A comparison of men with 1- and 2- year probation sentences. *Journal of Intellectual Disability Research, 42,* 346–353.

LOOMAN, J., ABRACEN, J. & NICHOLAICHUK, T.P. (2000). Recidivism among treated sexual offenders and matched controls. *Journal of Interpersonal Violence, 15,* 279–290.

MARQUES, J.K. (1999). How to answer the question, "Does sex offender treatment work?" *Journal of Interpersonal Violence, 14,* 437–451.

MARQUES, J.K., DAY, D.M., NELSON, C. & WEST, M.A. (1994). Effects of cognitive-behavioral treatment on sex offenders recidivism: Preliminary results of a longitudinal study. *Criminal Justice and Behavior, 21,* 28–54.

MARSHALL, W.L., ECCLES, A. & BARBAREE, H.E. (1991). The treatment of exhibitionists: A focus on sexual deviance versus cognitive and relationship features. *Behavior Research and Therapy, 29,* 129–135.

McCORD, J. (1978). A thirty-year follow-up of treatment effects. *American Psychologist, 33,* 284–289.

McGRATH, R.J., HOKE, S.E. & VOJITSEK, J.E. (1998). Cognitive-behavioral treatment of sex offenders. *Criminal Justice and Behavior, 25,* 203–225.

MOSELEY, J.B., O'MALLEY, K., PETERSEN, N.J., MENKE, T.J., BRODY, B.A., et al. (2002). A controlled trial of arthroscopic surgery for osteoarthritis of the knee. *New England Journal of Medicine, 347,* 81–88.

NICHOLAICHUK, T., GORDON, A., GU, D. & WONG, S. (2000). Outcome of an institutional sexual offender treatment program: A comparison between treated and matched untreated offenders. *Sexual Abuse: A Journal of Research and Treatment, 12,* 139–153.

PARK, A. (2002, July 22). What did the study show? *Time,* 32.

PERKINS, D. (1987). A psychological treatment programme for sexual offenders. In B.J. McGurk, D. M. Thornton & M. Williams (Eds.), *Applying psychology to treatment: Theory and practice* (pp. 192–217). Her Majesty's Stationary Office: London.

PROCTOR, E. (1996). A five-year outcome evaluation of a community-based treatment program for convicted sexual offenders run by the probation service. *Journal of Sexual Aggression, 2,* 3–16.

QUINSEY, V.L. (1984). Sexual aggression: Studies of offenders against women. In D. Weisstub (Ed.), *Law and mental health: International perspectives* (pp. 84–121). New York: Pergamon Press.

QUINSEY, V.L. (1986). Men who have sex with children. In D.N. Weisstub (Ed.), *Law and mental health: International perspectives* (pp. 140–172). New York: Pergamon Press.

QUINSEY, V.L., HARRIS, G.T., RICE, M.E. & LALUMIÈRE, M.L. (1993). Assessing treatment efficacy in outcome studies of sex offenders. *Journal of Interpersonal Violence, 8,* 512–523.

QUINSEY, V.L., KHANNA, A. & MALCOLM, P.B. (1998). A retrospective evaluation of the regional treatment centre sex offender treatment program. *Journal of Interpersonal Violence, 13,* 621–644.

RICE, M.E., HARRIS, G.T. & CORMIER, C.A. (1992). Evaluation of a maximum security therapeutic community for psychopaths and other mentally disordered offenders. *Law and Human Behavior, 16,* 399–412.

RICE, M.E., QUINSEY, V.L. & HARRIS, G.T. (1991). Sexual recidivism among child molesters released from a maximum security psychiatric institution. *Journal of Consulting and Clinical Psychology, 59,* 381–386.

ROMERO, J.J. & WILLIAMS, L.M. (1983). Group psychotherapy and intensive probation supervision with sex offenders. *Federal Probation, 47,* 36–42.

ROSENTHAL, R. (1995). Writing meta-analytic reviews. *Psychological Bulletin, 118,* 183–192.

SAGAN, C. (1992). *Shadows of forgotten ancestors: A search for who we are.* New York: Random House.

SETO, M.C. & BARBAREE, H.E. (1999). Psychopathy, treatment behavior, and sex offender recidivism. *Journal of Interpersonal Violence, 14,* 1235–1248.

SOLICITOR GENERAL CANADA. (2002). The effectiveness of treatment for sexual offenders. *Research Summary, 7,* 1–2.

STREINER, D.L. (1991). Using meta-analysis in psychiatric research. *Canadian Journal of Psychiatry, 36,* 357–362.

STREINER, D.L. (2002). The 2 "Es" of research: efficacy and effectiveness trials. *Canadian Journal of Psychiatry, 47,* 552–556.

TANG, J. (2002, October). Understanding and managing sexually coercive behavior. *Update: New York Academy of Sciences Magazine,* 2–5.

WORLING, J.R. & CURWEN, T. (1998). *The adolescent sexual offender project: A 10-year follow-up study.* SAFE-T Program (Sexual Abuse: Family Education & Treatment) Thistletown Regional Centre for Children and Adolescents & Probation and Community Services, Ontario Ministry of Community and Social Services: Toronto, ON.

WRITING GROUP FOR THE WOMEN'S HEALTH INITIATIVE INVESTIGATORS. (2002). Risks and benefits of estrogen plus progestin in healthy postmenopausal women: Principal results from the Women's Health Initiative randomized controlled trial. *Journal of the American Medical Association, 288,* 366–368.

Remediation

Panel Discussion and Peer Commentary

ROXANNE LIEB (*Washington State Institute for Public Policy, Olympia, Washington*): This conference offers a valuable opportunity to step back from the detail and noise of the day to day. Barbara Schwartz's paper succinctly reviews the past and emphasizes the relative youth of the field of sex offender treatment. She notes that over time the field has emulated popular mental health treatment practices, beginning with psychoanalysis and now concentrating on cognitive behavioral approaches. Since social policy often treats sex offenders as a special population, it is easy to lose sight that the accepted treatment interventions often closely follow general mental health practices. Similarly, current innovations in this field duplicate two new options for general criminal justice—the effort to recast crime as a public health problem and explorations of restorative justice. Schwartz outlines how these approaches are being applied to sex offenses, with another paper from Koss and Bachar describing a particular program in Arizona. English and her colleagues explore the use of polygraphs as a technological innovation in treatment and supervision practices.

As is often the case, the theoretical potential of these innovations is at a distance from a widespread application that is practical, fair, and cost-effective. Experiments, however, bring light to the shadows and allow us to discern if and how their reality can enhance individual and community lives.

Rice and Harris remind us of the value of precise thinking and scientific rigor as we strive to advance knowledge. Their paper summarizes the key studies from the literature on sex offender treatment, urging us to examine assumptions about which comparison groups are similar and which have hidden selection biases. They make a comparison to recent "knowledge reversals" in the areas of hormone replacement therapy and arthroscopic knee surgery: both instances where what was believed to be true was proven otherwise through careful clinical trials.

Becker and Hick's paper concerns juvenile sex offenders, pointing out that this population is not simply "small adults." They summarize an impressive body of research that describes important differences between adult and juvenile sex offender populations.

Finally, Lucy Berliner's paper steps outside preoccupations of research and treatment to examine the field's role in social policy development. Berliner reminds us of the harm caused by these crimes and urges sex offender experts to confront the difficult social policy questions, rather than standing aside and criticizing citizens and politicians for their efforts. She recommends several ways that sex offender experts can increase their effectiveness in the policy world.

R. KARL HANSON (*Department of the Solicitor General of Canda, Ottawa, Canada*): Sex offender treatment has changed considerably over the years. New treatments are introduced and once-common practices have fallen out of favor. Such

Ann. N.Y. Acad. Sci. 989: 441–445 (2003). © 2003 New York Academy of Sciences.

changes, however, have rarely been motivated by research findings, leaving observers to wonder whether any apparent evolution simply represents changes in fashion.

Evaluating sex offender treatment is difficult. The best single study of treatment effectiveness with sexual offenders, the Sex Offender Treatment and Evaluation Project (SOTEP; Marques, Day, Nelson & West, 1994) was initiated in the early 1980s and the final results are not yet available. The research and treatment costs were approximately $2.5 million for each year that the program was fully operational. It is unlikely that such a worthy experiment will be replicated any time soon.

The Collaborative Data Outcome Project (Hanson et al., 2002) was initiated in order to provide direction to future research. The first stage of this project was to define minimal standards for research and summarize existing findings. The next goal was to define a framework to guide future research efforts: how can a clinical setting with modest resources contribute to cumulative knowledge? One possibility is to establish a standard protocol in which settings could randomly assign sex offenders to two alternate treatments with near equal credibility. A single setting may treat only 10 offenders, but the contributions of 100 such settings could yield conclusions within a reasonable time frame (i.e., 5 years).

In many settings, research is considered a luxury. If treatment of offenders is going to advance, this attitude must change. Large numbers of sexual offenders are being treated the world over. No single group of researchers will provide a definitive answer to the question of treatment effectiveness. The treatments are sufficiently expensive, and the time required to detect recidivism is sufficiently long that progress will only come through collective efforts.

DAVID THORNTON (*Sand Ridge Secure Treatment Center, Mauston, Wisconsin*): I will comment on issues of randomization, management, and restoration and will close with a comment on listening carefully to all voices in the consideration of penalties for sex abuse.

Randomization: Research into the effectiveness of treatment designed to reduce sexual recidivism has been seriously handicapped by the difficulty of implementing random assignment designs in a correctional context and by the apparently low base rate of sexual reconviction. Lacking randomization, all studies are potentially subject to biases that may distort the results. The low base rate means that only very large samples will have the power to detect effects of the size treatment is expected to produce. To obtain clear-cut results it would be desirable to have at least 20 random assignment studies, each separating the main components of treatment through a factorial design, and with Ns of at least 200 for each condition. Unfortunately, there is virtually no chance of such a program of research's being funded in the foreseeable future. Rather, researchers have typically only had the opportunity of carrying out retrospective evaluation of existing services with the inevitable difficulty of finding ways of identifying untreated offenders who are sufficiently similar to those completing treatment to allow a meaningful comparison. In this context, the publication of Hanson et al.'s (2002) meta-analysis has generally been taken to mark a step forward in our knowledge. The authors devised ways of grouping the various methodologies used into categories that obtained quite different results. Thus, comparisons of treatment completers to offenders who drop out of treatment or who weren't offered it typically resulted in treatment completers' having the lower recidivism rate. In contrast, comparisons of treatment completers with those who were deemed not to need treatment typically resulted in treatment completers' having a higher recidivism rate.

These results have generally been taken to provide some encouragement for the idea that treatment can reduce recidivism. Rice and Harris do the field a service by striking a more cautious note. They point out that a comparison group composed of offenders not offered treatment will inevitably contain individuals who would have declined treatment or who would have dropped out had they begun. Of course, it will also include some individuals who would have been deemed not to need treatment. If the former groups may be higher in risk and the latter lower in risk, it is not clear whether the resulting combined untreated group is overall higher or lower on pre-treatment risk than those who complete treatment. My experience has been that sexual offenders who evade participation in treatment tend to be disproportionately general criminals, psychopaths, and those who categorically deny the sexual offenses for which they have been convicted, while treatment participants tend to be disproportionately nonpsychopathic "sexual specialists." Some attempt may be made to control for prior differences in risk between these diverse groups by using actuarial classification instruments like the Static-99 (Hanson and Thornton, 2000). Although this is certainly worth doing, we know that harder-to-measure psychological risk factors continue to have predictive value even after controlling for instruments like Static-99 (e.g. Thornton, 2002), and thus retrospective matching or statistical adjustments based solely on static predictors of this kind will not be sufficient to control for prior differences. Further debate needs to be held on what kinds of design, short of random assignment, suffice to provide meaningful data.

All this could be avoided, if, as Rice and Harris advocate, we were able to use stronger research designs in the first place. The most we are likely to achieve in the next decade, however, is a few more simple random assignment studies that compare treated and untreated offenders. Although this is certainly worth doing, it is not clear how useful the results will be. At most they will give an overall estimate of treatment effect, but they won't tell us which components of treatment are most helpful or how to improve treatment efficacy. An alternative, and probably more helpful, approach will be to work on the development of empirically grounded process models relating changes in psychological variables to reductions in risk. Research of this kind is both easier to implement than random assignment trials and less expensive since it only requires the collection of additional data alongside ordinary treatment delivery. Importantly, it also yields the kind of information that can guide the improvement of treatment methods.

Management: Several authors (Schwartz; English et al.; and Koss et al.) emphasize the need for integrating different agencies and services to produce effective management of sexual offenders. Schwartz argues for some form of triage in which risk assessment is used to divide offenders into categories requiring different degrees of management. This is certainly a rational response to the now established efficacy of actuarial instruments in producing groups with very different recidivism rates. It is certainly possible for correctional agencies to follow such a principle. The Correctional Service of Canada has done so for many years and a similar matching of provision to risk/need is being used in England. Schwartz suggests that a more thorough implementation of triaging would depend on the same principle's being followed by the courts and she argues for the establishment of sexual offender courts on the same level as drug or mental health courts.

The integrated management approach is most clearly exemplified in English et al.'s description of how postconviction polygraphy can be used to focus treatment and supervision decisions. They present data show that polygraphy leads to disclosure, not only of more victims, but also of a wider range of victims and more offense-precursors, than would otherwise be identified. They argue that risk management strategies that seek to limit offenders' access to potential victims or to intervene prior to reoffense need this more complete picture.

Sentiments on the use of polygraphy with sexual offenders are still quite diverse. Treatment specialists who have not used this method are generally cautious about it. Almost all those who have used it become advocates for its value. Anecdotally, the experience of using polygraphy is that it leads to much more disclosure than do other methods. Systematic studies examining this have been slow in coming, not least because practitioners have seen little point in seeking to prove what is for them obvious. Nevertheless, what is "obvious" is not always true and we could do with more studies that clarify the conditions under which polygraphy leads to better disclosure and the real clinical advantages that result. Additionally, enthusiasts for the method need to give thought to the consequences of polygraph errors. Even in laboratory studies the accuracy rate of polygraphy does not exceed 90%. Thus, some sexual offenders will pass the polygraph when they should have failed, while others will fail when they should have passed.

Restoration: The most exciting proposal in this session is the Restorative Justice model described by Koss, Bachar, and Hopkins. They highlight the difficulty the criminal justice model has in dealing with the bulk of sexual offenses, noting that the great majority of perpetrators exit the system with no effective preventive measures in place and after adversarial processes that often add to the victim's trauma. They describe an initiative that targets first known nonpenetration sexual offenses and sexual assaults involving minimal force, by perpetrators with no prior arrests or domestic violence calls. For this selected group, they describe a process of community conferencing in which the perpetrator acknowledges what he did, listens to the victim describe how she has been affected, and there is a mutually agreed-upon plan to redress the harm done and avoid repetition. Families and supporters of both the perpetrator and victim are involved, and what amounts to a year's supervision of compliance with the plan is provided. The perpetrator's incentive for taking part in this is avoiding the risk of a criminal record and sexual offender registration.

The details of this plan seem to have been carefully constructed in a way that integrates law-enforcement agencies with assessment and treatment specialists but greatly limits the involvement of attorneys. Potentially this strategy offers a better outcome for the victim, the perpetrator and the community. Of course, it is deliberately aimed at a narrowly defined group of offenders and offenses. However, there are an enormous number of these kinds of offenses so the potential benefit is substantial.

One complication for this approach lies in its focus on apparent first offenders. In reality some of these offenders will have committed many past offenses even if they have not previously been arrested. Arguably, however, this approach will at least be no worse for these cases than the likely criminal justice response would have been.

The Folly of Experts: Lucy Berliner provides an impassioned plea for liberal-minded experts to be less contemptuous of ordinary folk and ordinary politics, and of victims and victims' advocates, that have driven the creation of harsher penalties, sex offender registration requirements, community notification laws, and civil commitment. As she correctly points out, if the objective is better social policy, then there is no alternative to genuinely engaging with, and respecting, the ways in which these laws are created.

REFERENCES

HANSON, R.K., GORDON, A., HARRIS, A.J.R., MARQUES, J.K., MURPHY, W., QUINSEY, V.L. & SETO, M.C. (2002). First report of the Collaborative Outcome Data Project on the effectiveness of psychological treatment for sex offenders. *Sex Abuse: A Journal of Research and Treatment, 14,* 169–194.

HANSON, R.K. & THORNTON, D. (2000). Improving risk assessment for sexual offenders: A comparison of three actuarial scales. *Law and Human Behaviour, 24,* 119–136.

MARQUES, J.K., DAY, D.M., NELSOMN, C. & WEST, M.A. (1994). Effcts of cognitive/behavioral treatment on sex offenders' recidivism: Preliminary results of a longitudinal study. *Criminal Justice and Behavior, 21,* 28–54.

THORNTON, D. (2002). Constructing and testing a framework for dynamic risk assessment. *Sexual Abuse: A Journal of Research and Treatment, 14,* 137–151.

Implications of Public Health for Policy on Sexual Violence

KATHLEEN C. BASILE

Division of Violence Prevention, National Center for Injury Prevention and Control, Centers for Disease Control and Prevention, Atlanta, Georgia 30341-3724, USA

ABSTRACT: In the last ten years, researchers and practitioners have written about why sexual violence in particular should be viewed as a public health issue, and the importance of prevention of sexual violence. However, little has been written about how to accomplish this. In this paper I describe steps that could be taken using the public health approach to better achieve prevention of sexual violence. Most research and prevention related to sexual violence have focused on the individual and relationship levels. I discuss the importance of addressing all levels using an ecological approach (macrosystem, exosystem, microsystem, and personal history) and focusing more on prevention that addresses the societal and social roots of sexual violence. The paper concludes with some examples of potential preventive measures and policies consistent with a public health model.

KEYWORDS: public health; sexual violence; ecological approach; primary prevention

INTRODUCTION

Sexual violence takes a toll on victims, their loved ones, and society at-large. In the last few years, scholars in the field of sexual violence have begun to frame sexual violence as a public health issue (Becker & Reilly, 1999; Henry, 2001; Laws, 2000; McMahon, 2000; McMahon & Puett, 1999; Mercy, 1999; Post, Mezey, Maxwell & Wibert, 2002; Potter, Krider & McMahon, 2000; Saltzman, Green, Marks & Thacker, 2000). McMahon (2000) defines public health activities as "what society does to assure that conditions exist in which people can be healthy" (p. 28). A public health perspective focuses on prevention through health promotion (McMahon, 2000) and relies on science to identify and evaluate effective preventive strategies. It is a complement to the criminal justice response to violence, because a public health model emphasizes the importance of changing the social, behavioral, and environmental factors that cause violence, whereas the criminal justice approach traditionally has reacted to violence after it occurs (Mercy, Rosenberg, Powell, Broome & Roper,

Address for correspondence: Kathleen C. Basile, Division of Violence Prevention, National Center for Injury Prevention and Control, Centers for Disease Control and Prevention, Mailstop K60, 4770 Buford Highway NE, Atlanta, Georgia 30341-3724. Voice: 770-488-4224; fax: 770-488-4349.

kbasile@cdc.gov

Ann. N.Y. Acad. Sci. 989: 446–463 (2003). © 2003 New York Academy of Sciences.

1993). In this paper I present the rationale for viewing sexual violence as a public health issue, outline the public health model, highlight the ways in which sexual violence prevention fits this model, and offer suggestions for preventive efforts.

SEXUAL VIOLENCE IS A PUBLIC HEALTH ISSUE

Currently there is not one shared definition of sexual violence. The Center for Disease Control and Prevention's (CDC) National Center for Injury Prevention and Control (NCIPC) defines sexual violence as nonconsensual completed or attempted sexual activities, including vaginal or anal penetration; oral contact with the penis, vulva, or anus; intentional touching of a sexual nature; or noncontact acts of a sexual nature, such as voyeurism and verbal or behavioral sexual harassment. All the above acts also qualify as sexual violence if they are committed against someone who is unable to consent or refuse (Basile & Saltzman, 2002).

Sexual violence can be treated as a public health problem for a variety of reasons. First, sexual violence should be a public health concern due to the magnitude of the problem. According to the National Violence against Women Survey (NVAWS) conducted in 1995 and 1996 (Tjaden & Thoennes, 2000), 1 in 6 women and 1 in 33 men have experienced an attempted or completed rape in their lifetime, defined as forced vaginal, oral, or anal penetration. There were 302,091 women and 92,748 men who experienced completed rapes in the year prior to the survey. The incidence rate or number of separate victimizations occurring in the last year is even higher, because women on average experienced 2.9 rapes in the previous 12 months and men experienced 1.2 rapes on average in the last 12 months, translating to 876,064 rapes of women and 111,298 rapes of men (Tjaden & Thoennes, 2000). This survey and other research have shown that rape and other forms of sexual violence are largely "tragedies of youth" (Kilpatrick, Edmunds & Seymour, 1992, p. 3). The NVAWS found that 54% of all first rapes occurred to women before the age of 18, and almost half of these women were raped before age 12 (Tjaden & Thoennes, 2000). In the National Women's Study, Kilpatrick and colleagues (1992) found that 29% of all forcible rapes occurred when the victim was under 11 years old, and another 32% occurred between the ages of 11 and 17.

Second, sexual violence should be considered a public health concern because many of the consequences of sexual violence are health related. A public health approach treats all forms of violence as health issues because there are quantifiable physical and psychological injuries that result from them (Mercy et al., 1993). In the case of sexual violence, physical injuries can include vaginal trauma, broken bones, and bruises. Psychological injuries from sexual violence are also numerous and can include anxiety, fear, depression, posttraumatic stress disorder, and suicide ideation and attempts (reviewed in Crowell & Burgess, 1996). Sexual violence also increases women's long-term risk of health problems, such as drug and alcohol abuse, chronic pain, unintended pregnancy, and adverse pregnancy outcomes (reviewed in Heise, Ellsberg & Gottemoeller, 1999).

Third, implicit in the public health focus are the ideas that public health problems are preventable and that more emphasis should be placed on the front end before a problem begins or becomes widespread. Sexual violence is amenable to prevention. Public health underscores the importance of *primary prevention*, or preventing sexual violence *before* it occurs (McMahon & Puett, 1999). The public health approach combines a diverse group of scientific disciplines (e.g., sociology, psychology, medicine, and education) to create a multidisciplinary approach to prevention (Mercy and Hammond, 1999). In the last decade, the public health approach has been recognized as well suited in preventing multidimensional problems such as violence (Foege, Rosenberg & Mercy, 1995; Mercy et al., 1993). However, this approach can be a very challenging one for sexual violence prevention, as it involves what Mercy (1999) calls "having new eyes" to look at this issue. In other words, using this approach to address sexual violence involves considering sexual violence as a disease of the same magnitude as other diseases for which the public health model was developed to address.

THE PUBLIC HEALTH APPROACH

The public health model includes four steps (Mercy et al., 1993; Mercy & Hammond, 1999). In theory, information from each step is used to inform the next; however, in practice the four steps often occur simultaneously. The first step is *surveillance*. Traditionally, public health surveillance is the ongoing systematic collection, analysis, and interpretation of data on the incidence, prevalence, and risk factors of a public health problem. Data are reviewed in an effort to monitor and track a problem to determine who is being affected and if rates are increasing or decreasing, and to compare data across communities and over time (McMahon, 2000). However, applying the traditional mode of surveillance to sexual violence is problematic because many victims do not disclose their victimization to others, including potential sources of surveillance data. Often, surveillance relies on data that exist or are collected for another purpose. Thus, the information needed to address incidence, prevalence, and risk factors of sexual violence may not be available. For example, surveillance conducted through record reviews at hospitals is not likely to have specific information documented about sexual violence, unless the patient disclosed the information and the hospital staff chose to reflect it in the patient record. At present, their exists little traditional surveillance data on sexual violence other than Uniform Crime Report data, which is data on forcible rape and attempted rape reported to and compiled by participating law enforcement agencies and sent to the Federal Bureau of Investigation (FBI) (Kilpatrick, 2002). Conducting surveys is an alternative to traditional surveillance and can be a useful tool for monitoring and tracking sexual violence. This involves systematic data collection from a representative sample of the population of interest for analysis and interpretation. Surveys allow flexibility in the types of questions that can be asked and the level of detail of information that can be collected. Surveys may result in a better estimate of the magnitude of sexual violence because they allow more in-depth understanding of the problem and may reach more victims than traditional surveillance methods (Basile & Saltzman, 2002).

Identifying causes is the second step in the public health model and is accomplished through research to better identify persons at risk in order to inform preventive efforts. Researchers have examined factors that increase the risk for or protect one from sexual violence victimization or perpetration. Common methodologies used to identify risk and protective factors are cohort studies or case control studies.

Victim risk factor research focuses on characteristics that make victims vulnerable to sexual violence, but this research is distinct from victim blaming. Victim blaming mistakenly assigns responsibility for victimization to victims (e.g., if a woman was drunk when she was raped, it is her fault). While risk and protective factors are usually defined as individual level factors (e.g., previous history of violence or alcohol use), they can also be at societal or community levels (e.g., norms that promote violence, and hostile attitudes toward women).

The third step in the public health model is the *development and evaluation* of programs. This is a very important step in public health because it is where preventive efforts begin. At this step, surveillance and research are used to develop and test programs aimed at prevention. Evaluation is a critical piece of this step. Programs must be evaluated in order for users to be confident about them and before they can be adopted on a larger scale.

The final step in the public health model is *dissemination and implementation*. This involves communicating which preventive programs work based on evaluation of data and putting these programs into practice (McMahon, 2000). Dissemination of findings from surveillance and research activities is also important so that researchers, practitioners, and policymakers can know the scope of the problem, increases or decreases in its prevalence over time, and the most important risk and protective factors associated with it. Dissemination and implementation typically occur through mechanisms such as professional publications (e.g., refereed journal articles, reports, and books), media campaigns, or training activities. Dissemination and implementation are critical parts of the public health model because they could ideally lead to changes in policy.

TIMING OF PREVENTION, TARGET OF PREVENTION, AND THE ECOLOGICAL APPROACH

There are a number of different ways to categorize and describe public health preventive activities and programs. They can be categorized according to timing, that is, when preventive activities occur in relation to the outcomes of interest (e.g., before or after sexual violence has occurred), or by who receives the intervention (e.g., everyone or selected individuals). Finally, preventive activities can be grouped according to the level at which the focus is directed (e.g., individual or community). These categories are not mutually exclusive and many preventive efforts fall into more than one. For example, preventive measures that focus on everyone are often focused at the community level. Each of these different categorization schemes is described in more detail below.

Timing of Prevention

Traditionally, the public health approach has considered timing at three levels—tertiary, secondary, and primary. Applied to sexual violence, tertiary prevention involves trying to stop future violence by those who have a history of offending behavior, or for hard-core sexual offenders. For example, treatment programs for repeat or serial sexual offenders are a form of tertiary prevention. Secondary prevention focuses on those at high risk for offending as well as stopping recent sexual offenders from reoffending (Becker & Reilly, 1999; McMahon, 2000). An example is a program focused on youth with histories of physically violent perpetration and victimization who have not been identified as sexual offenders but who may be at risk, or a program focusing on newly identified youth sexual offenders. Primary prevention is the most ideal point of prevention, as it focuses on stopping sexually abusive behaviors before they start (McMahon, 2000). In the case of sexual violence, which has been documented as a problem of youth, it is critical that primary prevention start early in the life cycle. An example of primary prevention would be a school-based program instructing boys and girls on the harms of sexual violence.

These levels were originally designed for working with medical diseases like heart disease, where primary preventive efforts could be eating healthy foods (e.g., fresh vegetables and fruit) and exercising; secondary prevention might be focused on those at high risk for heart disease, like those with a family history and some early stage heart problems; and tertiary prevention would focus on preventing future complications among those people identified as having all the symptoms of heart disease. But these approaches do not work as neatly with social problems such as sexual violence. For example, sexual violence involves two main parties, offenders and victims, whose needs and vantage points are different. From a victim's perspective, treating an offender could be a form of primary prevention, because it will prevent potential victims from ever being victimized. From the reference point of the offender, any kind of prevention is secondary or tertiary. Furthermore, more than one offender can perpetrate sexual violence over the lifetime of a victim, which makes prevention ongoing and more complex. Even though this model does not fit sexual violence prevention perfectly, it is still useful in guiding efforts to prevent sexual violence. Public health's emphasis on early, primary prevention is particularly promising. Traditionally, the emphasis of those involved in sexual violence prevention has been working at secondary and tertiary levels, in part because the systems in place to help victims (rape crisis centers and hospitals) and prosecute offenders (criminal justice system) usually only reach them after the sexual violence occurs.

Target of Prevention

While not as commonly highlighted as the three levels discussed above, universal, selective, and indicated dimensions of preventive measures are helpful in further clarifying the public health approach to sexual violence prevention (McMahon & Puett, 1999; Mercy & Hammond, 1999) and may be more useful in designing prevention programs.

Universal preventive measures are those that focus on the community and larger society as a whole. Prevention that is universal is designed to aid everyone (or most everyone) in a given population. Examples of universal preventive measures that can be used to reduce sexual violence are media campaigns, reducing poverty levels, or providing parenting training for all parents. With *selective* preventive measures, the focus is preventing future violence by potential perpetrators, meaning those people that research identifies at high risk. Examples of selective preventive measures for the prevention of sexual violence are increasing adult mentoring of high-risk youth or treatment for those identified through research to be at high risk for offending. Finally, *indicated* preventive measures are designed for people who have already offended in an effort to prevent future violence.

The first two kinds of preventive measures, universal and selective, are the most critical to turn our focus toward, and most effective in meeting the objectives and goals of primary prevention.

The Ecological Approach

In addition to consideration of the timing and target of prevention, preventive efforts must consider the level at which to address the preventable risk factors. An ecological approach is helpful because it allows an examination of both microlevel and macrolevel variables in the prevention of sexual violence (Belsky, 1980; Heise et al., 1999; Heise, 1998; Mercy & Hammond, 1999). An ecological approach is a framework that combines personal, situational, and sociocultural factors to understand a problem such as violence (Heise, 1998). It includes the larger society, comprising those who are not directly affected by sexual violence. Four levels to an ecological approach used by Belsky (1980) to examine child abuse and neglect and later adopted by Heise (1998) to apply to violence against women are *personal history,* the *microsystem,* the *exosystem,* and the *macrosystem.* In the case of sexual violence, *personal history* includes the background of each individual involved in the sexual offense, namely, the victim and the offender. One example is if the victim or offender or both parties have a previous history of child sexual abuse. The *microsystem* involves the context in which the offending takes place. This level includes the relationship between the victim and offender and the specific dynamics around that relationship. For example, this could be a father–daughter relationship, an intimate partner relationship, or an acquaintance relationship, and each would have its own unique dynamics. The third and fourth levels are larger in scope. The *exosystem* is the social structures and institutions in which the microsystem is embedded. For example, the exosystem can include the neighborhood, the workplace, or social networks (Heise, 1998). In other words, the exosystem is the community and its social groups. For example, in the case of sexual violence, the community could be very isolating to those involved, both victims and offenders, or it could be supportive of the sexual offender (in the form of peer support for violence). The fourth level, the *macrosystem*, represents the larger society and culture, and the attitudes that pervade it. Components of the macrosystem include cultural norms and attitudes about women generally and about sexual violence specifically, the media, policies and laws, and the response from law enforcement to sexual offending.

Ideally, prevention efforts in the field of sexual violence would address all four levels of the social ecology. Although it is challenging to addresses all parts of the social ecology simultaneously, it is important to be cognizant of these four levels and the interplay among them.

EXAMPLES OF CURRENT EFFORTS TO PREVENT SEXUAL VIOLENCE

In this section, I discuss some of the main areas of focus in current sexual violence preventive efforts and tie the discussion of preventive efforts to the frameworks presented in the previous section, with particular emphasis on primary prevention, universal preventive measures, and the levels of the ecological approach. The current efforts highlighted below are by no means exhaustive. Rather, they represent examples of recent preventive efforts that target women only, men only, and both sexes. Generally speaking, there is a lack of evaluation of what does and does not work in the field of sexual violence prevention, so many of the existing preventive efforts should be treated as promising or potential practices until the field further clarifies what the best approaches are.

Preventive efforts have generally focused on the individual (personal history and microsystem) levels of the ecological framework, with less emphasis on the community and society at large (exo- and macrosystems). Programs have focused on preschool and elementary school ages (reviewed in U.S. General Accounting Office, 1996), middle and high school students (e.g., Foshee et al., 1998), and college age students (reviewed in Bachar & Koss, 2001). Some authors have pointed out that men, who constitute the larger majority of potential and real offenders, should be at the center of preventive work, as they are the ones who have the most control over the violence (Berkowitz, 1992). However, recent reviews by Lonsway (1996) and Bachar and Koss (2001) reveal that most preventive measures focus on changing attitudes of both men and women, while only a few preventive efforts target men only or women only.

Preventive efforts with women have been aimed at potential victims—in particular, how women and girls can modify their behavior in order to avoid sexual violence victimization. A victim focus has a political history. The field of sexual violence prevention would not exist today if it had not been for the grass roots movement of sexual assault advocates and victims/survivors who started the first rape crisis centers in the 1970s (Campbell, Baker & Mazurek, 1998) and lobbied to get the Violence against Women Act (VAWA) passed and into legislation (Valente, Hart, Zeya & Malefyt, 2001). Because of this history, this movement and the research and advocacy work that have resulted from it have had a largely victim-centered focus. Research has uncovered a great deal about victims' risk for victimization and revictimization, support and advocacy needs, coping and empowerment strategies, and health outcomes. It is important to continue to raise awareness of the risk of sexual violence victimization.

Research on how women can prevent sexual violence has included individual level focus on both resistance strategies to use during an attack (e.g., self-defense training) and avoidance strategies to minimize risk of attack (e.g., not going out alone at night, locking doors and windows) (Crowell & Burgess, 1996). However, avoidance strategies do not seem practical for victims whose offenders know them or live with them (Koss & Harvey, 1991). Further, avoidance plans will not have an effect on incidence rates as long as offenders exist, because they may only deflect the violence to another potential victim (Lonsway, 1996). Resistance strategies may have more utility. However, preventive efforts have yet to incorporate rape-resistance training (Bachar & Koss, 2001), even though resistance techniques, such as fighting back during an attempted rape, have been shown to be successful in resisting rape (Ullman, 2002; Ullman & Knight, 1992), even when the perpetrator and victim know each other (Clay-Warner, 2002). In sum, both avoidance and resistance strategies may be useful for some potential victims in certain circumstances, but teaching these as exclusive foci for rape preventive efforts may limit the ability for primary prevention of sexual offending, and could do harm in the process. For instance, both avoidance and resistance strategies put the responsibility on women to protect themselves and restrict their activities instead of focusing on offenders' behaviors. Furthermore, these strategies perpetuate fear in women and could lead to victim blaming if violence occurs when the strategies are not used (Koss & Harvey, 1991). Although these strategies are limited, researchers who find support for rape avoidance and resistance strategies view them as important techniques to prevent rape until the broader goal of primary prevention of rape occurs (Ullman, 2002). These victim-focused strategies need to be part of a plan that also includes violence prevention for perpetrators.

One example of a prevention program that has focused on both men and women is Safe Dates (Foshee et al., 1998). The Safe Dates program is a school-based ten-day curriculum used in middle and junior high schools (8th and 9th grades) in rural North Carolina that focuses on primary prevention of dating violence perpetration (including sexual violence) by changing norms around dating violence, decreasing gender stereotyping, and enhancing conflict management. In addition, a random subsample of participants, now in high school, is getting booster sessions. Another component of Safe Dates is community activities that promote secondary prevention of dating violence by offering services to adolescents in abusive relationships and training service providers. Early data indicate that this program results in a reduction in sexual violence perpetration on dates (Foshee et al., 1998). Safe Dates combines individual and relationship level prevention with exo- and macrosystem efforts to change universal social norms that condone dating violence.

The CDC's National Center for Injury Prevention and Control (NCIPC) is currently involved in planning a social norms campaign to address prevention of dating violence perpetration (including sexual violence) among 11–14 year olds (6th, 7th, and 8th grade students). The intent of the project is to examine the influence of peer groups on attitudes about dating violence and ultimately to change the social norms that allow dating violence to occur. This effort includes both primary and secondary prevention, as the intent is to reach this audience with prevention messages before norms and attitudes that support dating violence are firmly established. Adolescents 11–14 years old were chosen as the target of this campaign to maximize primary prevention and because there are few preventive programs targeting these early ages. Information gained from focus groups with adolescent boys and girls will inform the development of a comprehensive media campaign with elements that can be implemented at both national and local levels. Not only is this an example of universal prevention ultimately targeting all youth, but this example also includes all four levels of the social ecology, promoting individual, relationship, and societal level change.

The work of Berkowitz (1994) provides a good example of a sexual violence prevention effort with men. His program uses peer-facilitated groups of college men to examine the role that masculinity and peer pressure play in rape perpetration. The idea is to generate peer pressure against rape and discuss alternatives to stereotypical and sexist behavior. The intent of this program is to help men recognize their role and responsibility in the primary prevention of rape (Berkowitz, 1994). However, this program could also serve as secondary or tertiary prevention for some. Berkowitz's model addresses all four parts of the social ecology to some extent. It focuses on individuals, so includes personal history; it addresses the microsystem (relationships with women and with peers) and also deals with the exosystem issue of peer influence. This program also taps into the macrosystem, focusing on the sexist and stereotypical attitudes that perpetuate sexual violence.

GAPS IN SEXUAL VIOLENCE PREVENTIVE EFFORTS

As others have recently argued (Becker & Reilly, 1999; Henry, 2001, Laws, 2000; McMahon, 2000; McMahon & Puett, 1999; Mercy, 1999; Potter, Krider & McMahon, 2000), more attention should be given to primary prevention of sexual violence if real gains are to be made in decreasing this problem. Simply stated, stopping the problem before it starts should be as much a priority as providing services to victims and offenders. Furthermore, primary prevention is best accomplished by focusing on those who are responsible for violence—offenders (Laws, 2000; Berkowitz, 1992). Focusing on potential victims is important, but it seems counterintuitive to focus more attention on potential victims without addressing the existence of perpetration. In line with a public health model, a major effort should be to try to change offenders' behaviors, in addition to focusing on victims. Changing offenders' or potential offenders' behaviors should be more fruitful in efforts to decrease sexual violence than trying to change victims' behaviors.

Programs designed for women-only, mixed-sex, and men-only groups have attempted to promote awareness of sexual violence (see reviews in Bachar & Koss, 2001 and Lonsway, 1996). But the scope, the criteria used to measure success, and the timing of many of these preventive programs are often problematic. First, programs are usually too short in duration, and "success" is measured as attitude change immediately after program completion (Lonsway, 1996). Attitude change has to be an ongoing effort to be sustained over time. Regarding timing, programs often start too late in the life cycle to really accomplish primary prevention. Preventive efforts must start early and continue throughout the life cycle. There has been a large focus on college-age students. After earlier studies demonstrated that rape and sexual assault were huge problems on college campuses (Koss, Gidycz & Wisniewski, 1987), many colleges responded with prevention–education programs on their campuses (Bachar & Koss, 2001; Lonsway, 1996). These college programs are important and should be part of the preventive messages that students receive over their life cycle; but, as prevalence data have shown, many young people are already victims or perpetrators, if and when they reach college and get these prevention messages. Prevention messages at many developmental stages over the life span are important for prevention to be effective. There has been some movement to begin preventive efforts earlier in the life cycle, such as the regional work of Foshee and colleagues (1998) and the CDC's plans for a social norms campaign, but broader adoption of prevention messages throughout the life cycle is necessary.

There are several groups in society that should not be forgotten in sexual violence preventive efforts, but often are. For instance, the quantity of research and prevention of rape by husbands does not compare to the amount of focus on rape by other offenders (Yllo, 1999). In addition, little research and preventive efforts are focused on sexual violence perpetration or victimization among gay men and lesbians, elders, women of color, the disabled, and immigrants. Primary preventive efforts should not exclude these less studied groups. Other scholars have pointed to the important contribution cultural minority groups, in particular, can make in preventing sexual violence (Hall & Barongan, 1997).

There is little emphasis in sexual violence preventive efforts on the exo- and macrosystems (i.e., community and societal levels), with a few notable exceptions (e.g., Berkowitz, 1994; Foshee et al., 1998). More attention should be placed on incorporating these levels of the ecological framework into the efforts to end sexual violence (Mercy & Hammond, 1999; Heise et al., 1999). In addition to answering the question of why some individuals become offenders, other questions need to be asked: What is it about society and communities that helps to create and perpetuate sexual offenders and facilitate sexual offending? Do some communities have more sexual violence than others? If so, why? Data must be collected and compared across communities and over time in order to answer these questions.

By involving the exosystem, more community members can get involved in prevention. Included should be those in society who may not be directly affected by sexual violence, but are part of a society that allows it to continue. For example, in the case of child sexual violence, parents and other adults in the community could help identify potential cases of violence and increase general awareness about the issue, instead of waiting for children to disclose after the abuse occurs (Henry, 2001). Involving the macrosystem could mean reaching even more people. For instance, national campaigns against sexual violence in the media could affect rates of sexual offending by gradually influencing societal norms that condone sexual aggression. In addition, studies have shown that economic inequality is associated with community level violent crime (Sampson & Lauritsen, 1993), so decreasing poverty levels in communities might have an impact of sexual violence levels.

Involving the community and larger society in approaches to prevention has been employed in the prevention of other public health problems with some success. For example, a few decades ago automobile seat belt use was not common and not mandated by law. Today, mandatory seat belt use laws are the norm in the United States; however, states differ in their level of enforcement and penalties. As of 1996, 49 U.S. states (excluding New Hampshire) and the District of Columbia have passed a mandatory seat belt use law of some kind (Ferrini, 1997). Some states have standard enforcement, meaning that the police can pull a vehicle over because the occupants are not wearing seat belts (Ferrini, 1997). Mandatory seat belt use is a form of primary prevention of injury in motor vehicle accidents and is more accepted today than it was in the past, largely because the norms about wearing seat belts have changed through public awareness combined with changes in laws. Today about two-thirds of the population uses seat belts (Ferrini, 1997). Educational and media campaigns, and standard law enforcement practices around seat belt use have been shown to be associated with increasing usage rates (National Safety Council, 1996).

Another example of the successful involvement of society in a public health problem is smoking cessation campaigns and efforts. The CDC reports that almost 9 out of 10 Americans are exposed to environmental tobacco smoke (ETS), or second-hand smoke (Pirkle et al., 1996). A 1993 report from the Environmental Protection Agency classified second-hand smoke as a Group A carcinogen, meaning it is known to cause cancer in humans (Pirkle et al., 1996). The danger of second-hand smoke appears to have motivated nonsmokers to get involved in campaigns against smoking and in changing policies to create smoke-free environments. The creation of smoke-free environments in public places (e.g., workplaces, restaurants) sent the message that smokers cannot smoke in public, not only because it is unhealthy for smokers, but also because it is unhealthy for nonsmokers. The larger society of nonsmokers, not directly involved with the problem of smoking, got involved in the solution. While this example is not entirely primary prevention, it is an example of involving the larger society in preventing the problem. The same societal urgency needs to be established around decreasing sexual violence perpetration by involving the public in large-scale sexual violence preventive efforts.

AN EXAMPLE OF PRIMARY PREVENTION AND
UNIVERSAL MEASURES: STOP IT NOW!

While researchers and practitioners have written about the importance of primary prevention of sexual violence, few have demonstrated what this would or should look like. An organization called STOP IT NOW! is one exception.

STOP IT NOW!, founded by Fran Henry in 1992, is a national child sexual abuse public education, public policy, and research organization with the following mission: "to call on all abusers and potential abusers to stop and seek help, *to educate adults about the ways to stop sexual abuse, and to increase public awareness of the trauma of child sexual abuse"* (www.stopitnow.com). Italics are added here to emphasize the primary preventive components of this organization. This organization has worked to prevent child sexual abuse by employing different types of prevention and using all levels of the ecological model. STOP IT NOW! programs exist in Vermont, Philadelphia, Minnesota, the United Kingdom, and Ireland. Currently, the CDC is funding the evaluation of the Philadelphia program, and STOP IT NOW! is evaluating the Vermont program (Henry, 2001).

STOP IT NOW! has a few key premises. First, it uses the public health approach to prevent the sexual abuse of children, with a main interest in primary prevention. This is accomplished in part with a help line for potential abusers, friends and family of suspected abusers, and concerned community members. Another premise is the focus on adults. This is an example of a universal preventive measure because the intent is to try to stop child sexual abuse by getting adults from the community involved, rather than waiting for children to disclose. These adults may or may not be directly involved in the problem of sexual violence, but STOP IT NOW! wants them to be involved in the solution. Part of the rationale for involving adults was to take the burden off children to prevent their own victimization. Teaching children how to keep themselves safe is important, but that alone is not enough (Henry, 2001). Other writers have pointed to the importance of the role of bystanders and other witnesses of child abuse and not leaving the responsibility for deterring abuse only to the child (Feindler & Becker, 1994).

STOP IT NOW! involves adults in a variety of ways, such as public marketing campaigns, media activities, and community action. This organization believes that abusers can stop, and that offenders should be offered support in the form of treatment for their offending, while at the same time being held accountable for the violence. While not a perfect comparison, the efforts of STOP IT NOW! are similar to the efforts around second-hand smoking. Those working in the field of smoking and health were able to prove that smoke affects the whole society, not just smokers. By involving adults and using a public health model based on science, STOP IT NOW! is trying to demonstrate that child sexual abuse affects us all, and all should be involved in its eradication. Evaluations of STOP IT NOW! programs are ongoing, so it is not yet known how successful this approach is in decreasing sexual violence.

OPPORTUNITIES FOR PREVENTION

To reflect the importance stressed in this paper of moving toward the "macro" parts of the ecological framework, most of the suggestions presented in this paper are at the exo- and macrosystem level. Focusing on larger picture ideas, such as changing societal norms around this issue, may take a long time to accomplish. Many of the ideas that follow have not been tested, so at this time they should be considered starting points for how to incorporate primary prevention and universal measures into the work in this field.

Why are there very few, if any, public health, societal, or community messages about sexual violence? This question is especially pertinent when, as discussed above, there are so many messages about other public health issues, such as seat belt use and second-hand smoke (Laws, 2000). One answer is that sexual violence is still seen as a private matter, as shameful, and it is hidden, so there is stigma around this issue (Russell, 1984; Koss & Oros, 1982; Nathanson, 1989). There is a lot of shame, sensitivity, and embarrassment around sexual violence, which results in a society where perhaps it is easier to be a victim of attempted homicide or a car jacking, for example, than to be a victim of rape (Stout & McPhail, 1998). Coupled with the fact that it is sensitive, private, and hidden, sexual offenders have been shown to be fathers, uncles, other family members, intimate partners, friends, dates, and priests (Fisher, Cullen & Turner, 2000; Finkelhor & Yllo, 1985; Pierce & Pierce, 1987; Wiehe & Richards, 1995). Victims and others in the community very often know the offenders, which makes the issue too close to home and that much harder with which to deal.

One way to encourage involvement among society members in the prevention of sexual violence is to break the silence around sex and sexuality in general, to create a "norm of sexual integrity" (Henry, 2001) through social norms campaigns, social marketing, and other strategies. Henry (2001) defines sexual integrity as "sexual activity that is vital and life-giving and causes no harm," stating "we can't cultivate it if we can't discuss sex openly" (p. 12). Because of this inability to discuss sex in general, there is so much more difficulty breaking the silence about sexual violence. Sexual integrity is not meant to offend people's senses about sex and sexuality, but rather, to stop the norm of silence around sex in general, and around sexual violence in particular. Cultivating a norm of sexual integrity is not by itself sexual violence prevention, but it has implications for sexual violence prevention. It is an important step to change the way members of society think about these issues.

More specific to sexual violence prevention is educating the general society to know about warning signs of sexual behavior problems that could lead to sexual violence. A search on the World-Wide Web for "warning signs of child sexual abuse" almost exclusively provides information on warning signs among victims. However, warning signs of sexual behavior problems than can lead to sexual offending are numerous (www.stopitnow.com; Missouri Division of Family Services, 2002) and would be beneficial to the public so that community members can recognize and try to prevent sexual offending before it happens. On their Web site, STOP IT NOW! lists several of the warning signs of sexual behavior problems that could lead to child sexual abuse. Some examples include talking again and again about the sexual activities of children or teens, looking at child pornography, encouraging silence and secrets in a child, spending most spare time on activities involving children or teens and not adults, and talking about sexual fantasies with children (www.STOPIT-NOW.com). These warning signs do not necessarily mean that the suspected person is an abuser; rather, they should prompt closer attention. Educating the general public to recognize and acknowledge warning signs of unhealthy sexual behaviors and encouraging people in the community to come forward when they suspect these behaviors should change the norms. Changes in the social context should facilitate speaking up about this problem, allowing communities to pay closer attention and possibly avoiding sexual violence perpetration before it happens. Related to these goals, CDC's NCIPC is planning in the next year to fund a program to create statewide prevention collaboratives to promote the development and implementation of child sexual abuse preventive programs that focus on community responsibility in the prevention of child sexual abuse perpetration.

Educating the general public about societal norms, beliefs, and values that condone sexual violence by keeping it hidden or continuing to consider it normative are also important. Many studies have shown belief in rape myths (e.g., women secretly desire to be raped, women deserve to be raped if they dress provocatively) among certain segments of the population, such as males and blacks (Lonsway & Fitzgerald, 1994). Belief in rape myths has been associated with sexual offending (Malamuth, Linz, Heavey, Barnes & Acker, 1995). In addition, changing hostile attitudes toward women and sex role attitudes that condone aggression of men and passivity of women are equally important. Malamuth and colleagues also found that hostility toward women and mistrust of women, as well as support for the use of interpersonal violence to resolve conflict were related to sexual aggression (Malamuth et al., 1995; Malamuth, 2002). Again, challenging and trying to change gendered beliefs and negative attitudes toward women such as these must start at the level of the community and society, whose laws and norms passively condone violence and support keeping it silent. One example from a recent case study of a serial rapist is illustrative. Pino (2002) found that when prostitutes came forward and disclosed that they were raped, the police told them that not getting paid for a trick does not mean they were raped. This suggests a prevailing attitude among police that prostitutes cannot be raped (or if prostitutes are raped they are responsible for it), which stems from hostile attitudes and myths that certain women falsely accuse men of rape and deserve to be raped. These attitudes need to be addressed on a societal level in efforts to prevent sexual violence, because research indicates that they are widespread, not only held by members of law enforcement (for a review, see Lonsway & Fitzgerald, 1994).

The workplace seems to be an ideal setting for policies and other activities to prevent sexual violence. Explicitly stated, employee policies about sexual harassment and routine training about appropriate conduct in the workplace could be universal preventive measures used as part of employee orientation across the country. However, they presently exist in some workplaces only (Brown, 1999). Employee training for sexual harassment is important because sexual harassment is a form of sexual violence (Basile & Saltzman, 2002), is estimated to happen at work or school to one of every two women in their lifetimes (Fitzgerald, 1993), and has been associated with sexual violence (Cortina, Swan, Fitzgerald & Waldo, 1998) and dating violence (Wolfe, Wekerle, Reitzel-Jaffe & Lefebvre, 1998; Larkin & Popaleni, 1994). Training could serve as primary prevention if policies are taken seriously and enforced. Background checks before employment would also be beneficial, particularly for occupations that involve working with children. While background checks may not serve as primary prevention, they could serve as secondary prevention if identified abusers were forced to enter treatment. One venue for primary prevention of sexual violence could be through employee assistance programs (Henry, 2001). In many places of employment, employee assistance programs exist that address various personal problems that might hinder an employee's ability to do his or her job, such as drug or alcohol abuse. However, these programs do not address sexual behavior problems that are known to lead to sexual offending. If programs and policies like these existed in the work environment, society might begin to recognize that sexual offending is not a rare, unusual event that solely is perpetrated by a deviant few. Sexual violence is currently normative, as sexually violent behaviors are widespread and exist in a culture that promotes them (Berkowitz, 1994; Rozee, 2000; Schur, 1997). But sexual violence is also a largely hidden problem. By setting up policies to address it openly, it may be prevented and the norms that condone it may change (Henry, 2001). Taking advantage of the workplace for prevention efforts is another example of making community and societal level changes and affecting policies, as it is attempting to modify the structures and institutions in order to decrease sexual violence.

As suggested earlier, it is important to start prevention early in life. Promoting positive child development has broad benefits for the macrosociety and goes beyond sexual violence prevention. Scholars in the field have recognized the importance of promoting a positive parent–child relationship in efforts to prevent child maltreatment (Wekerle & Wolfe, 1993). Parent training seems to be critical to primary preventive efforts since early exposure to violence (witnessing violence or experiencing child sexual abuse) in the home is a major risk factor for sexual violence perpetration and victimization (Malamuth, 2002; Merrill et al., 1999; Messman-Moore & Long, 2000; Pierce & Pierce, 1987). In addition, research by Malamuth and colleagues (2002) has shown that a hostile home environment can set the stage for future rape perpetration. If parents are taught about positive parent–child relationships, child sexual abuse and other forms of violence might be prevented, both in the short term and long term when the children become adults. Parental training has shown promise in preventing child abuse and neglect (Gershater-Molko, Lutzker & Wesch, 2002; Guide to Community Preventive Services, n.d.; Kazdin, 1994) and could take place through home visitation by nurses to teach new parents, among other things, about healthy sexuality of children and sexual behavior problems.

Training on how to recognize signs of sexual behavior problems and potential sexual abuse victimization for those who work with children, such as doctors, nurses, teachers, and religious leaders, is also critical to child sexual abuse preventive efforts. However, training these groups must be suggested with caution, because the added issue of mandatory reporting is complex. This suggestion must go hand in hand with other policies that support and protect the victims (Henry, 2002).

As children grow to be teenagers, it is important to continue preventive efforts. Another possible approach that has taken place to some extent is primary prevention of date rape through awareness campaigns that teach young people about healthy sexuality (Freeman-Longo & Blanchard, 1998) and that sex that is not consensual is exploitative. More emphasis on primary prevention, targeting adolescents, similar to the social norms campaign described earlier and the Safe Dates program (Foshee et al., 1998), is needed to move closer to preventing sexual violence. Much of the prevention focus on college populations is due to the fact that sexual violence is a big problem on college campuses; but it could also be attributed in part to the fact that it is hard to gain access to children and teens, particularly to address sensitive issues such as sexual violence. This makes primary prevention in elementary and high schools challenging.

CONCLUSION

Using a public health approach to prevent sexual violence not only involves a different perspective or "having new eyes" (Mercy, 1999) but also involves having the patience to wait for change to occur. It will be worth the wait if there eventually comes a time when sexual violence is no longer a threat to our public and social health. Opportunities for primary prevention and universal preventive measures including all four levels of the social ecology abound, and they need to be developed and evaluated to see if they are effective. Involving society in the problem seems the most logical approach and has been successful with other public health problems. Responsibility for preventing this problem must include those who still do not want to talk about sexual violence or admit it exists. It seems plausible but must be demonstrated that primary prevention is more cost effective than other strategies. Stopping sexual violence before it starts could save millions of dollars in areas such as treatment costs, rape crisis services, prison costs, and lost wages. The average rape in the United States is estimated to cost $5100 in tangible, out-of-pocket expenses and $87,000 when a monetary value is attached to emotional distress and lost quality of life (Miller, Cohen & Wiersema, 1994). A more recent study by Post and colleagues reported that sexual violence costs over $6.5 billion per year in the state of Michigan alone (Post, Mezey, Maxwell & Wibert, 2002). Quantifying the cost effectiveness of prevention of sexual violence can be useful from a policy standpoint, as it can help communities and victims and their families build an argument for formulating policy aimed at decreasing the public health burden of sexual violence.

REFERENCES

BACHAR, K. & KOSS, M.P. (2001). From prevalence to prevention: Closing the gap between what we know about rape and what we do. In C. Renzetti, J. Edleson & R.K. Bergen, (Eds.), *Sourcebook on Violence Against Women* (pp. 117–142). Thousand Oaks, CA: Sage.

BASILE, K.C. & SALTZMAN, L.E. (2002). *Sexual violence surveillance: Uniform definitions and recommended data elements. Version 1.0.* Atlanta, GA: Centers for Disease Control and Prevention, National Center for Injury Prevention and Control.

BECKER, J.V. & REILLY, D.W. (1999). Preventing sexual abuse and assault. *Sexual Abuse: A Journal of Research and Treatment, 11,* 267–278.

BELSKY, J. (1980). Child maltreatment: An ecological integration. *American Psychologist, 35,* 320–335.

BERKOWITZ, A.D. (1992). College men as perpetrators of acquaintance rape and sexual assault: A review of recent research. *Journal of American College Health, 40,* 175–181.

BERKOWITZ, A.D., Ed. (1994). Men and Rape: Theory, research and prevention programs in higher education. *New Directions for Student Services Monographs, 65,* San Francisco: Jossey Bass.

BROWN, B.L. (1999). *Sexual harassment interventions.* ERIC Digest No. 206. Columbus, OH: ERIC Clearinghouse on Adult Career and Vocational Education. Available: http://www.ed.gov/databases/ERIC_Digests/ed429188.html.

CAMPBELL, R., BAKER, C.L. & MAZUREK, T.L. (1998). Remaining Radical? Organizational Predictors of Rape Crisis Centers' Social Change. *American Journal of Community Psychology, 26,* 457–483.

CLAY-WARNER, J. (in press). Avoiding rape: The effect of protective actions and situational factors on rape outcome. *Violence & Victims, 17,* 691–705.

CORTINA, L.M., SWAN, S., FITZGERALD, L.F. & WALDO, C. (1998). Sexual harassment and assault: Chilling the climate for women in academia. *Psychology of Women Quarterly, 22,* 419–441.

CROWELL, N.A. & BURGESS, A.W., Eds. (1996). *Understanding Violence Against Women.* Washington, D.C.: National Academy Press.

FEINDLER, E.L. & BECKER, J.V. (1994). Interventions in family violence involving children and adolescents. In L.D. Eron, J.H. Gentry, & P. Schlegel (Eds.), *Reason to hope: A psychological perspective on violence & youth* (pp. 405–430). Washington, DC: American Psychological Association.

FERRINI, R.L. (1997). Strengthening motor vehicle occupant protection laws: American College of Preventive Medicine public policy statement. *American Journal of Preventive Medicine, 13,* 401–403.

FINKELHOR, D. & YLLO, K. (1985). *License to rape: sexual abuse of wives.* New York: The Free Press.

FISHER, B.S., CULLEN, F.T. & TURNER, M.G. (2000). *The sexual victimization of college women* (NCJ 182369). Washington, DC: U.S. Department of Justice, National Institute of Justice.

FITZGERALD, L.F. (1993). Sexual harassment: Violence against women in the workplace. *American Psychologist, 48,* 1070–1076.

FOEGE, W.H., ROSENBERG, M.L. & MERCY, J.A. (1995). Public health and violence prevention. *Current Issues in Public Health, 1,* 2–9.

FOSHEE. V.A., BAUMAN, K.E., ARRIAGA, X.B., HELMS, R.W., KOCH, G.G. & LINDER, G.F. (1998). An evaluation of Safe Dates, an adolescent dating violence prevention program. *American Journal of Public Health, 88,* 45–50.

FREEMAN-LONGO, R.E. & BLANCHARD, G.T. (1998). *Sexual abuse in America: Epidemic of the 21st century.* Brandon, VT: The Safer Society Press.

GERSHATER-MOLKO, R.M., LUTZKER, J.R. & WESCH, D. (2002). Using recidivism to evaluate Project SafeCare: Teaching "bonding," safety, and health care skills to parents. *Child Maltreatment, 7,* 277–285.

GUIDE TO COMMUNITY PREVENTIVE SERVICES (n.d.). New findings prove early childhood home visitation prevents child maltreatment [on line]. Available: www.thecommunityguide.org/home_f.html

HALL, G.C.N. & BARONGAN, C. (1997). Prevention of sexual aggression: Sociocultural risk and protective factors. *American Psychologist, 52,* 5–14.

HEISE, L.L. (1998). Violence against women: An integrated, ecological framework. *Violence Against Women, 4,* 262–290.

HEISE, L., ELLSBERG, M. & GOTTEMOELLER, M. (1999, December). *Ending violence against women.* Population Reports, Series L, No. 11. Baltimore: Johns Hopkins University School of Public Health, Population Information Program.

HENRY, F. (2001, November). *A prescription for change on child sexual abuse.* Paper presented at the National Advisory Council on Violence and Abuse of the American Medical Association, Chicago, Illinois.

HENRY, F. (personal communication, May 6, 2002).

KAZDIN, A.E. (1994). Interventions for aggressive and antisocial children. In L.D. Eron, J.H. Gentry & P. Schlegel (Eds.), *Reason to hope: A psychological perspective on violence & youth* (pp. 341–382). Washington, DC: American Psychological Association.

KILPATRICK, D.G. (2002, January). *Making sense of rape in America: Were do the numbers come from and what do they mean?* Symposium conducted at the Centers for Disease Control Rape Prevention and Education Grant Program Regional Meeting, Atlanta, Georgia.

KILPATRICK, D.G., EDMUNDS, C.N. & SEYMOUR, A.K. (1992). *Rape in America: A report to the nation.* Arlington, VA: National Victim Center & Medical University of South Carolina.

Koss, M.P. & Harvey, M.R. (1991). *The rape victim: Clinical and community interventions.* Newbury Park, CA: Sage.

Koss, M.P. & Oros, C.J. (1982). Sexual Experiences Survey: A research instrument investigating sexual aggression and victimization. *Journal of Consulting and Clinical Psychology, 50,* 455–457.

Koss, M.P., Gidycz, C.A. & Wisniewski, N. (1987). The scope of rape: Incidence and prevalence of sexual aggression and victimization in a national sample of higher education students. *Journal of Consulting and Clinical Psychology 55,* 162–170.

Larkin, J. & Popaleni, K. (1994). Heterosexual courtship violence and sexual harassment: The private and public control of young women. *Feminism & Psychology, 4,* 213–227.

Laws, D.R. (2000). Sexual offending as a public health problem: A North American perspective. *The Journal of Sexual Aggression, 5,* 30–44.

Lonsway, K.A. (1996). Preventing acquaintance rape through education: What do we know? *Psychology of Women Quarterly, 20,* 229–265.

Lonsway, K.A. & Fitzgerald, L.F. (1994). Rape myths: In review. *Psychology of Women Quarterly, 18,* 133–164.

Malamuth, N.M. (2003). Criminal and noncriminal sexual aggressors: Integrating psychopathy in a hierarchical–mediational confluence model. *Annals of the New York Academy of Sciences.* This volume.

Malamuth, N.M., Linz, D., Heavey, C.L., Barnes, G. & Acker, M. (1995). Using the confluence model of sexual aggression to predict men's conflict with women: a ten-year follow-up study. *Journal of Personality and Social Psychology, 69,* 353–369.

McMahon, P.M. (2000). The public health approach to the prevention of sexual violence. *Sexual Abuse: A Journal of Research and Treatment, 12,* 27–36.

McMahon, P.M. & Puett, R.C. (1999). Child sexual abuse as a public health issue: Recommendations of an expert panel. *Sexual Abuse: A Journal of Research and Treatment, 11,* 257–266.

Mercy, J.A. (1999). Having new eyes: Viewing child sexual abuse as a public health problem. *Sexual Abuse: A Journal of Research and Treatment, 11,* 317–321.

Mercy, J.A. & Hammond, W.R. (1999). Preventing homicide: A public heath perspective. In M.D. Smith & M.A. Zahn (Eds.), *Studying and preventing homicide: Issues and challenges* (pp. 274–294). Thousand Oaks: Sage Publications.

Mercy, J.A., Rosenberg, M.L., Powell, K.E., Broome, C.V. & Roper, W.L. (1993). Public health policy for preventing violence. *Health Affairs, 12,* 7–29.

Merrill, L.L., Newell, C.E., Thomsen, C., Gold, S.R., Milner, J.S., Koss, M.P. & Rosswork, S.G. (1999). Childhood abuse and sexual revictimization in a female Navy recruit sample. *Journal of Traumatic Stress, 12,* 211–225.

Messman-Moore, T.L. & Long, P.J. (2000). Child sexual abuse and revictimization in the form of adult sexual abuse, adult physical abuse, and adult psychological maltreatment. *Journal of Interpersonal Violence, 15,* 489–502.

Miller, T.R., Cohen, M.A. & Wiersema, B. (1994). *Crime in the United States: Victim costs and consequences (NCJ Report No. 155281).* Washington, DC: U.S. Department of Justice, Bureau of Justice Statistics.

Missouri Division of Family Services. (2002). *Understanding and responding to the sexual behavior of children: the range of sexual behavior of adolescents.* Jefferson City, MO: Missouri Department of Social Services, Division of Family Services. Available: http://www.rollanet.org/~childlaw/miscdocs/sbcad.htm [30 July 2002].

Nathanson, D.L. (1989). Understanding what is hidden: Shame in sexual abuse. *Psychiatric Clinics of North America, 12,* 381–388.

National Safety Council. (1996). *Safeguarding the motoring public: The case for strengthening occupant protection laws.* National Safety Belt Coalition: Washington, DC.

Pierce, L.H. & Pierce, R.L. (1987). Incestuous victimization by juvenile sex offenders. *Journal of Family Violence, 2,* 351–364.

Pino, N.W. (2002, April). *A sociological study of a serial offender.* Paper presented at the annual meeting of the Southern Sociological Society, Baltimore, Maryland.

Pirkle, J.L., Fiegal, K.M., Bernert, J.T., Brody, D.J., Etzel, R.A. & Maurer, K.R. (1996). Exposure of the U.S. Population to Environmental Tobacco Smoke: The third national health and nutrition examination survey, 1988 to 1991. *Journal of the American Medical Association, 275,* 1233–1240.

POST, L.A., MEZEY, N.J., MAXWELL, C. & WIBERT, W.N. (2002). The rape tax: Tangible and intangible costs of sexual violence. *Journal of Interpersonal Violence, 17,* 773–782.

POTTER, R.H., KRIDER, J.E. & MCMAHON, P.M. (2000). Examining elements of campus sexual violence policies: Is deterrence or health promotion favored? *Violence Against Women, 6,* 1345–1362.

ROZEE, P.D. (2000). Sexual victimization: Harassment and rape. In M. Biaggio & M. Hersen (Eds.), *Issues in the psychology of women* (pp. 93–113). New York: Kluwer Academic/Plenum Publishers.

RUSSELL, D.E.H. (1984). The politics of rape: The victim's perspective. New York: Stein and Day Publishers.

SALTZMAN, L.E., GREEN, Y.T., MARKS, J.S. & THACKER, S.B. (2000). Violence against women as a public health issue: Comments from the CDC. *American Journal of Preventive Medicine, 19,* 325–329.

SAMPSON, R.J. & LAURITSEN, J.L. (1993). Violence victimization and offending: Individual-, situational-, and community-level risk factors. In A.J. Reiss & J.A. Roth (Eds.), *Understanding and Prevention Violence, Volume 3, Social Influences* (pp. 1–114). Washington, DC: National Academy Press.

Schur, E. (1997). Sexual coercion in American life. In L.L. O'Toole & J.R. Schiffman (Eds.), *Gender violence: Interdisciplinary perspectives* (pp. 80–91). New York: New York University Press.

STOP IT NOW! Available: http://www.stopitnow.com.

STOUT, K.D. & MCPHAIL, B. (1998). Confronting sexism and violence against women: A challenge for social work. New York: Addison Wesley Longman, Inc.

TJADEN, P. & THOENNES, N. (2000). *Full report of prevalence, incidence, and consequences of violence against women: Findings from the national violence against women survey* (NCJ 183781). Washington, D.C.: U.S. Department of Justice, National Institute of Justice.

ULLMAN, S.E. (2002). Rape avoidance: Self-protection strategies for women. In P.A. Schewe (Ed). *Preventing violence in relationships: Interventions across the life span* (pp. 137–162). Washington, DC, US: American Psychological Association.

ULLMAN, S.E. & KNIGHT, R.A. (1992). Fighting back: Women's resistance to rape. *Journal of Interpersonal Violence, 7,* 31–43.

U.S. GENERAL ACCOUNTING OFFICE. (1996). *Preventing child sexual abuse: Research inconclusive about effectiveness of child education programs.* (Rep. No. GAO/GGD-96-156). Washington, DC: U.S. General Accounting Office.

VALENTE, R.L., HART, B.J., ZEYA, S. & MALEFYT, M. (2001). The Violence Against Women Act of 1994: The federal commitment to ending domestic violence, sexual assault, stalking, and gender-based crimes of violence. In C.M. Renzetti, J.L. Edleson & R.K. Bergen (Eds.), *Sourcebook on Violence Against Women* (pp. 279–301). Thousand Oaks, CA: Sage Publications.

WEKERLE, C. & WOLFE, D.A. (1993). Prevention of child physical abuse and neglect: Promising new directions. *Clinical Psychology Review, 13,* 501–540.

WIEHE, V.R. & RICHARDS, A.L. (1995). *Intimate betrayal: Understanding and responding to the trauma of acquaintance rape.* Thousand Oaks: Sage Publications.

WOLFE, D.A., WEKERLE, C., REITZEL-JAFFE, D. & LEFEBVRE, L. (1998). Factors associated with abusive relationships among maltreated and nonmaltreated youth. *Development & Psychopathology, 10,* 61–85.

YLLO, K. (1999). Wife rape: A social problem for the 21st century. *Violence Against Women, 5,* 1059–1063.

Victim and Citizen Perspectives on Sexual Offender Policy

LUCY BERLINER

*Harborview Center for Sexual Assault and Traumatic Stress,
Seattle, Washington 98104, USA*

ABSTRACT: At any point, the "best practices" for managing sexual offenders typically derive from the prevailing social policy regarding such offenders. Social policy perspectives held by victims, citizens in the community, and sexual offender experts often are quite different, with victims, their advocates, and citizens supporting management strategies that are more harsh and restrictive than the strategies recommended by the experts. In this paper, these varying perspectives are discussed, and recommendations are made for ways in which sexual offender experts can be influential in shaping social policy.

KEYWORDS: sexual offender; sexual abuse; sexual crimes; social policy; child sexual abuse; victim advocate; rape; community notification

The last decade of the twentieth century saw heightened civic interest in the social policy response to sexual offenders. A public consensus emerged that sexual offenders were a menace to society and had for too long been permitted to remain in or return to the community and continue to victimize the innocent. Victims, their advocates and ordinary citizens successfully influenced legislative bodies to pass laws increasing the penalties for sexual crimes, "strike" laws that mandated life or extremely long sentences, special provisions applied to sexual offenders, such as registration and community notification, and civil commitment for sexually violent predators. Appellate courts have generally found even the most controversial of these laws constitutional.

Concern about sexual offenses did not begin in the 1990s. Rape victims began to speak out in the early 1970s, and the rape crisis movement was born. In addition to the development of victim advocacy and service programs, rape laws were reformed and protections for victims participating in the legal process were enacted. Examples include having different degrees of rape, removing the marital exemption, and barring the admission of victim sexual history. By the early 1980s child sexual abuse began to be recognized as a significant social problem. Programs and services for child victims proliferated. As had happened on behalf of adult rape victims, there

Address for correspondence: Lucy Berliner, MSW, Director, Harborview Center for Sexual Assault and Traumatic Stress, 925 9th Ave., Box 359947, Seattle, WA 98104. Voice: 206-521-1800.

lucyb@u.washington.edu

Ann. N.Y. Acad. Sci. 989: 464–473 (2003). © 2003 New York Academy of Sciences.

was legislative reform with regard to reporting and prosecution. For example, corroboration requirements were modified and special hearsay exception laws passed.

This period of reform clearly reflected the emerging recognition that sexual assault was widespread, caused serious harm, and that those who committed these offenses should be held accountable. The new focus beginning in the 1990s shifted from encouraging reporting and prosecution of cases onto consequences for those identified or convicted of sexual offenses. Citizens became more aware that most convicted sexual offenders eventually returned to the community and that in some cases they reoffended. Cases in which known sexual offenders committed new sexual crimes evoked outrage, especially when it appeared that action by the authorities might have prevented them from occurring. High-profile, very serious cases often served as the impetus for the passage of laws at the federal and state level.

THE DECLINE OF VICTIM AND OFFENDER SPECIALIST COLLABORATION

In the early years of identification and response to the problem of sexual assault, victim advocates and sexual offender treatment experts were allies. They made up a small group of professionals that shared in a commitment to raise awareness of the crimes, their impact, and the importance of undertaking a concerted societal response to victims and offenders. This was not only true at the policy level but there was often collaboration on individual cases between victim and offender treatment providers.

The close association between victim advocates and sexual offender experts has waned in recent years, in part as a consequence of successful social policy advocacy. As it became known that victimization was associated with many negative outcomes, more mental health professionals acquired expertise in treating the effects of victimization. Instead of referring victims to specialists, practitioners began to treat them in their more general settings. This is a positive development, but it means that many mental health professionals now treating victims are not participants in the formal and informal networks of victim and offender specialists that evolved over the preceding years. They are not necessarily persuaded that the two groups have common interests or that understanding and caring about what happens to sexual offenders is relevant to the care of victims.

Recent years have also seen a shift in child victim client mix. Anecdotally, many victim service providers report that certain types of case scenarios are now much less common. The classic incest case involving a family where one or more daughters is abused over a period of time, but that is otherwise functional, seems to have virtually disappeared. It is now more typical for clinical cases to consist of situations where children have been abused one or a few times by known but unrelated offenders. There is also evidence for an actual decline in intrafamilial sexual abuse since 1990.

Caseloads are now more representative of all sexual abuse situations. Most sexual abuse consists of a single or a few incidents committed by known offenders; long-term incest is relatively uncommon. Yet it was the latter cases that originally precipitated the close relationship between victim and offender service providers, because they often appeared amenable to psychosocial interventions and community-based treatment was the preferred outcome in many families.

Many early programs, such as Parents United, provided an array of services to victims, family members, and offenders. In other cases, informal alliances were formed between victim specialist programs and sexual offender treatment providers. As fewer and fewer of these cases were the typical fare of practitioners, the contact between victim treatment and offender treatment providers was reduced. The harsher societal response to convicted sexual offenders has also meant that sexual offenders who might previously have been eligible for community treatment alternatives are sentenced to prison terms. This has resulted in far fewer cases where victim and offender service providers have opportunities to interact.

In addition, practitioners who treat adult survivors see the worst possible outcomes of childhood abuse. Although most sexual abuse victims do not develop serious, long-lasting psychological problems, sexual abuse is a risk factor for various conditions that persist into adulthood. In most of these cases the offenders have escaped accountability; statutes of limitations have expired and it is too late to bring them to justice. Few offenders are willing to participate in reparative solutions such as acknowledging the harm and apologizing, paying for victim treatment, or going to therapy. These situations engender an especially negative view about the consequences of victimization and the intractability of offender denial and lack of remorse.

SOCIAL POLICY PREFERENCES OF VICTIMS, CITIZENS, AND SEXUAL OFFENDER EXPERTS

Sexual offender specialists and victim advocates agree that sexual assault is a serious social problem, deserving elevated attention. There is consensus on promoting a social climate that encourages reporting of sexual crimes and holding sexual offenders accountable. Where the divide has emerged concerns what should happen once sexual offenders are identified or convicted.

It is fair to say that in general victims, their advocates, and citizens are more supportive of harsh penalties, mandatory minimum sentences, and special provisions, and are more skeptical about the value of treatment than are sexual offender experts; sexual offender experts, on the other hand, tend to prefer greater flexibility in sentencing options, believe that expert assessment of risk should weigh heavily in confinement decisions, support programs and services for sexual offenders, and favor reintegration of sexual offenders into society with minimal stigmatization.

This disconnect is fueled in part by confusion about recidivism rates. Early efforts to heighten public concern and vigilance created the impression that reoffending was virtually inevitable without intervention and long-term monitoring. The imperative to lower supposed high rates of recidivism was used to rally victim and public support for treatment programs in the community and in prisons.

As is often the case with arguments for the seriousness of a social problem, the level of the risk was overstated. Base rates for recidivism among sexual offenders as a group are modest. But the public is now skeptical of the data and in addition is much less willing to take chances based on probabilities.

Punishment for the sake of punishment is a particular point of contention. Many victims articulate a desire for sexual offenders to suffer losses that are somewhat equivalent to what they have lost as a result of their victimization. Depriving sexual offenders of freedom is often seen as the closest available approximation. The shift toward determinate sentencing in the United States during the last two decades also emphasizes punishment for serious violent offenders. Under these schemes standard sentencing ranges are based on the seriousness of the crime and history of offending. A primary goal was to reduce sentencing disparities that occurred when judges had broad discretion and offenders who committed similar crimes received wildly differing consequences. Another important aspect of this social policy was a rejection of rehabilitation as the purpose of sentencing, and replacement with the principle of equitable sanctions that recognized the harm that was done by the offense ("just deserts").

VICTIMS AND CITIZENS ARE NOT ALWAYS OF ONE MIND

Despite the fact that social policy has become harsher and less flexible with regard to sexual offenders (as well as other criminals), victims and citizens do not have uniform opinions about what should happen to individual sexual offenders. There is often a discrepancy between views about sexual offenders in general and the known sexual offender. The belief that all sexual offenders should be prosecuted and severely punished can crumble when the accused is a family member or a person who does not fit the stereotype of a predatory criminal. It is not uncommon in sentencing hearings to see family members, coworkers, or pastors pleading for leniency for the offender. This phenomenon reveals that there is, at least at the individual level, a willingness among victims and citizens to consider individual characteristics and circumstances in determinations about what should happen to some sexual offenders.

Injustices may occur when the laws prescribe standard sentences or special provisions for all convicted offenders. Perhaps the area where there is the greatest concern involves adolescents convicted of sexual offenses. It is likely that most victims and citizens acknowledge that young teenagers should not be treated in the same way as older teenagers. Although the juvenile justice system still allows for rehabilitation as a major component of the system response, in many jurisdictions adjudicated teenagers must register as sexual offenders and are subject to community notification. It seems probable that victims and citizens would be receptive to more flexibility in this area.

Another type of sexual crime where sentencing options may seem appropriate are cases involving adolescent victims who are not coerced or who do not perceive themselves to be victims. When the age discrepancy is not large, there is not a pattern of involvement in such relationships, and the offender is not in a position of authority (e.g., teacher, priest, coach, etc), these offenses may be seen as transgressions of societal expectations or exploitation, but not necessarily as deserving of the same punishment as other sexual crimes.

The increasing number of Internet-related cases is also likely to provoke debate about the criminal justice response. Several situations raise social policy questions about how identified offenders should be handled. "Traveler" cases, those in which adolescents agree to meet up with individuals they have met on-line, most often involve no deception that the purpose is to engage in a sexual relationship. The documentation of the sexual communications by the youths and the absence of coercion or an authority relationship cast both victim and offender behavior in a different light than the more typical case of a highly vulnerable child who is at least subtly coerced. While these cases clearly represent exploitation on the part of the adult, there may be openness to handling cases of older teenagers who are "willing" victims differently than those that involve situations where the sexual contact is unwanted and the children acquiesce under pressure.

Sting "traveler" cases, in which law enforcement agents pose as teenagers, and child pornography cases are other potential areas for distinction. These situations raise questions about whether someone who has not actually victimized a child should be subject to the same penalties as a person who has. This is not to suggest that these behaviors are benign. For example, looking at or disseminating child pornography is a form of victimization of the children in the images. But these kinds of cases afford the opportunity to develop social policies that take into account different levels of societal sanctions.

INFLUENCING SOCIAL POLICY

When it comes to influence on social policy, the preferences of victim advocates and citizens are likely to prevail over those of sexual offender treatment providers and researchers. However, the expertise of sexual offender specialists is valuable in constructing a social policy response. A great deal of scientific and clinical knowledge has accumulated that can inform societal efforts to reduce sexual assault.

For this to occur a rapprochement between the two constituencies must emerge. There is reason to believe that the alliance between victim advocates and sexual offender specialists can be restored, at least in certain areas. Striving for closer association does not mean that it is necessary to have full agreement on all policies. However, sexual offender specialists who wish to have an impact on social policy must engage respectfully with victim advocates and citizens in the crafting and implementation of laws and policies.

Sexual offender specialists, like many other interest groups, have occasionally taken approaches that are counterproductive to increasing their influence on social policy. One major error is a negative characterization of victims, their advocates, citizens, or politicians. Sexual offender specialists sometimes refer to advocates as extremists or motivated by personal wounds, citizens as driven by hysteria or as vigilantes, and politicians as self-serving and pandering. Undoubtedly there are instances where there is truth to these kinds of observations, but as global descriptions they are offensive and inaccurate. It should not come as a surprise that policymakers will not be interested in incorporating the perspectives of individuals who denigrate them or their constituents.

At their core such attitudes reveal a startling lack of appreciation for the genuine fears of citizens whose primary motivation is a desire to protect women and children from known sexual offenders. Although the level of concern may not always be warranted, common sense dictates that moderating views does not come about by dismissing them out of hand. Sexual offender specialists weaken their position when they fail to ally with citizens on the common ground.

Another way in which sexual offender specialists reduce their impact is by appearing to believe that experts should have primacy in determining social policy. This is a common mistake made by academics who by their training place great weight on evidence derived from empirical research. As a result, they may take a superior attitude or become impatient when other considerations are given weight. Retribution for social transgressions is an example. Regardless of whether there is research showing that punishment deters crime, citizens overwhelmingly believe that it is fair to punish offenders as a way of conveying social norms and providing some measure of justice for victims.

Further, although academics may profess to be value-free, this is not always the case, and citizens are on to the fact that ideology often drives their social policy recommendations. A recent example is the reluctance of the academic establishment to acknowledge that longer sentences might be a factor in the decrease in crime rates that took place during the 1990s. From the perspective of citizens it is obvious that if young male criminals are taken out of commission during the high crime-committing years, they will not be victimizing the community while they are in jail or prison. Certainly crime rates are affected by other variables, but citizens recognize that this opposition to lengthy incarceration is not based only on data.

Finally, there is an appearance that sexual offender experts have a consistent bias in favor of social policies that have the effect of more lenient or preferential treatment for sexual offenders. When they diverge from the views of citizens, it is invariably in the direction that more sexual offenders should remain in the community or be released to the community, that treatment programs should be more widely available, and that sexual offenders should not be subject to what are perceived to be unfair burdens.

The example of registration is instructive. Specialists sometimes argue that because there is no evidence that registration decreases recidivism it is bad social policy. First, there is no requirement that laws be scientifically proven to achieve a goal before they are passed. But more importantly in this case, how onerous is it really for convicted sexual offenders to notify law enforcement of their address? From the perspective of virtually all citizens it is a minor inconvenience that an individual who has molested a child or raped a women should not find unreasonable. If law enforcement believes that knowing the whereabouts of convicted sexual offenders is useful, that is sufficient reason. When specialists make an issue out of registration, it comes across as advocacy on behalf of offenders.

As well, sexual offender experts compromise their credibility when they invoke the interests of victims only when it serves the purpose of advancing flexibility and leniency for offenders. Victims and their advocates notice that sexual offender specialists rarely publicly support longer sentences, community notification, or civil commitment.

THE CASE OF SEXUAL OFFENDER TREATMENT

There is disagreement among sexual offender experts about whether scientific evidence demonstrates that treatment for sexual offenders reduces recidivism. The most favorable interpretation of research results suggests a modest benefit. Despite the mixed research findings, in general, sexual offender experts have strongly advocated for sexual offender treatment in the community and in prisons. Sexual offender treatment specialists understandably believe that their efforts are making a difference, but in many cases they are treating low-risk offenders in the community where specialized treatment may be unnecessary to reduce recidivism. Some experts have advocated that all sexual offenders ought to be afforded state-paid treatment. Arguments for a cost benefit have essentially taken the position that avoiding even one instance of recidivism justifies the expense associated with treating large numbers of offenders.

In addition, specialists often advance other reasons why it is good social policy to have sexual offender treatment. Frequently, the fact that some victims do not want their offender to be incarcerated is offered as an important reason. Conveniently omitted is the fact that just as many if not more victims want sexual offenders to go to prison for very long sentences. Sometimes it is argued that sexual offenders who are sent to prison and not given treatment are at greater risk to reoffend. There is no evidence, however, for higher recidivism rates among offenders eligible for community treatment alternatives who are incarcerated.

THE CASE OF COMMUNITY NOTIFICATION

Many sexual offender specialists have spoken out against community notification. They argue that it is not proven to reduce recidivism, it potentially increases risk by subjecting offenders to stigmatization, it creates a false sense of security in citizens, it is arbitrarily singling out sexual offenders from other criminals, and it leads to vigilantism. Some of these arguments have merit. For example, there is no evidence that notification decreases reoffending. On the other hand, there is also no evidence that it increases recidivism. Citizens strongly support the laws; they do not report an increase in fears or a false sense of security. Incidents of vandalism or attacks on sexual offenders are rare.

These laws were passed because citizens overwhelming believe that the government is obligated to share information affecting their safety and that of their families. The origin of this type of law, now known as Megan's Law, was a situation in which a clearly dangerous sexual offender had to be released. Law enforcement was aware of this man's history and risk, but laws barred them from informing the community and two years later he reoffended in a heinous fashion. The community was understandably outraged that the government could know such important information and be unable to share it with citizens.

When Megan's Law was passed the federal government made state community notification laws a requirement for receiving certain federal funds. Since then courts have provided protections for offenders by ruling that notification must be based on risk, and some states require hearings where risk determination can be challenged. Instead of accepting the laws and recognizing the legitimacy of citizen concerns, many sexual offender specialists simply repeat anecdotes about the few cases of vigilantism and continuously advance their objections.

In fact, many states have successfully implemented community notification procedures that warn about the dangers of ostracizing or harassing offenders, and use the meetings as an opportunity to educate the community about the more common sexual offenders who may be family members or friends and how to protect them-

selves or their children from harm. The failure to capitalize on the potentially positive opportunities afforded by this social policy seems to reflect a negative view of
citizen capacities and advocacy on behalf of offenders.

THE CASE OF CIVIL COMMITMENT STATUTES

The most vociferous objections to recent social policy changes have been leveled
against the civil commitment statutes. Although the U.S. Supreme Court has found
the basic concept constitutional and sexual offender experts frequently testify in civil
commitment trials, many have expressed major reservations about the fairness of the
laws. Concerns range from fundamental disagreement with the Court's reasoning, to
questions about definitions of mental conditions, the science of risk prediction, a
worry that commitment is simply a ruse to keep these offenders off the street, and
that the expense of the programs and responding to legal challenges unnecessarily
consume resources that could be better spent.

These are all potentially legitimate concerns. Yet to a fair degree sexual offender
experts have exerted social policy influence on the implementation of the laws by
bringing their expertise to bear on the key issues of mental disorders and risk for future dangerousness. Most individuals who are committed are diagnosed with
paraphilias and are not just antisocial, actuarial risk-prediction instruments have become the order of the day, and highly regarded experts are developing genuine civil
commitment treatment programs in many states. In addition, experts are often involved in the screening process to determine which offenders are proper candidates
for civil commitment procedures.

But what about the problem the laws were intended to address? The first modern
civil commitment statute was passed in response to a situation in which a clearly
dangerous offender was about to be released and the authorities made an unsuccessful attempt to have him civilly committed under existing mental health laws. The
choices were to accept that there would occasionally be very dangerous individuals
returning to the community with no protection for potential victims or to craft an alternative. The courts have agreed that society has the right to have a mechanism to
invoke in such circumstances.

Sexual offender experts who oppose civil commitment often beg this question.
They sometimes suggest alternatives that cannot be applied retroactively (e.g., longer sentences), while at the same time opposing mandatory minimums, strike laws,
and extremely long sentences. If they support indeterminate sentencing (which also
cannot be retroactive), they worry that the laws will be too expansive in sweeping in
lower risk offenders. What is missing is a direct answer for the occasional problem
of a very dangerous offender being released.

One response would be to openly acknowledge that there is no way to prevent all
recidivism unless sexual offenders are routinely incarcerated for very long or life
sentences and to argue that the cost of some high-risk offenders reoffending on release is offset by the costs associated with alternative social policy options. Sexual
offender experts, like politicians, however, are often unwilling to engage in the concerted effort that would be necessary to build public consensus for this view.

Instead sexual offender experts generally criticize the civil commitment statutes,
and indirectly citizens and courts. The arguments often paint a skewed picture of

how the laws have been implemented. For example, it is not always mentioned that only a very small minority, perhaps 5–10% of about-to-be-released offenders are referred for civil commitment. Cost comparisons with incarceration are often made, but rarely is the comparison made to institutional treatment programs that are substantially more expensive than warehousing. Attention is called to states with substandard or inadequate programs when the focus could be on hailing the development of model programs that are releasing residents on less restrictive alternatives.

RECOMMENDATIONS FOR INFLUENCING SOCIAL POLICY

Not all sexual offender experts seek to be influential in determining social policy. Many researchers are content to test hypotheses and present data and leave it up to policymakers to make use of the results even if their decisions conflict with the researchers personal convictions. Practitioners may choose to operate at the individual case level and seek the best alternative available for specific offenders. For those who wish to make a difference at the level of social policy and laws, however, it is necessary to engage in the kinds of activities that can change social consciousness or produce legislative change.

In order to be a force in social policy, sexual offender experts need to reforge alliances with victim services, advocacy groups, and legislators. Advocacy on behalf of sexual offenders is untenable, and if sexual offender experts want to be seen as legitimately representing the interests of victims and citizens, they must engage with those constituencies in developing and promoting polices and laws. There are many examples of ways that sexual offender experts can advance their cause, and in many states sexual offender experts are integrally involved with the public policy process.

Specific strategies:

(1) Establish and cultivate relationships with key actors. Victim services and advocacy groups exist in most local communities, at the state level in all states and in national organizations; the same is true for child protection, law enforcement, and prosecuting attorneys.

(2) Be a resource to the community. Create opportunities to share clinical and scientific knowledge through offering in-service education or serving as a consultant. One component is willingness to talk to the media. This is especially important at the local level, where ongoing relationships can be established instead of simply providing a sound bite for a particular story that is usually about a single high-profile case.

(3) Enlist unlikely allies. It is often necessary that representatives of victims or the criminal justice system deliver the message. Invite them to visit treatment programs or incorporate them into the treatment process. Victim service professionals can help with victim impact or empathy enhancement sessions. Law enforcement professionals can explain laws and community expectations to offenders. The opportunity to observe or interact with sexual offenders who appear to be benefiting by treatment can help overcome skepticism. These professionals are far more likely to go to bat for treatment programs when they are in jeopardy, and will often have great credibility.

(4) Participate in development and implementation of policies. Get on the task forces and work groups that are often behind the passage of new laws. Attend the interdisciplinary professional networks where local decision making occurs. Be active participants in the community sexual offender management approaches that are now being developed.

(5) Provide quality assurance. Affirmatively seek ways to offer guidance to prosecutors, corrections departments, treatment programs, and lawmakers in areas where specialized expertise is especially relevant, such as risk assessment, specialized therapy, and relapse prevention.

CONCLUSION

Sexual offender experts can and should be important contributors to social policy regarding what happens to sexual offenders. There are many ways to enhance influence, beginning with forming and maintaining relationships with victim advocates, the criminal justice system, and legislators. Refraining from advocacy interpretations of data, offering feasible solutions, being a resource, and investing the necessary effort that goes with social policy development would go a long way. Most important, however, is showing respect for the concerns of citizens who by rights get to determine social policy.

After *Hendricks*: Defining Constitutional Treatment for Washington State's Civil Commitment Program

ROXANNE LIEB

Director, Washington State Institute for Public Policy,
Olympia, Washington 98504-0999, USA

> *Nothing compels a state to adopt a statute of this*
> *nature in the first place and many states have not*
> *done so, but a state that chooses to have such a*
> *program must make adequate mental health*
> *treatment available to those committed.*
> — JUDGE WILLIAM L. DWYER,
> *Turay v. Weston, 1999*

ABSTRACT: Washington State's law for sexually violent predators was enacted in 1990; since then, 14 other states have passed similar laws authorizing civil commitment for dangerous sexual offenders following their prison terms. Although the law has survived constitutional challenges at both the state and in the U.S. Supreme Court, a related set of court actions has addressed whether the treatment program is adequate. In 1994, the federal district court placed Washington's program under injunction and appointed a special master to ensure that the state improve deficiencies in the program. As of 2003, the federal court continues to oversee the state's program, with a threat of fines totaling several million dollars if the injunction terms are not met. Over an eight-year period, the special master delivered 19 reports to the court, documenting the program's deficiencies as well as its successes in meeting the court's orders. This article reviews these reports and court orders, detailing the court's requirements for an adequate treatment program.

KEYWORDS: sexually violent predators; civil commitment; adequate treatment program; Washington State

FIRST PROGRAM CRITIQUE: 1992

When Vernon Quinsey, Ph.D., visited Washington State's program for sexually violent predators (SVPs) in February 1992, the program had nine residents who had been civilly committed for "control, care, and treatment" to a special commitment

Address for correspondence: Roxanne Lieb, MPA, Director, Washington State Institute for Public Policy, 110 East Fifth Ave., Suite 214, P.O. Box 40999, Olympia, Washington 98504-0999. Voice: 360-586-2768; fax: 360-586-2793.
liebr@wsipp.wa.gov

Ann. N.Y. Acad. Sci. 989: 474–488 (2003). © 2003 New York Academy of Sciences.

center (SCC) inside a medium secure prison after completing their prison sentences (RCW 71.09.060). Quinsey, an international expert in sexual offender research and assessment, visited the program at the request of a state research organization charged with assessing the effectiveness of Washington's 1990 Community Protection Act.[a] This omnibus legislation had been proposed by a governor-appointed Task Force on Community Protection and was designed to remedy various perceived weaknesses in laws concerning sexual offenders. In particular, the law created a new form of involuntary commitment for dangerous sexual offenders who reached the end of their maximum prison term and were not suitable for confinement under the short-term provisions of state mental health law. This new form of civil commitment for a "small, but extremely dangerous" group of persons found to meet the definition of sexually violent predator was first enacted by Washington's legislature and later adopted by 14 other states (Lieb, 2003, p. 41). The law's focus on social control mechanisms following prison terms has been described elsewhere as a "third wave" of legislative and public attention on sexual offenders in the United States (Lieb, Quinsey, and Berliner, 1998, p. 53). As is often the case, this U.S. innovation in legal mechanisms for sexual offenders was precipitated by a horrendous crime. Washington's "trail of tears" leading to its SVP legislation has been described elsewhere and explored with particular care by the law's architect, David Boerner (1992).

At the time that Quinsey visited the SCC program in Monroe, Washington, it was located in a wing of the Special Offender Unit of the Department of Corrections (DOC). The state Department of Social and Health Services was responsible under the law for running the program, so the unit staff were all employed by the DSHS. Security, meals, and transportation were provided under contract by the DOC. The first person was committed to the program in October 1990; by the time of Quinsey's visit in 1992, three residents were engaged in the treatment program; the remaining six refused to participate. Quinsey identified what he described as two "very serious difficulties" with the program: one concerned the legislation itself, and the second concerned its implementation (Quinsey, 1992, p. 3). In terms of the underlying legislation, Quinsey noted that the ambiguous constitutional status of the law created "great uncertainty," and many residents were "simply waiting to see" if the law would be declared unconstitutional. "Everything is on hold until the legal issues are addressed more definitely," Quinsey concluded (p. 3).

Because the SVP law was imposed after, not before or instead of, a criminal sentence, Quinsey observed that it challenged the usual construct of treatment-oriented sentences. In his view, a front-end disposition, such as a sentencing option, was far preferable for "legal, ethical, and therapeutic reasons" (p. 3). Even so, front-end applications had been difficult for jurisdictions to apply in an effective and fair manner, leading to loss of political support and, in some instances, repeal. Because SVP statutes are imposed after completion of a criminal sentence, Quinsey noted residents have particular reason to perceive the law as "arbitrary and excessive," making it extremely difficult for program staff to form a "therapeutic alliance with an embittered clientele" (p. 4). Quinsey observed that many SCC residents saw

---

[a]The 1990 Community Protection Act directed the Washington State Institute for Public Policy to evaluate the effectiveness of state-supported programs for sexual offenders. The author works for the Institute.

litigation as their only route to release "or at least, quick release" (p. 4). Until some residents secured their release as a result of treatment-induced changes, Quinsey concluded "it will be extremely difficult to convince residents that a therapeutic release route is feasible" (p. 4).

In his report, Quinsey complimented the SCC treatment staff for their dedication and interest in creating a state-of-the-art cognitive-behavioral intervention program. Quinsey observed, however, that the statutory language did not "induce therapeutic optimism" because its preamble referenced a population that was unlikely to be cured (p. 4). To gain release, he noted, residents must convince a jury or court that their thinking/behavior patterns had changed such that they no longer posed a risk to the community. Quinsey questioned how treatment could be shown to alter the residents' mental diagnosis since their common diagnosis was "personality disorder," and most of the defining factors of this diagnosis are historical in nature (p. 4).

How then to improve the law? Quinsey recommended the state amend its statute to include a gradual release mechanism so residents who had progressed in treatment could be tested for release readiness in stages. Without such a mechanism, Quinsey advised, the law had a "fatal problem" (p. 5). In terms of program management, he observed that it was not wise to continue mixing residents awaiting trial with those who were committed for treatment, nor to mix residents participating in treatment with those who were not. In both instances, he predicted a negative affect on treatment participation.

Finally, Quinsey recommended that the state give "considerable thought" to the management and daily living patterns for those residents who were not progressing toward a stage of safe release, or not opting for treatment (p. 6). In these instances, he noted, long-term living arrangements were needed that offered opportunities for education, recreation, and personal development. "For most of these men," he concluded, "it is likely that secure perimeter security can be combined with considerable freedom within the institution" (p. 6).

Whatever the wisdom of Quinsey's recommendations, the state did not respond to the report by altering the SVP legislation or program structure. Given the uncertainty about the law's constitutionality, state leaders instead appear to have taken a "wait and see" attitude. The following year, 1993, the law passed its first major legal hurdle when Washington's Supreme Court found the law constitutional in a 6 to 3 ruling (*In the matter of the Personal Restraint of Andre Brigham Young, August 1993*). Because the law pushed traditional boundaries between civil and criminal law, legal experts were certain the case would ultimately be decided by the U.S. Supreme Court.

FEDERAL COURT INJUNCTION: 1994

The SVP law next made Washington State headlines in 1994 when a federal district court in King County found that the SCC treatment program violated its residents' civil rights. Challengers successfully convinced a jury that the 14th Amendment required that residents have access to mental health treatment offering a realistic opportunity for cure or improvement in the mental condition that caused the confinement. The presiding judge, William L. Dwyer, was an esteemed legal figure in the Northwest with a portfolio of landmark decisions, including a 1991 ruling that barred timber sales throughout the threatened habitat of the spotted owl.

Dwyer found that Washington failed to provide plaintiffs with access to "constitutionally adequate treatment" that offered "a realistic opportunity to be cured or to improve the mental conditional for which he was confined" (*Richard G. Turay v. David B. Weston et al.* No. C91-664WD, p. 2). Dwyer referenced trial testimony that had revealed that most of the program's clinical staff were inexperienced with a sexual offender population. "Training has been largely ad hoc, consisting primarily of lectures," without a supervising psychologist or psychiatrist available to staff for the majority of the program's operation (p. 3). Staff and residents were unable to assess treatment progress with any objective measures of improvement.

The court's injunction defined the steps necessary for Washington to bring the program into compliance with the constitution. Five injunction elements were specified:

- adopt and implement a plan for initial and ongoing training and/or hiring of competent sexual offender therapists;
- implement strategies to rectify the lack of trust and rapport between residents and treatment providers;
- implement a treatment program that includes all therapy components recognized as necessary by professional standards in comparable programs where participation is coerced, including the involvement of spouses and family members;
- develop and maintain individual treatment plans for residents that include objective benchmarks of improvement; and
- provide a psychologist or psychiatrist expert in the diagnosis and treatment of sexual offenders to supervise the clinical work of treatment staff, including monitoring of treatment plans of individual residents (pp. 4 and 5).

Following the June 1994 ruling, the state had until July 20 to alter the program to satisfy the injunction. On August 22, the court found the state's plans insufficient and ordered the parties to submit nominations for a "special master" to oversee the state's progress in meeting the injunction and offer expert advice to the state. Federal courts periodically use special masters to oversee court-mandated changes in public systems, including state boundary definitions, civil rights desegregation, and prison improvements (Feeley and Rubin, 1998, p. 75).

The person selected as Special Master, Janice Marques, Ph.D., brought strong qualifications to this position. Marques works as a manager in California's Department of Mental Health, previously directed a treatment program for sexual offenders at Atascadero State Hospital, and is a national leader in the field of sexual offender treatment. Her research on a treatment program for sexual offenders is widely regarded as the "gold standard" design on this topic (Marques et al., 1994).

THE FIRST YEARS OF THE INJUNCTION: 1994–1997

The Special Master's first reports to the court confirmed the injunction findings. Following a two-day visit in November 1994, Marques called particular attention to the "seriousness" of the lack of trust and rapport between residents and treatment providers. She observed that some difficulty in this regard was "inevitable" due to the nature of the involuntary commitment: "This is at best a challenging and difficult context in which to establish the trust and respect necessary for effective treatment" (p. 2). By this point, she reported, the program had a "four-year history of problems in this area" and both "staff and residents appear discouraged" (p. 2). Marques concluded that "significant improvements will not come quickly or easily" (p. 2).

In February 1995, the Special Master issued her second report and offered more descriptions and analysis of the SCC's difficulties (Second Report of Special Master, February 13, 1995). Marques noted that the "boredom, idleness, and impatience among most of the residents" was obvious, "as is their lack of hope regarding their chances for earning release through treatment" (p. 4). The staff, she observed, show "the strain of working in an environment in which their decisions are always challenged and their efforts criticized" (p. 4). Marques described the treatment environment as "particularly difficult and strained," and that the program was pervaded by a "litigious atmosphere" (p. 3) where nearly everyone is "involved in or affected by resident complaints, legal challenges and court actions" (p. 4). Marques urged the clinical team to work quickly to finalize the targets for treatment so that residents could see a "light at the end of the tunnel" (p. 5). She reported that none of the therapists or supervisors were certified as expert sexual offender treatment providers. (This certification was created in the same omnibus legislation authorizing the SVP law.) Although not required in the SVP law, Marques observed that treatment providers with this certification would "enhance the program's content and credibility" (p. 9). In terms of statutory remedies, Marques encouraged the state to pursue statutory revisions to authorize conditional release to the community following treatment (p. 5).

In the spring of 1995, the court received its third report from Marques. The report described progress on several fronts, including the hiring of a part-time, certified sexual offender specialist to lead the clinical team. The negative treatment environment was described as a continuing challenge: "there is still a long way to go before a positive treatment environment is established at SCC" (p. 6). Marques described the residents who actively refused treatment as "dominat[ing] the environment with their complaints and expressions of frustration" (p. 6). The fourth report (June 1995) describes a "very productive work period" (p. 5), with program changes that were intended to "limit interaction between those in treatment and those who are not." Persons who either were "actively opposing treatment" or "presenting significant management problems" (p. 3) were not allowed in the areas occupied by those participating in treatment. Marques noted that this separation, however, was not a complete solution, as treatment participants "continued to feel intimidated by some of the treatment refusers" and the refusers felt "frustrated and unduly restricted" (p. 7).

The legislative revision authorizing a conditional release provision was passed by the 1995 Legislature (Chapter 216, Laws of 1995). Marques observed that this legislation was "encouraging," but residents were unsure whether the required conditions "could ever be met" (p. 9). Marques observed that "it will be a major milestone in the program's development when the first resident, with the support and collaboration of the treatment staff, is released under these new provisions" (p. 10). In a few instances, individual courts in Washington released persons found to be SVPs directly to the community, requiring significant supervision and treatment elements. These persons usually resided in group homes with 24-hour supervision (DSHS press release, May 4, 2001).

In August 1995, Marques' fifth report placed significant emphasis on the treatment environment. Marques noted that this area of the injunction was the "most complicated and difficult" as it involved all residents and staff (p. 7). In her view, the "realistic goal" was a "healthy and humane environment at SCC, one in which effective treatment can occur," where those in treatment must not be harassed by other residents, and those not in treatment must have alternative productive activities (p. 7). Additionally, management of residents must be "guided by an overall set of rules that are fair, clearly communicated to the residents, and consistently enforced by the unit staff" (p. 7).

The negative SCC atmosphere, in Marques' view, was not the "result of staff incompetence or abuse;" she observed that staff had been "exceptionally resistant in the face of frequent criticism and threats of lawsuit" (p. 10). In her view, "some residents will never want to contribute to a positive environment at SCC and will continue to challenge the law, the program, and the staff on a regular basis" (p. 10). Treatment participants and refusers must be physically separated, she concluded, to create the possibility of a "cohesive, therapeutic environment" (p. 11).

From November 1995 through early 1996, several expert consultants visited the SCC at the request of Marques and offered recommendations. Her two reports during this time period concentrated on resident management issues and efforts to provide fair and consistent application of rules. A new position of ombudsman was established to assist with this goal, with selection made by both parties. Although counsel from both sides helped draft provisions regarding the position's role and authority, creating a structure to support a neutral role in the highly contentious environment was not easy.

The first ombudsman, Tamara Menteer, was hired in January 1996. Difficulties with the position emerged early; Marques' report to the court in July 1996 described the ombudsman's challenges in establishing trust and maintaining a neutral role. The ombudsman described her position to Marques as a "nearly impossible combination of tasks" (p. 8). Eventually, Menteer was terminated; her views became a matter of public record when she published an article about the SCC in a Seattle weekly newspaper (Menteer 1998). Menteer concluded that she found it "all but impossible" to remain neutral (p. 2); after her departure she founded an organization opposing continued punishment of sex offenders beyond their original sentence (Whitestone Foundation, 2003).

By 1996, the program's location as a separate wing in Monroe Corrections Center was clearly problematic. The space limitations made it difficult to separate the population according to their treatment participation, except in a superficial way, nor was there adequate room for recreational and vocational activities.

In 1997, Judge Dwyer visited the SCC and met with staff and residents. His subsequent October 1997 court order reinforced the program shortfalls identified in the injunction: (1) that staff needed experience working "under the direct supervision of an expert in the field;" (2) that "a community transition component…is not yet operational;" (3) that "treatment with a resident's family members has not yet been adequately integrated into the program, although progress has been made;" (4) that "each treatment plan…should broadly assess a resident's needs and skills beyond the offense behavior;" (5) that "each resident should be able to compare his program to objective measure of progress;" and (6) that "before the injunction is dissolved a structure for objective, external oversight must be in place" (p. 4). The order anticipated compliance by the end of six months. "What is required is not a plan," Dwyer wrote, "but a reality—the genuine providing of adequate mental health treatment to all SCC residents willing to accept it" (p. 4).

Dwyer found that the physical plant was a "serious obstacle to providing constitutionally adequate treatment" and prospects for compliance with the injunction would be enhanced by having the SCC move to a "better facility as soon as possible" (December 23, 1998, p. 5). As the state considered options for relocating the SCC, the range of choices appeared limited. The law called for a "secure facility" (RCW 71.09.060[3]); given the mental health treatment component, an obvious option was a state mental health hospital. Of the 14 states that passed SVP laws, 5 required that the program be located in a hospital setting (Lieb, 2003, pp. 46–51). Washington's history with its previous sexual offender treatment program, however, caused the 1990 Legislature to eliminate this option from the start.

Along with half of the states, Washington had earlier enacted special laws for sexual psychopaths; Washington's law passed in 1947 (Lieb, Quinsey, and Berliner, 1998, p. 59; Bowman, 1952, p. 38). Persons found by Washington's courts to be sexual psychopaths were committed to Western State Hospital near Tacoma or, to a much lesser extent, to Eastern State Hospital near Spokane. The Western State program operated under a model allowing residents more freedom as they progressed in treatment; at the final stage they had keys to their rooms. In the 1970s, the Western State program made headline news when a resident who escaped committed a rape and two murders. In 1979, headlines returned when a graduate who subsequently worked in the program as a therapist was found murdered in an isolated area. He had been shot by a man he was attempting to rape. Other bodies were found in this area, along with the discovery of sadomasochistic items in his apartment. In 1988, a resident on "furlough" committed a rape at knifepoint (Boerner, 1992, p. 552). Shortly thereafter the program was closed. Because of this history, the original SVP legislation specified that the program could not be located on the grounds of a state mental facility or regional rehabilitation center because "these institutions are insufficiently secure for this population" (RCW 71.09.060[4])).[b]

MOVING TO THE ISLAND: 1997

In late 1997, the state moved the program to McNeil Island Correctional Center (MICC), a medium-security prison located on an island off Puget Sound. The island, near Tacoma, formerly housed a federal prison, but in the 1980s the property was transferred to Washington State for use as a prison. As was the case in Monroe, the arrangement between the state Department of Social and Health Services (DSHS) and Department of Corrections called for the DOC to provide medical care, meals, transportation, and external security, while the DSHS was responsible for treatment. The Special Master's twelfth report, in 1997, described the advantages that the SCC superintendent expected from the McNeil Island location: "better program space;

[b]Lieb 1996, pp. 8–9.

greatly enhanced resources, including educational vocational opportunities; and proximity to Western State Hospital, which would allow SCC to share training and clinical resources with a major mental health program" (p. 11).

Most of these advantages, however, did not initially materialize. It was difficult for a mental health program run by the DSHS for less than 70 residents to negotiate terms with the DOC's management running a 1000-bed prison. Although the SCC program had experienced conflict with corrections managers in Monroe, the program was located within a "pod," and it was possible to influence this environment. The move to McNeil Island introduced a new set of variables because program space was not as self-contained; additionally, the injunction required the program to offer residents more opportunities for treatment and recreation, placing greater demands on the SCC to negotiate with the DOC.

The conflicts between the organizations centered on security issues. Prison regulations, for example, called for routine strip searches following a resident's visit with family and friends. Additionally, telephone calls were restricted to collect outgoing calls; a recorded announcement at the beginning of the call identified the caller as a prison inmate. When the federal court entered two court orders to end routine strip searches, prison management finally complied but also disallowed residents' use of the "big yard" due to perceived security threats. Clearly, these rules did not mesh with practices in the state's mental hospitals.

THE U.S. SUPREME COURT SPEAKS: 1997

In 1997, the U.S. Supreme Court settled the constitutionality of the SVP statute ruling on the Kansas statute that was modeled on Washington's law (*Kansas v. Hendricks*, 521 U.S. 346,369). The Supreme Court allowed states "wide latitude in developing treatment regimes [for sexual offenders]... and liability [on a claim for constitutional deprivation] may be imposed only when the decision by the professional is such a satisfactory departure from accepted judgment, practice, or standards as to demonstrate that the person responsible did not base the decision on such a judgment" (*Kansas v. Hendricks*, 521 U.S. 346, 368 n.4 [1997]).

The Special Master reported that the *Hendricks* decision precipitated a very difficult time for the residents, many of whom had expected to be released immediately after the decision was issued. Her twelfth report in the fall of 1997 described a "tense and negative" unit, with several residents "invested in the failure of SCC, including any of the program's efforts to improve trust and rapport" (p. 19). A second ombudsman had been appointed by this time, with an altered reporting structure so the person was supervised by a DSHS assistant secretary rather than by SCC management (p. 19).

The court's order in February 1997 acknowledged the state's progress in meeting the injunction requirements and described the newly appointed superintendent and clinical director as appearing to have the "credentials, experience, and energy needed to maintain a constitutionally adequate and effective program" (p. 3). Judge Dwyer indicated that he was nonetheless unwilling to release the state from the injunction because "more remains to be done" (p. 3). Dwyer restated the urgent need for a functioning community transition component as well as fuller integration of family members into the program. Additionally, Dwyer described the "treatment atmosphere and staff-resident relations" as the most difficult area of the injunction (p. 3). In 1998, Dwyer visited the relocated facility and determined that the standards for providing mental health treatment were "still unmet" (November 1998, p. 12). The trial testimony of an expert witness for the plaintiffs, Dr. Craig Harvey, is quoted in the order:

> The first is that, as I suggested earlier, the Department of Corrections very clearly dominates physically, administratively, procedurally, and psychologically the MICC and really in many significant ways encompasses the SCC. It is, for all intents and purposes, a prison. Feels like a prison, looks like a prison, and for the most part operates like a prison.
>
> In my opinion, in addition, in some not insignificant ways, the SCC residents actually have fewer, not more, liberties in comparison to the Department of Corrections prisoners. It is also my opinion that these things collectively represent impediments to any possibility that any significant therapy or treatment can be done under the present circumstances and in addition, because of the quality of life which is created there and the conditions that have been created there, ... present me with a concern about potential deterioration of people who are kept in the SCC under the current conditions. (December 23 order, p. 7).

The entanglement of the SCC with the prison clearly disturbed the court. Dwyer took significant issue with the MICC superintendent's request that the court defer to her professional judgment "about the needs of a prison" (p. 7). Dwyer pointed out that "the court has not ordered the DOC to do anything" (p. 6) and that SCC is "required by constitutional law *not* to be a prison" (p. 7). When the state argued that it was unclear what the court meant by directing "better meal and activity schedules," Dwyer's patience appeared strained as he described the obvious meaning: "meal and activity schedules that are more ample and more attuned to the rhythms of ordinary life, as contrasted with the artificial and restricted schedules that have prevailed to date" (p. 9).

In 1998, Washington State settled with 16 long-term SCC residents, paying each $10,000 for the inadequate mental health treatment plus $250,000 in legal fees. The state's attorneys made a strategic decision to stop defending the program's past conditions: "We are in a new place now and we have a relatively new style of treatment program," the SCC Assistant Attorney General stated to the press, "and we figured this is a way to move forward. (Porterfield, October 2, 1998, AI).

INCOMPATIBILITY OF A PROGRAM INSIDE A PRISON: 1998

In 1999, the U.S. Supreme Court agreed to hear a related SVP case, *Seling v. Young*. This case concerned whether the program's conditions of confinement were punitive and therefore violated constitutional prohibitions against *ex post facto* and double jeopardy. Again, many SCC residents hoped that this case would eventually bring them freedom.

The Special Master issued her sixteenth report in September 1999; by this time, the injunction had been operating for five and a half years. Marques described some conditions as improved, including one-third of the residents actively participating in treatment. Serious shortcomings, however, persisted, and the "prison's influence remains pervasive and damaging" (p. 12). A report in October from an independent group with a multidisciplinary focus, the Inspection of Care Committee, found deficiencies similar to those in the Special Master's report and characterized the program as operating "more like a correctional facility than a treatment center or program" (*Turay v. Weston,* November 15, 1999, p. 17). Dwyer's court order in November 1999 concluded that the only expected advantage of the program's relocation to McNeil that had materialized was "larger space with better views" (p. 11). He described the program as an "unwanted stepchild of a medium-security prison" (p. 16). Clearly, he was tired of waiting for compliance and decided to take action, finding the state in contempt of court (p. 20).

Dwyer identified three main causes for Washington's failure to achieve compliance:

- Inadequate resources: The "chief cause" was the state's failure to devote necessary resources to achieve compliance" (pp. 15–16). "Instead of doing what must be done, the state has treated SCC as an unwanted stepchild of a medium-security prison" (p. 16).
- Entrenched resistance to the injunction: "The defendants have fallen into a pattern of first denying that anything is amiss at SCC, then engaging in a flurry of activity to make improvements before the next court hearing, then admitting at the hearing that shortfalls of constitutional magnitude still exist, then returning to denial" (p. 16).
- The prison's dominating influence: "The placement of SCC within the perimeter of MICC continues to make it difficult to achieve a treatment-oriented environment."

Rejecting plaintiffs' requests to release all SCC residents as a remedy, Dwyer decided instead to impose financial penalties on Washington State. The sanctions were structured to create significant incentives for compliance: the state must pay $50 a day for each resident each day if the court's ordered improvements were not made, with payment deferred for six months. By this route, the judge put pressure on Washington's executive and legislative branches to invest in the law, both with resources as well as political will.

Washington's political leaders quickly responded to Dwyer's ruling. "When Judge Dwyer rules, governors jump" read the editorial in the *Tacoma News Tribune* (May 9, 1999). Within two days of the court ruling, Governor Locke declared his intent to ask legislators for $19 million to improve the program and authorized state officials to immediately spend a portion of this amount. Locke clarified the political stakes: "I ask the Legislature to join me in ensuring that the Civil Commitment program meets constitutional standards so that we are never forced to release dangerous sex offenders into the community without adequate treatment or supervision" (Carter, 1999, B2). That year, the program received an additional $3 million for staff hiring and training, and the Legislature budgeted $14 million for the first stage of a new stand-alone facility to be built on the island outside the McNeil Island Correctional Center (*Turay v. Seling,* May 5, 2000, p. 10).

Dwyer's November 1999 court order included commentary on the inherent difficulty of the SVP law. Although the statute is constitutional "on its face," Dwyer noted, in practice it "causes resentment and resistance because it reconfines, for an indefinite period, offenders who have served their sentence and have been released. Successful treatment of sexual offenders is no easy task even among those who voluntarily seek it; it is harder yet, by and large among those involuntarily committed.

But the difficulties have been recognized fully in the generous time already allowed for compliance, and at this point, on this record, do not excuse a failure to perform" (pp. 17–18). In terms of the relative policy merits of the SVP statute, Dwyer wrote that this question must be determined by the "public and the legislature, not the courts..." (p. 16).

As the SCC program hired staff and concentrated on improving treatment conditions, the Governor and legislative leaders tackled the statutory changes necessary to meet the court's order for a transitional facility in the community. The first efforts by the Department of Social and Health Services to locate transitional housing for individual residents resulted in front-page news when neighbors learned that the state planned to move a multiple rapist into a neighborhood. Local elected officials joined citizens to cry foul (Pacey, 2000, p. A1). The department then created a special task force to identify requirements for the facility and a process to identify and consider sites (Shrkorsky, 2000, p. A1; Washington State Department of Social and Health Services, 2002).

The task force identified several factors essential in site selection, including an average five-minute response time for law enforcement to reach the facility (DSHS, 2002, p. 17). This requirement made it difficult to site the facility in a physically remote location. As the department moved ahead in considering sites, each locality identified as a potential site responded with strong and immediate opposition. In each case, the argument followed the same pattern: Although we are sympathetic to the state's plight, our area is unsuitable and we already shoulder an unfair burden of the state's undesirable facilities—for example, mental hospitals, prisons, or work release programs.

In December 2000, the DSHS secretary authored an op-ed piece entitled, "We Can and Must Make This Sex Offender Program Work." The ten-year-old SCC program was at a "crossroads," Secretary Braddock argued, and "as a state and a society we will either follow through on the promise of civil commitment process for sexual offenders or we will risk losing the opportunity to continue supervising and treating these and future offenders after they are released from prison" (Braddock, 2000, p. B7).

IMPROVEMENT NOTED BUT INJUNCTION RETAINED: 2000

The May 2000 court order acknowledged the state's "genuine and sustained effort" to bring the SCC program into compliance since the contempt order was issued (p. 9). The seventeenth report from the Special Master described the period as "exceptional" (p. 9), noting that DSHS management had declared they would "make every effort not only to bring SCC into compliance with the injunction, but to build a model civil commitment program" (p. 2).

The court stated that "there is no doubt that this effort was caused by the contempt order" and "both sides have proposed findings" to this effect. "At all previous stages, the state agencies moved slowly, and often reluctantly, to make improvements. Faced with a sanction, they have moved with speed and determination" (p. 10).

As the injunction continued, the budgetary implications of sustaining a constitutionally sound treatment program at SCC became clear to legislative leaders. Seeing the long-term expense required by the SVP law, state fiscal leaders chose to create an alternative policy path for the future. In June 2001, 3ESSB 6151 was passed, establishing a prospective sentencing system for sexual offenders that maintained state controls over those determined to pose high risks. In doing so, the "pipeline" for potential SVP residents would eventually be significantly reduced for sex offenders sentenced after the effective date. "It has become very apparent that the costs of those residents at McNeil Island [have] become a drain," the House Republican's chief budget writer at the time stated. "Things just keep going up and going up with no end in sight" (Carter, 2000, p. 10).

After the next federal court hearing on the injunction in December 2000, Dwyer recognized the state's "genuine and sustained effort to bring the SCC program into compliance," noting that contributions of the SCC administration, the DSHS, the governor, and the state legislature (December 20, 2002, p. 8). "Conditions are much better," Dwyer wrote. The Superintendent, Mark Seling, was acknowledged in this order as providing "capable leadership" (p. 8).

Once again, the ombudsman had become a source of controversy. The court described the individual as a "conscientious and devoted advocate for the SCC residents"; however, his "partisanship" was hampering his effectiveness. Eventually, this person's contract was terminated (p. 10).

The 2000 court order directed that a separate facility was necessary for the SCC to effectively remove the prison's influence on the treatment program. Dwyer identified the program's continuing major flaw as the lack of a "step-down" facility. "Mental health treatment, if it is to be anything other than a sham, must give the confined person the hope that if he gets well enough to be safely released, then he will be transferred to some less restrictive alternative" (p. 11). Dwyer stated that the political opposition to these facilities, although "real and understandable," cannot justify a deprivation of SCC's residents' constitutional right to treatment (p. 7).

CONTROVERSY IN SITING A TRANSITIONAL FACILITY: 2000–2003

With the infusion of funds, the SCC's treatment program, as well as its vocational and recreational activities, were significantly expanded, and the Special Master's eighteenth report, in November 2000, described numerous accomplishments (p. 9). Similarly, her nineteenth report, in June 2001, described progress in these areas. Establishing a community transition facility remained the chief issue for the injunction. Also in 2001, the U.S. Supreme Court rejected the aargument that the State's SVP law "as applied" violated the Constitution (*Seling v. Young*, 2001). For SCC residents, this case had represented the last hope for immediate release through the courts.

In 2001, the Legislature directed all counties and cities to amend their comprehensive plans and development regulations for a Secure Community Transition Facility (SCTF). No jurisdiction elected to pursue the planning process; intead, some passed resolutions and ordinances to further restrict siting (*Turay v. Seling*, April 17, 2002, p. 13). The 2002 Legislature then passed ESSB 6594, preempting and superseding local laws and regulations and granting authority for the state to situate the facility if the counties do not plan for their location (Chapter 68, Laws of 2002). A "fair share" concept was incorporated into the law that requires counties that have committed the largest number of SCC residents to "take back a fair share of those who are conditionally released…"(DSHS, July 20, 2002, p. 2). Because more than 30 percent of the SCC residents have been committed from King County, the recent search for a transitional facility has concentrated on that area (DSHS, July 20, 2002, p. 2).

The process of situating a King County facility continues at the time of this writing. The facility is described in the press as "one of the most-despised public projects in recent local memory" (Ko, April 20, 2003). Public hearings have drawn thousands of protesters, with local elected officials leading the charge to fight locating the facility in their area (Barker, December 20, 2002). The law forbids location of the facility within "line of sight" of a "risk potential activity or facility." This definition includes schools, bus stops, day care centers and preschools, parks, trails, sports fields, playgrounds, recreational and community centers, synagogues, temples, mosques, and public libraries" (RCW 71.09.020 [11]). One proposed site was removed from consideration when a "fatal flaw" was discovered—that is, a school bus stop used by one child (DSHS, July 2002, p. 3). State officials plan to announce their decision sometime before the October 2003 federal court hearing on the injunction (Friederich, May 16, 2003, p. B3). The deferred sanctions in the case continue to accrue and will reach more than $6 million in the fall of 2003 (Friederich, February 6, 2003).

In 2002, the case was transferred to Judge Barbara Rothstein after Judge Dwyer's death from liver cancer. Shortly before Dwyer's death, Janice Marques stepped down from her seven-year role as Special Master. Judge Dwyer commended her for her valuable role in the case (*Turay v. Seling*, September 2001), describing her work and reports as "of great benefit to the court, the parties, the public, and to all institutions in the United States devoted to the civil commitment and treatment of persons found to be sexually violent predators" (p.1).

WHY HAS IT BEEN SO DIFFICULT?

Why has Washington's law faced such an arduous journey? Observers point to a variety of answers. Some believe the principal difficulties rest with the law, believing it to be an effort to further punish individuals under the guise of treatment. Others point to Washington's "pioneering" role with the statute and the fact that each step required the establishment of new legal ground.

Some onlookers criticize the state's legal strategy, characterized by Judge Dwyer as denial, followed by foot dragging, followed by denial. For some, politicians are the chief culprit because they embraced the law as a political solution in 1990 but never intended to fund and operate a full-fledged treatment program.

Although this article has focused on court decision-making, Judge Dwyer believed the central policy questions associated with the SVP statute belong elsewhere: "Whether better or more economical ways exist to prevent sex offenders from reoffending is for the public and state legislature, not the courts, to decide (*Turay v. Seling*, May 5, 2000, p. 6).

REFERENCES

BARKER, JEFFREY M. (2002, December 20). 200 oppose plan for sex offender facility. *Seattle Post-Intelligencer*.<http://seattlepi.nwsource.com/local100876_sexoffender20.shtml>.

BARISIC, SONJA. (2003, May 3). Miami man's 1973 nightmare inspires Viriginia sexual predator law, *Naples Daily News*. Florida. <http://www.naplesnews.com/03/05/florida/d929261a.htm>.

BOERNER, D. (1992). Confronting violence: in the act and in the word. *University of Puget Sound Law Review, 15*, 525–577.

BOWMAN, Karl M. (1952). Review of sex legislation and the control of sex offenders in the United States of America. *International Review of Criminal Policy* (January), 20–39.

BRADDOCK, DENNIS. (2000, December 19). We can and must make this sex offender program work. *The Spokesman-Review.com*. Spokane, Washington, B7.

BRADDOCK, DENNIS. (2000, November 17). Final siting criteria for secure community less restrictive alternative housing. Special Commitment Center, Health and Rehabilitative Services Administration, Washington State Department of Social and Health Services.

BRAKEL, S.J., PARRY, J. & WEINER, B.A. (1985). *The mentally disabled and the law.* (3rd ed.) Chicago: American Bar Foundation.

CARTER, M. (2000, March 21). Sex-offender center: 10 years of trouble. *Seattle Times*. <http://archives.seattletimes.nwsource.com/cgi-bin/texis.cgi/web/vortex/display?slug=sexx&date=20000321&query=Sex-offender+center>.

COSMILLO, LISA & DURAN, SARAH. (2000, July 17). Sex offenders' halfway house riles residents. *The News Tribune*. Tacoma, Washington.

DEPARTMENT OF SOCIAL AND HEALTH SERVICES, STATE OF WASHINGTON. (2002). Violation, penalties, and actions relating to persons on conditional release to a less restrictive placement. Olympia, WA.

DEPARTMENT OF SOCIAL AND HEALTH SERVICES, STATE OF WASHINGTON. (2002). Status report on the development of secure community transition facilities. Olympia, WA.

DEPARTMENT OF SOCIAL AND HEALTH SERVICES, STATE OF WASHINGTON. (2001, May 4). Sex offender placed in SeaTac home is sixth transferred by courts from special commitment center; family home and proposed secure facility at McNeil Island are options for releases. Olympia. <http://www.wa.gov/dshs/mediareleases/2001/pr01118.shtml>.

DI FURIA, G. & MEEKS, H.L. (1963). Dangerous to be at large—a constructive critique of Washington's sexual psychopath law, *Washington Law Review, 38*, 531–532.

DURAN, SARAH. (2001, February 3). State settles suit over sex offenders' treatment. *The News Tribune*. Tacoma, Washington.

FEELEY, MALCOLM & RUBIN, EDWARD L. (1998). Judicial policy making and the modern state. Cambridge: Cambridge University Press.

FRIEDERICH, STEVEN. (2003, May 16). State may miss predator deadline. *Seattle Post-Intelligencer*.

HACKER, F.J. & FRYM, M. (1955). The sexual psychopath act in practice: a critical discussion, *California Law Review, 43*, 766–780.

KO, MICHAEL. (2003, April 6). State official runs gantlet of anger, threats: His job is to take heat over sex-offender home. *Seattle Times*. <http://archives.seattletimes.nwsource.com/web/>.

LIEB, ROXANNE. (2003). State policy perspectives on sexual predator laws. In Bruce J. Winick & John Q. Lafond. (Eds.), *Protecting society from sexually dangerous offenders: Law, justice, and therapy*. Washington, DC: American Psychological Association.

LIEB, R., QUINSEY, V. & BERLINER, L. (1998). Sexual predators and social policy. In Michael Tonry (Ed.), *Crime and Justice: A Review of Research (*23, 43–114). Chicago: University of Chicago Press.

LIEB, ROXANNE. (1996). Washington's sexually violent predator law: Legislative history and comparisons with other states. Olympia, WA: Washington State Institute for Public Policy.

MARQUES, J.K., DAY, D.M., NELSON, C. & WEST, M.A. (1994). Efforts of cognitive-behavioral treatment on sex offender recidivism: Preliminary results of a longitudinal study. *Criminal Justice and Behavior, 21*, 28–54.

MENTEER, TAMARA. (1998). Throw away the key: The state's treatment of sex offenders poses dangers for us all. *Seattle Weekly*. <http://www.seattleweekly.com/features/9807/features-menteer.shtml.>*The Olympian.* (1999, November 22). State must treat offenders. (Editorial). Olympia, Washington.

PACEY, DOUG. (2000, July 19). Prosecutor, neighbors ask: Why put home for sex offenders here? *The Olympian.*

PORTERFIELD, ELAINE. (1998, October 2). *Seattle Post-Intelligencer*, A1.

PRAGER, I. (1982). Sexual psychopathology and child molesters: the experiment fails. *Journal of Juvenile Law, 6*, 49–79.

QUINSEY, VERNON L. (1992). Review of the Washington State Special Commitment Center Program for Sexually Violent Predators. Olympia: Washington State Institute for Public Policy.

Revised Code of Washington. (1957). 71.060.

Revised Code of Washington. (1985). 71.06.020.

SANDERS, ELI. (2000, July 18). Town upset over plan for rapist. *Seattle Times*, B1.
SAYLOR, M. (1988). The rise and fall of sex offender programs at western state hospital. Presentation to the Seventh Annual Research and Data Conference, Association for the Treatment of Sexual Abusers. Olympia, Washington.
Seattle Times, The. (2001, January 18). Treating sexual predators for release, not prison. <http://archives.seattletimes.nwsource.com/cgi-bin/texis.cgi/web/vortex/dislay?slug=preded18&date=20010118&query=sexual+predators>.
Seattle Times, The. (1999, November 18). Sex-predator program will change or go away. <http://archives.seattletimes.nwsource.com/cgi-bin/texis.cgi/web/vortex/display?slug=dwyred&date=19991118&query=sex-predator>.
Seling v. Young (2001). 531 U.S. 250.
SHUKOVSKY, PAUL. (2000, November 3). Criteria for sex offender homes. *Seattle Post-Intelligencer.* Seattle, Washington.
SIEGEL, B. (1990, May 10). Locking up "sexual predators." *Los Angeles Times,* A31.
Tacoma News Tribune. (2000, May 9). Limited reprieve for predator unit.
Tacoma News Tribune. (1999, November 21). Sex-predator center under new attack.
Tacoma News Tribune. (1989, May 23). System just couldn't keep suspect.
TASK FORCE ON COMMUNITY PROTECTION. (1989). *Final report.* Department of Social and Health Services, State of Washington, Olympia.
Turay v. Weston. Order and Injunction. United States District Court Western District of Washington at Seattle, No. C91-664-WD.
WASHINGTON LAWS. (1973). Ch. 142; *Revised Code of Washington.* 1989. Ch. 71.05.
WASHINGTON STATE INSTITUTE FOR PUBLIC POLICY. (1998). *Sex offenses in Washington state: 1998 update,* Document No. 98-08-1101, 24.
WASHINGTON STATE LEGISLATIVE BUDGET COMMITTEE. (1985). *Sex offender programs at western and eastern state hospitals,* Report No. 85–16.
WHITESTONE FOUNDATION. (2003). <http://www.whitestonefoundation.net/mission.html>.

Sexual Offender Commitment in the United States

Legislative and Policy Concerns

W. LAWRENCE FITCH

Forensic Services, Department of Health/Mental Hygiene,
Jessup, Maryland 20794-1000, USA

ABSTRACT: Fifteen states and the District of Columbia have laws for the special civil commitment of convicted sexual offenders who are about to be released from penal confinement and do not meet criteria for ordinary psychiatric civil commitment. As of summer 2002, nearly 2500 sexual offenders were hospitalized pursuant to one of these laws. An American Psychiatric Association task force declared that "sexual predator commitment laws establish a non-medical definition of what purports to be a clinical condition without regard for scientific and clinical knowledge," and thus "distort the traditional meaning of civil commitment, misallocate psychiatric facilities and resources, and constitute an abuse of psychiatry." It remains unclear how legislatures in states with these laws will respond to the U.S. Supreme Court's 2002 decision in *Kansas v. Crane* indicating that, absent a finding that an offender has "serious difficulty controlling behavior" (not an explicit commitment criterion in any state), commitment is invalid.

KEYWORDS: civil commitment; mental illness; sexual offender; sexually violent predator; paraphilia; forensic psychiatry

INTRODUCTION TO CIVIL COMMITMENT

Every state has a law for the civil commitment (involuntary hospitalization) of people with a mental illness. Generally reserved for individuals with serious psychiatric disorders like schizophrenia or bipolar disorder, these laws are used in most states only when an individual's symptoms become acute and place the individual at imminent risk of serious harm. Once a committed patient's symptoms begin to remit (and the risks abate), he or she ordinarily is discharged, typically with a referral for "aftercare" services in the community. Hospital stays for such patients rarely exceed 30 days, although some require rehospitalization periodically.

Most states also have laws for the special commitment of individuals charged with a criminal offense and found to be incompetent to stand trial or not criminally responsible (legally "insane"). Because the legal requirements for incompetency and

Address for correspondence: W. Lawrence Fitch, J.D., Forensic Services, Department of Health/Mental Hygiene, 8450 Dorsey Run Road, Jessup, MD 20794-1000. Voice: 410-724-3171; fax: 410-724-3179.

fitchl@dhmh.state.md.us

Ann. N.Y. Acad. Sci. 989: 489–501 (2003). © 2003 New York Academy of Sciences.

"insanity" are very strict, these laws, like those for ordinary civil commitment, are used almost exclusively for individuals with the most serious disorders. Individuals committed as incompetent to stand trial are discharged (and returned to court) as soon as their mental condition improves sufficiently that they no longer meet incompetency standards. Those who do not attain (or are deemed not likely to attain) competency in a reasonable period of time must be released or civilly committed under the state's ordinary civil commitment laws (*Jackson v. Indiana*, 1972). Individuals committed as not criminally responsible, in contrast, may experience extended periods of hospitalization, but even they generally transition to the community (typically on "conditional release") as their condition improves. The U.S. Supreme Court has ruled that individuals committed as not criminally responsible *must* be released when no longer mentally ill (invalidating a Louisiana statute permitting the continued hospitalization of such an individual on grounds of dangerousness alone) (*Foucha v. Louisiana*, 1992).

Finally—and to the point of this paper—15 states and the District of Columbia have special laws for the civil commitment of sexual offenders. When these laws first appeared more than 60 years ago, they targeted offenders who, although not seriously mentally ill (and, thus, not candidates for ordinary civil commitment or for findings of incompetency or "insanity"), were believed to have a "psychopathic personality" that caused their criminal behavior. Reflecting the "rehabilitative ideal" that characterized America's criminal justice system at that time (see Fitch & Ortega, 2000), these laws provided for civil commitment (for treatment) as a therapeutic alternative to jail or prison. An individual convicted of a qualifying offense and found to have the requisite psychopathology could be committed or sentenced, but not both.

By the 1960s, more than half the states had laws for the special commitment of "psychopathic" sexual offenders. Whether these laws fulfilled their rehabilitative promise, however, was never clear. In 1977, the Group for the Advancement of Psychiatry (GAP), in a tersely worded monograph, concluded that they did not: "First and foremost, sex psychopath and sexual offender statutes can best be described as approaches that have failed....The mere assumption that such a heterogeneous legal classification ["sex psychopath" or "sexual offender"] could define treatability and make people amenable to treatment is not only fallacious; it is startling....If the assessment of the statute in terms of achieving certain goals, for whatever reasons, leads to the conclusion that an experiment has not been successful, it should be halted" (GAP, 1977, p. 843). Released at a time when the rehabilitative ideal already was beginning to lose its appeal among criminologists and policymakers, the GAP study made a big impact. Within a decade, most states had repealed their special commitment laws, and in those with such laws still on the books, commitment rates slowed to a trickle (Fitch, 1998, p. 238).

Then, in the 1990s, these laws reemerged. Unlike their predecessors, however—laws that provided for civil commitment (for treatment) as an alternative to incarceration for convicted offenders—these new laws made no provision for commitment (or for treatment) until after an offender had served his or her criminal sentence and was about to be released from confinement. "Thus, their primary purpose would appear to be incapacitative rather than therapeutic. No one has suggested that these laws reflect a renewed faith in the power of psychiatry to cure sex offenders" (American Psychiatric Association, 1999, p. 12).

TODAY'S SEXUAL OFFENDER COMMITMENT LAWS

Of the 16 jurisdictions that currently have laws for the special civil commitment of sexual offenders, at least 14 pattern their laws on the law in Washington State. Enacted in 1990, Washington's law was the first of this new breed of sexual offender commitment law written expressly for the postsentence commitment of sexual offenders. Like so many of the laws that followed it, Washington's law was enacted in response to public outcry over a particularly heinous sexual offense committed by a recently released offender. Part of a larger package of legislation (the Community Protection Act), whose clear purpose was to protect the public from dangerous sexual offenders, the law not only established a scheme for commitment, it also increased sentences for most sexual offenses and required convicted sexual offenders to register with law enforcement authorities upon their release from confinement. (The law's registration requirement "also was the first of its kind and provided a template for legislation in other states and an impetus for federal legislation [the Jacob Wetterling Act, 42 USCA §14071 (West, 1997)] calling on all the states to enact sex offender registration laws" (Fitch & Hammen, 2003).

To qualify for commitment under Washington's law, an individual must be found to be a "sexually violent predator" (SVP). An SVP under Washington law is one who:

(1) has been convicted of or charged with[a] a "crime of sexual violence" (including forcible rape, statutory rape, indecent liberties by forcible compulsion or against a child under the age of 14, and other "sexually motivated" offenses); and

(2) "suffers from a mental abnormality or personality disorder which makes the person likely to engage in predatory acts of sexual violence" (Wash. Laws §71.09.020).

"Mental abnormality" is defined by statute as "a congenital or acquired condition affecting the emotional or volitional capacity which predisposes the person to the commission of criminal sexual acts" [Wash. Laws §71.09.020 and 030 (1990)]. "Personality disorder" is not defined.

SVPs become eligible for commitment only when their criminal sentence is about to expire (or, if found incompetent to stand trial or not guilty by reason of insanity of the criminal charges, when determined no longer to be eligible for confinement; or, if a juvenile, when no longer subject to confinement in a juvenile justice facility) [Wash. Laws §71.09.030 (1990)]. Before an individual can be committed, the state must prove that he or she is an SVP beyond a reasonable doubt [Wash. Laws §71.09.060 (1990)]. Committed individuals are placed in a secure facility on the grounds of a state prison. Perimeter security is provided by the Washington Department of Corrections. Clinical services are provided by the state's Department of Social and Health Services. The period of commitment is indeterminate: "until such

---

[a]In addition to indivciduals convicted of a crime of sexual violence, the law applies to (1) individuals charged with such a crime and found incompetent to stand trial or not guilty by reason of insanity, and (2) individuals found to have committed such an offense as a juvenile (Wash. Laws §71.09.030).

time as the person's mental abnormality or personality disorder has so changed that the person is safe to be at large" [Wash. Laws §71.09.100 (1990)].

Commitment laws in other states closely resemble the law in Washington. All target offenders approaching release from confinement, and all define the mental condition required for commitment in essentially the same terms. No state uses its ordinary civil commitment standard (e.g., dangerousness due to mental illness) for the commitment of SVPs. Indeed, statutes in several states include a preamble making clear that the law's purpose is to permit the commitment of individuals who would be ineligible for commitment under ordinary civil commitment law: "The legislature finds that a small but extremely dangerous group of sexually violent predators exists that do not have a mental disease or defect that renders them appropriate for the existing Involuntary Treatment Act....In contrast to persons appropriate for [ordinary] civil commitment, sexually violent predators generally have antisocial personality disorder features which are unamenable to existing mental illness treatment modalities" [Wash. Laws §71.09.010 (1990)].

RATES OF COMMITMENT AND RELEASE

A survey conducted during the summer of 2002 (hereinafter, the "2002 Survey") found that 2478 individuals were confined in SVP facilities nationally: 1632 were committed; 846 were confined pending a commitment hearing (Fitch & Hammen, 2002). States with the largest SVP patient populations (including both committed patients and those awaiting a hearing) included California (509), Florida (404), Wisconsin (246), and New Jersey (223). Massachusetts reported serving 260 patients, but 220 of them were committed under the state's old "sexually dangerous persons" commitment law, which was repealed in 1990 (except for provisions authorizing the retention of individuals previously committed under the law); only 40 patients were confined under the state's new law, enacted in 1999. Minnesota and the District of Columbia, the only other jurisdictions continuing to serve patients committed under first-generation sexual offender commitment laws, reported patient populations of 190 and 9, respectively. Other states reported the following numbers: 93 in Arizona; 185 in Illinois; 46 in Iowa; 78 in Kansas; 62 in Missouri; 9 in North Dakota; 58 in South Carolina; 0 in Virginia (law's implementation date delayed until 2003); and 164 in Washington.

In some states, the law allows for commitment of an SVP to outpatient treatment in the community—a "less restrictive alternative" to confinement (or "LRA"). In others, a committed individual can be transitioned to an LRA on "conditional release" after some period of commitment. Typical conditions of placement in an LRA include: compliance with treatment; leaving one's residence only with supervision; electronic monitoring; no use of drugs or alcohol; no access to internet pornography; and restricted access to "vulnerable populations" (Fitch & Hammen, 2002).

At the time of the 2002 survey, only 69 SVPs nationally were placed in an LRA: 36 in Arizona; 14 in Wisconsin; 9 in Washington State; 5 in Illinois; 3 in Kansas; and 2 in New Jersey. Some were committed initially to an LRA; others were placed in an LRA on "conditional release" after a period of commitment. In all, 82 people committed as SVPs (nationally) had been released from confinement. Most were placed on conditional release or "transitional release" (language used in Arizona to describe the status of the 32 patients placed in the state's single, freestanding LRA for SVPs). A few were released outright by appellate court (Fitch & Hammen, 2002).

COSTS

Costs associated with implementing sexual offender commitment laws include the cost of the end-of-sentence review (to determine whether an offender should be the subject of a petition for commitment), the cost of evaluations conducted prior to the commitment hearing, legal costs (attorneys' fees, court costs, other litigation costs), the cost of inpatient care and treatment, and capital costs (i.e., construction or renovation of facilities). In its second year of operation, California's sexual offender commitment program was allocated a budget of $47,393,000 (Fitch & Hammen, 1999). In 1999, the budget for Washington's SVP program was a "mere" $9.3 million (Duran, 2000, p. A9). Capital costs are not included in either state's figures, although both states have since begun planning for the construction of new facilities (Fitch & Hammen, 2003).

The 2002 survey of states with commitment laws found inpatient treatment costs (per patient, per year) ranging from $47,555 in Florida to $164,250 in the District of Columbia. In Minnesota, the state with the longest experience serving committed sexual offenders, inpatient costs were estimated to be $120,000. Other states reported inpatient costs as follows: $138,841 in North Dakota; $114,000 in California; $107,000 in Washington State; $100,000 in Wisconsin; $91,250 in South Carolina; $76,334 in Illinois; $75,000 in Arizona; and $54,666 in Missouri. In New Jersey, where patients are housed in a facility operated by the Department of Corrections (which has responsibility for the costs of room, board, security, and general medical care), the cost borne by the state's mental health agency is less than $17,000 per year.

The cost of serving an individual in the community is difficult to appraise, as there have been relatively few outpatient commitments ordered written to date, and the needs of individuals placed in the community vary so widely. In Washington State alone, the range extends from $25,000 to more than $400,000 (Seling, 2002). Kansas reports that it spends $100,000 annually for "transitional services" for SVPs in the community; Illinois reports an average of $80,000 for each of its five patients in the community; Wisconsin reports an average of $40,000 for its 14 (Fitch & Hammen, 2002).

Costs associated with the legal process are particularly difficult to determine. The clinical director of the Center for Forensic Services in Washington State estimates that court costs and "litigation costs" average approximately $35,000 per patient per year (D. Hamilton, personal communication, March 24, 2000). In response to a survey conducted in 1997, officials in Minnesota estimated that each commitment proceeding costs approximately $100,000, for attorneys and experts alone, not including other court costs (NASMHPD, 1997).

DIAGNOSIS

Perhaps the most hotly debated question concerning laws for the special civil commitment of sexual offenders is whether the people they are designed to commit have the kinds of mental disorders for which facility-level care and treatment is clinically indicated. The 2002 survey yielded information concerning the diagnoses of all patients committed in 14 of the 16 jurisdictions with these laws.[b] The survey determined[c] the number and percentage of patients in each state with any of the following conditions: "serious mental illness (such as would be common among patients committed under ordinary civil commitment laws)"; mental retardation; paraphilia (differentiated); and personality disorder (differentiated for antisocial personality disorder). Nationally, 12% of all committed SVPs were diagnosed with a serious mental illness. Four percent were diagnosed with mental retardation. Eighty-five percent carried a diagnosis of paraphilia, including 49% (of all committed patients) with pedophilia; 6% with masochism or sadism; 14% with exhibitionism, fetishism, frotteurism, or voyeurism; and 23% with paraphilia, NOS. Seventy-five percent of all committed SVPs carried a diagnosis of a personality disorder. Forty-eight percent (of all committed SVPs) had antisocial personality disorder (Fitch & Hammen, 2002). For state-specific information, see TABLE 1.

Clearly, many committed SVPs carry more than one diagnosis. The 2002 survey, however, did not examine how different diagnoses cluster. Therefore, it is not known, for example, what percentage of individuals with pedophilia also carry a diagnosis of antisocial personality disorder. Citing a 1999 study by Raymond et al., Fagan et al. recently reported that 60% of male pedophilic sexual offenders also meet criteria for a personality disorder, "the chief among them being obsessive compulsive (25 percent), antisocial (22.5 percent), narcissistic (20%), and avoidant (20 percent)." (Fagan et al., 2002, p. 2461). Although the prevalence of personality disorders (and particularly antisocial personality disorder) among pedophiles committed as SVPs is not known, the survey data and anecdotal evidence suggest it is higher than the prevalence Raymond et al. found among sexual offenders in general. If it is true, as many believe, that the diagnosis of antisocial personality disorder both raises an individual's risk of reoffense and lowers his or her susceptibility to treatment, then these findings say much about the purposes to which states are putting their SVP commitment laws.

PROFESSIONAL CONCERNS

Since their inception in the early 1990s, laws for the special, postsentence civil commitment of sexual offenders have aroused serious concerns in the professional community. Soon after Washington State's statute was enacted, the University of Puget Sound conducted a symposium on the new law, devoting an entire issue of its Law Review to an examination of the "dichotomies" at play when "predators and politics" come together (*University of Puget Sound Law Review*, 1992). The issue laid the foundation for an impassioned debate that continues to this day.

In 1994, the American Psychiatric Association established a task force to study these special commitment laws, which by then were beginning to take root in legis-

[b]Officials in Florida were unable to provide the requested information, and no one has yet been committed in Virgina, where the law's implementation date has been delayed until 2003.

[c]In some staes, the data provided represented the "best estimate" of the state official completing the survey.

TABLE 1. Diagnoses of patients committed (inpatient or outpatient) under laws for the special civil commitment of sexual offenders

Diagnosis	States															
	AZ (%)	CA (%)	DC (%)	FL	IL(%)	IA (%)	KS (%)	MA (%)	MN (%)	MO (%)	ND (%)	NJ (%)	SC (%)	VA	WA (%)	WI (%)
Serious mental illness	19	7	0	***	9	23	13	10	10	23	13	20	22	****	7	10
Mental retardation	5	1	0	***	2	0	4	3	10	14	0	2	2	****	9	9
Paraphilia	100	98	100	***	99	100	94	95	70	50	75	34	81	****	98	95
*Pedophilia	63	55	75	***	59	82	88	50	50	82	75	54	79	****	45	70
*Masochism/sadism	10	0.09	0	***	6	18	4	15	0	0	0	17	0	****	7	7
*Exhibitionism/fetishism/frotteurism/voyeurism	40	0.02	25	***	10	15	12	50	0	0	13	8	4	****	28	17
*Paraphilia NOS	56	43	0	***	37	18	14	***	0	18	13	35	21	****	60	25
Personality disorder	77	65	100	***	88	94	83	75	80	45	100	72	26	****	93	82
**Antisocial personality disoder	40	69	75	***	76	59	19	50	90	60	88	36	40	****	65	83

*Percentage shown represents the percentage of patients with a paraphilia who have the differential diagnosis indicated.
**Percentage shown represents the percentage of patients with a personality disorder who have antisocial personality disorder.
***Information not available at this time.
****Not Applicable (law not in effect).

latures across the country. In 1996, the task force released an interim report observing that the individuals these laws were designed to commit in many cases did not have the kinds of serious mental disorders for which inpatient psychiatric services were appropriate. The task force concluded that these laws employed psychiatric commitment as a "pretext for extended confinement that would otherwise be impermissible" and, thus, served to "distort the traditional meanings of civil commitment, misallocate psychiatric facilities and resources, and constitute an abuse of psychiatry" (American Psychiatric Association, 1996, p. 106). Three years later, in its final report, the task force declared: "[S]exual Predator Commitment Laws represent a serious assault on the integrity of psychiatry...[B]y bending civil commitment to serve essentially non-medical purposes, sexual predator commitment statutes threaten to undermine the legitimacy of the medical model of commitment....[T]his represents an unacceptable misuse of psychiatry" (American Psychiatric Association, 1999, pp. 173–174).

The National Association of State Mental Health Program Directors (NASMHPD)—an organization of Commissioners of Mental Health in each state—has taken a significant interest in these laws as well, conducting annual surveys for the last 6 years to assess legislative activity in different states and to monitor implementation efforts and legal developments in states with these laws. In 1997, NASMHPD released a Position Statement warning that laws for the special civil commitment of sexual offenders threatened to "disrupt the state's ability to provide services for people with treatable psychiatric illnesses,...undermine the mission and integrity of the public mental health system,...divert scarce resources away from people who both need and desire treatment,...and endanger the safety of others in those facilities who have treatable psychiatric illnesses" (NASMHPD, 1997, p. ii). Recognizing that, despite their warning, legislation was likely to continue in many states, NASMHPD included in its statement the following "guidelines" for legislatures bent on enacting statutes of this kind (NASMHPD, 1997, p. iii):

(1) If enacted, sexual offender commitment laws should be clearly distinct from ordinary civil commitment laws (to avoid any confusion of the two patient populations and, thus, minimize the stigma psychiatric patients might experience by their association with SVPs);

(2) SVPs should not be commitable to facilities with mentally ill patients (for the protection of the patients);

(3) SVP facilities should be administered and funded outside the state mental health authority (to maintain the mission and integrity of the public mental health system and guard against the depletion of resources allocated for traditional mental health services);

(4) If state mental health authorities are given responsibility for treatment, they also should be given a role in determining committability, treatment strategies, and length of stay;

(5) Laws should be narrowly drawn to capture only those offenders most in need of inpatient care and treatment;

(6) Treatment of SVPs should begin before their release from prison.

While subsequent legislation has accommodated some of NASMHPD's concerns, mental health agencies in states with these laws continue to be saddled with responsibility for providing (and funding) care for committed offenders, and their influence over commitment and release decision making is marginal, at best.

SEXUAL OFFENDER COMMITMENT AFTER *KANSAS V. CRANE*

As is discussed more thoroughly in papers by Professors LaFond and Janus, laws for the special civil commitment of sexual offenders have faced a variety of legal challenges. In 1997, the U.S. Supreme Court, in a split (5 to 4) decision, upheld the commitment of a Kansas man, Leroy Hendricks, who had the dubious distinction of being the first individual committed under Kansas's newly enacted SVP law (*Kansas v. Hendricks*, 1997). Mr. Hendricks was diagnosed with pedophilia. Hendricks conceded this diagnosis and admitted in testimony that he was unable to control the urge to molest children, stating that "the only way he could keep from sexually abusing children in the future was 'to die'" (*Kansas v. Hendricks*, 1997, p. 355). In appealing his commitment, however, Hendricks argued that his pedophilia was not susceptible to treatment and did not constitute a mental illness; therefore his commitment rested on grounds of dangerousness alone, in violation of the U.S. Supreme Court's ruling in *Foucha v. Louisiana* (1992). The Kansas Supreme Court accepted Hendricks' argument and found his commitment to be unconstitutional, observing as follows:

> It is clear that the overriding concern of the legislature is to continue the segregation of sexually violent predators from the public. Treatment with the goal of reintegrating them into society is incidental at best. The legislature concedes that predators are not amenable to treatment [under the state's ordinary civil commitment law]. If there's nothing to treat...then there is no mental illness. In that light, the provisions of the act for treatment appear disingenuous. [In re *Hendricks*, 259 Kan. 246, 258 (1996)]

The U.S. Supreme Court, however, hearing the case on appeal from this decision, expressed a very different point of view. Writing for the majority, Justice Clarence Thomas acknowledged that "dangerousness, standing alone, is ordinarily not a sufficient ground upon which to justify indefinite involuntary commitment....Proof of some additional factor, such as 'mental illness' or 'mental abnormality' [would be necessary]" (*Kansas v. Hendricks*, 1997, p. 358). He dismissed the notion, however, that the mental abnormality required must be one that was acceptable to the psychiatric community. "[W]e have never required state legislatures to adopt any particular nomenclature in drafting civil commitment statutes. Rather, we have traditionally left to legislators the task of defining terms of a medical nature that have legal significance" (*Kansas v. Hendricks*, 1997, p. 359). Moreover, he declared, an offender need not be treatable to be subject to commitment. He accepted the Kansas Supreme Court's finding that "treatment for sexually violent predators is all but nonexistent," but he wrote: "[W]e have never held that the Constitution prevents a state from civilly detaining those for whom no treatment is available, but who nevertheless pose a danger to others." Finally, and most significantly, Justice Thomas declared: "The precommitment requirement of a 'mental abnormality' or 'personality disorder' [in the Kansas SVP commitment law] is consistent with the requirements of these other statutes that we have upheld in that it narrows the class of persons eligible for confinement to those who are unable to control their dangerousness" (*Kansas v. Hendricks*, 1997, p. 358).

Although nothing in Kansas's commitment law required proof of an offender's inability to control behavior (as a prerequisite to commitment), in Hendricks' case, lack of control was established (conceded by the defense). Suppose it had not been. Would Hendricks' commitment still have withstood the Court's scrutiny? Did Justice Thomas mean to imply that all "mental abnormalities" or "personality disorders" render an individual unable to control his or her dangerousness? Or did he mean that, whether indicated by diagnosis or not, commitment in every case requires proof of such an inability? These questions lie at the heart of the Supreme Court's more recent ruling in the case of *Kansas v. Crane*, 2002).

Like Leroy Hendricks, Michael Crane was committed pursuant to the provisions of Kansas's SVP commitment law. At the time he was committed, Mr. Crane had just completed a five-month sentence for lewd and lascivious behavior. He had been charged with more serious crimes, including kidnapping and attempted rape, and in fact was convicted of these charges, but his convictions were overturned by an appellate court on technical grounds and, subsequently, Crane pled guilty to the lesser charge.

At Crane's commitment hearing, experts testified that he suffered from exhibitionism and antisocial personality disorder, and that these conditions rendered him a sexually violent predator, at risk for future offenses. There was no testimony (or finding) that Crane was unable to control his dangerousness, but the trial court committed him nonetheless. The Kansas Supreme Court overturned Crane's commitment on appeal, however, citing the state's failure to prove Crane's inability to control his dangerousness as required by *Hendricks*. "A fair reading of the majority opinion in Hendricks leads us to the inescapable conclusion that commitment under the Act is unconstitutional absent a finding that the defendant cannot control his dangerous behavior. To conclude otherwise would require that we ignore the plain language of the majority opinion in *Hendricks*" [In re *Crane*, 269 Kan. 578, 585 (2000)].

Kansas appealed the state court's decision, arguing that its rationale (that the state need prove individuals "completely unable to control their behavior") reflected a misreading of *Hendricks*. The U.S. Supreme Court granted certioarai, and in a 7–2 decision announced in January 2002, agreed with Kansas that "*Hendricks* set forth no requirement of total or complete lack of control" (*Kansas v. Crane,* 2002, p. 411). Some "lack of control" analysis, however, was required, the Court declared, lest the law be misused to commit "persons who are perhaps more properly dealt with exclusively through criminal proceedings."

> We do not agree with the state...insofar as it seeks to claim that the Constitution permits commitment of the type of dangerous sexual offender considered in *Hendricks* without any lack of control determination....[T]here must be proof of serious difficulty in controlling behavior. And this, when viewed in light of such features of the case as the nature of the psychiatric diagnosis, and the severity of mental abnormality itself, must be sufficient to distinguish the dangerous sexual offender whose serious mental illness, abnormality, or disorder, subjects him to civil commitment from the dangerous but typical recidivist convicted in an ordinary case. (*Kansas v. Crane,* 2002, p. 412)

The Court noted that 40–60% of male prison inmates have antisocial personality disorder and suggested that a law that would allow these inmates to be kept confined (after serving their sentences) under the rubric of civil commitment might invite commitment to be used as "a mechanism for retribution or general deterrence—

functions properly those of criminal law, not civil commitment" (*Kansas v. Crane,* 2002, p. 412).

Unresolved by the Court's opinion in *Crane* is the question whether diagnosis alone may suffice as proof of "lack of control." Does the Court's lack-of-control requirement simply represent an effort to distinguish individuals with a serious enough mental condition to warrant commitment, or does it stand as an independent criterion that must be established in every case? Must individuals who have schizophrenia (and are dangerous) also be shown to have serious difficulty controlling their behavior in order to be committed?[d] If not, what about individuals with pedophilia? In distinguishing Hendricks' (valid) commitment from Crane's, the Supreme Court described pedophilia as a "serious disorder," "a critical distinguishing feature [of which is] a special and serious lack of ability to control behavior" (*Kansas v. Crane,* 2002, p. 412).[e] The 2002 Survey discussed earlier found that nearly half of all committed SVPs are pedophiliac. Are their commitments validated by *Crane,* or, in the absence of specific proof of impaired behavioral control, are their commitments suspect? Finally, what of those individuals with "less serious" diagnoses? Seventy-five percent of all committed SVPs have a personality disorder. Nearly 50% have antisocial personality disorder. If an individual suffers from a disorder like pedophilia, which carries with it some impairment in behavioral control, but also suffers from antisocial personality disorder, must there be a determination which disorder accounts for the offender's propensity to offend? And if it is the latter, will commitment be permissible? Or would commitment under these circumstances amount to "a mechanism for retribution or general deterrence?"

As this paper goes to press, state supreme court decisions in Missouri and New Jersey have overturned commitments based on *Crane* [*Thomas v. Missouri,* 2002; In re *W.Z.,* 173 N.J. 109, 801 A2d 205 (N.J., 2002)]. Supreme court decisions in Wisconsin and South Carolina, however, have upheld commitments against *Crane*-based attacks (*Wisconsin v. Laxton,* 2002; In re *Luckabaugh,* 2002). Only the courts' varying interpretations of *Crane,* not the facts, distinguish these very disparate decisions. Inevitably, the U.S. Supreme Court will be called on to clarify its message in *Crane.* In the meantime, a number of states are implementing *Crane*-inspired requirements as a matter of practice (2002 Survey). In Wisconsin, for example, despite the state supreme court's ruling that no specific lack-of-control determination need be made, jury instructions have been modified to include "serious difficulty in controlling behavior" in the definition of "mental disorder," and officials report that evaluations now routinely address an offender's ability to control behavior. In California, although the intermediate appeals courts have upheld commitments against attacks based on *Crane* (see, for example, *People v. Williams,* 2002), the state attorney general has issued a directive to prosecutors always to adduce evidence of impaired control in commitment proceedings. The attorney general in Kansas also has advised prosecutors to adduce such evidence at trial and to request that an additional question (concerning lack of control) appear on the verdict form. Given the current uncertainty in the law, prudence, it appears, dictates conservative practice.

---

[d]If so, are ordinary civil commitment laws (none of which require evidence of impaired behavioral control) constitutionally suspect in light of *Crane*?

[e]Note that the Court also recognized Hendricks' admissions (that he could not control his urge to molest children) as evidence of his inability to control his behavior.

CONCLUSION

The current crop of sexual offender commitment laws in the United States represents an effort by the states to keep confined criminal offenders who remain dangerous at the end of their sentences. The extraordinary popularity of these laws in the 1990s may best be explained by sentencing reforms in the 1980s that had as their (unintended) effect the premature release of many dangerous sexual offenders (see Fitch & Ortega, 2000). These new laws, however, reflect only part of the effort states have made to "fix the problem." In many states, including some with these new laws, sentences for sex offenders have been increased (or made indeterminate) and new measures have been put in place more effectively to manage sexual offenders released to the community. Many states also have established (or enlarged) treatment programs for sexual offenders serving sentences in prison or on supervised release in the community. Accordingly, the pressure to use commitment as a means of assuring public safety may be lessening. Indeed, no state has enacted a new SVP commitment law since 1999.

Meanwhile, the states that have these laws struggle to provide meaningful services to a population of offenders who in many instances are exceptionally poor candidates for treatment. Most states have had little or no success moving patients through treatment and into the community and, as a consequence, face endless rounds of litigation. The U.S. Supreme Court's decision in *Crane,* although anathema to those whose sole concern is public safety, should be welcomed by advocates for treatment. Inability to control one's behavior may not be the ideal measure of treatment suitability, but at least it represents some effort to select for people with illness. It is only a beginning, however. Treatment advocates and civil libertarians together must continue their fight for reform if the medical model of civil commitment ever is to have legitimacy for this special population of patients.

REFERENCES

AMERICAN PSYCHIATRIC ASSOCIATION. (1996). *Task force report on sexually dangerous offenders.* Washington, DC: Author
AMERICAN PSYCHIATRIC ASSOCIATION. (1999). *Dangerous sex offenders.* Washington, DC: Author.
DURAN, S. (2000, April 9). Unfinished treatment. *News Tribune* (Tacoma, Washington), pp. 1, 8, 9.
FAGAN, P.J. et al. (2002). Pedophilia. *Journal of the American Medical Association, 288*(19), 2458–2465.
FITCH, W.L. (1998). Sex offender commitment in the United States. *Journal of Forensic Psychiatry, 9,* 237–240.
FITCH, W.L. & HAMMEN, D. (1999). Sex offender commitment: A survey of the states. Unpublished manuscript.
FITCH, W.L. & HAMMEN, D. (2002). Sex offender commitment: A survey of the states. Unpublished manuscript.
FITCH, W.L. & HAMMEN, D. (2003). The new generation of sex offender laws: Which states have them and how do they work? In B. Winick & J. LaFond (Eds.), *Protecting society from sexually dangerous offenders: Law, justice, and therapy.* Washington, DC: American Psychological Association.
FITCH, W.L. & ORTEGA, R.J. (2000). Law and the confinement of psychopaths. *Behavioral Sciences and the Law, 18,* 663–678.
Foucha v. Louisiana, 504 U. S. 71 (1992).

GROUP FOR THE ADVANCEMENT OF PSYCHIATRY (GAP). (1977). *Psychiatry and sex psychopath legislation: The thirties to the eighties*. New York: Author.

In re Crane, 269 Kan. 578 (2000).

In re Hendricks, 259 Kan. 246 (1996).

In re Luckabaugh, 568 S. E. 2d 338 (S.C., 2002).

In re W. Z., 801 A 2d 205 (N.J., 2002).

Jackson v. Indiana, 406 U.S. 715 (1972).

Kansas v. Crane, 534 U.S. 407 (2002).

Kansas v. Hendricks, 521 U.S. 346 (1997).

NATIONAL ASSOCIATION OF STATE MENTAL HEALTH PROGRAM DIRECTORS (NASMHPD). (1997). *NASMHPD policy statement on laws providing for the civil commitment of sexually violent criminal offenders*. Alexandria, VA: Author.

People v. Williams, 120 Cal. Rptr. 2d 11 (2002).

REVISED CODE OF WASHINGTON ("WASH. LAWS"). (1990). Chapter 71.09.

SELING, M. (2002). *Sex offender commitment in Washington State*. Paper presented at the Annual Meeting of the Forensic Division, National Association of State Mental Health Program Directors, Seattle, WA.

Thomas v. Missouri, 74 S. W. 3d 789 (Mo., 2002).

University of Puget Sound Law Review (Spring 1992). 15:3.

Wisconsin v. Laxton, 647 N. W. 2d 784 (Wis., 2002).

Emerging Issues, Policy Changes, and the Future of Treating Children with Sexual Behavior Problems

ROBERT E. LONGO

New Hope Treatment Centers, Summerville, South Carolina 29485, USA

ABSTRACT: Children and adolescents with sexual behavior problems are a growing national concern. While the field continues to make advances, we have much more work to do. We are working in a difficult and trying period for juvenile justice. It is a time when many are willing to give up on adolescents or punish them as we do adults. We have reached a point where many in our society do not know about, or care to understand, the complex issues that are the roots of violence and sexual violence in youth. Certainly their faith in the resiliency of youth has been tarnished. Nine critical areas that need to be taken into account when working with youth with sexual behavior problems are addressed. These areas include the unfortunate but continued trickle-down and use of adult-based treatment models to treat youth with sexual behavior problems, changes in juvenile law that have an impact on our ability to treat these youths effectively, the need for continued research in developing typologies for youths with sexual behavior problems and valid and reliable risk assessment scales, continued work with understanding and developing dynamic risk factors for sexually abusive youth, the need to develop better treatments for special populations of youth with sexual behavior problems, the need for a continuum of care, what constitutes best practice in treating youths with sexual behavior problems, the need for developing and refining standards of care, and the need for continued public education that supports prevention efforts to reduce sexual abuse by youth.

KEYWORDS: sexual behavior problems; sexual abuse; sexual violence; public health problem; adolescents; sexual predator; youthful offender

In this space, I can, at best, only summarize what I consider to be the current and emerging issues regarding children and adolescents with sexual behavior problems. The past decade has been one of many changes both politically and clinically in regard to this growing population of patients. I have worked in the field of sexual abuse prevention and treatment for 25 years, and during the past 10 years I have devoted

Robert E. Longo, MRC, LPC, Corporate Director of Special Programming and Clinical Training, New Hope Treatment Center, 225 Midland Parkway, Summerville, SC 29485. Voice: 843-572-3498, ext. 1130.

robl@newhopetreatment.com

Ann. N.Y. Acad. Sci. 989: 502–514 (2003). © 2003 New York Academy of Sciences.

my attention to working exclusively with adolescents. Currently, I work with both adolescents and young children ages 7–12 with sexual behavior problems.

The field of treating children and adolescents with sexual behavior problems began to grow during the early 1980s and experienced its most rapid growth in the 1990s (Burton, Smith-Darden, Levins, Fiske & Freeman-Longo, 2000; Bengis et al., 1999; Freeman-Longo, Bird, Stevenson & Fiske, 1995; Knopp, Freeman-Longo & Stevenson, 1993; Freeman-Longo & Blanchard, 1998.

Back in 1995, STOP IT NOW! brought public health thinking to the field of treating sexual abusers. By 1997, I and a few others advocated that the field of treating sexual abusers should consider sexual abuse as a public health issue, and we published that opinion in 1998 (Freeman-Longo & Blanchard, 1998).

Recently, organizations such as the Association for the Treatment of Sexual Abusers (ATSA) and the National Adolescent Perpetrator Network (NAPN) have also acknowledged the need to address sexual abuse as a public health problem. However, it was former Surgeon General C. Everett Koop who had the vision to look at all violence, including sexual violence, as a public health problem. In 1985, Dr. Koop wrote:

> Identifying violence as a public health issue is a relatively new idea. Traditionally, when confronted by the circumstances of violence, the health professionals have deferred to the criminal justice system. Over the years we've tacitly and, I believe, mistakenly agreed that violence was the exclusive province of the police, the courts, and the penal system. To be sure, those agents of public safety and justice have served us well. But when we ask them to concentrate more on the prevention of violence and to provide additional services for victims, we may begin to burden the criminal justice system beyond reason. At that point, the professionals of medicine, nursing, and the health-related social services must come forward and recognize violence as their issue, also, one which profoundly affects the public health ... Henry David Thoreau in his book, "Walden," wrote: "It is characteristic of wisdom not to do desperate things." I think we have worked with patience and wisdom. And hopefully the time of desperation is over.

As we move into the twenty-first century, the field of treating children and adolescents with sexual behavior problems faces many obstacles that might well be minimized or alleviated if we can begin to address the problem from a public health perspective. Keeping in mind the theme of addressing sexual abuse of children and sexual abuse by children as a public health agenda, there are nine critical areas I would like us to consider over the next few years and hopefully advance these areas over the next five to ten years.

THE TRICKLE-DOWN PHENOMENON

First, and probably most important, is the issue of stopping the trickle-down phenomenon from the adult field to the juvenile field. This phenomenon has been ongoing for well over two decades (Developmental Services Group, 2000) and has been destructive to the work we try to do with children. Unfortunately, we continue to erroneously view these children as mini-adults, mini-perpetrators, sexual predators, and the like.

Based on adult models, we often keep youthful patients in treatment longer than is necessary using adult-based models and treatment modalities that may even prove harmful to these patients. Chaffin and Bonner (1998) note that many adult treatments are controversial and may include involuntary treatments (i.e., phallometry, polygraphy, and arousal reconditioning) for purposes of public safety, rather than for rehabilitative reasons.

Unlike adults, children are still advancing in many areas. Developmentally, they are still developing physically, cognitively, and emotionally. While these patients must be held accountable for their behaviors, from a developmental perspective adolescents from the age of 13–18 are still dealing with their identity (their identities of self are still being formed), and they may experience role confusion. Even healthy youths are fine-tuning their sense and understanding about what it means to be responsible [thus, they can't drive until they are 16 (some states are considering age 18 for driving), vote or enter the military service until they are 18, and drink alcohol until they are 21]. We do not give children of this age the full complement of adult responsibilities, and we should not think that we can arbitrarily single out particular behaviors, criminal or otherwise, in order to selectively treat them as adults.

The field of treating adult sexual offenders does not take into account developmental stages and moral development. However, assessment and treatment planning for youth must take into account the patient's developmental abilities as well as potential developmental lags. Many if not most adolescents who have sexual behavior problems, also have learning disabilities that need to be taken into account. All systems, from judicial to mental health, need to take these and other factors into account when working with these cases.

JUVENILE LAW AND WAIVERS TO ADULT COURT

The second area of concern is the laws that have been developed and continue to be developed that (1) require youth to register as sexual offenders and participate in public notification, and (2) laws that waive juveniles into adult courts for committing sexual offenses. These laws place youth into the category of hardened criminals and all but destroy any opportunity for these patients to grow up and lead healthy, normal lives. As a result we now label young people as sexual predators, sexually violent persons, and stalkers. Registration laws, public notification laws, and laws that waive juveniles over to the adult system are but a few of the laws that need to be reviewed and addressed immediately.

While sexual crimes are horrific and serious behaviors, as professionals I believe we are obliged to look at these patients in the greater context of who they are and how these laws will impact them for the rest of their lives. Lawmakers do not take into account child development when their anger-driven causes enact such laws. When laws are being written, the creators do not work within a developmental framework. Recently the Supreme Court found that mentally retarded criminals should not be sentenced to death. The ruling was based upon the fact that this group of criminal thinks at a childlike level. That being the case, why would we want to treat children with sexual behavior problems like adults in adult courtrooms?

Legislators don't think in terms of causes and etiology, nor do many people in American society when it comes to punishing criminals. Seldom, if ever, do they think in terms of child development. Instead, legislators and the public repeatedly turn to the criminal justice system to solve the violence problem in America. However, the series of tougher laws passed each year to address violence, and to guide the criminal justice system, do not address the underlying causes of violence or sexual abuse. In most cases, children who bring guns to school, do so because they do not feel safe and secure. Children and adolescents do not rape and molest because they believe it is the right thing to do. Their reasons for engaging in such behavior are complex and not completely comprehendible at that age.

Unfortunately, a growing number of states have enacted laws that severely punish youth, and now all states have laws that can waive youth to the adult criminal justice system. In the state of Connecticut, for example, a 14-year-old can be waived to adult court and sentenced to serve time in an adult prison. On July 25, 2001, an article in the *New York Times*, written by Sara Rimer and titled "States adjust adult prisons to needs of youth inmates," noted that "the number of youth admitted to adult prisons doubled in little more than a decade to 7,000 in 1998 from 3,400 in 1985.... There were 9,100 offenders under 18 in adult jails in 1997."

The following are excerpts from a *USA Today* article by Michael P. Brown dated January 1998 and titled: "Juvenile offenders: Should they be tried in adult courts?"

> The present-day controversy surrounding waivers appears to be a consequence of at least two factors converging. First, the definitions of childhood and age-appropriate behavior are in a state of flux... Violent juvenile crime has increased by nearly 70% since 1986... the "get tough" approach to dealing with law violators—as seen throughout the criminal justice system—increasingly is being applied to juvenile offenders as well...

> While it is true that waivers have been in existence for more than 70 years, they are used more today than in the past... This has drawn attention to how society's response to juvenile offenders is changing from primarily being oriented toward rehabilitation to increasingly becoming prone to subjecting juveniles to conservative criminal court practices. Every state and the District of Columbia have at least one provision (some states have as many as three) to waive certain juveniles to criminal court. Juveniles may become "legal adults" through judicial waiver, prosecutorial discretion, or statutory exclusion.

> A judicial waiver involves the juvenile court waiving jurisdiction over a case and sending it to criminal court for prosecution. In all but three states, juvenile court judges have been entrusted with the power to waive juveniles to criminal court.

> Age and offense seriousness traditionally have been the criteria by which juveniles are waived to criminal court. Twenty-one states and the District of Columbia have no minimum age requirements for transferring juveniles to criminal court. Among the remaining 29 states, minimum age requirements range from as young as *seven* to 16. The largest proportion of cases waived to criminal court are serious crimes such as murder; offenses involving serious personal injury (such as aggravated assault); property crimes; public order offenses (such as disorderly conduct, obstruction of justice, and weapons offenses); and drug offenses... Moreover, some states permit juveniles to be waived if their current charge is a felony and there is evidence of prior felony convictions. Furthermore, most states have a provision that allows juveniles to be waived to criminal court if there is reason to believe that offenders are not amenable to treatment.

What we must keep in mind is that punishment is not prevention. I believe the criminal justice system must play a role in sexual abuse prevention and treatment, and that we must hold criminal sexual abusers accountable for their behavior. I do not believe that all sexual abusers should be handled alike, because not all sexual abusers are the same. A one-size-fits-all approach will not work with youth at risk. Some adult sexual abusers may need to be imprisoned for life; however, the majority of children and adolescents with sexual behavior problems can be safely and effectively treated in the community once they have been assessed and determined to be a low risk.

TYPOLOGIES AND RISK ASSESSMENT

A third issue is the need for funding to continue and complete the work now being done to develop a typology of adolescents who sexually abuse and to establish validated risk assessments for both children and adolescents with sexual behavior problems. Initial typology research is nearing an end. However, once a proposed typology is established, further research will need to be conducted to validate the proposed typology.

Having a proposed typology will further assist the field in developing the necessary risk assessment tools for assessing adolescents. Currently there are several scales being investigated: the J-SOAP (Robert Prentky), the ERASOR (James Worling), the J-RAT (Phil Rich), and the Protective Factors Scale (Janis Bremer). While these tools all show promise, further research is necessary to further develop and validate them.

At this time there is no typology of children (ages 12 and under) who sexually abuse or have sexual behavior problems, nor is there a validated risk assessment tool to use with patients in this age group. With the growing number of programs treating children, this is essential for advancing the field.

DYNAMIC RISK FACTORS

The fourth point, which is related to both typology and risk assessment noted above, is the need to develop dynamic risk factors for children and adolescents who sexually abuse. Some of the previously mentioned risk assessment scales include dynamic risk factors, but these are not comprehensive. Because children and adolescents are still in developmental stages, there are multiple treatment areas and concerns, and thus multiple dynamic risk factors for which we can track progress.

Some of the dynamic risk factors that are recognized include (1) attitudes toward offending, (2) negative peer influence, (3) emotional self-regulation, (4) general self-regulation, (5) intimacy deficits, and (6) resistance to treatment.

Gail Ryan (in press) notes, "risk assessment and treatment models based solely on unchangeable risk factors in the past are likely to over-estimate risk, as well as missing important opportunities in treatment to change what is changeable. By balancing offense specific interventions with preventive interventions to increase healthy functioning, outcomes may improve, and iatrogenic risks may be reduced."

Ryan proposes that in working with youth with sexual behavior problems we need to consider three types of risk factors: (1) static (e.g., permanent disabilities, family of origin, early life experience), (2) stable (life spanning) risk factors (e.g., temperament, intellectual potential, physical attributes, heritable neurological characteristics), and (3) dynamic risk factors (e.g., situational, cognitive, emotional, and behavioral factors that may change throughout the individual's life).

There is no doubt that many of these risk factors have their origins in child maltreatment. Child maltreatment and child neglect play a significant role in the etiology of violent and sexually abusive behavior. We have reached the point in our understanding of violence and sexual aggression where we can no longer ignore childhood maltreatment as a critical problem and crucial treatment area for our patients. Child abuse and neglect, and now domestic violence, have been repeatedly demonstrated to affect child development. Maltreatment has been demonstrated to play a role in the etiology of aggressive conduct problems (Ryan et al., 1998).

Children are resilient, and by addressing dynamic risk factors we can promote better healing and recovery in our patients.

SPECIAL POPULATIONS

The fifth factor is the need to put more focus on special populations within the field of assessing and treating children and adolescents with sexual behavior problems and sexual aggression problems. Of specific importance is the need to develop new programs and enhance existing programs that treat female children and adolescents. Most sexual offender treatment programs were developed for adult males and that lead to "trickle down" for programs treating adolescent males. The needs in treatment for males are different for girls in several areas. Gender-specific programming is important for working with female patients. There is growing literature that tells us there are significant differences between boys and girls, that they advance through the stages of development differently, and that there are differences cognitively and emotionally between young boys and young girls (Robinson, 2002). The growth of these programs has been sporadic, and at present, Alex Guarrbana (2001) notes that there is a lack of gender-specific programs for adolescent females.

Another special population we need to continue to pay attention to, and develop more resources for, is children and adolescents with sexual behavior problems who have serious learning disabilities, and/or are developmentally delayed/disabled. This includes programming for those patients who are diagnosed with mild retardation to those who suffer from profound retardation. Often, this type of patient is most difficult to place. Community-based programs are often reluctant to take these patients, as they are difficult to manage and treat.

Professionals must continue to think differently when working with youth. Age, developmental and contextual issues, learning abilities and styles, etiology of the patient's problems, cultural issues, spirituality, and gender differences must all be taken into account when we work with youthful patients. As we move into this millennium, we should not be using models and treatments for youth that were developed for adults. Instead, we should be developing programs that work with the areas outlined above, while being sensitive to cultural issues and attempting to blend our American culture and traditional methods of treating youth with their individual cultures (Lewis, 1999).

CONTINUUM OF CARE

The sixth issue we need to address is the need for all states to develop a continuum of care in treating children and adolescents with sexual behavior problems. This is not a new idea. Steve Bengis (1986, 2002a, 2002b) noted a need to provide a continuum of care for sexually abusive youth and proposes the following continuum:

(1) Self-help groups and "hot lines" for support.
(2) Out-patient services, including abuser-specific assessments and treatment and other more traditional clinical services, i.e., individual therapy.

(3) Day programs with vocational or educational emphasis.
(4) Out-of-home options, including specialized foster homes (preferably without other children present), and/or mentor homes.
(5) Community-based group homes and half-way houses.
(6) Unlocked, intensive, community-based residential placements.
(7) Locked-secure correctional and mental health programs.

In reworking Bengis's concept of a continuum, I would propose the continuum be expanded to include:

(1) Self-help groups and "hot lines" for support.
(2) Prevention programs.
(3) Diversion programs.
(4) Psychoeducational-based programs.
(5) Out-patient services, including abuser-specific assessments and treatment and other more traditional clinical services, i.e., individual therapy.
(6) Day programs with vocational or educational emphasis.
(7) Out-of-home options, including specialized foster homes (preferably without other children present), and/or mentor homes.
(8) Community-based group homes and half-way houses.
(9) Specialized transitional (step-down) residential programs.
(10) Unlocked, intensive, community-based residential placements.
(11) Secure, intensive, residential placements.
(12) Locked-secure correctional and mental health programs.
(13) Locked-secure correctional facility.

Bengis also states that in using such a continuum, we should pay attention to the following criteria as a guideline for placement of patients:

(1) The placement should correspond to the level of risk posed by the patient.
(2) The level of client risk should be determined by examining both (a) the client's level of self-control (the bottom-line acting-out that the placement has been designed to contain), and (b) the staff–client ratios present on-line to contain these behaviors.
(3) Whenever legally possible, movement along the continuum should be based on the competency level achieved by the patient.
(4) Required competency-levels should correspond to the level of internal control required for safe placement at each level of the continuum.
(5) Initially, patients can be referred to any level of the continuum that corresponds to their diagnosed level of risk. However, decisions regarding movement to less restrictive placements should be competency based.
(6) The entire continuum of care should use the same sexual abuser–specific assessment and treatment criteria. While specific placements may emphasize different aspects of sexual abuser–specific treatment (e.g., one program may emphasize learning the assault cycle and another may emphasize arousal reduction), all placements should adhere to the guidelines established by the National Task Force on Juvenile Sexual Offending (1993). Sexual abuser–specific treatment that takes place in other than out-patient settings, i.e., residential or day programs, should incorporate sexual abuser–specific milieu treatment. As such, all staff in those placements

should be trained: (1) to provide abuser-specific interventions as part of their work on-line with youth; (2) to integrate the basics of abuser-specific treatment into interventions that do not involve sexually abusive behaviors; and, 3) to integrate abuser-specific issues into vocational and educational curricula. Programs that offer specialized assessments and specialized groups, but that do not provide specialized milieu treatment, should not be considered sexual abuser–specific programs.

(7) Whenever possible, caregivers should remain consistent as a youth moves from one level of the continuum to another (i.e., probation officer, caseworker, therapists).

(8) Placements along the continuum should be evaluated (1) by professionals trained in both evaluation methodology and abuser-specific assessment and treatment, and (2) according to sexual abuser–specific criteria agreed to in advance by evaluators and those being evaluated.

(9) The continuum should include long-term self-help and require a community relapse-prevention component.

(10) Day programs and educational placements should be thoroughly integrated into the continuum of care and be required to provide sexual abuser–specific treatment.

(11) All youth placed in programs anywhere along the continuum should receive pre- and postabuser-specific evaluations. These evaluations should be the basis for initial placement and for discharge to less restrictive settings. These evaluations should also screen the patient according to more traditional clinical criteria (i.e., thought disorders, clinical depression, ADHD, other neurological criteria).

(12) In other than locked settings, failure to meaningfully participate in treatment over reasonably appropriate periods of time should be "grounds" for discharge from a program. Ideally, such a discharge would also constitute violation of probation and/or court orders and subject the youth to placement in a more restrictive and/or locked setting. For youths who are not court involved, such discharge should also result in placement in a more restrictive setting. In locked correctional settings, treatment should be considered a privilege. Youths who refuse to meaningfully participate in treatment over reasonably appropriate periods of time, should be discharged from treatment groups and allowed to "serve their time." Within the confines of appropriate human rights criteria, such youths should receive minimal institutional privileges until such time as they agree to meaningfully participate in treatment groups. They should also be required to serve the maximum sentence imposed by a judge. The option of participating in treatment should be available to these youths at any time during their incarceration.

BEST PRACTICE

Seventh, we have yet to firmly establish what constitutes best practice in treating children and adolescents with sexual behavior problems. Although the number of programs for youthful offenders grew rapidly during the first half of the last decade, juveniles have been the focus of sexual offender treatment for at least twenty years (Freeman-Longo et al., 1995). While the field is not new, conceptualization of what constitutes effective treatment for this population is still evolving (Hunter & Longo, in press).

As noted earlier, the trickle down of clinical approaches used with adult sexual offenders, has occurred with little regard for developmental and contextual issues that need to be taken into consideration in treating adolescents; or evidence that the areas of therapeutic focus are relevant for the juvenile sexual offender population, e.g., deviant sexual arousal (Freeman-Longo, 2002; Hunter, 1999). Most often, treatment techniques and modalities used in treating adult sexual offenders have been directly applied to juvenile sexual abusers, or modified only slightly to make materials more easily understood, without taking into consideration learning styles and multiple intelligences (Gardner, 1983). High levels of confrontation still abound in many programs, with little regard for the potential impact these approaches may have on youths with histories of abuse and neglect.

The majority of juvenile sexual offender treatment programs have generally adhered to a traditional adult sexual offender model. Standard interventions include the teaching of relapse prevention and the sexual abuse cycle, empathy training, anger management, social and interpersonal skills training, cognitive restructuring, assertiveness training, journaling, and sex education (Freeman-Longo et al., 1995; Becker & Hunter, 1997; Hunter, 1999; Burton et al., 2000). Questions about the appropriateness and effectiveness of these approaches in the treatment of juveniles makes imperative the full development and testing of juvenile-specific intervention programs (Hunter & Longo, in press).

The use of a holistic/integrated approach (Longo, 2001; Hunter & Longo, in press) blends traditional aspects of sexual abuser treatment into a holistic, humanistic, and developmentally consistent model for working with youthful sexual offenders.

A focus group meeting of professionals held on March 10, 2000 in Washington, DC, addressed many of the concerns the field of treating juveniles with sexual behavior problems faces, and also noted that the sequencing of treatment was also important to overall program efficacy (Developmental Services Group, 2000). Current models using cognitive–behavioral treatment appear to be most promising regarding exoffender-specific treatment, but it was also noted that treatment for these patients must go well beyond treating just the "sexual" problems and it needs to address "growth and development, social ecology, increasing health, social skills, resiliency, and incorporate treatment for the offender's own victimization and co-occurring disorders."

STANDARDS OF CARE

The eighth issue concerns standards of care for the assessment and treatment of children and adolescents with sexual behavior problems. It was not until the late 1980s that the field of treating sexual offenders considered the development of standards of care. The first effort came out of ATSA with the publication of its handbook for members. Since then the handbook has been revised several times to its current version (Association for the Treatment of Sexual Abusers, *Practice standards and guidelines for members of the Association for the Treatment of Sexual Abusers,* 2001). While this handbook is quite comprehensive, the focus is much more specific to adult sexual offenders than for children or adolescents.

In 1990 Coleman and Dwyer proposed a set of standards for care for the treatment of adult sexual offenders. These standards were later revised and updated in 1996 (Coleman et al., 1996), and they were most recently revised and updated for a third time in 2002 (Coleman et al., 2002). These standards are specifically focused on adult sexual offenders.

The first effort to specifically address the assessment and treatment of juvenile sexual offenders was not a standard of care, but rather a guideline for working with these patients. The National Adolescent Perpetrator Network convened a group that is referred to as the National Task Force on Juvenile Sexual Offending, which published its first report in 1988 (National Task Force, 1988), which was later revised in 1993 (National Task Force, 1993). Efforts are currently underway to revise the 1993 report and publish the third version. However, as noted earlier, this document and its contents is not considered a document that sets a standard.

In 1996 the National Offense-Specific Residential Standards Task Force was developed, and over the course of three years this small, independent group researched, developed, and published standards of care for the residential treatment of juvenile sexual abusers (Bengis et al., 1999). This was the first successful attempt to produce and publish standards for juvenile sexual abusers.

While there have been several independent efforts to establish standards of care, there is no national standard that is endorsed by a national agency or organization. Thus even the independently published standards today are not enforceable or endorsed by a single national organization.

PUBLIC EDUCATION AND PREVENTION

The ninth and final point is, again, not a new concept. The idea of preventing sexual abuse has been around for a long time, but most efforts were secondary and tertiary prevention efforts. It was not until the mid-1990s, however, that organizations such as STOP IT NOW![a] made headway into getting the general public to view sexual abuse from a primary prevention standpoint (i.e., preventing the would-be sexual offenders/abusers from ever assaulting his/her first victim). Another recent organization devoted to preventing sexual abuse is Stop Child Molestation.[b] More recently, there has been a move not only to address sexual abuse from a prevention standpoint, but also as a public health issue (Freeman-Longo & Blanchard, 1998). As noted earlier, STOP IT NOW! championed this effort, and now organizations such as ATSA endorse this concept, and ATSA now has a public policy statement suggesting that sexual abuse is a public health problem.[c]

Now, books are being written on this subject (Freeman-Longo & Blanchard, 1998; Abel & Harlow, 2002). Unfortunately, in this author's experience and in talking with other authors of similar material, no large publishing houses were willing

---

[a]http://www.stopitnow.org
[b]Stop Child Molestation group. http://www.stopchildmolestation.org
[c]http://www.atsa.com/pppublichealth.html

to publish them, and authors have to publish their ideas and concepts with smaller publishing houses, or self-publish their works. It is my understanding that this reluctance is based upon publishers believing that the general public is not ready for such books.

Freeman-Longo and Blanchard (1998) note:

> Using the public health model, there are three levels of sexual abuse prevention—primary, secondary, and tertiary. The goal of primary prevention is to prevent sexual abuse before it occurs. Primary prevention puts responsibility on the would-be abuser not to sexually abuse others. Primary prevention invites those who believe they have a problem to seek help and treatment, promoting a message of hope and recovery.
>
> The goal of secondary prevention is to teach people how to avoid becoming a victim. In its most familiar forms, secondary prevention consists of child sexual abuse prevention and awareness programs in schools, and rape awareness, prevention, education, and self-defense classes. Although crime prevention programs and efforts are valuable, secondary prevention programs place the responsibility for sexual abuse prevention on the potential victim. Another form of secondary prevention identifies "at risk" individuals who may be susceptible to becoming abusive or to be abused and intervenes to reduce that risk.
>
> The goal of tertiary prevention is to stop the abuse from continuing. This may involve treating victims of sexual abuse and teaching them ways to avoid and/or prevent sexual abuse from happening again. Treating sexual abusers and helping them learn ways to not sexually abuse again is another form of tertiary prevention. While treatment is a valuable and worthwhile effort, the problem with this level of prevention is that it occurs after someone has been abused or after the abuser has already caused victimization.

They go on to say:

> Canadians, along with Australians and New Zealanders, make reference to restorative justice, transformation justice, and satisfying justice. All are quite similar and argue in support of greater victim and community involvement. Just as important is a diminished emphasis on adversarial court proceedings that increase tensions and do little to heal victims or abusers. Reconciliation and restitution are important components of most of these programs. Mediation is encouraged. Punishment is seen as a measure of despair that has little to do with justice and even less to do with healing the injured parties. Whenever reasonably possible, it is the desire of community justice teams to keep offenders in the community where "reintegrative" shame can be experienced. Abusers are expected to face the pain and humiliation brought on by their crimes and not have incarceration serve as an escape.
>
> Citizens are re-empowered when the courts allow them the initiative for alternative sentencing. This becomes a labor-intensive process in which citizens must meet victims and abusers and participate in sentencing, treatment, and probationary responsibilities.
>
> At a smaller level, some communities participate in family group conferencing. This approach to crime tends to bring smaller numbers of people together than do community-based programs. Usually the victim, the perpetrator, and their families come together to mediate solutions outside the courtroom. The goal is to connect or re-connect the abusers to family and community. Abusers may thereby feel more guilt, but at the same time, are less alienated. Always the ultimate goal is the restoration of social bonds and the reintegration of each affected person back into the community.
>
> These are truly revolutionary approaches to justice. Yet, most have their origins in ancient aboriginal traditions that are being revisited and reworked to address the crimes of today. The solutions for the future have been right behind us where we are least inclined to look. It is time for us to investigate the solutions that other nations have developed. They offer us great hope.
>
> … society can move in a more responsible direction regarding sexual abuse prevention. To reduce sexual abuse in America, citizens must work on preventing it from occurring. Prevention requires public education. We believe this is best accomplished by addressing it as a public health issue. Using a public health model holds tremendous promise

today for reducing sexual abuse in America tomorrow. Prevention is not punishing a behavior after it occurs. Prevention is stopping the problem before it occurs.

SUMMARY

Children and adolescents with sexual behavior problems are a growing national concern. While the field continues to make advances, we have much more work to do. We need to foster and promote concepts such as restorative justice, transformative justice, and prevention. We must address the issues noted in this paper and other issues related to working with sexually abusive youth.

We are working in a difficult and trying period for juvenile justice. It is a time when many are willing to give up on adolescents or punish them as we do adults. As professionals our most difficult task very well may be to develop and maintain a perspective of who our patients are and remember that we do this work for our children and to help our upcoming generations.

We have reached a point where many in our society do not know about, or care to understand, the complex issues that are the roots of violence and sexual violence in youth. Certainly their faith in the resiliency of youth has been tarnished. They have taken a hardened and calloused view of treatment. It is a time when we as professionals who work with these children are being challenged in ways we have not been challenged before.

Despite what will feel like an uphill battle for the next few years, I suggest we continue our work, which is both necessary and important. In the process, it is my hope that the issues addressed in this paper will get the necessary attention and support professionally, financially, and politically.

REFERENCES

ABEL, G.G. & HARLOW, N. (2002). *The Stop Child Molestation Book: What ordinary people can do in their everyday lives to save three million children.* Philadelphia, PA: Xlibris Corporation.

ASSOCIATION FOR THE TREATMENT OF SEXUAL ABUSERS. (2001). *Practice standards and guidelines for members of the association for the treatment of sexual abusers.* Beaverton, OR: ATSA

BENGIS, S.M. (1986). A comprehensive service-delivery system with a continuum of care for adolescent sexual offenders. Shoreham, VT. Safer Society Program.

BENGIS, S.M. (2002a). *A state-of-the-art continuum of care for youth who engage in sexually abusive behavior.* Unpublished manuscript.

BENGIS, S.M. (2002b). *Principles guiding the development of a competency-based continuum of care for sexually abusive youth.* Unpublished manuscript.

BENGIS, S., BROWN, A., FREEMAN-LONGO, R.E., MATSUDA, B., ROSS, J., SINGER, K. & THOMAS, J. (1999). *Standards of care for youth in sex offense-specific residential programs* (National Offense-Specific Residential Standards Task Force). Holyoke, MA: NEARI Press.

BROWN, M.P. (1998, January). Juvenile offenders: Should they be tried in adult courts? [Electronic version]. *USA Today.* www.usatoday.com

BURTON, D.L., SMITH-DARDEN, J.P., LEVINS, J., FISKE, J.A. & FREEMAN-LONGO, R.E. (2000). *1996 Nationwide S: A survey of treatment programs & models serving children with sexual behavior problems, adolescent sex offenders, and adult sex offenders.* Brandon, VT: Safer Society Press.

CHAFFIN, M. & BONNER, B. (1998). "Don't shoot, we're your children": Have we gone too far in our response to adolescent sexual abusers and children with sexual behavior problems? [Editor's Introduction]. *Child Maltreatment, 3*(4), 314–316.

COLEMAN, E. & DWYER, S.M. (1990). Proposed standards of care for the treatment of adult sex offenders. *Journal of Offender Rehabilitation, 16*(1–2), 93–106.

COLEMAN, E., DWYER, S.M., ABEL, G., BERNER, W., BREILING, J., HINDMAN, J., KNOPP, F. H., LANGEVIN, R. & PHAFFLIN, F. (1996). Standards of care for the treatment of adult sex offenders. *Journal of Offender Rehabilitation, 22*(3–4).

COLEMAN, E., DWYER, S.M., ABEL, G., BERNER, W., BREILING, J., EHER, R., HINDMAN, J. LANGEVIN, R., LANGFELDT, T., MINER, M., PFAFFLIN, F. & WEISS, P. (2001). Standards of care for the treatment of adult sex offenders. In M. Miner & E. Coleman (Eds.), *Sex offender treatment: Accomplishments, challenges and future directions.* Binghamton, NY: The Haworth Press.

DEVELOPMENT SERVICES GROUP. (2000). *Understanding treatment and accountability in juvenile sex offending: Results and recommendations from an OJJDP focus group.* Prepared for: Office of Juvenile Justice and Delinquency Prevention Training and Technical Assistance Division, Inc., 7315 Wisconsin Avenue, Suite 700E, Bethesda, MD 20814.

FREEMAN-LONGO, R.E., BIRD, S. STEVENSON, W.F. & FISKE, J.A. (1995). *1994 Nationwide survey of treatment programs & models: Serving abuse reactive children and adolescent & adult sexual offenders.* Brandon, VT: Safer Society Press.

FREEMAN-LONGO, R.E. & BLANCHARD, G.T. (1998). *Sexual abuse in America: Epidemic of the 21ˢᵗ century.* Brandon, VT: Safer Society Press.

GARDNER, H. (1983). *Frames of mind: The theory of multiple intelligences.* New York: Basic Books.

GUAMBANA, A. (2001). Staff training: Gender-specific differences. *Juvenile Accountability: News & Views,* OJJDP, *3*(1), 3.

HUNTER, J.A. (1999). Adolescent sex offenders. In V.B. Van Hasselt & M. Hersen (Eds.), *Handbook of psychological approaches with violent offenders* (pp. 117–130). New York: Plenum.

HUNTER, J. & LONGO, R.E. (2003, in press). Relapse prevention with juvenile sexual abusers: A holistic/integrated approach. In G. O'Reilly & W. Marshall (Eds.), *Handbook of clinical intervention with juvenile abusers.* New York: Wiley.

KNOPP, F.H., FREEMAN-LONGO, R.E. & STEVENSON, W.F. (1993). *Nationwide survey of juvenile & adult sex offender treatment programs & models, 1992.* Orwell, VT: Safer Society Press.

LEWIS, A.D. (Ed.). (1999). *Cultural diversity in sexual abuser treatment: Issues and approaches.* Brandon, VT: Safer Society Press.

LONGO, R.E. (2002). A holistic approach to treating juvenile sexual abusers. In M.C. Calder (Ed.), *Young people who sexually abuse: Building the evidence base for your practice.* Dorset, England: Russell House Publishing.

LONGO, R.E. (2001). *Paths to wellness: A holistic approach and guide for personal recovery.* Holyoke, MA: NEARI Press.

NATIONAL ADOLESCENT PERPETRATOR NETWORK. (1988). The report from the National Task Force on Juvenile Sexual Offending. *Juvenile & Family Court Journal, 39.*

NATIONAL ADOLESCENT PERPETRATOR NETWORK. (1993). The revised report from the National Task Force on Juvenile Sexual Offending. *Juvenile & Family Court Journal, 44*(4).

RIMER, S. (2001, July 25). States adjust adult prisons to needs of youth inmates. *New York Times.* www.nytimes.com

ROBINSON, S.L. (2002). *Growing beyond: A workbook for sexually abusive teenage girls— Treatment manual.* Holyoke, MA: NEARI Press.

RYAN, G. & ASSOCIATES. (1999). Web of meaning: A developmental-contextual approach in sexual abuse treatment. Brandon, VT: Safer Society Press.

RYAN, G. (2002, in press). *Static, stable and dynamic risks and assets relevant to the prevention and treatment of abusive behavior.*

Index of Contributors